Slow Fade T

SLOW FADE TO BLACK

The Negro in American Film, 1900-1942

Thomas Cripps

Oxford University Press

Oxford   New York

Oxford University Press

Oxford   New York   Toronto
Delhi   Bombay   Calcutta   Madras   Karachi
Kuala Lumpur   Singapore   Hong Kong   Tokyo
Nairobi   Dar es Salaam   Cape Town
Melbourne   Auckland   Madrid

and associated companies in
Berlin   Ibadan

Library of Congress Cataloging-in-Publication Data
Cripps, Thomas.
Slow fade to black : the Negro in American film, 1900–1942 /
Thomas Cripps.
p.   cm.
Originally published: 1977.
Includes bibliographical references and indexes.
ISBN 0-19-502130-4
1. Afro-Americans in motion pictures.   2. Afro-Americans in the
motion picture industry.   I. Title.
PN1995.9.N4C7   1993
791.43′6520396073—dc20   93-6520   CIP

To Alma Taliaferro Cripps

To Alma Taliaferro Cripps

Preface

Historical facts never speak for themselves, or at least not until the historian has imposed order upon them. Thus there is a constant tension between the fugitive details of history and the historian's urge to impose a systematic meaning upon them. On the one hand, as Werner Sombart has said, where there is "no theory" there can be "no history." On the other, Stendahl tells us that "the truth may be found only in details." This book, like most works of history, falls somewhere in the middle.

In general the book is a social history and proceeds from two distinct perspectives on the history of American culture and society. First, there would be no need for the book were it not for the peculiar American racial arrangements in which a highly visible yet numerically inferior "black" group has been customarily, and often legally, ostracized from, exploited by, and occasionally patronized by, a numerically and politically dominant "white" group. Black history in the American sense, then, is the history of a racial relationship marked by antipathy, antagonistic cooperation, and conflicting loyalties which W. E. B. DuBois once characterized as the "twoness" of American life.

Second, many of the ideas and strategies in the book stem from concepts proposed by historians and critics of popular culture for whom popular art is an expression of deep seated values and attitudes which may be studied variously as social data, collective myths, and artistic genres. Although this book is about the slow growth of Afro-American impact on motion pictures, the fact that most of it is taken up with a *struggle* for hegemony over the medium of film precludes the formulation of a theory of black genre film. That, it is to be hoped, will be taken up in a later volume. For the moment, suffice it to say that the discussion is informed by a reading of many students of popular culture, the relationship between audience and filmmaker, and the anthropological bases of communication—among them Herbert Gans, John Cawelti, Russel B. Nye, Andrew Tudor, Will Wright, and Christian Metz.

These matters of race and popular culture over a period of three-fourths of a century of interaction between black and white filmmakers and their audiences not only have contributed to a unique American cinema but to an understanding of the breadth of American cultural history. As John Kouwenhoven has said in a book on the arts in America which ends with a provocative chapter on architecture—"Stone, Steel, and Jazz": "We cannot understand either the limitations or the achievements of [American] civilization if we continue to think of it solely as the product of Western European culture, modified by the geography and climate of the New World." In movies too Afro-Americans affected the medium even though they could not control it; that is what the book is about.

Because this book is taken up so much with the *pre*conditions of strong black interest in movies, the growth of power sufficient to alter movie images, and the growth of a cadre of black film creators its emphasis is broadly social rather than focused on the black film genre that would *eventually* emerge. I have tried to borrow concepts from scholars whose work emphasizes the breadth of culture such as Basil Willey's *The Seventeenth Century Background* in which he quotes T. S. Eliot on criticism: "In attempting to win full understanding of the poetry of a period you are led to a consideration of subjects which at first sight appear to have little bearing on poetry."

As this manuscript slowly grew into a book two interesting works on black movies appeared. Donald Bogle's very personal "interpretive" history, *Toms, Coons, Mulattoes, Mammies & Bucks* (New York, 1973), although lacking detailed citations, provides a witty portrait of black actors at work in Hollywood. Daniel J. Leab's *From Sambo to Superspade: The Black Experience in Motion Pictures* (Boston, 1975) follows the progress, or lack of it, toward "positive images" of Afro-Americans on the screen. Unfortunately, the timing of the gestation period of the publication of this book prevented me from making use of their ideas.

Acknowledgments

My earliest inquiry into the subject of this book began more than a dozen years ago. Over the years the staffs of many libraries gave generous assistance, among them the Doheny Library of the University of Southern California; the Special Collections and Theater Arts libraries of the University of California at Los Angeles; the Bancroft Library of the University of California at Berkeley; the libraries of Stanford University; the Library of the Academy of Motion Picture Arts and Sciences in Hollywood; the Feldman Library of the American Film Institute at Greystone, Beverly Hills; the departments of Manuscripts and Iconography of the Wisconsin State Historical Society; the Lamar Library of the University of Texas at Austin; the Ohio Historical Society; the Chicago Historical Society; Butler Library of Columbia University; Mugar Library of Boston University; Beineke Library of Yale University; and Founders' Library of Howard University.

Certain libraries provided continuing openhanded service over a period of many years so that I must give special thanks to Jean Blackwell Hutson and Ernest Kaiser of the Schomburg Collection of the New York Public Library; Joel Sullivan of the Manuscript Division of the Library of Congress; William Forshaw and Marian Bell of the Enoch Pratt Free Library of Baltimore; Paul Meyers of the Performing Arts Branch of the New York Public Library; and Walter Fisher, Virginia Richardson, and Florine Williams of Soper Library of Morgan State University.

Patrons of film archives impose a burden upon the repositories far greater than that required for using a book or even a manuscript collection. Each student requires not only personal attention to queries but his research requirements include expensive editing tables and projectors. Nevertheless, film libraries the world over have provided unstinting services for which I am grateful: James Moore of the Motion Picture Section of the National Archives; Dave Chertok of Sherman Grinberg Library; the Fox-Movietone Library; der Staatliches Filmarchiv der Deutschen Demokratischen Republik, Berlin; Erique J. Rebel of Nederlands Filmmuseum; Jacques Ledoux of the Royal Film Archive of Belgium; Per Calum of the Danish Film Museum; Roger Holman and Jeremy Boulton of the National Film Library and the British Film Institute; and Larry Karr and Larry Klein of the American Film Institute.

For their favors and personal attention over several years I am especially grateful to Frank Holland of the National Film Library in Aston Clinton; George C. Pratt and James Card of the International Museum of Photography in George Eastman House, Rochester; John Kuiper, Paul Spehr, David Parker, Patrick Sheean, Barbara Humphreys, Harriet Aveny, and Joe Balion of the Motion Picture Section of the Library of Congress; Eileen Bowser of the Museum of Modern Art; and Stephen J. Zito of the American Film Institute.

The research progressed because of leads and other assistance provided by Buck Harris of the Screen Actors Guild; Bob Thomas of Associated Press, Hollywood; Professors Frank Gatell and Paul Worthman of UCLA; Walter Burrell, then of Universal Pictures; Professor Russell Merritt of the University of Wisconsin; David H. Shepard of Blackhawk Films, Davenport, Iowa; Gordon Hitchens and Lorenzo Tucker of New York; and Professor Robert V. Haynes of the University of Houston. For allowing me to view films and other materials I am indebted to Paul Coss and David Beddow of the Westinghouse Broadcasting Company; Dave Dixon of the Canadian Broadcasting Company, Vancouver; Paul Killiam of Killiam Shows; John H. Baker, Columbus, Ohio; Ernie Smith of Bolton Landing, New York; Professors Norman Holmes Pearson and Standish Lawder of Yale; Sammy Gertner of the Enoch Pratt Free Library; Nate Zelikow; and Robert Stendahl of East Gary, Indiana. For permission to use materials in the James Weldon Johnson Memorial Collection at Yale I am grateful to Mrs. James Weldon Johnson and Poppy Cannon (Mrs. Walter White). For insights into Hollywood which cannot be expressed adequately in a footnote I owe appreciation to George P. Johnson, Bill and Peggy Walker, Carlton Moss, Stanley Kramer, Joel Fluellen, and Ben Maddow (the latter three in long telephone conversations).

At several stages the work was supported by a grant from the Yale-Harvard-Columbia Intensive Summer Studies Program, four grants from the Morgan State College Faculty Research Committee, two sum-

mer grants from the American Philosophical Society, a fellowship of
the American Council of Learned Societies which, along with a sabbati-
cal leave through the courtesy of the Trustees of Morgan State University and Presidents Martin D. Jenkins and King V. Cheek, enabled me
to write for a year, and finally the George P. Hammond Prize of Phi
Alpha Theta.

Various drafts of the manuscript profited from readings in whole or
part by David Parker of the Library of Congress, Stephen Zito of the
American Film Institute, Dean Philip Butcher of Morgan State University, and J. R. Lyston of Essex Community College. A less obvious debt
is owed to Professor August Meier of Kent State University and Professors Louis R. Harlan and Horace Samuel Merrill. If this book is read-
able, they must share credit for its merits because of their years of
friendly, witty, incisive criticism given to many pages of my earlier
work. My editor at Oxford University Press—Sheldon Meyer—clarified
issues and caught many errors. But neither they nor other contributors
to the book are responsible for its remaining flaws.

I am grateful for permissions to quote verse and lyrics from the fol-
lowing works: "Jazzonia," from Langston Hughes, *The Weary Blues*
(New York: Alfred A. Knopf, Inc., 1926, 1954); "Lift Every Voice
and Sing," words by James Weldon Johnson (Copyright Belwin-Mills
Publishing Corp., New York); "Africa Smiles No More," words by
Grant Clarke and Walter O'Keefe, from *Golden Dawn* (Copyright
Warner Brothers Music, Los Angeles); and "Remember My Forgotten
Man," words by Al Dubin and Harry Warren, from *Gold Diggers of
1933* (Copyright Warner Brothers Music, Los Angeles).

There is no way to measure the impact of research and writing upon
one's family. My children—Ben, Alma, and Paul—have tolerated my
absences, my pursuit of data and movies, and my lone hours at the
typewriter with unfailing good will and good humor. My wife, Alma
Taliaferro Cripps, has contributed her energy, skill, patience, and
loyalty without limit, and without expectation that I could find an adequate way to express my thanks for our life together. Our book is all
I have to offer.

T. C.

Baltimore, Maryland
July 1976

Contents

Slow Fade To Black

SLOW FADE TO BLACK:
AN INTRODUCTION

In the spring of the war year of 1942 a page-one bannerline in the show business trade paper *Variety* proclaimed BETTER BREAKS FOR NEGROES IN H'WOOD. The news marked a watershed in the history of American racial arrangements that would have far-reaching implications for future social change. A century of dominance of Southern racial metaphors in popular entertainment had come to an end. Movies, cartoons, mass-produced graphics, Tin Pan Alley music, and other popular diversions stopped depicting Afro-Americans as accommodating, contented, comic figures. The nation's most persistent social problem would now begin to receive the artistic recognition it had heretofore been denied.

In 1942, after many years' running fight, delegates of the National Association for the Advancement of Colored People and the heads of several Hollywood studios met and codified some social changes and procedures. The studios agreed to abandon pejorative racial roles, to place Negroes in positions as extras they could reasonably be expected to occupy in society, and to begin the slow task of integrating blacks into the ranks of studio technicians. The agreement directly affected only a tiny cadre of Hollywood Negroes, but the implications for the future were boundless. This book describes how this historic moment came about by tracing the role of blacks in film over its first half-century. Four themes are interwoven in the text: the survival of black performers within the motion picture industry; the growth of black protest against the worst Hollywood racism; the fitful underground movement to create an independent black cinema; and the movement to make the art of the film speak forthrightly to issues generated by the dualistic American racial system.

Historians have either studied film as an art pristinely aloof from the society for which it was made or have recounted the "progress" of racial liberalism in Hollywood while ignoring the social reality behind it. Hollywood films were written, directed, and produced to fit current American values and tastes. This whole expensive and complex structure allowed little role for blacks, a relatively small minority in a social system dominated by whites. Related to this was the myth of the "melting pot" that permeated the nation's consciousness before World War II.[1] It was the way that Americans learned to accept and tolerate the ethnic differences of new European immigrants of the turn of the twentieth century. Such tolerance was not extended to the differences of highly visible black Americans; indeed, quite the contrary. Blacks were tolerated only as long as they accepted their inferior status.

From its very beginnings the film sharpened the distinctions between black and white experience and excluded Afro-Americans from the screen. (Only the first primitive movies, which were limited to unedited recording of visual reality, allowed blacks a role.) Three great traditions of American popular culture came immediately to the screen—the western with its roots in wild west shows, the melodrama with its roots in traveling repertory companies, and slapstick comedy with its roots in ethnic vaudeville—all of which allowed only marginal black contributions. Later genres of American cinema—musical comedy, gangster film, and "screwball" comedy—helped perpetuate racial exclusivity in keeping with social custom.

Afro-Americans suffered a major disadvantage during the three decades of silent film. So much black entertainment had a strong musical element and depended upon audience reaction and participation for full effect. The absence of sound restricted the black actor's range. Black movie audiences did try to make up for this lack by rhythmic shouts, clapping, foot-tapping, and yells of encouragement to the heroes on the screen.[2]

Of all the social forces playing upon Afro-Americans the most difficult to weigh (because it is so often denied) was the effect of American liberalism. For all its drift, American democracy held out the promise of a better life for blacks. Conflicts and tensions built because of the persistence of racism and because change was not great enough. Many blacks, especially those who wrote for the popular press, responded in several ways. First, they overestimated the unity of white society that so rarely acted in concert on racial matters. Second, blacks flocking to northern cities brought with them a kind of cynical optimism. In nationwide black organizations there was a strong drift toward embracing American values and a rejection of black nationalism.

In the early twenties Hollywood could offer no mythic or artistic expression to blacks fragmented by the urban experience. Hollywood continued to draw on the old Southern stereotypes of Negroes as happy, lazy workers on the plantation. How were black artists and actors to respond to this situation? Were they to reject Hollywood completely? Or would they try to assimilate and work for the seven-year contract as their white counterparts did? For the most part blacks followed the second course, and black audiences, too, preferred the slick Hollywood product to "race" movies ineptly produced by blacks.

It must be said that black actors in Hollywood were not traitors to the race. The general drift of Hollywood was liberal, and held out a promise of change that blunted black criticism over the decades.

Indeed, by the end of the Great Depression, popular taste had become more sophisticated and no longer was willing to accept so readily the old Southern stereotypes that Hollywood was offering. Black protests against these stereotypes were having their effect, too. Blacks were soon making Hollywood careers as character actors. Progress continued slow, but all-black Hollywood films appeared, and individual black actors gained recognition through excellent parts often relatively free of racist overtones. Each lapse by the studios that followed these advances invoked louder protest, and so the pattern developed, much as the larger Negro struggle developed on the broader national scene.

It must be remembered that the actual social changes in American life lagged behind Hollywood movies. This is why the meetings of 1942 were important: they codified and publicized social gains that had been made in Hollywood.

Such black gains were largely the result of white patronage and white liberalism. Where was the black enterprise to develop its own people's film talents? Such enterprise did exist, but it operated underground, inadequately financed, plagued by technical inadequacies and inexperience, severely hampered by problems of distribution and publicity. The heroes of this movement—the Lincoln Company, Oscar Micheaux, the Colored Players, Reol, Ralph Cooper, and George Randol; their white "angels" such as Harry and Leo Popkin, Bert and Jack Goldberg, Alfred Sack, and Robert Levy; and such white directors as Harry Gant and Harry Fraser of Hollywood, and the German émigrés, Edgar G. Ulmer and Arthur Dreifuss—attempted to speak directly to black audiences.

Unfortunately black audiences failed to respond as black filmmakers hoped they would. The black middle class found their films to be ridiculous in their imitation of white norms of behavior, while many poorer blacks must have strained unsuccessfully for a glimpse of themselves. As they settled in their seats at the Dunbar or the Booker T., they often laughed in the wrong places and itched for the Hollywood feature that would appear in fifty-nine minutes. They knew black sheriffs and millionaires did not exist in real life. Meanwhile in Europe such American expatriates as Paul Robeson, Josephine Baker, and Lewis Douglas appeared in movies that dealt with racism by making Negroes part of an international proletariat nurtured in Marxist dogma. Afro-Americans found little identity in such a role, so these films, too, were rejected by black audiences.

Perhaps the most illuminating element in the black struggle for an indigenous cinema was the attempt of the Negro press to create a black aesthetic. Such writers as Lester Walton, Harry Levette, and half a dozen more wrestled with the duality—the "twoness," as W. E. B. Du-Bois put it—of American racial codes as they impinged on the cinema. Was the Negro to be a unique American with an "eternal tom-tom beating in his breast," or was he to be a "lamp-blacked Anglo-Saxon"?[3] By 1942 the critics had turned away from race movies and now supported Hollywood and the NAACP as the most effective means to bring about proper depiction of blacks on the screen. The keenest of these writers recognized that, for all their symbolic value as black enterprise, race movies tended to acquiesce in segregation, place white cupidity off-limits as a theme, rehash many stereotypes for which Hollywood had been blamed, set black against black, and imitate white movies.[4]

Blacks, thus, demanded to be treated as immigrants rather than as Indians or Orientals. This became the implicit black position by 1942. The last thing they wished was a rash of demands for censorship that would return them to the sterile years of the teens when blacks, like Orientals in later years, disappeared from the movies simply because studios wished to avoid conflict. Asians, save for interludes when war fever heightened fears of "the yellow peril," slipped into a dull run of sentimental celebrations of filiopiety. Indians, too, except for occasional massed attacks on wagon trains and iron horses, passed into noble, dignified oblivion. Perhaps because they bought more tickets than any other identifiable group and because many of them came to own the movie industry, immigrants received a friendly treatment in films, even before America at large accepted them. If there was a failure of cinema art in the years between *The Romance of a Jewess* (1908) and *The Jazz Singer*, which punctuated the end of the silent era, it was in the kindness that strangled any artful rendering of the harshness of urban immigrant life.

In sum, to understand the history of Afro-Americans in the history of the cinema is to see a race in tension with white society, in conflict with itself and its own ideals, in a quest to overcome historic disabilities, and moving slowly toward a viable cinema identity and an honest contribution to Hollywood movies. Its most significant achievement—significant, perhaps, because it was so improbable—came in the summer of 1942. With pejorative images driven from the screen the medium was free to allow blacks to contribute when the old Southern stereotypes of blacks ceased to be accepted as Hollywood practice.

The 1942 agreement accomplished far more than allowing a few blacks to appear in roles that were not overtly racist. It changed the whole tune and nature of Hollywood's response to the Afro-American's role in film and, by extension, in American life as well.

Chapter One

THE UNFORMED IMAGE: THE AFRO-AMERICAN IN EARLY AMERICAN MOVIES

During the first ten years of commercial cinema, starting in 1895, Afro-Americans through luck and accident appeared on the screen in a more favorable light than they heretofore had done in theater or fiction. Indeed, they portrayed a range of roles[1] far more varied than American society would grant them in everyday life. Unfortunately for Negroes, whites slowly acquired technical and financial control over the motion picture industry and combined the many tiny studios into a nationwide system. Blacks soon all but disappeared from the screen.

Most early Negro appearances in film followed the Southern stereotypes of the wretched freeman, the comic Negro, the black brute, the tragic mulatto, in keeping with literary and theatrical tradition. The primitive techniques of early cameras made it difficult to convey these stereotypes, though, and so visual reality often appeared despite the filmmakers. For one thing editorial cutting did not exist until 1903, so there could be no real screen narrative.

Meanwhile in primitive movies some blackface figures made a strong impression. A cameraman "shooting" the 9th Colored Cavalry had no way of cutting to blacks serving mint juleps under a Southern moon. They were black troops and had to appear as such. Location shooting—the filming of pictures on actual sites rather than stage sets—further gave a tone of authenticity to images and prevented distortion.

Years passed before the medium moved beyond simple novelty. Each film of the 1890s was a loop of pliable celluloid about fifty feet in length, fixed upon a series of pulleys and sprockets. The strip was inside a box into which the viewer peered at the "moving" pictures as he handcranked the mechanism. The earliest subjects provided an exciting glance at something in motion: trained bears, the hustle and scurry of a Chinese laundry, a Sioux Indian dance, Annie Oakley firing a Winchester—anything that provided immediate visual stimulation.[2]

Audiences had been prepared for the cinema by more than a half-century of playing with visual toys and the record of numerous experiments and demonstrations of motion in photography: Eadweard Muybridge's capturing the galloping motion of Leland Stanford's horse in Palo Alto, the Zoopraxiscope demonstrated at the Columbian Exposition of 1893, the projection device presented at the Cotton States Exposition of 1895, and W. K. L. Dickson's experiments at the laboratories of Thomas A. Edison where the Kinetoscope, originally a device to be coordinated with the phonograph, emerged in 1891.[3] In the spring of 1896 it was projected on the screen at Koster and Bial's Music Hall in New York. Gradually the flickering images replaced live vaudevillians in the hearts of audiences.[4]

The urban audiences themselves were as new as the technology. Many of them were recent immigrants who not only carried no baggage of racial lore, but were insulated from Southern literary racism by their own illiteracy, and were receptive to the cinema, which, like vaudeville, demanded little knowledge of English. Cities accommodated to the presence of blacks and immigrants, while the countryside exhibited nativism and condoned lynching. In cities the older forms of entertainment, the minstrel shows and tent shows, slowly declined as movies first merged with, then replaced, vaudeville.[5]

The audiences soon grew to millions. All day in the Lower East Side of Manhattan along Houston Street immigrants trickled into movie houses, while children wheedled tickets from parents and passers-by. Inside they were "rapt and entranced" before the brief screen stories. In the darkness a cry would ring out at Indians on the screen: "Das Wildes und grausames Volk!" Not so far away in Greenwich Village the crowded balcony looked like a "Tuscan Hill town." In the Bowery one resident bought a ticket every night but hated the occasional "dago show" that slipped through the informal censorship of the house managers. The small nickelodeons could run four shows every hour for a thousand viewers, and in some neighborhoods there were rows of them with gaudy fronts and shrill barkers—all largely unavailable to Negroes.[6]

Long before popular journalism accepted the new immigrants, vaudeville was putting forth ethnic characterizations on stage. Vaudeville troupes proudly advertised themselves as "The Two Irish Lords," "a consistent carnival of crisp Celtic comedy," or any one of a half-dozen other ethnic billings. Buster Keaton, Charles Chaplin, Ford Sterling—indeed, most comedians—learned their trade in ethnic theater, or, like Mack Sennett, whiled away afternoons watching vaudeville and burlesque. So when movies came to the immigrant warrens they drew upon a tradition that contributed to "creating a community of city dweller, by establishing norms of taste and behavior."[7]

Lester Walton of the black New York *Age* noticed early on that Negroes had no such visible past that whites could draw upon. Instead, Southern literary tradition shaped black images, chiefly because whites knew nothing about blacks. It did so through the sentimental racism of popular melodrama, the infiltration of Yankee literary life by genteel Southerners, the sentimental *Uncle Tom's Cabin* road shows, and the early infusion of moviemaking with Southern lore.

Southern black metaphor as it came to the melodrama limited blacks to the roles of venerable retainers, comic servants, clever octoroons, confidantes, bodyguards, boon companions, and obstreperous *enfants terribles*. From Aphra Behn's *Oroonoko* in the eighteenth century to the 1845 production of Anna Cora Mowatt's *Fashion*, blacks acted out the values of the master class, and with Horseshoe Robinson's servant they barked at the Redcoats: "Don't yer come to 'buse me; I am a native American nigger."[8]

Whatever modest power Harriet Beecher Stowe brought to *Uncle Tom*, it served blacks no better. Three generations of sentimental veneer laid on by scores of road companies blurred the Abolitionist message. No Negro played the title role for over a quarter-century after its first performance in 1853. Gimmickry soon replaced black drama. One company manager boasted of his "scenic production" in which "some novelties some good comedy has been written in" along with thirty drops and a "moving river double decked steam boat plantation allegory etc." in a magnificent setting "using no house stuff [*sic*]." By the 1890s Charles Frohman produced *Shenandoah*, David Belasco staged *Heart of Maryland*, and Julia Marlowe appeared in *Barbara Frietchie*, all in the tradition of Southern lore. Some of the most powerful early attempts to deal with race on the screen sprouted from nineteenth-century sources, including Uncle Tom and the star-crossed mulattos of Dion Boucicault's *The Octoroon* and George Sheldon's *The Nigger*.[9] Even the song slides used to encourage audiences to sing derived from "Darkies Dancing by the Light of the Moon" and other Southern lore.[10]

The dominance of Southern themes in drama was matched by a Southern literary revival in New York. Even though the hothouse plant that was the Southern mystique could not survive in antique purity in Northern cities, its purveyors moved there. Thomas Nelson Page, Benjamin O. Flower, Silas McBee, J. C. Hemphill, and other Southern journalists and editors not only lived in the North but moved in élite circles and served on the nation's genteel magazines. They remembered the Negro only as they had been taught and passed on the lore to their Yankee friends. Before he entered movies, for example, William Selig of Chicago managed "a genuine fast black show" in the South where he met the dignified Negro vaudevillian Bert Williams, whom he recalled only as a "yellow boy" with a "deep, wide, open watermelon expanse of mouth."[11]

At the same time Negroes, both intellectuals and urban masses, shared an indifference to the cinema. Because of their deep puritan fundamentalist roots, black churches eschewed film as needless frivolity. Organized Negro groups such as the Afro-American Council and the American Negro Academy struggled for survival against injustices. Not until the spring of 1909 would fragments of the Niagara Movement and the Constitution League join with other blacks and liberal whites to form the National Association for the Advancement of Colored People, and not until 1915 would its house organ, the *Crisis*, speak to a national black audience on the subject of the cinema.

Contributing to the black apathy toward cinema was an apparent lack of a usable past. Even the tradition of minstrelsy gave Negroes no sustenance because white imitators had usurped its forms and cast aside its roots in stick dances, bones, strings, shuffles, "dancing all over," plantation walks, and "patting juba." After Daddy Rice of Louisville popularized minstrels through his traveling blackface shows, only a few famous Negro acts—Josiah Henson, Madame Sissieretta Jones—competed with the large white troupes such as Dan Emmett, the Christy Minstrels, and Lew Dockstader. At the turn of the century the more truly Negro musical comedy of Rosamond and James Weldon Johnson, the Oberlin graduate Will Marion Cook, and Bob Cole appeared in New York. The new format—black and urban—abandoned the stylized turns of white minstrelsy, added a farce plot, and introduced ragtime to the lyrics of Negro writers such as Paul Laurence Dunbar, but it could offer nothing to the silent screen.[12]

In the absence of a usable past blacks depended on urban pluralism and the tolerance it produced, along with the sheer primitiveness of movie technique, to preserve them from distortion at the hands of white producers. For ten years they survived, especially in reportorial footage, suffering less than in other media but unable to create a black cinema from scratch.

This broad black imagery survived only as long as moviemaking consisted of no more than a single camera upon a tripod, recording the objective reality before it without artifice, staging, or editing. Even as rudimentary cutting began to allow characterization, early Negro roles hewed closer to vaudeville depictions than to Southern literary forms.

By any count, the number of blacks on the screen was tiny, but at least for a few years they used the primitive anarchy of the early independent, often piratical, producers as a field for black expression.

Among the first Negroes to appear on film were a group of West Indians who appeared in a series of short pieces shot for Edison Kinetoscopes in 1895. They danced, bathed, and coaled ships in film uncorrupted or altered by editing. Many relatively benign, vaguely anthropological vignettes followed, including a few Indian subjects. Occasionally in the 1890s there were demeaning bits such as Edison's *Watermelon Contest* in which four grinning Negroes wolfed melons and spat seeds with a will.[13]

The Spanish-American War in 1898 brought black soldiers to the screen. In *Colored Troops Disembarking*, black men with weapons in hand marched down a gangplank on their way to Cuba. Another Edison film, *The Ninth Negro Cavalry Watering Horses*, was one of the earliest cinematic records of troops on the march, and one in which Americans saw crisp armed black men outside their prescribed "place." Black troopers in smart order pass before a fixed camera shooting at a cloudless sky broken by a single tall pine. Other catalogues featured *The Battle of Mt. Ariat* with the "famous 25th Infantry, colored," and the *Colored Invincibles* fighting with "as much zeal as their white brothers."[14] Only five years later, by the time the campaign to "pacify" the Philippines caught the attention of Americans, things had changed. To celebrate that aspect of the war Edison reenacted a *Rout of the Filipinos* in which white soldiers bang away at a retreating brownskinned adversary. For blacks who could not find themselves in a campaign in which they actually took part, it was one of the first instances of white editorial control over a filmed racial statement.[15]

In a pet project of Edison a sharper deviation from racial typing appeared, with disarming surrogate Negroes in blackface allowed both aggressive and sexual roles. Edison had hoped to use minstrelsy in a test reel which was to synchronize sound-on-cylinders with film. In one of the reels the blackface minstrels act out the traditional forms, with endmen in striped pants waving tamborines, but in another, *Minstrels Battling in a Room*, a white man in light clothing contrasts with the dark makeup of the minstrels who pummel him with a bottle. In still another, *Sambo and Aunt Jemima: Comedians*, two handsome Negroes coyly kiss without gross racial overtones.[16]

Soon after the turn of the century, films began to grow longer and make use of cutting, selecting, and editing shots for various visual and narrative effects and for simple character developments. Usually dated from the release of Edwin S. Porter's *The Great Train Robbery* in 1903, narrative development had been emerging even earlier, and by

Edison's *The Morning Bath* (©. Thomas A. Edison, Inc.), like many topical films, recorded raw unedited reality. (International Museum of Photography at George Eastman House, hereafter GEH)

1905 had become a minor art. As white men learned the craft of the cinema, blacks would find it less hospitable, but for the moment at least there were roles for blacks other than the plantation slavey or the mulatto rotting in freedom. The worst problem for blacks remained exclusion from the seats of power. An aggressive black was usually enacted by a white man.

By 1905 the old Negro stereotypes came back to rival the black soldiers of the summer of 1898. Catalogue writers who described the hundreds of films in release described their products as though they had learned nothing and forgotten nothing since the first "darkey" stories. The pages were thick with chicken thieves and crapshooters, and their appeal was to the "proverbial" and the old fashioned, one catalogue urging its wares because "these darkies are of the 'Old Virginny' type." Compared with the days of movie infancy, the films were a deluge. Selig, for example, advertised *Interrupted Crap Game*, a story of "darkies" who neglect their game to pursue a chicken; *Prize Fight in Coon Town*, depicting "two bad coons"; *A Night in Blackville*, "hot stuff" with "two coons" out with their "best babies"; and so on through the pages. *Chicken Thieves* or some variation on the theme appeared in several catalogues, the most typical featuring a "colored dominie" who joined in the feast just before the denouement under the muzzle of a shotgun. Another catalogue entry pleaded authenticity because "all coons like chicken." Worse still, one catalogue listed a movie depicting "the catching, taring [*sic*] and feathering and burning of a negro for the assault of a white woman." Another catalogue featured Porter's *The White Caps*, a story of hooded vigilantes, "the advance guard of civilization" who preside as "a drunkard and wife beater is given a good coat of tar and feathers." A few of them burlesqued racial violence, reducing it to comic surrealism, as if this would make acts such as lynching somewhat more acceptable. One of them featured a black preacher whose feast on stolen chickens is interrupted by the shotgun blasts of a posse, while another ended with a comic dynamiting. These films presented blackface surrogates for Afro-Americans who bore a striking resemblance to later animated cartoon characters—impervious to explosions, car crashes, and physical abuse. For white audiences, consciously or unconsciously, they provided the opportunity to act out their racial anxieties while remaining aware that these films were not really in earnest.[17]

Nevertheless humane and dignified black figures continued on screen. As technique matured, a few melodramas reached the audience that had been raised on a diet of traveling repertory shows such as *Uncle Tom*. And the continued sales of topical footage preserved blacks as objective reality. Edison's West Indian subjects survived—among them a demure Afro-Carib dance in prim frocks—and in 1903 he released an authentic *Ballyhoo Cakewalk* featuring ten coolly strutting black dancers.[18]

At least one of these early films (according to Georges Méliès's catalogue) used surreal ambience to heighten its black presence. *Off to Bloomingdale Asylum* (1902) suggested a white man's nightmare-confrontation with an allegorical "bad nigger." An omnibus driven by four Negroes is stalled by its bucking horse. The blacks are kicked, fall to the ground, change into white clowns, pummel each other, and at last change into a huge black man. When he refuses to pay his fare the conductor sets fire to the omnibus, and the bulky Negro breaks into pieces, thus saving the white from having to face a self-willed black.[19]

Compared to black roles in other media the range was boundless. Although most films made no demands on their white audiences to accept blacks in any but the most traditional situations, a few went a step further. In a brief Edison vignette of 1903, *The Gator and the Pickaninny*, a patently fake alligator swallows a black child. The surprising ending, not indicated by its cryptic title, has a fatherly black man in makeup chop open the gator with an ax and free the child. In Edison's *A Scrap in Black and White* two boys, one black, one white, pummel each other without a clear decision, although the climax is a knockdown by the black boy, who hovers menacingly over his white victim. By mid-decade some documentaries depicted the masculine figures of black sandhogs entering their airlock to work under a river. In

The stylized clowns of *Off to Bloomingdale Asylum* (© G. Méliès, Inc.), identified in catalogues as "Negroes," reveal the historian's risk in relying uncritically on written documents. (GEH)

a brief bit of Atlantic City ballyhoo a Negro bandmaster led the resort's fiftieth anniversary parade.[20]

But by far the most striking single artifact of the primitive era was the shaping of the old melodrama *Uncle Tom's Cabin* into the first of a number of well-wrought motion pictures. For several years Edwin S. Porter had ground out his quota of footage of fires and hurricanes in the Edison studio. Then he began analyzing the films of Georges Méliès and noticed their narrative use of editing and cutting. He put his observations to work in four close-packed years from 1902 to 1906, creating, among hundreds of titles, *The Life of an American Fireman*, *The Great Train Robbery*, *The White Caps*, and *Uncle Tom's Cabin*. At fifteen minutes, or a thousand feet, *Uncle Tom's Cabin* was one of the longest and most expensive American movies up until that time. Fourteen settings carried the story. Porter's Tom was a white man in

From earliest times *Uncle Tom's Cabin* (© Thomas A. Edison, Inc.) provided a traditional vehicle for bringing black images to the screen. (Library of Congress)

blackface, and his production owed more to sentimental melodrama than to Mrs. Stowe. Yet, there for audiences to see were the cruelties of slavery; a black man's selfless courage in defense of the pregnant slave, Cassie; Tom's familial devotion; and finally a safe prediction that Lincoln would free the slaves.[21]

There was no reason to expect the film to take on the values of a black aesthetic, but Porter managed to infuse it with some of the Abolitionist fervor of Mrs. Stowe's original in spite of a *non sequitur* steamboat race between the *Natchez* and the *Robert E. Lee*, and a troupe of cakewalkers, debts to the gimmickry of the old road shows of *Tom*. Most important, it stimulated a run of cinema *Toms* from 1909 through 1927, each one restoring some of the vigor of the original. Sam Lucas, a black actor, performed in one, and finally in Universal's production in 1927 blacks and whites quarreled over Charles Gilpin's unwillingness to read sentimentality into the part, resulting in his replacement by

James Lowe, whose reading restored some element of black manhood.[22]

At its most bumptious the cinema provided the perfect medium for expressing energetic, competitive machismo. The astonishing presence of an occasional black in such a role was a measure, no matter how statistically small, of the breach with traditional black typing. One of them, *Everybody Works but Father* (1905), a vehicle for a Lew Dockstader routine, featured two versions, one black, one white, of a family that rebels against its rocking-chair-bound father.

Imagine a dim room behind a small store front, straight chairs squeaking a bit, a flickering screen, the whirring of a projector—a movie theater in 1904. A gruff Dutchman is seated in a sparsely furnished room. A Negro servant woman enters, carrying a bucket of ale. She pours a glass for the man, and standing behind him, she takes a long swig on the bucket. He turns and angrily hurls his glass at her. In the blink of an eye, no pause to consider consequences, pure rage her only response, she dumps the bucket over the white man's head.[23] Then, after a few dark seconds of intermission as "leader" flows through the projector gate, two smartly dressed black men approach a small cluster of Cau-

A Bucket of Cream Ale (© American Mutoscope & Biograph Co.) derived from vaudeville style, thus permitting black vengeance behind the comic mask. (Library of Congress)

casians as they await their turns at the stall of a sidewalk drink-vendor. They are contemptuously refused service. Later, the second of the blacks, imposing in hat and cape, bribes three kids to blacken the vendor's face as she naps under a kiosk in the parklike setting. As she awakens, passers-by inexplicably laugh at her, spank her, and harry her from the park. The chase builds into a frantic romp through the streets, and ends only when the gleeful whites drench her with seltzer bottle and watering hose.[24] The vendor learns the viciousness of racism by becoming black and experiencing it firsthand. No one knows how popular such films may have been, but they provided a remarkable variety of black attitudes.

Although the fiction film soon resumed traditional forms, the reportorial film continued to offer strong black figures. Two new forms of documentary film made their appearance in the decade after 1905: the boxing film and the exotic travelogue. Both may have enjoyed far more popularity than the first primitive pictures, and both survived the coming of the cinema enactment of the Civil War.

The most exciting black appearances on film were Jack Johnson's boxing pictures. Johnson's presence was a kind of iconic celebration of the "bad nigger" who flaunted white values as he battered a train of white opponents. He provided the excuse for federal attempts to ban boxing films from interstate traffic. Not until the day of Joe Louis would black fans have such an athlete with which to identify. One of the surviving pictures, Johnson's fight with Stanley Ketchell in 1909, set Johnson's effortless, cool right hand against his opponent's flailing, awkward misses. At the knockout Johnson stands, arms akimbo, leaning on the top rope, letting the crowd noise roll over him. Johnson's fights with Ketchell and with Jim Jeffries in 1909 and 1910 touched "racial pride," according to trade papers, and brought a strong black presence to audiences from the inaccessible sites of the bouts. Kalem, one of the earliest studios to produce westerns, added to the Johnson legend with a movie biography "from the baby in his mammy's arms to the full fledged gladiator of the fistic arena."[25] Johnson's prowess triggered the search for a "white hope" to dethrone him, and in turn, a pair of parodies of white ineptitude against black boxers, *The Night I Fought Jack Johnson* and *Some White Hope*. In both the blacks were portrayed by whites, yet in each the overawed white opponents make comic business from their fear of a Negro, one pursuing the referee rather than face Johnson, the other escaping the Negro by being rudely awakened from what was only a nightmare bout.[26]

Generally, topical reportage about Africa rendered black subjects with anthropological detail because the makers had not the benefit of editorial cutting. They faithfully captured not only tribal ritual that would become a cliché of later movies but the motley look of African towns with their black policemen, bourgeois merchants in fezes, tunics, and frock coats, and a scattering of Islamic turbans. The pictures of the safaris of Theodore Roosevelt and Paul J. Rainey showed blacks and whites alike toting burdens, a distinct breach with social convention of later jungle movies. They were so successful as to stimulate both the contrived movies that exploited the zoo of the Selig Polyscope Company and the faked depictions of Theodore Roosevelt's famous safari in 1909. Racism, when it emerged, was in in the eye of the reviewer such as the *New York Times* man who patronizingly admired the hunting skill of the "savages" in *The Military Drill of the Kikuyu Tribes and Other Native Ceremonies.*[27]

To calculate the impact on the American public of a handful of these films is difficult. There is no sure way to measure frequency of exhibition because film was sold rather than rented; rights to exhibit were sold for unlimited reruns; and piracy further blurred the box office data. Moreover, scholars are not agreed on the effectiveness of film as a teaching medium. Nevertheless these movies did represent a modest breach in traditional Negro stereotypes.

But after 1908 or so conditions within the movie industry changed. Unfortunately for the audiences the range of racial experience depicted on the screen narrowed, perhaps reflecting the continuing inability of filmmakers to render controversial, evolutionary, topical issues on film.

American racial arrangements had never had a completely uniform character. Even during the days of slavery thousands of blacks never experienced the institutional cruelties of the plantation. Many lived on small farms, working in the fields beside their owners, and a quarter of a million of them worked in a factory system. In places such as Baltimore there were more free Negroes than slaves. During postwar Reconstruction racial injustice persisted. For every black representative in Congress or a state legislative there were thousands of ex-slaves who lived in the Carolina lowlands and the Louisiana rice lands in conditions little different from slavery. To this day historians are not agreed on the origins of racial segregation, one group tracing it back to slavery, another finding it a late "capitulation to racism" and a social substitute for bondage.

In the decade bridging the turn of the century Afro-Americans reached the nadir of their fortunes in America. The franchise in the South gradually conformed to the "Mississippi plan," a system of legalistic entanglements that victimized poor, migrant, rural, illiterate blacks by denying them the ballot box. In support of the new arrangements was a covert system of nightriding and terrorism, not under the direction of an omnipotent Ku Klux Klan but merely any casual, mundane clique of "white caps" avenging a presumed rape or merely burning off the crops of the county's richest black farmer.

But then, coincident with the development of movies, social changes occurred that were difficult to report much less comprehend. Booker T. Washington's Tuskegee Institute, numerous farmers' institutes, and the National Negro Business League, pointed toward a parallel black economic growth under the benevolent tutelage of friendly whites. Through the nadir, black literacy increased, along with property ownership. Republican Party political appointments remained high and probably increased even in the ranks of Southern postmasters, customs collectors, land officers, and internal revenue collectors. The ranks of Tuskegee's commencement speakers were thick with alumni who had scored in the white man's game of temporal wealth. Scattered through the North was a thin network of urban black bourgeoisie faithful to Washington's way. His critics who felt he was selling out the race for short-run economic gain tended to come from an articulate Yankee literati: William Monroe Trotter, editor of the Boston *Guardian;* W. E. B. DuBois, Harvard's first black Ph.D.; and others. But their criticism was blunted by the well-publicized black gains. Black churches grew in numbers and wealth. The black press widened its influence. Lynching and mob violence appeared on the wane. The black migration away from the South held out promise of a better life for Negroes in the future.

The uneven pace of change divided blacks for and against "Bookerism." If lynching declined in incidence, urban "race riots" increased; if black wealth increased, it failed to keep pace with white; if blacks trekked away from Southern oppression, Yankee cities stifled hope in new ways; if political appointments seemed glamorous evidence of Republican goodwill, the two friendliest Republican Presidents, Theodore Roosevelt and William Howard Taft, bent their energies toward building a "lily white" party in the South. That Washington was a celebrity and patronage broker more than a political force may be seen by the events following two bloody racial incidents in the summer of 1906. Republican Presidents had always given jobs to Southern black politicos as a reward for services to the party and as a sign of the party's roots in the antislavery crusade and in the politics of Reconstruction. But in 1906 a severe riot ravaged the black neighborhoods of Atlanta and an unsolved shootout broke the peace of Fort Brown, Texas, where newly arrived black soldiers were quartered. In the first case Roosevelt refused to use the voice of the Presidency to condemn racial violence and in the second case, despite black protests, he and his Secretary of War, Taft, discharged without honor scores of black troopers who had protested their ignorance of the identity of the bush-wackers in Texas. In both instances Washington and his followers were helpless to change the Presidential decisions.

Thus, coincident with the refinement of moviemaking technique great changes had shaken black and white society alike. Gradually the first urban black protest organizations began to contest for ascendancy with Washington's old-style accommodation approach. Washington had frequently participated in ceremonial governors' conferences and meetings with Northern philanthropists, but the new Negro leadership actively worked with white peers in such organizations as the NAACP. The founding of the Urban League testified to the view that new prob-lems—job discrimination, shabby housing, residential segregation—de-manded new solutions. But because the sources of movies were nos-talgic and because blacks struggling among themselves for hegemony expressed no clear voice, moviemakers continued to derive racial themes from dated white sources.[28]

Indeed, the racial question proved to be the only subject of movies in their second decade that did not accommodate to urban tastes. Some studios—Vitagraph was one—were thought to specialize in capturing city scenes. By 1909 many small companies—Kalem, Biograph, Vita-graph, Essanay, Lubin—took the first step toward breaking Edison's early patent monopoly, toward shaping national distribution systems, and toward squelching foreign competition. Their new Motion Picture Patents Company with Wall Street-backed Biograph as senior partner attempted to control the market, thereby driving their competitors westward to Southern California, where they took advantage of the rough photogenic country, the sunny shooting days, the cheap land dangled by Los Angeles boosters, and proximity to Mexico, where they could flee from police and patent lawyers. The removal westward carried them away from their immigrant roots in Eastern cities and away from the new black ghettos.

As their product improved, studios became more conservative in their artistic perspective because they worked for increased middle-class ac-ceptance, even replacing "nickelodeons" with new theaters so as to win the genteel trade. Indeed, many pioneers never pushed beyond their early creations and never found new sources of inspiration. In-stead they clung to melodrama, genteel Shakespearian themes featuring famous actresses such as Sarah Bernhardt, and the handy imagery of minstrelsy.

The first black presence on primitive movie screens resulted from the limits of editorial control over film. After 1908, as filmmakers gained increased control over their material, the role given blacks

changed. Movies still rarely ran for more than a few minutes, but form
and content changed as directors became masters of editing, cutting,
and rhythm.

Biograph's *The Fights of Nations* in 1907 represented a transition,
both in its cutting technique and its depictions of blacks. While certainly not a masterpiece of cutting, it strung together a strand of ethnic
pairs who fight in presumably characteristic styles; Latins with knives,
Jews with guile and gestures, Scots with highland swords, and so on.
The blacks in "Sunny Africa, Eighth Avenue" slash each other with
razors over a woman, and pause only to watch what was probably the
first authentic filming of jazz dance. Only the Negroes are missing from
the finale in which harmony reigns over all groups—even Indians—as
they pass under a flag-festooned proscenium. The point is obvious: all
are welcome under the American sun except blackfolk. Less obviously,
Motion Picture World failed to notice the absent blacks and found all
the peoples "well represented."[29]

Film now turned more often to heavyhanded old-style race humor
and even an occasional location-documentary, such as Edison's *The
Pickaninnies* (1905), Essanay's *Dancing Nig* (1907) featuring the
"well-known fact" of Negro rhythm, Lubin's *How Rastus Got His
Pork Chops* (1908), Pathé's *How Rastus Got His Turkey* (1910), Vitagraph's *A Georgia Wedding* (1909) with its "reasonably true" Negro
grotesques, Edison's *Uncle Tom Wins* (1909), and the carefully selected old blackfolk shot in Rome, Georgia, for *King Cotton*. Such
traditional black scenes were mentioned in the trade papers: a *Motion
Picture World* review in 1909 described a moderately innocent racial
incident as "a fat nigger woman slips with a pail of water."[30]

Even so, blacks continued to have a wide range of roles despite the
trend. By 1910 Thanhauser and other studios had hired black contract
players. And drama and comedy still occasionally turned on the fact
of race rather than its burlesque. Edison's *The Colored Stenographer*
(1909) milked comedy from a suspicious white wife who brawls with
a black charwoman whom her husband has placed at his desk to conceal
his blonde secretary. The last Negro troopers to appear in films before
World War I were in *The Tennessee Guards*. Black rage was allowed
full range in *The Slave's Hate*. And amongst the innocuous servants of
Ruy Blas and others, Dion Boucicault's famous standard, *The Octoroon*, appeared on film at least twice. If the old melodrama depended
on the tragic mulatto stereotype, at least its author, inspired by the
success of *Uncle Tom's Cabin*, had in 1859 helped invent her from the
whole cloth of slavery.

The most striking drift toward a narrow racist approach appeared in
films of Africa, largely because editorial control won its battle over

authenticity of location. After 1910, save for a few documentaries such as Gaumont's *Life in Senegal* (1910) with its "little black boys hard at work on their studies," and Pathé's *Tuaregs in Their Country* (1909), which attempted to display "African beauty," the trend was toward drama. The best of them made Africans into variants of Kipling's *Gunga Din*, the Hindu waterboy who gave his life for the British Raj. Griffith himself made *The Zulu's Heart* for Biograph. In it the Zulus are deterred from attacking a Boer wagon when one of their number kills three of his fellows in defense of the whites. The fadeout is on the Zulu, who clasps to his breast a doll given by the grateful Afrikaners. The comic version, *Rastus in Zululand*, enlightens Rastus by having him see the superiority of European culture over African. *King of the Cannibal Islands* sketched another popular theme, the white man who survives the threat of a primitive culture. Gene Gauntier's *Missionaries in Darkest Africa* (1912) for Kalem treated kidnapping, miscegenation, and eventual suicide by a missionary's remorseful daughter. *Voodoo Vengeance* (1913) celebrated the British breakup of a nascent Mau Mau conspiracy. *The Zulu King* (1913) was a comic version of the white god, or henpecked John Smith who becomes king of the blacks while in flight from his wife, thereby getting a laugh because "the white man comes out on top" through "the beautiful stupidity of the aborigines and how easily they were conquered by modern tact and wit." One of the best was *The Kaffir's Gratitude* (1915), whose title character, with no investment in the outcome, saves a white fortune in diamonds from a "social parasite" with the zeal of a slave defending the master's plantation.[31] Even comic intentions would not allow many role reversals such as that in *Queen for a Day*, in which a missionary and his daughter are saved from Zulus when their maid assumes the native throne and helps them escape. The times required that even Othello's "swarthy features . . . not be mistaken for those of the African type."[32]

By 1915 the most striking trait of the jungle movies was the dull impotence of their blacks. In 1914 Edgar Rice Burroughs had responded to studios' interest in his *Tarzan* stories by inserting a movie-rights clause in his book contracts, but his Anglo-Saxon lord of the jungle would have to wait for a postwar revival of African vigor. Meanwhile Louise Glaum and Charles Ray capered through *Forbidden Adventure* (1915) with black boys hunkered down in atmospheric corners as functionless as toadstools. Selig's *A Night in the Jungle* in the same year further betrayed the genre by having the sole aggressive African fall victim to a tame leopard improbably trained to protect whites against black intruders. The European scenes were tinted angry red and the African in passive blue-green.[33]

Between 1910 and 1915 the drift toward older black stereotypes proceeded apace, although the reason was not wholly clear. External relations between the races had begun to rise from the nadir: casual violence declined, indexes of black wellbeing seemed better, blacks organized more effectively, and interracial committees flourished. The sole factor absent from earlier years was the coming Golden Anniversary of the Civil War with its attendant emphasis on reunion and disregard of the Abolition movement.

For whatever reason, the range of black roles contracted to the point that the most obvious black identity was ignored. Some films toyed with the iron taboo of miscegenation through comic cautionary tales that sidestepped the central issue by using trick endings and confused identities. In *Black and White* a white girl darkens a rival's skin with a potion but suffers remorse when she is herself blackened and suffers the advances of a black butler. *The Valet's Wife* was one of many prankish tales hinging on substituting black babies for white. In *Mammy's Child* a jealous white girl on a jaunt to a park trades her doll for a Negro baby, at least until the black mother cancels the deal with a baleful stare. A similar theme ran through *Cause for Thanksgiving*, one of a series of "Sonny Jim" comedies produced by Tefft Johnson. Jim trades his turkey to little black Lily Ann for her baby brother, Rastus, because her family has a surfeit of children but no holiday dinner. Thus the only way to breach taboo was to contrive and to torture ordinary love, hate, conflict, and identity and to rest plots on quirks.[34]

Simultaneously, Afro-American family ties, machismo, and loyalties disappeared from the screen unless as were connected with whites. A strain of childhood egalitarianism was tossed aside in *Sonny Jim at the Mardi Gras*, in which a black mother whips her daughter after Jim has taken her hand-in-hand through the Luna Park steeplechase to the beach. Black transvestism was the subject of a gaily mounted burlesque, *Florida Enchantment*, in which maids of two families staying at the Ponce de Leon Hotel take magic seeds which change their sex and spoil their family's lives. In the resulting romp only a single actual Negro appeared. *Colored Villainy* by Keystone was no more than a blackface farmer's daughter joke at the end of which a local boy wins the girl from the "colored traveler." In *Swami Sam* by Vitagraph an edge of black masculine aggression is dulled and made comically ambivalent by a fat black matriarch. The swami is a classic ghetto hustler, duping cops and neighbors with equal cunning. In garish robes and turban, surrounded by Tarot symbols, he foils a raid by hypnotizing the cops, exposes a police spy "in drag," and prepares for a final assault with drawn pistols. But in the end he is caught by a tough black laundress

Although some black images in early cinema deviated from Southern lore, films such as Mack Sennett's *A Colored Girl's Love* (© The Keystone Film Co.) revealed the persistence of blackface idiom. (Author's collection)

who barges in fearlessly to claim her past-due bills and drags him off to the terrified police.[35]

Meanwhile Afro-Americans remained powerless as producers became more alert to the opinions of their white audience. Legend had it that the black vaudevillian Bert Williams failed to raise backing for filming his routines, failed to interest bookers in "a few" one-reel experiments, and had a Brooklyn opening blocked by a white mob. In Jacksonville whites threatened to throttle a Kalem production unless the studio ceased making such movies as *Florida Crackers*. And Bill Foster, a legendary black pioneer filmmaker, faltered and sought capital from white sources. The black critic of the New York *Age*, Lester Walton, later Minister to Liberia, bristled at the publicity for a lynching movie: lobby-card copy on Sixth Avenue reading "Hear His Moans and Groans, Price One Cent!" and in the Bowery it was billed as "educational." In both cases he called for a black community protest that never came.[36]

It is difficult to attribute causes to the seeming decline in black fortunes after 1910. Harlem and its equivalents elsewhere had only just opened up, and maybe the beginnings of the ghetto system contributed. Perhaps, as many blacks thought, the resumption of Democratic power in Congress in 1910 and in the Presidency itself in 1912 brought a return of Southern values to the national scene. The Golden Anniversary of the Civil War revived old white prejudices, and blacks were seen once more as slaves. Black intellectuals themselves became celebrants of a deeper meaning of the anniversary in pageants of massive proportions. But for most Americans the celebration touched depths of feeling which reinforced their long-founded racial prejudices.

Americans gave homage to a lost pastoral virtue and purity. No better image could be found for depicting rural innocence than the Old South, whose "Lost Cause" had fallen victim to the industrial might of the North. It was an easy step from here to an apology for slavery. Moreover the new Southern gospel came coated in soldierly duty, filiopiety, and personal courage that seemed lacking in the Northern war effort. Recently urbanized Americans celebrated the war through a nostalgic haze that allowed them to believe it had been fought for the abstract principles of union and states' rights rather than for the emotional and moral issue of slavery. The mood appeared on film in the spring of 1909 when President Taft greeted the joint encampments of the Confederate veterans and the Grand Army of the Republic at Petersburg, Virginia.[37]

Intersectional reconciliation became a national theme as the anniversary approached, and accordingly, black roles in the cinema that focused on the Civil War necessarily retraced worn ruts. The acceptable Negro became a loyal slave, the sacrificial goat in the ritual of the reunion of the sections, a wistful icon of old ways, steadfast in the defense of his master's home and family, obligated by the logic of the situation to reject Yankee promises of freedom, and finally, resolute in rejecting black brothers in blue uniforms and those who had fled from farm to town.

Because most movie directors kept abreast of popular tastes, a single figure cannot be isolated as a leader of the trend. But D. W. Griffith fit the role so well it was as though he had been sent from Central Casting. He brought together in one mind an abiding suspicion of city life, a sentimental bias toward "right-thinking Negroes," a childhood love of Victorian narrative, an apprenticeship in traveling stock companies, a reverence for a genuine Southern war hero among his antecedents, a good sense of his mother's Protestant morality, and most of all, a keen feeling for the South, its travail, its burden of race, and its rural inferiority.

Poverty drove Griffith's family from the farm to Louisville and the

young man into an austere life of odd jobs relieved by his attraction
to the life of the stage, first by watching Julia Marlowe and other famous performers, then by cadging small roles, and finally by joining
the Nance O'Neill stock company. He married an actress and moved to
New York, where in 1908 he began writing, acting, and eventually directing for Biograph movies on Fourteenth Street. Like most films, his
were short and topical pieces on themes of race, immigration, urban
problems, Indians, labor, suffrage, and the place of women, with
forays into classics such as *Ramona* and *Trilby*. His heroes were often
vague Jeffersonian individualists pitted against officious authoritarian
snoops such as cops and reformers.[38]

At first his pictures were indistinguishable from the common run,
but soon he synthesized his social and artistic vision into a mature expression that caught the eye of the prestigious *New York Drama Mirror* and provided the occasion for the first movie review ever in *The
New York Times*. He borrowed, invented, and learned pacing,
strengthened the narrative ability of the medium, and adopted the conventions of melodrama to the grammar of the film. Not that he alone
transformed the cinema; his gift for bombast and self-advertisement
only made it seem so. Nevertheless, his unique mind-set made him the
most credible interpreter of Southern and black experience on film, at
least to a generation wanting relief from the clatter of urban change,
with the result that the new Negro of the cities was drowned in the
martial vision of Griffith's Southland. Five of his last Biograph films
were set on plantations, and only two, *The Honor of His Family* and
The House with the Closed Shutters, in 1910, hinted that Southern legend and reality conflicted. This metaphor of Southern tragedy which
he developed and with which he infused his epic, *The Birth of a Nation*, helped to firmly etch the outlines of Negro character in film long
after its fidelity to American realities had passed.

The broad outlines of Southern visions of the past were already well
known to Northern readers through the dominance of Southern regional writers. It only remained for Griffith, Ince, and other moviemakers to synthesize the Civil War into a cycle of heroic Southern
cavalrymen, gentle but iron-willed women, Yankee infantrymen un-
aware of the chivalric rituals of war, all brought together in the end by
an intersectional marriage of former enemies.

"Ben's own life was not worth as much to him as the happiness of
Colonel Frazier and his small family." The line might have come from
scores of movies, but it was from Griffith's canon of Civil War melo-
dramas released between 1909 and 1911, of which *In Old Kentucky*,
The Battle, *His Trust*, and *His Trust Fulfilled* typified the genre. *In
Old Kentucky* opens on three white men and a blackface butler as a

father and son swear allegiance to the Confederacy while the second son hangs back. The butler rubs his hands with glee as the rebel son thrashes the laggard. Loyalty to family, personal courage, impulsiveness, and love of region are Southern virtues with which the Negro identifies. As the picture enlarges to the wider view of war (with an early "pan" shot) the sons take opposite sides. At the end the wounded rebel son, after eluding certain capture and death, and the returned Union officer hesitantly embrace and shake hands while wrapped awkwardly in the folds of both their flags. In a reprise of the opening the black butler looks on with approval, needing no investment in the situation in order to give his love to whites.[39]

In the two years after, Griffith turned out more than a half dozen Civil War dramas (still a tiny portion of his total output), each one exploring corners of Southern life and moving toward a total vision, with three of them—*The Battle, His Trust,* and *His Trust Fulfilled*—serving to rough out trial images, shots, and cuts for his eventual masterwork, *The Birth of a Nation.* Griffith not only played all the Southern chords but added his own flourishes so that a reviewer found *The Battle* "has in a more than ordinary degree that pleasing Biograph characteristic of throwing the spectator into the very heart of things." He opened the war with a big scene, "the dance before the departure," dressed the sets with strong forms and textures, and toned down the florid stage style of acting. He gave strength and bearing to the Southern woman waiting out the battle. The battle itself he fought out behind low redoubts, flags aflutter, preserving the human scale by cutting to a boy who bolts and runs to his mother, who teases him into returning to the smoke of the lines where, among the milling men, he becomes a dangerously exposed ammunition bearer. The last cut is to her, and we know she is proud. Only the black figures remain to be sketched in.

His Trust and *His Trust Fulfilled,* released several months earlier in two parts because of lingering doubts of the staying power of audiences, supplied the black imagery. In keeping with the myth, a Southern officer goes off to war with the field hands cheering and the house in the charge of the dutiful servant, George. After the soldier dies in battle, George hangs his sword over the mantel, thenceforward assuming to a striking degree the white male duties to home and family, even at great personal risk defending the homestead against rude Yankee marauders who put it to the torch. George saves widow, daughter, and sword from the flames, takes them into his own house, and with "his savings" continues protecting them, "true to his trust." His wickedest enemies are Griffith's favorite bugbears, the rowdy town blacks of Reconstruction, grinning under their high hats. At the fadeout the

His Trust and *His Trust Fulfilled* (© American Mutoscope & Biograph Co.) were among several early exercises by D. W. Griffith derived from his childhood exposure to Southern lore. (Library of Congress)

daughter is safely educated and married off to an English cousin, and George, bent and woolly-headed, receives for his lifetime of toil a single grateful handshake from a white man.

Apart from the veiled and probably unconscious sexuality in George's behavior, his fealty, his ardor in the absence of personal gain, and his treasuring of white expressions of gratitude, all formed the outline of blacks on screen for years to come. More than any other director Griffith gave future moviemakers a model, a cinematic language, and a rich romantic tradition that would define an Afro-American stereotype. He was the bridge between nineteenth-century Southern melodramatic and literary tradition and the new art of the cinema. The cycle of Civil War movies to which he contributed narrowed the range of black roles on the screen because his special blending of Southern mystique and the craft of cinema eventually moved motion pictures from their old anarchy toward a centralized system of art and industry that Negroes could not penetrate. Porter, J. Stuart Blackton, Thomas

Ince, and other innovators who might have contributed a converse black imagery burned themselves out while Griffith remained at the height of his powers.

For Afro-Americans nothing could have been worse than the reunions, intersectional lovers, grizzled veterans, intertwined flags, blue and gray bunting, and loyal darkies. Every trait seemed an abandonment of the Abolitionist heritage and the legacy of the Republican Party to sectional harmony graced by approving hat-in-hand Negroes. The rush of movies commemorating the Civil War destroyed the chance for a humane treatment of Negroes on the screen. Instead, they restored Southern lore to the screen and taught a new urban generation a false nostalgia.

Varied plots ended in ritual sameness. In *The Empty Sleeve; Or, Memories of By-Gone Days* a one-armed veteran in the Grand Army of the Republic daydreams of the war, "and as a fitting climax we see a Union and Confederate soldier clasping hands." In another the Southern maiden knows "her brother leads the grays" as surely as "her lover leads the blues," and at the end there will be an embrace when the Yankee "returns for his Dixie girl." *A Reconstructed Rebel* fights against Honduran rebels in defense of the American consulate with the same vigor he brought to the Lost Cause. In *Days of War* two brothers, wartime enemies, embrace. In *A Flag of Two Wars* an old Confederate dies penniless, leaving his sword and flag to his son, a hero in Cuba whose troops "salute the two flags with equal reverence." *The Suwanee River* offers the mood of the popular song cast over the era of Reconstruction as a "fiery" Southern lad and a Northern girl on adjacent plantations meet clandestinely with the aid of a black "uncle." A last reunion comes when the boy returns, rich, to redeem the estate from the auctioneer's gavel.[40]

The steady stream of films reassured audiences of the sincerity of the Southern cause by presenting it in sacrificial terms. *A Girl Spy* "consecrated her entire life to the cause of her beloved Southland." Another girl shoots her Yankee lover *For the Cause of the South*. Death sanctified loyalty in such images as "the vacant chair" in *The Soldier Brothers of Susannah* and its variation in *The Only Veteran in Town*. Some of these were filmed in the homey air of the South, such as Photoplay's *The Littlest Rebel* and five Gene Gauntier pictures.[41]

Black characters gave their lives and fortunes for the cause of scores of white Southerners. *The Confederate Spy* set the mood. It opened on a pastoral plantation homecoming as slaves, "happy, contented, and well cared for . . . joyous as a bunch of school children," led by old Uncle Daniel, greet their new mistress coming down the lane. War comes, ruining the scene, but old Daniel defends the place against Yankee marauders when he is not spying and running messages through the swamps, at last saving the day "for massa sake and little missa." A trade reviewer loved every moment. "Much good can be done by presenting to those who know nothing about such scenes a reproduction of them," he wrote. "Perhaps in that way a better understanding of the Southern people can be disseminated."[42]

The next year *Hearts and Flags* offered Uncle Wash, who protects Colonel Dabney's daughters from Yankee foragers even after they use him to batter in the door. A Union captain saves the day and returns after the war to seal political reunion with his marriage to one of the girls as Wash looks on. In *Mammy's Ghost*, Mammy has her white ward rattle a chain in the attic to persuade Yankee searchers that a ghost rather than a wounded rebel is in the attic. In *A Special Messenger* a girl spies for the Confederacy secure in the knowledge that her black butler is nursing her wounded lover. *The Judge's Story* is a flashback told by a "mammy" in which a Negro defendant saves the Judge during the war and earns "the rest of his days in happiness and

Hearts and Flags (© Thomas A. Edison, Inc.), one of scores of movies that celebrated the Golden Anniversary of the Civil War, revived traditional Southern black roles. (GEH)

comfort" rather than in jail. In *Uncle Pete's Ruse* black Pete, "the only cool and collected person on the premises . . . saves a hidden rebel soldier from Union eyes by painting smallpox on the family."[43]

The rattle of sabers and gunfire continued on screen through the election year of 1912 when Woodrow Wilson brought the Democratic Party and Southern ideals back to the capital. Sambo, the black servant in *The Soldier Brothers of Susannah*, typical of this happy breed, feeds his homecoming master, who is thin from eating "no count vittles up Norf." Uncle Mose and old Mammy in *None Can Do More* and *Old Mammy's Secret Code* both die in their master's causes, he while freeing his master from Yankee prison, clutching a picture of Lincoln to his bosom, "loyal to his savior, but even more loyal to his master," and she by suffering execution as a spy after using her laundry line to signal in code from inside Grant's headquarters. An entire black family guard the plantation from Union troops in *The Informer*, as they sneer at the "false brother" who joined the Federals. Even the suicidally tragic mulatto may die in the cause, as she did in *A Gentle Volunteer*. By 1914 *In the Fall of '64* extended the loyalty to the entire slave quarter whose inmates concealed a Confederate officer from the Yankees. Freedom was not their ambition. One of them, Old Mose in *The Old Oak's Secret*, finding his new freedom unbearable, hides his master's will with its manumission clause in a tree.[44]

The cycle of war movies shaped the outlines of heroism and villainy in purely Southern terms. Few pictures featured Yankee heroes save for those who moved South after the war. To live in the North was to experience misery and bad food, remedied only by an eventual recrossing of the Ohio or the Mason and Dixon Line. Southern "heavies" were foreigners or declassé overseers, never slaveholders or their slaves. Black heavies, when they appeared, were either town Negroes or mulattoes. Jim, the loyal slave in *A Slave's Devotion*, for example, rebels not against the institution of slavery but only against his cruel overseer. He runs not for freedom but to evade the overseer and his dogs, and finally, as a Confederate runner, dies saving his old master. Lew Dockstader, the old minstrel, played the title role of *Dan*, the servant-friend whose life is spoiled by the cruel overseer who hopes for war so as to win the master's daughter during the turmoil. We know he is evil because Dan finds him "preaching freedom and riches to the negroes." *Old Mammy's Charge*, "The Sweetest Southern Story Ever Told in Pictures" according to its ad-mats, carries Mammy northward with her newly married mistress. Soon both parents die, leaving Mammy to struggle against the courts, who wish to take custody of their orphan. At last the old grandfather comes in search of his daughter and takes Mammy and child southward "where peace and comfort await them."

The titles rolled on, with no deviation from the well-worn racial roles.[45]

The celebration of Southern virtue and Negro fealty to it made Abraham Lincoln into no more than a spearbearer, or at best an icon of sectional conciliation. In Vitagraph's literal dramatization of Julia Ward Howe's *The Battle Hymn of the Republic*, Lincoln, rather than the vessel of God's wrath, is a passive Christlike figure before whom emancipated slaves kneel. The line-by-line rendering of the song ignores the phrase "to make men free." In *Lincoln the Lover* he is seen only through his love for Ann Rutledge and in the end through the wistful gesture of a "darkey servant" who tiptoes up to the President dozing before a fire and "looks a moment lovingly at his master." Reviewers seldom took note of the underlying racial themes in movies about Lincoln.[46]

If film, through Griffith and other pioneers, provided succeeding generations of urban Americans with a rural Southern racial imagery that had only marginal relevance to their lives, then it will be instructive to examine the same art as it treated other racial and ethnic groups. Indians, European immigrants, Mexicans, Asians, and gypsies experienced disparate fates, but, save for the shabby Mexican and gypsy treatments, they were only slightly better qualitatively than that accorded Negroes. Mexicans, gypsies, and Orientals remained aliens by virtue of color, culture, and geographic remoteness, inspiring no artistic or popular cinema tradition except for their use as heavies. Therefore only Indians and Europeans provide continuing comparison and contrast with the Afro-American cinema figure, the former as a dense symbol of obtuse resistance to assimilation, the latter as a case of the highest expression of the American polyethnic dream caught in Emma Lazarus's poem cast in the base of the Statue of Liberty: "Give me your tired, your poor . . . ."

Like the Negro, the Indian cinema metaphor emerged from older literary genres, but also took form as a result of United States government policy toward the tribes. For years the fundamental Indian law had been the famous Dawes Act, which encouraged assimilation while, unfortunately, allowing exploitation of the Indians. The new act, sponsored by Congressman Charles H. Burke of South Carolina, recognized the difficulties inherent in marrying the two cultures and postponed the rights of citizenship until such time as the Indians had demonstrated their economic self-sufficiency within the American legal code. The resulting system combined the worst of the reservation system, the Bureau of Indian Affairs bureaucracy, the isolation of the tribes on marginal land, the ambivalent educational programs, and official footdragging. The final defeat of the Indians in the West led white journalistic "muckrakers" in turn to exalt the Indian. Literature and

popular entertainments reflected the concern in the themes of dime
novels and wild west shows. At the same time bourgeois Easterners
turned to western travel, conservation movements, and the new-
founded Boy Scouts of America for emancipation from urban life.
From the speeches of President Theodore Roosevelt to the movies
of "Broncho Billy" Anderson, the West and its Indians caught the
imagination of America. Coincidental with the rage for Indian lore,
the movie studios moved westward where the rough golden hills and
pristine sunlight of Southern California stood ready to become background for a thousand "westerns."[47]

In no time the Indian-as-noble-savage, symbolic of a disappearing
rustic America, came with a rush to the screen, coincident with and
perhaps even contributing to the decline of black portrayals. The
Indian films were at least as numerous, perhaps more so, than the
Negro films. The salient difference centered on the presumption
of an ancient Indian culture. White cameramen in the earliest days of
Edison shot *Buck Dance* with ringing fidelity to their subjects, a gesture they never made toward black life, which they saw as an imitation of white culture. The insistence on authenticity cast the Indians
as cultural opposites to whites.

With great success the Indian movies mined the veins of miscegenation, the tragedy of mixed blood, the merit of betraying brothers. Gradually, the good Indian, a domestic version of Kipling's Gunga Din,
emerged as a stereotype. Indians sometimes complained to the Bureau
of Indian Affairs of the growing stress on race war, but to no avail.

In the few years before the Civil War boom Indian movies began
to dominate the screens. One-third of all productions were westerns.
When Carl Laemmle broke with the Motion Picture Patents Company
and founded the studio that later became Universal, his very first film
was *Hiawatha*. D. W. Griffith saw one of his earliest works, *The Red
Man and the Child*, receive praise in the prestigious *New York Dramatic Mirror*. Red Wing, Mona Darkfeather, and other Indians regularly appeared on the screen. By 1912 Bison, Broncho, Domino, and
Kay-Bee, all releasing through Ince, maintained a permanent cadre
of cowboys at Inceville, near Venice, California, complete with a
ranch and an Indian interpreter. Charles Inslee, who had played Indians even before the studios followed the sun from Fort Lee, New
Jersey, regularly received fan mail addressed to "The Lone Indian."
Literary and theatrical tradition had trained up a generation of eager
fans. The cowboy actor William S. Hart was the finest example. His
attitude toward Indians was reverential. Of a childhood encounter he
recalled, "I worshiped the little Indian girl," and of her mother he
wrote, "I cannot call her a squaw." The whole tone of the movement

was moral. They were "women's pictures," brim-full of harried virgins of Victorian literature, with Indians providing both conflict and a contrast to white hypocrisy.[48]

In contrast to their treatment of Negroes, who suffered a slow attrition of power during the cycle of Civil War movies, motion pictures from 1909 onward ennobled Indians into demigods who shimmered in natural virtue that illuminated the effete corruption of "civilization." They were heroic figures whose tragedy was their wistful inability to survive within white culture or to prevail outside it. For the entire history of cinema Indian roles never ranged beyond these clichés.

No amount of white duplicity could alter the historical fact of Indian defeat; therefore when cultures clashed, Indians suffered. No amount of acculturation could bring Indians closer to white ideals. One of the first of the genre to dramatize this was *Call of the Wild*, which opens with a graduate of Carlisle School for Indians falling in love with the daughter of an army officer. When she rejects him, he first kidnaps her, then realizing his drift away from his tribal roots, releases her and symbolically rips off his white clothing. The theme was repeated in Pathe's *Back to the Prairie:* "Disabused and in conflict with the usages of a society for which he was not born, Red Fox returns to the primitive life of his fathers.[49]

The Indian-as-marginal-man rarely survived with his life or his culture. Moviemakers tried to achieve authentic representation of Indian culture on the screen in order to have it die, like Byron, crippled and finally broken against a foreign culture. Griffith's *Broken Doll* exercised all parts of the myth. A white girl and an Indian girl become friends when blanket-Indians come to town one day. The white girl gives the Indian a doll as a token, "the first kindness" in their friendship. The sets testify to Griffith's urge to do justice to Indian life: well-selected exteriors, apparently authentic dress, family and tribal blocking of the players. His town sets, on the other hand, are wooden and stagey, speckled with rootless white idlers. When Indians and whites eventually clash, the chief smashes the doll, symbolically marking the breach. When the Indian child later retrieves it she is starkly alone in a wide shot, as though caught between the cultures. Griffith cuts back and forth from doll to angry warriors, in effect acting out the child's dilemma. The balance is broken when "the child goes to warn her new friends" of an Indian attack. Her shots still place her in isolation, in contrast to the war party's solidarity. As she warns the whites, the next cut is to the broken doll in the center of a low, tight closeup of the Indians riding toward and over it. The audience learns through the doll that the races must remain pure in order to survive. The last shot is on the Indian maid, shattered by her cross-cultural experience, head bowed, then painfully looking up, perhaps lost in prayer before the broken doll who has taught her that love cannot cross racial lines. The ending became a cliché in Indian movies: it was they who must die to prove a point.[50]

Griffith did not invent the model, but his rendering of it clearly revealed the artistic dead end of the genre. Cross-cultural conflict merely provided an excuse for a ritual reenactment of Indian defeat. Assimilationism, because it was socially unlikely, was an excuse for death but not tragedy, like the death of a devoted dog.

Indian life became by definition inferior, rejected alike by Indians, whites, and those who had the clearest opportunity for choice, the halfbreeds. Even Helen Hunt Jackson's fictive cry for reform of Indian policy, *Ramona*, when it became a movie, lost its reformist edge in Griffith's hands and made Indian defeat seem to one reviewer a "natural selection."

Sometimes the Indian hero faced rejection by both worlds. *The Curse of the Red Man* follows an Indian fresh from scholarly and athletic triumphs at Sherman Institute for Indians to his homecoming at which "his tribe ostracizes him." He finds his education "is useless when pitted against the superstitions of his people," drifts off the land, and "meets the curse" of drink. The end comes in a flash of color from cool blue to a stark yellow shot of the Indian, solitary against the light on a rocky desert crag. Griffith's *Iola's Promise*, with Mary Pickford in the title role, places an Indian maid between the white "cut-throats which formed the scum of the old Southwestern desert" and her "savage and turbulent tribe." Finally she makes the "supreme sacrifice," dying in the act of bringing a nugget to a prospector who had jilted her. "If I cannot stay with you, and be one of the cross-heart people," she says, "then I will bring you the little stones with the yellow specks." In *The Arrowmaker's Daughter, Indian Blood, Red Hawk's Sacrifice, An Indian Legend,* and *The Yaqui Cur* Indians warn whites of tribal attacks, die for the cause of white men, or otherwise reject Indian life. In the latter instance the Indian embraces Jesus, the "Big Love Man." Few plots followed that of *The Paleface Brave* into the core of Indian life.[51]

Indians, if they knew of movies, were at a loss as to a response. Most of the pictures favored Indian life; only inference carried the viewer to their patronizing core. Indeed in the late summer of 1914 when a delegation of Chippewas descended upon the White House in protest of Selig's *The Curse of the Red Man*, a trade-paper correspondent replied sharply, pointing out that its character of a drunken, antiheroic graduate of Sherman Institute for Indians was in fact "Willie Boy," the Indian who shot a white man and became prey of half a dozen desert sheriffs. A remake in 1967, *Tell Them Willie Boy is Here*, demonstrated the immutable, stylized icon from which Indians could never deviate. The only differences between 1911 and 1967 were in giving Willie Boy his true name and in admitting the white sheriffs' motivations as fear that the manhunt would spoil William Howard Taft's visit to the West.[52]

By 1914 the motion picture industry yearned for middle-class respectability: nickelodeons tailed off; movie palaces grew in staid neighborhoods; the "trades" shaped producers' opinions away from the "insanity, murder, and self-destruction" that seemed to typify movies; Universal, Adolph Zukor, and others moved to California just as the Italian spectacle *Cabiria* opened in New York in a "legitimate" house complete with a full orchestra.[53] Art, industry, and moneymaking soon combined into a powerful force.

Beginning in 1915 Afro-Americans became the only racial minority capable of mounting a campaign against this force. The social struggle to shape cinema into a democratic art form became theirs. Negroes fell between Indians and immigrants in American racial arrangements —ambivalent, caught between slavery and freedom. Unlike Indians, they had already absorbed American culture; unlike immigrants, they could not expect to be absorbed by it.

Immigrants in the movies fared better than in actual life because moviemakers could not afford to offend potential ticketbuyers and because immigrants (first Irishmen, then Jews) slowly took over the industry. Every stage of moviemaking from production to ballyhoo and exhibition felt the impact of the "new Americans." D. W. Griffith's largest moneymaker of his young career was *The Romance of a Jewess* (1908), a little gem of a picture that played on the tensions between Jew and Gael on their road to becoming Americans. A trade paper complimented Kalem, dubbing it "O'Kalem" for its successful exploitation of Irish themes. Trade reviews often included an estimate of a picture's impact in ethnic "nabes" (neighborhoods), a gesture never offered to blacks and Indians. "Is bound to be an enormous draw wherever Irishmen are found," was a typical guess by *Kinetogram*. Before Jewish migration westward *Photoplay* identified "The Dominant Race: The Irish Who Propel the Production Side of the Photoplay Business." House managers exercised an informal censorship in order to suppress films that might offend their immigrant customers. One of Mack Sennett's first comedies for Keystone, *Cohen at Coney Island*, was recut and patched to accommodate ethnic opinion.

Many early movies simply used already established ethnic designations and dress to create a mood or situation from which a comic incident would unwind. *Alphonse and Gaston Helping Irishman, How the*

Dutch Beat the Irish, Lady Bountiful Visits the Murphys on Washday, and *Happy Hooligan Surprised* all were invocations of popular fiction, cartoon, or vaudeville figures rather than racial types. In *Murphy's Wake* men in gaelic hats and keening women pray over the presumably dead Murphy, who rises from his bier to quaff a flagon. In *Cohen's Advertising Scheme,* a Jewish tailor gives a coat to a passing tramp, only for the viewer to see that the coat advertises a fire sale. The fade-out is on Cohen dancing a jig and rubbing his hands. With many ethnic types, however, pejorative traits were balanced with admirable ones. In the 1906 movie *The Black Hand,* a patently Italian butcher helps apprehend *Mafiosi* kidnappers. As early as 1907 the maturing of the technique that helped destroy black figures on the screen served to preach the ethic of the melting pot and a mutual respect for group differences.[54]

Melodrama possessed immigrants of human emotions never allowed Afro-Americans. Griffith's *The Romance of a Jewess* caught the tension surrounding the decision to marry a *goy.* *In Little Italy* was heavy with stereotyped gestures, wine, and passion, yet it attempted to capture ghetto life. A title card in *The Child of the Ghetto* reads: "Rivington Street: The Strugglers." By depicting the squalor of the city such films became tributes to the fortitude of the immigrants. In *The Story of a Rose* Guido scrimps, brings his wife to America, and after her death, cares for his daughter who is poor, crippled, but happy amid her roses; *The Detectives of the Italian Bureau* are "courageous and honest men of Italian birth . . . rounding up and punishing Italian criminals"; a Jew neatly avoids a German and an Irish flimflam team and collects a reward in *Levi's Lucky;* a Rabbi and his daughter are reunited in *The Jew's Christmas,* in spite of her marriage outside the faith. *Bimberg's Love Affair, For the Wearing of the Green, A Story of Little Italy, The Colleen Bawn,* and others carried the stream along to the eve of the Great War, when American interest in Europe would increase. Here and there an Anglo-American such as Griffith would identify a character as "a black hand dago," but usually the Europeans received sentimental, if patronizing, treatment.

In contrast, environment changed nothing for Bert Williams; in his movie he was *A Natural Born Gambler.* To compare the status of blacks and immigrants on the screen one need only see one of the many movies on the theme of exchange of babies. In Biograph's *Mixed Babies* the Goldsteins, the Fogartys, the Spiggetos, the Schultzes, along with "Mrs. Rastus Johnson and her little Ebenezer," lose their children at a department store nursery, with the humor at the expense of the blacks.[55]

The exceptions to the rule of temperance toward foreigners centered on gypsies, Orientals, and to some degree Mexicans. Films featuring cross-cultural themes involving them and native Americans usually ended unhappily for the non-natives. In *Rescued by Rover*, for instance, a dog saves a boy from gypsy kidnappers, and in *The Gypsy's Warning* death prevents an interracial marriage.[56]

Mexicans, like gypsies, lacked the close-packed unity of the eastern ghettos and took on cinematic traits of inferiority. When they were not merely "greaser" heavies, they chose self-sacrifice for the wellbeing of the *gringos* in their lives. In Griffith's *Greaser's Gauntlet* the Latin hero survives a melange of gypsies and Chinese and, though spurned and falsely accused, rescues the heroine from kidnapping. Broncho Billy Anderson's *The Mexican's Faith* featured a Mexican who molests a girl who "Returns Good for Evil" by rescuing him from lynching. He becomes her devoted servant and in turn rescues her. *Tony the Greaser* saves the cowhands from an attack by Mexican *insurrectes* and dies "surrounded by the respectful cowboys and soothed in last moments by Mary's kind administrations."[57]

Orientals added an ingredient to the racial formula in that they were nonwhite yet, unlike Negroes, came from a well-known culture. The movies reflected this by romanticizing Oriental culture through fatalistic stories placed in stylized settings. Biograph's *The Hero of Liao Yang*, for example, traces a successful Japanese mission against the Russians. But once within the forbidden city of American culture the Oriental reverted to type, either the sacrificial victim or the exotic primitive. He becomes a *Hindoo Fakir* in outrageous garb or a murderer who kills his English master for his estate in *The Mystery of Brayton Court*. Or, as in *The Heathen Chinee and the Sunday School Teachers*, he decadently induces prim matrons to "go native" by smoking opium. The title character of Griffith's *That Chink at Golden Gulch* saves the whites from a bad end by tying up the heavy in his shorn queue, which renders him *declassé* among the Chinese. In the end he leaves the village, comforted with the knowledge that white men had cheered his selfless act.[58]

And so the world's newest medium of expression avoided coming to grips with the central issues of race and group, "the problem of the twentieth century," in the words of W. E. B. DuBois. Instead, the increasingly middle class audience preferred easily accepted melodrama and slapstick essays into racial tension. Because certain dramatic racial conflicts such as those involving the insular gypsies appeared not to lend themselves to becoming allegories for American social conflict, they passed into disuse. After the sentimentalizing of the immigrant and of the Indian experience only Afro-Americans were left as a possible artistic source. And yet as moviemaking moved westward the probability that segregated blacks would make a contribution was further reduced.

Not until 1915 would a black voice speak effectively to the question of the social impact of movies, and for many years it would remain more a political than an aesthetic voice. The trade paper *Motion Picture News* praised Lester Walton's efforts to rally his black readers against racist movies. He had needled them by contrasting their reactions to those of the Irish and the Jews who had by their political pressure driven the "stage Irishman" and the "stage Jew" from American theatres. In the case of Negroes, he thought, there was even more urgency for change because whites knew enough of European life to ignore ethnic types, whereas they knew nothing of Afro-American life except "the disgraceful antics . . . of white actors under cork."[59] But at that moment he was asking too much of a people marked by bondage, recently escaped from a hostile South, and scattered through still small ghettos. The occasion for raising black consciousness would be the release of Griffith's *The Birth of a Nation*, at once a major stride for cinema and a sacrifice of black humanity to the cause of racism.

Chapter Two

THE YEAR OF
THE BIRTH OF A NATION

In the spring of 1915 the small New York office of the NAACP received a wire calling attention to the release of D. W. Griffith's new and spectacular movie entitled *The Clansman*. Having had its première on the West Coast, it would soon make its way through Washington and thence to New York, taking on the new title of *The Birth of a Nation*. West Coast NAACP was deeply worried, and New York Negroes soon saw why.

The Birth of a Nation departed from the short vignettes of former years and in a single stroke synthesized all of the devices and advances developed in the first generation of cinema. Like many earlier films it came from a literary source, but it also profited from close cooperation between its original author, a screenwriter, and Griffith. Although not among the first films shot in California, it was the first to exploit the rich variety of the western landscape. While scores of little movies had retold the epic of the Civil War, only *The Birth of a Nation* reached a scale that gave it larger meaning commensurate with the fifty-year anniversary of the Civil War.

But the most important new stroke came from the brush of the press agent. *The Birth of a Nation* was dressed in the trappings of celebrity. Seats at the Liberty Theatre on Forty-second Street sold for two dollars. A forty-piece orchestra supported the film, which ran two or three hours longer than the average movie. Leading Americans in politics, religion, and philanthropy testified to its power, artistry, and historical accuracy. President Woodrow Wilson, a professional scholar and historian before his entry into politics, praised its fidelity to the sad days of Civil War and Reconstruction. George Foster Peabody, a philanthropist who had given much to Negro causes, gave it his reluctant endorsement, a position in which he was joined by numerous clergymen. Their testimony appeared in metropolitan newspapers in film advertisements far larger than usual.

Blacks, though, saw no art; they saw the retelling of Reconstruction history as a Gothic horror tale haunted by black brutes. The movie appeared as black status had deteriorated. Lynching persisted in the rural South as life in Yankee cities worsened. Black sharecroppers remained trapped while black migrants wasted in the cold daily round of poverty. Republicans abandoned their black clients even as Wilson brought Southern Democrats into his coalition. Even the reforms of the urban progressives seemed to be for whites only. Despite the Negro's rising wealth and literacy and the emergence of black reformers, the Wilson years seemed to celebrate racial discrimination, residential segregation, closed ballot boxes, and Jim Crow accommodations. As conditions worsened, blacks struggled among themselves, dissipating protest that might better have been directed at white institutions.

Yet black racial consciousness had sharpened. Not only did Northerners challenge the leadership of Booker T. Washington; they became increasingly aware of the power of direct action. Now a black élite led an urban mass. For example, as early as 1900 the all-black Citizens' Protective League emerged from the élite group as a response to white riots against the blacks along Eighth Avenue in New York. With the founding of W. E. B. DuBois's Niagara Movement, William Monroe Trotter's New England Suffrage League, and later national bodies such as the NAACP, a national web of black organizations took shape.

Through the medium of the black press a complementary black aesthetic began to take form. At first negative, merely crying "Hooray!" at the news of the folding of an American blackface show in London or crowing when a black such as the Reverend A. J. Carey was seated on the Chicago censor board to screen movies for racist themes, the movement grew positive. The New York Suffrage League began offering a prize for a best scenario. Columnists such as Lester Walton of the *Age*, who enjoyed exposing blacks who participated in racist movies, urged Negroes to make motion pictures of their cultural events. Walton spread the word of Carey's work to New York, praising him for uncovering a bit of racist titling in which exhibitors called the same picture *One Large Evening* in the ghetto and *A Night in Coontown* in white houses. The most famous black school, Washington's Tuskegee Institute, circulated a promotional movie. And most important of all, 30,000 spectators at the New York State Fair watched a black pageant,

"The Star of Ethiopia," which celebrated black achievement on the fiftieth anniversary of emancipation.[1]

Too late to affect the content of *The Birth of a Nation* or any other movie, the growing racial consciousness at least provided the platform to challenge the monopoly that white filmmakers enjoyed. Even before the shock of the film's release there were stories of all-black film companies and their occasional productions.[2] No longer would blacks be silent while white men in black masks paraded across movie screens. Their newspapers thenceforward raged whenever white moviemakers flirted with racism. Impatient intellectuals urged protest, suggested forming Negro film companies, went against the liberal tide and demanded censorship of racial slanders. Their outrage fused with that of the young NAACP, which began a half-century career of lobbying in Hollywood studios.

Until the release of *The Birth of a Nation* the races never confronted each other on equal terms, the rulers versus the aggrieved. The whites were like the two salty veterans of the Java trade in *The Sultan's Dagger*. As they search for the filigreed kris of Dipa Negra one of them wonders about the natives' hostility. His companion replies:

> They're all like that toward whites. Blest if I can see why. The natives have never been so well off as since the Dutch took hold of things two hundred years ago, but they hate white skins in spite of the fat years that go with them. They're harmless, but hostile as a sheathed dagger.[3]

Griffith caught the crest of the Civil War wave just before it broke. His timing was perfect: Westerns and other popular genres lapsed into a round of "quickies" and formulas after their first flourish. Even though studios ground them out so rapidly that "the promiscuous carrying-off of little girls by Indians is assuming the proportions of a national calamity," exhibitors and trade papers "noticed no feverish enthusiasm" and decided audiences "were tired of them."[4] The way was clear for the splash to be made by the release of *The Birth of a Nation*.

The picture should have been little different from dozens of movies that preached old verities. But Griffith had slowly expanded his control over the medium with here a wide shot of a horizon in *Ramona*, there a well-composed crowd sequence in *The Battle*, an occasional closeup, a narrative use of an "iris," a slow, intuitive accretion of cinematic devices.

Coincidentally, Frank Woods, a film critic and a writer for Biograph, had written a draft of a script from Thomas Dixon's unsuccessful dramatization of his novel *The Clansman*, a nightmare of interracial brutality, rape, and castigation. Pacifism, sectional harmony, racial

In contrast to Griffith's sentimentality, Thomas Dixon's racial ideology took a more violent form. (Mezzotint from Thomas Dixon, *The Clansman* [New York, 1907 ed.], facing p. 232)

paternalism, rural virtues, all of the larger American values received a rude twist from Woods's script.[5]

At its opening as a stage drama in 1906 Dixon himself gave an intermission speech in which he explained his hopes for *The Clansman:*

> My object is to teach the north, the young north, what it has never known—the awful suffering of the white man during the dreadful reconstruction period. I believe that Almighty God anointed the white men of the south by their suffering during that time . . . to demonstrate to the world that the white man must and shall be supreme.[6]

The play had received good notices and enthusiastic audiences during its Southern run. But several Southern dissenters attacked it. A prominent minister labeled it a "disgrace" and pleaded "for God's sake, the negro's sake, and our sake, give the negro a rest from abuse." The Governor of Alabama called it a "nightmare" and a flogging of a dead horse. Newspaper critics granted its impact on audiences but condemned it as a moneygrubber and a "riot breeder." One reviewer noticed its split personality, which spouted love and race hatred from the same platform, and concluded that Dixon, who "never was well balanced," had "gone crazy."[7]

Dixon's blatant racism was itself not unusual. What struck many Afro-Americans was the casual way it was accepted by Northerners as it made its way out of the South into the Middle West and eventually to New York. Dixon, proud of his creation, later peddled it around the motion picture companies, one of which, Kinemacolor-Clansman Corporation, folded before he could use the scenario which Frank Woods had written for him.

It was Woods who arranged a meeting between Griffith, who had read *The Clansman*, the angels, and Dixon in Harry and Roy Aitken's West Seventy-fifth Street apartment in New York. Estimates vary, but Dixon sold his idea for between five and ten thousand dollars and a royalty. Griffith agreed to a collaboration, and the two of them worked in Mutual's loft in Union Square after Griffith's shooting day ended.

Shortly after the Christmas holidays of 1913 they left for the West Coast.[8] Several Southerners in the company contributed to the ambience. Henry B. Walthall, a Virginian who played "the little colonel," was a true believer in the Southern faith. Lillian Gish, Griffith's favorite actress at the time, had "pity and understanding" for the South and would have said nothing to mar the happy days. Those like Miriam Cooper, who thought the Southern mood a mite silly, bit their tongues and went to work. Among the blacks Madame Sul-te-Wan sat closest to Griffith, both personally and professionally. A fellow-Kentuckian, she admired and loved Griffith, who responded by promoting her from a menial to an actress.[9]

They worked through the summer and into the fall of 1914, raising capital as the need arose, and finished shooting in October. Griffith was transformed by the task, perhaps catching some of Dixon's revivalist fervor. Only his cameraman, Billy Bitzer, was hesitant. To him, "It was just another sausage after all," and besides, "How would you show it in the South?"[10]

The West Coast atmosphere reinforced Griffith's and Dixon's traditional Southern values. Remote from urban life, they romanticized the Old South, while the many California blacks used in the militia and crowd sequences, grateful for an opportunity to work, did nothing to break the spell.

The replication of Dixie extended even to the segregated barracks in which the black extras lived. Looking on approvingly were the Civil War veterans who lazed on the knolls between the "takes" in which they were riders. Jimmie Smith, a cutter from Alabama, told tales of an election in 1868 when whites stayed away to prevent "a war of the races" while blacks marched in battalions to the polls to the tune of crackling rifles and whistling stray shots. Griffith looked for actors who were "children of the South" and whose "faces are full of trust and innocence and beauty." Among them were a descendant of Charles Carroll of Carrollton, a son of a Confederate general, and others. Dixon returned the favor by announcing he would allow only a son of the South to film his work. The South was the phoenix rising from the ashes of defeat to make "a better and more wonderful victory in the building up of a clean, tolerant and beautiful new world." The real enemy, Griffith thought, was the "intolerance that was not satisfied till we had poured the best and most beautiful blood of our entire altar before his feet."[11]

The land itself contributed to the setting. Far out in the San Fernando Valley, stretching from the Universal lot across from the Provenencia Rancho, southwestward to Cahuenga Pass, into Orange County toward Fullerton and Whittier, northward to Ojai in Ventura County, where it was easier to rent horses, made scarce by European war, and finally to Calexico, where the company shot footage of cotton fields after a rattling midnight train ride, the company worked in pastoral isolation.[12]

After a winter of cutting and editing, the final product with its benign Southern agrarianism, sentimental piety, and easy racial paternalism seemed far less racist than Dixon's novel. A mulatto leader of some power in the film was crafted from a "big buck nigger" in the novel. The carpetbag governor, nameless in the movie, was named William Pitt Shrimp by Dixon. A sexual assault seemed less vicious in the film. The film was often paternalistic where the novel had been racist.[13]

In the final print the titles piously open on a plea for freedom of speech so as "to show the dark side of wrong, that we may illuminate the bright side of virtue," and a jeremiad against war. The opening shot reveals real Negroes, not blackfaced actors, brought in the bondage which "planted the first seed of disunion." The other side of the institution of slavery is somehow made to be seen as stern Abolitionists currying the favor of blacks. Early in the film the Stonemans of the North and the Camerons of the South are seen as friends across sectional lines, basking in a life that "runs in a quaintly way that is to be no more." Black kids frolic under the eyes of benevolent whites and kindly darkies.

Before the Civil War, upon the first visit of Austin Stoneman to Piedmont, house servants furtively peer from back rooms, fearing Yankees; Negroes in long shots work in cotton fields, interrupting their twelve-hour day only for their two-hour dinner break; in town other blacks caper and frolic for the visitors. When war flares and Southerners march, Negro slaves cheer them on—a scene rehearsed in *The Battle*. The horror of the race war spurred by the two demons of slavery and abolition is first seen as black troops raid the streets of Piedmont under the orders of their white captains. A title reminds the audience that it was in South Carolina that the first black troops entered the war, one of many historical footnotes that lend credibility to the movie. An ominous black trooper stands on a porch while white women cower in the cellar below and a loyal mammy throws water on a fire set by the raiders—the implication is clear: good Negroes may save the day from bad niggers.

Back in Washington the conspiratorial mulatto housekeeper of Austin Stoneham, the fictional rendering of Congressman Thaddeus Stevens, is curt and rude to Senator Charles Sumner, her presumed benefactor. In a bit of type-casting, she tears her dress and licks her hand in an erotic gesture; Stoneman, entering and touching her bared shoulder, is treated to a teasing withdrawal. Thus another black heavy is added to the plot: the ambitious mulatto trying to rise above her place.

When Lincoln appears it is as the benefactor of good Negroes. Conversely, when his policies differ from the position of the moviemakers he is made to seem the reluctant dupe of insidious Cabinet ministers who fairly snatch the Emancipation Proclamation from his hesitant hand, in order "to enforce the rule of the coming nation over the individual states."

With the beginning of Reconstruction Stoneman argues with Lincoln against a policy of clemency for the defeated South. But under Lincoln the South happily begins rebuilding under the old social system. Eager darkies pick up their tools with a will while the best Southern women open up their mansions as boarding houses.

Only the gentle hand of Lincoln stays the dark powers standing nameless in the wings. Thus after his authentically staged assassination, offered as another tribute to the authors' veracity, good Southerners mourn, "Our best friend is gone," while Stoneman's mulatto housekeeper grasps his arm and whispers fiendishly, "You are now the greatest power in America."

Many theatres would put an intermission at this point—on the brink of the coup by the forces of misrule. Nestling down into their seats for the second part, audiences read a caveat against anticipated charges of racism: "This is an historical representation of the Civil War and Reconstruction Period, and is not meant to reflect on any race or people of today." Trailing after this invocation comes a string of impressive footnotes from Woodrow Wilson's history of the United States. "Adventurers swarmed," they claimed, as enemies of both races arrived in the South "to cozen, beguile, and use, the negroes." Blacks quickly took office, knowing nothing of authority but "its insolences." Congress toppled Southern civilization in a callous effort to *"put the white South under the heel of the black South."* Power in Washington shifted to an uncrowned king residing in a "strange house on Capitol Hill" presided over by a mulatto mistress, while white men, roused by self-preservation, formed "a great KuKluxKlan, a veritable empire of the South." The core of the message spreads over six consecutive titles uninterrupted by a single shot.

Blacks stream in and out of the corridors. One of them, Silas Lynch, soon to be Lieutenant Governor in Piedmont, bows to Stoneman, who ostentatiously intones, "Don't scrape to me. You are the equal of any man here." The revolution is confirmed as the old Abolitionist Sumner is forced to make social obeisances to the gloating mulatto mistress. Sumner pleads for a more temperate policy, but Stoneman insists on making Lynch the peer of Southern whites by having him assume power over the South. "Sowing the wind," the title announces. Beneath the surface level of politics smoulders the real question, revealed as Lynch leers at Elsie, Stoneman's young daughter.

In the South Carolina Legislature black actors portray a dissolute, riotous band of politicos: barefooted, drinking in the chamber, gotten up in garish clothes. In the galleries stand the silent, intimidated whites, helpless before the cheers of the black majority. Lynch, the black gallery, and the legislators join in the jubilation at the passage of a law "providing for" racial intermarriage.

Next, on the personal scale, we see Lynch making overtures to Elsie Stoneman; then we cut to Cameron watching white children scare black children by hiding under sheets. The title fairly cries out: "The inspiration," and Cameron forms the KKK, ostensibly to throttle black anarchy.

The incident that binds the themes together is what black militants called "the Gus chase." Gus, "a renegade Negro," approaches Flora Cameron, "the little sister," as she goes to the spring. As she frolics through a glade there are cuts to squirrels framed in an iris. Thus the Negro becomes a predator about to pounce upon a harmless animal. Indeed, as the shortened shots increase the tension his posture lowers into an atavistic skulk. He quickly proposes marriage, supports his suit by mentioning his promotion to captain, and when she starts, assures her that he will do no harm. But her rebuff and flight will allow no audience to consider it anything less than a rape. At the climax she leaps over a cliff to her death, while Gus scuttles like a land-crab over the rock.

Meanwhile, coarse, jocular town Negroes celebrate the black party's

The Birth of a Nation's mulatto villains who, according to the producers, used the disorders of Reconstruction to climb above their station, outraged blacks but aided the film's box office success. Here Silas Lynch (George Siegmann) covets Elsie Stoneman (Lillian Gish) as a sexual symbol of his new arrogant power (© Epoch). (Academy of Motion Picture Arts and Sciences)

triumph; Lynch persuades black yeomen to throw down their tools; overdressed town hangers-on dance the streets; idlers cadge free supplies; and black soldiers push the Camerons off the sidewalks. Even the urge to power is made to seem an African fault: "Lynch [is] a traitor to his white patron, and a greater traitor to his own people." Grinning blacks tote picket placards through the streets. Some signs like "40 Acres and a Mule," having obvious historical roots, are juxtaposed to fanciful legends such as "Equality Equal Rights Equal Politics Equal Marriage."

The cause of this malaise blows on the winds from the North. The Freedmen's Bureau is "The charity of a generous North misused to delude the ignorant." And a faithful black mammy confirms the point when she speaks to a Northern Negro: "Yo' northern low down black trash, don't try no airs on me!" kicking him in the pants for punctuation.

Amidst the travail of "outrages," denials of the ballot to dignified old Southerners, biased Negro juries, insolent black soldiers, and a

The corrupt alliance of carpetbagger and Black-and-Tan regimes disfranchised the old planter class, Griffith argued, thus justifying the rise of the Ku Klux Klan. But organized Negroes were quick to point out willful distortions, such as placing in the same frame historical facsimiles like the sign expressing black hopes for "forty acres and a mule" beside such patent frauds as a placard demanding "equal marriage" (© Epoch.) (Academy of Motion Picture Arts and Sciences)

crescendo of disorder, only a few verities prevail: old faithful blacks, staunch Southern women, and the heroism of the Klan. The ritual of the Klan weds the clans of old Scotland to the Southern cause by quenching a fiery cross in a Confederate flag soaked in the blood of the dead Cameron.

The climax builds with rapid cutting from the orgiastic shots of blacks to the steady rise of Klan strength. Finally the Klan "tries" and convicts Gus of the rape and executes him, dumping his body on Lynch's porch while spreading the word abroad that they will "disarm the blacks." But Lynch raids the Cameron house, finds Klan robes, and arrests the old patriarch of the family. The blacks spit upon him as he is paraded before them in the streets. In a comic interlude it is the old mammy and her husband who pull off his rescue and flee to an old house in which two Yankee veterans eke out a meagre life.

Meanwhile Lynch, "drunk with wine and power," orders preparations for a "forced marriage" to Elsie. Finally the audience may see the double standard of Stoneman. Black power is acceptable to him in the South, but when one of his Negro henchmen courts his daughter his Anglo-Saxon heritage will permit no assent. By then the whites, helpless behind their shutters, their town in the hands of the "crazed negroes," can be saved only by the Klan.

As the shots grow shorter the tempo picks up. The tiny hovel of the Yankee veterans is surrounded by black troops; Elsie is bound and gagged in preparation for her marriage; Stoneman faints; the defenders of the hut prepare to bash in the skulls of their women with clubbed pistols rather than submit them to the Negroes.

Then the Klan rides into town, frees Elsie, and at the last possible moment rescues the little band. The next cut is to blacks throwing down their weapons and scurrying away.

As though to provide a reason for this orgy of violence, terror, racism, and paranoid fantasies of white sexual inadequacy, the next sequence slowly fades into a monstrous allegorical figure of Mars who dissolves to "The Prince of Peace." Through a split screen the audience may see Ben Cameron and Elsie reunited on a rise at the edge of the ocean. The coda at once embraces pacifism, Christianity, Klan terrorism, and the virtues of the white race in a fasces of love and beauty.[14]

The foregoing is not a fair recapitulation of *The Birth of a Nation* because it focuses on what Negroes saw at the expense of what critics saw. Audiences were swept along by broad shots of wheeling cavalry ranks, the puffs of field pieces firing into the advancing lines of infantrymen, vignettes of heroism such as that of the Southern officer who reaches the Union earthworks despite the firepower that has withered his ranks and futilely spikes a six-pounder with his flagstaff, and depictions of the foragers and skirmishers who roamed the countryside, burning and spoiling. The effect was not created merely from historically correct shots but through the blare of the orchestra, the pacing of the narrative, the easing from the grand design into the human scale, the clear characters set off from each other by costume, "business," and plausible motivations. The poet Vachel Lindsay found it a "picture of crowd splendor" in which the "Ku Klux Klan dashes down the road as powerfully as Niagara pours over the cliff" with "mobs splendidly handled, tossing wildly and rhythmically like the sea."

Unfortunately, thought Lindsay, Griffith gave his art to retailing "the Reverend Thomas Dixon's poisonous hatred of the Negro," rather

than the works of less wrathful Southerners such as Joel Chandler
Harris, Harry Stillwell Edwards, George W. Cable, Thomas Nelson
Page, or Mark Twain.[15] And that is what blacks saw. They would have
none of the compelling beauty, rich narrative form, painterly composition, or complex visual imagery. For them it was a rough and cruel
racist slander upon Afro-Americans during Reconstruction, and therefore they owed nothing to the tradition of opposing censorship.

On February 8, 1915 the completed film opened at J. R. Clune's
Auditorium in Los Angeles, where it ran throughout the year. In
a few days the company sent another print to New York for a preview. There, with a few dozen witnesses scattered through a dank,
empty building, Dixon saw it for the first time. Harry Aitken and
Theodore Mitchell, a candidate for press agent, were also present.
Dixon crept up to the empty balcony from which he would escape if
it proved a flop. But then the music came up and he was swept along.
Afterward an uproar greeted his descent to the lobby. It was then, he
remembered, that he shouted across to Griffith that its tame title should
be changed to *The Birth of a Nation*.[16]

The principals knew they had an exciting motion picture, and they
divided forces to exploit the film. Griffith, set up his own independent
company to handle his royalties. Dixon tried to disarm impending criticism by eliciting endorsements from prominent Americans. The Aitkens set about jacking up prices and promoting its New York opening
at the Liberty Theatre, where Dixon's play had run ten years earlier.

Dixon wangled an interview with Woodrow Wilson in the White
House on the strength of their days as graduate students together at
Johns Hopkins University, and persuaded the President to screen the
movie in the White House on February 18 as an example of a new
communications medium. At the end Wilson intoned: "It is like writing history with lightning. And my only regret is that it is all so terribly
true." Early the next morning Dixon cadged another interview from
his fellow North Carolinian, Secretary of the Navy Josephus Daniels,
as a prelude to meeting the crabby Louisianian Chief Justice Edward D.
White, who grudgingly consented to a screening only after Dixon told
him it was about the Klan. Griffith meanwhile had booked the ballroom
of the Raleigh Hotel and invited a number of congressmen.[17]

Even before the film reached New York the NAACP secretary,
May Childs Nerney, began sending out pamphlets by the thousand
to the smallest of towns, compiling a list of pending state censor bills,
and dogging the exhibitor for preview tickets. She reminded members
that as a drama *The Clansman* had stirred riots in Philadelphia and
offered that 1906 event as a legal basis for blocking the openings.[18]

Thus, if Dixon's motive had been to develop the race consciousness of the white North, he failed miserably. Instead, the two most enduring by-products of *The Birth of a Nation* would be, first, a stimulation to the cinema as an art form, and second, a heightening of black awareness and identity that far outstripped Dixon's wildest hopes for white people.

Early in February, less than a month before the announced New York opening, blackfolk began a nationwide campaign to rally brothers and allies against the movie that few eyes had ever seen. Days ahead of the New York première black Angelenos 30,000 strong sounded the call. Both the Los Angeles and the San Francisco branches of the NAACP unsuccessfully brought pressure upon their city fathers, eliciting from the black *California Eagle* the wishful but premature page-one banner: "CITY COUNCIL BY UNANIMOUS VOTE PASS RESOLUTION WHICH WILL BAR THE MOVING PICTURES OF THE CLANSMAN SHOWING IN THIS CITY."[19] Through the spring the paper kept up a barrage of attacks on Griffith's version of Reconstruction, urged and praised excisions of the film made by the San Francisco municipal censor, and encouraged the delegation of a Negro Welfare League that called upon the mayor of Los Angeles. By March the West Coast secretary understood the nature of the enemy and the reason blacks would probably lose their fight. It was "a masterpiece," he wrote, "and, from an artistic point of view, the finest thing of its kind I have ever witnessed," a fact liberal whites could not forget as their adherence to principles of free speech weakened their solidarity with Negroes.[20]

Meanwhile, the Epoch Corporation, which was to be distributor, mounted an unprecedented advertising campaign that magnified the impact of the movie. Advance sales, reserved seats, an orchestral accompaniment, monster billboards of nightriders in Times Square, posters scattered through suburban train stations, special trains from Connecticut and New Jersey, robed horsemen riding the streets— all the arts of ballyhoo and publicity were brought to bear on a single movie.[21]

At first the NAACP could expect no help from whites. Their generally held view of the excesses of Reconstruction did not differ from Griffith's. Besides, in intellectual circles cinema was beginning to take on serious aesthetic overtones that precluded the use of censorship as a tactic. Even as *The Birth of a Nation* entered its opening run German emigré Hugo Munsterberg attempted to shape a grand theory combining psychological perception and aesthetics in his *Photoplay: A Psychological Study* (New York, 1916). From a poetic point of view poet Vachel Lindsay took *The Birth of a Nation* itself as a model for his cinema theories. "Art by lightning flash," he called it. Editing produced a kind of visual music with its own rhythm and logic. Cutting

LIBERTY THEATRE 42d Street, West of Broadway

EVENINGS at 8:45 SHARP. 25c, 50c, 75c and $1. Loge Seats, $2.
SATURDAY MATINEE, 2:15 SHARP. 25c, 50c, 75c and $1. Loge Seats, $2.
OTHER MATINEES at 2:15 SHARP. 25c and 50c. Loge Seats, $1.

ALL SEATS RESERVED

HOUSE REMODELED ACCORDING TO SCIENTIFIC ADJUSTMENT OF FOCAL REQUIREMENTS

BEGINNING WEDNESDAY NIGHT

MARCH 3d

AND TWICE DAILY THEREAFTER INCL. SUNDAYS

The Mightiest Spectacle Ever Produced!

D. W. GRIFFITH'S Picture Production which will Startle the World!

A RED BLOODED TALE OF TRUE AMERICAN SPIRIT

LOVE & ROMANCE MIDST HISTORIC SCENES.

COMEDY WHICH RELIEVES THE THRILL OF ADVENTURE

GRIPPING HEART INTEREST AND SOUL STIRRING EMOTIONS.

See This Masterpiece

TOO GREAT FOR COMPARISONS.

CONCEIVED, INSPIRED AND CREATED IN AMERICA.

THE EXPRESSION OF GENIUS IN A NEW REALM OF ART.

A COMPOSITION OF NATIONAL FIGURES WITH THE UNIVERSE AS ITS BACKGROUND

Rich in Historical Value

THE MOST REALISTIC AND STUPENDOUS VIEW OF STIRRING EVENTS IN THE DEVELOPMENT OF OUR COUNTRY.

FOUNDED ON THOMAS DIXON'S FAMOUS NOVEL AND PLAY

THE CLANSMAN

SYMPHONY ORCHESTRA OF 40

☞ SEATS NOW

18,000 PEOPLE
3,000 HORSES
8 MONTHS
IN THE MAKING
COST
$500,000.00

The advertising campaign for *The Birth of a Nation* gave as much pause to black leaders as its strong racial theme.

from closeups to crowd scenes made for "panoramic drama." "Thus the white leader . . . enters not as an individual, but as . . . the whole Anglo-Saxon Niagara." Audiences, he thought, became mobs "for or against the Reverend Thomas Dixon's poisonous hatred of the Negro." And yet he thought the film "a wonder in its Griffith sections."[22] Unfortunately for blacks, on the one hand, few viewers could distinguish between Griffith's art and Dixon's ax-grinding; while on the other, few liberals could reject constitutional guarantees of freedom of speech by advocating censorship of racism. The result for the NAACP was a climate in which they could expect little success.

Politically, too, the tide ran against the NAACP. The federal government had once been on the verge of plunging into film censorship, but except for the racially-motivated strictures on the importation of boxing films there were no statutes regulating content. But on the state level a few investigations connected movies—specifically, nickelodeons —with urban vice and led to state censor boards in New York, Kansas, Maryland, Ohio, and a number of municipalities. But most film censorship fell under the purview of the National Board of Censorship of Motion Pictures, later called the National Board of Review, a private body created by producers who hoped to give movies respectability as family entertainment and to overcome the reputation of nickelodeons as vice dens. Even though it was private, the board was admired by public censors because it was said that most exhibitors abided by its decisions. The veteran, urban-progressive Frederic C. Howe was the chairman of the board. He had given testimony before the House Committee on Education and helped sway government away from public censorship.

As March 3, the New York première approached, blacks stood alone, with no connections in critical circles, no friends amongst the ascendant Democrats, the device of censorship lost to them, and with only the Mayor's office open to appeal. Even then, Epoch's case was served by the President's endorsement of the film, which Dixon brought from the Washington screening. Worse yet for blacks, the screening at the National Board of Review on February 20 was punctuated by wild applause. With little expectation of opposition, Epoch advertised the opening.[23]

Heartened by a few cuts won on the West Coast, the NAACP went to work in the few days before the première. Through the *New York Age* and the NAACP house organ, the *Crisis*, they demanded similar cuts in the New York print, resting their case on stories of race riots in Philadelphia on the occasion of the stage production of *The Clansman*, on the rumor that the Board had split its first vote to approve the picture with chairman Howe dissenting, and on hearsay that leering

Negro closeups survived. When the cumbersome board of 125 agreed to a few deletions, the NAACP pressed on for a total elimination of the latter half and demanded that Negroes screen the picture.

As the première approached, the Negroes learned what they had suspected all along: the motion picture business was a closed lily-white preserve from which they could expect nothing. The liberal Howe grudgingly allowed the NAACP two of a promised ten tickets to a March 1 screening, with the proviso that whites use them. The Negroes pressed against the barriers by attempting to squeeze two light-skinned Negroes into the segregated preview. The board retreated and stopped answering mail just as the Negroes brought suit to enjoin Epoch from opening. The board relented, admitted that earlier segregation had been unofficial, and offered to allow three white members of the NAACP—Jacob Schiff, Jane Addams, and Lillian Wald—to see the picture.[24]

After the preview the NAACP intensified its polemics against the film's racism, filed criminal proceedings against Griffith and the Aitkens, circularized the movie industry with the case against Epoch, and demanded the local commissioner of licenses stop the film as a nuisance. Intimidated, the board consented to another review and induced Epoch to accept two more cuts. Oswald Garrison Villard, one of the founders of the NAACP, pressed on by refusing advertising for the picture in his New York *Post* and by printing Jane Addams's caustic review in which she saw the movie as "a gathering [of] the most vicious and grotesque individuals he [Griffith] could find among the colored people, and showing them as representatives of the . . . entire race." She, like Wilson, had mistaken verisimilitude for reality.[25]

The NAACP not only had stalled Epoch's drive to get the board's seal on its picture but had succeeded in rallying black and liberal opinion all over America in a phalanx that would have been impossible without the movie as a *cause célèbre*. On the local scene they tried to bait the police into shutting it down. Nationally, they solicited help from the journalist Ray Stannard Baker, the producer Lewis Selznick, and other famous Americans. Then they sent copies of Francis Hackett's stinging review in the *New Republic* to 500 newspapers, marking the first time either side used a critic's aesthetic standards.[26]

After the board gave its approval the NAACP still nagged at them for names and addresses of the members and pressed Mayor John Purroy Mitchel of New York to stop the film in the interest of "public decency." They brought delegations of clubs and churches to the City Hall where the Mayor, fearing a riot, refused them a license to parade. W. E. B. DuBois of the *Crisis*, Fred Moore of the *Age*, Rabbi Stephen A. Wise, Villard, and other NAACP members, delegates from the Negro and white clergy, and the Urban League overflowed into the outer halls of the Mayor's office. Mitchel denied he held statutory power over the film and droned through a recitation of excisions and riot warnings that had already been made, thus disarming the delegates, who then withdrew.[27]

The Mayor's statement split black protestors into two groups—those who wished to quiet down the dispute for fear of boosting ticket sales and those who wished to press the fight. The militants extended outward from NAACP circles to Lester Walton of the *Age*, who not only demanded black effort but hinted darkly that the greed and racism of moviemakers would have been easily thwarted if the Jews and Irish had been the maligned. On the other side of the deep fissure was the "Tuskegee machine," Booker T. Washington's accommodationist coterie who had reached the Mayor ahead of the NAACP through the efforts of Charles W. Anderson, a recently dismissed federal officeholder. Often antagonistic, but at times cooperative with Northern liberals, the Tuskegee group chose this occasion to embarrass "the Vesey Street crowd"—Anderson's epithet for the NAACP—and "take the wind out of their sails" by demonstrating Washington's influence with powerful white men. So, not only did the picture enjoy its première, but blacks suffered the internal recriminations that often marred their efforts to unify against racism.[28]

But the deepest fissure cleaved black from white. Whites flocked to the Liberty Theatre. Reviewers, even the most sensitive, accepted the logic of the picture, believing that its reverential treatment of the tragedy of the South could not be racist because Griffith depicted both good and bad Negroes. Predictably, many white Southerners agreed with a preacher who praised Griffith's version of "ten years of hell" at the hands of "venomous half-breeds" and "hordes of ignorant blacks." Negroes were astonished, however, at the chorus of Northern liberal whites who joined in. Friends of the Negro such as philanthropist George Foster Peabody, Governor of California Hiram Johnson, critic Burns Mantle, explorer Richard Harding Davis, novelist Booth Tarkington, and social reformer Dorothea Dix accepted the movie as an accurate rendering of freedmen who mistook "license for liberty." To notice, as did S. S. Frissell, a friend of the NAACP, that "in the worst parts of it the negro is painted no worse than a bad white man" was to miss the central point that blacks were "bad" because they were black. Moreover, for every resolute white such as Jane Addams, Mary White Ovington, and Florence Kelley of the NAACP, dozens of others thought the cause more futile than right. At the very beginning of the fight the NAACP had abandoned an effort to persuade financier Otto Kahn, whose brother, Felix, owned a piece of Mutual Film Company, the producer of *The Birth of a Nation*, to change parts of the film. Many other whites were outflanked by their own feelings for constitutional guarantees that militated against censorship. The NAACP's tactic of rallying liberal white Southerners resident in the North failed miserably. Lester Walton grew impatient with the critic of the *Chicago Tribune*, who claimed *The Birth of a Nation* as the greatest movie ever made. Walton granted, "While this may be true, the fact remains that the photoplay is vicious, untrue, unjust, and has been primarily produced to cause race friction in Northern cities."[29]

For blacks the endless niceties of opinion seemed to press their white friends into the same frame with their white enemies. Thomas Dixon punctiliously insisted that he hated not blacks but rather "the pollution of our race by the infusion of Negro blood," an historically "unassailable" position that Lincoln himself would have admired. Besides, he argued, if violence tinged his work, it had at least "put the fear of God into the heart of every evil doer." He claimed, "The only objectors to it so far are a Negro Society [the NAACP] which advises its members to arm themselves and fight the whites and to make 'mongrel marriages.' "[30]

Toward the end of March the NAACP's New York campaign ground to a halt. But by April the NAACP had made its presence felt. Three stages marked its progress: political organization, a position on the sticky subject of censorship, and a clearer aesthetic ideal. "Nothing has so helped to unloosen the energy and to stimulate the cooperative support of the colored people of this country as this attack on their character and place in history," said an NAACP report to the members. The same writer also reached a black position on censorship. "All forms of censorship are dangerous to the free expression of art," he granted, but wherever a censor board existed, "it was our right and our duty to see that this body acted with fairness and justice."[31] The third stage, the actual attempt to create a black cinema achievement, would await the defeat of the campaign against *The Birth of a Nation*.

For the moment the NAACP turned its attention to Boston, where *The Birth of a Nation* would open a second front. A few cuts in the film in New York had whetted the appetites of blacks for another fight. The *Amsterdam News* set the mood of the Boston struggle with a headline: "ORGANIZE! ORGANIZE! ORGANIZE!"[32] What happened in Boston would inspire similar drives throughout the year, indeed, for years to come. Branches all over the country not only contributed but also added their support to contests in Kansas, Ohio, and elsewhere. In one instance the NAACP cooperated with the Urban League by paying young boys to distribute pamphlets through theatre queues under the gaze of threatening police.

Boston—"Freedom's birthplace," the home of William Monroe Trotter's militant *Guardian*, and the liberal Boston *Post*—opened the attack on *The Birth of a Nation* from both pulpit and press even before the picture arrived. Mayor James Curley understood grassroots politics and granted a hearing in the opening blare of Tremont Theatre advertising.[33]

Curley allowed both sides full expression, perhaps hoping they would burn themselves out so that he would not need to act. Griffith footnoted his work with historians and offered $10,000 for proof of distortions. Early in the game the NAACP judged Curley to be "a democratic and very kindly Irishman," even though they suspected him of lack of sympathy with their demand for censorship. The Epoch group won the opening rounds largely because they trapped Moorfield Storey of the NAACP into admitting he had not seen the film and because other NAACP delegates seemed "shaky" and buried in their notes, and prone to interrupt the proceeding. At last Curley touched off the rage below the surface of the meeting when he straddled, promising to cut the picture while admitting his powerlessness. "Bosh," carped one of the NAACP group who thought Curley to be shamelessly "playing to the colored galleries" and no more. The blacks tried everything during the short-fused session: they hissed a mention of Wilson, urged the banning of the film under the laws governing boxing movies, cited shots of race hatred and "sexual excesses," invoked the Women's Christian Temperance Union, and read letters from Rabbi Wise, Jane Addams, Ovington, and other liberal whites. At one point Curley, piqued at the growing mountain of redundant testimony, asked if Macbeth tended to incite feeling against whites. Storey bristled and charged the Mayor with representing "the other side." The meeting broke up amid Curley's denials, Griffith's insistence on filming "history" as he saw fit, and an offer to cut a few shots.[34]

Curley made good his offer, and the movie opened on April 10 with the chase scene, several leering Negroes, the marriage sequence, Stoneman alone with his mistress, and the South Carolina legislature excised, as concessions rather than acts of conscience or requirements of law. During the second week the *Post* began to take the Negroes' side despite Epoch's considerable advertising space. Its writers reported the murderous moods of New York audiences, discovered that Curley's predecessor had banned *The Clansman* in 1906, and chided the producers for using clergymen as "authorities" in the ad copy.[35]

Then toward the end of the week the small black community of Boston made its strongest stand, taking to the streets for a direct confrontation. Two hundred police turned out when a group of blacks attempted to buy tickets at the segregated theatre. Active in the melee was Trotter, who had cut short a lecture tour. In the lobby he railed against the discrimination, then as the heat rose a cop hit him, and other policemen poured in and arrested ten blacks. A few blacks managed to get inside and at the death leap smashed an egg against the screen and tossed a stink bomb into the crowd. Outside, brawls sputtered in the street.[36]

The next day a wild, hooting crowd gathered at Faneuil Hall, where a crowd of blacks heard Trotter castigate Curley for his betrayal of Negro voters. Michael Jordan of the United Irish League chipped in with an attack on Wilson, and the old Abolitionist Frank Sanborn added a few words. On Monday the blacks marched up Beacon Street to the gold-domed State House, singing "Nearer My God to Thee." Trotter and sixty others pressed inside, while perhaps two thousand waited grimly on the steps. Hurriedly, Governor David Ignatius Walsh and Attorney General Henry Attwill thrashed out the limits of their authority to deal with the film, as moderates led by Booker T. Washington's friend and high ranking black officeholder, W. H. Lewis, reached them ahead of Trotter, revealing the continuing stress within black ranks. Reluctantly, they allowed Trotter to speak from the steps, while the Governor disarmed his impact by promising to ask the legislature for a law prohibiting inflammatory material. Then he ordered the police to stop the show because the gathering was *prima facie* evidence of the movie's power to breach the peace.[37]

Satisfied for the moment, the Negroes called off a demonstration at the Tremont Theatre. But again, marginal success produced friction within black ranks. Trotter used the occasion to squeeze in a bitter denunciation of "colored traitors," meaning Lewis, and by extension, Booker T. Washington and his moderate National Negro Business League, which, Trotter claimed, had issued a conciliatory statement that the movie was "historical and would have good effect." For their part the moderates thought the demonstrations had "suffered from too much Trotter."[38]

Yet, unlike the tag end of the New York fight, the blacks of Boston, even the extremes of Lewis and Trotter and their white allies, had been brought together by the exhilaration of direct action. Also, despite the failure to break the run of the film, they had forced whites to deal with a black united front, had created a model for the future, and had shown how the New York office could nurture local leadership. To stand together across the street from the Robert Gould Shaw monument, with its dedication to the brave black troops of the Civil War, and to catch a glimpse of the Crispus Attucks monument through the trees on the Common, to sing "The Battle Hymn of the Republic," to raise two hundred dollars, was to act in a new drama in the theater of the streets. "The colored troops fought nobly," a witness reported.[39]

Black solidarity in Boston opened up new vistas as blacks were able to make both aesthetic and political demands upon whites. Militants and moderates each made a contribution, the former more political, the latter unexpectedly more aesthetic. The Boston militants burned most of their energy in the cause of the "Sullivan bill" that would create the censor board. Emmett J. Scott, a central figure in the Tuskegee group, would lead a black movie through to completion long after the NAACP dropped out.

In Boston the moderates played a cool hand forced upon them by their own inner factionalism and by Washington's urge for anonymity. They necessarily faced *The Birth of a Nation* as an aesthetic problem because politically, Washington could barely control his Boston branch of his National Negro Business League. Two members, it was reported, intended to endorse the film in Washington's name, providing the basis for Trotter's charge against W. H. Lewis. Washington could do no more than make a vague effort to fight the picture on Southern ground and to send out "sermonic material" on request to black communities beleaguered by the film. He feared direct action in Boston because he remembered when Negroes had been hired in 1906 to protest *The Clansman* as a promotional gimmick, so he contented himself with words of praise for the "Negroes [who] are a unit in their determination to drive it out of Boston."[40]

Washington quickly moved to the aesthetic problem of creating a black alternative to *The Birth of a Nation*. In the spring he knew only that he could not join Griffith in shooting a prologue about Tuskegee because he could neither trust Griffith nor associate himself with the "hurtful, vicious play." He had been interested in cinema for years and as early as 1909 had engaged filmmakers to shoot promotional movies of the campus and its programs. With the arrival of Griffith's epic, Washington renewed his interest and opened negotiations for repurchase of the old rights to not-very-profitable footage shot in 1913. By summer he and Scott pursued a project with Universal, and finally, just before his death in November, he began to view his own popular autobiography, *Up From Slavery*, as a "counter-irritant" to *The Birth of a Nation*.[41]

Meanwhile the debate plodded on in Boston, obscuring the movement toward a black cinema, diverting black attention from art toward politics. Late in April, having failed to block the run, blacks put pressure on the legislature. As a result the Sullivan censorship bill became law, Epoch tacked on a bland prologue about Hampton Institute, and several whites—among them George Peabody and Senator Wesley L. Jones of Washington—publicly turned against the film.[42]

The debate over the question of censorship revealed the special black position that was shared by many white ethnic minorities. They modified the general principle of freedom of speech on the ground that roles which depended on exaggeration or burlesque seemed to slander the whole race, and therefore society had an obligation to protect its minority members from outrages to which only they were subject by virtue of their uniqueness. Most Boston newspapers took a traditional view, which the producers capitalized upon by quoting in massive advertisements in opposition to the Sullivan bill, which, they claimed, would "assassinate dramatic art in Massachusetts." At a meeting in the First Unitarian Church, Charles Eliot of Harvard, W. H. Lewis, and others thrashed out a means of separating art from propaganda, *The Birth of a Nation* in their view being the latter. Most whites tried to draw a line short of "absolute freedom" but could not agree on "mischief" or a "travesty of history" as the benchmark. Others rejected the Negro contention that Griffith's view of Reconstruction was biased. Rather, the paternalists among them thought, "It is not an attack on a race, but only reveals conditions that should create admiration and sympathy for what the colored race have accomplished since the days of Reconstruction." An occasional Negro such as George L. Knox of the Indianapolis *Freeman* complicated the issue by endorsing the depiction of slave loyalty and the "love the 'black mammies' had for young white soldiers."[43]

The black position could be established only by confrontation; whites surrendered only under attack. Dixon bore much of the responsibility for the external clatter of *The Birth of a Nation*. He boasted of giving inspiration to it, of financing it, of titling it, of seeing it through production crises, of beating its drums with the zeal of a seasoned advance man, of giving it much of its personality as an event. He scored his finest coup by capitalizing on the President's *imprimatur* after the film's screening in Washington. Late in the year Dixon still believed the film was "transforming the entire population of the North and West into sympathetic Southern voters," and as he put it to Wilson's secretary, it would *"revolutionize . . . every man in my audience into a good Democrat!"* For a while Dixon's racism and naïve politics immobilized Wilson. He did not wish to abide by his endorsement, yet he could not appear bullied by agitation. Finally he allowed his secretary, Joseph P. Tumulty, to "leak" the President's disapproval of the "unfortunate production" in a letter to Representative Thomas Thacher of Massachusetts, but far too late, for Dixon had commercially exploited the President's name for more than three months. Belatedly blacks had forced the President toward the position of the liberal urban weeklies who had long since denounced Dixon as a "yellow clergyman" who had perverted Griffith's genius to specious ends.[44]

By midyear Negroes had made substantive gains, but serious weaknesses remained. First, their aggressiveness moved white producers to suppress black roles rather than to alter them to new demands, thus reducing black appearances on screen. Second, the black cinema industry began to grow fitfully. Third, political gains generated more pride than substantive change, driving the NAACP into a generation of pressure against not Hollywood but *The Birth of a Nation*, and thus making Griffith's movie into an eternal bugbear that wasted black effort and money. The glories of spring and summer of 1915 in Boston were ephemeral in the long run, for the censor board that blacks helped create turned against them and gave its approval to *The Birth of a Nation*. As the year dragged on, the NAACP's *Crisis* could only impotently record minor success with glee and failures with cynicism. The defeat of the NAACP in New York and Boston was reflected in the bulging cash boxes of Epoch, Dixon, and Griffith.[45]

Everywhere the discipline of Boston broke down into scattered skirmishes, while black leaders wished for the great days of unity. A black alumnus of Hampton Institute who had been in Boston caught the wistful mood. "As I looked over that vast crowd of Negro men and women," he wrote, "this thought came to me: this is a united people though in the minority and they are going to win." He dreamed of a meeting of Washington, DuBois, Trotter, and Bishop Alexander Walters at which "a race of ten millions of Negroes would be united." Only then, he thought, "a Nation would *really* be born" which would unite as equals with "the best blood of the white race."[46] Instead of the alliance of the NAACP and Tuskegee, though, every black community seemed to offer its own easily smothered tactics.

May Childs Nerney tried to preserve a solid front of ideological and tactical consistency by mailing out a thick packet of reviews, model letters, and clippings so that each NAACP branch had a running start when the movie came to town. But unlike the Boston affray, the nationwide campaign was a negativistic assault during which the *Crisis* crowed:

> The latter half has been so cut, so many portions of scenes have been eliminated, that it is a mere succession of pictures, sometimes ridiculous in their inability to tell a coherent story.[47]

In many cities—Pasadena, Chicago, Wilmington—the NAACP fought with varying results for censorship, but their strongest victory was in Chicago, where the support of Mayor "Big Bill" Thompson helped them seat a black preacher on the censor board. In Cleveland and Pittsburgh the campaigns were leavened with liberal white organizational support. In Des Moines, Philadelphia, New York, and elsewhere censorship was tied to antiriot ordinances. DuBois even considered asking the Anti-Slavery Society to take up the film with the Lord Mayor of London. At its worst the campaign resulted in publicity for the picture. In one case—Oakland—the exhibitors bribed a defunct black organization to boycott the picture as a publicity device. Nevertheless by year's end the distributors could exhibit the picture almost anywhere they wished.[48]

So black leaders knew in 1915 that blind advocacy of censorship was a dead end. No matter how many new members flocked to the NAACP, how many flagging branches blossomed or new ones sprouted, how many whites were converted or scared by the new black unity, how many producers backed off from the subject of race, in the final battle censorship was a rearguard action rather than a direct assault on racism in American life.

Indeed, the campaign may have contributed to a slow attrition of black roles on the screen while drawing attention away from all-black alternatives to white productions. Already the innovators of the experimental DeForest Phonofilm system had attempted to record the postminstrel black musical achievement on film.[49] But instead of a black cycle of cinema, all blacks disappeared, as a result of NAACP protests against pejorative roles and white producers' feelings that black protagonists were out of the question. In the absence of a clear choice, however, blacks persisted in their campaign against *The Birth of a Nation*.

Few whites understood what the furor was all about. In some cities white ministers argued that the picture was downright friendly toward "the great Negro race, a race which has contributed so much to our culture." The Aitkens lived out their lives in Waukesha, dreaming of the day when they could do a soundfilm remake, puzzling over the bankers' reluctance to support them, and as late as 1954, crabbed with age, Dixon and Griffith dead, they sat by the telephone waiting for an "angel."[50]

Griffith himself professed shock at Negro resentment of his work. "That," he said, "is like saying I am against children, as they were our children, whom we loved and cared for all our lives." Puzzled, he listened as his black maid, troubled and tense with emotion, blurted out, "It hurt me, Mr. David, to see what you do to my people."[51] Caught between the saddened old Negro and the aggressive new Negro, Griffith lived out his life learning nothing and forgetting nothing.

White friends of the black cause knew little more. The dogged black pursuit of censorship slowly lost the ear of the philanthropic white liberals within the NAACP. Indeed, DuBois himself fretted over the course toward censorship. Still no one seemed able to get off the tiger's back. Small breaches with Southern lore went unnoticed in the heat of the moment. Thomas Ince's ambitious melodrama *The Coward* (1915), starring Charles Ray, admitted the possibility of less than valiant Southerners and featured a black man who affected the plot. The cowardly son of a lordly planter enlists in the army only at his father's pistol point and as quickly deserts. Rotting in disgrace in his room, comforted only by the servants, he hears of Yankee plans and, cowardice overcome, he speeds to warn the Confederates—his escape covered by a black servant who shoots a Union trooper. But neither the ungallant rebel nor the Negro who had acted—misguidedly by later black lights—in the interests of his homeland was noticed by black or white activists.[52]

The worst single evidence of black inability to take a new direction appeared with the release of Edward Sheldon's old melodrama *The Nigger* (1915). William Fox released the picture only a month after *The Birth of a Nation*, thereby arousing blind rage amongst blacks, demands for its suppression, a wasteful error in judgment on the part of the NAACP, and still another sputtering campaign. Despite its title the movie was an indictment of intemperance and intolerance that could be seen as a charge of racism against whites. Philip Morrow (William Farnum) is a "wet" gubernatorial candidate and liberal enough to attempt the rescue of a black lynching victim. Then his whole life is diverted from the course of public service. His opponents dredge up his Negro lineage through a lightskinned grandmother. He becomes a "dry," persuaded that race riots are motivated by whiskey-inflamed passions. But no matter, for he loses his wife, serves out his term, and chooses "a new life of lonely self abnegation, with a past to forget and an ancestry to forgive."[53]

Putting aside the obvious patronizing reference to pedigree, the film may be taken, at least in part, as a tragedy brought on by mindless racism, a testament to the influence of environment over genetic heritage, and a sermon against alcoholic excess rather than against the frailty of one race. Indeed, a few blacks, among them the editor of the Washington *Bee*, took such a position, and some NAACP members themselves "failed to discover anything which in the opinion of the Legal Redress Committee would bring it under" antiracism ordinances.[54]

Nevertheless, by April the New York office of the NAACP was flooded with ominous warnings, suggestions as to tactics, and boasts of blocking the showing of the film. Through the summer the NAACP allowed local campaigns to progress. In Cleveland, for example, Harry Smith's militant *Gazette* compared the picture with Atlanta's Leo Frank lynching case and persuaded Mayor Newton D. Baker to ban *The Nigger* from the city's screens. In Toledo blacks stacked an interracial committee five to three and blocked the film "as a play reflecting on the Negro." By late summer advertised openings failed to materialize in several cities, and here and there cautious exhibitors changed its title to *The Governor*. But the scattered successes against *The Nigger* provoked little of the enthusiasm which surrounded *The Birth of a Nation*. Even in Cleveland NAACP members quarreled over Sheldon's play, some granting the point that it stressed a rape by a black drunk, an episode ending with a lynching, but others insisted that the mulatto governor's achievements were those of a Negro, even though he was presumed white through much of the plot.[55]

In the face of indecision and a resulting waste of resources May Childs Nerney, who bore the burden of the summer's correspondence, redirected attention away from the movie. "Dr. DuBois and I do not think Sheldon's play, 'The Nigger,' objectionable," she wrote to the NAACP branches. "A friend of mine went to see it and says that it shows the other side, that is, the white man's responsibility for existing conditions, and the motives for such crimes as are commited by colored people are shown in every case to be drink and not race." Some of her correspondents not only agreed but praised the film for its possible salutary effect on bigoted whites.[56]

Unfortunately for blacks they could not so easily cut free of harrying *The Birth of a Nation*. Soon point-scoring tactics began to outweigh the original goal of suppression; caution about giving publicity to the picture was cast aside. The NAACP recruited new members and branches in the name of fighting *The Birth of a Nation*. "ANOTHER FEATHER IN THE BROTHERHOOD'S CAP" blared the California *Eagle* when an opening was momentarily thwarted by a protest. Richmonders claimed the protest would result in a "branch for you all." One of the faithful in Atlantic City thought it would "help to place the name of the Association before a great many persons." In Trenton protest served to "revive interest in the work . . . and to make Herculanean [sic] efforts to increase our membership." When zeal generated rivals, local branches snubbed them. "The so-called vigilance committee does not meet with the approval of our Branch," wrote a San Francisco officer. "They are giving the picture too much publicity."[57] Nonethless the NAACP had done its job and was entitled, perhaps, to a puffed chest and a bit of aggrandizement. Censorship meant a modicum of black control over the third largest industry in the United States.[58]

Unfortunately, the great melodrama of good versus evil—the NAACP against Epoch—drew attention away from the task of making black movies, and through the next three decades wasted an inordinate amount of black money and energy. By then *The Birth of a Nation* had become a tempting and easy target, sluggish under fire, timid and given to appearances in dank church basements and seedy Ku Klux rallies.[59] The trade papers credited its occasional high grosses to its free publicity. The costs to blacks—tactical, financial, and psychic—were enormous. Each new generation of NAACP branch officers knew they risked being labelled as against freedom of expression. Thus through the years they needed to demonstrate to courts and to police that *The Birth of a Nation* constituted a clear provocation to disorder, a case that rested on Boston in 1915. When they could not reach the courts they marched in picket lines outside even the artiest of little film societies who revived it for its artistic merit. The finest mind in the ranks, DuBois, could only lamely assert that "We are aware now as then that it is dangerous to limit expression, and yet, without some limitations civilization could not endure."[60]

If the strategy had paid off, the message of the medium of protest would have been, in the words of a 1918 NAACP press release, that "A new type of Negro . . . has long since, except in the backwoods stage, supplanted the shuffling, flat-footed, watermelon-eating, hat-in-hand stage monstrosity." But branch presidents found it too easy to concern themselves with *The Birth of a Nation*, which could swell their membership rolls, rather than the larger question of the blacks' role in the movies. The worst possible solution resulted from the misshapen policy: the movie became an icon of racism, worshipped by racists largely because of the reputation given it by the NAACP. With the coming of the so-called Hays Office self-censorship system, the studios abandoned black roles altogether rather than choose between the wrath of the NAACP or what they thought would be unsalable black heroes.[61]

The branches themselves felt the strain in the form of increasing dissent. In Boston, the scene of old victories, Trotter's friends came to see the NAACP as a stealer of thunder rather than as a saviour. By 1921 Lester Walton, the sharpest newspaper critic in black New York, lectured the NAACP for its negativism and for the continuing publicity it gave to Griffith's film.[62]

Every protest seemed dogged by the threat of disaster. From time to time the Klan capitalized on the publicity by announcing the production of a new film that would outdo Griffith. They and Dixon each completed at least one undistinguished, overpublicized picture. In New York in 1925 the NAACP nearly fell into a trap by attacking a revival of a poor hoary racist tale called *Free and Equal*, only to guess at the last moment that the exhibitor *wanted* them to protest as a boost to ticket sales.[63]

The year 1930 brought another crisis for the NAACP when the new distributors put a sound track over *The Birth of a Nation* and rereleased it to a whole new audience. By then the movie seemed treacly, but sound would give racism a new dimension. So, despite Walter White's admission that "Unfortunately, the picture does have merits as a work of art," the ritual of première-versus-protest dragged on. White and the Southern white liberal Will Alexander sent letters of protest to Will Hays, who dismissed them, feeling that the picture would have only a small audience of admirers of classic cinema. Torn between raising a clamor that would benefit the movie and letting it pass, he hoped unnoticed, White at last decided to ask the branches to deal with local exhibitors and clergymen in their offices rather than on the street. The waning of the glamour and the sense of movement grated on some of them and caused them to plead for "a little more notice in your *Crisis*." Under pressure from the predominantly white American Civil Liberties Union, the official NAACP line argued that *The Birth of a Nation* was not art but mob incitement, a position gradually supported in the thirties by increasing clinical evidence that motion pictures indeed affected the behavior of children, and by the ranting of Thomas Dixon, bitter and idle in Raleigh. Through the years of the depression the NAACP trod more softly, but it never clearly deviated from its course of suppression.[64]

Not until World War II would the NAACP begin to get over its terrible linkage to *The Birth of a Nation*, at last admitting it had reached the point of diminishing returns and shifting its energies to the more profitable course of forcing contemporary, rather than dead, Hollywood to end its racist production practices. By then the original producers had declined into crabbed old age—Dixon in Raleigh, the Aitkens in Waukesha, Wisconsin, and Griffith in his hotel rooms—although the three old men could still trigger knee-jerk reactions by the NAACP with such fanciful projects as a color and sound version to be shot as a rival to *Gone With the Wind*. During the depressed thirties blacks became the darlings of the Communist Party so that NAACP picket lines regularly drew white radicals who gave an unwarranted Marxist identity to the blacks and threatened to coöpt the issue. By 1937 the NAACP had drifted from suppression toward awarding favorable citation to movies such as John Ford's *Hurricane* which contained anti-racist messages. But the ACLU still grumbled. In 1939 Arthur Garfield Hays offered ACLU resources to any exhibitors who felt victimized by an NAACP demonstration. Roger Baldwin of the liberal white group told Roy Wilkins that the power to squelch a racist film opened the way to those who would block a pro-Negro picture. By 1940 most viewers of the film were members of university clubs and film societies, and they resented the NAACP's interference with their studies.[65]

At last, after a half century, the NAACP abandoned its crusade against *The Birth of a Nation* and returned to a point of view advanced

by DuBois in 1915. He granted then that Griffith was a "mighty genius" against whom protest was pointless. Instead, he argued, Negroes
should forget "the cruel slander upon a weak and helpless race" and
turn with a will to creating their own aesthetic tradition. To this end
he personally mounted an ambitious pageant, *The Star of Ethiopia*,
which celebrated black African roots.[66]

Despite its outliving its potential gain for blacks, the campaign against
The Birth of a Nation had been the dawn of a new day. It provided the
first occasion on which black men, long organized into local groups,
stretched their muscles across the nation. It reminded them that the
"progressive era" had been for whites only and had ended in Jim Crow
government, lynching, and the seedtime of a new Ku Klux Klan. It
provided a model against which to test white racism. It turned the attention of a few Afro-Americans toward cinema as a means of expression. It became a useful rhetorical weapon in any negotiation over film
content and casting. In short, it provided black assimilationists with a
black weapon. But in the short run it also stimulated a distinctly black
nationalist gesture, a black cinematic rebuttal to *The Birth of a Nation*.
It was released in 1919. It was *The Birth of a Race*.

Chapter Three

TWO EARLY STRIDES
TOWARD A BLACK CINEMA

The Birth of a Nation had swiftly aroused blacks. Griffith's picture had produced hasty decisions, nationwide protests, and more direct action than anyone in the black leadership had ever contemplated. Blacks never debated whether to stand and fight it, but rather *how*. But after a spring and summer of litigation and lobbying, to fight in courts and streets seemed to be no more than wasted motion.

A few protestors attempted to create an indigenous black cinema in response to *The Birth of a Nation*. The little circles of blacks barely knew of each other, so wide had the diaspora spread them. And indeed, even their ambitions differed: an NAACP committee wishing merely to use a major studio's facilities to produce an antidote to Griffith's movie; a Tuskegee Institute group hoping to make an independent picture with white resources in Chicago; and the Lincoln Motion Picture Company in Los Angeles, attempting the first halting steps toward an all-black production center which would turn out examples of a well-wrought black aesthetic. They shared the common goals of producing movies with black investments in the plot-lines, black characterizations with humane dimensions, dramatic conflict based upon the facts of American racial arrangements, and a conscious effort to make the tools of the filmmaker speak to black needs. Together they represented the first measurable black efforts to challenge the white monopoly over the art of the cinema.

What made them so important was the optimism of their creators, who rested their faith on an ever-growing black urban audience and, to a lesser degree, on a long history of black economic nationalism. Afro-

Americans had been moving off the land in the South since the nineteenth century, at first to Southern cities and then to the North. After the turn of the century loosely scattered Negro neighborhoods began to coalesce into ghettos as a result of growing white antipathy and real estate practices and a few black real estate enterprises such as Phil Payton's Afro-American Realty Company in New York. Later in the late teens these ghettos acquired a degree of prosperity, due to the demand for black labor for wartime production. Economic and social institutions serving the newly arrived throngs increased rapidly. Estimates of movie theaters alone ran as high as 600 even though refugees from Southern black fundamentalism kept a sabbath which often stretched from Saturday night through Sunday, thus stunting the potential audience.[1]

The presence of a black urban audience was a precondition for the development of a black cinema aesthetic, and thus a means of freeing black leaders from the pursuit of censorship. The black masses brought the black élite around to an old response to oppression—a parallel black economy serving the needs of its community. In this sense all-black companies producing "race movies"—films made for the black audience —served the same function as the ante bellum free Negro hotelman, barbers, and undertakers, at least that sector of them who served a black clientele. Gradually after the Civil War black newspapers and a few urban trades followed the tradition, with the NAACP and Tuskegee and other putative film producers trailing after.

As early as the summer of 1915 with *The Birth of a Nation* furor at its height, the principals independently of each other began to move toward a cinema, rather than a censorship, alternative. The first of them was the NAACP, or at least May Childs Nerney and a scenario committee that included the white social worker Mary White Ovington and the black editor of the NAACP's house organ, W. E. B. DuBois. By early May they opened negotiations with Carl Laemmle of Universal, a maverick who had broken the monopoly of the motion picture patents trust by moving to a huge complex beyond Cahuenga Pass on the edge of the San Fernando Valley in Southern California, where he could turn out pictures beyond the purview of patent lawyers and courtrooms.[2]

Although DuBois dropped out early to pursue a similar project on his own, the others opened substantive conversations with Elaine Sterne, a Universal scriptwriter who would help them shape *Lincoln's Dream*, a celebration of black progress. She was trotted around Chicago and New York while the committee agreed to read "a sketch of the scenario —or plot or whatever you call it."[3]

The insurmountable obstacles to their entering into an agreement with Universal were their fear of breaking the anonymity of the members and of losing money. They preferred to remain apart in the role of consultant, but the cagey Laemmle wanted them to put up $50,000 of an expensive budget. Ovington was never able to raise more than $10,000, to be matched by Universal's $60,000. Despite Elaine Sterne's efforts the Association refused to commit its resources to making a movie, although they agreed to a reading of a rough-draft scenario before the Boston branch by the historian Albert Bushnell Hart. When by June there were still NAACP officers who "threw cold water" on the proposal, Sterne began to search for another backer.[4]

Meanwhile in Tuskegee, Alabama, Booker T. Washington and his personal secretary, Emmett J. Scott, began to search in earnest for a black-controlled motion picture production. Together they had become familiar with the ways of white folks, not only by directing the world-famous Tuskegee Institute but also through their connections with Republican politics, dozens of Negro newspapers, their National Negro Business League, agricultural improvement associations, and their propaganda mill, which pumped out articles, speeches, and books promoting Washington's program of self-help, black economic development, and job-training. Scott dabbled on the side in moneymaking schemes, attempting to open Southern territory to Yankee-made products—safety pins, vacuum cleaners, automobiles, hosiery, and so on—most of which failed, punctured by letters insisting "it would be necessary for us to close any contract under consideration with a member of the Caucasian branch of the human family."[5]

Both Scott and Washington knew something of motion pictures, the former from having inquired into stock purchases, the latter from having negotiated the rights to shoot movies on the Tuskegee campus. Then during the crisis over *The Birth of a Nation* in Boston one of Washington's allies in the National Negro Business League had discussed with Griffith the likelihood of shooting a conciliatory prologue to his epic, and Washington himself negotiated the repurchase of rights to the old campus footage. For the moment Washington remained aloof from all such offers and allowed Hampton alone to supply Griffith with film.[6]

But by the end of May, Elaine Sterne, perhaps tiring of NAACP indecision, began to cultivate the Tuskegeeans. Still, she was remiss in her appointments and pessimistic enough to tell Scott through Rose Janowitz, an intermediary, that "she was about ready to drop the photo play about which we talked because the support she wanted had not been forthcoming."[7] So Scott and Washington turned to Amy Vorhaus, an author with connections at Vitagraph. As a counterforce to *The Birth of a Nation* she proposed an updated *Uncle Tom's Cabin* that would use the medium to teach men that "prejudice is a conservative reaction and an ill-founded habit." Scott went to New York to pick up the new thread, but mutual suspicion and bad faith caused them to draw apart.[8]

The dream of a great black action against *The Birth of a Nation* flickered out. By late summer Sterne turned again to the NAACP, feeling they were capable of rousing a large audience and fearing "the Griffith crowd were actually planning to do something of the sort with the active support of *Tuskegee!*"[9] From a twelve-reeler the movie had shrunk to five reels to be titled *Lincoln's Dream*. Still the NAACP motion picture committee could not pry money from its white liberals.

Meanwhile Scott tried to rally the principals for one last meeting in New York to "find out how much unity of purpose and cooperation there can be." As a result of the meeting he concluded that the best bet lay with H. C. Oppenheimer, a Hollywood figure who thought it wise to bring Tuskegee and the Thomas Ince Studio together. Happy at the thought of getting clear of the two women, Scott pursued Oppenheimer for a few weeks, turned cool, fished briefly for new producers, but finally gave up because he "did not feel there was a square deal all around." Mary White Ovington clung to hope for a few more weeks, guessing that the "prejudice of the Southern members of the firm" accounted for the failure. Finally Laemmle withdrew after having failed to receive any matching funds.[10]

With the fading of *Lincoln's Dream* Scott and Washington had learned the dangers of competing in the world of white finance. No amount of negotiation and discussion seemed able to affect the decision-making process. White funds, capital, equipment, and personnel by their nature seemed to freeze out black enterprise. Thereafter the two Tuskegeeans looked at other less impenetrable resources: stock purchases, acquiring portable projection equipment to screen film outside normal channels, shooting a movie in Tuskegee, and reviving their thoughts of a filmed version of Washington's autobiography, *Up From Slavery*.[11]

Sifting his files, Scott opened correspondence with Edwin L. Barker of the Advance Motion Picture Company of Chicago, this time with a difference. Scott determined that a Negro would dominate the arrangement, and he mounted a three-pronged campaign to ensure his goal. First he offered Barker the motion picture rights to *Up From Slavery*, thus stamping the movie with "not only Dr. Washington's personal strivings, but also the strivings of the race climbing up from the tragic period represented by slavery in America." Second, he offered a "package": a strong theme of racial interdependence, himself as writer-consultant, Tuskegee and its campus, a promotional tie-in with Washington's publishers, and, most important of all, "that indefatigable something which I shall call *the colored man's viewpoint*." Third, he promised an alliance with the six hundred National Negro Business League chapters and his connections with over one hundred black newspapers which would "be harnessed to the publicity . . . in the interest of the photoplay." It would cost, he archly wrote, fifteen percent royalty, a monthly stipend, and an expense account.[12]

Unfortunately for Scott and the entire Afro-American people, Washington died before Barker could reply. Still the opportunistic Scott signed a contract a month later. *Lincoln's Dream* was dead, but Scott's dream lived on. The film's title was to be *The Birth of a Race*.

If Scott's scheme had worked, a black company would have broken the Hollywood monopoly and kept open the door of hope for aspiring black moviemakers. Only two small flaws marred the arrangement. Scott had unwittingly given Barker the right to sell his interest to a third party unbound to Scott's conditions, and in his haste to avoid an overbearing white company Scott had taken up with a Lilliputian.

But enthusiasm concealed the hollow center even as false starts consumed more than eighteen months until September 1917. A glowing prospectus promised money to investors with encouragement from a pantheon of rich white and black celebrities including Julius Rosenwald of Sears and Roebuck, Governor Frank O. Lowden of Illinois, Robert Russa Moton of Tuskegee, Fred Moore of the *New York Age*, solicitous Southern whites, the National Negro Business League, and several black clergymen and physicians. To a man they believed the movie would emerge as an inspirational black statement with a plea for mutual respect between the races. The black academies of the South pledged their support, the Selig Polyscope Company would shoot the movie, the famous black singer Harry Burleigh would supervise the music, and the achievement of the Negro race from bondage to freedom was to be the theme. So said the prospectus.[13]

But again the black cause was betrayed, not only by the confusion of variegated leadership but also by the weak financial position of the company. Weakness encouraged chicanery and mismanagement, which for two years was camouflaged under periodic stockholders' newsletters. By the spring of 1918 William Selig's company had spent $140,000 on the half-finished production. Selig, Rosenwald, and others backed out, leaving the field to Giles P. Corey, a Chicago stockbroker who was arrested under the so-called blue sky laws for fraudulently promoting stocks. Daniel Frohman of New York, a veteran vaudeville producer, took over and completed another portion of the film in Tampa, a vast biblical sequence which bore no relation to Selig's footage. By then the blacks felt control slip from their grasp. More Negro footage was left in the cutting room when the producers again shifted emphasis to take advantage of the rising war fever.[14]

So shabby was the whole operation that the trade paper *Variety* found scant evidence of shooting when it investigated. But worst of all for blacks, Barker told the paper that the movie would not be about the Negro at all and that Scott was no longer a scenarist. Amidst denials the company staggered through final production work in Tampa.[15]

The première was an even more grotesque defeat for blacks than the long charade of production. In November 1918 deep in the inside pages of *Variety* the backers announced the opening in Chicago. To assure a good house they cozened the investors into buying ten-dollar tickets, this while they still juggled theatres and patched together a release print. Finally, a month later, they opened at the fashionable Blackstone Theatre, where friendly local critics fancied they saw a "truly great," "clean, sincere," picture that was "worth seeing" even if it was a bit long. The trade papers, nevertheless, refused to avert their eyes. To them the blacks had every right to feel enraged and cheated by a pastiche of two movies edited into one pictorial, rambling, falsely pious mélange that ignored its racial premises to the point that "the spirit of the picture's preachment went glimmering when the producer and the scenario writers had the little white boy trounce the little colored boy." The worst blast of all came from *Variety*. "In the most fashionable theatre in America," it grumbled, "the most grotesque cinema chimera in the history of the picture business had its debut, and in all probability its demise." Angrily the reviewer told the tale of the stockbrokers hustling the race angle "largely to the colored folk on South State Street." In an effort to retain anonymity, the producers shortened the credits, even inking over names in the program. For the blacks it was a "terrible waste," a patchwork of "gorgeous settings run alongside shoddy drops," great chunks told in printed titles, pointlessly spectacular scenes placed next to cheap stock shots, redeemed only by a Biblical prologue that "dominates the cheap and uninteresting story as the Rockies would dominate Coogan's Bluff."[16]

The black defeat went largely unnoticed even in the Afro-American press. But a young Negro mailman in Omaha took careful note of the "mammoth swindle." George P. Johnson, along with his brother, Noble, a frequent player in Universal pictures, had already formed the Lincoln Motion Picture Company in order to avoid such dubious dependence on white financiers. Up to this time they had remained small and undercapitalized, with Noble running the studio in Los Angeles while George acted as part-time booker in Omaha. The miserable reports on *The Birth of a Race* coming in from his managers induced the Johnsons to press on with their work.[17]

From the beginning there was little to encourage the small company: no army of black investors, no account books revealing a black audience. Only the awareness of a growing black urban audience, of the failure of censorship as a tactic, and of the stillbirth of *The Birth of a Race* buoyed their hopes. "White" movies still offered little gratification to black viewers. Indeed, a judge in a censorship case suggested that blacks had no recourse against racism in movies save the "silence of contempt." Early black pioneers went largely unrecorded, even in the black press: the legendary Bill Foster, Bert Williams's two movies for Biograph, the attempt by a Negro company to produce Harrison Dickson's *Saturday Evening Post* "darky" stories with the assistance of Clarence Muse, the entry of Isaac Fisher, editor of the magazine *Negro Farmer*, into the ranks of producers.[18] So for the Johnsons no usable past was offered up as a predictor of success.

In spite of the inauspicious omens the brothers Johnson set out in the summer of 1915 "to picture the Negro as he is in his every day life, a human being with human inclination, and one of talent and intellect."[19] More than any other enterprise had even attempted, the Johnsons carried the notion of a black aesthetic to its limits as a social force. Unlike the efforts of Emmett Scott and the NAACP, the efforts of the Lincoln Company sprang from black roots in Los Angeles, and their idea spoke to blacks rather than to whites. The first production was a small sign that the black community of Los Angeles had reached the size and self-awareness to support such a risky enterprise. The *California Eagle* regularly featured such headlines as "CENTRAL AVENUE ASSUMES GIGANTIC PROPORTION AS BUSINESS SECTION FOR COLORED MEN." Along the avenue there was a Booker T. Washington Building, two hotels, an employment agency, two newspapers, a confident Watts Colored Independent League, a Dahomey café, a tough NAACP branch, a black baseball league—in short, a swagger and bourgeois pride that concealed vestiges of an oppressed past such as the porters' and redcaps' news column and the want ads for cotton pickers in Calexico.[20]

The self-confident black bourgeoisie took pride in Los Angeles, contrasting it with Bakersfield, "strictly a Southern city." They sometimes won Jim Crow cases in California courts. Occasionally they moved to other suburbs such as Pasadena and boasted of such victories as entering a black float in the Rose Bowl parade. They spent holidays in Santa Monica and complained bitterly when doors closed against them. Their grudges against enemies took the form of political defeat for the mayor, whose administration had announced "the color line has been drawn in the ocean at Santa Monica." And most important, they rid themselves of the factionalism that harried Negro communities in the East. Marcus Garvey's Universal Negro Improvement Association, the Tuskegee

Industrial Welfare League that formed the basis of the Urban League, the fraternities and alumni associations all received equal glowing treatment in the black press. Their individual wealth seemed to one white critic far higher than the estimate of *The Negro Yearbook*.[21]

In the midst of this rebirth of black culture in western soil the Lincoln Motion Picture Company sprouted. Noble Johnson, caught up in the white movie world, was a plunger who risked money and the security of his regular character roles with Universal to start the company. His conservative, even stuffy, brother George, stayed behind in Omaha and distributed the movies from there. Their first movie reflected their audience; its title was *The Realization of a Negro's Ambition*.

James Burton, a young Negro Tuskegee graduate, is working on his father's farm. Saying goodbye to his family and girlfriend, he heads west. In the California oil fields he is denied a job because he is black, but he saves the boss's daughter when her two-horse rig bolts, and as a consequence is given a job and later the opportunity to prospect for oil. He is welcomed home as guest of honor at a lawn party marred only by a few local gossips who stand between him and eventual good

The Realization of a Negro's Ambition, like most Lincoln productions, boosted black bourgeois goals. (George P. Johnson Collection)

fortune. At the end of his training, persistence in the face of odds and fineness of character win him an independent income from oil and the hand of his best girl. His life fades out on ambition realized, a happy family, and a place in the country.[22]

So ran the modest two-reeler that was Lincoln's first production. Trite by critical standards, it nevertheless represented a black perspective. Tony Langston, Lincoln's booker in Chicago, snapped it up and also agreed to take their future output. To him the Chicago market was merely the first in a national network of black houses.[23] Audiences would be able to see for themselves that Negroes could surmount discrimination by a bit of luck and pluck in the manner of the Horatio Alger stories.

In August 1916 the Johnsons added another ingredient to the prototypal black hero with *The Trooper of Troop K*, an ambitious but brief piece shot on location in the San Gabriel Mountains depicting the exploits of the Afro-American cavalry against the Mexican Carranzista

Jimmie Smith served the Lincoln Company as hustler, actor, agent, and promoter to the end. Here he appears with Beulah Hall in *The Trooper of Troop K*. (Jimmie Smith Collection)

army at the battle of Carrizal in June 1916. Noble Johnson starred as the shiftless Negro who becomes the redeemed hero, the mirror image of the Hollywood Negro.[24]

In Chicago Langston was ecstatic. Now he could sell movies to the exhibitors who had been chary of all-Negro movies because of "the junk that had been foisted upon them" in the past. Glowing press releases preceded its run everywhere. At Tuskegee 1600 students exulted in its quality and its black theme. In New Orleans it ran in black and white houses and in many dates drew "record breaking crowds." In Omaha Johnson essayed his first première, using Negro lodges, bands, and well-heeled black bourgeoisie.[25]

In their early years the Johnsons' major problem remained the gnawing lack of capital. Gross receipts were never enough to pay for the next release. Consequently, in 1916 Johnson made one grand effort to enlist the black business community by wangling a screening at the annual meeting of the National Negro Business League in Lincoln Electric Park in Kansas City. Perhaps it was Emmett Scott himself, eager to learn the lore of movies, who encouraged Johnson to bring a print of *The Realization of a Negro's Ambition*. He depicted Lincoln as a staunch force standing in the face of white blindness to black aspiration. Unfortunately for the company, Johnson probably raised little capital from the conservative body, although they supplied him with a number of useful, effusive press releases plugging the movies.[26]

Unswayed by limited capital and buoyed by the friendly reception in Kansas City, the company acted to improve its position and to capitalize on its early success. To avoid the pitfalls suffered by the NAACP and *The Birth of a Race* company, Johnson started a clipping file on the black movie companies so as to expose frauds and curtail wasteful spreading of meagre capital. Strapped by the paucity of release dates in white-owned theatres, he attempted to build a network of personal friends across the nation to serve as bookers. Later he would move to Los Angeles so they could merge production and distribution under one roof. In the process they created a new black institution in the midst of a rich, aloof white world, although secretly they nursed fears that "the brother is not up to times in handling such fast business as the Moving Picture Business call for."[27]

In a short while George Johnson's file swelled with prospectuses, clippings, and press releases from the little black companies that promised so much and produced so little. Bill Foster was a good example. A clever hustler from Chicago, he had been a press agent for the Williams and Walker revues and Cole and Johnson's *A Trip to Coontown*, a sportswriter for the *Defender*, an occasional actor under the name of Juli Jones, and finally a purveyor of sheet music and Haitian coffee. He

may have made the first black movie, *The Railroad Porter*, an imitation
of Keystone comic chases completed perhaps three years before *The
Birth of a Nation*. Foster, like other inmates of the file, occasionally
tried to hook on with Lincoln. "I am at a standstill," he once wrote,
"waiting for something to turn up."[28] The worst exploiters of blacks
were not the honest hustlers like Foster but rather men like Luther J.
Pollard, the black boss of Ebony Pictures, who espoused race pride in
their publicity sheets throughout the war years but then ground out
the traditional black stereotypes. Gleefully the men of Lincoln recorded the news of one of Pollard's pictures that was canceled in a
Chicago house because it was "degrading" to the race. Other small
newly formed black companies, fed by audiences of northward urban
migrants, were fearful of departing from comedy, intimidated by the
demands of drama, and never rose above retailing annual black events
such as the Howard-Lincoln football game.[29]

It was the Johnsons' organization that most reflected their talents and
set them apart. They tapped the most enduring resource in Negro life,
their personal friends scattered in a wide skein over the country. Tony
Langston of the *Defender*, Robert L. Vann of the *Courier*, and Romeo
Daugherty of the *Amsterdam News* were the foremost in a cadre of
journalists who acted as bookers, promoters, and spies on the other
companies. To break the white monopoly on distribution they created
an all-Negro exchange, printed their own advertising handouts to ac-
company each release, and made their own preview slides. They even
discussed with Universal the opening up of 650 Middle Western houses
for *The Trooper of Troop K*. In some towns they felt so strong they
insisted on a full week instead of the customary split week. As quickly
as possible they stopped "wildcatting," that is, carrying films around
the country as though they were hairbrushes, counting the house, and
moving on in the morning. "I have always been leary of the man with
the thing under his arm," Langston explained. "I learned this along
with the Jews, and you know that they are the last word in smartness
when this game is concerned."[30] By 1917 with only two pictures in
release they had exchanges and press agents in most of the ghettos of
America. Their most imaginative tactic outstripped white Hollywood
in its search for a profile of its audience. Exhibitors received a survey
sheet asking for house size, ratio of black and white patrons, names of
the local black press, thematic and topical preferences, and, most striking, a request for a comparison in audience response to Noble Johnson's
work in Lincoln and in Universal productions.[31]

Still, in the best of circumstances Lincoln felt the pinch of meagre
resources. In the midst of the World War its marginal position could
be seen starkly against the backdrop of successful white moviemaking.

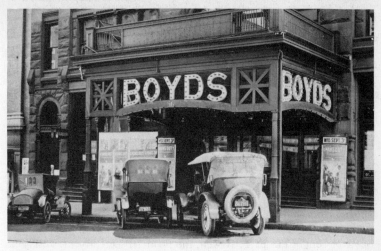

Boyd's Theatre in Omaha played Lincoln movies. (George P. Johnson Collection, UCLA)

Metro had its Loew's releasing arm, Fox its West Coast Theatres, and so on. Where they neither owned nor operated theatres they applied the pressure of oligopoly through the device of "block booking," that is, requiring the purchase of a group of poor films for the privilege of buying one moneymaking picture. Lincoln had only its chain of part-time bookers, with George Johnson himself still working a full shift in the Omaha post office between stints for Lincoln. Even as the studios moved and expanded, the assembled officers of the Lincoln Motion Picture Company met on the balcony of Smith's Drugstore on Central Avenue.[32]

That Lincoln remained largely frozen out of the seats of power may be seen in its failure to win a contract to shoot newsfilm of the black troops in France. Even when Emmett Scott became an assistant for Negro affairs to Secretary of War Newton D. Baker, Johnson was unable to crack the white monopoly. Scott, busy with running down black soldiers' complaints of discrimination and lynching, probably paid little heed to the quiet, olive-skinned postman from Omaha who visited his office. At best, George Johnson thought the wartime Committee on Public Information should have shared its funds in proportion to the American racial constituency for the purpose of getting honest film of black troops in action. In addition, to avoid "some humiliating farce . . . staged by either white directors and actors or inexperienced colored actors," he proposed a black assistant in the Washington office; a Negro Bureau staffed by Noble Johnson, R. W. Thompson of Scott's office, and representatives of two other black film companies, Quality and Dunbar Amusement; and finally a national "Advisory Board of Representatives of the Negro Race" to be staffed by an interracial committee.[33] Instead of a Negro bureau, a lucrative contract, and good documentary film for ghetto audiences Lincoln lost out and was forced to buy stock footage from the French Government, after one last desperate flying trip to New York attempting to raise money for the venture.[34]

Still in urgent need of funds, Johnson took what seemed to him a gamble—a leave of absence from the Omaha post office. On the same journey that brought him to the War Department he continued in a wide arc through the Northeast, pleading with black capitalists to support the only black motion picture company in Los Angeles. Besides Scott he sought out E. T. Atwell, the financial secretary of Tuskegee; an attorney for Madame C. J. Walker, the richest of black women; a brace of black bankers; Robert L. Vann of the *Pittsburgh Courier;* and Robert Levy, the white angel of the black Lafayette Players and the Reol movie company. In Levy's case, refusal stemmed from two successive blows to Lincoln's hopes: his awareness of Universal's insistence that Noble Johnson cease making race movies, and possibly Reol's hope to penetrate the South with a series of white-financed pictures.[35]

Ignored by rich blacks, throttled by the big white companies, Lincoln stumbled through the war by making a bit of newsfilm of black sports and western scenes. In their optimistic moments they hoped for daily grosses as high as $400, but by the war's end economic recession had plummeted them to $75 for two-day bookings. Anxiously, they watched a young rival, Oscar Micheaux, a black man from the prairie, begin his quarter-century career as a one-man motion picture company, while from another direction they feared "the Jews are making ready an attack upon the Negro field in the Movies."[36]

By 1920 Lincoln had reached a plateau of race consciousness and grew timid and blind to further development. For example, the brothers quarreled over Micheaux. George entertained thoughts of a merger on the strength of the youngster's two unsuccessful but promising movies, while Noble felt a Micheaux story was a "little too advanced . . . for us yet and unless we would change it so decidedly that it would hardly be recognizeable we could not expect much support from white houses."[37]

Lincoln lost way in the competition from many quarters, yet the Johnsons found it awkward to spread their risks by a merger. Postwar conditions had brought whites into the business, along with young enterprising blacks like Micheaux. When George Johnson reopened the question of a merger of black moviemaking with Robert Vann of the *Courier* as a focus, Vann would have nothing to do with them. With Noble Johnson gone, at the behest of Universal, the company seemed to need an infusion of new ideas. Vann did not trust George Johnson to produce them and insisted on Micheaux as a partner.[38] By midsummer the merger of Lincoln's experience, Micheaux's youth and energy, and Vann's nationally famous publications failed to materialize. Lincoln and Micheaux continued as rivals for capital, distribution outlets, and advertising space.[39]

Because they were a *succes d'éstime* in the black world the Lincoln men probably stimulated the small beginnings of some of their rivals who emerged during the war years. Mere rivalry, however, was not the worst of it. Not only did rivals siphon off and divide the limited pool of capital; they failed to develop the perspective of the Lincoln pictures, whose plots had emerged out of black institutions, dreams, and a sense of community. Lincoln managed in *The Realization of a Negro's Ambition* and in *The Trooper of Troop K* to show the relevance to the Negro world of the hard Yankee truths of the puritan ethic of work. Shiftless Joe, the trooper, was redeemed by it; Jim Burton used his "Negro's ambition" to overcome discrimination. Most of the companies operated at the lowest level of a black aesthetic, merely presenting Negro images on a screen, often little different from their counterparts in white movies. Rarely did they depart from comedic forms, and practically never did the black protagonists have a stake in the denouement.

Ebony Pictures' *Black Sherlock Holmes*, for example, was little more than a nonwhite comic rendering of Conan Doyle's hero. Based in Chicago, the company could not draw on the experience picked up by Noble Johnson in his work for Universal. Besides, most production details were in the hands of white men nominally under the black J. Luther Pollard.[40] In another Ebony film, *Spying the Spy*, the "hero," probably played by Sam Robinson, is introduced in such a comic manner as to destroy the point of a black presence: a headline in the *Ebony Examiner* blares "SAMBO SAM CAPTURES SINGLE HANDED A NEST OF SPIES." Then we iris-in as Sam pins his clipping up beside his other triumphs. He exits from a wide shot of his room to the street where follows the white "heavy," Herman Schwartz, to the White Eagle Laundry in which spies are making cartoon-caricature bombs. Sam captures Schwartz in a laundry bag and delivers him to his chief, who sits under a benign portrait of Lincoln. There Schwartz literally becomes as black as his name implies, insisting, "I am a respectable colored gentleman." Undaunted, Sam in a comic deerstalker and rainshedder follows

two blacks to the "Coffin Club," where the scene degenerates into a
rehash of Negro fears of skeletons. Finally Sam captures a spy, and the
movie irises-out to its end. The movie muddles the central theme of
a black spychaser by inconsistently using "Sambo" as the hero's name,
placing him in a shabby milieu, and retreating from the implications of
the black pursuit of a white heavy. It remained a white movie because
it ignored, even in its own comic terms, the aesthetic problem of the
black hero's role.[41]

Most of such products drew the wrath of the Lincoln men trying to
rise above comedy. They resented their white crews, their "small
time" performers, and their dependence on comedy. In private Langston would grumble: "I know most of the Shines with them and they
don't count for much." When the white Democracy Photoplay Corporation hired the Negro actor Sidney P. Dones as a front for their
Democracy or a Fight for Right, a "Smashing Virile Story of Our Race
Heroes," Johnson scribbled on their brochure "pretty weak stuff." On
another occasion a Lincoln informant checked on a promising all-black
Othello to be done by Delight Films, a white company pretending to
be black, and reported "the whole place looks like a swindling joint."
Advertising further enraged them. Such items as a pamphlet beginning
"Colored people are funny," set their teeth on edge.[42]

By the end of the war there were so many small black companies
that overextension and overproduction resulted. There were thousands
of feet of black heroic soldiers, for example. Charlatans and "good
race men" competed in the same markets, each claiming "to offset the
evil effects of certain photoplays that have libeled the Negro," "to
bring about interracial understanding," "to show the better side of Negro life," and "to inspire in the Negro a desire to 'climb higher.'"
Those in the South and West labored under the worst conditions of
scant capital, poor equipment, and bumbling technicians. Scores of
them printed glossy brochures on which George Johnson noted "no
records of any film produced." Even those that boasted a famous name
in the credits, such as Jack Johnson's in *For His Mother's Sake,* could
expect attachments of negatives in lieu of back rents. Most of them
had no assets save the endorsement of a well-known politician or
preacher, a promise to make "clean, inspiring, unprejudiced" movies,
and a hint that ten percent profits could be had. When a movie received praise, a company could afford only one print, which they
would sell for a quick gain rather than exhibit on percentage. Distraint
affected even the best of them such as *A Giant of His Race,* whose
backers lost a print in a sheriff's sale even though they had grossed $700
in a week's run in New York. And worst of all, to earn their money
the exhibitors inflated prices for their black customers on the ground

that "in a colored theatre no matter if its a 2, 3, or 5 reeler with colored actors it's a feature." Then there was the bottom rail, the companies that subsisted by buying the "outtakes," the discarded footage of more solvent companies, and the outright frauds who promised a spectacular train wreck costing $80,000 only to have the customer discover stock shots from older movies. There were also white failures such as Mark Dintenfass, who, having failed in larger white markets, opened a small studio in Jacksonville in order to make Negro movies in a marketplace already beset by tiny margins, cutthroat competition, limited outlets, and empty pockets.[43]

The black press, led by Lester Walton of the *Age*, praised the "strides" made by black companies and gave them "credit and encouragement," but such a conscientious critic never glossed over the sloppy cutting and misspelled titles that even able attempts such as Douglass's film of Paul Laurence Dunbar's *The Scapegoat* suffered from. Worse, though, were the whites such as Harrison Dickson who purveyed their films based on "life-long association with all sorts of Negroes." Walton devoted an entire column to Dickson's adaptation of his own *Saturday Evening Post* stories in which he has black doctors speak in a patois which proved Dickson "unconscious of the fact that there are thousands among us who possess dignity, education and refinement."[44]

In the push-and-shove of such a dense market, and with the splintering of its merger with Micheaux and the *Courier*, Lincoln needed to make a good picture that would reestablish it in the postwar scene. Also, with Noble Johnson's departure for Universal, they needed a new star. But again the awful problems of competing in a wildcat field were revealed. The Johnsons made a movie entitled *A Man's Duty*, starring their new actor, Clarence Brooks, which they expected to be up to their standard. But even with pitifully low salaries and a ratio of exposed film to usable footage under the barest minimum of 2-to-1, they still reached $5000 before advertising costs, forcing them to hand out press releases which desperately hustled the company's securities "before this stock is offered to white clients." Even though the film received good notices at splashy openings in Oakland and Atlanta, becoming the first Negro movie to run two days, it still managed to gross only $100 per day.[45]

Lincoln's achievement of première status revealed yet another barrier to black cinema. To demand loyalty to the race from the black world was an anomaly in the larger American economic system. The plight of blacks seemed to require communal rather than competitive activity. Competition seemed wasteful and debilitating, especially with the market sprinkled with hidden white backers and exploiters. Yet the need to outdo rivals finally led Johnson to his grandest gesture that was to

establish Lincoln as the epitome of black cinema: a grandiose Los Angeles première for *A Man's Duty* at the Trinity Auditorium designed
to heap up a bit of working capital. Ordinarily a Hollywood première
brought together all the tools and talents of the press agent in a glittering manufactured event which would capture the attention of journalists whose stories in succeeding days would assure the commercial
success of the movie. For Johnson, though, patchwork would have to
do. And yet searchlights, heralds, posters, programs, advertisements,
and press releases carried the company to heights it would never again
reach. A personal appearance by Clarence Brooks, dancing on stage by
Anita Thompson, songs by A. C. Bilbrew's Quartette supported by an
orchestra, all suitably underpaid, gathered enough for Lincoln to clear
$700 for the evening. But more than anything it convinced the com-
pany it could outdo the efforts of its competitors.[46]

In its motion pictures Lincoln had successfully incorporated every
device made popular by Hollywood and yet had not compromised its
emerging black aesthetic. The message of these movies was clear:
Blacks had every right and capability of participating fully in American life. No barriers save those erected by the white man stood in the
way. Aspiration fulfilled in *The Realization of a Negro's Ambition*,
the redemption of the soldier's life in *The Trooper of Troop K*, the call
of duty in *A Man's Duty*—all in the plotty, sentimental style of the day
drew the Afro-American into the midst of life.

At last Lincoln determined to explore the very fibre of racism in
America with a treatment of "passing" and the tensions between the
racial castes. George Johnson himself came west to work on the script
and to begin the task of mounting a glamourous première. The difficult
theme, always a sore spot amongst blacks, implying a rejection of Negro values and a traitorous surrender to racism, had been frequently
debated in black circles. To introduce it into movies might reach a
new level of black cinematic consciousness and a maturity of craft
that only Oscar Micheaux would rival. In addition to thematic values
the company introduced the gimmick of using members of the wealthy
black set of Los Angeles in bit roles, with the realtor Booker T. Washington, Jr., most prominently featured. Along with the tragic cross-
cultural theme the film blended western locales with an interior comedy
of manners. The eclectic approach was designed to introduce production values that would enable them to command "the necessary high
rental of $100 per day." The broad range would also "keep away from
too much heavy dramatic action, as our actors have not the experience
at this time."[47]

To get a return on the investment Johnson attempted an even more
grandiose première at the Trinity. Success that it was, it would also

demonstrate that the company was bound to a cycle of planning production and release which left it no time for an ambitious, artful effort. Lincoln came into the week of the opening carrying a budget of $8000, its highest ever. To get it back, Johnson rented the Trinity for a split week, hired "10 of the prettiest girls in town" to sell tickets at $1.50 top prices, and spread advertising through the black and white newspapers. On opening night he stretched streamers across the street, hired a footman to open car doors, created a singing and dancing prologue, and gathered a claque of newspapermen and Hollywood actors. As the crowd gathered, two buses brought the performers up to the door for a grand entrance. His backer was overwhelmed and encouraged him to sponsor similar premières in black and white houses across the country.[48]

And yet the enormous effort produced no viable results. The glamorous opening of *By Right of Birth*, including printing, rentals, lights, music, commissions, and fees, ran over $1000. And still, after a week of strain and donated labor the company cleared only a few dollars.[49] Furthermore, the contrived tinsel of a première could not conceal the fact the house was dark two days later. There simply was not enough spending money in black Los Angeles to sustain more than a split week, even after a strenuous promotional effort.

Nevertheless, at the peak of their careers the men of Lincoln had demonstrated a will beyond endurance, a sense of black identity beyond the NAACP calls for censorship of odious Negro roles, and acumen above Scott's naïve adventure with the *Birth of a Race* company. They had also revealed that independent black filmmakers had a lonesome road to go to overcome the handicap of a film exchange no larger than a few friendly newspapermen and a "ma-and-pa" office in Omaha. White companies not only had distribution centers, regional exchanges, and bookers, but even while their money was tied up in current releases they could still confidently expect loans from the Bank of America and other staid institutions. No black company had that expectation, not even Oscar Micheaux, who later would substitute his own traveling for Lincoln's thin web of exchanges.

A glance at Johnson's own figures is instructive. He boasted that some titles grossed $25,000, a sum belied by the fact that there were never more than five release prints to cover the entire country. Moreover, daily average rentals in the early years were only $25. So taking Johnson's most optimistic dream—$100 per day average and a negative cost or "nut" of $8000—each print would have to go through fifteen two-day openings as successful as the Trinity premières in order to make a profit. Roughly Johnson would need seventy-five black ghettos whose residents would turn out for a race production that was technically less than adequate.[50] The best-kept records, those for 1921, reveal the struggle in detail. From a strong $4000 in the urban Northeast, with a top in Chicago of $350, they went down the Eastern coast earning $2300, topped by Augusta's $175; moving to the Middle West, they slumped to $1248 with lows near $10; then with a rash of dates during the dog days of summer they took in $2295 through Texas, Oklahoma, and the Southwest, closing out the summer (when most white theaters closed) in the deep South, where they did a surprising $3300 but with lows down to $6 per day. For such a period, however, overhead and expenses ran to nearly $3000, which, when added to production costs, meant at best a highly marginal enterprise.[51] And there was no mention of such untold hidden costs as low pay, donated effort, uncompensated overtime, small and overworked crews, and the absence of the luxury of elaborate sets and frequent retakes. With the missing production values caused by stinting budgets, this put the angle of selling the films purely on the basis of racial pride. There was no way to get clear, ever.[52]

The burden of surviving under such conditions proved too much. The postwar depression, coupled with a raging influenza epidemic, drove the company over the edge. It expired after producing a one-reel documentary of the black 10th Cavalry on post at Fort Huachuca, Arizona, where, even with the cooperation of the Army, the producers were so pressed by expenses on location that they apparently patched together the shortened two-reel movie from an original script of six reels. In a last-ditch effort they escorted a local Garveyite and a delegate from First Kinematograph in Japan through the rented studio in the hope of opening up new markets.[53]

Lincoln failed in spite of its expertise, proximity to Hollywood, and ties to the Negro press. But Johnson counted at least thirty black companies who folded without producing a single picture. Others staggered along on the largesse of white backers or rented newsfilm to lodges by the foot. Few of them ever reached the stage of actual production. Too many depended on some single-shot race angle. Anita Bush, for example, journeyed to the all-black town of Boley, Oklahoma, where she made a black western that, along with the company, quickly disappeared from view, unable to derive sustenance from the virtue of claiming to be the first black Western. A halting success such as Sam Langford's *The Brute* would start a rash of rumors that Charles Gilpin or some other famous Negro actor was going into pictures. Here and there a small provincial company such as Gate City in Kansas would emerge. As is typical of most artifacts made for a limited audience, none of the films made during this period has survived.[54]

Understandably, almost predictably, the Lincoln Company, the first and clearly best black effort in motion pictures, ground to a halt. If nothing more, at least the company had provided a black aesthetic statement where otherwise there would have been a void; it had demonstrated possibilities without falling victim to the snares suffered by the NAACP and Emmett Scott. The motives of all three enterprises, give or take a few grains of profiteering, were the same: to bring black images to the screen. This the Lincoln Company achieved in the face of problems that would outlive them. Those within the black microcosm were already changing. In the beginning the black press had so generously praised all black enterprises that many investors of the race were suspicious of the self-congratulation with which the capital-hungry companies indulged themselves. Also, future cinema companies would need to combine better Booker T. Washington's notion of a separate black economy with white financial assistance, that is, the use of white money while preserving black control of ghetto enterprise. Of all the black film producers of their day, the Johnsons came closest to Washington's ideal. As to a black aesthetic, their movies appeared as dark reflections of white models, very much in line with the optimistic assimilationism abroad in the black ethos of the World War period. To ask more was to imagine a Charles Waddell Chesnutt novel, scenario by George Johnson, directed by Noble Johnson, financed by more than the ghetto could supply, yet with a black hand on the reins, and finally screened for an eager, critical black audience and a curious, appreciative white one. In the thick of life the Johnsons did what was possible.

Waiting off-camera was the creator of the next stage of black aesthetic refinement beyond the plateau of race consciousness reached by the Lincoln Company. Oscar Micheaux, already tested by a couple of early exercises, would move from his prairie roots among white people and begin a lifelong, inchoate, insular exploration into every glint and facet of life in the dualistic American racial system. Of all the black producers Micheaux would most exemplify the spirit of the Johnsons in the years between the Great Wars.

Chapter Four

BLACK AND WHITE
IN HOLLYWOOD

To manufacture movies a complex white oligopoly grew, with a cautious eye on its cashbox. Blacks, laboring under the failure of *The Birth of a Race*, the eventual demise of the Lincoln Motion Picture Company, and the near-parodies of white movies produced by small black companies, could offer no countervailing voice.

In the next twenty years Hollywood movies lost their sharp eye for urbanization, immigration, and ethnic assimilation into American life. They abandoned not only blacks but their entire social vision. Hollywood was insulated from the East, with its urban social problems, by nearly a week's railroad journey, and once settled in the Los Angeles sun filmmakers often felt equally remote from local centers of life. Los Angeles was not a city in any conventional sense. It was more a checkerboard of suburbs loosely connected by electric railways and later private automobiles following the courses of multilane freeways. If Los Angeles lacked a center, its sprawl also encouraged extreme social segregation.

The many small producers who followed in the wake of Laemmle's IMP company became through mergers a half-dozen giants. Their decisionmakers soon stretched all the way back to New York offices. Furthermore their distance from ordinary American life forced them to abrogate some of their power, especially with respect to depicting racial themes.

This meant that the only film role for Afro-Americans was to serve powerful whites and to act as models for screen characters. The resulting dependent class of blacks were never able to deal with the studios as equals. Blacks found they could not compete in this world. They had become court jesters, living not in the castle but on a minor fief stretching south from Los Angeles to Watts.

By 1920 Hollywood was little different from the rest of America in the substance of its racial attitudes, and its movies reflected much of the racial temper. And yet many conditions of American life were magnified and distorted in the Los Angeles area. Climate and terrain would allow the growth of rambling suburbs years before they grew elsewhere. Electric interurban railways, then later freeways for thousands of automobiles would tie together the homogenized stucco and pink neighborhoods into enclaves of cultural and social segregation. Status in the large studio hierarchies determined income, neighborhood, and social circles even more rigidly than such structures in other cities.

A calculated "boosterism" advertised the virtues of life in Southern California and attracted a steady flow of new immigrants to the area. Recent victors over San Diego for primacy in Southern California, the Angelenos basked in the Mediterranean climate and purveyed it to the frustrated and displaced native white Americans in the East. In the years from 1890 to 1920 the Los Angeles Chamber of Commerce encouraged wide-spread speculation in land. Racially restrictive covenants in real property deeds assured that the distant suburbs would be a white man's country. Uninvited, the blacks also came, growing from 1250 in 1890 to almost 50,000 by 1930. Black Los Angeles soon became as sharply defined as "darktown" in any Southern industrial city. The flat dry Los Angeles basin further shaped racial caste barriers, for whites lived on the golden slopes and ridges and blacks in the hot depths.

As population grew, electric railways stretched outward from the streets of the old Spanish pueblo, not only pulling together the suburban communities but creating new ones. By 1920 the area from Santa Monica on the west deep into Orange County on the south was connected to the urban core. A white rider could reach work in a movie studio on the cars that ranged even beyond Hollywood through Cahuenga Pass all the way to Universal City on the San Fernando slope, while only one line served the thousands of blacks strung out in little bungalows along Central Avenue toward Watts. After 1906 a decision to annex the "Shoestring District," a narrow strip of land that permitted Los Angeles to legally be joined to San Pedro harbor—with the heaviest shipping, the densest freight lines, the dirtiest refineries, the most pungent rubber tire plants—linked the black ghetto to the harbor.

But the assurance that blacks would live on the fringes of the most ruinous industrial area did not mean they would benefit from the jobs. Many industries, because of the same transport system that encouraged suburbanization, were able to decentralize and be near their white workers. Automobiles moved to Long Beach, oil to El Segundo, aircraft to Santa Monica, steel to Torrance, movies to Hollywood and the San Fernando Valley, all safely away from the black community locked into the marginal, poorly drained, or otherwise unsalable land stretching through the dull haze and yellow flats of the basin.

As the automobile created the ascendancy of private transportation, black isolation amounted to near imprisonment. White communities in the hills, barely visible to blacks through the graying smog, built wide boulevards that testified to their wealth and power. Central Avenue, the main street of Watts, on the other hand, remained narrow, crowded, and thinly topped. In the next generation freeways replaced streetcars, forcing blacks to buy cars they could not afford in order to reach jobs no one else wanted.[1]

The result was a black community as surely in the grip of white exploitation as any Southern black ghetto. In such a closed world Negroes were soon polarized amongst themselves. Too scattered and unorganized to protest movie depictions, too busy surviving in what by Eastern standards seemed a promised land, too proud and worshipful toward the few blacks who crashed the motion picture industry, they were able to have little or no impact on producers. Within the industry black actors often feared to contribute their opinions to the moviemaking process because they were so vulnerable and easily replaced.

Meanwhile, within the industry other forces mounted to contribute to the making of the Hollywood Negro as a ritual type in American movies. The movie industry consolidated its power into a small group of omnipotent corporations built on the rim of the Los Angeles basin distant from the blacks in the bottoms. By the end of the Great War this change from many tiny independent producers to a monstrous oligopoly was complete.[2] Mergers began even before the war when Famous Players and Jesse Lasky united and began releasing their pictures through Paramount. Such an arrangement became the model for the industry, to be followed by the distributors and exhibitors all over the nation who joined in protective leagues. Many of the oldest companies closed their doors under pressure from the giants. Kalem, Triangle and Selig, the last major Chicago production unit, along with Thanhouser, the first to hire a black player, all folded. A nationwide influenza epidemic, the strictures imposed by war, and the fumbling readjustments to peacetime accelerated the changes.

To survive, the studios used their new power to cut production and control volume. The one-reeler went the way of the kiwi. Consolidation brought shock waves of unemployment and retrenchment.[3] A relatively few expensive pictures replaced the hundreds of "programmers"

Early blacks in Hollywood played comic butlers on locations that later black stars would purchase as residences. (Author's collection)

formerly ground out every few days. As the more than seventy studios fell to a handful, the old, cheap moviehouses gave way to "picture palaces" designed to appeal to a more staid middle-class audience. Some of the gaudy barns could hold 5000 viewers. None of them, from the Regent at 116th Street and Seventh Avenue in New York to Fox's Moorish temple on Peachtree Street in Atlanta, was intended for blacks.[4]

Producers sought to guarantee a market for their increasingly expensive products by giving first preference to theatre owners who would show only the films of one company, then later insisting on exclusive booking. Exhibitors retaliated by forming into their own guilds as a countermeasure to the studios' growing power. As a peacetime boom stoked by optimism drove up revenues, ticket prices soared to a dollar. Along with grosses negative costs also rose to nearly $100,000 with length regularly reaching up to nine reels. A few of the biggest stars such as Charles Chaplin, Mary Pickford, and Douglas Fairbanks attempted to cling to their money and share power by forming United Artists, but the big studios and their bankers generally prevailed.[5]

Even after the major companies had formed, occasional economic shocks wracked them. To cushion the shocks they resorted to award-ing preferred playing times to pet theatre chains who booked exclu-sively with one company—"block booking" that allowed accountants to predict a more stable income—and selling "paper" advertising mate-rials. The competition became so vicious that Paramount's agents in the Southern states were nicknamed "the dynamite gang." Slowly the major companies followed the course laid by Adolph Zukor and Para-mount. They made films and rented them to distributing exchanges owned by themselves.[6]

As movies became more expensive, producers grew more cautious about risky themes. A costly production of *The Ten Commandments* laced with hokum would be a far safer enterprise than, say, Griffith's *Intolerance,* with its complicated plot, rhythm, and social message. Bet-ter to avoid invention, imagination, and controversy. The more adept at making such movies the producers became, the less likely they were to take risks. Their audiences came to expect lavish pap, and even stopped attending cheap program movies which offered no elegant production values. Well-mounted, smooth, cleverly paced, authenti-cally detailed historical and costume dramas, exotic melodramas, pietis-tic religious movies, and slick renderings of modern novels and plays made up most film fare. To assure a return on the investment every effort was made to bleed out social comment. Laurence Stallings's and Maxwell Anderson's antiwar play *What Price Glory?,* for example, became almost a celebration of warfare. Like the old *intendants* of the king, the Eastern bankers sent supervisors to the studios to oversee their investments and to insure that they made "entertainment the pub-lic wants." The directors gradually lost control over the content.[7]

As each new economic cycle caused a further step toward conglom-eration and homogeneity, even morals became subject to regulation in order to ensure increased ticket sales. Just after the war, with pro-duction at a low ebb, the Famous Players comedian Fatty Arbuckle became entangled in a sordid case of rape and murder. The studios hired Will Hays, a stuffy Republican warhorse, as a so-called czar who would regulate the moral tone of movies thenceforward. His code of acceptable behavior further narrowed the range of possible cinema topics. It specifically prohibited miscegenation between the white and black races, so there was no clear way to write a scenario in which a black protagonist appeared or one in which any deep relationship could occur across racial lines.[8]

Movies came to reflect the taste of a few strong men—Irving Thal-berg and Louis B. Mayer at MGM, Zukor and Lasky at Paramount, the brothers Warner, and so on. At Columbia, for example, Harry Cohn boasted that he could tell whether a picture was good or bad by the itch of his buttocks during a screening. Authoritarianism, excess fat, sycophancy, and nepotism replaced youth and flexibility and produced caution and dullness, raising still another barrier between producer and audience.

Creative artists felt thwarted and either emigrated or succumbed. Sergei Eisenstein, the famous Soviet director, left Hollywood without ever beginning an intended biography of Toussaint L'Ouverture starring Robeson.[9] The conservative search for the tried-and-tested would hardly ever lead toward Negro themes. Even serious documentaries about African life would be followed by exploitative corruptions such as *Ingagi*, shot on location in California and featuring a lurid, fleeting hint of sex between a gorilla and a white woman.[10]

Underlying the whole Hollywood organism was the supportive fabric of hierarchical race relations with blacks in conflict with the quiet deep-seated racial prejudices of the workers in the studios. Job, status, residence, social circles were defined, as in the rest of America, by race. The important difference was that in Hollywood such arrangements became the premise upon which moviegoing Americans reinforced their racial attitudes. Powerless darker races lived far down in the Los Angeles basin away from the centers of studio vitality and power. Thus whites throughout the motion picture industry cleaved to racial policies and attitudes shaped in a lily-white world. The most prominent black figures viewed by whites were servants and entertainers and the unctuous shoeshine boys and hustlers who clutched at the fringes of power at the studio gates.

A promotional movie designed to show off the facilities of the Ince Studios reflected the daily round of life in Hollywood. The audience sees a wide shot of the great white Thomas Ince Studios panning past huge barnlike stages, shops, dressing rooms, and offices. All white faces. Cut to a pleasant residential street. A Filipino houseboy says goodbye to his master, a movie star on his way to Inceville. A few shots carry him to the studio. There a liveried black porter in a pillbox cap fingers the mail at the gate. Cut again to the star, Louise Glaum, as she ends her day with tea on the lawn, served by a stately Negro in a white uniform.[11] White symbols of work, power, and creativity were set against servile blacks, mute and smiling in the background, mindful, as far as anyone could tell, only of a fallen napkin, a stray postcard, or an unshined toe.

White Hollywood, isolated in private houses, rested on the backs of black servants as a natural order of things, but more than that, white was separate from black at every stratum of life. In the old days a star might ride the streetcar to Edendale to work or pass lunchtime with the motormen lounging amid the orange groves and church spires that dominated Hollywood and Vine. Even then, however, few stars looked down in the basin toward the poor. Charles Chaplin was asked by a worried friend to discontinue his walks southward toward the ghetto, and soon he too took up the life of beach parties in Santa Monica. Only Oriental servants and an occasional movie star such as Sessue Hayakawa and his wife, Tsuru Aoki, could live in the Hollywood Hills. Sam Baker, the Negro boxer, could not even call for his white coworkers in their Hollywood apartment without arousing a protest from the manager. Even the Anglo-American and Mexican poor felt remote from brownskinned men. Most poor whites felt insecure and strained by long hours, oppressive labor practices, and the danger of having a scarce job wiped out by a retrenchment or the accident of a laboratory fire; so blacks, to them, would have been more a threat than anything else.[12]

The closest social relationship between blacks and whites was that of master and servant. In the silent era Chaplin had Kono, his Filipino houseboy; Ronald Colman his "boy"; director W. S. Van Dyke his "colored houseboy," Napoleon, who sat at home with the dog "waiting to hear from their master"; and so on. When producer Joe Pasternak came to Hollywood in 1926 he was urged to get a car and a Filipino butler as a sign of his status. By the 1930s Mae West's maid, the accomplished actress Libby Taylor, played her role both on and off screen, fussing over the bathwater, the breakfast, and her employer's moods. Marie Dressler remembered the texture of show business success as "sitting in the luxury of my apartment at 1566 Broadway with a maid and a Jap cook, waiting for the manicurist to do my hands and a hairdresser to arrange my hair."[13] Even on the set Negroes were never professionals. If they served as actors, assistant directors or casting directors, they were identified as lackeys. Gracing every set were errand boys; and when the actors worked in a "tank shot," Negro maids rubbed protective oil on their bodies.[14]

Overt racism fell into disrepute along with the Ku Klux Klan in the 1920s. But vestigial racism could not help but survive in the closed Hollywood air. Not necessarily calculated or conspiratorial, it was simply normal intellectual baggage, a casual manner of whites toward blacks. Social relations, humor, jobs rested on it. When Edgar "Blue" Washington acted in Tim McCoy's silent westerns it was expected that his title would be "handyman" and that whites would play pranks on him. On one location they placed snakes in his bedding and laughed at "the blue streak as Blue Washington lit out across the plains." During the bizarre events surrounding the murder of William Desmond Taylor, a silent film director, whites in the Mack Sennett studio hazed a butler by taking him through a cemetery only to have the scene ruined for them by his crackling laughter at *their* absurdity. In her gaudy evangelist shows in Hollywood Aimee Semple McPherson regularly reenacted the Negro's plight in America, complete with crapshooter on stage. Racial jokes continued as part of the repertoire of stage comics. At its best it was merely capricious. With equal vigor W. C. Fields could thrash a man who referred to a "nigger" in the presence of his domestics, pay off his cook's mortgage in an impulsive gesture, and yet die leaving his estate to an orphanage for white boys. The system appeared at its worst when "the studio would have to pay off the outraged husband of a Negro lady who had been violated by a certain director."[15]

On the set crewmen habitually referred to black lights as "niggers," and makeup men boasted of their ability to heighten racial stereotypes with their craft. Martin and Osa Johnson, presumably sensitized by their careers as documentary filmmakers, could describe their South Pacific subjects with "ugly faces—eyes with scarcely any pupils, flat noses . . . coarse, rapid gutteral speech. . . ."[16] And even though Negroes began to break down casting barriers in the 1920s, many white men still took the prominent black roles.

Blacks as victims had few options. The stars such as Ethel Waters (who did not reach Hollywood until the end of the silent era) took as much money as they could. The maids and butlers assumed a diffident protective coloration or laughed it off, preferably at the expense of whites. Sometimes they developed a professional flippancy that annoyed their white employers. One cook enjoyed bursting into the drawing room to announce, "You folks better hustle to dinner if you don't want the stuff to get cold."[17]

From the earliest days race was steeped into every corner of life, from the "nigger" in the scenario marginal notes written for the sound version of *The Birth of a Nation* to the simplistic "how-to-write-for-the-movies" books that taught young fans the racial code. Some merely warned their readers to "stay away from censorable themes," while others defined the traits of racial stereotypes. One of the earliest lessons in comedy writing appeared in 1913 and featured a "shiftless, worthless, fat negro" whose eventual good fortune brings him quantities of chicken, pork chops, melons, and "other things dear to a darky's heart."[18] Jack Warner remembered a most ironic tale of racial prejudice that revealed a Negro market for films and white blindness to it. Young and pinched for funds, Warner rented a reel of negative to a Negro, attributing the reverse shading to the actors' race. The Negro billed the movie as "First Negro Movie Stars" and, according to Warner, "had the box office jumping for three weeks."[19]

The absence of black opinion, except for an occasional writer such as Wallace Thurman in the early 1930s, allowed whites a smug confidence in the accuracy of their views. *Variety*, for example, reported in 1923 that Griffith "has long urged the idea . . . that this generation is ready for a new Uncle Tom," basing his conclusion on the success of his scared Negro character in *One Exciting Night*, which he believed had done well in the South. Even then he forgot that a clever sleuth in the movie was a black African.[20]

Along with incidental racism, and in part the cause of it, Hollywood nurtured a Southern mystique. Many blacks and whites had drifted from the South to California and found work in the studios, and their beliefs colored life in the movie colony.[21]

In the studio offices the pattern held. Executives such as Harry Rapf and William Selig came from traveling minstrel shows. Y. Frank Freeman, for years with DeMille and Paramount, was born in rural Georgia. And the Southern theatre chains, competing for the limited Southern dollar, trained the sharpest practitioners in the business: men such as Steve Lynch of Paramount; Edward Kuykendall, a former president of the Motion Picture Producers Association; and Sam Katz of Paramount's Publix Theatres. Directors of the stature of King Vidor, Clarence Brown, and W. S. Van Dyke were proud Southerners. The close connections encouraged cooperation with Southern exhibitors, and occasional splashy Southern premières. Almost any Southern theme required a native white consultant, and they leavened the city with their racial tales. One of them told the story of a Texas Christian University football player who, in the days of Kenny Washington, Woody Strode, and Jackie Robinson, eluded three black tacklers of the UCLA team, at last falling before a white tackler and muttering, "Dr. Livingston, I presume."[22]

The air was so heavy with casual racism that the foreign colony unavoidably breathed it in. Salka Viertel, one of the many European immigrant screenwriters, loved the long rides out Pico Boulevard to the shimmering, irridescent seashore at Santa Monica, but she felt hurt by the growing racism of her circle. When she hired a black maid, the German actor Emil Jannings refused to dine in the presence of "die Schwarzen." Worse, her own son, angry and spiteful at not making the football team, screamed at her, "You dirty foreigner!" Next, she thought, he will call me "Polack"! She felt alone because of the false liberals who "sit around their swimming pools, drinking highballs, and talking about movies while the wives complain about their Filipino butlers." Greta Garbo, who eschewed flashy luxury, succumbed to the point of having a Negro drive her old Packard. The English especially seemed not only to accept American racial mores but to delight in them, reveling in "a marvelous colored band," or the voices of "coal black mammies . . . telling you how much they love you" over the car radio.[23]

Between the wars there was little overt interracial hostility—nothing to bring racial prejudice to a conscious level. Liberals were punctilious toward the feelings of minorities; there were even acts of personal sacrifice and courage, but they effected no general changes. Ronald Reagan's father, for example, forbade his children to see *The Birth of a Nation* and slept in his car rather than stay in anti-Semitic hotels. Fred Astaire proudly boasted of appearing on the same vaudeville card with Bill Robinson. Famous blacks such as Robinson never stepped from their public roles of smiling entertainers, so there was scant criticism of things as they were. Jews, on the other hand, curtly took up the challenge of anti-Semitism. When Mary Pickford, for example, attributed the rise of Hitler to Jewish avarice during the dreary Weimar Republic, she faced a stiff rebuttal from the actress Carmel Myers.[24]

Even more revealing of racial postures was the point at which art and life became one: the publicity campaign for MGM's *Trader Horn* in 1929. The small company on location in Africa had been beset by misfortune, the rumored death of an actress, and disappointing footage, so that for retakes and promotional uses they brought Mutia Omooloo, a young African who had given a sensitive performance in the movie, back to California. From his arrival onward his every wish was treated as a savage eccentricity. Segregated on the studio lot, he was made to seem fey because of his Islamic kosher demands, his sightseeing and wandering on Central Avenue, and shopping in five-and-tens. Feminine companions for him became the assignment of a studio toady who doubled as pimp. Misunderstandings up and down the avenue resulted in bickering and violence, ending in a wild chase through Culver City; a confrontation with Irving Thalberg, the head of production; hospitalization and eventual escape; down to the very night of the première at Grauman's Chinese Theatre, complete with Africans in loincloths in the lobby. There, even his balking at the segregation of the women he escorted was taken as no more than African orneriness. At no time was he taken seriously. The studio research department even forgot the names of the tribes, eventually labeling them "Gibboneys" and "Joconeys" after Cedric Gibbons and J. J. Cohn, two studio executives.[25]

Blacks observing Hollywood from deep down in the basin knew the social structure of the movie colony was unfair and corrupt, and yet the ills of the Afro-American could not be traced directly to it, nor could the motion picture industry be characterized as more racist than any other American institution. In fact the well-known liberal politics and philanthropy of many of the stars would not allow movie people to stand as a hateful enemy. The point is that at its *best* the system still placed Negroes below the salt. Thus a whole black world grew up south of Hollywood, remote, oppressed, and yet in the twenty years between the wars incapable of well-focused response to racism in the movies.

Furthermore, divisive elements within the ghetto contributed to the persistence of the racial system. Oppression encouraged the growth of a a stratified black society, which divided black attention away from protest against discriminatory practices. Central Avenue north of Watts in the 1920s throbbed with life: dense, varied, sought after by white habitués of "hot-colored" clubs, carved by industrial zoning, and yet the center of the black middle class. For a black visitor it seemed as though the servants of the stars came alive only in the jazzy sessions of Sebastian's Cotton Club in Culver City. Simultaneously the growing and slowly stratifying ghetto included the families of the Beaverses, the McDaniels, and the Dandridges—the future black stars. Louise Beavers was already appearing in neighborhood social entertainments. The black *Eagle* straddled between urging black solidarity and the breaking of white barriers, applauding all manner of black enterprise from the local chapter of Marcus Garvey's Universal Negro Improvement Association to the latest effort to raise capital for "race movies."[26]

Black Californians further blunted their pressure on whites because they had taken on some of the traits of white "boosterism." From promoting "the beautiful city of Watts" as "the coming Negro town of California" it was only a short step to boosting the home-grown stars of ghetto clubs, and from there a shorter step toward acquiescing in some of the demeaning roles forced upon them. Black papers reported the gossip of Twelfth and Central as though it were Hollywood and Vine, and generally they supported the aspirations of the few Negroes in the studios. More automobiles, crowded street corners, new young stars such as Carolynne Snowden at the Cotton Club, Stepin Fetchit flaunting his wealth, feeding the love-hate blacks felt for him, angry complaints that Hollywood distorted black identity in such movies as Cecil B. DeMille's *The Ten Commandments*—all contributed to the tempo of the black West Coast.[27]

Yet beneath the vibrant activity and black camaraderie was a vague uneasiness. Movie roles were only resumptions of old Southern roles. Blacks were still dependent upon whites for jobs, status, and security. To do sixty-eight weeks at the Cotton Club, win a featured role in *In Old Kentucky*, dance in von Stroheim's *Merry Widow*, attend cast parties, have a dressing room on the MGM lot, a roadster and a maid, and best of all, a five-year contract was still, at bottom, to be beholden to powerful white men and to be replaceable by any one of the sleek young "foxes" in the chorus line. That was Carolynne Snowden's story, but it could have been the life of any black actress in Hollywood.[28]

Success meant puffed press releases to disguise the wide spaces between jobs. It meant a hard journey from Omaha for Julia Hudlin, who saw an old Lincoln movie and quit her job as a social worker for a try at Hollywood. After six years of struggle she became a personal maid to the movie star Leatrice Joy, and later "secretary" to Dolores Del Rio. When her employer went to Europe the blacks had a farewell party of their own on Seventeenth Street. Other women, like Anita Thompson, a young black New Yorker who shocked her social set by taking a fling at show business, chose to stop short and leave Los Angeles before falling into the slough of servant life. Mildred Washington survived as a "Creole Cutie" in Sebastian's between roles in *Uncle Tom's Cabin* and *In Old Kentucky*. Even good performances brought few new roles, and many clung to their menial jobs or to ghetto hustling. Zach Williams, after moving from Louisiana, did two gemlike bits in *Yankee Clipper* and *The Merry Widow* as a cook and an archly flippant dandy, but between jobs he faced long dry spells spent hanging on the fringe of the sporting world along Avalon Boulevard. Even at their best, black careers ended with no more than a friendly obituary praising a long succession of "mammy" roles.[29]

Rather than make the rounds of the casting offices and agents, Negroes clustered in a little cadre along Central Avenue from the Dunbar

If blacks failed to hang on in Hollywood playing servants they might become servants, like Julia Hudlin here ministering to Dolores Del Rio. (George P. Johnson Collection)

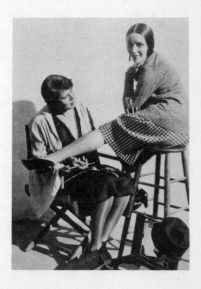

Hotel in the forties northwards into the teens toward the Lincoln Theatre and toward Hollywood. Studio scouts scanned the avenue looking for likely specimens and invited the most physical types to "cattle calls"—mass invitations to try out for spots in the coveys of natives in jungle movies.

Between jobs they supported themselves through regular jobs with City of Los Angeles agencies such as the highway or the water department. Like longshoremen at the morning shape-up, they hung on the corners at the Dunbar and Smith's drugstore, to see and to be seen. Only Stepin Fetchit and a few other contract players retained agents.

Once a job was secured, the actor would hope to be picked up on Central by a studio bus. If not, he rode the electric railway up Central Avenue past midtown onwards to Hollywood Boulevard, where he caught a bus westward to Columbia, Fox, or Warner Brothers. The unluckiest rode all the way through Cahuenga Pass to Universal City. The best duty to all was at MGM because there was only a short ride up Central to broad Washington Boulevard and westward to Culver City. After the coming of sound, commuting worsened because of a black migration southward into Watts and Compton coupled with a drift of studios away from the congestion of Hollywood and Sunset Boulevards.

Because casting directors preferred types rather than talent, success was measured in the number of hours, days, or weeks rather than in the quality of roles. Therefore the black actor counted himself lucky to pick up his $3.50 per day as an extra, and aspired to no more than that. Indeed, a speaking part could easily lead only to another "cattle call" rather than an interview for a substantive role. If the hurt and frustrated actor eventually chose to marry, the economic rigors slowly drove him toward the waterworks and the highway gang. Not that whites were not sometimes defeated by the system; rather, blacks never won. Geography, automobiles, stratification, and segregation saw to that.[30]

Trained, overqualified actors also suffered, like the child actors in Hal Roach's *Our Gang* series who found slurred, rather than precise, speech a *sine qua non* for winning a part. Roberta Hyson in 1929 lost her first tryout for the same reason. Teresa Harris, trained in music at the University of Southern California, measured out her career in bits. Evelyn Preer, a veteran of the Lafayette Players and understudy to Lenore Ulric in the Broadway production of *Lulu Belle*, supported herself between jobs at a saloon in Long Beach and on radio station KFOX. Others drifted into music, became agents, or, like Lawrence LaMar or Ruby Berkeley Goodwin, caught on with black newspapers.[31]

At the top of the black world was a cadre of doctors, lawyers, pharmacists, and officers in the Golden State Mutual Insurance Company, but black actors derived no sustenance from them because white producers turned to another élite of sorts for advice on racial matters, for gangs of "extras," and for the unctuousness that so many whites expected from blacks. These were the studio Negroes. Two of them in the 1920s, Jimmie Smith and Charles Butler, worked outside the plants recruiting extras along Central Avenue. Others worked inside. The two most famous were Oscar Smith of Paramount and Harold Garrison of MGM. Both were nominally bootblacks, but they also ran elevators, hustled errands, fingered mail, and delivered messages. Sometimes they cadged small roles, as did Smith in the 1928 version of *The Canary Murder Case.* Smith came to the studio just after the World War as a valet to Wallace Reid, whose will provided that he be given a shoeshine stand in perpetuity. Garrison was known to blacks as an assistant director, but to whites he was "Kid Slickem," the bootblack. Both Smith and Garrison held flimsy power over blacks because of their

At Paramount the studio bootblack, Oscar Smith, cadged more roles than many trained performers. (George P. Johnson Colection)

Accomplished actors such as George Reed and Teresa Harris, here on the set of *Hold Your Man* (© Metro-Goldwyn-Mayer Distributing Corp.), displayed their talents by accommodating to the status quo. (George P. Johnson Collection)

modest influence among whites. But, like everything black in Hollywood, their power was quickly eroded at the end of the 1920s when the studios turned to the new Central Casting Corporation and their black agent, Charles Butler, for players. So tenuous was the situation then that Jimmie Smith, who had brought James Lowe to Universal to replace Charles Gilpin on the set of *Uncle Tom's Cabin*, took his protégé to England in search of fortune rather than cling to the fringes of power.[32]

With the coming of sound, the Negro began to receive more attention from Hollywood. The occasion for centralizing casting coincided with a wave of interest in Negro life reflected in the release of King Vidor's *Hallelujah!*, Fox's *Hearts in Dixie*, and the black bits in revue films designed to show off the new soundfilm systems. There were some who saw the era of sound as the apotheosis of blackness because, they believed, the Negroid voicebox recorded with greater fidelity

than the Caucasian. And yet at the crest of this wave blacks still had
not gained much recognition. Shortly after the fad began, Harry Levette started a column, "Gossip of the Movie Lots," for the Associated Negro Press. It revealed both the breadth of the stream and the
dead end to which it ran. Week after week he noted the jobs Negroes got: 600 for retakes and location shots for Ernest B. Schoedsack and Merian Cooper's *Four Feathers*, 200 more for a big production
in Hollywood, still more for retakes on *Trader Horn*, studio shots for
Hearts in Dixie, and so on. A bannerline in the *Amsterdam News*
flashed: "MOVIETONE BECKONS HUNDREDS OF NEGRO AUDIENCES." On
soundstages in one week blacks worked in Buck and Bubbles musical
shorts, retakes for *Hallelujah!*, plus the scattered others totaling 200.
And yet, except for Stepin Fetchit in his shuffling stock character, no
black star with a continuing following emerged.[33]

Stepin Fetchit and the lesser players together, consciously or not,

Extras such as the former slave here teaching James Murray and Helene
Costello how to dance on the set of *In Old Kentucky* (© Metro-Goldwyn-
Mayer Distributing Corp.) contributed to a conservative ambience.
(George P. Johnson Collection)

acted both as a conservative force and as a palliative for black rage. Their foolish public roles and conspicuous consumption made them appear richer and more powerful than they really were, so blacks adored them even when they may have winced at the flunkeys' roles that paid the bills. Fetchit cruised Central Avenue in his big car with "Fox Contract Player" lettered on its side, claiming as his title "The King of Central Avenue." Because of his professional needs, Fetchit never revealed any inner dignity to whites for fear of undermining his public image. Only with black friends did he reveal the pleasure he derived from his season ticket to the Hollywood Bowl symphony series. To a white reporter he hewed to type, insisting, "If you put anything Ah says in the papah, it might be wise to kind of transpose it into my dialeck." Except for Spencer Williams, who wrote stereotyped scenarios of Octavus Roy Cohen stories at Christy Studios, there was no black voice inside the studios to deny the universal nature of Fetchit's type.[34]

Negroes, in such a shabby corner even in good times, became the first victims of the rollback of production induced by the Great Depression. With revenues shrinking, the studios dropped the blacks. By the 1930s the good black roles had come and gone. The myth of the resonant Negro voice box echoed hollowly. Fetchit was let out of his contract. Duke Ellington, taking a brief turn in an Amos 'n' Andy movie, was hungry enough to call it a "crowning point." In the slump even Al Jolson in blackface looked good enough for the *Amsterdam News* to claim "that every colored performer is proud of him."[35]

All the gains made by black professionals in the late 1920s and the early sound era had no direct support from the Los Angeles Negro community. All roles were counted equally as "progress." Within the studios Negroes never had the opportunity to protest either the emphasis on Fetchit as a type, or the way he and other blacks were dropped as soon as the depression started. Actors who broke into the movies on the basis of one slim talent or, worse, one stereotyped trait, found life the harshest, for they were easily replaced. Even the cumbersome, noisy machinery needed for sound-on-film hurt in that it reduced mobility and encouraged a rash of comedies-of-manners and flippant, talky stories that allowed little room for the traditional roles of black servants.

Clarence Muse and Willie Best exemplified the new order. Best was one of several Negro actors who played Fetchit-type roles. For a while he was even billed as "Sleep 'n' Eat." Inexperienced, he remembered strolling along Central Avenue amidst the soft-drink stands, strip-zoned apartments, and the Father Divine Café, when at Forty-first he caught the eye of a white man cruising in a big car. Scared at first that it was a

Room at the top was for only a few stars like Stepin Fetchit. (The State Historical Society of Wisconsin)

Even a star like Willie Best was obliged to "offer to caddy" for white star Charles Winninger. (Author's collection)

policeman, he bolted. Eventually he landed an RKO contract. Later, surrounded by the florid colors of his apartment, decorated by buying from the poor black stores on the street, steeped in the smells of hamhocks and mustard greens, Best sipped a glass of icewater and pondered: "I often think about these roles I have to play. Most of them are pretty broad. Sometimes I tell the director and he cuts out the real bad parts. . . . But what's an actor going to do? Either you do it or get out."[36]

Muse came from other circles with formidable credentials: a dabbler in the law at Dickinson Law School, experienced on the stage with the Lafayette Players in New York, and a witty writer and composer. Yet for him, power amounted to no more than being able to work regularly. Despite the decline of the Central Avenue boulevardiers he acted, he served "as an expert in the making of pictures employing colored talent," and wrote dialogue and an occasional song and script and newspaper column. He never saw his work as degrading or racist, and eventually he condemned Walter White and the NAACP for hurting black chances to "build ourselves into" the movie industry by seeming arbitrary protest against Hollywood racism. In other words he advised Hollywood in the art of preserving the traditional black images, especially with his work on *Hearts in Dixie*. His contribution to the status quo extended even to the point of amusing the white cast of *Fury of the Jungle* (in which he played "Malango") by doing dialect routines with his pet goose. His conservatism was further supported by his popular Negro dude ranch, one of many sidelines Hollywood Negroes employed in order to survive.[37]

Another force that paradoxically contributed to black pride and community while supporting the rigid racial order of Hollywood were the *grandes dames* of the ghetto, a social élite who gave without stint to help the race while at the same time supporting their style of life by playing traditional roles as domestic servants. Louise Beavers, Hattie McDaniel, Teresa Harris, Libby Taylor, Lillian Yarbo, Marietta Canty, and others carried both their stock roles and their selfless lives in their baggage—inseparably. For the twenty years between the wars their parties and fundraising "affairs" graced the inside pages of the black press: McDaniel's soirees and Canty's work with the established charities, Sunday schools, and the Sojourner Truth Home were forerunners of Lillian Randolph's favorite club, the Benevolent Variety Artists.[38]

Black actors read and wrote the columns in the Los Angeles *Sentinel* analyzing "Why Negroes Live Better in Los Angeles." In short, their well-deserved pride in what they did *off* screen allowed them to ignore the impact of what they did *on* it. They were proud that they had kept open the door of hope in Hollywood.

Those with the choice simply lived materially better lives, as did many of the black men who survived by playing the hapless jungle men in Tarzan movies, always hoping for a better role next time. Below them were the hundreds who never read a line on camera and who measured success by the scattered two- and three-day jobs as dress extras. Put together they represented a strong conservative force. Protest against demeaning roles generally came from outside their circle and sometimes split the community into "pros" and "non-pros." From the actors' viewpoint, to protest traditional black roles would only drive Negroes onto relief rolls. Not until the growing race consciousness of the war years would the two groups think of mending the fissure between them. Even then Fetchit could argue that he had paved the road for later blacks because his stereotyped behavior had made white audiences readier to accept black behavior.[39]

Hence at a time when white Americans living in cities were encountering more and more blacks, Hollywood continued to use old stereotypes to depict blacks. The social concerns of early movies had long since faded, victims of escapist entertainment values. "The Vitagraph was always urban in its outlook," a critic wrote of one of the old Eastern studios. "Its sentimental stories were the stories of the city streets and tenements." Seldom would the later Hollywood product evoke such a comment.

The grateful blacks who regularly appeared in movies and lived on the fringe of the industry were in no position to offer protest or even honest observation. They paid their dues for the right to work by keeping silent. There were few liberal white voices of protest because the Eastern Jews who were most powerful in the industry were neither the radicals in the garment trade unions nor the rich philanthropic Germans of New York and Chicago but Europeans who had only recently arrived as penniless immigrants. And often their racial advisers were *goyim* drawn from their Southern theater chains.

Finally, almost every racial opinion or decision was confirmed by the trade papers and box office returns. The isolation of Hollywood would not have been possible without the faith studios placed in box office returns from the South. These, coupled with a few previews in safe suburbs such as San Bernardino and Riverside, provided the final justification for certain kinds of racial depictions. And in the absence of audible black protest such data strongly reinforced attitudes formed from observing local conditions in Los Angeles. Bankers, investors, and producers, by relying on limited evidence, fell into patterns, cycles, and types of movies, all designed to sell. In a short time they came to accept box office receipts as the sole criterion of success. Thus the myth blossomed that the Southern market would predict the success of racial themes not only in the South but the North as well; for if a picture would not sell in the South, it might not sell in the North. Besides, Southern profits, though smaller than those of other regions, might carry a movie out of the red. The Southern box office became a monolithic creature that predetermined racial images on the nation's screens.[40]

Yet, the movie industry was as blind to true conditions in its markets as it was to the true feelings of blacks in Los Angeles. Studio men had no accurate data from the South, misread much of what had been gathered, ignored other omens, and failed to appraise the shift in American racial attitudes, a trend they might have contributed to rather than retarded. Generally, the movie trade journals, even while subscribing to the myth, held Southern grosses in such contempt that *Motion Picture Herald* reported no box office receipts south of the Ohio River. *Variety* used only five Southern cities as "keys," or samples, with only two, New Orleans and Birmingham, reported for the lower South. The Southern cities always compared unfavorably with the North, sometimes with one or two New York houses earning more than the entire South. At Christmas 1923 the best New Orleans theater grossed $3400, while the Capitol in New York announced a profit of $50,000, this while the best Birmingham house regularly fell below $1000 per week. *Variety* often hazed New Orleans for its plight. Headlines claimed the city was the "CHAMP BAD PICTURE TOWN," "FLOPPING ONCE MORE AS USUAL," where "BUSINESS IS BAD AND SOMETIMES BADDER."

Nearby in Covington in 1925 a theater manager, desperate to fill seats, accepted empty beer bottles at the gate, earning only $23 and 1812 empties.

Throughout the 1920s in the South there was a dreary round of excuses for low box office returns: hot weather, dog tracks, state fairs, free concerts, and, later, night baseball. Even movies with Southern themes failed. In the depression conditions predictably worsened. Rural, ill-kept wooden theaters frequently burned. By the 1930s radio and roller derbies joined fairs and carnivals as drains on ticket sales. At its best the Southern economy remained bound to one crop, causing managers to complain, "When crops fail, the box office takes a licking." Another economic quirk was the six-day week. While many Northern cities gathered good gates on Sunday, Southern laws either banned shows or took inordinate percentages of the grosses for the charities, censor fees, and entertainment taxes that were used to placate fundamentalist preachers. Such impedimenta acted as fixed costs, along with legal fees incurred in testing blue laws. Southern censorship in its capriciousness and arbitrariness proved to be another burden. A few censors in Memphis and Atlanta served as guides for many states.[41] The Strand in Birmingham went three straight weeks setting record lows and by the end of 1932 only one house in all of New Orleans was in the black. Warners ended the silent era by announcing the closing of its Southern chain because of isolation and other "operating problems."[42]

Obviously there was no way of tracing low grosses to racial themes. Trade reviewers, in fact, were often wrong in making such predictions. *Variety* was astonished to learn that despite presumed Southern anti-Semitism, *The Cohens and the Kellys* did $11,000 in Baltimore in 1926. Even expensive hard-ticket movies such as DeMille's *The Sign of the Cross* were unpredictable in the South. In New Orleans in 1933 it made less than a horror picture-vaudeville double bill. In short, inconsistency ruled, and movies neither made money in the South nor followed clear enough patterns to warrant using the region as an indicator of national racial attitudes.

Negro themes were equally immeasurable. The trade papers could not even count the segregated black audiences who were obscured by using the euphemism "drawing population" to mean "white." When early sound films stimulated a rash of Negro pictures such as *Hallelujah!* and *Trader Horn*, they did well in Southern dates.[43]

When occasionally movies captured some of the reality of the black world, executives learned the wrong lessons from the box office returns. In 1929, a year after Harry Pollard's *Uncle Tom's Cabin*, King Vidor's *Hallelujah!*, shot on location in the South, using an all-Negro cast, neatly caught the piety and enthusiasm of rural religion, while only occasionally lapsing into stereotyped gamblers and mammies. The film did well even in New Orleans; and in Memphis, Baltimore, and other Southern towns it ran without comment. Yet the cycle of films it stimulated included the old stereotypes.

The extent of Hollywood inflexibility may be seen in a cursory survey of the roles played by the "Hollywood Negro." As the black world in the 1920s grew more aggressive, demanding, and unified through the NAACP, the Universal Negro Improvement Association, the Urban League, and the "buy-where-you-can-work" campaigns, the Hollywood Negro grew more stylized and fictive. From 1915 to 1920 roughly half the Negro roles reviewed in *Variety* were maids and butlers, and 74 percent of them were known in the credits by some demeaning first name. In the 1920s servile roles reached 80 percent of all black roles. By the 1930s they had dropped by half, but casting policy still restricted Negro roles by allowing Cab Calloway, Lena Horne, and other performers to appear only "as themselves" with no investment in the plot. Such billing accounted for 15 percent of Negro roles. Added to these were the nameless hordes of painted tribesmen who fell before the stout arm of Tarzan.[44]

In other words, not until the 1930s did Hollywood notice blacks and their increasing dissatisfactions with American life. But the most remarkable blind spot of all was revealed in the trade papers, which regularly reported black *and* white concern with ghetto life. The trades reported a plethora of bustling, popular, thriving black activity in other media without taking notice of its possible uses in cinema. Powerful drama, exciting musicals, racially integrated vaudeville and burlesque, and even black theatrical activity in the South were often heralded by banner headlines. Yet the ferment and the vigor were lost on moviemen. They failed to notice the rage for Negro theatre that began as early as 1918 when William Smith, a Philadelphia theatre manager, pointed out that the success of Harlem's Lafayette Theatre should be taken as a demand for more of the same. The famous *Shuffle Along*, with book, music, and lyrics by blacks, came to Broadway in 1921, triggering a movement for an all-Negro opera company. In the same year Charles Gilpin toured the South in *Emperor Jones* without incident. "NEGRO ACTORS ARE FLOODING BURLESK," croaked *Variety* in 1925 as Gus Hill of the Columbia Burlesk Wheel created six all-Negro and mixed cast companies that toured as far south as Baltimore. Vaudeville also boasted fifteen weeks of all-black shows and a black circuit. By 1933 Chicago played four all-black shows at once, with the Mills Brothers returning for an unprecedented seventh run. When talent grew thin, the boxers Jack Johnson and Battling Siki went on the road.[45]

Within a short time variety was joined by the drama. In 1925 white critics praised Paul Green's *No 'Count Boy* for its acting, which came from "inspiration and painstaking preparation" rather than the presumed natural acting ability of Negroes. A year later Paul Robeson opened in *Black Boy*, adding to his already imposing artistic stature. In one season, 1927, there were eight black companies on Broadway, some of them also on the road. A year later Wallace Thurman's playbill for *Harlem* included a glossary of Negro patois for the convenience of its white audiences. As box office grosses swelled, radio joined the trend.[46]

The demand overflowed to Europe, starting with companies of *Shuffle Along* and the many editions of Lew Leslie's *Blackbirds*. Another review, *Dover to Dixie*, starring Will Vodery and Florence Mills, "scored a veritable triumph [and] . . . Every number was violently encored." Josephine Baker ranged from the Folies Bergère to clubs to drama to movies such as Maurice DeKobra's *Siren of the Tropics* and Marc Allegret's *Zou Zou* with Jean Gabin. French playrights followed the trend with such productions as Sacha Guitry's *Blanc et Noir*, which focused on an interracial triangle. Nonetheless, *Variety* set American cinema apart from life by finding a French drama, *The Black Ace*, "unsuitable for America . . . since it places the negro in an unbiased light, almost idealizing him."[47]

The boom, still unnoticed by Hollywood, brought changes in the ghetto. Black theaters were chronically short of film. Counting variety and cinema the number of these houses rose to nearly 1,000 after World War I, with Chicago in one year opening three new ghetto houses totaling 8000 seats. Critics in the black press grew more demanding of Negro drama, acting, and production values as though to ask the second mile of their black brothers on the stage at the crucial moment of climbing ambition.

For all the yeasty activity, Hollywood clung to its myth of the darky maid, propped by faith in the Southern box office. Trade paper reviewers continued to predict failure for black movies in the South or explained away success as an aberration, while ghetto exhibitors cried for more film to the point of threatening to shorten their week. Rarely would *Variety* endorse a movie with Negro roles as "sure fire for any audience."[48]

Instead, the movie industry continued to depict the old metaphorical Negro. As late as 1930 *Variety* urged readers to catch Al Jolson's sluggish failure, *Mammy*, as a glimpse of a dying earlier day, and yet studios ground out still later versions of the same minstrel genre.[49]

The reliance on haphazard data could not alone support Hollywood's decisions with regard to racial themes and types. The Hollywood Negro—amalgam of eternally smiling servant, living sacrifice to white ambitions, rootless toady with no life of his own, witless jungle man—

emerged from the total experience of white men in Southern California. Isolation from changes in American life, from the Negro world even on its own Central Avenue, and from its own audience, the leaden rigidity of the large studio system, the underclass of grateful blacks who were forced into silence in return for movie roles—all these factors allowed moviemakers to view the world through the prism of the mythical Southern box office. Its distortion of American values let the executives feel that the tastes and prejudices of the white South were at the core of their own decisions. Most of all, in the years after Griffith this isolation provided them the luxury of believing in their own creation, the "Hollywood Negro," who populated their motion pictures long after he had lost his ephemeral connection with the real world.[50]

Chapter Five

THE SILENT HOLLYWOOD NEGRO

The decade after D. W. Griffith's *The Birth of a Nation* brought bad times for the Negro on the screen, not so much because of that motion picture but because a newly awakened urban black yearning for better things made the black images seem more old fashioned, irrelevant, misleading, and maddening than ever before. The social forces unleashed by the war carried new ideas into the social fabric of American life. With changes would come freedom from old images and myths, especially those related to race. Soon whites, if not willing to change racial arrangements, were at least less able to prop them up with the visual images of rural tradition. Afro-American life itself became more urban, politically aware, organized, and demanding. But for the moment and until the mid-twenties Americans were reassured that under the turmoil lay the bedrock of old verities. Generally, liberalized sexual codes, women's behavior, other signs of social change, were one with pious hymns to the old ways. Thus when black consciousness burned hot, movies offered no fuel, not even for the modest changes that whites had already accepted.

E. M. W. Tillyard in his *Elizabethan World Picture* wrote of a society which needed to "tame" new facts by fitting them to older forms. America must have been this way after the wrenching shifts brought on by the World War, and movies provided a medium through which taming could be managed. Especially for blacks who were unrepresented in the seats of power, this meant continuing grudging tolerance of a white man's Negro on the screen, a tamed image having little to do with changing social reality. Black soldiers, labor organizers, Pan-

Africans, Zionists, cool cats, intellectuals, all the blacks who broke the old molds in Northern ghettos, were unseen on the nation's screens. In spite of the montage of new Negroes a sense of order and the rightness of things demanded that only the old stereotypes be trotted out across the screen like Jeremy Bentham, dead, stuffed, and wheeled out for board meetings of the London School of Economics. Aunt Jemima, Uncle Ben, George the Pullman Porter grinned from their advertisements, eternally giving of themselves, reassuring white men that nothing had changed. Darkey stories rehashed at white parties, anxious queries to diffident maids, and wistful attendance at oldtime minstrel shows reinforced belief. In Tillyard's words these old forms could "on the one hand express the idea of order they so longed for and on the other serve as a fixed pattern before which the fierce variety of real life could be transacted and to which it could be referred."[1]

The roots of change had penetrated deep into prewar intellectual groups, which challenged the old order and brought an "end to American innocence." The psychologist William James, the "progressive" educator John Dewey, and other academics questioned old truths. Their relativism was reflected in the growth of environmentalism—the notion that experience, not genetics, determined human capacity—in John B. Watson's "behaviorism," and in the naturalism and realism which appeared in the work of American novelists. Materialism triumphed over religion, frankness over convention, and cultural relativity over chauvinism. Optimism was in the air. "In 1919 the tomorrows seemed vaster," said the writer John Dos Passos. "We were at bottom fundamentally optimistic, and we were gay crusaders," recalled Joseph Wood Krutch of his days on the Fabian *Nation*. "The future was bright and the present was good fun at least."

New ideas encouraged new freedoms, especially for women. Men and women in greater numbers attended universities and the new junior colleges. By 1914 the liberated woman had already become "the flapper" who read widely, dressed in freer clothes, danced in public, and discussed sex. The movies celebrated such trends with interesting works such as William C. DeMille's production of Zona Gale's *Miss Lulu Bett*, the countrywoman who throws over the traces of drudgery.

Within communities of obvious ethnic identity there was even greater variety as some clung to old ways, some exploited new conditions, and still others did their best to assimilate Anglo-Saxon ways. In Chicago's Italian ward, for example, behavior included outward migration, upward mobility, poverty, and the marriage of crime and ethnic politics brought off by Big Jim Colosimo.

As urban institutional life expanded, personal life narrowed to small circles of family and neighborhood, for whom mass media provided increasing draughts of sensationalized social data in print, on film, and on airwaves. So sometimes change faced resistance from these little cores of stability. For example, conservatives fretted over liberal sexual mores. Similar fears were reflected by the prohibition of alcoholic beverages, the federal action against radicals during the "red summer of 1919," and the repression of blacks returning from the Great War during the same riot-torn season.[2]

Negroes, traditionally consigned to the bottom rung, broke the surface of white life before whites in the mass were prepared to accept them. The Harlems of America contained all the ingredients of general American life. Along with the dull brown slums and the grubby, chanting storefront churches that prayed for them with the tang of old Southern meetinghouses, there were trim, tweedy blacks on the Sugar Hills, polishing their cars until they could see themselves in the Simonize finish. Somewhere between the work-oriented black bourgeoisie and the ground-down poor were the successful hustlers who had gone to school in the city streets. Like Alex Pompez they were equally at home in the numbers game—the poor man's gaming room or stock market—in the sporting and entertainment circles—Pompez backed the New York Cubans baseball team—and in middle-class parlors.

Now and again, when they paid attention, whites caught a flash of this life through glimpses of show business, bohemia, and news stories of black protest, all of which revealed the black world as a distorted, exotic mutation of what jazzmen referred to as the "square" life. Jazz, or "nigger music"—the term belongs to the black *Chicago Defender*— came to whites through Paul Whiteman's genteel rendering of George Gershwin's proto-jazz *Rhapsody in Blue* in New York's Aeolian Hall. From the rage for primitive art that followed popular anthropology it was an easy step for white intellectuals to find parallels in Harlem life. Carl Van Vechten, Mabel Dodge Luhan, and Ridgely Torrence celebrated and patronized the blacks they found there. More than ever, white aggression produced black self-defense. With the Ku Klux Klan just past its peak, the NAACP defended the right of a black Detroit dentist to defend home and family in a hostile white neighborhood even to the point of killing an assailant, a nearly unheard-of event before the war. And the flippant black press—the *Courier*, the *Defender*, the *Journal and Guide*, the *Afro-American*, the *Sentinel*, the *Eagle*, the *Age*— recorded it all.

And yet withal, blacks gained nothing in the white man's cinema except through such accidents as the decline in taste for ante bellum and Civil War melodrama, which depleted the ranks of old retainers and loyal servants who had shuffled through the genre. The Hollywood Negro, shaped as he was by life in the movie colony rather than by the stuff of city life, served as a tamed image and a drag on the thrust of black demands. As late as the mid-1920s major Negro roles went to white men in blackface. Not until after 1925 would a small cadre of Los Angeles Negroes replace the old white actors.

The years between 1915 and 1925 constituted the laying of a ground for later change that would not be clearly manifest for blacks until the eve of the Great Depression. W. E. B. DuBois's famous editorial in the *Crisis* demanded "a sterner, longer, more unbending battle against the forces of hell in our own land. We *return*. We *return from fighting*. We *return fighting*. Make way for Democracy! We saved it in France, and by the Great Jehovah, we will save it in the United States of America, or know the reason why."[3] A. Phillip Randolph and Chandler Owen's socialist *Messenger* evoked white hysteria. But black intellectuals were confident. The war had brought a decline in constitutional support for Jim Crow laws despite Woodrow Wilson's Southern political commitment, the army had appointed Emmett Scott as an assistant secretary for Negro affairs, blacks demonstrated for a federal anti-lynching law, and postwar race riots shocked Americans with the news that racial problems were no longer, if they ever had been, a purely Southern question. Most of all, newly migrated Negroes experimented with social organizations such as the NAACP, the Urban League, and Marcus Garvey's zionist Universal Negro Improvement Association. A more demanding black press chronicled the changes.

Early on, the Hollywood studios aspired to longer pictures with literary themes that would appeal to middle-class audiences. Vitagraph claimed its pictures "will not only draw record crowds, but will bring Higher Class Patronage at Higher Prices." *Les Miserables, The Life of Moses, Oliver Cromwell, A Tale of Two Cities,* and themes from grand opera and Shakespeare—"high art films," Vitagraph called them—came to the picture palaces that had replaced the old storefronts. As the need for working capital increased, banks began to exercise a conservative influence over the content of motion pictures. Prestige and higher grosses encouraged the development of "stars"—actors whose identity and charisma sold tickets and who thus came to command high wages and approval of scripts that would continue to show their talents in most favorable lights. Mary Pickford was "America's Sweetheart"; Theodosia Goodman became Theda Bara, the incarnation of "Arab Death"; and male stars such as Douglas Fairbanks, Charles Chaplin, William S. Hart, and Rudolph Valentino brought acrobatics, comedy, western life, and exotic romance to the screen, and incidently provided another powerful voice in determining theme and content of their movies. The demands of quality encouraged the trend toward mergers. A model union was that of Adolph Zukor and Jesse L. Lasky, independents who joined with W. W. Hodkinson's Paramount and later with the Publix chain of theatres. Many more combines followed. The combinations put a premium on profit, shifting artistic control from the director to the producers and other studio supervisors. Scripts were subject to hierarchical approval, even for writers of the stature of F. Scott Fitzgerald.[4]

In their urge to tame the new demands made by changes, the studios hired Will Hays to create a model of pious rectitude that included the American success myth, stratification along lines of wealth, secure segregation of the races, and relations between the sexes suitable for family viewing in a code of "Don'ts and Be Carefuls" that guided producers. At first a nervous reaction to moralistic critics of the industry, the Hays Office provided a conservative brake on creativity after 1922. It also prohibited ethnic name-calling and miscegenation in a well-meaning gesture that effectively barred blacks from any roles calling for serious relationships with Caucasians. Thus no studio depicted black despair, poverty, neglect, outrage, caste, or discrimination. Instead Hollywoodians sentimentalized social forces and made their own Jewish and Irish assimilationist comedies on the order of Anne Nichols's *Abbie's Irish Rose,* a bittersweet parody of the strains of a Jewish-Irish marriage that was so frequently milked as a theme that its author could not win a plagiarism suit because the court held the worn plot to be in the public domain.[5]

The immediate institutional barrier to fuller presentation of Negro life on the screen was the absence of a friend at court. The most liberal Jews who managed the studios had no way of knowing how to render black life honestly. Even if they were aware of the reams of copy *Variety* devoted to black entertainments, they still resided in remote California after the exodus from the old studios in Fort Lee and the Bronx. As to their artful use of immigrants as movie topics, they testified from experience and from the opinions of the many resident Roman Catholics, both Italian and Irish, in the studios. Frank Capra at Columbia, Eddie Mannix at MGM, Winnie Sheehan and the Protestant Darryl Zanuck at Fox, and Marshall Neilan at Mayer's early studio gave counsel to the Selznicks, the Goldwyns, and the Lessers. Negroes, on the other hand, had as friends at court only white Southerners, such as Steve Lynch and Y. Frank Freeman at Paramount and King Vidor at MGM. On specific cases such as *King of Kings* Cecil B. DeMille consulted with the well-known Jesuit Daniel Lord, thus further cementing the connection between church and studio, later made permanent with the founding of the Legion of Decency in 1933. Gentile counsel and Jewish authority was the most frequent division of labor, a point not lost on Frank Whitbeck, an MGM publicity man who once called his

boss a "fat Jewish s.o.b." only to be warned that if he wished to remain
in show business "there is no such thing as a *Jewish* sonofabitch." At
the top were the Jewish bankers: Goldman and Sachs for Warners;
Kuhn and Loeb for Paramount; S. W. Straus for Universal; and the
Italian founder of the Bank of America, A. P. Giannini. Together the
entire arrangement soon made it impossible for Negroes to enter the industry. They lacked capital, experience in newly specialized crafts,
and, most important of all, "contacts."[6] Furthermore, directors had developed the art beyond what any pariah Negro might absorb from
outside the circle. The pioneer geniuses Griffith and Thomas Ince, the
pictorially graceful Maurice Tourneur, the authoritarian Erich von
Stroheim, and the commercial successes—Cecil B. DeMille, Allan Dwan,
Herbert Brenon, James Cruze, and Frank Lloyd—took giant strides forward from the old two-reelers.

What the foregoing story meant for Afro-Americans was exclusion
from all but a few traditional roles, and a few newly developing roles
as atmospheric furniture, at least until the late twenties. Artistically,
except for Griffith's *Birth of a Nation* and Colin Campbell's *The Crisis*
for Ince, the Negro rarely inspired whites. And worse, plummy Negro
roles often went to Europeans trained in blackface vaudeville, this despite the view of one visitor to Hollywood who felt Negroes were
"better actors" and "so easy to find." Even a fine script such as Laurence Stallings's *The Big Parade* spewed such gratuitous gibes as "The
coon begins to apply the lather."[7]

The cinema lagged behind plodding liberal drift and presented social
change only after it was no longer controversial. The Negro press was
puzzled not so much by Hollywood's intransigent racism as by its persistent irrelevance, omissions of recent black life, and the fact that it
no longer evoked laughter or pleasure from urban audiences. At first
black protesters were unorganized, active only on a national scale, not
involved in neighborhood action against white exhibitors. They were
still learning the uses of urban neighborhood structure, newspaper cru-
sades, and economic boycotts.[8]

Black tactics consisted of building a voice within the black community, encouraging black movies, and praising good roles and honest
casting in white movies. The movement grew from the Negro press in
mid-America, the *Courier* and the *Defender*, and the Los Angeles press,
and spread to New York, where Lester Walton stoked the movement
by blasting the blackface tradition, protesting the rash of anti-Asian
racism, complaining of segregated theaters, praising Negro music and
Ridgely Torrence's *Three Plays for a Negro Theatre*, and urging race
unity. But not until 1920 or so did whites begin advertising ghetto
houses in black papers. And even then they used only cuts, mattes, and

The horse trainer of John Ford's *Kentucky Pride* (© William Fox) was an instance of an earthy new type, often uncredited, which departed slightly from Southern tradition. (Author's collection)

D. W. Griffith's *The Idol Dancer* (© David W. Griffith, First National) provided one of many cattle calls—this time in Florida. (Author's collection)

Boxing trainers, like Jerry Peterson as Smoke in *The Great White Way* (© Cosmopolitan Corp.), presented more urban black roles and brought them closer to the action. (Author's collection)

Transported to another century in *The Love Mart* (© First National Pictures, Inc.), Raymond Turner played Poupet serving Gilbert Roland's Jallot—leaving the role unchanged. (George P. Johnson Collection)

press releases from the pressbooks intended for whites. For some time to come, then, blacks felt a lack of power, influence, and impact on white media. And yet, even the conservative pundit H. L. Mencken told the executive secretary of the NAACP that the old racial arrangements could not last because "fighting back" would change blacks into a force for further change.[9]

For the moment blacks could count on only a small erosion of the old Southern metaphor and then largely because of a shift in urban taste away from the Civil War and the ante bellum South. Imperceptibly, newer black roles allowed a modicum of ambiguity, a subliminal denial of the root premises of racism. Horse trainers, boxing trainers, convicts, and jungle men, because they were rejections of Southern high-church racial formalism, shaped a tacit, half-revealed, fuller Negro psyche. Horse trainers were more than Toms; the knowledge implicit in the role opened the way for more plot involvement. Boxing movies gave off a hint of egalitarianism. The jungle men, though vanquished, at least provided dramatic conflict by fighting white men. And finally, a few whites such as Robert Flaherty and Ernest B. Schoedsack with a flair for capturing anthropological truth on film would bring new dignity to darker peoples in *Nanook, Chang*, and other forthright forays into other cultures.

At a secret, perhaps unconscious level, even to the blacks' presence who created it, there was looming ambiguity in the new black characterizations that could not be contained within the crumbling limits of the old stereotyped roles. The jungle man who fought with shield and spear had the mean marks of the hated and feared "bad nigger." His spear was his razor. Under every Tom's mask was a Staggerlee, the mythic sexual hero of Negro lore, grimacing under the smile of the "good nigger." And as though he were the black heart of Joel Chandler Harris's whitened Brer Rabbit, behind the dutiful shuffle of every Stepin

Fetchit was the glibly hostile "signifying monkey" of Afro-American hagiography.

In the worst of times this was the best that might be expected. Fortunately for Negroes the five years before *The Birth of a Nation* had produced the glut of Civil War movies that soon reached perverse heights, faltered, and died. At first the black press compared all racial typing with that of *The Birth of a Nation* and welcomed "as flowers in May" the few black roles that departed from it, ignoring further questions of aesthetics. With increasing urbanization and remoteness from Southern roots, a war for "democracy," and rising black awareness, conservative racial imagery would have to take some other form.[10]

With few exceptions the Civil War movies were as alike as sausages. Deviation from the formulas, especially the intersectional lovefeast, brought warnings from the trade press. "One of the scenario problems of the day is to write a Civil War story that will not offend that considerable population south of Mason and Dixon's line," observed *Motion Picture News*. And yet each ritual reenactment of the torn families, the fetishistic tales of the officer caste, the love affairs sacrificed to war, the loyal slaves, the crass Yankees, the déclassé overseer-villains, even in fine films, grew remote from the real urban world. Not only were white Americans less responsive; Afro-Americans no longer remained uncomplaining. The bankruptcy of Southern ancestor worship was evident in declining box office receipts and even in popular screenwriting textbooks. One of them claimed the old types "are gradually going out of fashion," while another added that if a fledgling author had no better inspiration it would be "much better not to send it out."[11]

No better example of the waning of the Civil War as metaphor-for-union may be found than Colin Campbell's production of Winston Churchill's *The Crisis* (Ince, 1916), chiefly because it was such a well-crafted piece. Neatly composed, almost painterly frames, a fine fidelity

An athlete at the end of his career might, as George Godfrey did in *Old Ironsides* (© Paramount Famous Lasky Corp.), catch on for a few films. (George P. Johnson Collection)

to period, and some departures from hackneyed themes could not save it from dwelling on the statistical rarity of families divided, of blacks caught in cardboard roles. It served to reveal the irrelevance of the war as a usable past. It opens and closes on a colophon of crossed rival flags and a cut to Lincoln striking the fetters from a kneeling Negro. From there the story drifts to ante bellum days set in striking period scenes in which two families "have their daily quarrel over slavery." Campbell's picture granted honest disagreement over the question by having the Southern daughter ask her father at a slave auction to "buy Mrs. Scales' quadroon, Hester, for me," only to have the young Yankee, Brice, buy her to prevent the breakup of a Negro family. When war comes, the sequences are in flattering imitation of Griffith, tinted in red, but from Sherman's side at the siege of Vicksburg. The strain of war is contrasted with the good-natured haggling over Lincoln and slavery. Lincoln's climactic death is made to seem a sacrifice for the sectional union symbolized as well by a marriage. Throughout, Negroes appear in the customary roles, but they are less obsequious than Griffith's movie blacks, and there is even a strong black woman whose courage prevails in the face of war.[12] However, the genre rarely allowed even a well-made movie to rise above cliché.

When movies focused on the ante bellum South without the war as dramatic conflict, the situation was even less imaginative. The most gothic of the tales was Triangle-Kay Bee's *The Bride of Hate* (1916), in which a Southern doctor avenges a hurt by promoting a love match between his enemy and a light-skinned slave he has won at cards. Later he reveals her identity and drives his enemy to drink and death. "Exhibitors below the Mason and Dixon line had better watch out," a reviewer warned. New Orleans became a popular locale because white actresses such as Pauline Frederick and Lina Cavalieri could be used as Creoles. Kentucky replaced Virginia as a location, thus allowing a shift to hillbillies. Then there were exploitations such as that of the baseball player Ty Cobb in *Somewhere in Georgia*.[13]

While the films of the Old South declined, Negroes faced racial typing from another quarter, the movies that emerged from the popularity of Edgar Rice Burroughs's Tarzan stories. His work rested on a firm base of nineteenth-century exploration and curiosity about the new anthropology and remote peoples, leavened by the safaris and hunts of Theodore Roosevelt and other public figures, and recent booms in conservationism and in western camping. Earlier movies had featured expeditions and primitive attempts at shooting tribal life and wild animals and their fakes and parodies. Burroughs's contribution was a white hero lowered as a *deus ex machina* into the jungle, where, in the author's racist scheme, he learns to use its lore with greater effect than the natives. At that, awkward problems of racial ambiguity emerged because black men fought with a white for power—no matter how faltering—and moved dangerously close to being "bad niggers." As a result Tarzan's cinema locale in time gradually shifted away from Africa.

Nevertheless, in its two spurts at the beginning and at the end of the twenties the trend survived hopelessly inept writing, grubby production values, and decreasing fidelity to Burroughs's original conception. The cycle began in the late teens when Burroughs, a failed plunger in minor schemes, salvaged the movie rights to his jungle stories, and after receiving a feeler, sold one to Selig, in whose "zoo" it would be shot. The first picture, *The Lad and the Lion,* disappointed its author but stirred his hopes to bring Tarzan to the screen.

Even before its release Burroughs sold the rights to Tarzan to Bill Parsons, a Chicago filmmaker, who took a company to Louisiana in order to match locations with earlier shots taken in Brazil. Even though they exhausted their cash and lost their hero to the U.S. Army, they completed the film using Otto Linkenhelt—Elmo Lincoln—a yeoman actor in Griffith's troupe. Again, Burroughs brooded over violations of his ideas, but the result soared above his expectations.

The savior of the picture was Harry Reichenbach, the first of the flamboyant press agents. His campaign caught the attention of urban Americans who seemed starved for rustic romance and adventure. Shamelessly he registered an ape at New York's Knickerbocker Hotel, sent engraved invitations to first-nighters, instigated fan clubs, and splashed ads in the newspapers invoking some of the sex fantasies underlying the urge for jungle pictures. See the "abduction of the white girl by the apes," they cried.[14]

Tarzan of the Apes, though neither racially nor artistically advanced, offered patrons a curious respite from urban pace, while pointing the way to future evasions of racial conflicts in the plots. Burroughs's success had rested not so much on chauvinistic and invidious comparisons of whites with other races, but more on his faith in the average man's capacity for overcoming adversity with common sense. Indeed, his first *nom de plume* was Normal Bean. The movies from the very beginning were equally subtle, and appealed to a self-satisfied racial cockiness rather than hyperaggressive racism. The critics noticed in the first Tarzan film a trend that carried through to the end of the cycle in the days of television: a focus on animals and wholesome jungle ambience in contrast to the decadence of civilization. The resulting avoidance of pejorative racial comparisons meant that Africans could be expected to disappear from the plotlines except as atmosphere furniture. Unlike earlier jungle pictures, Tarzan featured only one African role.

Instead, *Tarzan of the Apes* cast racism as mere Anglophilia, a respectable wartime point-of-view, and political conservatism in the form of regard for the British class system—or at least for Lord Greystoke, the nobleman of Burke's *Peerage* who became Tarzan, the nobleman of nature. Burroughs's sources were the travel writings of Henry M. Stanley, who glamorized for American readers his trek through Africa, and Kipling's Mowgli, the shrewd *indigene* of *The Jungle Book*. So the first premises of Tarzan's heroic superiority remained below the surface along with, for example, his notion of the faculty of imagination. "The beasts know it not, the blacks only a little," he wrote, "while to one in a hundred thousand of earth's dominant race it is given."[15] The resulting ambiguity could not conceal the fact that implicitly inferior tribesmen resisted the "lord of the jungle," thus calling into question the very superiority upon which Burroughs had rested his hero's stature.

As though fearing the black rage beneath the surface of the cardboard black heavies, the producers cheapened, then abandoned Burroughs's concept and eventually moved Tarzan out of the jungle into urban settings and into tropical lands unpopulated by blacks. Except for the earliest soundfilm versions, never again would they recover the fidelity or their large audiences. The sequel, which failed to reach the half-million-dollar gross of its predecessor, featured a uniformed maid as the most prominent black in its stills, and drew the wrath of Louis Reeves Harrison, one of the most distinguished of early critics, for abandoning its jungle roots for an urban setting. By 1918 Burroughs had been edged out as holder of exclusive rights and sold the character to Numa Pictures, a division of Artclass, a producer of programmers, which employed an inexperienced Tarzan, Florida locations, and a plot that opens on an ocean liner bound for France and ends in Paris. Samuel Goldwyn bought and distributed it as best he could and barely survived the critics' estimate that "the novelty is lost in the latest release." Succeeding silent Tarzans strayed as far from black Africa. National Film Corporation's 1920 serial muddied the racial imagery by starring the Polynesian Kamuela Searle as Korak, son of Tarzan, pitted against Arab heavies. By 1921 the first cycle ended with two heavies from *Mittel-europa*, one a Bolshevik, and plots which were tangled in squabbles over Greystoke's title. The last serial brought back Lincoln and broke from the ranks of the cheap "state rights" films into full national distribution. But *The Adventures of Tarzan*, as it was titled, lacked dramatic racial conflict: a few black bowmen help drive off Arab marauders, and a black child appeared as a "Tonto" figure whom Tarzan patronizes by leaving him with the women to "shoot bad mens with spit fire sticks."

Thus by 1921 Tarzan had become no more than a commuter, flitting through the jungle ghetto on his way to work in the city, averting his eyes from black concerns, and in conflict with urban Europeans. No Tarzan for the rest of the silent era could overcome the resulting banality, nor could writers solve the problem of the place of the armed black warrior in white men's movies about Africa. Blacks thus were able to gain only insofar as minimal gestures toward verisimilitude required black men to play Africans. But by the time of Tarzan's revival in the late 1920s the productions of FBO, Numa, and Universal (the first major studio to release a Tarzan film) focused on athletics, and chose such famous athletes and stuntmen as Indiana football star James H. Pierce, stuntman Frank Merrill, and physical cultist Joe Bonomo for their title roles. Heavies were descendants of white pirates, Arab raiders, or Waziri tribesmen led by Boris Karloff in blackface. Generally, critics ignored them, audiences gave them modest support, and black reporters praised every "cattle call" and casting assignment they generated.[16]

Both derivatives and predecessors of the genre were also racist not in their depictions of blacks but in their omissions. The studio jungles were thick with the lives and plots of white men with blacks as atmospheric furniture rather than "bad niggers" in conflict with white invaders. Selig's *A Night in the Jungle* (1915), for example, had the gunbearers hie off to the bush while a laggard paws at the white woman on the verandah, eliciting only a mild threat that he would be "severely punished." It was hardly evidence of Africans as serious antagonists, and, indeed, they soon disappeared from subsequent last-reel reunions, dramatic conflicts, and from animal pictures save as occasional fodder. In Louise Glaum's vehicle *The Leopard Woman* (1920), she impetuously orders her lover killed, remorsefully wishes him alive, and when a Negro dies in his stead, "Madame is overjoyed that Culbertson escaped." Fox's *The Jungle Trail* (1919) offers a white "god" who rules a tribe after "his great strength wins him their worship," a gimmick topped by *A White Barbarian* (1923), a British picture featuring the "Songora tribe, who possess a white royal family."[17] Thus through one device or another blacks disappeared except as casual objects.

Gradually during these years the Hays Office taboos on darkskinned heavies and on miscegenation supported and codified dramatic relationships until only two means survived by which studios could use exotic locales and nonwhite peoples. First, the locales could be Polynesian, thus using white actors playing, like Marie Antoinette at Versailles, at being primitive, trading on the lore of Robert Louis Stevenson, Daniel Defoe, and Captain Cook, and thus eliminating aggressive black figures. Second, the heavies could be halfbreeds whose worst traits resulted from bad blood rather than racial identity. This accommodation, conscious or not, allowed the playing out of dozens of tragic mulatto

themes, cross-cultural conflicts, and love affairs across racial lines, all
of which was accomplished without the Negroes whose presence in
America contributed to white fascination with race.

Freedom from racial taboo encouraged redundancy and eventual
carping by the trade press at "the South Seas hokum, such as undressed
native maidens and heavy atmosphere." Repetition resulted in absurdity
such as Clara Kimball Young's daughter of a French derelict in Abys-
sinia, "Le Fille Sauvage," who was raised in a leopard skin, takes a
French lover, passes as the reincarnation of the Queen of Sheba, and
at last, being white withal, "it all ends in a clinch." The taboo could be
broken in *The Tiger's Claw* (1923) because the brownskins are East
Indians, thus allowing an American dambuilder to marry a halfcaste
only to suffer the destruction of his work at the hands of her old suitor,
"a Hindoo magician, who sees his power over the natives waning."[18]

At the top of their form audiences appreciated the sandy exotics in
an innocent way even when they were preposterous productions of
ridiculous novels such as Edith M. Hull's *The Sheik*, which starred
Rudolph Valentino, and popular Broadway hits such as *White Cargo*,
which stirred a cycle of tropical pictures. Spectacles such as Fairbanks's
The Thief of Bagdad (1924), with its aura of a rich, dense Oriental
culture, its grand sets by William Cameron Menzies, its atmospheric
use of Anna May Wong, So-jin, the "passing" Negro, Noble Johnson,
and its black eunuchs, was an exciting, athletic exercise in the genre
which drew wide praise.[19]

Box office success encouraged white goddesses who built careers on
lightly clad brownskinned roles. The earliest and most archetypal was
Theda Bara—fobbed off as an anagram for "Arab Death." "Kiss me, my
fool," she said in *A Fool There Was*, William Fox's near-burlesque of
Kipling's poem about a female "vampire" who consumed men and their
fortunes. Her success as a "vamp" led to gaudy press conferences attended by "Nubian" servants and to forty movies before the rage
burned out.[20]

Her successors were blonde good-bad girls even more remote from
their brownskinned sources: Betty Blythe as *The Queen of Sheba*, the
swimmer Annette Kellerman as *A Daughter of the Gods*, and the
erotic dancer Gilda Gray as *Aloma of the South Seas*. Herbert Brenon's
Kellerman picture ran to extravagant proportions, on location in Jamaica, and in a studio set replica of a Moorish city with a soaring
minaret from which the star dove into the sea. Money, stars, sex, and
critical acclaim testified to the popularity of the genre. Mary Pickford,
Lenore Ulrich, Pauline Frederick, Lina Cavalieri—everyone tried at
least once to be a white exotic primitive.[21]

With Negroes safely off the screens the variations were endless, embracing a minor revival of Indian movies that allowed dramatic conflict to develop around themes of interracial sex without fear of intrusion by the awkward presence of blacks. "The taint of Indian blood" was the theme of such pictures as Douglas Fairbanks's *The Half Breed* (1916), *One Eighth Apache* (1920), and the creaking melodrama *The Heart of Wetona* (1919), in which the white suitor saves the halfbreed maiden from ritual deflowering. Interracial love surfaced in *The Squaw Man* and its sequels (1913–1931); *The Woman God Forgot* (1917), a tale of Montezuma's daughter and one of Cortez's officers; and programmers such as *The Red Woman* and *The Red Red Heart* (1917–1918). With fears of miscegenation dampened by the segregation of blacks there was less need to resort to trick endings such as that of *The Scarlet West* (1925), in which an educated Indian "saves the garrison from a treacherous Indian attack, gives the girl to the young white lieutenant . . . and returns to the haunts of his forefathers." Indeed, the times inspired ambitious failures such as Paramount's *The Vanishing American* (1925).[22]

The blacks' only consolation was in the knowledge sprinkled through the *Sentinel* and the *Eagle* that they were getting "extra" work, honing their tools with slim experience, and developing a tight little cadre of ready and willing black actors. But that would be slow in coming. Even vocal and direct-action protest, the oldest of black tactics in the early twenties, seemed fruitless compared to the results achieved by Jews in their protests against DeMille's *King of Kings* and the Indians in their recruitment of Secretary of Interior Ray Lyman Wilbur to fight against "being exploited in aboriginal roles."[23] For the moment blacks did what was possible in the isolation of California: jungle men, servants, substantive roles for a few as exotics, and on the lowest rung, cattle calls.

Show business for whites and blacks alike had always been an avenue of upward mobility, but not the movies. Whites came to the hills of Hollywood to succeed; blacks came incidentally: Madame Sul-te-Wan, Noble Johnson, Onest Conley, Zach Williams, Spencer Williams, Raymond Turner, the Shackelford twins, Floyd and Lloyd, and occasional boxers such as George Godfrey. A few, like Carolynne Snowden and Louise Beavers, were Californians or childhood migrants. Others came from black companies such as the Lafayette Players, with a little dramatic training and wide experience in musical performing, a pattern that worked to fix blacks in exotic character roles that led nowhere. For example, Benny Ayers came to Hollywood from Troop C, 10th United States Colored Cavalry, and survived as an exotic in *South of Suva* (1922) and *The Leopard Woman* (1920). Sam Baker gave up boxing for a career in the mid-1920s—*The Thief of Bagdad, The Road to Mandalay, The Sea Beast, The Missing Link,* and *Louisiana.* Oscar Smith moved from Wallace Reid's valet to studio bootblack to valet roles, to Djikki the Senegalese soldier in Paramount's *Beau Sabreur* (1927). Webb King worked in the studios and with the black Lincoln Company but gave up and took jobs with Los Angeles County. Sulte-Wan came from a cloudy past in Louisville, deserted by her "Hindu" father, drifting in and out of circuses and Negro vaudeville, to Hollywood and an introduction to her fellow townsman, D. W. Griffith. Their enduring friendship, deeper, some say, than the badinage with which they kidded each other, led to *The Birth of a Nation* (she spits on the old Colonel), to seven years with Griffith, a series of Negro comedies with L-KO in 1920, and scattered other jobs, none fine enough to prevent her from confessing, "I get bitter sometimes because I don't work long enough to buy a handkerchief."[24] Like blacks everywhere they seemed on the surface frozen between idle despair and gratitude for small white favors.

Of all the blacks Noble M. Johnson exemplified both the plight and achievement of the Negro actor. His boyhood in Colorado prepared him to be a stuntman and an animal trainer, both of which stood him in good stead during dry spells in a career that stretched from Lubin in Philadelphia to Hollywood and John Ford's *She Wore a Yellow Ribbon* in 1949. His coppery-bright skin and square features opened up a wide range of roles that allowed him to obliterate his racial identity in white circles while receiving praise from the black press. His position with the Lincoln Company gave him temporary independence from Universal, yet he had regular roles in Universal's B-movie series, *Bull's Eye, Red Ace* and *Red Feather Specials.* His credits in the better pictures seemed endless although small: "a renegade cowboy," a Mexican, and so on. Through the mid 1920s they included *Adorable Woman, Leopard Woman, Kismet, The Four Horsemen of the Apocalypse, Robinson Crusoe, The Courtship of Miles Standish,* and *The Ten Commandments* (as the bronze man). In one year he appeared in nine movies including *Flaming Frontier, Aloma of the South Seas, Manon Lescaut, Lady of the Harem,* and *Ben Hur.*[25]

For blacks in the 1920s Johnson's career was a kind of victory within a context of despair, a black presence that went beyond menials to substantive roles. His sinister brute and hulking Lascar, forever emerging from below decks, skulking over the banyan roots, peering from behind the filigreed door of the seraglio, fingering his dirk, his assegai, or his kris, cut a new notch on the measuring stick of black attainment. Unfortunately for Negroes, Johnson could no do more; his bright skin permitted him to avoid Tomming, but it made no demands on white audiences. The more Negroid actors, on the other hand, could not in-

Of all the men of Lincoln, Noble Johnson was the most successful moon-lighter in such films as *The Most Dangerous Game* (© Radio Pictures), *Son of India* (© Metro-Goldwyn-Mayer Distributing Corp.), and *Moby Dick* (© Warner Brothers Pictures, Inc.). (Author's collection)

dulge in such symbolic assimilationism. For the Williamses, the Shackel-
fords, Floyd and Lloyd, and George Reed success meant praise in the
black press for the quantity rather than the quality of their parts and
a bit of admiring gossip about their middle-class lives.[26]

If Afro-Americans derived scant profit from the offhand racism of
commercial movies, they at least gleaned beneficial side effects from
the new genre of documentary pictures that popularized cultural relativism. Indeed, the documentaries were an indicator of the changing
norms of popular American racism. For years factual film had offered
no more than strung-out shots connected by lame, humorless titles—at
least until young Robert J. Flaherty, the son of Irish immigrants, came
out of the rough country near Iron Mountain, Michigan, where he
had grown up amongst the Indian villages and Canadian mining camps
that provided the visual sources of his later naïvely anthropological
film work.

Flaherty was the first filmmaker to bring a "sociological imagination"
to the recording of the lives of darker peoples. He let the images speak
for themselves, yet he was unafraid to contrive, if contrivance added
to versimilitude. For years white men had been fascinated with the rimlands and the outbacks and the brown men who live there, but only
Flaherty caught them on the wing in *Nanook of the North* (1921) and
Moana (1925). Gone were the ringed noses and tattoos that ran
through the clammy stream of old movies that had ignored family,
gods, and dignity. Whites were forced to see darker peoples as real
men through Flaherty's "innocent eye."[27]

Flaherty's work mirrored the problem of honest black movies. He
shot and processed film without altering Eskimo culture, even while
enlarging igloos, introducing heaters, and taking the men away from
the hunt. Yet Hollywood was no more interested in such loving fidelity
than it was in shooting authentic Negro life. Revillon Frères, the fur-
riers, financed *Nanook*, but even then, distribution of such flinty stuff
was problematical, especially in competition with the mindless *curiosa*
Martin and Osa Johnson brought back from their gawking trips to
Africa and Borneo. After making the rounds of the screening rooms
Flaherty finally sold *Nanook* to Pathé.

Later he sold the idea of *Moana* to Jesse Lasky, who had been im-
pressed with *Nanook*'s European sales and wanted a safe replication.
To Flaherty *Moana* was a record of Samoan life, timeless as "a frieze
on a Grecian urn." To intellectuals it was the embodiment of Frazier's
The Golden Bough. But to Lasky it was a plotless "turkey," and after
half-dozen unheralded previews he quietly released it hoping for a
small, safe return. Thus ended Flaherty's "epic of race." His next project, for Irving Thalberg of MGM, ended as a bloated Hollywood

junket to Tahiti, complete with crackling radios, movie stars, and disputes with his Hollywood collaborator. The Hollywood producer's feel for the subject was expressed at a preview of *Moana:* "Boys, I've got a great idea! Let's fill the screen with tits."[28] Flaherty's sensitive film promoted no revolution and at its best found only limited runs in small houses and eventually schools. And yet his intuitive, personal feel for the relativity of cultures exposed, as clean as a blade, such visual evidence of humanity and dignity that it weakened the ability of racism to survive.

Nevertheless, in the noisy 1920s it was like a remote, half-heard echo. The studios did little to follow his course. At Paramount Ernest B. Schoedsack and Merian C. Cooper made *Grass*, *Chang*, and *Four Feathers*, each movie moving a step away from documentary toward melodrama. *Chang* ran well on Broadway for a few weeks in 1927, but its Laotian story was lost on the black students at Hampton Institute, who, without waiting for it to begin, used its screening as the occasion for a rebellion against their puritanical administration. Small independent distributors could afford only the dull cans of film brought back by expeditions to Africa. They were poorly edited glimpses of animals interrupted by bits of pygmies and staged dances: *Gorilla Hunt* (1926), *Through Darkest Africa: In Search of the White Rhinoceros* (1927), *Simba* (1927), and *The Bushman* (1927), which *Variety* found "just another animal picture, this time without the real thrill shots which 'Chang' and others of this style have led the public to expect." The era closed with the preposterous fake, *Ingagi*, a legendary gorilla who allegedly kidnapped a white woman.[29]

Thus the rich cinema tradition of the mid-twenties had given little to blacks and had tended to segregate them through artifice and through Hays Office policy. In turn, for most of the tag end of the silent era the black press had the sticky dilemma of pressuring studios to abandon pejorative stereotypes while at the same time standing for the principle of keeping a black presence on the screen. A not uncommon result was a frequent split between California Negroes and the NAACP, each taking a different side, the former praising the number of black jobs won, the latter attacking their substance. Caught between the persistent irrelevance of the older metaphors and the lack of new images, blacks made small contributions to Hollywood films.

At their very best, most black roles were no more than symbols of the plight or status of white principals. How should black critics respond, for example, to Triangle's *Mr. Miller's Economics,* a picture in which the seamy side of life is symbolized by images of a Negro laundress and "a little Jew tailor"? Or Universal's *The Cohens and the Kellys in Atlantic City* (1927)? When Cohen goes to jail his fate is symbolized by being seated next to an elegant, natty black man, perhaps a hustler or policy banker; and when he escapes his diminished status is again illustrated as a Red Cap intimidates him with a glare.[30]

These were the years when even tiny victories for Negroes were infrequent. Children's movies with black roles became egalitarian. Black actors slowly got more work, with more substance, more lines, and more variety. Blackface declined noticeably.

And so each new ambiguity, contradiction, deviation carried black characterization farther away from the old types, probably without the conscious participation of whites. The earliest example was that of Bert Williams. For years he had been admired by whites and worshipped by blacks as he mugged and capered his way from turn-of-the-century Negro revues to the famous Ziegfeld Follies. In the mid-teens as Biograph faltered through its last days Williams went up to the Bronx studio and made two vignettes, *Fish* and *A Natural Born Gambler*, both based on the old types but infused with a bit of humanity and a little of the "bad nigger." But if Williams's Follies role was intended as a comic, loosely fluid contrast to "Anglo-Saxon straightness," Biograph's bookers would have none of it, fearing "the Southern territory would resent and would not exhibit the pictures of a Negro star."[31]

Perhaps they feared the truth under his mask. In *Fish* he is a loping, friendly country boy, tangled in apronstrings and farm chores while itching to be his own man. To do this he fishes through a comic routine and hawks to the whites. He is gauche and lazy, but also the hustler who must sell the fish as it grows warm and stale. In *A Natural Born Gambler* he is deep within Negro circles unseen by whites—the sly treasurer of his black lodge and major domo of the perpetual card game in its "library." He must struggle to preserve his place in the lodge, win the game as honestly as necessary, and avoid raid, arrest, and trial at the hands of whites. He is leader of blacks, enemy of convention, the "bad nigger" for all who could see through his darkey makeup.[32]

Bert Williams's short career on the screen was like a starter's pistol in the race for varied Negro roles. His two last pictures constituted a Negro beginning. The result was not an end to racism, but at least an increase in the racial ambiguities inherent in the new urban metaphor of the "good-bad nigger," the whole man whom Griffith had kept separated in good and bad characters. For example, in the new urban scene Negroes often delivered the punchlines of the humor with an underside of wisecracking resentment. The erotic symbolism of "jazz age" movies, in which whites imitated Negro life, presented a white version of mythic Negro sexuality for which white Southerners lynched men.

A good example of the complicated ambivalence was not black at all but, according to Sam Goldwyn, "one of the best pictures ever produced" at his studio. In *Jubilo* (1919) Will Rogers played a drifter who sings a ditty describing his plight as if he were "the darkey" who stayed on and held the land while "the massa" fled after the Civil War. The best sequences were rough-textured rural scenes haunted by cuts to the song, with Jubilo winking roguishly, a black soul peering from inside his white skin. He sings

> Massa run, ho, ho;
> Darkey stay, hah, hah,
> In the year of Jubilo.

as he flees the scene of a train robbery, knowing that a drifter, like a Negro, would be the first to be arrested.[33]

Sometimes racial ambiguity appeared in dream sequences, as in the two boxing comedies released in the year of *The Birth of a Nation*. In *Some White Hope* Donald McBride played Hiram Limburger, a boastful *schlehmiel* who dreams he has a match with the Negro champion, "Lam Bangford." He is saved from a nightmare beating when his wife drenches him with a bucket of water. *The Night I Fought Jack Johnson*, with its floating, striped-jacketed boxers who end their bout with a dance, brought white and black together in combat within a dreamlike setting. The dreams were an egalitarian parody of black-and-white relations in the only situation that would make equality plausible. A parody of jungle movies, *Pa's Family Tree*, begins as a burlesque family discussion of Darwinism after which Pa naps and dreams he is in the jungle flirting with a fat blackface woman and receiving a brusque shove from a black cook. He, like the boxer, is saved from cannibals by a timely reminder of conditions in the real world: Ma arrives as white queen of the tribe and saves Pa from becoming *pot au feu, garni*.[34] Although these early aggressive black males appeared in dream sequences or in blackface, they brought to the screen a strong "bad nigger" that was not possible in the old days.

Women and children found easier access to white movies because American racial lore found black women benign, unthreatening, and earth-mother wise, and black children prepubescent boon companions. Still they, too, took on urban depth and ambiguity. Almost in the smoke of 1915, in Lloyd Ingraham's *Hoodoo Ann* (1916), the child-woman title character has her maid-confidante, Black Cindy, help her fulfill the conditions of a curse so that "the wedding of Ann is the funeral of the hoodoo." In *Mr. Miller's Economics* (1916) "a colored washerwoman with a liking for pretty clothes whether she owns them or not" reenacts the self interest of a slave stealing from the big house. She needs a dress suit for her husband's appearance at "the Afro-Aryan

Ball" and to step a bit out of the squalor of a "typical negro shack."
From such unthreatening beginnings black women's roles became
stronger as the subsurface ambiguity emerged from the "bad" slave in
conflict with white society. In a few years she surfaced in DeMille's
Manslaughter (1922), one of the cycle of pictures mourning the loss
of old morals in the midst of effete urban life. Leatrice Joy plays the
daughter of the idle rich who kills a cop and is convicted of manslaughter after the prosecutor who loves her charges the jury thus:
"The overcivilized mad young set of wasters—to which this defendant
belongs—must be STOPPED! Or they will destroy the Nation—as
Rome was destroyed when Drunkeness and Pleasure drugged the
Conscience of its Young!" A flashback depicts the Barbarians entering
an orgiastic Rome while a lone Negro stands among the defeated. The
cut is to the woman whose conviction also is symbolized by Negroes:
in her first day in jail one mauls her while unceremoniously taking
her measurements; the other, a black jailbird, leads a chorus of derision
at one of the fallen mighty. Whites, low and high, knew their status
by how blacks treated them.[35]

   Black children slowly emerged from white comic fantasy toward
Southern childhood egalitarianism. One of the earliest was Mack
Swain's comedy, one of a rash of mixed-baby situations, *By Stork Delivery* (1916), in which outraged black parents chase after their kidnapped baby crying, "They done stole our little Washington." Before
1915 they might have gladly traded their baby for a turkey. Slowly
the kids firmed into Hal Roach's *Our Gang* series and its imitators. The
earliest predictably did the least justice to blacks. One child actor began with the name of Joffre Pershing Johnson, shortened it to Sambo,
and earned good reviews playing types such as Ebenezer Eczema Abraham White in the early "Baby Marie" Osborne series. Another gang
picture, Dave Fleischer's *Busting the Show* (1920), offered a "blackface
comedian" whose mugging stole the show in the kids' backyard theater presentation of "The Grate Nigger Bucking Wing Dancer." Gradually in Roach's two-reelers the Negro became a peer of the whites.
Sometimes Farina or Sunshine Sammy or Stymie were the butts of
racial jokes—falling into the flour barrel, and so on—but in many pictures they were protagonists. By 1927 in *Me and My Dog* Allan Hoskins (Farina) had replaced Ernest Morrison as the central black figure.
In a jangling series of events he loses his lunch to the gang's dog, loses
the dog to a crooked ventriloquist, reduces a snobbish dog show to
chaos, and pursues his dog to the dogcatcher. Failing to meet the fee to
recover the dog, he pathetically agrees to let the local bully punch him
at the rate of twenty-five cents per sock. The other kids join in and
rout the bully. When they hear—mistakenly—of the dog's death the

reaction shot is Farina's as he expresses grief for the gang. Only a few
dialect bits and a reference to chicken mar the egalitarian tone. Blacks
were grateful for the gesture. Morrison appeared in *The Negro Yearbook*, and Hoskins and Stymie Beard became the subjects of friendly
gossip about their income, travels, road shows, even to the point of an
elaborate plot by the *Amsterdam News* to get exclusive interviews in
Harlem away from prying white reporters.[36]
After the women and children, the next step over the weakened
barriers was the growth of incidental roles for Negro males. The oldtime roles atrophied further with a shift in taste. "WHAT THE PUBLIC
DEMANDS TODAY IS MODERN STUFF WITH PLENTY OF CLOTHES, RICH SETS,
AND ACTION," said a 1918 wire from Paramount in New York to Cecil
B. DeMille. "NOTHING PRIOR TO THE CIVIL WAR SHOULD BE FILMED." The
result for Negroes was slow expansion of both quality and quantity of
their work and possibly at some level a heightened awareness on the
part of whites that blacks were more than they had seemed in the past.
As early as the mid-1920s the trade papers published stories of impending productions of all-Negro pictures.[37]
The range of black roles seemed boundless despite the persistent
bias toward servants and exotics. White writers, consciously or not,
found ways to allow them more humanity and wit, and each new role
lent a further hint of the ambiguity hidden beneath the Negro stereotype.
They appeared in exotic locales in such pictures as Kleine's *The
Ruby of Kishmoor* as both sides of the "good-bad nigger." Rufus the
servant is a reassuring presence to the whites in the melodramatic pursuit of the gem through a pirates' nest in Jamaica and an attack by Negro "loungers." In one of the jungle movies, *The Lion's Mate* (1924),
"Nedra, the half-breed Chief" adds a tinge of interracial rivalry in a
struggle over tribal politics. *The Three Must Get Theirs* (1922)—Max
Linder's parody of *The Three Musketeers*—employed race as a probably unconscious device to point up racism. As the principals duel and
cavort through the bedrooms of a sixteenth-century French town one
of the sleepers, an incongruous Negro, pops awake, forcing the viewer
to ask himself why it was surprising to find a Negro in a white world.
The conundrum ends with a wide shot of three black strolling jon-
gleurs in period costume.[38]
The taboo against black male aggression fell into disuse, beginning
with the days of the boxing dream sequences of the teens. The World
War itself fed the movement with the Creel Committee motion pictures of black troops, Goldwyn's *Too Fat To Fight* (1919) with its
black soldier, and Griffith's war film, *The Greatest Thing in Life*, in
which a black soldier gives his last drop of water so that his white

buddy may live.[39] Boxing itself brought changes in typing. Racetrack habitués and trainers could be black because of the flavor of farm, animals, and servility. But boxing was different, and reeking of sharp practice and city streets. Two popular B series, *Leather Pushers* and *Flying Fists*, both used Negroes. The latter starred the lightheavy-weight champion Benny Leonard and his "black shadow," who shared negotiations and decisions, plotted ring strategy, shared bad moments with Benny, and kept jazzy time on a snare drum during training. In *Jazz Bout* he saves the day by inspiring faltering Benny in the late rounds with hot riffs on his drum. Benny wins and gets the girl, with the black trainer crooning "I Got the Knockout Blues." With blacks in close relationships with white characters even servant roles turned flippant, causing *Variety* to look askance at George Reed's black porter in *Red Lights*, who cries out in court, "Get out 'er here, you miscolored white trash."[40]

Other Negro roles stretched the whole range of behavior to lengths that only a few years before would have been not only impossible but incomprehensible. One of Buster Keaton's most neglected pictures, *Seven Chances* (1925), followed the progress of a young man who must marry in order to inherit millions. Among the eligible brides who have answered an ad and are conducted through the rousing chases and confrontations is a striking black woman whose quiet presence comically surprises the suitor, who approaches her from the rear, and quietly shocks the eye when she coolly appears at the church. Black flippancy dominated one of the last blackface roles, that of Tom Wilson as Sambo in Harry Pollard's *California Straight Ahead*. The fast-paced plot followed a playboy across the continent in a kind of land-yacht in an attempt to prove his ability to support himself. Along the way the blackface valet operates the vehicle as a dining car and a rolling penthouse in which he handles everything: cooking, managing daily crises, and eventually, steering the romance to its union. It is the tradi-tional role made large, manipulative, and humane in spite of itself. The vestigial trappings of the old metaphor include a rabbit's foot and an outsized razor, yet they seem more humanly comic within the larger dimensions of the black role. At one point he perks up a flagging dance, and the whole rhythmic black stereotype takes on humane freshness as he says to his feet: "Come on smokin' puppies, show yo' nationality!" Whenever the old servile roles recurred, they were somehow different and larger. *The Woman God Changed* (1921), for example, was told in flashbacks by a Negro maid.

Variety caught onto the changes and encouraged them. Its review of *Love is an Awful Thing* (1922) praised "Douglas Carter, colored,

[who] contributes some especially subtle Bert Williams touches of light humor that are most welcome," while complaining of the "spook stuff" and the "quivering negro servants" that seemed to be a "needless extension" of the old style.[41]

To understand the full scope of Afro-American growth on the screen the decline of D. W. Griffith is instructive. If his life had been a well-made play written by a Negro writer, the heights of *The Birth of a Nation* and *Intolerance* would have been its climax. The declining action would have been his fitful career afterwards, interrupted by his grand reaches for the stars such as *Broken Blossoms*, *Way Down East*, and *Orphans of the Storm*. Denouement would be his last lumbering attempts to deal with the Negro on the screen, *One Exciting Night*, *His Darker Self*, and *The White-Rose*. No one understood any longer what he was trying to say; the coming of urbanization baffled him; his sad life paralleled an upswing in Negro fortunes.

Not that blacks calculatedly fed off his corpse. The old Southern racial myth simply fell of its own weight once its original purposes, premises, and social context were removed, as, indeed, they had been in Northern and Western cities. If social myth sustained and explained things as they were, then change, ever so slight, sometimes rendered myth bizarre and sterile. Even the fine hand of Griffith, who believed the myth deeply, could not save it from barrenness. His final stumbling essays into it revealed *its* hollow core, not his, and may have contributed to others abandoning it.

One Exciting Night appeared in 1922 at the ragged end of the cycle of Southern pictures and expressed the genre at its worst. Griffith's scenario, under his pseudonym of Irene Sinclair, failed to render Negroes accurately because of his old habit of presenting "both sides" of the Negro in two characters, a Manichean conceit that denied the screen any fully sketched black character. By 1922 the trades found it the "veriest hokum."[42]

The tangled story takes Agnes Harrington from her birth "in sombre Africa" to her adopted home in Kentucky where a dual struggle ensues as her stepmother attempts to marry her off while bootleggers seek a cache of money. The climax follows two murders, after which the family is locked in a manse during a violent storm and the murderer is revealed as the suitor in the arranged marriage. The two sides of blackness pervade the story. Romeo Washington is played in blackface by Porter Strong as the terrified servant whose antics liven the storm sequences. The obverse is "Black Sam," once a servant to Agnes's mother in Africa, who comes to America, joins the bootleggers and becomes the instrument through which Scotland Yard improbably finds her true identity and enables her to claim her fortune and marry her lover. In Griffith's eye black character can be seen only in the contrast between the sober "Kaffir, the dark terror of the bootleg gang," the sleuth who "in his own primitive way" leads the Yard out of its bafflement, on the one hand, and the emasculated Romeo on the other.[43] The resulting fragmentation ruined an interesting dramatic premise.

From every direction Griffith felt the wrath of black and white critics. The Pennsylvania censor objected to the word "nigger" and to violent and erotic bits. D. Ireland Thomas in the black *Chicago Defender* denounced it and insisted, "We've got to stop making this kind of film," and either get an honest black image on the screen or "a Race picture." Even a wellwisher complained. "What has happened to you?" he wrote to Griffith. "Are you losing your sense of values. . . ? Do you stop to think that the negro foolishness appeals only to the empty-headed and to the negro patron it gives only pain as you make him as a race ridiculous?" Angrily he dismissed the picture as "a mongrel." It did only "fair business." At Boston's Tremont Temple, for example, "The weekly grosses never ran very big, but large enough to cover the house rental."[44]

The next year Griffith completed *The White Rose*, a tale of the Evangeline country peopled with servile blacks, an old "auntie," and a crapshooter, all save one in blackface. Again Porter Strong played a black servant, "Apollo." Again Griffith gave the Negro two "sides." This time the positive side consisted of the blacks who shelter an outcast, defiled white girl in their humble cabin until righteousness triumphs. Again critics turned on Griffith and dismissed his "mawkish sickening sentimentality," his refusal to take ideas from "the trend of the day," his "jumbled and pointless" plots, his morbid attachment to "the attacking, raping, or wronging of the defenseless girl." He was in their view in "isolation, surrounded by minor advisers, [a] genius out of touch with the world." Eventually Griffith pulled back from the stock Negro roles so that even his gemlike soundfilm biography of Lincoln, full of flinty, rough frontier textures, included not a single Negro appearance.[45]

The clearest signal of change in the larger world and in Griffith was *His Darker Self*, a picture so unworthy of his talent and so remote from prevailing taste he could not pull it together. At the release of *The White Rose*, *Variety* offered his estimation of American society:

> This generation is ready for a new Uncle Tom, and his experience with the darky character played in "One Exciting Night", and with the public reception of his new story of the Southland confirm him in his desire.

The new picture was to be a vehicle for Al Jolson as just such a Negro in blackface, but they hit snags in the form of the death of Porter Strong and a long run of Jolson's current play. *Black Magic* or *Black and White*—its working titles—finally broke down from bickering between Griffith and the producer, Albert L. Grey. After Jolson broke their flimsy verbal agreement and fled to Europe, unhappy with himself in the role, Grey found a new star, Lloyd Hamilton, changed the title, and reduced Griffith to an adviser. More than a year later in 1925 they were still trying to salvage it by cutting it to a two-reeler despite complaints from their impatient bank and its being "difficult to work into shape."

John W. Noble finally finished *His Darker Self,* and it opened quietly in New York's tiny Cameo, complete with powerful black ambiguities that would have been impossible in Griffith's old pictures of the rural South. Except for Hamilton's blackface disguise the black roles were cast for Negroes. Unconsciously white writers gave them rough edges, glowering faces, heavy dimensions, and motives that drove them to chase and even physically maul whites. In the movie-ghetto, blacks ruled supreme, and they had a clear investment in the outcome.

Old Eph has unknowingly been smuggling whiskey for black Bill Jackson, a dance hall owner. After a police raid Jackson, believing Eph to be an informer, frames him in a bogus murder. Bill Sappington, Eph's white fishing partner, who has aspirations to be a detective, decides to help and in order to pursue the investigation disguises himself in blackface. From his first confrontation with black bouncers at Jackson's Black Cat saloon he is deeply into a black void. Tough black bruisers intimidate him in tight one- and-two-shots. Cakewalkers cruise the dance floor. Revelers bubble over. Waiters glide with cool skill between the customers. A light-skinned girl makes a pass at Sappington. The bouncers toss out a drunk. Bill Jackson, tough and ominous, gives him a job as a bouncer.

For all the world the funky scene resembles Langston Hughes's "Jazzonia":

> In a Harlem cabaret
> Six long-headed jazzers play.
> A dancing girl whose eyes are bold
> Lifts high a dress of silken gold.

A neat thread of humor runs through the sequence. Sappington's collar steams as he dances; his match lights spontaneously; a cocktail shaker hanging on a coattail churns its contents into butter; the black girl, pursuing the hero, says of his disguise: "I jest know you is a outdoor man—you is so sunburned." When he is discovered he flees a threatened knifing to a wide shot of a river baptism. "Come in, Sinner,"

cries the preacher, "and be washed whiter than snow." The comedy
turns on skin color, but the racist derives no special pleasure from it.
The shot is heightened by a score of black church women in authentic
white dresses. Finally, washed white, Sappington manages to pull the
threads together, free Eph, and marry happily. Such strong, black imagery was astonishing in a picture that began in the hands of D. W.
Griffith. It was as though the Negro freed from the plantation could
not be tamed, for benign obsequiousness gave way to balky and threatening city blacks, the hated loungers of Griffith's *Birth of a Nation*.
The film at last reflected in distorted, half-seen form something of what
Alain Locke meant by "The New Negro," perhaps moving the *Times*
man to grumble at Sappington's incongruous references to the Negroes
as "smokes," and a black *Courier* writer to see the Griffith-Jolson split
a symptom of flagging movie racism.[46]

Racism in motion pictures did not end with the unwitting victory
of black imagery over white directorial control. But such attempts at
depicting Negroes on the screen destroyed the monopoly of the old
rural darkey stereotype.

To sustain the movement away from black stereotypes other changes
would occur in the fabric of society, in both worlds, black and white.
In Los Angeles each new Negro acting job added to the wealth and
stability of the Central Avenue thespians. Among the whites, only
Jolson and Tom Wilson survived among the blackface actors. The
studios took halting steps toward measuring audience responses to
their products. A *Courier* critic believed, "Film producers are at last
learning that the true Negro type, whether for pictures or stage, cannot be reproduced through blackface impersonators." Al Jolson, he
correctly observed, "seriously doubted his ability to register as well
upon the screen as upon stage." By 1924 the *Afro-American* boasted
that not a single day passed "in which some race actor was not at work,"
to the tune of more than five hundred casting calls for the year.[47]

Afro-Americans had started the decade in the streets with their angry
protests of *The Birth of a Nation*. They sharpened their racial consciousness during the "red summer" of 1919, flirted with black Zionism
during the Indian summer of Marcus Garvey, and came into the mid-
1920s more aware, more unified, more urban than they had been at
any other time in the decade. In March 1925 Alain Locke, the first
black Rhodes Scholar and a professor of philosophy at Howard University, put together his famous Harlem number of *Survey Graphic*
magazine, thus registering for white readers "the transformations of
the inner and outer life of the Negro in America that [had] so significantly taken place in the last few years." Every branch of art and life
was represented in the magazine and the book that followed—all, that

In the early twenties traditional roles changed little. In *The Ne'er Do Well* (© Famous Players–Lasky Corp.) Jules Cowles appeared in familiar black-face. (Author's collection)

is, save motion pictures. Not until the publication in 1927 of Monroe Work's dense *Negro Yearbook* would movies appear in serious black writing.[48]

Black attention to the screen was equally slow abuilding: from early "plugs" for Negro actors and their movies, to encouragement of the coming all-Negro companies, to rumbling campaigns against the periodic revivals of *The Birth of a Nation*, to strong pleas for readers to see rare documentaries such as Crusader's *Tuskegee Finds a Way Out*.[49] As early as 1917 Lester Walton of the *Age* had begun to hone a black aesthetic with a social focus by judging New York theater for its relevance to Negroes and the fidelity with which black roles were written and rendered. Other blacks in other towns joined in. Negro war veterans in Washington picketed *The Birth of a Nation* with placards asking, "We represented America in France. Why should 'The Birth of a Nation' misrepresent us here?" It was only a short step to using drama and dance for social ends, whether through the performances of the Lafayette Players in Harlem or organizing a "simple and dignified" benefit performance of Nathaniel Dett's *Juba Dance* at Carnegie Hall, or a songfest of slave songs by the women of Harlem's Salem Church.[50]

Poverty and the rural Baptist tradition kept blacks out of moviehouses. But as more Negro houses turned away from vaudeville toward movies the black press received advertising from the white exhibitors, while Walton and his colleagues—Floyd Snelson of the *Courier*, Romeo Daugherty of the *Amsterdam News*, and others—plugged movies so that early apathy gave way to the Chicago *Defender*'s insistence that "we must break into this game."[51] The result was that by 1925 blacks were far more prepared to make demands on white filmmakers and to make their own movies.

Change had occurred on racial frontiers in large measure because of the conditions shaped by urbanization, although contacts between the races remained minuscule. Each new Negro removed to a Northern city represented one less who would grow up in the Southern mold. Each new victory of substance or of attitude resulted in a higher level of black demand. Each interracial contact opened the way for another. As early as 1921 a *Times* critic condemned *Shuffle Along* in part because of its stereotyped rhythms "popularly supposed to be inherent in the negro." Even in Europe, German censors and rightist press quarreled over the film *The Black Pest* for its "false and exaggerated accusations against French colored troops." Alexander Woollcott asked whites to move forward further by ceasing to patronize and pity Negroes by "slumming" in the theaters of Harlem but instead protest the Jim Crow balconies in white houses. A *Times* editorialist approved of the Hays Office prohibitions against pejorative national typing in order to "keep down needless and harmful prejudice."[52] On the occasion of a revival of *The Birth of a Nation* a *Times* editorial called for more "patient and sympathetic treatment" of Negroes before the Communist Party exploited racism. "There have not been lacking signs since the war that the race consciousness of the American negro has been awakened," it noted. The actor Arthur Hohl, appearing in *White Cargo*, gave an interview that appeared in the *Courier* in which he confessed his liberalism. "Here I am trying to be a good American in private life," he said, "while in Leon Gordon's new play I am compelled to imagine myself a Negro-hater eight times a week."[53]

Taken together the events made no revolution in American racial arrangements, but they did reflect a dulling of the edge of racism. Although discrimination in jobs and housing remained, Negroes shared a portion of the bullish economy. Taking one thing with another the movies reflected the glacial shifts. The Civil War had disappeared from the screens; jungle men had become clichés; blackface actors survived only on the pull of nostalgia.[54]

Slowly the Ku Klux Klan and other overt bigots fell from power to burlesque. In the midst of the boom for Negro revues, films, and drama the Klan's own film, *The Toll of Justice*, bogged down in reshooting and recutting. Of all such efforts the greatest defeat came in 1924 to Al Woods, who resurrected an unreleased ten-year-old picture shot in the old Ince studio. *Free and Equal* was a crude gesture at depicting the corruption that would surely follow the mixing of the races. The story is the dream of a lightskinned Negro who "passes." A militant exhorter for Negro rights, he accepts an invitation to dwell in the house of a liberal white judge. Eventually there is a murder that demonstrates the point "that Booker T. Washington is right—the Negro must stay in his place." The picture perished in New York in part because *Variety* warned exhibitors:

> There is no chance for the picture to get a nickel anywhere. It is not only old fashioned but so crudely done that the Sunday night audience laughed it practically out of the theatre—this while Woods stood around counting the take, only then learning his movie was "just so much junk."[55]

Even if a moviegoer in 1924 could stroll Broadway and catch Noble Johnson in *Cannibal Island* or the "stupid colored man" in *Dixie Handicap*, the NAACP and its liberal white allies, the polyethnic urban audience, and the freewheeling rhetoric of the "jazz age" held out the promise of a better future. One autumn night in Calhoun City, Mississippi, as a movie flickered on a country screen showing a comic black maid masquerading for her mistress, the bride in a wedding, a raging white man leaped from his seat, clawed his way to the screen, and began slashing at it with a knife.[56] In the next few years he would have many more opportunities to vent his rage.

If a moviegoer watched the growth of a black cinema imagery through the twenties, Negroes would seem to have gained far more in artistic stature than any other group. By the 1920s immigrants, Orientals, and Indians developed into stock figures, irrelevant to industrial America except as romantic icons. Each had been a part of the American experience, but in turn each had atrophied in the hands of screenwriters into wooden figures of assimilationist sentimentality, tragically vanishing aborigines, and inscrutable menace. During the decade Indians disappeared from westerns. After a few protests to President Wilson Orientals lost their rough edges and became smooth, tolerable villains, wizened sages, and tragic halfcastes. Only immigrants persisted as mythic expressions of open-handed assimilationism, teaching its values even as the government repudiated the myth by closing its shores to further immigrants.

Compared with Negro imagery on the screen, Orientals suffered from redundancy, melodramatic convention, and eventually the tackiness of the Bs. Even more than blacks, their fortunes rose and fell, touched by external fates such as California racism and shifts in American foreign policy, and sometimes modulated by the old Western romance with Eastern culture. They were the silent menace, the yellow peril, "an enemy within our midst," a nemesis of xenophobic William Randolph Hearst. So outrageous was Hearst's melodramatic serial, *Patria*, with its misused beauty, Irene Castle, its oily Mexicans, arch Japanese conspirators, and pious call for preparedness against greedy nonwhite foreigners that President Wilson found no "history written in lightning" but only insults to allies and neighbors. The Senate and Wilson cowed Hearst into some decent elision, but still it opened in New York and made a ragged run. Somehow Japanese militarism and Chinese revolutions evoked images of *Tsing Fu, the Yellow Devil* who "forces his intentions" on white women, and of tong men who kidnap white children, and of—luckily for America—California Legionnaires who break up a ring of Japanese cutthroats. Occasionally the racism boiled so hot that *Variety* complained, as against Frank Borzage's 1922 production of Peter B. Kyne's *Pride of Palomar*, because "the anti-Japanese feeling is here expressed in pretty raw terms."[57]

As in the case of black imagery on the screen, only a few attempts at art crept in among the racial monuments. A handful of well-wrought art directors' creations such as that of William Cameron Menzies in *The Thief of Bagdad* struck reviewers. One group of sets seemed like "works of art," another like "animated Japanese prints," and so on. Then, like a tawny rivulet through a blue stream, there was the career of Sessue Hayakawa and his wife, Tsuru Aoki. Together they dragged Orientals out of the ranks of the heavies, for nearly two decades fighting for better roles, risking breaches of contract, giving human dimensions to *The Tong Man* and other stock creations, even though in the end *Variety* concluded, "No one has yet been able to make him a romantic figure in American or any other Occidental surroundings." The best of the lot came in 1919: D. W. Griffith's *Broken Blossoms*, a delicate, evocative film of Thomas Burke's overstated tale "The Chink and the Child." The fog of Limehouse, Richard Barthelmess's wistful role as a Chinese pacifist come to redeem the wartorn Occident, Henrik Sartov's painterly cinematography, an original score, tinted film, and a big New York première were brought off so well that *Variety* winced at the "Chinese propaganda." Even so, not until Pearl Buck's day in

Hollywood in the thirties would the heart of Chinese life appear in a major picture. Until then American audiences rarely saw more than the demimonde of insidious halfcastes, lustful kidnappers, vicious tongmen, and wispy Madame Butterflies played by a tiny cadre of Asians such as Sojin, Anna May Wong, and James B. Leong:[58] In the end, along with Charlie Chan, Earl Derr Biggers's shrewd Chinese detective, they slipped into the ranks of the programmers, into artistic and social irrelevance.

Indians provided another social metaphor to compare with Afro-American imagery. The western frontier had been one of the first movie metaphors to appear wholly out of American experience. Yet after the Indian had served a generation of viewers as a ritual loser in the white man's conquest of the frontier, he lapsed into cliché and disappeared. If losers could not be plausible heavies, they became patronized "vanishing" Americans, an accurate reflection of federal policy from the days of Helen Hunt Jackson's exposé of white exploitation, *Ramona*, through the assimilationism of the reservation law and the destruction of integrative rituals and tribal life by means of the boarding school system. Gradually dramatic conflict came to grow out of mixed bloods. An Indian would die in the snow, lacking "the strong purposes and undying obstinacy . . . that would lead a white man to ultimate victory." But the halfbreed would die caught between two cultures, possessed of a "white mind" but lacking "the hitting power, the stamina, the comeback of the white."

First National's masterpiece of special effects, Willis O'Brien's *The Lost World* (1925), compared the unconscious differences in the two images. The lone Negro in an exploring party is a "game and loyal black," while the heavies are "nearly all half or quarter breeds —mongrel mixtures of all shades and colors," including one who is "almost white" and "cursed with enough education to make him a malcontent." DeMille's *Squaw Man*, his third version, carried the taboo— "The barrier between the Indian and the Caucasian that can never be crossed"—to its conclusion in tragedy. But thereafter Indian life, its cup of culture shattered, offered nothing to Hollywood. In the programmers of Hoot Gibson, Tom Mix, and Jack Hoxie no Indians at all appeared—only, in the words of Mrs. Mix, "plenty of action, a simple plot, a very white hero, an impossibly incorrigible villain, a number of dangerous schemes to be foiled, and a helpless heroine to be rescued at the last moment." John Ford's career moved from B westerns to the epic *The Iron Horse* (1925) with barely a glance at redmen. Only Colonel Tim McCoy, a nondescript actor with a sure knowledge of Indian lore from his own life on the frontier, used movies to say, at least, that "uprisings were not wholly the fault of the red men."[59]

Compared with Indians, then, Afro-Americans remained on the ground as a live and growing presence, suppressed but capable, someday, of breaking out. The Indian as metaphor could never be more than symbol of defeat in the celebration of white manifest destiny.

By the 1920s immigrants as a metaphor of American faith reached the crest of a sentimental wave, while blacks watched from the sidelines, unwelcome and still believing in the American dream. Yet with American irony, the immigrants paid the price of assimilation in the form of deteriorating ethnic cultures while Negroes slowly sharpened their sense of urban group identity. The myth of the "melting pot" strengthened even as xenophobia closed the gates to future migrants. The myth required European roles to lose their rough edges, to "Americanize," to succeed by following the path of the Hollywood producers themselves. Thus any story of "a 'Wop' immigrant" ended with his cultural suicide, often under pressure from organized immigrant societies.[60]

From George Beban's *The Italian* in 1915 to *Clancy's Kosher Wedding* in 1927 dramatic conflict gave way to comic peacemaking. The latter movie opens on the assumption that "there are three races here, Irish, Jewish, and innocent bystanders," and ends with the pious homily that "the sun can't shine in Ireland when its raining in Jerusalem." From honest treatment of the tension between groups the studies gave in to pressure, gave artificial representation to each group, "sidestepped anything which might be repugnant to the Irish race" or any other lobby, mixed a pastiche of elfin, whimsical, amiable brawlers. It was as though the studios wished, instead of good notices for artistic merit, trade-press guesses that "for an Irish neighborhood house this picture is about perfect." Presiding over the maudlin cycle were the Irishmen at court such as Leo McCarey and John Ford, who, like many children of immigrants, carried in his baggage a romantic vision of the old sod that tinged his pictures. At its height the cycle brought the groups together through a marriage of Gael and Jew. The short step from melting pot to marriage altar began in the first decade of the century and reached full stride with Anne Nichols's widely panned but long-running *Abie's Irish Rose* and its many imitators. By 1926 she had generated a "Sidewalks of New York craze" in *Variety*'s argot. Jesse Lasky's stars and money and Victor Fleming's direction redeemed her bad play and gave life to the epic that began by streaming past the Statue of Liberty and ended with an intergroup marriage. It also started the flow of *Cohen and Kellys* programmers; *Nize Baby, Schlemiel*, and other exploitations; *Humoresque*, Fanny Hurst's tale of an immigrant violinist; *The Golem*, Paul Wegener's imported medieval Jewish myth; *King of Kings*, Cecil B. DeMille's "hard ticket" biblical pastiche; and *The Jazz Singer*, Al Jolson's treacly rendering of a cantor's son who breaks orthodoxy only to return in the last reel for a filiopietistic *Kol Nidre*.[61]

But unlike the remote and Oriental motifs and the vanishing Indians, the ethnic pictures held out an unconscious and bitter message for blacks. Like *The Fights of Nations* a quarter of a century earlier, many of the immigrant pictures in their opening sequences placed blacks in the thick of urban life, but in the end they remained outside the circle. The movies seemed to say that America was a promised city in which whites could live in harmonious diversity, while for blacks they promised only enough to blur the appeal of race nationalism and Zionism.

Chapter Six

UNCLE TOM WAS
A "BAD NIGGER"

When *Uncle Tom's Cabin* came to the screen in 1927 for one of its periodic revivals, many Negroes saw it as the highest achievement of blacks in the cinema. The success of a new film of Mrs. Stowe's classic was also a tribute to a slowly dawning fact of cinema life. During the years of the decline of romantic Southern literature no new sources of black experience came into the ken of white writers. Consequently, black thematic material on film was not only arrested, but even regressed. So in the absence of a black artistic force in tension with a white system, Tom stood alone as a surrogate "bad nigger," a Staggerlee in mufti. As George Johnson, a chronicler of Tom's growth on the screen, recalled, James Lowe, the actor in the 1927 film, "became 'Uncle Tom' in the flesh," suffering "degradation" and "gross insults" on the set until "he took on the God-like character." But the whites on the sets also learned a new dimension of the urbane Negro, for Lowe's silent humility lasted only "until one day it became generally known on the gigantic set that the Christ-like Lowe could be aroused and that he was a dangerous 'nigger' when aroused." Whatever had happened, *Tom* again became a vehicle for teaching whites, as he had in his first appearance in 1852.

The great black exodus reached floodtide during the twenties. Harlem, Chicago's South Side, the northwestern cores of Baltimore and Washington filled with black Southerners. There Negroes remained marginally employed, with a strong economic matriarchal base, with some of the old *noblesse oblige* of Southern life replaced by wages-for-service. Segregated black warrens further removed them from white contact and encouraged the expression of sides of Afro-American personality long muted by the demands of Southern etiquette.

The old Negro imagery of Southern literary tradition no longer fit as snugly as it once had. In his urban habitat the Negro found life a bit like Frederick Douglass's day as a slave in Baltimore. On the eastern shore of Maryland he lived under the threat of the lash, but in Baltimore he hired out as a ship-caulker, walked to work, lived away from the eye of the boss, and saved enough cash for a train ticket and freedom in New Bedford. Even the air smelled freer, he thought. The free city Negro scared whites. D. W. Griffith made him the bugbear who threatened life itself, and found support amongst the historians who had blamed the excesses of Reconstruction on him. To fearful whites he was the overtrained mulatto, inured to the conceits of freedom but unchecked by the reins of Puritan rigor.

The situation appeared in microcosm in the motion picture studios. In Hollywood white contract writers could not consciously observe blacks, and only one Negro, Spencer Williams, a writer of Christy two-reelers, worked regularly. A few Southerners in the culturally isolated studios remembered shimmering days of childhood, and when hired as consultants, they propped their legends. The result was that Hollywood created modern Afro-American roles in the framework of older received wisdom.

Nevertheless, ambiguities inherent in city life insured that the old metaphorical darkey of Southern lore would not survive intact. Blacks began to suffer on the screen more from the invisibility imposed by liberal white writers, made timid by their ignorance of Negro life, or embarrassed by their lack of alternatives to old-fashioned Southern lore. Moviemen were helpless to translate the new Negro into artful or mythic truth. Unconsciously, white writers sketched in roles not only unavoidably ambiguous in themselves, but with gaping holes to be filled by the "business," the "takes," the expertise of the black actors who would read the lines. To render Negro life more faithfully some studios even hired blacks as consultants, or "assistant directors," as they were called in the black press. And here and there executives released trial-balloon announcements that they intended to make movies about Negroes. Uncontrolled then, many black roles would symbolize the irony and cynicism of urban life, and movies, in spite of themselves, would play upon the urban ambience.

As Southern racial lore silted over and black lore remained segregated, the only available literature possessed of a strong black persona remained *Uncle Tom's Cabin*. Abolitionist in tone, filled with black escapers and rebels, its hero, Tom, a strong character, Mrs. Stowe's work would have to be the source not only because it was familiar literature that had been done before, but because it provided an alternative to Southern racial logic. The last ingredient, if one could be found, would be a Negro actor who could bring humanity to the title role without letting whites in on the secret until it was too late to change.

Blacks and whites alike were ready for a strongly mounted *Tom* because he provided a common focus for right-thinking liberal nostalgia. For blacks he was a tragic figure from the time of troubles in bondage; for whites he represented their best thoughts concerning race relations and equality. Besides, Tom could open a window on a rural past, a simpler time which could be appreciated by harried urbanites. As a reviewer put it in a friendly review of *Tarzan* in 1918: "We are, all of us, tired of looking at society, sex, allegorical and historical pictures." If "the lost generation" or "the jazz age" or "the roaring twenties" seemed hyperbolic and fragmented metaphors for Americans, the country, nevertheless, had become citified, "deadpan," hero-seeking. *Tom* certainly was not Babe Ruth or Charles Lindbergh, but he was a black image, which seemed to grant the point that self-conscious, urban blacks no longer, if they ever had, conformed to the outlines of Southern imagery—and that the country needed a new black hero.

The new temper could be seen in the greeting *Tom* received from blacks. By its release in 1927 the style and substance of city life had obliterated some of the premises of ideological racism, while a number of urban black leaders represented examples of the new Negro. Replacing Booker T. Washington's circle were urban blacks such as Marcus Garvey of the zionist Universal Negro Movement Association and A. Philip Randolph of the pioneering Brotherhood of Sleeping Car Porters, in addition to leaders of the veteran outfits like the NAACP and the Urban League. If the white leaders of the Republican establishment refused to yield to black demands for, say, an antilynching bill, at least strong black figures appeared in the social frieze. The black press had matured into a nationwide network capable of reporting on the growing urban black community: city papers such as the *Courier* and the *Defender* reached large regional audiences and enjoyed the services of national black news networks. Most important of them as far as *Tom* was concerned was George P. Johnson's Pacific News Bureau, which fed Hollywood gossip and movie-lot job statistics into the black press. In white circles *Tom's* debut would be covered not only in the low-circulation trade papers but in critical reviews and features in daily papers as well as the tinselly prose of the first generation of colorful fan magazines. Therefore a strong *Uncle Tom* could expect a black and white audience who understood him more clearly than any since Mrs. Stowe's novel appeared in 1852, and might finally eliminate the caricature he had acquired in years of sentimental road shows.[1]

Nevertheless, there were no open doors to Hollywood. It was true that the motion picture industry appeared to the world as the embodiment of American culture, but so few of its great moments had come from American sources. By the late twenties no wave of artfully mounted epics of the Civil War had followed Griffith's lead.

A glance at the situation in Hollywood in the years surrounding *Tom's* making in 1927 will be useful. First, the black acting corps grew. Joining the veterans Sul-te-Wan, Zack Williams, and Noble Johnson came Ernest Wilson, the Shackelford twins, Floyd and Lloyd, Raymond and Martin Turner, and George Godfrey. Along with George Johnson's Pacific Coast News Bureau came Harry Levette and other black writers who covered the movie colony. The work had a kind of pathetic quality because of the need to puff up even the smallest jobs as gratification both to the struggling actors and their black fans. A small role would invariably be greeted thus: "Raymond Turner, the clever colored actor who made such a hit in Richard Barthelmess's 'The Patent Leather Kid,' has been singled out by First National for feature bits in future pictures."[2] The busiest of the actors were the kids in *Our Gang.* By the late twenties they crowded their lives with personal appearances, welcomed by mayors, trailing a retinue of parents and managers, commanding $5000 per week, torn by the demands of the black and white presses.

The finest hour for a Negro actor came in 1927 when Noble Johnson appeared as an "apache" in the Paris of Louis XV in *When a Man Loves,* Uncle Tom in the Duncan Sisters' production of *Topsy and Eva,* a Lascar ship's cook in *Vanity,* and an exotic in *The King of Kings* in addition to his roles in western Bs. He had three Los Angeles openings in the same summer at the Forum, Grauman's Chinese and the Egyptian.[3] He prevailed as a kind of victor over oppression, a versatile black presence where there would have been none before.

The difference between blacks and the whites was expectation. Negroes could only aspire to pictures as a capstone to an athletic career, or as a reward for being a dutiful studio toady or a coppery-skinned exotic. Stardom was for whites only. Even the major primitive roles still went to whites such as Annette Kellerman, Richard Dix, and Lon Chaney. The erotic dancer Gilda Gray, for example, was the temple vestal rescued by Clive Brook from a life of abomination in Goldwyn's *The Devil Dancer* (1927). Racial taboos became ironclad because the whites, as surrogates for exotics, simultaneously evaded prohibitions against miscegenation, disarmed racist criticism of interracial roles, and denied the roles to Negroes. Any deviation brought *Variety* to the defense of the rigid Hays code, thus drawing a prudish veil over any kind of black masculinity beneath the simple visage of the native. Of

The Slaver, a "quickie," *Variety's* critic wrote: "Dynamite angle through a negro tribal chief on the coast of Africa making a deal with a dissolute white sea captain to buy a white girl. Supposed to be 'squared,' " he explained edgily, "by a negro cabin boy sacrificing his life, saving the girl from the black nabob." Rare was a role like Blue Washington's tribal chief who kills a Boer in *Passion Song* (1928).[4]

Generally blacks remained exotic atmosphere for white plots even though the rough hulk of racial ambiguity peered through. Tod Browning's flair for the macabre and Lon Chaney's for weird makeup combined to bring a good example, *West of Zanzibar*, from stage to screen. "Deadlegs," a magician, rots in Africa for eighteen years waiting his chance to punish the man "who made me this thing that crawls" and overawing the natives with remnants of his old magic act. At the end he goes on a native suttee pyre in his daughter's stead as she and her suitor flee the frenzied tribesmen, chilled by the glistening Negro who approaches the verandah, muttering, "We come . . . get white girl." The texture of the jungle is maintained by shots of a wizened chief, flickering voodoo rites, shimmering black warriors, and two fat black dancers. Yet to the end, there is not a single memorable closeup of an African; they provided only the flavor of locale.[5]

In the years before *Tom* the exclusion of blacks from jungle movies petrified into unbending taboo. All relations between human beings needed to be denied—even hatred, which would have been an allegorical statement that blacks had some reason for hatred. On Broadway and for a brief fling in the movies evasion took the form of declassé halfcaste women. In *East of Suez* she was half Japanese; in *White Cargo* she was Tondelayo, a "half negro" who does not appear until the first act curtain, and then largely as an omen-motive of what it is like for white men to "go black—to succumb to native life." Tondelayo dies not for the murder of her husband, but in order to show that a "nigger" cannot escape white man's law. Such a play was too strong for the screen. The Hays code proscribed it. Thus blacks, even in jungle movies, could not substantively effect white characters.[6]

Even the pioneering work of Robert Flaherty led nowhere for Negroes. *Nanook* pointed to the increasingly plotty *Grass*, *Chang*, then to Frederick O'Brien's *White Shadows in the South Seas* complete with white movie stars, and the few high moments of his and F. W. Murnau's *Tabu*. The end came with Schoedsack and Cooper's *Four Feathers*. Like its predecessors, *Grass* and *Chang*, it began on location, this time in the Sudan, with authentic shots of "fuzzy wuzzies." But more and more A. E. W. Mason's romantic novel took precedence over fidelity, and the final retakes were in Southern California using hundreds of Negroes from Central Avenue in one of the largest cattle calls

ever. To the black press corps such a picture was not anathema but
rather a chance to excel. Two hundred Los Angeles Negroes worked
in the picture and were proud of the fact, especially after Tod Browning told a black reporter they were "the most uniform collection of
splendid physical development I have ever seen," a living embodiment
of those "who live outdoors constantly battling with nature." John
Murray was part of their pride because he was 96 years of age, had
been General Joseph Wheeler's slave, and now was independent and
employed.[7]

The murky by-product of Flaherty's genius, the "animal pictures,"
persisted, growing more corrupt and dull with each new release. Yet
as late as 1929 black newspapers advertised the pictures, suggesting a
yen for anything black on the screen. *Gorilla Hunt* (1926), *Through
Darkest Africa: In Search of the White Rhinoceros* (1927), *The Bushman* (1927), and *Simba* (1927) spun out their capering pygmies and
legendary beasts, eventually to canned music and synchronized prattle.
Jango, (1930) a patent fraud, came to light when two Harlem Negroes
struck for higher pay at the Long Island location.

Worst of all, the animal movies not only failed to depict African life
authentically and honestly; they became elaborate unconscious allegories for the "black brutes" of white Southern folklore. *Ingagi* (1930),
ostensibly the result of the Congo expedition of "Sir Hubert Win-
stead," asked its audiences to accept "semi-simian women guarded by
apes" and a ritual sacrifice. Sexual ambiguity peers through *Ingagi's*
fakery when a gorilla comes to carry off his woman-sacrifice as the
whites bang away with rifles. The net result was a pastiche of shots—
neat, clean village streets peopled by bustling Africans set against hollowly false titles fobbing off the legend of the gorillas and the sacrifice
"which, in the superstitious minds of these natives, protects them from
the raids of these beasts." In one sequence there is a wide shot of the
whites' tent, a cut to Africans frolicking in a stream, a tight shot of an
alligator that is too clearly lighted to be the "quick-and-dirty" footage
demanded by shooting on locations in available light, then a cut to the
natives in full flight. In other words, the story of black fear is told
by a white cutter at his workbench rather than by a cameraman in
Africa. A year later, too late to matter, the Federal Trade Commission
investigated the company and blocked further distribution because of
its use of stock shots, deceptive ads, and Los Angeles locations.[8]

With the decline of the Civil War, the ante bellum South, the jungle,
and the rimlands as inspirations for movies, there was little reason to
expect the growth of a black presence on the screen. Nonetheless, the
age of silent film closed with more promise than at any time since the
war. The slow build of minor roles, slowly departing from the old

types, increased the number of black actors. DeMille and others received friendly encouragement rather than rage from the black press whenever they dropped hints of impending black productions. DeMille's 1926 trial balloon for an all-Negro movie of DuBose Hayward's *Porgy* in the *Amsterdam News* read: "The picture will portray the human everyday life of the American colored man, his joys, [and] his sorrows."[9]

As movies grudgingly opened to blacks in small ways they gradually became human on the screen. The old metaphor still reappeared with each chestnut such as David Belasco's *The Heart of Maryland*, even to the extent of using Myrna Loy as a mulatto. Still the new Negro came on the screen as confidante, friend, ally, and most significantly, as enemy, in a wide variety of new films.

One of the best because of its sybaritic waterfront air, set against the plush brocade of the urban rich, was Donald Crisp's *Vanity* (1927). Noble Johnson played Bimbo, the ship's cook—a role that surely would have gone to a Latin type earlier. Rich, preening Barbara Fiske (Leatrice Joy) of San Francisco, pampered by servants, talks on a flowered telephone to her fiancé, Lt. Van Cortland (Charles Ray). Before marrying she has a fling at the "Recreation Hut" where in the jubilation following the Armistice she meets a rough sailor, Happy Dan Morgan (Alan Hale), who takes her to his ship. His crude song establishes the erotic mood:

> For she knifed me one night
> 'Cause I wished she was white,
> And I learned about women from 'er.

A cut, and we are in a tight shot down the hatchway where, hulking upwards like a great beast rising from the ooze, Bimbo, sweating in sailor's stripes, glowering with his bad eye, grinning at Barbara, is the model "bad nigger." Morgan hurls him back down into the galley and turns on Barbara, now helpless, with the brown man below her only hope. Bimbo rises again from his slough and wrestles the sailor while Barbara stares. Terrified, she seizes a gun and shoots Bimbo, no one able to guess whether her greater fear is of Bimbo's blackness or Morgan's intentions. Humbled by the experience she flees home where, with the first humane act of her life, she saves a thieving servant from discharge. In the brief climax of *Vanity* American audiences saw black and white characters involved with each other and changed by the experience.[10]

In the same year *In Old Kentucky* provided a far more conscious break with stereotyping. John M. Stahl's picture used Charles Dazey's play to depict the South after the Great War. The hero returns from the war broke and drunk, only to recoup the family fortune by riding his old cavalry mount in the Derby. The new environment could not contain the old servant types. Stepin Fetchit and Carolynne Snowden played them and broke the mold by having a clear love affair—a sexual relationship denied the Hollywood Negro during the 1920s. Both performers knew what they had done and proudly boasted of it for the rest of their lives. When vestiges of the old types survived sometimes, white critics voiced their disenchantment with them: "You may or may not struggle to keep a straight face when a negro eats a pie three sizes too large," wrote the *Times* man of the comedy in *In Old Kentucky*. At the same time the black press never took Negro actors to task for accepting the roles but instead reported their antics on set, their teaching whites the Charleston, their salvation from the Cotton Club chorus by signing film contracts.[11]

Uncle Tom's Cabin had become the inevitable vehicle for Hollywood's new concern with black subjects. The abolitionist tract, being familiar to blacks and whites alike, transcended the barriers between the races. Its credentials as an inviolable classic, a popular road show and melodrama, and a box office success narrowed the potential field of conflict over content and interpretation. It had been filmed several times before with success. In 1902 Edwin S. Porter had made a stagey film of fourteen tableaux based on the melodramatic Tom shows that leaned heavily on Tom's slavish love for Eva. Tom's popularity led to remakes every few years—Thanhouser in 1909, Imperial in 1913, in 1914 starring the Negro actor Sam Lucas, and in 1918 J. Searle Dawley's version for Paramount, shot on location in Mississippi with white Marguerite Clark as both Topsy and Eva. Occasionally Tom became a touching bit of sentimental business in a larger picture. Artcraft's *When Do We Eat?* (1918) took a group of stock company players through their small-town, sentimental renditions of Tom shows. Another one, *Little Eva Ascends* (1922), brought a slight moan of *déja vu* from the *Variety* reviewer who complained of "too much time being devoted to the performance of 'Uncle Tom's Cabin.'" As late as 1925 Universal released a two-reeler, *Uncle Tom's Gal*, with Edna Marion in roles of Topsy, Eva, Eliza, and a farmer's daughter attached to a second-rate movie company filming a Tom show. A year later *Our Gang* appeared in *Uncle Tom's Uncle*. In all, the important common ingredient was a warm, nostalgic, glowing spirit. Friendly white nostalgia coupled with black knowledge of the original Abolitionist intent of Mrs. Stowe's novel established it as the perfect vehicle for interracial amity and a prestigious stroke that would move Carl Laemmle's studio into the front ranks. Universal in 1926 began a steady stream of press releases about their new production of *Uncle Tom's Cabin*.[12]

White Hollywood seemed ready for a new departure. *In Old Kentucky* scored a hit without complaint or incident in spite of its black lovers. DeMille sniffed the air with undisguised enthusiasm as he craned about for an omen favorable to the production of a cinema *Porgy*. The trades applauded the fading of many old stock characters as films moved outdoors and away from melodramatic sources. "Clumsy housemaids seem to have gone out of style," *Variety* carped. Another reviewer found a B jungle movie no more than a childish "phantom of the past." And a theater writer called for a movie reprise of the Toussaint Players' all-Negro production of *Goat Alley*.[13]

Afro-American intellectuals and journalists responded in kind. In the late twenties they slowly established a role for themselves in America: they chose both racial integration *and* racial pride. This allowed them to embrace the race consciousness of the West Indian Marcus Garvey, the American sense of "two-ness" described by DuBois, the black economic base taught by Washington, the two-handed reach of the "Harlem wits" who wrote from within the ghetto outwards, and the direct assault on racism demanded by the NAACP.[14] "The quickening conscience of the nation will not consent to go on living forever on the basis of a lie," wrote Dean Kelly Miller of Howard University. "The relation of the Negro will become firmly established on the basis of equality or . . . inferiority. Which it shall be, will depend upon the Negro himself." James Weldon Johnson's song, "Lift Every Voice and Sing," caught the mood of race awareness and became "the Negro national anthem" as it spread to black churches everywhere:

> Sing a song full of the faith that the dark past has taught us,
> Sing a song full of hope that the present has brought us,
> Facing the rising sun,
> Of our new day begun,
> Let us march on till victory is won.[15]

The mood of the late twenties gradually bent black critics and fans toward the Hollywood product and away from support of black cinema achievement, eventually driving Oscar Micheaux and other black filmmakers into bankruptcy or idleness.[16]

They complained that whites would never move off the dead center of *Oroonoko* and blackface minstrelsy, and took note of "the lack of pictures with Negro characters teaching Negro ideals" which forced them to "witness those with Nordic casts or none at all." The result, according to Kennard Williams in the Baltimore *Afro-American*, was that "much subtle injury is done the race by the establishment of the thought, unconsciously, it is true, but none the less mischievous that 'All White is Right.' "[17]

Still, the black press ran countless stories that set Hollywood's cupidity against its "progress": First National announced the signing of Charles Gilpin, the original *Emperor Jones*, to play Tom; at MGM "Racial Types Lend Reality to Latest Chaney Pictures"; Romeo Daugherty complained of Harlem's lily-white projectionists union, of the radio networks' hiding black actors behind European names, and took note of protests directed at the whites playing black roles in Broadway's *Lulu Belle*, which used blacks only for "atmosphere."[18]

In the spring of 1926 Universal began location shooting for *Uncle Tom's Cabin* in Plattsburg, New York, with Harry Pollard directing and Charles Gilpin in the title role. All the resources of a great studio, a proven director, the Hollywood stars Ernest Torrance and Colleen Moore, and America's greatest black actor would be given over to mounting an ambitious film. But the studio objected to Gilpin's aggressive reading of *Tom* and, according to gossip, to his drinking. He was let out of his contract, and immediately Jimmie Smith, hustling to survive in black Los Angeles, edged his client James Lowe, an athletic vagabond who had started in Universal's *Blue Streak* series as a black sidekick of the white cowboy hero, into an audition and eventually the role of Tom, which he gave a "more brilliant reading" than any of his rivals.

By year's end the company had moved to Natchez for locations on a river steamer and on the waterfront. During shooting Edna Rosalyne Heard, a Santa Monica music teacher, sang background and counseled Pollard on elements of Negro culture. Later Madame Sul-te-Wan joined the cast. The *Amsterdam News* cheered the Southern sojourn: "Never before has the Southern Negro had the good fortune to be selected to take part in a clean cut motion picture." Every Negro actor, it sang, "should be proud of the opportunity which is his to help portray conditions as they were in the days of oppression." Back in Universal City optimism swelled so that the studio announced that not only would they make Uncle Tom but also a series of Octavus Roy Cohen's stories of the South—"Negro stories played by colored actors"—and a production of Florenz Ziegfeld's long-running musical *Showboat*, with its powerful voice of the black deckhand, Joe.[19]

The picture was expected to cost over a million dollars, to be regained with Broadway drumbeating, but it stalled in the cutting room, losing ten reels and setting back the opening until October. Even then nine cutters sweated out another dozen reels and brought it into New York at fourteen—less than half its intended length. In Los Angeles, at the cavernous Pantages Theatre, Universal tried to disguise flaws and sell it as a "hard-ticket" road show with the new synchronized sound, and an appearance by Laemmle.[20]

In the end, if Negroes felt any gain, it was in the fact of black participation. The impossible length, the quarrels with Gilpin, the misfired New York opening all cooled interest in the project and exposed it as a mixed achievement. Location shooting removed the patina of Southern romance that had crusted over its message. But the difference between Lowe's view of Tom and the sentimental Toms of the old traveling shows, even the silent cinema Toms, was not as wide as Lowe's friends contended, even though Mrs. Stowe's Abolitionist message was probably stronger than it had been in years. *Variety* forthrightly praised the brief focus on the black lovers, George and Eliza, ignoring the white casting that made them vestigial fossils of the blackface era. Even after the New York opening cutters still patched together yet another "improved version." In London, Negroes heard, it went so badly that the exhibitors mounted a "lavishly produced Negro plantation prologue" starring Lowe himself in order to cover its flaws. In the South it was banned outright in Birmingham because *non sequitur* shots of Sherman's invading Union Army made it "unfit for Birmingham and the South." The Negro press grew edgy enough toward it to begin boosting Noble Johnson's version of Tom in an otherwise worthless rival called *Topsy and Eva*. As though to point up black reservations, Lowe and Smith left Hollywood for New York and then a smashing tour of Europe, intending to carve as much meat as possible from Tom before Europeans realized he was a turkey.[21]

The picture plodded on for over two hours, spinning out three plots and a comic line. The story follows first George Harris and Eliza, whose intended marriage is scotched by George's master. Uncle Tom and the Harrises are thrown together when Tom's kindly master decides to sell him and the Harrises' son to cover debts. Eliza flees across the ice with her son to a kindly Quaker. The Dred Scott decision provides the legal means for returning them, forcing George to swim for freedom alone and Eliza to near-suicidal frenzy at the thought of her child's sale. Tom is lifted from certain sale "down the river" by the intervention of Eva and her father, the Yankee Augustus St. Claire, who buys the old slave. Black, comic Topsy enters as Eva's child-servant who proffers a bit of levity before the maudlin deaths of Eva and her father. Tom is auctioned off to the cruel Yankee, Simon Legree, along with Eliza, who is brought to the house to usurp the place of Cassie, an older mulatto who improbably is revealed as Eliza's mother. The women flee, retreating to Legree's attic, where they hide while Tom is beaten to death, to the end silently concealing their hideout. Legree happens upon them but dies in drunken apoplexy, permitting all to be reunited at the end. So winds the picaresque plot through years and miles too improbable with coincidence, too laden with Yankees to effectively indict the Southern "peculiar institution." Nevertheless, after years of a happy South basking in the fruits of a benign slavery Tom was barbed enough to earn censorship in parts of Dixie.

Despite all its faults that cutting could not redeem, the picture spread wide a vision of blackness that had not been seen in years. Lowe's Tom, while not abandoning the accretion of sentimentality that had crusted like barnacles over Mrs. Stowe's character, restored some of his strength. All of the tools of shooting and cutting were marshalled to give him stature. And the discrete, rambling structure gave him proportionally more presence because white roles were either like St. Clair —fleeting bits of cardboard—or like Legree—throwbacks to prairie-town melodramas. But neither Lowe consciously nor Harry Pollard unconsciously imparted more than the materials would allow. Yet, all things considered, white Southerners grumbled, Yankees exulted, and blacks felt their cause represented as well as possible.[22]

Black journalists plugged the movie throughout its production and into release, overcoming disenchantment with its concessions to Southern white sensibility. Universal admitted that the United Sons and Daughters of the Confederacy had forced cuts of cruelty, shifted the onus for slavery to the Yankee Legree, to the point of showing "northern troops coming to the rescue of slaves suffering under northern cruelty." But D. Ireland Thomas of New Orleans emphasized the unprecedented black contribution. Calvin Floyd, despite his pique at vestiges of blackface style, thought that "all through it the Negro is shown to splendid advantage" and so powerfully that even whites applauded "each time a slave scored a point." For him, Lowe seemed caught in midair between a "superb" performance and old-fashioned "humility [that] makes you want to give him a swift kick." But all things considered, Floyd thought the total effect was inspirational:

> If a Negro ever felt like doing something to try to elevate his people he ought to feel like it when he sees the eternal hope in the old slave's eyes in his darkest hours.

Finally, if the lingering view of slavery seemed "humiliating to the colored spectator," he could console himself with the knowledge that Lowe took $500 of white men's money for every working week. The *Amsterdam News* welcomed the picture into Harlem at Christmas, and stoked a new Negro rage for cinema.[23]

If *Uncle Tom's Cabin* failed blacks it was as an omen for whites to read. It brought a strong black figure artfully to the attention of whites, but unfortunately the studios chose a safe policy of reproducing Universal's success rather than pushing beyond it. Even though they had bucked Southern opposition and the threat of box office losses,

Uncle Tom's Cabin (© Universal Pictures Corp.) featuring Gertrude Howard and James Lowe, broadened black social roles from life in the slave quarter to . . . (George P. Johnson Collection)

even though the trades reported good grosses, even though it opened in the South without incident, the picture failed to start a cycle.[24] Universal itself did no more than attempt to patch together a six-reel sequel using the outtakes. Lowe, in spite of the critical praise, received only a few feelers from Fox and MGM, and finally left for a tour of Europe. Gilpin lost his second job at Fox, and George Reed risked his career by refusing to replace him, an event that led blacks to believe that the studios simply refused to pay top dollar to Negro players.[25]

The studios seemed to turn backward. After their success in *In Old Kentucky*, Carolynne Snowden was entrapped by maid roles and Stepin Fetchit began to ossify the demeaning traits of his screen character. Two studios merely dusted off old Tom shows and rereleased them. Another announced a series of two-reelers, *Baby Jewels*, based on Octavus Roy Cohen's *Saturday Evening Post* "darkey" stories.

The worst of the spinoffs from Tom was *Topsy and Eva*, a rival already in production at the release of Universal's picture, because it revealed the insuperable obstacles Afro-Americans needed to overcome in Hollywood. The whites at United Artists were not so much vicious as they were sentimental and ignorant of black criticism.

On the oceanside of the San Gabriel Range, south of Universal City, such a crew of well-intentioned, invincibly ignorant whites gathered to make a movie. Rosetta and Vivian Duncan were clever San Franciscans who knew nothing of the Negro world but much of the minstrel tradition from which they had fashioned their blackface sister act. Lois Weber was an alert white director who quit when she learned she would not be allowed to shape a serious drama from the Duncans' vaudeville act. The studio brought in Del Lord from the ranks of serial directors. After he "made a mess of it" the exasperated producers turned to Griffith, who had an itch to do a Tom show. Griffith gave it ten days in which he reshot, recut, and patched it into a pathetic, regressive, burlesque of his racial beliefs. The result was an old-fashioned tribute, not to Tom, but to Tom shows. The trades found it tolerable, although by the time of its opening in the Duncan Sisters' hometown the studio brought in Mary Pickford's cutter, still trying to save it. "Kiddie matinees" was its level, according to *Variety*, which also guessed its grosses flowed from the Duncan Sisters' personal appear-

Life among the planter class (© Universal Pictures Corp.). (Author's Collection)

Universal's *Uncle Tom's Cabin* changed James Lowe, here receiving children's applause at a London benefit, into an international star—at least until the studio ran out of Negro roles for him. (Jimmie Smith Collection)

Unfortunately for blacks, *Uncle Tom's Cabin* (© Pathé Exchange, Inc.) stimulated as much parody as imitation. (Author's collection)

ances with the picture. In its final form it was no more than a hoary racial joke relieved only by Noble Johnson's staunch effort to preserve Tom's dignity, and a tinge of environmentalism that had crept into Topsy's role. The Duncans saw her as a black child forced to act in a grotesque comic way and affected by the beatings that had driven away her "goodness."[26] Thus, in spite of the celebrity of Tom, the basic social organization of Hollywood prevailed and predetermined the thrust of the Negro movies. No black writer intruded, the director who objected was let out, and Griffith's racial cant found its way into yet one more American film.

And, yet, too much had happened to Americans. The old imagery, the Negro as metaphor for an idyllic, long-gone pastoral ideal, could stifle the artistic presentation of the new Negro, but it could not prevent the striking variety of Afro-American roles. The breadth of black imagery grudgingly widened.[27]

After years of conservatism movies began to catch up with social change by creating some Negro roles that were far more assimilationist than would have been possible in the actual life of the twenties. In one of his first pictures, *Beggars of Life*, William Wellman adapted Jim Tully's picaresque tale of hobo life to the screen. Louise Brooks played a young girl who accidentally kills her brutal foster father. Richard Arlen's hobo helps her escape to the dangers of hobo jungles and the brutality of "Oklahoma Red" (Wallace Beery). Along the way Edgar "Blue" Washington, a sometime Los Angeles policeman, appears as Mose, a black wanderer who joins the pair in their struggle. Throughout their brief alliance he is their equal and their champion. When Red and Arkansas Snake fight over the girl, it is Mose who knocks a knife from the Snake's hand. He is the train-wise hobo who can elude the railroad police and miraculously forage for food. As a sick tramp sinks down on his deathbed he cries out to Mose: "Hey, black man, where's your hand? I'm afraid." All that remains of the old time Negro are two comic bits with chickens and a brief flicker of pulling back—scared— from the corpse. In their final moments together Mose and Red dress a corpse in the girl's clothes and set it afire in a boxcar in order to let the girl escape to Canada. Mose covers the escape by elaborately "tomming" the police. Even so, despite Washington's central role, *Variety* took no notice of his presence.[28]

At Paramount Cecil B. DeMille, who never did complete his intended production of *Porgy*, introduced a Negro into a symbolic role in *Old Ironsides*, a ritual celebration of American virtues in which a black man was included. George Godfrey, an enormous black boxer who left the ring feeling white champions evaded his challenges, played the ship's cook on board the frigate *Constitution*. The ship's career up to the battle of Tripoli forms the plot thread. Off the Saracen forts the cook joins a dangerous night landing party that contributes to the reduction of the forts and the eventual triumph of American arms.[29]

Both on and off camera cracks in the old molds were more apparent. In many small roles and in their perquisites blacks received much the same treatment other actors expected. Carolynne Snowden had her own dressing room next to the stars on Erich von Stroheim's pictures. Stepin Fetchit stayed in the commandant's guest house when he came to Annapolis to work in John Ford's *Salute*. His personal dresser was a bit player named John Wayne. Monta Bell's *Man, Woman, and Sin* (1927) establishes Gilbert Roland's hardscrabble beginnings by having him live in a cul-de-sac behind the rich kid's house. There black children intently play around the fire hydrants; an old man sits on his steps and strums a banjo to himself; a cut is to a dark-skinned woman leaning out her window and taking the air. Von Stroheim in *The Merry Widow* established the slick Manhattan roots of a troupe of entertainers by using a brash, cigar-smoking Negro company manager, a role missing from Ernst Lubitsch's sound version. In brief dance flashes Carolynne Snowden contributed to the casual, swinging life of Paris. She remembered similar appearances in *The Wedding March*, *The Gilded Butterfly*, and other films. In *Queen Kelly* Stroheim attempted an allegorical black mass with an African priest, verger, and a clutch of prostitute-vestals which did not survive to a release print. The work increased at such a rate that Central Casting maintained a Negro section under Jimmie Smith's successor as Central Avenue's roguish hustler, Charles Butler.[30]

The most direct exploration of the question of assimilation, at least in its newer version after the evasive years of Creoles, Polynesians, and mistaken identities of the melodramas, was Josef von Sternberg's synopsis, *The King of the Cannibals*. Unproduced, it still revealed the new possibilities considered by Hollywood studios. Originally written for the German actor Emil Jannings, it was the tale of a West African "black King, who by dint of body and brain and pride of race controls the black earth." It opens on the ritual of selecting his mate with its giant pulsating drum that "is the soul of black Africa." Soon a beached exploring party intrudes, and the blacks who have never seen white men are convulsed with laughter. The stock white opening, the proferring of baubles, is scorned by the king. The whites are saved only when one lights a match and another kills a snake with his pistol. The king hesitates, not from fear, but from realizing "that there were things for him to learn and to acquire which are outside his ken." He leaves with the whites, first setting in motion the great drum that would insure that "his love for Africa and the black man be kept alive in his heart."

In London he is confused by white society and makes his way to a Negro cabaret, where "negroes have gone to hell because of the white man's sins" and where he is rebuffed by a black dancer and learns the stigma of blackness in the white world. A halfbreed mulcts him of his money, "and his nobility vanishes in proportion to his acquiring the traits of the whites." He soon drifts into the prize ring, where he becomes a champion, wallows in high living still dogged by his desire for the dancer, and finally is imprisoned after a riot in the cabaret. The halfbreed hopes to assume his mantle in Africa after learning the king has been broken by prison and released as a stoker on the ship taking the decadent London blacks back to Africa. His humiliation ends as he hears again the pulse of the great drum. Machismo restored by Mother Africa, he defeats the halfbreed, takes the dancer as his queen, and regains the throne, "the black king of the black earth."[31]

The press releases were thick with such dreams and experiments, but the studios could not budge off the dead center of *Tom, Our Gang,* and the fresh blacks of *Beggars of Life* and *Man, Woman, and Sin.* The first stride into black themes would have to wait for the threatening, experimental, and panicky first days of soundfilm when the studios were willing to try anything in order to gain an edge in the new game.

Warner Brothers had been staggering along even during the prosperous twenties; otherwise they might have been less prone to experiment with the new sound system called Vitaphone. Edison's synchronized discs, DeForest Phonofilm, and other innovations had proved momentarily impractical. But beginning in 1926 with a few short pieces, *The Adventures of Don Juan,* and then *The Jazz Singer,* sound became part of a reluctant revolution. By coincidence the Negro world experienced "an upward turn" that show business of the 1920s had vaguely promised. Even before the self-conscious social awareness encouraged by the depression of the 1930s, blacks had begun to crack the racial system in many small ways. In Washington, for example, Kelly Miller, Dean of Howard University, served as Vice-President of the newly formed Community Chest. Also in 1928 the Social Science Research Council called together delegates from eighteen social service and interracial organizations to discuss the statistical data on race relations. Segregation in the capital began to crumble in small corners, ranging from the police department's annual children's Christmas party to the Young Communist League's 1932 dance. Each new change revealed the racism next to be defeated. A Negro platoon of the Fire Department, an innovation in 1919, was exposed later as a device for curtailing Negro recruits. Black and white joined in common protest against the injustices of the famous "Scottsboro boys" rape case in Alabama. The National Theatre broke its Jim Crow policy for a special performance of *Green Pastures*. Similar changes could be found in Boston, Chicago, New York, and elsewhere.[32]

The Hollywood Negro not only made no revolutions but may have reinforced the racial status quo. But at least the movies after 1925 began to reflect some of the agonizing, slow social changes on the American scene. For Hollywood the next step would be a brief flash of blackness on the screen when sound became a medium to express Negro music and dance—and when whites and blacks alike believed in the briefly current myth that white voices recorded poorly and black beautifully.

Another plain indicator of the relative polishing of racial attitudes and tastes under urban pressures at the end of the decade was the declining number of pejorative movies of Oriental life, of the trend away from Indian heavies, and of the continually sweetening immigrant ideograms. Japanese naval rivalry joined the persistent Chinese revolutionary turmoil in the daily press, so the old Chinatown melodramas with their trapdoors and murky alleys rattled against the reality of social and political change in Asia. By the end of the decade the worst of the hoary villains, Sax Rohmer's Dr. Fu Manchu, in his opposition to whites, is given genius, guile, and, ultimately, humanity; for no matter how nefarious his schemes, at bottom they rest solidly on plausible antiimperialist revenge upon the British for killing his family during the Boxer Rebellion. Oriental heavies declined in numbers until the revival of Oriental sentimental romances in the 1930s as a result of the popularity of the missionary's daughter and novelist, Pearl Buck, and her imitators.[33] Thereafter, until the war fever of the 1940s, Asian themes, at least in major movies, tended toward verisimilitude.

With the waning of the tradition of darkened doorways and glinting daggers of old Chinatown, the most persistent racial discrimination for Asians rested on the demands of the box office which resulted in plum roles for whites. James B. Leong, Sojin, Tetsu Komai, and others rarely received well-rounded roles, and Hayakawa and Wong eventually moved to Europe. Instead, in big movies and in Bs alike, marketable white players such as Warner Oland, Edward G. Robinson, Myrna Loy, and Sidney Toler received the meaty roles. On the other hand, the total number of roles waned under pressure from the liberal press. *Variety*, for example, regularly condemned the "villainous . . . Chinese chop suey magnate [who] . . . could have been left out," the "lurid lobby billing playing up Oriental mysticism, yellow peril characters and the . . . mysterious Orient," the "labored melo," the "tried and true hokum," the "celluloid libel," the "exaggerated artificiality," and so on.[34]

Indians went into similar eclipse once the studios had exhausted the mythic imagery of the frontier. Benign presentments of the Indians' "side" such as Richard Dix's *The Vanishing American* of 1925 resulted in box office failure. Culture conflicts appeared as struggles between Indians and white renegades, halfbreeds, or crooked trading post agents rather than true clashes of cultures, and they usually ended in empty rituals of false conciliation. By 1927 *Variety* noticed that "the Indian, once the partner of the film cowboy, has largely disappeared."[35]

Predictably, European immigrant groups remained closest to white assimilationist ideals. Because of this, the sentimental movies of immigrant life celebrated Americanization in ways that could never include nonwhites. In dozens of movies Jewish filiopiety, Irish whimsy, and Italian passion adapted to American life. John Ford made three Irish films in one year, and late in life still remembered a favorite shot from one of them: "the Gaelic cross, with the people passing in front of it."[36]

The myth of the melting pot excluded Afro-Americans. By the end of the silent film age they had scarcely bettered their position, for they remained excluded from all but the periphery of assimilationist movies. If the myth of the melting pot held no relevance for them, and if strong figures such as *Tom* seldom appeared, then their predominant contribution to Hollywood cinema was as furniture and atmosphere. Thus for the moment creative Negroes in the cinema could only look on from the Hollywood sidelines or turn to independently produced all-black cinema—the "race movies."

Chapter Seven

THE BLACK UNDERGROUND

The Hollywood feature film enjoyed fifteen years of refinement following the innovations of *The Birth of a Nation*. The same period offered Negroes little. The reasons were clear. At their most well meaning, white movies never really touched the Negro world. That market was supplied by a thin stream of movies created by blacks for black audiences. Stifled by short capital, muddled by the tangle between cultural nationalism and NAACP assimilationism, stunted by lack of outlets, rendered comic by inexperience and artlessness, exhausted by the unending pursuit of "angels," the all-black cinema failed miserably. Yet its purveyors could not turn off their efforts, for to do so would have been to admit that in the twentieth century only white men could teach the freedmen. So the all-black companies survived travail, white infiltration, inept production and unheralded releases. Their ambition never wavered, although it often outstripped their capacity and their potential.

If the Lincoln Motion Picture Company seems an antique reminder of black effort in the teens, the benchmarks of the 1920s would be the films of Oscar Micheaux. His ambition had far greater strength than his pedestrian cinema achievement. Yet he, the Colored Players Corporation, and a cluster of tiny companies that rarely survived the printing of their prospectuses formed an underground cinema that attempted a black aesthetic to fill the vacuum left by Hollywood. They did not fail so much as they were overwhelmed by the impossible.

Ever since the days of Lincoln and *The Birth of a Race* Negroes had made fitful gestures toward a black aesthetic cinema tradition. Imposing obstacles appeared at every turn: the opposition and infiltration of the white majority, black apathy and inexperience, lack of facilities, and, as Lincoln learned in the harshest of lessons, woefully inadequate distribution exchanges and theaters. In contrast, during the silent era the white companies in Hollywood strengthened and expanded. Moreover, hurdles for blacks were raised higher by the same optimistic assimilationism that helped to stifle Garveyism. Every Negro gesture toward supporting the black studios was a pessimistic vote against the ultimate equalizing of the wealth and institutions of American life. Besides, white money, expertise, and skills combined to make most of the all-black pictures cooperative efforts between black and white. Negro movies, then, became a misnomer for all of the producers except those in the independent mold of Oscar Micheaux; and he too would eventually recover from bankruptcy by borrowing from white sources. The result was uneven, and yet the small movement provided ghetto audiences with black imagery beyond the Hollywood Negro. For many blacks they taught a toughminded, doctrinaire, bourgeois competitiveness—perhaps unrealistic for "the brother on the block" but nonetheless an optimistic statement that blacks could aspire and sometimes even win the game. The patent racial chauvinism provided an aesthetic balance to the racism of the Hollywood Negro. Finally, the trend gave needed experience and exposure to a generation of performers, actors, and exhibitors.[1]

The most tangled problem of aesthetics was the need for a mythic figure. Critics had already begun to see the larger-than-life mythic quality of the cinema beyond its form and expression as art. Hence, movies presented a sometimes unstated conundrum for black filmmakers because whites to one degree or another had assimilated the core values of American life and had developed mythic heroes to symbolize the values. For those on the bottom rung as on the top, movies were something one experienced in the dark, where fantasy, escape, the will to power could all play in the mind's eye. The dream of success was at least plausible. Most blacks firmly sat in the low wallows of American life, mired in segregation and discrimination, while astride the heap were the tiny black bourgeoisie on "strivers' row." The great myths did not fit as cleanly. For them as audiences to root for the cavalry against the Indians, Tarzan against the tribes, Douglas Fairbanks over the vizier was an anomaly. From another quarter the middle class was always threatened by breaking the cup of identity, of becoming whitened by success. Already middle-class blacks and whites were more like each other than were middle- and lower-class blacks. Thus merely to bronze white images and make them stand for black would make them ludicrous. The agonies of turning to Mother Africa for inspiration had already been demonstrated by Garvey, the South still encouraged flight rather than inspiration, and the ghetto was too bitter to contemplate; thus there always shimmered the temptation to make mirror images of white movies. Therefore success itself might be a false god for Negroes.[2]

By 1920 no black alternative to Hollywood emerged because the Negro moviemaker could only look to the two failures, the Lincoln Company and the *Birth of a Race* Company, in addition to a few ragtag black-fronted producers of "quickies" of the genre of *A Black Sherlock Holmes* and *Spying the Spy*. Their best contribution had been to give another twist to the ambiguous "good-bad nigger," the Nat Turner behind the grinning mask. Lincoln's forte was the micrometer-perfect reproduction of mirror-image black heroes who woo and win by the last reel, a parallelism of values induced by the baggage of white technicians, producers, directors, and writers in the train of all the black companies. It was a reenactment of the American paradox: no matter how unbending the racial caste lines, blacks and whites came together in antagonistic and reluctant cooperation, and each marked the other's life in unnamable ways. Still, good or bad, they provided a rallying point for cultural nationalism that no amount of Negro-laden Hollywood productions would invoke. In the black papers an all-Negro movie elicited praise and encouragement for the company, sometimes a plug for the sale of the stock outstanding, and a friendly or even an exuberant review.

The only black objections to the race movies came from Romeo Daugherty and Easterners who saw the pictures as impediments to real progress in a bootless game with white giants. "Micheaux," Daugherty wrote in 1925, "is in the same boat in which Marcus Garvey found himself when he tried to bring out a daily paper to compete with the O'Fays." In other words, they needed audiences, not doctrinaire racial nationalism. Noble Johnson liked to think he would not work in a picture unless he thought it broad enough to reach whites, while Luther Pollard, whose Ebony Film Corporation was largely a creature of white investors, wrote that when any Negro film scored in a white theater "he feels good because he knows it helps."[3]

During the years of World War I no clear challenger rose against the Lincoln Company. Oscar Micheaux was still going door-to-door in the prairie raising capital, while white companies with a few blacks on the letterhead as a sop to Negro exhibitors experimented with race comedy. The Committee on Public Information under George Creel released a dribble of War Department footage of black troops to black companies. Negro lodges and other groups screened their parades and outings, and numberless little groups issued prospectuses and press releases without ever turning out a motion picture. Lincoln was a giant in such a setting, with its $75,000 capital pool, its president and star, Noble Johnson, its distribution outlets centered in Omaha, its regional managers and their connections with black newspapers. The only other groups with such stable assets were Robert Levy's Reol Company, whose strength came from the all-black Lafayette Players, the Harlem theatre group for whom Levy was also an "angel"; and the Frederick Douglass Film Company of Jersey City under the direction of Traverse Spraggins.[4]

Like the men of Lincoln, the Douglass company wanted to fill the screen with strong black success images. Its pictures were calculated to offset the "evil effects" of *The Birth of a Nation*, to bring harmony between the races without puffing "the value of one race at the expense of the other," "to show the better side of Negro life," and "to inspire in the Negro a desire to climb higher." Their first attempt became their continuing model, *The Colored American Winning His Suit* (1916), but their inability to get bookings and to heap up capital while waiting for the grosses to come in created the same problems that often stalled Lincoln. By the end of their first year their sole outlet in the South failed to deliver enough revenue to warrant continuing the contract. Their only answer was a cooperative arrangement with Lincoln to book Eastern dates in return for Lincoln's covering the West for Douglass.

Black movies provided a reinforcement to growing postwar race consciousness by providing the newspapers with a visible example of the race's enterprise, talent, and demiurge for success. Douglass's first release spurred the New York *Age* to enlarge its space given to movies, up to then circumscribed by Lester Walton's love of the stage. At first Douglass received only a nodding notice that its state rights were for sale—no reviews, no advertising—while the Lafayette Theatre consumed the columns. But by the spring of 1917 Walton praised the company, its competitors, and the hundreds of Negro theaters as "a move in the right direction."[5]

With the release of Douglass's adaptation of Paul Laurence Dunbar's *The Scapegoat*, Walton became a harsh critic who still encouraged the company, in Dunbar's words, to "keep a pluggin' away." But he gibed at the discontinuity and the gratuitous use of dialect titles for two Negro doctors, darkskinned enough so that there was "no identity problem" to be solved by dialect. Nevertheless, the picture seemed the "best to date" and deserving of "great credit and encouragement" because of its good grosses at the Regent in Baltimore, the Howard in Washington, and in Northern dates.[6]

In the midst of the war effort the movement lost momentum, perhaps because the rigors of war compounded the already insuperable obstacles to black moviemaking. So several of them turned to the Creel Committee for salvation, figuring that by acquiring films of black soldiers they could cut costs, invade white theaters, and enter the peacetime market from a position of solvency. After George Johnson's unsuccessful negotiation with Emmett Scott, the Eastern companies, with whom Scott was probably more familiar, received rights to the government film. Luckily, in a way, the film revealed the invidious racial attitudes of white writers in the Signal Corps, thereby stimulating the eventual resumption of black film production. Nevertheless, the black bargainers acquired some fine footage as well. Lincoln's film, purchased from the French government; shots of the 369th Negro Regiment totaling twelve monthly two-reel shows released by the newly formed Toussaint Exchange; and Douglass's films of blacks from combat to homecoming processed from script to screen by a Negro were among the batches of Army film released to blacks. The piquant pleasure of seeing staunch black figures on the screen packed the Lafayette when the feature length *From Harlem to the Rhine* shared a bill with Harlem's 15th Regiment Orchestra. Applause rattled through the house as Bert Williams, Jim Europe, and other familiar soldiers appeared, and increased as the camera followed the 15th into the line and eventually to their occupation of Germany. Later *Our Hell Fighters Return* (1919) showed them marching up Fifth Avenue and home to Harlem. Of all the critics Lester Walton took the greatest care to distinguish between French film, which presented the Senegalese as soldiers who "helped save the 'white man's civilization,' " and Hearst-Pathé footage, which focused on a black soldier baffled by the French language, a mock discussion of the relative safety of the army and navy, and a Negro officer calling another "niggah." Walton, "tired of being maligned," railed at the Creel Committee for the insult.[7]

With the end of the war the pattern of Negro migration became more clearly northern, and Lincoln, committed deeply to the West with its cinematic technical facilities, was remote from both capital and audiences. By the early twenties they expired, while the survivors clustered along the East Coast. The postwar optimism spurred a nationwide revival of black cinema riding the waves of the exodus, of race consciousness, of the spreading Harlem Renaissance, and of a slow accretion of new urban wealth. From that platform Negro film production leaped forward from the small beginnings of the teens. Two score motion pictures were made in 1921 alone from studios in California through Texas to the East. Where no films appeared there were glowing prospectuses and press releases. "COLORED MOTION PICTURES ARE IN GREAT DEMAND," claimed an *Age* headline late in 1920, as Walton urged support of ghetto houses, twitted black Petersburg for letting its theater go under, and plugged Douglass and Micheaux, who had come to New York.[8]

The difference between black East and West seemed almost a parody of the white movie system: money and power in New York, glamour and bravado in Los Angeles. Black Californians, more like Rotarian boosters than good race men, were urged to see Reol's production of Dunbar's *Sport of the Gods*, not for some deep black chauvinistic reason but because it played to "overflow" houses in New York and Chicago (although, belying the blurbs, the Philharmonic Auditorium booked it for only a one-nighter). "No tragic race issue is involved; no tiresome sermon preached," boasted the *Eagle* of a black western.[9]

Their most persistent struggle, indeed their black *raison d'être*, was for control of the product. Sidney P. Dones, a gadfly in black theatrical circles, made *Injustice*, a seven-reel western which Walton of the *Age* castigated for its unctuous pretense that the Red Cross was racially integrated and its putting ghetto patois in the mouths of Negro collegians. Angrily, Dones blamed, then sued, L-Ko, the white studio to whom he had assigned distribution, for its cutting butchery and its low sales. To him it was "the usual attempt of the white man to shape anything dealing with the race question according to his prejudiced notions."[10] J. Luther Pollard's black comedies in this regard were like Andy Razaf's most socially pointed lyrics, which simply never appeared among his Blackbirds Revues—they reflected the danger of accepting white support. Because whites backed Pollard, his comedic line scarcely differed from the whites' and was redeemed only by the fact of a black presence. Yet that alone was enough to induce revenue-hungry Lincoln to bid for distribution rights.

An example of a possible victim of the endless bargaining for power may have been the films of the Democracy Photoplay Corporation, a white Middle Western firm with a capital of $110,000 and a goal of a million. Its major figures included Sidney Dones, the whites, and Thais Nehli Kalana, a descendant of Queen Liliokulani of Hawaii. Their contribution to the war effort was *Democracy, or a Fight for Right* and *Loyal Hearts* (1929), the latter being "a Smashing Virile Story of our Race Heroes in the Great World's War in France." Like DuBois's famous editorial in the same year, the picture announced that in exchange for the black soldiers who fought bravely "The Negro Now Appeals for Fairness in the Name of Humanity." Yet, despite the racial chauvinism and the social criticism of the heralds, Walton complained that the rankling segregation within the Red Cross was glossed over. It was as though the tension within the black-and-tan company was revealed

in the glowing racial ambitions of the advertising, which contrasted
with the equivocal evasions of the film itself. In the end the company
could muster only eight release prints.[11]

So, Negroes hesitantly turned to movies, held back by the fore-
knowledge that they were a white man's medium and by vestigial remains of rural Baptist fundamentalism. But through 1921 a mild boom-
let in black pictures swelled, and for the first time the conservative
black bourgeoisie joined the movement. In Washington, for example,
Walter Pinchback, manager of the Republic and the Lincoln on stylish
black U Street, put legendary W. C. Handy in as orchestra director of
one and black violinist Joe Douglass in the other, and visited New York
to book pictures and learn the methods of running a big luxurious
house. In Kansas City the white-owned house that screened Micheaux's
movies had a thousand seats. The McAvoy in Buffalo promised to run
race pictures "when possible to obtain them." C. Tiffany Tolliver
opened a Negro exchange in Roanoke. In New York the Lafayette
asked as much as fifty cents to see Reol's *Sport of the Gods*. Coincident
with the expansion, by 1923 white moviegoing slumped, particularly
in the South, so the prosperity soon attracted white owners who bought
into the Lafayette in New York and the Dunbar in Philadelphia.[12]

The Negro community was caught short-handed by the new demands. For money they tried Julius Rosenwald, the Chicago merchant,
while Micheaux went door-to-door soliciting. In a nationwide exercise
in underdevelopment they spun wheels in dozens of false starts or
turned out journalistic miscellany. In Los Angeles, for example, "Kid"
Herman gathered footage of the opening of a black hospital and an
NAACP meeting. By 1922 the Renaissance Film Company had released
its third picture featuring the Harlem Y, the Booker T. Washington
Sanatarium, the Imperial Elks Lodge, a covey of rich black women,
and Marshall Foch's farewell to the black 15th. "What a pity that *same*
company cannot get busy with the *right* thing," complained a friend of
Emmett Scott in 1919, after he gave up the fight and tried to get a job
with DeMille.[13]

In a wave of race solidarity mixed with an urge to shape an aesthetic,
as each production went into release, the Negro press grew friendlier
toward the black enterprise, yet more sharply critical of the results.
With each new picture a tradition developed with which to make comparisons, and to reveal progress against the benchmarks along the way.
D. Ireland Thomas, the Johnsons' old booker and promoter with Lincoln, in the *Chicago Defender* spun out the lessons he had learned in
the old days: it was not enough to cast out the old stereotypes; "exploitation" had become necessary. In the teens the exhibitor merely
opened his doors and blacks came to a race picture. But in 1922 "The

people [were] not flocking into theatres any more just because it is a
Race picture," he announced. "They have to be shown that it is a good
picture."[14]

Leigh Whipper, an actor who had worked for Griffith, carefully
analyzed Ben Strasser's all-Negro *His Great Chance* as an example of
how-to-do-it, sorting out the good shooting from the sloppy cutting
while attempting to inspire his readers with the legend of Bill Foster,
who had supposedly shot the first all-black picture in 1912. To Whipper the key was that each example of black cinema "will pave the way
for a higher standard of films among us." Such serious criticism remained a thin stream, and sometimes went no further than dutiful
cheerleading. In the *Defender*'s overenthusiastic pages the Norman
company's *The Green-Eyed Monster* became "one of the most spectacular productions ever shown at a local house"; while the *Pittsburgh
Courier* exaggeratedly praised Edna Morton as "our Mary Pickford"
for her work in eighteen pictures, black and white.[15]

The friendly press and the loyal audiences gradually encouraged a
nationwide bubbling of tiny companies and frothy ambitions: the
Unique Film Company in Chicago; the Reol in New York; Micheaux,
by then in Chicago; Lincoln, still surviving in Los Angeles; Andlauer
in Kansas City; Lone Star in San Antonio; Ben Strasser in Winston-
Salem; and more. Most of them floated on a wave of good intentions,
but only a few struggled into production.[16] Thus most of the artifacts
of the black filmmakers may be seen in only fleeting glimpses—a "still"
here, a fragment of script there, and only rarely a complete motion
picture. Their ambitions rather than their achievements reveal their
story.

In the early days Emmett Scott and the Johnsons unsuccessfully
searched for blacks who would join the fight against Hollywood. But
the first, cocky, eager black movie "manufacturers" merely clogged
the market with glossy prospectuses and promises, chewed up the thin
stock of venture capital, and made audiences cynical of their inept
products. And even though their movies must have smacked of the
escharotic black world, and many Negroes rushed to see them, competition often strangled the little studios. Besides, the worst of them were
"just novels using a colored cast instead of white." And even the best
of them, the energetic Lincoln, staffed by a black actor trained up as
a director by Lubin in Philadelphia, a malleable white director, a national booking office in Omaha, and connections with the *Defender*,
the *Courier*, and other black papers, failed after the great postwar influenza epidemic.[17]

All over the land their products flashed up like clinkers from a blast
furnace—without reason or prediction, thrown up by random subsur-

face forces—incredible in their variety of source and theme. Among the lost and poorly distributed achievements were Dr. A. Porter Davis's *The Lure of a Woman,* the first Negro picture produced in Kansas City; Oscar Micheaux's one or two titles every year; Pollard's Ebony two-reelers; Eureka's New York-made *Square Joe,* featuring the black boxer Joe Jeannette; Monumental's intended monthly bulletin in the manner of the large white studios; the films of the three Texas companies, Cotton Blossom and Lone Star both of San Antonio, and Superior Art Productions of Houston, which turned out a locally released title in 1921; Norman's *Crimson Skull,* shot in the all Negro town of Boley, Oklahoma; and many more. Occasionally as a curiosity, *Billboard* or one of the other white trades would ask a Negro to review one.[18]

Their products hewed to no type. Micheaux, who anchored his canon in the no man's land of the lightskinned mulatto, also produced a boxing story starring Sam Langford, an exposé of the Ku Klux Klan, and a folksy tale of the sodhouse frontier. Ebony ground out its old-fashioned comic darkeys. Sidney P. Dones, "the Henry Walthall of the Colored Race," according to his notices, did *Reformation* (1920), a black temperance tract written by a white man.

If entrepreneurs had only stayed in the studios! Instead, men burned themselves out and exhausted capital and good faith by plugging scores of little pictures that never appeared, or were buried in narrow graves dug by poor distribution and the wasteful failure to muster more than one or two prints. By 1921 there were two dozen companies, most of them without a single title in release. Their chronicler was George P. Johnson of Lincoln. When his own company folded under the weight of the influenza epidemic, he began a crabbed life of clipping news of the little companies, muttering to himself at their failures. They were everywhere: Gate City in Kansas; C. B. Campbell in Pensacola; the Colored and Indian Film Corporation in New York, which tried to bring together the great stars of the Negro stage for *Uncle Remus's First Visit to New York;* and more. Nothing seemed to go well in the early 1920s. Colored Feature Photoplays, for example, capitalized at $125,000 with each share par-valued at a dollar, but its own officers held no more than $250 of the issue. Blackburn Velde got a picture into release starring Jack Johnson, only to have the negative seized for alleged nonpayment of rent. Constellation Film Corporation started in late 1921 with a glowing prospectus and a black front led by Charles W. Anderson, the nationally known Republican and ex-internal-revenue collector for Wall Street; a nationally known lodge official; and a black preacher. Still they could not come close to their goal of two

million dollars in fresh capital. The movement inevitably attracted
hustlers as well as black hopefuls. In 1924 a St. Louis promoter raised
money by collecting advances on fares to Hollywood where Negro
subscribers would star in *Jingle of the Jungle*. It was difficult to tell the
grifters from the race men because both unabashedly employed gimmickry over substance. William H. Clifford, a sincere black entrepre-
neur, could not resist claiming that his movie would rectify the distortions of history, rescue the Negro from playing "a fool, a criminal or
a mere menial," and "break the shackles of our fettered brethren and
sisters." Unfortunately, the company spent its last day before shooting
in the trivia of "oratory, reading of the play and the financial founding
of the company" rather than in blocking shots. Among the most promising failures was the company founded by Harry Pace, partner of the
composer W. C. Handy and the force behind the successful Black
Swan "race records," who wanted to bring the popular revue *Strut
Miss Lizzie* to the screen with synchronized music.[19]

Most of the black companies behaved like proliferating little black
storefront Baptist churches weakened by their own competition with
each other. Whites, to oppress them, needed do no more than collect
the rent on time. Others were more like smart hustlers who lived by
their wits on the streets, producing nothing, but turning an occasional
trade, and surviving without bringing pain upon the brother on the
block. The most dedicated of them was Bill Foster's company. He began in Chicago in 1912, produced *The Railroad Porter* and other films
in the Middle West, moved to Los Angeles and tried to raise $25,000
with the encouragement of an officer of the black Golden State Insurance Company, scattered a four-page flyer, and finally in 1929 appealed
to the NAACP for support. As with so many of the black companies,
George Johnson had cryptically typed at the bottom of his file: "There
is no record of this Company haveing [sic] made any productions."[20]

No center could hold under such anarchy unless newspapermen effectively urged race solidarity. By the mid-twenties, they were not up
to the task. Except for a general willingness to print notices of new
companies, they failed to give direction to the movement. The Lincoln
Company had wedded self-interest to George Johnson's creature, the
Pacific News Bureau, so that Lincoln received far more coverage in a
black press greedy for "boilerplate" to fill its pages. Furthermore,
Johnson had enlisted Romeo Daugherty, Tony Langston, D. Ireland
Thomas, and other journalists as flacks and bookers. In those days even
Micheaux's *chutzpah* could not overcome Lincoln's early lead. After
Lincoln faltered, black attention turned not to Micheaux but to white
Hollywood, in part because Johnson, Harry Levette, and others began

covering the major studios in a rush to support the whites' hesitant steps toward better use of Negroes. In turn studios like MGM began sending them regular mailings and even exclusive Negro stories.[21]

Few Negro writers followed the early trailmarks of Lester Walton toward an indigenous cinema. The most serious national attempt was more noteworthy for its ambition rather than its success, and for its reach into other corners of black life. Except for Lincoln's gesture toward enlisting the National Negro Business League during the teens, many of the moviemen seemed like hustlers on the perimeter of middle-class circles. Yet, Johnson, and Robert L. Vann of the *Pittsburgh Courier* in 1921 patched together a national dream-union of themselves; W. C. Handy's partner, Harry Pace; a disused Jersey studio; and the black Memphis politician Bob Church—all to be unified under the aegis of a new black magazine, the *Competitor*, to be published by Vann. "Moving pictures," said the *Competitor*, "have become one of the greatest vitalizing forces in race adjustment, and we are just beginning." On the occasion of the opening of Micheaux's *The Symbol of the Unconquered*, a cautionary tale in opposition to "passing," his picture was made to seem a symbol of the goals of all-black cinema, to teach "impressive lessons on the folly of color, both within and without the race."[22] Outside of New York, the press agreed with the goals. Kennard Williams in the Baltimore *Afro-American*, for example, asked readers to combine "sensible support of Negro producers like Micheaux" with "organized protest" against Hollywood movies. Even when lofty ambitions were unmatched by competence and pictures were "amateurish to a flagrant degree" and "cheaply staged," the black press charitably pretended that "faults and virtues are about evenly divided."[23]

Unfortunately, the proposed national union of moviemen with the black bourgeoisie died in infancy, a victim of regional snobbery. An *Amsterdam News* critic who judged all-black movies lame and inept beside Hollywood pictures resented them and granted them no support:

> White theatre managers in Harlem have from time to time played the Oscar Micheaux pictures more from a mistaken idea of a sentiment which they feel they should exhibit in a colored community than because of the worth of the pictures. With an opportunity of viewing the best things along picture lines, it is hard to expect colored people to accept these Micheaux pictures here in Greater New York and Northern New Jersey, and they don't. . . .

> In those sections where the opportunity for witnessing the best along theatrical lines does not exist, these Micheaux pictures would no doubt be considered the real ziz, but when it comes to competing with what our people are accustomed to see here, they are passé.[24]

Such Harlem impatience signaled a continuing division in the Negro world between those exhibitors who rented Tom Mix and Bill Hart westerns because "the Colored people were crazy about these two stars," and those who adopted the homily that "no picture draws like a good Race production."[25]

Early on, black filmmakers faced one last trouble besides the divisions within the black world: a small white movement within the major studios to turn out funny, disarming little Negro comedies that could siphon off ticket sales from indigenous black productions while entertaining whites as well. They depended on variations on Southern local color, parodies of white literary figures such as Sherlock Holmes, "spook" stories, all based on "the matchless active humor of the race," and the legacy of "the agreeable black-face act." Like Octavus Roy Cohen and Harrison Dickson they created a black world without the core of empathy that might have given them human dimensions.[26]

Throughout the postwar decade these movies reached for both markets by striving for a tone of harmless innocence rather than keen-edged racism. Beginning with Keystone's blackface farmer's daughter joke, *Colored Villainy* (1915), they included Arthur Hotaling's "three Zulu comedies" shot in Jacksonville for Lubin, L-Ko's razor-toting *Barber of Darktown* and his "dusky belle," Mack Sennett's "coontown lovers" in *A Dark Lover's Play*, and by 1921, the best of them, Harrison Dickson's series for Pathé.[27] Shot on location in Dickson's hometown of Vicksburg under the eye of accommodating black advisers nourished by white sentimentality, *The Custard Nine* was typical. It was a sketch of Virgil Custard, a dandy in "Darktown's four hundred" who leads Vicksburg's black baseball team through a farcical excursion leavened by phony tickets and a railroad strike.[28] The genre survived until the age of Amos 'n' Andy, who appeared in two early talkies and a cartoon.

Thus in the beginning of the twenties race movies seemed trapped between their white imitators and their black critics, ritually acting out the "two-ness" of life in white America, and baffled by the same tensions that divided blacks into integrationists and nationalists. But gradually the growth of black wealth and literacy combined with emerging white liberal voices pulled Afro-Americans toward the ideals of integration and individual aspiration, thereby dampening the appeal of Garvey's Zionism as well as the strain of economic nationalism buried beneath Booker T. Washington's pious accommodationism. Thus in the milieu of the twenties the black movies became a social absurdity, for they created a black world without whites in which, therefore, black divisiveness and bungling rather than white cupidity consigned Negroes to the bottom. The pictures, awkward and sloppily cut, were doomed to an uneven contest against Hollywood. The loser's share was measured out in split weeks, single-shot dates and infrequent runs in the big chains, so that, again, black was made to seem shabby. Scuttling along, barely making their "nut," they were shaken out of the market when bad times hit at the same time that the white majors survived by trimming fat, firing relatives, closing a few grind houses, and paring production schedules. Eventually the black press accepted Hollywood ads and plugged white pictures because the ads earned money, press agents' "boilerplate" was free and filled the columns, and the growing numbers of Negroes in Hollywood movies seemed a vindication of black social strategy.

Consequently, except for the movies of Oscar Micheaux, the most prolific and original of the all-black producers, who will be treated *sui generis,* the bulk of the 1920s movies appealed to Negro audiences for the hope they offered that racial integration and personal aspiration were compatible, feasible social goals for middle-class blacks. Indeed, poor blacks on the street were often heavies who deserved the denouements that fell in on them.

So many of them never rose above white models, and therefore never carried their aesthetic beyond a black investment in the plot. The Norman Brothers' *Scarlet Claw* (or *Crimson Skull*) (1921) was like all westerns except for its locale in Boley and black stars Bill Pickett and Anita Bush.[29] *Injustice* (Democracy, 1919), *The Burden of Race* (Reol, 1921), *A Giant of His Race* (North State, 1921), *The Green Eyed Monster* (Norman, 1921), *Spitfire* (Reol, 1922), *The Call of His People* (Reol, 1922), and *As The World Rolls On* (Andlauer, 1921) played on the theme of bourgeois aspiration, each in its own way. Their marginal differences—usually mere gimmicks—never interfered with the message. In one Jack Johnson was a *guru* of athletic and romantic success for a young protégé, in another a black chemist finds a gasoline substitute, another hero wins a mail-route contract and the girl, and still another dramatized the educational theories of Booker T. Washington. All illustrated in the last reel "the possibility of the individual endeavor and reward of a character of the Negro race." Even a film in which "passing" is the theme, *The Call of His People,* rejects the fraud, but not for an intrinsic black reason but for the more general, white reason that it was "the quality and not the color of a man that counts."[30]

At a lower level they imitated white westerns; flogged the dead horse of *The Birth of a Nation;* provided work for Percy Verwayen, Edna Morton, Lawrence Chenault, Sherman H. Dudley, and other veterans of the Negro stage; adapted to the screen black classics such as Paul Laurence Dunbar's *The Sport of the Gods* and "white" classics such as *Ten Nights in a Bar Room;* or, later, hashed out detective fiction in *The Flaming Crisis* (Monarch, 1924), *The Midnight Ace* (Dunbar, 1928), and others. The worst of them exploited Negro actors such as Sidney Dones, and the racism of whites such as Leslie T. Peacocks, who combined in 1925 to do a two-reeler featuring "Charley Chocolate," "Douglas Darkshanks," "Mary Picklefoot," and "Gloria Swansdown."[31]

All the while, they sputtered and misfired as Hollywood slowly opened its doors to Noble Johnson, Carolynne Snowden, Madame Sul-Te-Wan, and Stepin Fetchit, the cadre of Negro performers who drew black ticketbuyers toward white movies. The result was that one after another they expired. Only the Lincoln Company up to 1921 built more than two movies on a foundation of black money. Reol and others that produced more than a single title necessarily accepted white money and control. Moreover, each new black figure in Hollywood and on the New York stage during the black Renaissance deprived the black companies not only of their talent but of their reason for existence. Only lack of talent or extreme race chauvinism would drive Negroes to serve in the outbacks of Boley and Jacksonville, strangled by the paucity of money, audiences, technicians, and equipment.

Only one Negro producer broke the pattern. Oscar Micheaux's prairie roots, querulous personality, curious racial theories, and financial ties to his own publishing firm supported him against adversity. For twenty years he carried the movement in the face of apathy and mockery; in spite of an amateurish, almost naïve artlessness. Like the comedians Jerry Lewis and Harry Langdon and the tragedian John Barrymore, he suffered for want of a firm hand to lend discipline to his craft. Eccentrically, he could ascend to peaks of bizarre excess and then insert unmatching cutaway shots. He would create a mood with a fine backlighted shot; then his limited budget would force him to cut to a lame, ill-lighted mistake that would have ended on the cutting room floor of a major studio. It was as though Dunbar or Langston Hughes published their first drafts without benefit of editing, their flair and genius muffled in casual first strikes. If the Lincoln Company was a black mirror image of the organizational system of MGM, then Micheaux was the black analogue to a white independent like Sam Goldwyn.

Micheaux's early life ran in striking parallel to that of W. E. B. DuBois, and both men, standing on the frontier of race, looked with fine acuity into the hidden crannies of racial mores. Both grew up in rural, largely white, communities where, despite cool distance, they were patronized and subsidized. They differed in that DuBois moved into the thick of racial struggle while Micheaux moved from Illinois to the South Dakota prairie. Despite an apparently erratic education, he recorded his life in a first novel, *The Homesteader*, which, after he marketed it himself from door to door, formed the basis for his first movie. The motif running through his book and subsequent tales and movies centered on the strain of color caste in America.

He might have lived out his days as a book drummer but for a used copy of *The Homesteader* falling into the hands of the Johnsons in Los Angeles. Through the summer of 1918 they engaged in a fitful correspondence of deals and counterdeals in which Micheaux first proposed they make a movie of *The Homesteader*, then decided to go it alone when they would not make it into a big eight-reeler. Starting from scratch, in the old Selig studio in Chicago, he would shoot and cut it and open it in New York in less than two years. In that short time he moved beyond the faltering Lincoln men, who still shot only on Sunday while awaiting the opening of new facilities.[32]

Micheaux exuded the rattling *chutzpah* of a black Sammy Glick, a "rough Negro who had got his hands on some cash," according to the prim men of Lincoln who were scared enough of him to keep a spy in his office. To the end, they disapproved of his style, his gambling, his cavalier disdain for creditors and his spats with the censors, everything but his eventual $100-per-day rentals. He packed his wife home to mother in order to give free play to his deals and dreams. He roamed the prairie around Sioux City like a country drummer, hustling stock in his own motion picture company to the white farmers who had supported his publishing venture.[33]

His brassy methods shaped *The Homesteader* into an event that other black producers envied. He landed the fine veteran of the Lafayette Players, Evelyn Preer, to give support to the rookies and amateurs who would make his epic of "the great American Northwest" and "the race question." He whipped up a purple campaign to sell it, proclaiming, "Nothing would make more people anxious to see a picture than a litho reading: 'SHALL RACES INTERMARRY.' "[34] In between selling stock, recruiting, scattering rumors that he had sold a book to Metro and Triangle, and pushing his work on white bookers, he wrote a script of six hundred shots and four hundred titles. By the end of summer, 1918, he began to learn his craft. He learned to prefer interior shots because "the most subtle things go on in doors [sic]," and he began, like Alfred Hitchcock or Eisenstein, to typecast. "Good face—bright complection with good hair and my kind of Chin," he wrote of one actor. His quick march from apprentice to studio chief outraged George Johnson, who smugly reported that his company was sprinkled with white men "except where the money was."[35]

With the release of *The Homesteader*, Micheaux's confidence became boundless, and his grosses equaled the $5000 "nut" for his next

Oscar Micheaux's early work *The Homesteader* derived from his youth on the prairie. (George P. Johnson Collection)

project. Few blacks could ever say as much. His stock prospectus named him president, novelist, and scenarist of the "Micheaux Book and Film Company" and placed the offices in New York, Chicago, and Sioux Falls. His next picture, *Within Our Gates*, based on the famous Leo Frank lynching case, was to be paired with a book and sold "as witnessed by the author." The flyer overflowed with glittering claims of "conflict, great emotion, sacrifice, intrigue—and a tense love situation," and a promise to follow the lead of the white companies in forging a chain of outlets for his pictures. The two betrayals of tacky reality were his statement that road shows would receive his "personal direction," a euphemism for his slogging the country with the film under his arm, and his order for only four release prints.[36]

Micheaux needed every glimmer of optimism. Like the Lincoln men who preceded him he faced the terrible odds of booking against the white chains. He soon discovered that he could slip pictures into black neighborhoods of Southern cities only in the slack summer, when it was so hot the majors shut down much of their operation. From late

May through July he could count on only one-night stands and split weeks, with only one full-week run in New Orleans and only one re-booking, in Atlanta.[37]

The Lincoln men were torn between awe of and contempt for his endless energy. In Omaha Johnson received a warning from a fretful Micheaux employee:

> MICHEAUX STATES MAKING YOU PROPOSITION   DONT ACCEPT BELIEVE ME I AM FOR YOU AND IN A POSITION TO KNOW HIS UNBUSINESSLIKE METHODS BEYOND COMPARISON   HAVE HIM BOOKED SOLID UNTIL MIDDLE JULY BUT CANNOT STAND HIM ANY LONGER[38]

Within Our Gates opened in January, 1920, in Chicago and Detroit starring Evelyn Preer, Lawrence Chenault, and Charles D. Lucas. The sensational melodrama of Southern lynching was so vivid that blacks and whites alike in Chicago fought its release by the censor board as conducive to "race riot," possibly accounting for its poor reception. Micheaux blamed Negroes for the slow sales and weak distribution. "Our people do not care—nor the other race for that matter, for propa-ganda," he complained, but he still expected to do movies that "leave an impression."[39]

Micheaux had reached the verge of stability, needing but a stroke of press agentry to carry him past the ranks of Lincoln, Ebony, Reol, and the others who had made one film or so and then faded under the bur-den of "flu" ravages, isolation in the West or in Boley or Jacksonville, or loss of the enthusiasm of white owners. His chance came when he teamed Evelyn Preer with the black boxer Sam Langford in his third film, *The Brute.* His entry into New York, in contrast to his first foray with his picture under his arm, rivaled Lincoln's thoroughness.

The Brute opened in New York in the late summer supported by nine prints, every one "in action" in both North and South; by a strong package of lobby cards and stills; and by the teamwork of Micheaux and his brother, who in concert were able to promote the New York opening while cutting and polishing their next film. The prerelease campaign drew enthusiastic audiences who cheered the boxing se-quences of Langford. And even though Lester Walton gave it his mixed blessing, grousing at its dives and crapshooters but admitting the audience's excitement, he predicted that "movies are destined to take the lead in catering to the present insistent demand for the production of plays written by Negroes and produced by Negroes."[40] Even though he did not specifically endorse *The Brute,* the message was clear: Mi-cheaux had arrived.

But most important, Micheaux's boundless energy and dogged per-sistence had shown that the staggering burdens under which race

Only Micheaux—as here in *Within Our Gates*—risked treating lynching as a theme. (George P. Johnson Collection)

movie-makers labored could be overcome, at least in the short run. In the cutting room they had known there was "something lacking," a half-expressed feeling for the flaws of "race movies": the bad lighting concealed action, the unmatched textures marred shots made under varied conditions, the jerky rhythms worked to false climaxes, and a "poorly staged" fight sequence ended with a silly closeup of a glove "as large as a pillow."[41] Every one of these problems could have been corrected by shooting at a higher ratio of exposed film to usable film, by retakes, and by using a master cover-shot from which to cut to varied angles and to closeups. None of the black filmmakers could afford the luxury of a cutter who could edit a bad shot and control pacing and texture merely by good selection, but at least the Micheaux group knew the problem and gave their attention it.

Outside the studio and the lab, Micheaux seemed more at home among the tangled activities necessary to pull off a glittering première. During the summer when prerelease excitement flagged, perhaps because of the disastrous *Within Our Gates,* Micheaux rushed to New York to sell dates, to Omaha to patch relations with Lincoln, to Chicago and Fort Lee for more takes, then to a meeting with James Weldon Johnson, DuBois, and Charles Waddell Chesnutt to promote a movie of the latter's novel, *The Conjure Woman*—and seemingly between gasps for breath tried to get "somebody to go abroad in the interest of our pictures," all the while dreaming of a chance to "take the players to Cal. to produce all winter."[42] At last he fought through offers of dull midweek dates; demands for "paper," raised prices, and a supporting two-reeler; and complaints against "race propaganda" and too "realistic" lynching sequences.[43]

By summer's end Micheaux clearly led moribund Lincoln, Robert Levy's price-cutting Reol, and the other race movie producers. If *The Brute* was less than a critical success at least Micheaux had departed the ranks of those who had failed to survive their second picture. His rise brought black cinema regularly to the Eastern ghettos. Together he and second-ranked Reol represented nearly half the total output of "race" studios. He could get $500 per engagement in the urban houses: the Lincoln (Cincinnati), the Comet (St. Louis), the Vaudette (Detroit), the Daisy (Memphis), the Regent (Baltimore), the Dunbar (Washington), and the Royal (Philadelphia); and in New York's Lafayette he once cleared $2000 on a gross of $10,000. Not counting the Negro YMCAs and schools that formed the backbone of the revenues of some black producers, Micheaux listed more than fifty cities in which he could net $150 to $500 per title, and by then he tried to release four every year. Still, though he earned $40,000 in 1920 and hoped for $100,000 in 1921, he was not beneath taking $25 for a one-nighter in Mound Bayou or Arkadelphia. Indeed, his "bread and butter" was down home in the South, where he had more dates than in the North. With the shift of bookings to the East and the South, California-based Lincoln folded, a circumstance that puzzled George Johnson as he complained of the Negroes who "always have money to eat dress and go where they want to go . . . [including] the colored ball game every Sunday," but would never go to a Negro movie.[44]

With the death of the Lincoln Company Micheaux felt threatened by only one source of rivalry with whom he would struggle for the rest of his life:

Levy and many other Jews who are making negro pictures, going under negro producers, which they can afford to do because . . . they let the pictures go for what ever they can get out of them, too there

are so many bad colored pictures on the market who are letting the
exhibitors set the price on their pictures [because] . . . the exhibitor
finds that the colored people will come to see a rotten negro picture as
quick as they will to see the best one. [sic][45]

In other words, at the peak of youthful success Micheaux found another disturbing anomaly in the black situation: not only could white
men invade the field profitably; the very goal of a well-patronized all-
Negro cinema seemed a dead end because it reached a seemingly un-
critical audience. Blacks simply did not see *themselves* on the screen—
even the screen of Oscar Micheaux. Mere black presence on the screen,
reflecting bourgeois white aspiration, no longer was enough. The cinema remained a silent disused tool. Lester Walton knew this perhaps
better than did Micheaux.

Unfortunately, since neither black critics nor audiences nor whites
knew for certain Micheaux's intentions, at the height of his powers he
faced hostility from Negro circles. For example, *The Brute* roused no
black pride despite the use of Sam Langford as an icon of black machismo in combat against lynching. Southern police shut it down as "a
very dangerous picture to show in the South," although no whites were
likely to see it. But black audiences did little more than cheer its boxing
shots. In Chicago its opening was ruined by a nasty fight with the local
censor who wanted no racial violence on the screen only months after
the city had faced the worst race riot in American history. But black
critics spoiled the work more than white legalism. In Chicago a black
reviewer obscured the movie with a shot-by-shot synopsis punctuated
by pious moralizing. "I didn't mind that," he said of a love affair, "but
the story was not elevating." He pleaded that the producer would see
the light. "No Mr. Micheaux," he wrote. "Society wants a real story of
high moral aim that can apeal [sic] to the upbuilding of your race."
Many perceptive blacks neglected cinema. Lester Walton, like so many
metropolitan critics, never forgot his love of the stage. Floyd Snelson,
for example, titled his fresh column in the *Courier* "Theatrical Comment" in a Pittsburgh nearly barren of theater. Moreover, as the twenties rose out of the slough of postwar depression, radio, professional
sports, and "race records" captured valuable attention and newspaper
space from black movies. At the top of black society among the intellectuals the cinema received even less support. Kelly Miller, Dean of
Howard University, addressed his syndicated column to "Harvard and
Hollywood," comparing the circus-funeral of Valentino as an example
of the decadence of American society with the quiet death of President
Eliot of Harvard. The worst sting must have come from the friendly
reviews black critics granted Robert Levy's production of Dunbar's
The Sport of the Gods. In contrast to *The Brute*, the *Defender* thought

In *The Brute* Micheaux learned how to combine melodrama with sound exploitation technique. (George P. Johnson Collection)

it "a stirring melodrama of the underworld . . . of pathos, romance, and love . . . that stands unequaled for its entertainment value."[46]

As the mid-twenties approached, Micheaux found the price of survival to be a continuing struggle to define his ambitions and to win over a skeptical black audience. Neither the groups dominated by whites nor the ephemeral producers who died aborning needed to work out an aesthetic position. In fact young, unfocused Micheaux felt no pressing need for an aesthetic until it was thrust upon him by success. For example, his *The Symbol of the Unconquered* (1921) was a mindless scattergun that was to be part of "one of the greatest vitalizing forces in race adjustment," a promoter of racial understanding, an indictment of the KKK, a "thrilling and realistic" melodrama, a lesson in "the folly of color, both within and without the race," a love story, a quest for oil-bearing land, and a pointed assault on "passing" Negroes.[47]

Gradually in the years following, he broke the pictures down into unified themes, but they attracted less and less attention from press and fans. And when he was short of cash he was not above an occasional exploitation of gullible Negro audiences. *Within Our Gates*, his treatment of the Leo Frank lynching case, reappeared a year later as *The Gunsaulus Mystery*, a "whodunnit" probably patched together from old "outtakes" or merely retitled and rereleased. The press, when it took notice, remarked on the size and enthusiasm of audiences rather than on the film's artistic merit, and by 1923 his spring release generated only eleven lines in the New York *Age* and a split week at the Douglass. His production of T. S. Stribling's *Birthright*, a demonstration that racism persisted even for black Harvard men, appeared in a small ad but received no plug at all in the columns. By then George P. Johnson had changed his name to George Perry, and opened his Hollywood Negro news service that grew more assimilationist with each new integrationist gesture of the white studios.[48]

By the middle of the decade Micheaux's achievement was his survival in the face of adversity. As the other companies slowly expired, he moved to Yonkers, where he not only kept his group working but developed Shingzie Howard as a new star and produced two Chesnutt novels, *The Conjure Woman* and *The House Behind the Cedars*, and possibly a burlesque on Marcus Garvey—*Marcus Garland*.[49]

Nearly all of Micheaux's films are lost. If one of the silent pictures must stand for his canon it would be *Body and Soul* (1924), both for what it said and for the response it evoked. The picture represented the highest level of achievement for Micheaux. For the first time he wrestled with the nature of the black community, without recourse to shoddy devices, overdressing in the good cloth of Dunbar or Chesnutt, or interracial sensationalism. The theme allowed full play to his racial consciousness. To his stable of new stars he added Paul Robeson, fresh from triumphs on the white man's stage and football fields at Rutgers. The result was a rich black imagery that never materialized in other survivals of the 1920s and a modest accommodation with black intellectuals. For years black leaders, including Booker T. Washington, had railed against "jackleg" preachers who exploited the deep religiosity of poor blacks who settled in cold ghettos and turned to the charismatic churches as visible proof that their old Southern rural lives still had meaning. In *Body and Soul* Micheaux not only exposed cultist parasites but also advertised the promise that blacks could organize against the bootleggers and gamblers in their midst.

Not that Micheaux worked out all the themes in lonely isolation. To the contrary, his first print submitted to the New York censor board presented the preacher as the embodiment of unredeemed evil, with not a single redemptive quality in the black community. The New York censors would not tolerate it for much the same reason the NAACP would have given.[50] So Micheaux recut it and fabricated an elaborate and confusing sequence which allowed the ingenue to awake and find that the preacher was a covert spy assigned to break up a bootlegging ring. If blacks could make movies in isolation, they still could not release them until white eyes had approved them. Furthermore, whites seemed to have developed a sensitivity to racial slurs that escaped the cavalier Micheaux.

The second version, bearing white fingermarks, may have given rounded dimensions to Negro life. The balance demanded by the censor board broadened the scope of the conflict and forced the characters into protagonist-antagonist tension. In the case of Paul Robeson's preacher, it enlarged the role into complex parts. In a dual role he brought power to the gambler's cynical smile and to the preacher's practical piety. Micheaux gave him tight closeups that tilted up to capture a virility long missing from black figures. Robeson fairly oozed the strength and sexuality of enthusiastic religion while at the same time giving off the hard, ominous energy of the "bad nigger" gambler. For Robeson, it was one of the few occasions when he cut free of white direction and bridged the deep fissure in the black world between the venal, erotic Staggerlee and respectable black bourgeois. His power carried him above the necessarily confused plot and allowed him to make a sensitive measurement of black character in American life.

Micheaux too reached high. In spite of the stagey, unmatched cutaway shots inherent in low-budget shooting, the garbled plot, and the broad comedy relief, he pulled off a modestly successful black movie. The exteriors had the rough and unpainted texture of Auburn Avenue, Beale Street, or some other black Southern promenade. The sets reinforced the dichotomy of the roles with simplistic, yet effective tricks. In the main saloon set a *Police Gazette* cover gazed down like a broad wink, while a benign portrait of Booker T. Washington set the tone of bourgeois ambience in the ingenue's home. In the end Micheaux contrived his way around the New York censor board by shifting Robeson from venal preacher to cool detective, at once tricking the audience into expecting a white man's "bad nigger," and symbolically turning away from the hoary stereotype.[51]

The plot in its probable final form follows preacher Isaiah T. Jenkins through a hot, dry Tatesville, Georgia, "blind tiger"—a rural speakeasy—where he is bribed to tone down his temperance sermons. The heavy is Yellow Curly Hines, a light-skinned hustler from Atlanta who is in town recruiting for Cotton Blossom's Shoulder Shakers. Cutting to the church, Jenkins exhorts the dozen elders and fidgeting women, interrupted by a flashback to his time in jail. Here the confused recutting muddles Robeson's schizoid role. Is he preacher or detective or jackleg? Back and forth, we follow the preacher, archly half-smiling, through a card game with Yellow Curly, to a rousing, shouting, clapping sermon improvised over the motif of "Dry Bones in the Valley." From the amen corner a woman shouts she has been washed whiter than snow in the blood of the lamb. Too late to be fully effective, the preacher's urban doppelganger emerges as Black Carl, the detective who modestly pleads for the hand of a young girl in the flock. The tempo mounts when the mother misses the savings she has hidden in the family bible. The end ambiguously interrupts a bloodhound chase in pursuit of the preacher, who presumably inspired the theft, whereupon the young girl awakens from the nightmare "bad nigger" to an apparent rosy, married future side-by-side with his bourgeois incarnation.

Depending on which version a viewer saw, the picture reached beyond the capacity of Hollywood. Either the picture was an exposé of a social condition deep within, and relevant to, only Negro circles; or it used the medium of the dream-flashback to sketch an allegorical black figure alternately dominated by his two sides, the prim role of bourgeois aspiration according to the rules of the game and the arcane black hustler for whom the game has been a fraud. It seemed to say that the survival drive of Afro-Americans living under oppressive conditions may almost casually choose either route as an escape. The dense life of the ghetto with its many alternative life-models, close-packed upon each other and in competition, had never appeared before on film.

There is no way of knowing whether *Body and Soul* revived the black cinema movement, but it surely arrived coincident with sanguine conditions. By the mid-twenties black communities had become better organized and more self-conscious, and the movies reflected the new awareness. Micheaux not only survived the decade but increased the social thrust of his pictures. His *Spider's Web* (1926) treated the love-hate relationship between the ghetto and the "numbers game"; *The Wages of Sin* (1929) analyzed the strains of urban life upon the black family; *Birthright* (1924) followed a Negro Ivy Leaguer southward to minister to his people's needs. Gradually the translucent watermarks of the middle-class ideologies of personal aspiration and of black solidarity tinged his films.

The ranks of the producers thinned as the old one-shot companies passed and their places were assumed by more sound operation such as the Colored Players and the Dunbar Company. To the old burden of undeveloped distribution the new companies added the fresh problem of soundfilm, a doubly expensive technological innovation because it

In *Easy Street* Micheaux made use of
Richard B. Harrison who had made
a mark on the legitimate stage. (Lorenzo Tucker Collection)

Micheaux's *Wages of Sin* featured "the black Valentino," Lorenzo Tucker.
(Lorenzo Tucker Collection)

required investment both in production and exhibition of films. Underneath, other future headaches could barely be discerned: the gradual increase in Hollywood Negro roles, the drift westward of black actors such as the Lafayette Players, and the growth of Hollywood advertising in the black press, all of which seemed to rebut the *raison d'être* of race movies.

Nevertheless, the remaining twenties on the eve of soundfilm brought Negro movies to yet another plateau, although still far below Eisenstein, Pabst, Lang, Lubitsch, Von Stroheim, Cruze, Whale, and other creators who contributed to and exploited the riches of Hollywood and other cinema centers. The issue for Negroes remained not aesthetics but social function, in the manner of Soviet art. Indeed, Eisenstein's excesses—often ignored by friendly critics—his bourgeois heavies darkened into near gargoyles, the silly posturing of his Soviet heroes of the people, bore striking caste-marks like those of Negro movies. But at least "race movies" began to deal with life from a blacker perspective.

The Harlem Renaissance still bubbled like a freshet through the land, even though it cut no permanent watercourses. *Shuffle Along* and the other black revues bloomed as "indigenous drama,'' according to Theophilus Lewis who thought they were a signal to abandon totally white forms. Black writers tangled with their white angels over social content. Amy Ashwood-Garvey searched for black angels for her musical even as films of the activities of her husband's UNIA were shown in New York halls. "RACE ACTORS ALL THE RAGE IN LONDON, PARIS, AND BERLIN," a *Courier* bannerline reported. Black performers and exhibitors came to admire their growing and appreciative black audiences, a Washington booker claiming he had never lost money on a Negro picture. George Johnson thought the time had come for Negro companies to produce movies in packages so as to tide themselves over the dry spells. Regional papers such as the Norfolk *Journal and Guide* joined the chorus of praise. Actors and their pictures trailed encomiums like foxtails on car fenders: the "greatest of all colored pictures," the "world's greatest Negro actor," and more. In addition to the continuing feature film production the good times helped renew interest in comatose black newsfilm. Famous Artists of Los Angeles intended a biweekly newsreel with themes selected by the editor of the *Eagle*.[52]

In the spring of 1926 the Colored Players moved from Washington to Philadelphia, where they assembled a pair of pictures in the pungent tradition of black cinema. Their *Ten Nights in a Barroom* and *Scar of Shame* are the surviving strokes of silent black artists. Not only did they join Micheaux in the thinning ranks of serious producers of "race pictures"; they used Lawrence Chenault and Shingzie Howard, two of his favorite actors, and Charles Gilpin. Sherman (Uncle Dud) Dudley, a black impresario of Washington, fronted for the white angels and crew hidden behind the Colored Players.[53]

Their first film, *A Prince of His Race,* played on the theme of mother love beset by conventional melodramatic circumstance. Their unsuccessful attempt to update and blacken *Ten Nights in a Barroom* into a modern parable groaned under the burden of the antique script and of the florid stage style of Charles Gilpin—probably freshly fired from Universal's *Uncle Tom's Cabin.* Nonetheless, it was a sincere attempt to relate to a unique black social problem. Prohibition had made it fashionable amongst whites to drink *verboten* whiskey as a social protest, but for blacks prohibition had a bitter side. The stability of black neighborhoods suffered from segregated white saloons and nightclubs, violence-prone white bootleggers, and white slummers. Moreover, the decline in quality of ghetto life must have encouraged frustrated blacks toward alcoholic escapism—with booze far worse than that served in Harlem's segregated Cotton Club.[54]

The finest hour of the Colored Players was *Scar of Shame.* Despite its stilted manner this 1927 film made one of the most effective statements of Negro aspiration stunted by the gritty rot of the ghetto streetscape. The *Amsterdam News* singled it out as "a new standard of excellence."[55] The picture placed the black thrust for "the finer things" against the drag of the coarse, grinding ghetto that cheats the hero of beauty and virtue. To reach for the prize, it seems to say, is to pull a comet's tail of poverty and brutality. The hard world of the streets makes brutes and hustlers of smart blacks with a will to live. They are the unassimilable "bad niggers" who can never leave the darkened doorways of the ghetto demimonde, but whose guile permits them to survive in cool style. Unfortunately, the picture stumbles when it asks the Negro to rise above the life of the streets because it draws a veil over the external forces that made the slum what it is. Thus the hero, Alvin Hilliard, can end his suffering only by opting for white culture and rejecting black. Hilliard's decision, because he is a musician, is cast in musical terms: in order to escape the ghetto he must become a teacher of stuffy "white" music. His landlady smugly predicts he will be "the leading composer of our race."

Alvin Hilliard, alone with his music, observes Louise, a beautiful lightskinned girl who lives under the heel of a sadistic father. They meet and enjoy a wistful romance for a few weeks of ephemeral happiness in Alvin's world of neat, dull furniture. Set against their drive for "the finer things" are the exteriors of the grey street, paper-strewn and strung with rough, musty storefronts. Out there, Spike, the black saloon owner and hustler, lives by a hard code. He leads Louise's drunk

By the end of the twenties attention shifted to the Colored Players and their star, Lucia Lynn Moses. (Library of Congress)

and broken father to help him ruin her marriage so he can keep her in his sphere. The marriage to Hilliard is already strained by his furtive reluctance to introduce her to his mother, knowing his mother feels the girl is beneath "our set."

The polar opposites of black life appear as equally evil. The rough violence of the streets and the color-caste snobbery of the mulatto élite both destroy Negro aspiration. Louise is pulled from one to the other through an improbable ruse by which the heavies send Alvin to his mother's suburban home while they force Louise into a sordid liaison with Spike. The two evils of caste and street are opposed by cutting from the liveried butler at Alvin's mother's place to Spike, the "bad nigger," who is at least not trapped into the vulgar display and class fetishes of the mulattos. He is evil, but no *more* so than the race traitors in the suburbs.

Louise is hurt by Alvin's shame for her low caste, and she runs off with Spike to a life in the black underworld. In quick succession Alvin wounds Louise, is convicted, jailed, escapes, and takes up a new life as a piano teacher, while Louise begins a scarlet career as Spike's cabaret singer. The old lovers meet years later after Alvin falls in love with a pupil from his own station in life, whose father, a *roué*, has an affair with Louise.

Here the film fails to survive its tangled plot. The point has managed to peer occasionally through the interstices of the rickety busyness of the surface action. How shall it end? Should not a blatant cautionary tale remain true to its principles and have the starcrossed lovers at last embrace across the lines of caste as a lesson to Negroes and as a covert repudiation of American racial arrangements? No. The lovers meet and part, and Louise, realizing she is "a victim of caste," kills herself, allowing Alvin to step over her corpse and marry into his proper station.

If the denouement seems a heartless retreat from using the melodramatic conflict to make a strong plea against class snobbery, at least *Scar of Shame* displays unconscious strength. At its worst the picture is a betrayal of its title, for, if there is a "scar of shame," Alvin is left unmarked by it, and presumably rises to the heights of music with his mannered, brightskinned bride on his arm. Louise, on the other hand, must fall, the title tells us, because the ghetto will pull her down, marked by her dark skin, which does not entitle her to a ticket out. But our eye tells us only her father is dark and she is nearly as light as Alvin, thus revealing the truer fact of black life: that suffering may befall anyone, without regard for color. Another bit of unwritten verisimilitude is the inference the audience may make that Negroes must strangle each other for a few crumbs from the white American table, but again the point is thrown away. Like all "race movies," by excluding whites *Scar of Shame* blamed the victim for his plight. The implicit environmentalism of Alvin's crying out for "the finer things" is, then, no more than a throwaway line. Almost as accidentally, the false goals of the shingled suburbs appear as a Victorian clutter, set against the clean lines of Philadelphia's Georgian rowhouses and the spare, flat planes and chiaroscuro rooms of the black poor. The goals of the script seem violated by the fine camerawork, which becomes a tacit plea for Negroes to redeem the ghetto rather than trade its close-knit character for the bland insularity of the suburbs. But all of this seems unconscious. The movie fails because its surface action repudiated what the camera forced into the mind's eye.

The crew on the picture revealed the nagging issue beneath many race movies: besides Dudley and the cast all were white Hollywood journeymen—writer David Starkman, director Frank Peregini, and cameraman Al Ligouri. And according to the star, Lucia Lynn Moses, blacks contributed only their presence:

> I never saw a piece of paper. I did everything they said. And that's all. . . . I never took any directions from anybody colored. . . . It was always the two white fellahs.[56]

White tutelege or not, if the best of the black films muddled its message to its audience, then the coming of depression, costly technology, new techniques, and a liberal threatening Hollywood promised only to shut down "race movies." In the late twenties nothing they produced seemed to catch fire. Even Micheaux, in 1927 now the dean of the black producers, hyperbolically plugged his latest release as "the first really big film with a cast of colored players," as though neither her nor his audiences remembered his having done anything memorable. Exploiters retailed rereleases and hustled cheap shots of lodge meetings and parades. Rising costs made new companies dependent on white sponsors. By 1930 the largest Negro houses in New York were still among those unwired for sound—nearly four years after the first Vitaphone release. By then the only black soundfilm was a "synched" French film featuring the expatriate Josephine Baker.

The end of the era came when Micheaux went into voluntary bankruptcy. His brother moved to Dunbar, where with $10,000 in white money he helped shoot *The Midnight Ace* in the old Vitagraph studio in Brooklyn. Micheaux himself fled to New York, probably to keep from relinquishing hold on his prints so that he might use the fruits of reruns to get back on his feet. Thematically the last movies of the period slumped into cheap melodrama, and enough tired stereotypes crept in that *Variety* felt obligated to explain them away to prospective bookers as aberrations of Negro taste. Dunbar's *Ace* was a stock melodrama in which a woman must choose between cop and crook; Micheaux's own *Thirty Years Later* rested on the old gimmick of hidden racial identity and a Negro who "becomes proud of his race"; *The Witching Eyes* played on a Haitian "evil eye"; Micheaux's *The Millionaire* transported Celia, "a siren" and "the concubine of the 'Lizard,' " a master criminal, to the Argentine in a plot "chock full of action, thrills, romance and intrigue." The most fanciful of them, Richard D. Maurice's *Eleven P. M.* (*ca.* 1928), was a curious failure that attempted to weave together threads of black urban experience with a Gothic tale of reincarnation. "Find my kid and educate him so he doesn't grow up like me," a dying hustler says to Sundaisy, a light-skinned streetsinger of vaguely Polynesian cast. In the end Sundaisy, moved by revenge, returns from the grave as a superimposed dog and kills the heavy in partial fulfillment of his early pledge.[57]

And so, by the end of the silent era, momentum had shifted to Hollywood because the blacks were either trapped in the dying art of silent drama or they were too poor to raise funds for soundfilm, a medium which showed flaws more harshly than silent film had. Hollywood's all-Negro musicals *Hallelujah!* and *Hearts in Dixie* in the early sound period further weakened the market for "race movies" and drove blacks toward imitation of Hollywood models, drill-team tapdancers, and gangsters that passed for social comment. Micheaux and the others had made a largely lost contribution to Afro-American life with inadequate materials and skills by recording some of the excitement and tension of the Negro world. Until "race movies" could recover from the dual shock of the Great Depression and soundfilm, the only source of

Of all the "race movie" producers Micheaux displayed the best advertising paper. (Lorenzo Tucker Collection)

By the end of the twenties Micheaux's *The Millionaire* (© Oscar Micheaux) strayed from purely racial themes. (Library of Congress)

black imagery to deviate from Hollywood orthodoxy would be "the indies"—*Variety*'s term for independent producers here and abroad who reached a small, dependable audience of "art film" fans who went to tiny houses—"sure seaters" in *Variety*'s argot—such as New York's Cameo and Baltimore's Little Theatre.

Chapter Eight

TWO CHEERS FOR THE INDIES

In the transition years when sound films were replacing silent films, black cinema had one of its richest periods of development. Its films were called "indies," for they were independently produced movies either made abroad, in disused studios in the East, or by a few California mavericks who used the facilities of major studios in exchange for rent, subsidies, or promises of eventual release through chains. Because the indies were not part of the Hollywood establishment, they could take risks, reach into experimental areas, and cater to audiences untrammeled by stereotypes induced by fear of loss of box office revenue.

Thus with the irony implicit in American racial arrangements, Negro cinema hopes were placed in the hands of a random group of white independents whose work would be highly praised and yet would be unseen by most moviegoers. Economic depression had killed off (temporarily, in Micheaux's case) the black producers, leaving the field to this most improbable lot of whites who, if they failed to light the way to a black future, would at least provide guidelines for later black filmmakers and students.

In order to observe the special plight of the indies and their black players, it will be useful to follow three of them: the Meschrabpom Company of the Soviet Union, Kenneth Macpherson's Pool Films in Switzerland, and Dudley Murphy, a director of indifferent reputation and a roguish eye for Negro life who eventually made three interesting black films.

Until the race movie companies could recover from their economic shocks, blacks owed their screen image, at least in its most favorable light, to these mavericks. In the tag end of the silent era they provided the last clear artistically rendered black imagery on the screen. Their works remain today among the finest depictions of Negro life and style.

Not that Murphy, Macpherson, and Karl Junghans (sometimes Carl Younghans), the German director who would try to make a "race movie" in Russia for distribution in America, were household names to Afro-Americans. They were much more like paintings discovered in an attic or lost manuscripts that touched only the generations who followed them. Moreover, none of them could be expected to rise above the ruck of racism. And yet, by exalting presumed Negro traits they gave them fresh meaning and beauty.

Negroes of the day knew little of them. Walter White, a major figure in the NAACP, like many Afro-American intellectuals, paid scant attention to movies, suspected the motives of their makers, expected little from Hollywood, and turned to Europeans for the redemption of the medium:

Perhaps in time we may evolve to the point where moving pictures producers and distributors may have the intelligence and courage enough to utilize the excellent material . . . written about the Negro by Negro and white writers.

He wrote to a white intellectual:

I am not hopeful of this for some years to come. Perhaps the only way such a picture could be done probably would be through its production by a European company and then brought to America with the accolade of European success.[1]

White had hit upon the irritant—the box office. A few whites such as Van Vechten and Julia Peterkin had always rendered the black experience tolerably enough to rate praise from flattered Negroes. But studios shied from them as box office poison.

Of the early cinema Negrophiles Murphy was the most unlikely *and* the most successful. He had led an undistinguished career adapting short stories to the screen, writing fragments of sequences, and directing some. Except for Gloria Swanson's *The Love of Sunya* (1927) they were light comedies such as *High Speed Lee, Stocks and Blondes,* and *Jazz Heaven,* chiefly for FBO, the reorganized Robertson-Cole studio that would become Radio-Keith-Orpheum, the cinema branch of Radio Corporation of America. He once stepped outside the studio and joined the painter Ferdinand Leger in making an *avante garde* short, *Ballet Mécanique,* which was well received in cultist circles. And in 1928 he negotiated with Van Vechten for a movie of Negro life.

Like many whites in artists' circles he had a zest for Harlem glitter and boasted of his Negro connections and of liaisons with black women.[2]

The pieces fell into place: Murphy's raffish notions of Harlem; his access to RKO's sound equipment of its parent, RCA; the studio's eagerness to join a growing two-reeler cycle; the slump in Harlem Renaissance activity that momentarily freed W. C. Handy, J. Rosamond Johnson, and other black contributors; the coincident availability of Bessie Smith, Jimmy Johnson, and Jimmy Mordecai as performers; and the black musicians' urge to perpetuate the popularity of Negro folk music that had swelled in the 1920s beyond the limits of "race records." The ingredients were the finest of the genre. Handy consented to use his *St. Louis Blues* as a title song. Mordecai was a lean and cool exemplar of jazz dance. Bessie Smith, thirty-five and at the height of her powers, made an unprecedented appearance. J. Rosamond Johnson, who had written "Lift Every Voice" with his brother, served as arranger and provided a choral background. Quality marked even the minor players. Isabel Washington, sister of Fredi, who would debut soon, appeared briefly. Murphy himself fleshed out a story and directed at RKO's Gramercy studio.[3]

Racism itself seemed to work in their favor because the National Board of Review waived objections to the erotic overtones of the final print, in part, Abel Green of *Variety* guessed, because of its presumed authenticity. Green checked his story with a former manager of Harlem's Savoy ballroom, who told him that close embraces on a Negro dance floor were a sign of betrothal rather than lasciviousness. In any case, white censors averted their eyes and gave it a seal, and thus a far wider distribution than it could have otherwise expected if it had been a sexy white picture.[4]

The result was the finest film of Negro life up to that time. The Johnson brothers had always felt that middle-class Negroes were chary of depictions of seamy ghetto life, and whites could have easily offered a liberal chorus of support for prettying it up. Instead, they all allowed Bessie Smith's raspy timbre and moaning blues to come through. Moreover, the musical choruses supported rather than stifled the blues idiom. No one cared whether the smoky ambience would be taken by whites as evidence of "how Negroes really are." The low budget contributed to its success. The script called for an establishing shot in Beale Street in Memphis, but the picture opened merely on a stairwell crap game, thus avoiding the temptation to include irrelevant stock shots. The black actors in the sequence give the scene, not to the shooters as Hollywood well might have, but to a comic janitor-hustler who takes a cut of the "action" as payment for keeping it from "the white man [who] pays me to keep this place clean."

The spare, economical story flashes on in seconds. Jimmy (Mordecai) coolly enters the game with a bankroll obtained from his woman, Bessie. As he rolls, her rival, the St. Louis woman, rubs the cubes on her hip for luck, and he wins. "That's a pretty yeller woman, you know they're liable to do anything," he says in praise. They go to Jimmy's room—"Bessie just pays for it"—where she tries to bid him away with the promise of a "roadster." Bessie, monumentally proportioned, broad, dark face scowling, enters and fights for her man. And having won, she offers him the soft wheedling of a whore to her pimp: crawling on the floor, clinging to his leg, counting the blessings she gives him, accepting a casual kick, and finally reaching the gin bottle, she croons, "My man's got a heart like a rock cast in the sea" into a slow dissolve to a saloon. At the bar a tight closeup catches her dark, mournful face as the band slowly picks up the beat and the room vibrates in chorus with her song. The rhythmic cutting from Bessie to the crowds, with the "St. Louis Blues" over all, breaks with a cut to Jimmy's gliding, dancing entrance as he cajoles Bessie, takes her money from her stocking, and with a broad grin, exits with a sneering flair, leaving Bessie in a tight closeup on a last blue note.[5]

In every instance old stereotypes took on new dimensions. The janitor looks to "the man's" interest, yet shares allegiance with the black shooters. A sociologist could accept the tight, in-group struggle of the two women, and perhaps pick the "yaller gal" as victor. Mordecai's dancing hustler, like Gary Cooper's westerner, imitated his own life style. Bessie Smith teetered on the edge of alcoholic decline, her voice enriched but not yet broken. The musical contributors scored a jazz-and-blues idiom and fit it to movies. Textured lighting and rhythmic cutting set off Murphy's spare direction in a perfect vignette of a facet of black urban life.

In terms of advertising and booking, it proved a failure. Hollywood, still testing the water, refused to plunge in, even after the trades reviewed it favorably. Its awkward length forced it onto the bottom of a two-page spread plugging *Bulldog Drummond*. Trade reviews were peppered with misinformation. For example, Handy's song, not Johnson's, was labeled "the Negro national anthem." But *Variety* wanted to rescue it for wider audiences and found it "pungent with tenseness and action and replete with Aframerican local and other color." Abel Green went so far as to apologize to his white readers for the story that was only true to the life of "a certain strata of black folk as it is to the white trash."[6] Any two-reeler suffered from awkward programming and indifferent advertising; *St. Louis Blues* carried in addition the burden of timid bookers.

Within the year Murphy followed up his *success d'éstime* with a second effort for RKO. Again, his own sense of Negro life would not carry him beyond the jazz scene, but his *Black and Tan* fantasy succeeded in reaching the Negro press. The *Amsterdam News* bubbled with praise for the mood inspired by Duke Ellington's "half savage, half tender" title composition, combined with the "stark realism" of Harlem folk life, tenements, and saloons.[7]

And yet the *Amsterdam's* focus revealed the terrible odds against a fine black film in competition with Hollywood. When *Black and Tan* opened it was buried under a Ruth Chatterton comedy and a Ken Maynard western for a split week, to be followed by Paul Whiteman in the lily-white *King of Jazz.* Nevertheless Murphy's picture offered testimony to the hopes of a small coterie of whites such as music publisher Irving Mills, who wished to broaden the audience for black music and brought Ellington to RKO's attention.[8]

The audience at the Sunset on Harlem's west side saw Duke Ellington plugging away on his music in the face of adversity. He sits at the piano in the halflight, working with his cornetist as two movers attempt to repossess the piano. The movers—one of them was probably Edgar Connor—bumble through a comic routine that in a white movie might have enraged organized Negroes. The piano is saved when Fredi Washington enters, with light skin, high cheekbones, almond eyes—no more than a "Tondelayo" in Hollywood—and plies the men with gin. Her tragedy is love for her man rather than that of Hollywood's tragic mulatto. She dances to support Duke's composing, and they both know her heart will not tolerate the strain. The shot ends on the mottled greys of the room as they are drawn closer and he plays the composition to which each has given. The cut is to his hands so the camera may pull back and place them in a nightclub. The seedy saloon, with its drill-team chorus boys in tails against a fake South Seas drop, is sketched in with short, jazzy cuts. Fredi's act is in the manner of Josephine Baker —the bright-skinned primitive in grass skirt and tiara. The cuts leap from a flashing mirror to her contorted face to a camera under the glassy floor to her swoon and the chorus boys who cover her with ritual feathers. A cut carries them to the bare rooms where mournful black faces and tense hands strain in anxiety over her shadowy bed. "Duke," she whispers, "play the 'Black and Tan Fantasy.'" The music segues from spirituals into the fantasy as the camera pulls back to off-focus closeups of her tearful face under the glinting light and to Duke's face as he plays out the song. She dies as a woman in command of her life, neither black matriarch nor tragic halfcaste. Her light skin becomes irrelevant.[9]

Even with a touch of the maudlin, Murphy's movies were fine and black, yet their impact was negligible in box office grosses and bally-

hoo. His own career did not pick up appreciable momentum until he
began his long-deferred pet project of shooting Eugene O'Neill's *The
Emperor Jones* in 1933. And that would await a union of the principals,
coincident with a major studio's willingness to lease its disused East
Coast facilities.

Until then Negro performers busied themselves in a cluster of promising, though eventually fruitless, foreign projects, as if in answer to
Walter White's expectation that blacks should expect cinema art only
from across the sea. Sergei Eisenstein from deep within his artistic
sense, Carl Junghans on orders from the Communist Party, and Kenneth Macpherson from a fascination with blacks as visual icons all began hopeful movies using Negro themes and actors. Unfortunately,
the foreigners found obstacles that Walter White never anticipated,
and only Macpherson completed his picture. Like Murphy, he would
show an initiated group the possibilities of Afro-American cinema, but
no more.

Kenneth Macpherson made one of the most artistically wrought motion pictures employing Negro characters ever created. Like Murphy
he brought together the finest talent and rose above the racial lore of
his day. The difference between them centered on motives. Murphy
sought the main chance; Macpherson wanted to distill and refine the
juices down to the finest brandy, and deep in his own cellar drink it
with his friends. Thus he marked no royal road to a black future because only a handful of *cinéastes* saw his movie in their film society
sessions. His little group in Territet, Switzerland, lacked organization,
money, and artistic definition. They kept in touch through their little
magazine, *Close Up*, which from 1927 through 1933 spread the surety
that they could purge cinema of commercialism, bring it to bear on
social problems, and shape it into a universal language. The rich husband of the poetess Winifred Bryher, his co-editor, kept them going.[10]

Among the problems discussed in the pages was racism, to which
they devoted an issue in 1931. The Marxist critic Harry Alan Potamkin
drew an analogy between Jews and Negroes, finding them hurt badly
on the one hand by cinema racism and on the other by Yiddish and Negro pictures that were spoiled "because there is not sufficient training
or cinematic insight." Nothing, not even Vidor's *Hallelujah!*, satisfied
the circle. And from Vidor's low ridge of "spuriousness" and "senti-
mentalism" it was all downhill to the fake jungle documentaries filled
with "the unauthoritative, the supercilious, the patronizing, the wisecracking" stuff of "Nordic art."[11]

They formed Pool Films, through which they would produce
"jagged" visual poems filled with "tension" and "vague symbolism." In
1929 they attempted to enlist the American Negroes Langston Hughes,

Walter White, and Elmer Carter of *Opportunity*, who sent a perfunctory article on all-Negro movies. Hughes stalled. White hung back awaiting the completion of *Hearts in Dixie*, about which he had heard the worst and from which he expected nothing because he too accepted the powerful myth of the Southern box office.[12]

In February 1930 Macpherson wrote to Eslanda Goode Robeson and discussed the shooting of a film while Paul Robeson was in Europe on a concert tour. Almost between trains they hoped to schedule a few days shooting. For the Robesons it was to be a forgotten interlude at Lake Lemans, filming and lazing in the cafés as relief from the tour.[13]

Borderline was the title of the picture that would test their racial and cinematic theories. Macpherson had worked on it for a year before writing Mrs. Robeson, and he was eager to start. The Robesons would break off their hectic tour in the spring while Macpherson blocked in the shooting script. They would sweep into Montreux from London's Albert Hall on March 21 or 22 and be gone for Berlin by the 29th. Then Macpherson and Bryher would have enough "one-take" footage with which to splice their complex montages. Eslanda was excited. "Paul says he is entirely willing to work hard and fast at the film," she wrote. "And of course I am. We will do all we can on this end to prepare." In her mind's eye she saw it through to glittering release in Europe's capitals.[14] Indeed, when they reached Switzerland everything went perfectly, even to the point of wringing good performances from the literary figures, among them Hilda Doolittle, who acted the roles in the manner of Eisenstein's typecasting. The Robesons were Pete and Adah, the black intruders in the staid white lives of Astrid and Thorne. The result was to be a poetic sketch of life "on the cosmic racial borderline," with Robeson as a many-layered symbol of blackness. The finished film hewed to its intended lines. A thin plotline held the visual experiment together. Peter works in a small-town café when, unknown to him, Adah returns from a fling. Thorne and Astrid are set apart by memories of his old love for Adah. Gossip and malice hound the blacks. The two whites quarrel, and Astrid dies accidentally. The town turns on the blacks. Pete goes to Thorne's flat where they at last feel hatred dissolve as they became aware that the village's enmity has poisoned the air and made them instruments of its hate. Pete leaves, "a scapegoat for unresolved problems, evasions and neuroses for which the racial borderline has served as justification."[15]

The film was a visual experiment in lights and shadows, and a comment on racism. The village is to be "cleansed and hallowed by their passing," so black imagery becomes virtuous and white evil. Thus Astrid stirs the gossip in the bar, carps at the "niggers," quarrels with her lover, and calls him "niggerlover." In contrast, the Robesons appear innocent of petty hatred, standing clean against the light sky, spare treetops, and white water. Cutting back to the inn, the mood is artificial and crackling with racism muttered by an old harridan. In a tight closeup a white woman pours wine into the mouth of a sot. The rhythm of the cutting is a counterplay between natural blacks in repose and snarling whites. Foreshadowing the climax is an allegorical cut to a white drinker spilling his bloodlike wine into a sodden ashtray. When black meets white, Robeson coolly fingers a bedspread, stolid in the face of invasion, while Thorne slouches, intimidated by Pete's calm. Back in Thorne's room, Astrid's death at the end of a nasty fight is told with a cut to an ink bottle spilling into an ashtray. In the days that follow, the bar livens, traffic increases, Pete and the bargirl play at being exotic primitives in a mock romance. But nothing can be the same. From a playful knife in the girl's mouth, the cut is to a bloody knife in a pan of water; idyllic exteriors are spoiled with flashbacks to the bloody room; an old woman stirs in the fireplace as the fires of hell; the Negroes leave. The barflies abjectly mutter farewells, and one of them tosses aside a last rose. In the end it is the white world turned upside down, the Negro made whole, the European idiom reordered with black the symbol of virtue and white the incarnation of evil. Black purity stands against European decadence, "sordid calculation and unbridled jealousy."[16]

Yet for all its fine traits, *Borderline* remained a curiosity that demonstrated the snags of independent European production. Even though it had broken with a racial past, distribution was impossible, and Robeson's presence happened in a vacuum. As Murphy's work was buried in the two-reelers, *Borderline* never reached beyond the *cinéastes*. The makers needed the connection with the Negro audiences that they had attempted to reach with their letters to White and Hughes. Instead, trade papers and critics condemned with faint praise the "beautiful photographic compositions" which were "to the detriment of clarity." More socially minded critics had fewer reservations and found it "a symphony in black and white," and a "lash of the whip in the face of understanding humanity." A continental viewer went so far as to praise it as "perhaps the greatest that has as yet been produced." But the trades thought audiences could not accept it. Still, Pool Films hoped for a continental run, and even an American première until misunderstandings in customs, the threat of censorship, and the anticipation of only a tiny audience of "intellectual circles" in only a half-dozen cities dampened their ambition.[17] So the picture became no more than an unmarked grave for a stillborn achievement.

The events surrounding *Borderline* would have shown to any observer that European style and point of view could offer little to Negro

Americans. What passed for racial liberalism was often no more than a worship of presumed primitiveness. Black Americans were lionized more than understood. Or, later, they became pawns in international diplomacy that went beyond race. And if anything, European production increased problems of distribution.

Nevertheless, black Americans had carried on a romance with Europe that stretched back to the tours of the Fisk Jubilee Singers and Sissieretta Jones in the nineteenth century, and to the black expatriates Florence Mills and Josephine Baker and their exported revues. Some few Negroes may have seen French quasi-documentaries such as Leon Poirier's *Cäin*, shot in Madagascar, his *L'homme du Niger* with Harry Baur, or Marc Allegret and Andre Gide's *Voyage au Congo* (1928). And Josephine Baker's pictures, such as *The Siren of the Tropics* for Allegret, received a limited American release. At least French racism, although it rested on primitivism, did not include slavery and Uncle Tom in its baggage, and it revered black American expression such as *le jazz hot*. Only later would the failures of Robeson, Richard Wright, and Melvin Van Peebles steer Negroes away from Europe as a cinema source.[18]

Long on "star quality" and short on talent, Josephine Baker moved from the ghetto squalor of St. Louis, and deserted American revues—wisely, for she became a lifelong darling of French literati. Negro Americans were proud of her reputation but found her films hard to take. The worst of them was *The Siren of the Tropics*, which burned the fingers of everyone who touched it.

The fame of the picture may have come from J. A. Rogers's friendly review after a Paris screening. Though he granted it was no more than "the old story of the native girl who falls into hopeless love with a white," he liked the sequences in which she comes to Paris, dances for some children in a park, is spotted by an impresario, and as respite from her upper-class French life embarks on a stage career. Later the Associated Negro Press found it so distressing as to label its American importer, Jack Goldberg, a false friend of the race for bringing to New York a shoddy, inept clinker that "renders the Negro ignoble."[19] Theophilus Lewis, the most acid of the Harlem critics, found *la Baker*'s dancing a travesty and the picture a throwback to *The Perils of Pauline*. "Miss Baker will never crash the films in a big way," he concluded, "unless King Vidor enters her life." Unfortunately, no one listened. The New York Urban League used the opening of the film as the occasion for a benefit, complete with press releases that characterized the Maurice DeKobra script as Baker's autobiography.[20]

Meanwhile French pictures that clearly breached racial etiquette remained undistributed, perhaps because of negative reviews in the trades.

Two fine French filmmakers, Robert Florey and Sacha Guitry, made
a comedy of manners, *Le Blanc et le Noir,* in which a childless wife
sends for an unseen singer in her garden, who then slips into bed in the
darkened room. The resulting child is, unknown to her, black. The
cuckolded husband saves the marriage by placing the baby in an orphanage and adopting a white baby. The light-comic document on race
elicited a prim response from *Variety:*

> Striking instance that morals are a matter of geography. Story goes big
> in Paris, but in America, no audience would stand for it, even if
> slipped in unnoticed.

Croix du Sud (1932), a Pathé film shot in Africa and Joinville, featured
not only miscegenation, but an African chief who rejects his white
woman for a black. *Variety* found it equally unrewarding.[21]

The final barrier to Negro success in Europe was political. If the
United States government disapproved of a picture, pressure could be
brought even against the most Marxist of states. The most maddening
episode seemed at first the surest bet to strike a blow for black social
cinema. The Communist Party, after its initial celebrity as the savior
of blacks in the Scottsboro case, embarked on an ambitious adventure
in Negro circles, culminating in the campaign of James W. Ford for
Vice-President of the United States in 1932. In the spring before the
election he returned from the Soviet Union with a vague charge to
raise a company of black actors who would journey to Russia to make
a movie of American racial life. The *Amsterdam News* gave it a
friendly play because presumably the Russians were above stereotyping, and they had also pioneered in the use of crowds of amateurs "to
show mass movements rather than to exploit the heroics of the individual." Ford in the beginning hoped for one hundred blacks, but the lack
of expense money soon dwindled hopes, numbers, and seriousness. One
of the presumptive thespians was the guest of honor in a rent-party-like
gathering at Small's Paradise which ran on for so long the guests drank
up all the profits. Nevertheless, Ford, Henry Lee Moon, then a young
newsman, and the West Indian Communist W. A. Domingo formed a
fundraising committee. By summer famous show business Negroes and
a cadre of left-liberal whites helped raise enough to send twenty-six
Americans to work for the Meschrabpom Film Company. The League
of Struggle for Negro Rights and other groups tendered a bon voyage
party for Langston Hughes, Moon, Ted Poston, Loren Miller, and
other Negro intellectuals, among them a core of Communists.[22]

Not until the *Bremen* had landed them in Europe and they reached
Leningrad by rail could they see the thin reed to which they had become attached. Carl Junghans, a German, had been engaged to direct

a script written in an improbable and remote style. Like later "race movies" every modest jump of the plot called for an interlude of singing, yet few of the Negroes could carry a tune. In the workers' paradise, all of them were without overalls. Hughes, who was to be a script-doctor, found it laughable and disillusioning. The script bore the handprints of a German, a Russian, and an Afro-American. Hughes had not heard of the trip until he reached California on a lecture tour, and, though he was warned to be disappointed, he went along. On board the *Bremen* he immediately noticed that Wayland Rudd and Sylvia Garner were the only experienced actors. No one was a worker in the Soviet sense. The contracts and the script were both in Russian, so they stalled for a fortnight awaiting a translation.

Black and White, the working title, was an epic of the black and white workers of Birmingham. But it was shot through with silly errors. At last Hughes received permission to weed out the burlesques, including a white mill owner who dances with his black servingmaid, a lynching that is advertised over the radio, a Negro who calls for Yankee help over the radio, and a crusade of Northern workers who rush southward to join their black proletarian brothers.

Hughes was torn between laughter and tears at the chore laid out before him. As summer passed and they at last moved toward Odessa to shoot the picture, the rehearsals grew more ludicrous. Of the whole group only one "shimmy-sha-wobble" dancer could sing a note. As ineptitude slowed the work, the director searched for a looser, darker-skinned member to replace the wooden, light-skinned actor assigned to play the tragic lynching victim, and settled on Ted Poston, whereupon one of the American Communists cried out: "What has Ted Poston done for the class struggle that he should have the honor of being lynched?"[23]

Then they caught rumors, including some in the New York *Herald-Tribune*, that the film was to be shut down. No one clearly saw why, but gradually they discerned that Stalin would abandon the project in order to smooth the way for eventual Soviet diplomatic recognition by the United States. Apparently Colonel Hugh Cooper, the American builder of a Soviet dam, and Ivy Lee, a Rockefeller representative and a friend of Stalin, persuaded the Russian leader to call a halt. "Comrades, we have been screwed," Moon announced to a protest meeting of the blacks in their hotel. Moon had been ill and lingered in Moscow while the others sojourned in Odessa, and had heard the story in the capital. Studio executives fobbed off prepostrous excuses: Soviet cameras would not shoot Negroes, they were all "unsuitable" types, there were not enough Russian Negroes for mob scenes, and so on. The blacks squabbled over whether to protest but gave in, in the face of the lame script and the black Communists who were obligated to defend the Russian action. So in the end they received a summer abroad, a few chores as European "stringers" for American newspapers, some expenses, and a few insights into Soviet authoritarianism. One of the company began to enjoy barking "Fuck the GPU!" in order to see English-speaking Muscovites blanch.

Except for two or three Communists, the company slowly straggled back to America and to an angry, divisive winter in which party members set about identifying and castigating villains, chief among whom were Moon and Poston, who exposed the Communist charade in the pages of the *Amsterdam News*. To party faithfuls, Moon and Poston were contemptible homosexuals and "misleaders." At first the black press had wanted to believe the Communists; they had needed to see it as a white plot "to alienate the affections of the Negroes for the Soviet Union." But soon they printed not only the participants' outraged tales but W. C. Chase's cartoon depicting a Russian and American lyncher in embrace as the Russian pushes in a Negro's face.[24]

The Russian episode had held out hope for Negroes because of the feeling that the Soviet Union stood against oppression. As early as the 1920s they had produced a few "agitprop" antiracism movies. So it was an easy matter for the Americans in the summer of 1932 to miscalculate the Russian will. The episode added to the evidence that Negro Americans could expect nothing from Europe. For a Frenchman to admire jazz or to emulate a black style of life was at bottom to reach no higher than American racial attitudes. Soviet political waffling was little different from American filibustering. And even if a European product survived, the distribution problems were insurmountable. Thus, in the four decades after 1930 Europeans would produce black movies, but their lower range would be worse than American films and their high mere curiosities.

There remained one remote possibility for black nationalists who demanded more rapid change and black control of it: independent production so good that regular distribution channels would bid for it, a combination of a strong black presence among the performers or writers, a dollop of white venture capital, and brisk business at the gate. Blacks would assume a share of control outside the studio monoliths, and they would reach the bookers that had been unavailable to Oscar Micheaux.

One clear example occurred in early 1933 as the sun set on the returning Soviet stragglers. It involved, with supreme racial irony that could happen only in America, the finest living black actor-singer, a white director with a yen for Harlem nightlife, the greatest living American playwright, a sharpening of the NAACP urge toward racial

Stalin's cancellation of *Black and White*, an intended indictment of American racism, outraged and embittered the Afro-Americans who had made the long journey to the Soviet Union in good faith. (Amsterdam News, October 5, 1932)

integration, a depression-ridden white studio eager to hire out its disused facilities, a white writer with a good ear for poor black patois, two
neophytes in the movie business who had made a bundle of cash by
distributing an arty German movie, and a black press willing to watch
the offspring of such a complex union with an open mind.

The way to that future was pointed by *The Emperor Jones* more
than any other single picture. Its literary basis was a strong gothic play
by Eugene O'Neill, who wanted to see the movie into production, and
who acquiesced in several cinematic changes. Its protagonist was to be
Paul Robeson. The director was Dudley Murphy, then confidently
ready for his next Negro subject. DuBose Heyward, the author of
Porgy, which blacks and whites alike flattered by erroneously calling
it a "folk drama," wrote a jazzy prologue. Having completed its West
Coast studio, probably short of cash, and on the edge of bankruptcy,
Paramount-Publix gladly opened its surplus Astoria studio.[25] At the
same time, Negro intellectuals drifted toward naturalistic drama, abandoned the "reluctance on the part of colored people to see what they
consider lower phases of Negro life," and granted that some sensitive
whites might write realistically of Negro themes.[26]

All of the principals worked easily together. After meeting with
them at his southern estate, O'Neill allowed Murphy and Heyward to
adapt his materials. Robeson trusted O'Neill's feelings. At the top of
the pile two eager promoters, John Krimsky and Gifford Cochran,
backed their first American film in the beginning of an intended career
of high risks and low returns. Everything fitted neatly. Heyward's prologue gave humane black dimensions to Brutus Jones, the Negro railway porter who becomes a Carib king. Harlem's oppressive poverty
and fearful in-group aggression tinged the opening. Jones's easy way
with rich whites and his confident mien gave him a realistic competitive edge for which his later court is a reasonable fantasy extension.
J. Rosamond Johnson's score divided the picture into four movements
and motifs: African, to Gullah, to Harlem jazz, to Voodoo, a sure-
handed attempt to symbolize a long race-memory.[27] The rest of the
cast was superb, from white Dudley Digges as a conniving courtier to
Jimmy Mordecai, Frank Wilson, Fredi Washington, and Ruby Elzy.
The climax of Jones's death becomes a black social variant of the in-
evitability of Greek tragedy given new meaning through an artful use
of environmentalism. The marquees departed from custom by giving
top billing to a Negro.

Robeson's Jones overawes the picture and gives it heroic dimensions.
The crapshooters and pretentious, overdressed courtiers who are
named for the rail stops on Jones's old run, the voodoo drummers, and

the "bush niggers" surrounding the court appear as plausible figures rather than extreme stereotypes. Also, the combination of gothic ambience and naturalistic acting artfully rendered the broad stereotypes unnecessary. When Jones dies in a revolt, he is not a Pullman toady or a high-roller under the stairwell; he is a black king dying in pain and rage at his demeaning fall.[28]

At the box office the film confounded the dire predictions, doing well in nervously booked Southern dates, topping its week in a Western date, and running well in Harlem. Audiences loved it, save for the reserved black bourgeoisie and J. A. Rogers. To balance his review the *Amsterdam News* ran Ted Poston's favorable piece as well. White middlebrow weeklies agreed; and the *cinéastes* of *Close Up* thought it "heavensent." The ads lagged behind their subject by emphasizing "Gin Gals Dice," but all things considered it was an impressive debut of blacks into independently produced and financed feature films outside the confines of Hollywood and crafted with finer stuff than that of the race movies.[29]

The most important fact of its entry into American cinema was that, whatever its merits as a work of film art, its white director, Dudley Murphy, pleaded with Walter White to screen it before the NAACP, partially from motives of disarming adverse black press comment. But also he asked "if [White] saw fit to recommend the film as a sincere work of art." White held back from overtly endorsing the picture but assured Murphy that he did not agree with the carping of some of the black newspapers. In turn, White asked young Roy Wilkins of his staff to observe the "significant" box office success of the picture and to prepare a story on the NAACP's reaction to it. He gave Wilkins permission to develop as part of the press release a statement in which the NAACP gave its sanction to Krimsky's campaign "to break into the South with the picture."[30] Eventually, organized Negroes shaped the idea into an annual ritual by giving yearly awards to Hollywood movies—often under the rubric of "brotherhood."

Thus, racially oriented movies from independent producers and from overseas had scant impact on mass American audiences, but they served as indirect inspirations and models. Unfortunately, their remoteness, both geographically and intellectually, served as barriers to widespread distribution. In their own time they could contribute no more than a "fading effect," in the words of the social psychologists, to the dominant stereotypes. Paul Robeson, for example, would spend the rest of his decade-long career making independent pictures in Europe attempting to recapture the dense integrity of *Borderline* and *The Emperor Jones,* and to destroy the historical Southern Negro.[31] In a few tight

circles of intellectuals the independents had made a few blacks aware
of the possibilities, although they would wait in vain through the thirties for equal developments in popular movies.

Besides, the Jazz Age and the Harlem Renaissance had come to an
end, and Negroes had lost some of their cachet in white intellectual
circles, so that, all in all, few Afro-Americans viewed their prospects
with equanimity. If outrage and demands increased along with New
Year's Day optimism in the black press, substantive reasons for real optimism seemed to decline. Langston Hughes could only look back wist-
fully and wonder:

> We were no longer in vogue, anyway, we Negroes. Sophisticated New
> Yorkers turned to Noel Coward. Colored actors began to go hungry,
> publishers politely rejected new manuscripts, and patrons found other
> uses for their money. The cycle that had charlestoned into being on
> the dancing heels of *Shuffle Along* now ended in *Green Pastures* with
> *De Lawd.*

Walter White transferred the feeling of malaise to the cinema. "Because the producers of moving pictures must depend upon a nationwide distribution which includes the South," he wrote in 1929, "it is
almost impossible to start off with the presentation of anything but
the old stereotyped concepts of the Negro."[32]

The only salvation might be a longshot wager, the new soundfilm
that had intruded upon silent film and stirred a myth in Negro circles
that Negroid voices recorded with higher fidelity than white. "I do
not see how they are going to keep the Negro from achieving a permanent place in the movie world so long as they have talkies," wrote
James Weldon Johnson, as though giving up on the esoteric indies. "I
myself have noticed that their voices record much better than white
voices."[33]

Chapter Nine

"BETTER THAN WHITE VOICES"

In 1927 Afro-Americans flashed upon the Hollywood screen briefly. Like a long string of Chinese firecrackers, all-black two-reelers exploded erratically. These films brought the best of Afro-American vaudeville, vernacular dancing, and the more commercial forms of jazz to film. Also, because they required little investment and because the risk of failure and its impact on their careers was borne almost exclusively by the black performers, the studios could grind them out regularly.

There is no way of proving that they were popular. In any case, these shorts continued to be made throughout the 1930s, which indicated Hollywood believed there was a continual audience and market of some size. They brought to the screen the best of Negro popular entertainment and jazz-related music. Black musical revues and stage shows vibrated with galas, blues shouters, gospel singers, scat singers, flash dancers, and lindy hoppers; and for those in small towns off the main circuits there were "race records" featuring Sister Rosetta Tharp, Ma Rainey, and Mamie and Bessie Smith.

In keeping with past racial arrangements, the technical basis of the movement remained in the hands of the white corporations with the closest affiliations to the record companies, which had already been retailing these versions of black music to white listeners. Vitaphone had exclusive contracts with Victor, Brunswick-Balke, and other disc producers that allowed them to turn out more than one hundred "shorts" shot in and around Manhattan. Western Electric and Warners had concluded their agreement as early as 1925, after which they began shoot-

ing in the Manhattan Opera House, where the acoustics were good and
the stiff musical vignettes demanded by the bulkiness and immobility
of the cameras seemed plausible. Soon after, Fox bought into its own
system, Movietone.[1]

By October 1927 *The Jazz Singer* had demonstrated the possibilities
of the new medium. Al Jolson played the son of a cantor in a plot
thick with sad Kol Nidres embellished with sentimental Southern songs
and jazz bits derived from Negro life.[2] Within months all the majors
bought licenses to use the new sound systems. Production reached four
per week for Vitaphones alone. Each new release in turn demanded an
enormous investment in wiring the theaters for sound, running as high
as $20,000 for a large house, with a total of $12,000,000 in installations
for 1928 alone.

Blacks were incapable of such an investment, and not until 1931
would Micheaux be capable of a "talkie."[3] Not that they did not try.
As early as the spring of 1929 advertisements appeared in the black
press soliciting a million dollars for the Tono-Film Corporation, run
by Paul Robeson, jazzman Noble Sissle, and composer-arranger Will
Vodery. Their plans included singers such as Ethel Waters, Josephine
Baker, Adelaide Hall, and Cora Greene. In California Bill Foster resurrected his hopes of cracking the motion picture industry, this time
through soundfilm. "We have no separate art," he wrote, putting aside
black music. "We are no different than the American white man." But
he called for race unity and initiative in order to use "our great opportunity to show the world what we can do."[4]

Although nothing came of the glowing words, Foster began to cir-
culate the myth on which a brief flash of black exposure on the screen
would be built. He claimed that "tests proved one great outstanding
fact—the low mellow voice of the Negro was ideally suited for the pictures." Added to his musical comedy attainments "the peculiar ability
of the Negro" altered the ground rules of Hollywood stardom, Foster
insisted, so that "he fits right into the new age." The black press from
the Mississippi to New York encouraged him, agreeing that " 'TALKIES'
OPEN NEW AVENUES FOR PROFESSIONAL ACTORS IN MOVIES."[5]

Foster went to Hollywood and dashed himself against the system.
"The Negroes fight me harder than the whites," he grumbled, "they
are all from Texas and Okla. Thinks everyman from the east is a crook
[sic]." Yet even when whites bungled in Foster's opinion, he felt
frozen out:

> The white man has fell flat trying to Produce a real Negro show as he
> has always did. Harts of Dixie and Hallulga. the Big Producers are
> afraid to produce a big Negro Drama. the South will resent it. Boy-

cott their pictures, would thow the Business into Politic. one told me
If the Negro wants Big Pictures of Negro life of today they will have
to produce them themself. [sic]

Bitterly he struggled, "trying to get somewhere in this Business as a
Producer" of "Pictures That Talk-Sing-Dance Reflect Credit," because
"if a colored producing co dont make the Grade now it will be useless
later on after all the Big Co.s get merged up—they will set about con-
trolling the Equipment then the door wil be closed [sic]."[6]
Foster's morose estimate was correct. He could hardly prevail in the
face of studio consolidation, a sharp decline in race movies, and major
sponsorship of all-black productions and two-reelers featuring blacks.
The temporary result was a mélange of conflicting changes in the
way Negroes appeared on the screen. For one of the rare moments in
its history the motion picture industry would leap ahead of its audience's tastes and opinions. Blacks on the screen would become whole
and rounded. Some studios would consult them with the care and politesse formerly reserved for organized Catholics and Jews. Black critics
began to find more merit in the Hollywood product than in that of
Micheaux or Dunbar. White Americans were more conscious of black
life in all its aspects than they had been before—from Amos 'n' Andy on
radio, through the Scottsboro case, to the increasing pressure brought
by the NAACP.[7] There was increased pressure and litigation, demands
for black history in schools, pressures against urban Jim Crow, conflicts over housing, increasing competition in sports by teams such as
the Renaissance team, which defeated the white "world" champion
Boston Celtics, and the increasing militance of such organizations as
Harlem's Colored Merchants Association.[8]
Ever since the great days of the Williams and Walker revues, black
stage productions followed the course of Miller and Lyles and their
white successors such as Lew Leslie downtown to the white houses.
Serious racial drama often came from the fertile minds of whites such as
Paul Green, Jim Tully, DuBose Heyward, and Julia Peterkin.[9] The
white critic Burns Mantle mourned the resulting black inability to "get
together on some form of revue that would be a real credit to their
race" instead of playing to whites. "There is nothing worth imitating in
white revues," he concluded, but "there is a lot worth creating for the
colored shows." The black answer, urgently integrationist in tone, was
symbolized by the columns of Lawrence LaMar, whose entertainment
column in the *California Eagle* covered *black* performing in *white* media, and the sidebars of George Johnson's Pacific News Bureau coverage
of such integrationist matter as "Big Crusade Against Racial Screen
Insults."[10]

And so, black and white writers mutually patronized each other and believed that amity would defeat prejudice as soon it became profitable. Signs of harmony were rampant. When Ernest Lubitsch called Clarence Muse's revival of *Run Little Chillun* "one of the finest pieces of direction I've ever seen," Muse in turn claimed, "Hollywood's not prejudiced; they'll buy anything that's successful. So I say we've got to give them something that's good." Already, he thought, he had helped end the worst of Negro dialect stereotypes by simply refusing to coach actors. James Weldon Johnson went so far as to believe white writers on black themes could be judged on their merits, especially since so many black writers and audiences displayed "reluctance . . . to see what they consider lower phases of Negro life." Indeed, it seemed that for every black director who struggled to make the point that American theatrical tradition was "not complete without the Negro contribution" there was a critic who agreed with Bishop W. J. Walls that Amos 'n' Andy, *Green Pastures*, *Porgy*, and Wallace Thurman's *Harlem* were no more than "the jazzy, staccato, expression [and] commercialization of primitive weakness."[11]

In the heady air, most black observers of the cinema wagered on the good intentions of Hollywood whites and urged Negro performers to look to soundfilm as an avenue of aspiration. *The Jazz Singer* generated "sobs . . . heard all over the theatre" in Harlem because of its "sympathetic interest in Negro life." But the press also alerted blacks to "the production of movietone musical shorts which will be produced in the Jersey plant of the Fox Film Corporation" which would likely have openings for blacks.[12]

Black performers and a few white directors such as Dudley Murphy and Monte Brice developed a tenuous mutual trust. These collaborators produced the richest and finest work to date by blacks: the two-reel "short subject." Brief and involving little risk, pungent and tangy, like a local colorist's short story rather than a major novel, the shorts were intended as showcases for talent that seemed not to fit the Hollywood mold: directors sharpening their tools, cutters anxious to try new ideas outside the routines of major production, contract players gaining seasoning.

The earliest of the black talkies, Christie Comedies' version of the Octavus Roy Cohen stories, hewed closest to traditional Southern forms. Starting as early as 1928, even before *Hallelujah!* and *Hearts in Dixie* were in the can, Al Christie of Paramount had sent a company southward for location shots and signed Spencer Williams, a young stocky black veteran of World War I, to write continuity. Williams's craft and wit, combined with his ability to squeeze honest black roles into the crevices of white movies, enabled him to build a long career,

Cheap short films provided an opportunity for experiment, but the earliest such as Al Christie's *Melancholy Dame* (© Paramount Famous Lasky Corp.) merely used black players such as Roberta Hyson and Spencer Williams (who also wrote scripts) in white stories. (GEH)

at first with Christie, then with the majors, punctuated by occasional all-black pictures, and finally with the television team of Amos 'n' Andy. As a prerequisite of success the black press played up his commodious office and glamorized him as author of the first black talkie. He was a gadfly who wrote, directed, and acted, appearing in each of the Cohen stories: *The Melancholy Dame, Oft in the Silly Night, The Lady Fare, Music Hath Charms,* and *The Framing of the Shrew.* In addition to Williams, several of the Lafayette Players appeared, among them Evelyn Preer, Edward Thompson, and Roberta Hyson. Christie released them through Paramount and gave them strong play in the trades, "as the Class of the Market," and a novelty accepted by white Southerners.[13]

The series treated Negro "high society" in Birmingham. The hero of *Melancholy Dame,* for example, was Permanent Williams, a cabaret owner whose wife, Jonquil, is jealous of his attentions to Sappho, an entertainer. Despite the booming business Jonquil wants her fired. The entanglement grows, leavened by threats of violence. In *Music Hath Charms* the same cabaret is the set for similar contretemps between Florian Slappey, Zenia Sprowl, Sam Ginn, Lawyer Chew, Roscoe Griggers and other denizens over who shall lead the band. The story of *Oft in the Silly Night* departed from the formula and offered a cross-class love affair between a black chauffeur and the daughter of his employer. A trade reviewer found it "a fine attraction for key theatres and those houses whose audiences appreciate clean comedy without custard pies and slapstick."[14]

The strange combination of Octavus Roy Cohen and Spencer Williams introduced a striking amount of Negro lore to the screen. It was as though the two Southerners (Williams came from Louisiana) hammered out a motif based on the tension between their black and white points of view, yet promising white Southerners no threat to segregation of the races. One of the later pictures, *Brown Gravy*, opened on "Ev'ry Time I Feel de Spirit" and "Joshua Fit de Battle ob Jericho," two traditional Negro songs that most whites knew. The singing was presented as a rehearsal for a contest of choirs in Memphis, a common black social event. The character of a charlatan medium of the occult played for comedy, a black woman deeply suspicious of black men, a gaudy lodge named "the Knights and Ladies of a Better Worl'," all parodied qualities of Negro life: the institutional looseness of black religion, the tough matriarchy encouraged by economic necessity, and historically dense fraternal life. At their worst the scripts simply grew remote from what Williams knew and closer to what Cohen must have fancied, as, for example, when the black bourgeoisie sounded like cotton choppers.[15]

Whether the pictures would prevail as black statements or as white men's creatures depended on who controlled the medium and whose motives survived in the purest state. As an example of their conflicting interests, Roberta Hyson, a fugitive from the nightclubs awaiting a chance to do the "serious, soulful side to Negro life," was signed by Cohen for the comic "character I had in mind."[16] The resulting compromise of values apparently provided more entertainment than offense.

At the same time Pathé signed Bill Foster and the vaudeville team of Buck and Bubbles to produce a rival series of black two-reelers. Foster went beyond his nominal duties as script-doctor and made the first black assault on the lily-white unions by demanding a black cameraman. Over at Fox, Will Vodery was signed to the largest contract ever for a black musician as supervisor of their soundtrack music.

For the first time in years black leaders gave support in their public writing, stirred more by the release of a pair of all-Negro features than by the shorts. But several of them, including Walter White of the NAACP and Elmer Carter of the Urban League, tried to define a black role that stimulated self-respect and race-consciousness. The Urban League organ *Opportunity* even praised Charles Butler's Jim Crow department of Central Casting. Kenneth Macpherson culled the opinions for an all-Negro issue of *Close Up*. The notion that movies could become potent factors in changing racial attitudes received a modest support from educational psychologists whose work pointed toward the possibility that stereotypes were recalled longer and with more intensity than factual data. The intellectuals encouraged both Negro and white filmmakers, although White predicted that good black films probably would have to come from Europe.[17] The good gray *New York Times* joined in with criticisms of movie racism. King Vidor, Lon Chaney, Alexander Woollcott, and other whites chimed in their approval of "the Negro [as] one of the greatest actors by nature."[18]

The movies revived black dilemmas of aesthetics; for while there was white monopoly over cinema production, the rage for blacks on the screen—nearly a decade after a similar rash in theater—was made possible by black music. For years Negro intellectuals and leaders had been divided by the sticky aesthetic problem presented by black music: Were Negroes uniquely musical and rhythmic? Did their music come like the wisdom of the Talmud from deep within the soul of a chosen people? Or was their music merely the fossil of work songs and chants on the New Orleans waterfront? Most of the time the argument simmered beneath the surface of the Negro world, some disclaiming both the central importance and the quality of "nigger music," while others embraced it as "the gift of black folk."

But with the coming of sound-on-film white men, the controllers of the motion picture industry, became the arbiters and filters of Negro music on the screen. Because it rested so much on improvisation and the heat of the moment, rather than scripting or scoring, jazz-on-film allowed the fullest black expression. Even then blacks who conformed to white models and easily took white direction survived. Stepin Fetchit would get more work than Bessie Smith; Louis Armstrong more than Duke Ellington; Bill Robinson more than Charles Gilpin.

For example, Aubrey Lyles and Flournoy Miller sold imitations of their first 1921 stage success, *Shuffle Along*, with its comic Negro bootleggers, to MGM. *Jimtown Speakeasy* opens on a boy tap dancing to a guitar in a Negro dive. The dialogue introduces a "pickaninny" doing a "Charleston"; malapropisms like "dat lady renounced dinner," "ignorancer," "condiculous"; a brandished razor; a parody of blues sung by the "Shufflin' Along Four"; and a number in drag. Miller and Lyles

enter and go through some stagey camouflage of their purchase of il-
licit whiskey hidden in a cigar box:

STEVE: When you go past that policeman on the corner, don't let
them cigars leak.

SAM: Look here, what did you want to tell that man I was crazy
for?

STEVE: I didn't tell that man you was crazy, he knowed it.

SAM: Just to show you how crazy I is, I wants my half of the
money right now.

STEVE: What money?

SAM: The money the man just spent over the counter.

STEVE: You can't get it. That would be breaking the disagreement.

SAM: I wants my half of the money after each purchase.

· · ·

STEVE: You can't get it. Now wait. I'se the boss around here.

The bit ends with a refugee from burlesque: an elaborate argument
over who owes what to whom founded on the "revision" and "mul-
sifying" of the figures. At the end they smash the bottles, fearing a
police raid, only to learn with exaggerated sadness that the siren was a
passing ambulance. In another Miller and Lyles script the comedians
appear as *The Mayor of Jimtown* and the police chief, in dialect, with
neither official able to spell "cat." The farce ends with their "famous
boxing dance number" to Irving Berlin's *Ivy*.[19] The dialect made it
tolerable to whites, but the evasion of the police was a classic black
conflict situation.

By the summer of 1929, with the nation's economy still riding the
crest of the bull market and Hollywood jubilant over the heady success of soundfilm, the studios used such two-reelers to experiment with
both music and with Negroes. "COLORED PEOPLE IN MANY SHORT
TALKERS" was the *Variety* headline announcing the trend. They ranged
in fidelity from the Christie productions of Cohen's comedies to Columbia's use of Mamie Smith, "the foremost exponent of the 'Blues'
type of song," in *Jailhouse Blues*. The studio's advertising copy treated
her with studied reverence:

It takes extraordinary talent for a negro man or woman to gain any
measure of success as a public entertainer. MAMIE SMITH, by reason of her ability to interpret the soul of a people whose rampant
spirit of gaity and joy of living could not be dimmed by adverse circumstances, ranks with the leading music artists in widespread popularity.[20]

The black presence on the screen was overwhelming, at least in the little world of the two-reeler. Ford Lee Washington and John Sublette —"Buck and Bubbles"—contributed their version of Hugh Wiley's Saturday Evening Post stories in Pathé's series, *In and Out, Foul Play, High Toned, Darktown Blues, Darktown Follies, Black Narcissus, Honest Crooks,* and others. The plots hung on threats of jail, "high-yaller mamas," and other stock situations. But they also included the efforts of the pair to get jobs in the office of a booker, to thwart thieves, to win a wrestling match with "a high-hat Jamaica Negro" while smashing baggage on the Memphis run—all interlarded with flash-dancing and singing. Effectively they had, by their presence, imposed black themes and situations on the white man's screen. Other shorts featured both commercial and jazz music, rendered by black bands. Possibly the implied segregation of the situations, threatening no one, allowed white reviewers to accept blacks on the screen. The trades, despite an occasional barbed complaint "that the lines spoken by the colored boys are sometimes lost because of the natural sing-song delivery that is typical of the race," found them "pleasing" with "plenty of pep" and "sure to get response from any audience," thus rejecting the conventional view that black pictures would not sell.[21]

The right wing of the trend depicted life in the Old South as a passive, crooning accommodation to slavery. Tiffany released one-reelers featuring the Forbes Randolph Kentucky Jubilee Singers, such as *Slave Days,* which was "for lovers of real darky melodies." But the trades noticed they offered "nothing particularly new with the usual old Southern cabin setting, and the black boys harmonizing outside the door." One of them, *Cotton Pickin' Days,* opens on a wide-shot vignette masked by foliage; cabins and rough fences appear in the middle distance; crooning field hands are heard over all; cut to a cabin interior and a boy with his dog; another cut to a medium-shot stagey exterior, all hands around the fire crooning; a placid mule frames the right edge; a child pouts in the arms of its black mammy. With the scene established, the cutaways are to the Forbes Randolph choir singing old favorites like "Give Me That Old Time Religion," "Camptown Races," and "Way Down Upon the Swanee River." The harmony was more barbershop than black Baptist shout, and the total effect was barren of strong black imagery.[22]

The trades were especially ecstatic over Jules Bledsoe and other black performers. Columbia ad copy stressed Bledsoe's credentials as a performer on the stage in *Deep River* and *In Abraham's Bosom.* Bledsoe, whose booming voice had earned him the role of Joe in the Broadway production of *Showboat,* was one of several performers whose style lent itself to the most old-fashioned themes. He did shorts for

Columbia with a lack of spirit that become customary in the most conservative examples of the genre, yet the white reviewers liked his singing of "Old Man Trouble" and "Wadin' in the Water" and praised his work "as only a negro could sing it, and probably only Bledsoe among negroes."[23]

The difference between the style and flair of the conservative and the contemporary shorts is perhaps no more than quixotic. But one distinction may be found in their scripting and working conditions. The old-fashioned themes seem more carefully staged, more tightly directed, and possibly more formally scripted. On the other hand, the more urbane themes occur in more freewheeling productions, into which, therefore, blacks might inject more of themselves. In some cases they were lifted directly from old black revues.

If shorts indeed took their black atmosphere from the gaps in the thin scripts that allowed blacks to improvise, then Vitagraph's script for Miller and Lyles's *Harlem Knights* was a model case, for it ran on for only two paragraphs, at least in its copyright version. Their *Midnight Lodge* (1930) also allowed nuances of Negro life to come into play. The barely sketched ambience must have been fleshed out by the blacks on the set. The establishing shot opens on the meeting of a black lodge as the members sing "Get on Board Little Children," followed by the ladies of Mt. Nebo Baptist Church singing, "There is No Hiding Place," after which a wispy plot trails, no more than a lame burlesque joke really, in which the treasurer wishes himself struck down if he is lying about the theft of the lodge funds. In like fashion, later titles reflected the same casual scripting, each one admitting the possibility of a larger black contribution—ad lib and perhaps unconscious.[24]

By 1932 the *Melody Makers* series joined the ranks of the conservative shorts by using Stephen Foster's works as background for shots of the humble blackfolk whose "cares and joys" he had recorded. Instead of a freewheeling romp through a jazz piece, a narrator intones over the humming blacks, "Everywhere the darkies gather, nay whitefolk too. . . ." The unbearable acting and stereotyping from an earlier day crushed even the spark of sentiment that had made Foster worthwhile. The whites constantly went "to the quarter" in order to listen to the slaves as "My Old Kentucky Home," "Old Black Joe," and "Oh Susannah" spilled forth. Among the entire black segment of company only Frank Wilson received an acting credit.[25]

As long as shorts survived, like a dull thread running through a bolt of cloth, the antebellum crooning darkies perpetuated the Southern stereotype. If this style had been the only one generated by the shorts, the genre would have been a waste of film. But a more urbane black musical tradition ran parallel to the old Southern images. One of the most striking, for its rarity alone, was *After Leben* (1929), which featured James Barton, the veteran white actor who had led a kind of double life as a vernacular jazz dancer from whom Bill Robinson supposedly learned "his stuff." In front of a cabaret set and a poorly blocked audience Barton teaches a group of lindy hoppers how to dance and justifies his high reputation among critics with a final delicate and disciplined rubberlegs routine. Because of Barton's virtuosity the black contribution was minimized; nevertheless the dance routines were pioneering efforts.[26]

The best of the early black shorts were those that sketched the urban scene, or at least stylized it in musical terms. As the new Negro emerged on the musical screen the old types became more difficult to contain. The old Southern levee scenes soon gave way to more and more jazzy urban blacks. In the short run, the trend was at its most noisily evident in animated cartoons, perhaps because the sketched figures were no more than surreal surrogates for human figures. Replacing the old Southern pastoral motifs and their black props were new forms which allowed the ambiguity of the "good-bad nigger" to seep through the fissures left by the crumbling of the old types. For example, Louis Armstrong appeared in Paramount's *I'll Be Glad When You're Dead, You Rascal, You* (1932) as a skin-clad half-animated figure in hot pursuit of "Betty Boop," an erotic cartoon version of the twenties flapper. The lyrics of the song tell a lurid tale of a friend who has moved into Louis's apartment and taken possession of his wife and his gin. But the figures on the screen belie the song by having Louis as a jungle man fly through the air, singing and blowing choruses on his trumpet while pursuing the tiny, fragile, white figure of Boop. Armstrong, whose career rested firmly on the two props of musical genius and the ability to get along with whites, came across as a "good-bad nigger," singing about a lecherous friend while ambivalently pursuing the cartoon figure of a white woman.[27] In a similar cartoon of the same vintage Cab Calloway is seen as a physical reality, while Boop again appears as a cartoon. Calloway, backed by his own orchestra, sings the title song, "Minnie the Moocher"—hardly a term a flashy Negro male would use toward a white woman in real American life. The ominous black presence is sharpened even more because Boop has a companion, Bimbo, a mindless, doglike character, clearly black; so even if she escapes the reality of Calloway, whose band is intercut rhythmically with the cartoon, she is accompanied by the ambiguous sexual-racial presence of Bimbo (then a slang term for prostitute). As late as 1938 Betty Boop's animated figure still appeared with Negro actors in varying predicaments of muted sexual aggression. It was common to fill programs with shorts, so an extensive audience, largely white, must have seen the surrogate blacks who pursued Boop.[28]

Unfortunately for their quality the black animated images suffered when they were removed from a musical idiom. *Felix the Cat*, the *Out of the Inkwell* series, Walter Lantz's *Uncle Tom's Cabin*, and others merely traded on burlesques and stylizations of the oldest forms of Southern black depictions.[29] Others exploited connections with or similarities to already derivative materials like *Amos 'n' Andy's Wrasslin' Match*, an animated cartoon in silhouette, or their imitators, Pete and Repeat, in *Seven 'n' Eleven*, a one-reeler about two hobos who capture a convict. Still others milked laughs from parodies of spirituals or of the sunny South—"mammyland," as it was called—or exaggerated the shuffling, splay-footed maids in striped stockings who were nemesis to MGM's devilish mice, Tom and Jerry, or merely played the reassuring Mills Brothers' voices over a bouncing ball. The mundane, easy normality of it all made sharply barbed racial pejorative unnecessary, so the cannibals and their razors pursuing Tom and Jerry in MGM's *Jungle Jam* were rare. The most famous and in some ways the most typical was Walt Disney's *Who Killed Cock Robin?* (1935), which opened at Radio City Music Hall billed equally with Robeson's *Sanders of the River*. Its color, animation, and musical style earned it a place on the National Board of Review list of ten best films. The colorful twist on the nursery rhyme was larded with satires of the famous, including Stepin Fetchit, who appeared as a brown figure suspected of the murder and manhandled by two cops in the form of glowering blackbirds. But like most cartoons its quality depended upon caricature of black *life* rather than of the mere physical figure as in cartoon of white celebrities. Unfortunately for their Afro-American critics they persisted long into the forties and enjoyed a revival during the war when a Hungarian animator, George Pal, adapted the Southern motifs to a new technique of employing puppets—"Puppetoons," he called them—for animation sequences. His *Jasper* series prevailed over Negro protests and survived on the strength of its winsome pickaninny, Jasper, his protective mammy, and her enemies, a hustling black scarecrow and his wisecracking partner in crime, a glib crow, who devote their days to filching and grifting watermelons and pies.[30] Together, they strode through a trail of venal deacons, ghosts, dialects, grins, and song.

But despite their survival powers, the cartoons were only a minor thread of black culture in shorts. Through the depression decade of the 1930s the musical shorts persisted as a strong black genre which featured the Mills Brothers, Don Redman and his orchestra, Cab Calloway, Louis Armstrong, Eddie South, Leon Abbey's orchestra from

France, Jimmie Lunceford, the Hall Johnson Choir, Duke Ellington, Ivie Anderson, Bessie Dudley, Ethel Waters, Chick Webb, Jimmy Mordecai, Noble Sissle and Eubie Blake, Cora La Redd, and dozens more. Their ultimate impact may have been only as a subliminal presence; nevertheless they helped reshape the black cinema image. The most cheaply done of the shorts still offered talented, cocky, prepossessing Negro figures to a white audience which until recently had been presented only with Southern stereotypes of black life.

At their best the black shorts said something of the malaise of blacks torn between life down home and in the city. One of the finest was Vitaphone's *Yamacraw* (1930). Murray Roth's direction, James P. Johnson's music, and Jimmy Mordecai's performance transformed the stuff of *Cotton Pickin' Days* into a real sketch of the black dilemma. The establishing shots open on a cheap silhouette of a cabin; the shot narrows to an old man smoking and a black earth-mother serenading a child; the shot pulls back to a cardboard cutout of the farm, distorted in the manner of the German expressionists; lovers clasp in anxiety over the man's decision to leave the farm for the city; shadowy hands reach up in mournful religious ecstasy; the lovers walk hand-in-hand down the hill, intercut with two-shots of their strong faces; a crane shot carries the viewer up as Mordecai sings "Yamacraw," hefts his suitcase, and departs for a city made stark and angular by the darkened sets; a nappy-headed dancing girl picks him up in a whirling montage; caught up in the jangle of the metropolis, he returns her embrace, but soon looks to the country and the cabin in a ritual reenactment of what many urban Negroes felt about their hard journey to the city. *Film Daily* shed its professional reserve and pronounced it a "jazz symphony of Negro life that is arresting in movement as well as dramatic in idea."[31]

Such musical fables erratically reached for more than they could grasp, but the best of them managed to carry bits of black life and character like flecks of lint on their shoulders. Even though direction was in the white hands of pedestrian hacks such as Roy Mack and Joseph Henabery, they nonetheless were suffused with a black ambience because the loosely scripted vignettes depended in varying degree on black improvisation. Mack ruined *Smash Your Baggage* (1932) with malapropism and mannerisms, requiring trumpeter Roy Eldridge to point his instrument upward in phony ecstasy, a gesture he held in contempt. Yet, in spite of Mack's interference, the picture caught the frenzy of busy redcaps in Grand Central and their tight-knit fraternity. When the treasurer of the Brotherhood loses funds at dice the thin plot provides the excuse for the driving beat, the flash dancing of jiving jitterbugs, and a rubberlegs routine led by a top-hatted hoofer—the

The best short films used not only black players such as Fredi Washington, here in the tragic *Black and Tan* (© RKO Productions, Inc.), but black music such as Duke Ellington's. Ellington stands over her with director Dudley Murphy and novelist Carl Van Vechten. (GEH)

performers in the climactic benefit-revue. The busy short provided gigs for a half-dozen usually segregated black acts.[32]

When contrived premises and clumsy settings marred the shorts, their music still carried them. *That's the Spirit* (1932) placed the veteran Flournoy Miller and Mantan Moreland in a ghostly pawnshop as nightwatchmen, with Miller in white lips and whiney accents, and Moreland literally leaping out of his shoes. Both of them had often either parodied the old folk beliefs in witchery and voodoo, but usually in the noisy privacy of ghetto theaters where audiences laughed with knowing gusto. But organized Negroes bristled because in white theaters they would be taken not as stock figures of black burlesque but as reportage. Therefore such movies mollified black critics only so long as they provided an excuse for the music. In this case, Noble Sissle redeemed the film with "Tiger Rag" and "St. Louis Blues," punctuated with scat dancing that seemed to astonish the bandleader himself.[33]

Another example of the way in which black presence often prevailed over white direction and writing was Henabery's *Barbershop Blues* (1932). It sketched the camaraderie of a black barbershop, accented by the flash dancing of the Nicholas Brothers to the beat of Claude Hopkins's band, well-chosen Harlem exteriors, hustlers pushing sweepstakes tickets, and the rhythmic rag-snapping of the Nicholases as bootblacks. The thin plot ends with a bright new shop won on a bet. "Some hot music" is the only script note on the finale, yet the band uses the three words as an excuse to tear into "Mystic Moon," "St. Louis Blues," "Trees," "Nagasaki," and "Loveless Love."[34] Sometimes complex facts of Afro-American life were muddled or distorted, although often without spoiling the musical sets. In *A Rhapsody in Black and Blue* (1932), for example, the matriarchy that rose as a function of male unemployment and the blues sounds of the "race records" were made to seem mutual enemies. Sidney Easton and Victoria Spivey played an out-of-work husband and an overbearing wife. She resents his hanging about the house, beating time to his records, and at last at the height of a spat she skulls him with a mop handle. His counter-aggression is in his unconscious fog, where Louis Armstrong in royal robes blows a strong reprise of his Betty Boop short. Easton's wife, frustrated because he has shut her out of his fantasy, ends the routine by smashing his record—his machismo—over his head.[35]

Good and bad, the shorts lasted until the 1940s, at their worst as plotless vaudeville fillers which traded on the fad for "nut jazz" such as Cab Calloway's zany, mock-abandoned scat songs like "Hi De Ho," and at their best as legendary visions to which some famous artists had given a few moments of song and dance. If in most cases jazz on film proved too static unless redeemed by rhythmic cutting, once in a while a bright one like Vitaphone's *Black Network* (1936) shone through the strictures of the film medium. It featured Nina Mae McKinney in her declining years and the Nicholas Brothers ascending in a neat story of blacks who try to create a radio show. Another, *The Symphony in Black* (1935), acquired a mythic aura because of its arty lighting, symphonic style, an appearance by the tragic Billie Holiday, and a turn by Earl "Snakehips" Tucker. Nearly all great black performers appeared in them: Ethel Waters in *Bubbling Over*, Sissle and Blake in *Pie, Pie, Blackbird*, the Hall Johnson choir in *Syncopation Sermon*, Bill Robinson, Dusty Fletcher, and Muriel Rahn in *King for a Day*, Adelaide Hall in *The All-Colored Vaudeville Show*, Calloway in *Hi De Ho*, and Eunice Wilson in *Dixieland Jamboree*. Toward the end of the cycle the shorts broadened to include overseas black culture, at least in the work of Katharine Dunham, a lithe dancer who couched her show business career in scholarly terms. In 1940 she did *Carnival in Rhythm*, a celebration of Afro-Cuban tempi, with the black modern dancers Archie Savage and Talley Beatty.[36]

Finally, on the verge of World War II, Afro-Americans lost their most favorable opportunity to dominate short film production. Fritz Pollard, the black football All-American from Brown University, fronted for a new piece of hardware that might have revived musical film as a means of black expression. "Soundies" or "Phonovision"—the trade names varied—was a system of film loops back-projected on a jukebox screen that required a comparatively small investment, which Pollard might have marshalled. But many exhibitors, fearing the competition, "militantly opposed" the process, and it had only a brief vogue. "The ofays," recalled Pollard, acquired the few black holdings so that all that remained was an undistributed pile of finely honed jazz numbers in front of shoddy drops. In one of them Fats Waller sits, hatbrim up, noodling a cadenced "Yeah, yeah, the joint is jumpin'" as backup to a reed-slim dancer with processed hair and a bottle on his hip. In others he ripped through his trademarks "Ain't Misbehavin'," "Honeysuckle Rose," and "Your Feet's too Big," always under a widebrimmed hat and flanked by sleek "foxes" in bare midriff or satin. In another Louis Armstrong blew out his favorites "Shine" and "I'll be Glad When You're Dead." Mickey O'Daniel tore through a driving dance introduced by Fetchit in a striped zootsuit. Dorothy Dandridge did a parody of Josephine Baker. Fat, raspy Jimmy Rushing sang a gritty "Take Me Back, Baby" in front of Count Basie's band. Ellington relaxed with a drink and a cigarette while Ivie Anderson sat in a windowsill doing "I Got It Bad and That Ain't Good." But the false ring of a "happy Harlem" and the poor production values spoiled spontaneity and left the blacks in the cold again.[37]

In the end, the great surge of Afro-Americans into short films subsided and the bubbling optimism of the early days of sound film dissipated. The work of bringing Negroes to the screen was put into the hands of Vitaphone's dance director, Roy Mack, who had never done a complete movie, and Joseph Henabery, who had a long, dull career that ended in the jerry-built Columbia studio. As a result, black shorts received scant acclaim, awards, or measurable audience attention. Even when audiences enjoyed them, there was always the threat that Negro style might, in the wrong hands, lapse into racist cliché. They became a haven for the waning stars like Nina Mae McKinney and Stepin Fetchit. On the one hand critics ignored them; on the other, black audiences seemed to find little of substance under their musical surfaces, at least in comparison with the Hollywood feature films.

The achievement of the shorts may be compared to the precious art of the tap dancer. Tap dancing has disappeared from the jazz scene, reappearing only in stunted form as a sweaty "single" in the middle segment of a television revue, just before the second commercial. Billie Holiday made a short once, a good one—and yet she herself barely remembered it. "It gave me a chance to sing a song—a real weird and pretty blues number," she recalled. "That was the good thing about the part." But afterward, nothing. "I don't know if anybody else saw it, but we never did. It was just a short subject, something they filled in with when they couldn't get Mickey Mouse. We'd have had to hire a private detective to find out where the hell it was playing."[38]

Chapter Ten

BLACK MUSIC
WHITE MOVIES

In 1928 MGM and Fox started production on a line of musical feature films that paralleled the development of the shorts, with the exception that the feature films attempted to reach beyond mere recording of Negro show business achievements so as to depict a sensitively stylized, densely packed Afro-American social order. The two studios departed from custom with two well-mounted all-black celebrations of life, *Hearts in Dixie* and *Hallelujah!*, each of which in its way was an artful, humane depiction of black Southern life and its spoilage by urbanization. These attempts to render black life on the screen increased white awareness of its depths. At their best they cast blacks in tragic terms, and at their least, in winsome fables. In black circles, especially among intellectuals, the films drew forth some of the first forthright principles of black cinema aesthetics, for they helped, through the polarization of this opinion, to define the nature of the black role in movies.

If the films failed to generate a crackling string of bright successors, they nevertheless thrust themselves upon the attention of black and white critics so forcefully that thereafter their memory survived as a litmus test of the quality, and even progress, of black cinema imagery. In fact, it might be argued that they once and for all dragged serious black critics away from the "race movies" and toward Hollywood as the final source of black aesthetic redemption. Early on, some black intellectuals had labeled as false friends of Afro-America those whites who persisted in distributing "race movies," believing they demeaned the entire black world by taking them for a race of easily gulled bumpkins.

The black themes started slowly, held back by studio conservatism, the burden of new investment in sound equipment, and the fear of economic depression. But a white Texan with the improbable name of King Vidor and an impressive list of films to his credit had always "nurtured a secret hope" to bring Negro life to the screen. "The sincerity and fervor of their religious expression intrigued me, as did the honest simplicity of their sexual drives," he thought. "In many instances the intermingling of these two activities seemed to offer strikingly dramatic content." But before 1928, when they heard rumors of a similar picture in the works at Fox, the MGM executives had always waved him aside. Then they looked more closely at his lists of striking scenes—his river baptisms, cadenced preachers, banjos, country dancing, and urban blues. Even so, Vidor bypassed the studio when he returned from a European vacation and went directly to Nicholas Schenck, chairman of the board of Loew's, MGM's parent company. And despite his zeal and his credentials the studio heads extracted a promise from Vidor to match their investment with a piece of his own salary.[1]

From the very beginning the studio involved a few blacks in the production. The race press regularly received and printed releases designed, as never before, for its special readers. To enrich Vidor's vision of Southern Negroes, MGM assigned Harold Garrison, their black major domo, as assistant director. And Vidor's earliest planning included consultations with James Weldon Johnson, then executive secretary of the NAACP.[2] Gradually the white press as well took up the black theme in their trade papers, annuals, and gossip columns.

Meanwhile at Fox *Hearts in Dixie* matured from a proposed two-reeler, William Fox's sentimental tribute to the Southland, into a full-length feature. Winfield ("Winnie") Sheehan had been given the routine assignment, but upon seeing the impressive rough cuts he asked the studio for a story that would hold the vibrant music; whereupon they commissioned a script "treatment" from Walter Weems, an old Southern minstrel man. Next they asked the New York office to comb Harlem—the stock Hollywood solution to a black casting problem—for a big black voice to carry the developing film.[3]

Having started first, Fox leapt ahead. Even before they found a big name they began their shooting schedule. At first they had auditioned Charles Gilpin, in spite of his troubles on the set of Universal's *Uncle Tom's Cabin*, but soon his "carelessness and crankiness" disenchanted them. His successor, George Reed, lacked the requisite persona and failed to generate a following of black fans, perhaps because he had seemed a part of a plot to dump the more outspoken Gilpin. Finally, Sheehan literally bumped into his star, or, more precisely, brushed him with his car fender at the studio gates where Clarence Muse, the veteran of the Lafayette Players, had been hanging about waiting for a cattle call. Muse's deep baritone won the role of Nappus over the only other candidate, Tony Lucas, the brother of old Sam Lucas.[4]

The result was a great leap forward for Sheehan's project. By the summer of 1928 he had shut the doors to the sound stages, thus muffling gossip about the progress of the "Dixie" picture. Inside the studio gates the mood and tone of the picture took on a racial logic as inexorable as a Greek tragedy, an extension of Griffith's old Manichean good-bad sides of the Negro psyche. Having signed Muse as the dignified Nappus, Sheehan and Paul Sloane, the director, turned to one of their favorite black players, the veteran Stepin Fetchit, for the tragicomic Gummy. Perhaps they selected him because of an ad he took in a trade paper offering himself as "a convincing, unexaggerated original or modern negro . . . that will meet the approval of the Board of Censorship and the patrons of the North and South," a role he shaped on the road in "southern towns that wouldn't allow other members of his race to enter the town."

By the early days of 1929 the film had grown from a two-reel "sausage" into Fox's major production for the year—a self-conscious attempt to revolutionize American attitudes toward the Negro. The unstated ambitions of all the black performers in the shorts seemed to come together in one grand picture. The opening graphics and mats timidly avoided mention of Negroes; but soon a full page ad appeared in *Variety*, a "mammy" selling flapjacks turned up in a première theater lobby, and five stills graced a single page of the Sunday *New York Times*. Generally, however, the image of the film remained muted, and its distributors made few extravagant claims for it. Even in the black press, perhaps because the ad men were unsure of their ground or because they had no idea whether they had captured an aesthetic prize or had slandered Negroes, the ads hinted at no social message and claimed only a faithful rendering of "the old songs and spirituals," a bit of comedy and dance, "and a tear or two."[5]

When *Hearts in Dixie* opened early in the spring it far exceeded the hesitant claims of the advertisements. Indeed, it was among the best feature-film treatments of Afro-Americans precisely because it filtered the human dimension of Southern Negro life through the flawed prisms of Weems's script, the direction of Paul Sloane, and the choreography of Fanchon and Marco, a team of ex-vaudevillians and dance entrepreneurs. Thus, although the surface data seemed to exemplify Southern white norms of racial segregation, the superiority of white science over

The best sound films tried to capture a bit of black life as in *Hearts in Dixie*
(© Fox Film Corp.). (The State Historical Society of Wisconsin)

black folk wisdom, and the justified place that blacks held on the bottom rung of life, the film still clearly deviated from old ways. Clarence
Muse, the best evidence, gave Nappus a quiet patriarchal dignity—
floridly so at times—which emerged from his inner values rather than
from an Uncle Remus's conventional native wit. Even Gummy, Fetchit's lazy Negro, is touched with tragedy and spirit as well as buffoon-
ery. And most important of all, dramatic conflict flows from a situation
in which blacks have a clear investment so that the characters strain
against circumstance, grow in self knowledge, and positively alter their
group identity. Thus in the thick of Southern black life action flows
from black ambition, not white instigation.

The plot of *Hearts in Dixie* was simple: a tale of old Nappus, a black
tenant who scratches a meagre living from worn soil; his daughter
Chloe, wife to shiftless Gummy; and their two children, Chiquapin and
Trailia. The prologue focuses on the universal problem of getting a
living as the A. C. Bilbrew Choir sings "This Cotton Wants Pickin' "
over the establishing shots of a cotton field. The slow rhythm of the

cotton delta is set against the cadence of black picking and chopping.
The work is shared and is relieved by song and chant in gray, rough
sets that make real the oppressive life. The blacks are not happy but
merely well-worn into the routine. At the end of the day the chiaroscuro scene and the jazzy beat of dance in the sand flats provide release from the grind. Fetchit himself bursts the bonds of his stock role
and makes the lazy Gummy come alive in a fluid sand dance. A crane
shot sweeps the crowded scene. A cut carries into the cabin where
beautiful, careworn Chloe sees to the children. She sleeps a bit and
dreams of a black cat, an omen that brings swamp fever to her and to
Trailia, forcing Nappus to choose between the white doctor or the
conjure woman. In rich lights and darks with striking panache he persuades the doctor, the film's only white, to come to the cabin. Fore-
shadowed by a dance-ritual, Nappus and the doctor come upon a voodoo rite that Gummy has allowed to be chanted over his dying family.
Gummy slumps in a grief that Fetchit's fans might have found surprising in him. Later he began to settle into his comic rut as his roving eye
picks out a new wife who baits him with her high tolerance of his laziness, a gift she withdraws once they are married. Even then, Fetchit's
Southern Negro is well used as a metaphor for the defeated Southern
black male, a fate Nappus hopes to spare his surviving grandson.
Gummy remains the ruined male unable to work in his own interest
except under the lash of his new wife's tongue. Meanwhile Nappus is
driven to sell his possessions in order to send his grandson northward to
study medicine so he can return to aid his people.

Only a few false notes sound. Nappus's crisply trained voice rattles
against Gummy's back-country drawl. The Negroes rest a little easy
under their burdens. The voodoo woman is a mere patsy for the white
doctor's arts to expose. Gummy grows too fast from a slow-moving
plausible Southerner into a cardboard, shuffling marplot. Still, the picture is faithful to its ambience within the limits of Weems's imagination, and Bernice Pilot, Zack Williams, Bilbrew, and the rest give intelligence and craft to their roles.[6]

The picture had a shattering impact. Audiences and critics hailed it
as the leading edge of change. The modest two-reeler had become a
celebrity and a reason for carrying on the trend started with the black
shorts, MGM's *Trader Horn,* and a few other titles. Every innovator
took heart; every hack took notes. The "Dixies" had arrived and altered the black face of moviemaking in Hollywood.

The critical reception for *Hearts in Dixie* was overwhelming. The
toughest black writers, those with knee-jerk hostile reactions to *any*
white production, cast off reserve and praised it. When the NAACP
held back, a proud cast member needled their timidity. The picture

Trader Horn (© Metro-Goldwyn-Mayer Distributing Corp.) enriched the jungle film genre with the quiet presence of Mutia Omooloo who shared the screen with Harry Carey and Duncan Renaldo at the height of the rage for black musicals. (Nederlands Filmmuseum)

spoke to a spectrum of racial opinion, including blacks to whom it was an oasis in a racist desert and liberals who thought its sometimes saccharine empathy a promise of better days for the benighted. *Whom* they praised revealed *what* they believed. Mordaunt Hall, the *New York Times* critic, for example, singled out Fetchit as the leading gatherer of applause and laughter; while the *Amsterdam News* blessed Muse for his forebearance, which "far excels the low comedy" of Fetchit. His Nappus was a "sterling work" pressed from the mold of Booker T. Washington that succeeded "in putting over the moral that nothing the colored man has was obtained without hard work."[7]

Nevertheless neither black nor white viewers took notice of the missing ingredient in the dramatic conflict—the oppressive system that had put the blacks on the bottom rail. But that would have been asking too much. For Hall of the *Times*, for example, it was enough that the film "shows how the talking picture has produced opportunities for people to whom the whole matter of the cinema is an untrodden field." Blacks would probably have agreed. Indeed, that was the sense of Muse's attack on the NAACP. He reminded them that *Hearts in Dixie* was to be a cheap two-reel experiment to determine whether the differing tastes of blacks and whites could find a common ground. "This is a game we must build ourselves into," he claimed as he asked blacks to be "enthused" enough to demonstrate the box office power that would result in their "heading productions."[8]

Outside of New York the white press joined in the praise, although for different reasons. Llewellyn Miller of *The Los Angeles Examiner* was touched only by Fetchit's ability to evoke Negroes and "their simplicity, their love of a good time." Indeed, for every paper that praised "understanding presentations of their problems" set against "flashes of their joys and ambitions" there was another paper that found only "the entire colored race, lighthearted, ready with its songs, dances and laughter." In between were the neutralists who wished it well for its "double novelty of Negro players and movietone which makes its appeal," or as one critic wrote, its "dearth of pseudo-Nordic coating."[9]

Opposition to the picture was rare. Walter White of the NAACP stood apart and privately looked to Europe for eventual respite from racist movies. The small, white left-wing centering in the editorial staff of *Close-Up* saw no essential change in the ancient stereotypes. The critic for the black *Chicago Whip*, who had never surrendered the black right to regard white enterprise with suspicion, found it diverting, and preferred Fetchit's bravura moués to Muse's "overacting." His friendly opinion was not altered by the nagging fret in the back of his mind "that the picture, in the cotton scenes and acted in the southern dialect and customs was degrading."[10]

So in the spring of 1929 *Hearts in Dixie* repeated for a broader appreciative audience the lesson of the black two-reelers. A strong black presence, within the limits imposed by coexistence with a powerful majority, could affect the art of the cinema in spite of a script written in traditional Southern racial metaphor. The question remained as to whether the momentum could be sustained in the face of scarce material, indifferent audiences, uncomprehending studios, and the strength of other popular movie cycles. Already the power of two-reelers burned out for lack of thrust and for lack of persistent black inspiration.

The vehicle that would eventually carry the black imagery needed the additional baggage of a dense urban black metaphor. Even in *Hearts in Dixie* the denouement came with Nappus's sure knowledge that the way out was through the lore of the city to which he sends Chiquapin. Yet the spirit of *Hearts in Dixie* was missing in following "problem" pictures. Within two years Muse appeared in *Dirigible* for his friend, Frank Capra, as a servant on the fringes of a grand white enterprise of sailing a dirigible over the South Pole. Later he appeared in a Warner Brothers' production of Michael Curtiz's *Cabin in the Cotton*, an evasive indictment of the exploitation of sharecroppers. Despite a hint of interracial cooperation against the planters, Muse's strong black man was hampered by blindness, and he seemed shrunken compared to the resolute white croppers.[11]

Then King Vidor's *Hallelujah!* followed *Hearts in Dixie* and outdid it in deep-felt sensitivity for Negro life. By looking deeper into American racial arrangements, including the process of urban migration, it also exposed greater tension and hostility. The timid secrecy of *Hearts in Dixie* gave way to splashy preproduction news releases concerning the progress of *Hallelujah!* And yet Vidor kept it close to his original ambitions, at least as far as studio and black community pressure would allow. In the black press there was general support for the MGM project, less on its merits than on their assumption that the best qualities of *Hearts in Dixie* would be improved in a second seemingly sincere attempt.

Although Vidor could not beat Fox into release, he at least had won his three-year battle to make a picture based on "his own observations in Texas and elsewhere of the everyday life of the Negro." And if it had been knowledge of Fox's Negro project that had spurred MGM to action, then at least Vidor at a single stroke had overcome the studio opinion that "a picture like that will attract too many Negroes to the theatres, and the whites will stay away," and had dampened down trade paper opinion that the movie would be no more than oppressive, unappealing, revenue-stifling social propaganda.[12]

Moreover, Vidor brought yet another quality to his project: he knew enough of Southern black life to realize his ignorance. So in addition to the MGM writer Wanda Tuchock, who knew nothing of blacks, he also took on Harold Garrison, a black employee of the studio who was given the title of "assistant director," at least in the releases to the Negro press. With Garrison in tow, even if their lines of observation of Negro life curved from different approaches, they were at least tangential. Together they would tell the rich story of the pristine Southern Negro rather than "the Negro who apes the white man." And in so doing they would go into the country and shoot its beauty and place the black man in it. Only then could Vidor reach into the contrasts of the black city where *Hearts in Dixie* had averted its eyes. Only there would they find the deep sources of conflict in the black soul under the layers of white man's civilization where even "the polished Negro . . . possesses, under the surface, the rhythm and abandon, the love song and laughter of those in a primitive state."[13]

If such a premise seemed doomed to racist distortion, blacks bided their time, in part because of Vidor's energetic campaign to recruit authentic types in the manner of the Soviet director, Sergei Eisenstein,

Hallelujah!'s black assistant director, Harold Garrison, in cap on left.
(Wanda Tuchock collection)

and in part because *Hearts in Dixie* had raised slightly their hopes for
good works from Hollywood. If anything, they feared for Hollywood's will to produce *Hallelujah!* rather than whether they could
overcome Vidor's tunnel vision of black Texas life. Black performers,
indeed, fought each other for the good roles in the brief season of
Northern city tryouts. After Vidor's press releases, in which he cast
himself as a sympathetic Southern observer who had "a great feeling
for the black people," Negroes hurried from New York and Chicago
nightclubs, from the ranks of black workers, and from "on the street"
to auditions. "FILM FAME BECKONS AND HARLEM IS AGOG," the *Times*
reported.[14]

Trailing *Hearts in Dixie* by several months, Vidor at last finished
casting and started up production in the late summer of 1928. If artless
and overt racial stereotyping still cast a pall over the project, it was because of the clichés of the press agents rather than because of Vidor's
idea. Daniel Haynes, the male lead, had earned a diploma from an élite
Negro college, but the press flacks reported only his ability to register
primitive religious ecstasy, an apparent consequence of his life as "an
itinerant preacher." The women in the cast, whether trained actresses

or vaudeville troupers, were described as "dusky belles," and were characterized, like Nina Mae McKinney, as "a jungle Lorelei," or like the luckless Honey Brown, who eventually took sick, as a "colored Clara Bow." The recruiting of Harry Gray revealed the cool eye with which some black critics observed the antics. In the white press the patriarchal Gray was called "Dad" and reported to have been a North Carolina slave "discovered" either on the street in New York or preaching in a Chicago church. But to the blacks on the *Tatler* he was a fool who "struts around Harlem in a plug hat and cutaway coat reminiscent of the days when minstrelsy was in flower."[15]

Nevertheless, as the company moved southward to Memphis for location shots, they undermined the old black style as well as Southern etiquette. Several years earlier on a Mississippi location trip actress Mary Astor learned first-hand of white racial aggression in a black church when a white Mississippian, in courtly deference to her, shouted to a pew of Negroes: "Move ovah theah, niggah." But in 1928 Honey

The black craftsmen of *Hallelujah!* (© Metro-Goldwyn-Mayer Distributing Corp.). (Wanda Tuchock collection)

Brown, with Wanda Tuchock in tow, barged right into a department store and began trying on clothes. Even though back in the antique air of the Peabody Hotel she rode the freight elevator, she had shaken the local norms. The *Memphis Commercial Appeal* went further in encouraging the project by attacking Eugene O'Neill and Vachel Lindsay's "questionable theory" of black atavism in their *Emperor Jones* and *The Congo*. "The southern negro cannot go backward," an editorialist argued, because "the Afro-American" was a newly minted creature moving away from primitivism. Furthermore, the paper insisted, calling on the evangelist Billy Sunday as witness, black theology was spiritually richer than "impersonal" white Christianity. The Southern reporters went so far as to forgive breaches of racial etiquette on rural locations in Hernando and across the river in Arkansas because Vidor and the blacks were Southerners bent on truly capturing "the negro living in the environment that he is accustomed to and loves so well." Although Vidor's deference to his black advisers, Harold Garrison and the local preachers whose flocks he used, rattled white onlookers, usually they were delightedly bemused rather than outraged, as on the day he gave Fanny Belle DeKnight her cue by calling her "Madame."[16]

In fact, the honest white Southern gawkers in their way seemed more forthright than the Hollywood whites who presumably knew better but ambivalently embraced popular racism from casual ignorance and mental laziness. The same columnists who praised Vidor for his effort to carry Negro life beyond "Carl Van Vechten's select literary circles" by making a Southern black *Nanook of the North* saw the cast on the set as no more than a motley of blacks "clustered about the card tables, gambling, crap-shooting, losing, winning, calling drawly greetings to one another, shuffling nervous dancing feet between scenes." To Hearst's Louella Parsons they were:

> Dusky belles, tall young black-skinned boys, plump mammies and pickaninnies . . . swarming about the Metro-Goldwyn-Mayer lot, giving it the appearance of a California Harlem, or a real "down south" plantation.[17]

Back in Hollywood Afro-American culture touched the picture in a final crucial step after hiring Garrison, casting in the ghettos, hearing black Southern counsel, and observing life under the eye of the white South. Neither technology nor studio executives permitted effective sound recording on location. This meant every foot of film of the flats of Ten Mile Bayou, the upper reaches of the Yazoo Delta, and the dirty redbrick ribbon of Beale Street needed to be cut to match sound back in Hollywood. Irving Thalberg felt a commitment to the picture not only as proof that music could carry a narrative but as a prestige picture whose losses MGM would write off as its contribution to cinema art. He even financed keeping the company assembled for retakes. Yet, except for the addition of an Irving Berlin song, he released it as Vidor wished. Moreover Vidor had been encouraged to develop his pastoral setting through the use of painterly composition of frames and distortion of sound in the manner of the German expressionists. Music, then, formed the whorl that held them fast to the same center. Every foot of film would be "synched" to black music. On location a metronome kept time for, say, a pan shot of cotton pickers *and* the camerman shooting them, so the lens would fall on a singing face over which sound could be dubbed weeks later. It was as though a crew of whites learned to shoot and cut on the beat of black music or suffer an impossible chore later in the lab.

Even so, monstrous editing problems surfaced. There were no editing machines—"moviolas"—so they matched sound with motion through signals between projectionist and editor, marking the frames as they went. On wide shots and even medium shots they laboriously dubbed "wild sound," distorting crackling branches into cracks of doom, bird twitters into omens, puddles plopping underfoot into drumbeats. The strain unbalanced them. Vidor watched a berserk cutter hurl a reel against the unspliced strips hanging against the wall like a beaded curtain, and fall sobbing in the tangles of weeks of work. Black performance and music were wedded with Vidor's art and technical skill—to create the highest achievement yet in depicting black life within the strictures of the white man's movie colony.[18]

The strongest black objections would not be directed against the Southern sequences but against the studio-shot urban wickedness juxtaposed with rural piety. Here white stereotyping and black bourgeois outrage clanged together. Vidor's appreciation of Negro life extended only to its pristine rural forms. Wanda Tuchock had known only one Negro in her entire life in Colorado before moving to Southern California. Garrison, grateful for his job, would have said little to disabuse them of their notion of the life he knew so well. Daniel Haynes, Nina Mae McKinney, William Fountaine, and the others were troupers whose experience included not only the genteel bourgeois round of life but also tours in *Chocolate Dandies*, *Shuffle Along*, *Rang Tang*, *Africana*, and *Brownskin Models*. Together they created a shabby side of black urban life that affronted some organized blacks, as well as the black moviegoer who could tolerate stereotypes in the darkened privacy of the Apollo or the Alhambra where "there ain't nobody but us colored folks" but who vaguely resented such a production in the hands of white moviemakers *and* white audiences.[19]

Thus the unique movie that eventually opened simultaneously in Harlem and Midtown was a tangle of ambivalence, of black art, of white sense and white gaucherie, of producers' courage and exhibitors' timidity, of black praise and black damnation. It suffered not because it was bad, but because no one knew what to do with it. In the South shortsighted bookers predictably shied from it. In Chicago itself the big Balaban and Katz theater chain would not book it until after its long run at a little independent house.[20]

Hallelujah! opens on Zeke, a cotton tenant, taking the family crop to market, a sequence rich in the tone and shading of a rural South bound to the graying cottonlands through the muted rhythms of black religion. In town Zeke finds a harsh, cruel ghetto livened by the figure of bright-eyed, lazy-legged Chick, the dancehall hooker. She and her lover, Hot Shot, edge Zeke into a crap game, a steep loss, and a fight

A stylized celebration of black life in *Hallelujah!* (© Metro-Goldwyn-Mayer Distributing Corp.). (Author's collection)

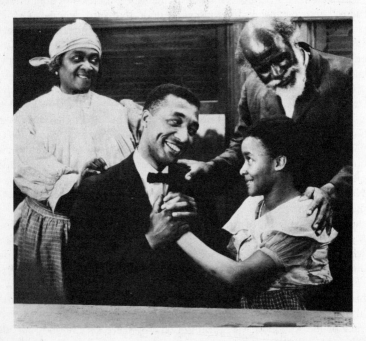

that ends with his brother's death. (Most of the shots in this section were studio interiors remote from black locations, and here blacks winced at Vidor's inability to tame the ghetto world to the artistic insight from which he had shaped Zeke's rural roots.)

In atonement for his brother's death Zeke becomes a preacher. Tall and lean with a commanding presence, he dominates revivals and meetings etched with angles and planes of light and shadow that point upward like a cubist's gothic window. Against the lights and darks, black hands reach and clutch in rhythm with the ancient music of the spirituals. In the heat of the moment of a mass baptism by a river dotted with the white-clad figures of pious black women even Chick is converted— in her fashion. The subliminal sexuality of emotional religion magnetizes Zeke, who deserts his country girl for Chick, with Hot Shot following in sullen jealousy. Chick, cramped by the country life, and confusing desire for Zeke with getting religion, resumes her old life until Zeke finds her with her gambler, harries them to Chick's death, and strangles the dandy-smooth Hot Shot, escaping amid the ominous crackling of brush and reeds of the swamps. The wild sound foreshadows Zeke's eventual capture and sentencing to a chain gang. In the end he returns to home, family, country girl, and rural roots.[21]

Critics everywhere, black and white, echoed praise while urban blacks showed vague unease. In New York Richard Watts found it "one of the most distinguished and exciting motion pictures ever made," and others agreed. The *Post* called it "truly great"; the *World*, "a daring departure from its timid predecessors." Elsewhere effusive praise was joined by occasional patronizing comments. Edwin Schallert of *The Los Angeles Times* thought it "barbaric, weird, fantastic" and "oddly fascinating and sometimes oddly repellent." Hearst's paper in Los Angeles printed Parsons's estimate that it was no more than a faithful recording of "the colored folk, [who were] curiously susceptible to religion." Pasadena, Detroit, Baltimore, Boston, Chicago, Portland— wherever it played critics grew hyperbolic. In Baltimore the reviewer in the staid Baltimore *Sun* chided local bookers for delaying its opening and running it at a tiny arthouse. Elsewhere in the South exhibitors outdid themselves in selling the picture. In Salisbury, North Carolina, Negro preachers and academics previewed it. Savannah showed it to civic leaders so as to disarm their hostility. Other towns used publicity stunts to insure its running without incident. The Louisville *Courier-Journal* asked readers to admire both the "natural" Negro and Haynes's "well-trained" voice. At its worst, white newspaper criticism focused on "the primitiveness of Africa and the comparative civilization of negro life along the Mississippi" or "the keen insight into the character of the old time plantation negro." The fan magazines *Screenland, Motion Picture*

Classic, Screen Secrets, and *Photoplay* weighed in with friendly feature stories. The middle-brow *Literary Digest* summed up the favorable criticism with an unpatronizing white recognition of Negro cultural uniqueness that was itself unique. Not only was Vidor's film "something new under the sun," but also a positive statement that "the Negro is as different from the rest of us as we are from the Russians, the Germans, or the French."[22]

Few white critics found fault with the picture, although *Variety* lost its usual glibness because its reviewers struck such opposing postures. In sum, it warned provincial bookers that *Hallelujah!* was part of the "popularization" of an urban tendency "to glorify the primitive negro life of the south and the emerging race consciousness and intellectual vigor of the colored people." It would therefore have dubious value, *Variety* argued, "for the everyday white person detached from the liberal movement that centers in New York City." Not that it was not a fine movie depiction of "simple," "primitive," and "supernatural" Negro life; it just would not sell tickets.[23] Then by year's end *Variety* came around by giving play to stories of box office grosses that "vindicated" courageous bookers. Only on the political wings did hostility run strong. The Marxist critic Harry Alan Potamkin found it a cheap gesture at evading black bourgeois criticism by maligning only the "lowly." And in England, where no American reader intruded, the conservative James Agate merely huffed in contempt. "Personally, I don't care if it took Mr. Vidor ten years to train these niggers; all I know is that ten minutes is all I can stand of nigger ecstasy," he wrote. "I am completely tired of expositions of the negro by whites."[24]

Negroes, on the other hand, were torn by the ambiguous social significance of *Hallelujah!* They knew too much. The external evidence surrounding the picture must have set them on edge: there had to be an angle. Blacks had already been divided by casting decisions that had left the losers embittered. They also knew that the black Congressman Oscar DePriest had been trotted about the studio in return for a friendly endorsement. They recognized that Fetchit had already stereotyped his role in *In Old Kentucky* into a permanent role beyond which *Hallelujah!* would need to move if "progress" were to be made. And they knew the gossip of the movie lots—Nina Mae McKinney, who played Chick, had almost quit after a grip called her "nigger." At a white opening Harold Garrison was herded to the Jim Crow gallery, where, according to *Photoplay*, he "probably [is] just as happy, for he appeared with a broad smile, his dusky friends, and a tuxedo and a green fedora hat." And early on, blacks noticed that white reviewers appeared to misread the responses of Harlem audiences.[25]

With the release of *Hallelujah!* Negroes needed to debate in public.

The main thrust of black opinion had shifted: first away from apathy, then away from censorship, and then away from the insular ground of "race movies." But to take white men's movies seriously meant that blacks chose to contend with Hollywood rather than to build black cinema. Indeed, "race movies" suffered thematically whenever white movies made some gesture toward racial justice. All-black movies in the 1930s would become more of an enterprise of exploitation, more dominated by white entrepreneurs, more patently offering mirror images of white bourgeois models of assimilation, and eventually less appealing to the black critics who had once seen them as hopeful signs of race solidarity. Even Micheaux, the *beau sabreur* of the movement, brought Frank Schiffman and Leo Brecher, white officials in the Apollo Theatre, into his post-bankruptcy company, an event reported without a raised eyebrow in the black nationalist *Negro World*.[26]

The broad central stream of black opinion took its lead from Congressman DePriest's approval of the picture as a sign of liberal progress. It was as though the end of the silent era opened the medium to Afro-American expression in music and dance and subsequently to all forms of performing. If show business was an analogue to American life, then Negroes could expect liberal gains in American life. And *Hallelujah!* was the optimistic ritual celebration of the good future.

DePriest stood next to Bill Robinson in the glare of lights at Harlem's Lafayette Theatre, preconditioned to praise the picture as a consequence of his visit to the studio during production. As Robinson introduced the cast and the congressman, "Crackling applause suggested a group grown politically conscious of itself." DePriest rose to speak at a spot between the bright lights of 125th Street and the more somber 135th with its famous Harlem YMCA, Harlem Hospital, and branch of The New York Public Library, with its Schomburg Collection. To the happy, jostling, sharply dressed crowd he proclaimed: "We are standing on the threshold of civic and cultural emancipation in America. Tonight we have seen how far our race has progressed culturally and artistically since the Emancipation Proclamation." Later he wired MGM congratulations for having "opened a new field" for Negro expression.

The NAACP organ, the *Crisis*, joined in the praise, focusing on the drama and the use of expressive hands to capture the mood of black religion, this despite W. E. B. DuBois's discomfiture upon being seated on a side aisle. The most prestigious brain in Negro circles, DuBois, variously a Pan-Africanist, a propagandist for social equality, a sometime economic nationalist, and quasi-independent editor of the *Crisis*—his opinion mattered. He found it an important contribution to American life, false only in the absence of oppressive whites who caused black malaise. Despite his unease at the "lurking comedy" behind a white mask of sincerity, he praised "the scenes of religious ecstasy [which] rise to magnificent drama, unexcelled in my experience and singularly true to life." In Chicago the aggressive *Whip* fell into line and grudgingly admired the theme and acting. As to those black "numbskulls" who found fault with the picture, the *Amsterdam News,* fearful of scaring Hollywood into retreat from its black cycle, warned them that they sang in unison with the racist Southern exhibitors who had passed a resolution condemning Negro movies.

James Weldon Johnson, although cool to the picture, appreciated the better jobs it gave the Negro acting fraternity. And the actors confirmed his judgment, as they eagerly plugged their product. Harry Gray promised to sell millions of tickets as a sign of faith in all-Negro movies. Daniel Haynes agreed with Johnson that "slowly rising from 'atmosphere' to small 'bits' and parts in which he proved his worth and ability the Negro has finally broken through the shell of apathy and indifference and emerged in the light on the screen."

The dissenters weakened their position by appearing to demand not art but propaganda that would ignore the worst conditions of black life, and soon it was clear that they stood as a minority. The *West Indian News,* the organ of a tiny urban élite of emigrés, granted the picture many merits but quarreled with the image of the Negro as "a weakling, a degenerate; a base ignorant being given to debauchery." Such a vision of whites, the *News* claimed, would never appear on the screen. Besides, Vidor should have "presented the struggles of the Negro race and boosted their accomplishments." Other critics attacked not only the film but Vidor's crass motives and Negro gullibility as well. White ethnic groups, they said, would not have held still under the slander, and they offered the wrath spewed against Sinclair Lewis's *Elmer Gantry* as a case in point. The *Whip,* despite its grudging admiration for parts of the picture, summed up the dissenters' cavil:

> A subtle vehicle of race prejudice, it is a diabolical insinuation upon the religious integrity of the Baptist church, it is a contemptible portrayal of the weaknesses and misfortunes of a lowly people . . . and holds up colored people of our country to disgust, jeers and disrespect.

Another version of Vidor's inadequacies held that he missed the nuances of ghetto class structure and thereby misplaced his emphasis. A black clergyman granted the menace of "the careless, shiftless, and criminal type of Negro [who] is too conspicuous among us" but felt Vidor had failed to suggest the constriction in the ghetto that threw together the black bourgeoisie with the daily threat of hustlers and criminals. However, such critics stopped short of blaming white oppression for criminality and merely pointed to the low element's "pernicious habit of attempting to put himself on equality with other Negroes," those who had presumably demonstrated their right to be assimilated.[27]

Black criticism notwithstanding, cinema had achieved a number of benchmarks that in some ways moved beyond the general racial attitudes of the white audience. Not since the days of unedited novelty footage a quarter of a century before had Negroes crossed the screen with such vigor, with so many nods to black cultural roots, with such an appreciative black audience and curiously attentive white one. As if in signal of a new day, blacks deserted the all-black cinema that had helped them through the dry twenties in favor of the promise held out by *Hearts in Dixie* and *Hallelujah!* Together they were oracles announcing the end of the Southern literary monopoly on Afro-American metaphor and imagery in fiction and in cinema.

Unfortunately, in the short run the conservative studios failed to carry their early success into a fully matured cycle. The bulkiest roadblock appeared in the figure of Al Jolson, whose sentimental minstrelsy in *The Jazz Singer* must have been taken as the sole reason for the picture's success. Although Warner Brothers would come to know the limits of the appeal of this genre for urban audiences, in the bright months after the coming of sound they miscalculated and encouraged Jolson to repeat his saccharine routines in sequels such as *The Singing Fool* (1928), *Mammy* (1930), and *Big Boy* (1930). *Mammy* appeared in a haze of innocent nostalgia through which derivative black life filtered. With Irving Berlin's and James Gleason's musical comedy, *Minstrel Days,* as a source, the studio pretended no authenticity; thus the picture was no more than an honest excuse to milk Jolson's popularity.[28]

Big Boy was another matter. Riding the crest of the black wave, its white writers and director Alan Crosland hubristically asked their audience to accept Jolson not as a blackface minstrel but as a genuine Negro. He was Gus, the faithful jockey in long service to Bedford Stables. In every situation in the joyous life of the stablehands' quarter, the waiters' post in a slick restaurant, the tack room just off the racetrack paddock, Gus wisecracks but knows his humble place and appreciates it. If he seems too calculating, it is always in the master's interest, and if he oversteps he remembers to "yessir" obsequiously. A flashback allows him to recall the old days with a few spirituals. His only breach with Southern etiquette is a handshake in the winner's circle after he boots home his master's horse. Thus blacks were taught their place in life, a bit of their history, and a sample of their music by a company of white writers and a singer under cork. Only in the last moments are we allowed the evasive demurrer that it is all a game: a shot of Jolson pirouetting into white as "himself," and we learn that it was all a sales pitch for the new musical he wants *us* to invest in. As he betrayed blacks in the picture, so in the end he betrays the audience by denying everything.[29]

As Jolson revealed the barrenness of minstrelsy for urban audiences, RKO's *Dixiana* (1930) revealed the dense impossibility of putting Southern romance on the screen. Even though the studio went the second mile in assembling a package of Bill Robinson's dance sequences, Bebe Daniels's "star quality," the first original musical script ever commissioned, some bits of the Lafayette Players, and expensive color-film sequences, the writers found no fresh themes in the South. The gulf separating Southern history from American egalitarian drift proved too wide. It opens across a spread of cottonland along the reach of a river, with blacks bending under their tasks. The next shot carries up the broad lawn to the big house, where a solitary slave primps the grass. The frame settles on two planters, father and son, who quarrel over whose slaves can sing better and which slaves love their master more. Putting aside a few bright bits, a picture so remote from historicity, even that tinged by Southern legend, had nothing to offer modern Americans. Black life, indeed the South itself, intruded only as a fanciful stage set littered with old racial baggage.[30]

Not that the Southern scene stood alone in its thematic barrenness. Despite the early success of black musical shorts, Negroes remained largely segregated from musical bits except for occasional specialties. Both white vaudeville and European music hall tradition shut the door in the face of black performers. One of the earliest musicals, David Butler's *Sunny Side Up* (1929), played on the conflict between elegant Southampton and the happy squalor of the Lower East Side, while blacks played jazz in insular quarantine in the corner of a single sequence. Even the early musical revues designed to show off the studios' rosters of stars offered only small bits by Carolynne Snowden and Ethel Waters.[31]

The most frightfully inept failure of the period pointed up the inadequacies of older genres for interpreting the new Negro. Ray Enright's *Golden Dawn* (1930), once a play with music by Oscar Hammerstein II and Otto Harbach, took place in a British East Africa ruled as a condominium with the German Army during the Great War. Far from resenting their joint colonial status, the blacks rest easy in "peaceful subjection" under the heel of the black matriarch, Mooda; a black overseer, Shep, who wields his whip as a scepter; and Dawn, the albino priestess—the triune surrogates for European forces. The plot hangs on a quadrangular rivalry with Dawn the objective of a British soldier, black Shep, and Mulunghu the tribal god. The resulting hybrid is characterized by a flashback revealing that Dawn is the child of a white trader, the unintended comic style of Noah Beery's blackfaced Shep speaking in Southern dialect, and the climax in which the Briton reduces the "bad nigger" Shep into a cringing "tom." The denouement of the busy plot comes when the Europeans, who are "no match against a frenzied multitude of blacks," are saved as Dawn renounces her tribal god in favor of the white man's god and accepts her white origins, thereby, presumably, bringing rain to the parched kraal and saving the British Army from certain destruction.

Under Beery's cork and the improbable gimmick of Dawn's flashback revelation the barest bits of awareness of a black presence peered through the lyrics. "Gone are the golden days," begins a chorus which ends on:

> Woe! Since the white man came
> Sewing [sic] the seeds of shame,
> Harvesting war,
> Oh! With her million trials
> Poor Africa smiles no more!

Even then, most of the other songs stumble, as, for example, "The Whip Song," which is done in dialect, Mulunghu's song, which dwells on the god's yen for Dawn's "white body and the blue of her eyes," and Dawn's trilling about "him, I call my Bwana." Besides, the last shot falls not on Africa but Dawn's shipboard honeymoon with her British Tommy.[32]

Afterward, few memorable bits of black music or life appeared. In 1933 Lewis Milestone's *Hallelujah, I'm a Bum*, with an urbane script by Ben Hecht, placed the faltering Jolson in a good role as the leader of Central Park hobos played by the black dwarf Edgar Connor, Harry Langdon attempting a comeback, and Chester Conklin playing out the string. Amidst the Rodgers and Hart music, they romped through a froth of egalitarian whimsy and leftist drivel.[33] Eddie Cantor's humdrum comedies for Sam Goldwyn, *Kid Millions* and *The Kid from Spain*, both made decent use of incidental blacks, in the former as ragamuffins whom Cantor treats to a Technicolor celebration in an ice cream plant, in the latter by using Connor as a bullfighter's assistant. The *Amsterdam News* then predicted that Connor would "ascend the niche in the cinematic world vacated by Stepin Fetchit."[34] Mervyn Leroy threw away an opportunity to make a clear statement of black despair in *Gold Diggers of 1933*. He had Etta Moten sing "Remember My Forgotten Man," an evocative song that sketched the plight of the war veteran discarded by the depression, thereby recasting the mood of the wisecracking movie toward social awareness. From a rainy window she sings:

> Remember my forgotten man
> You put a rifle in his hand
> You sent him far away;
> You shouted—Hip Hooray!
> But look at him today!

Then we lose her as the chorus picks up the refrain:

> . . . forgetting him, you see,
> Means you're forgetting me
> Like my forgotten man.

But Moten sang in silhouette, and the special point that a Negro would have brought to the song was thrown away.[35]

In succeeding years a few bits appeared, good and bad, but in the absence of a Negro voice in Hollywood, none plumbed depths of black life. Moten a year later sang a segregated "Carioca" in *Flying Down to Rio;* the Marx brothers rattled off a parody of "All God's Chillun Got Wings" in their anarchic *Duck Soup* (1934); Jolson staged a burlesque of *The Green Pastures* in his *Wonderbar* (1934), and a year later Fred "Snowflake" Toones sprinkled Jolson's *Go Into Your Dance* with standard malapropisms; genuine black gamins frolicked in the spray of a fire hydrant, inspiring an elaborate water ballet by Busby Berkeley in *Footlight Parade* (1933); Fred Astaire paid touching homage to "Bojangles" in *Swingtime* (1936).[36]

But the briefest routines required careful segregation of the sexes, even patently blackface bits such as Bill Robinson's duet in *Cafe Metropole,* which was cut after black press protests, and Martha Raye's bit with Louis Armstrong in *Artists and Models,* which irritated the Southern press and *Variety.* "It's that 'Public Melody Number One' sequence," said *Variety,*

> done in a frankly Harlem setting, with Louis Armstrong tooting his trumpet against a pseudo-musical gangster idea. While Miss Raye is under cork, this intermingling of the races isn't wise, especially as she lets herself go into the extremist manifestations of Harlemania torso-twisting and gyrations. It may hurt her personally.[37]

Necessarily, then, the most persistent racial product of thirties musicals was the canon of amiable Bill Robinson and the child star Shirley Temple. "Discovered" by Fox's Winfield Sheehan after a brief career in short comedies, she got a small part in *Stand Up and Cheer,* an optimistic froth based on an idea of Will Rogers for resurrecting the nation's morale in the dog days of depression, complete with Fetchit as a mumbling running gag. *Variety* praised the "sure-fire, potential kidlet star," and Fox paired her with Robinson in *The Little Colonel, The Littlest Rebel, Curly Top,* and 1938's expensive *Rebecca of Sunny-*

brook Farm. A surefooted, one-take craftsman, she mastered Robinson's famous staircase dance, and their resulting series never failed to return a million dollars. "Uncle Bill doesn't tell her feet where to go," said Bojangles. "Her heart, it tells her." Yet if Negroes winced at Bill's company manners that got him work, they relished his footwork.[38] The pair's two archetypal movies were *The Littlest Rebel* and *The Little Colonel.* The ante bellum traits unfold in ritual order: white-topped servants, coarse Yankees, genteel Southern officers. Robinson the butler pursues the interests of his master, fends off marauders, holds together the household, leads Temple's father through the swamps, and appeals to Lincoln for his pardon. He does a time-step to cover an escape and again to raise fare for the trip to Washington. The latter picture, from Annie Fellows Johnston's children's book, added Hattie McDaniel as a mammy, a cadre of black children for Temple to command, and a Negro baptism.[39] But they all seemed farther than ever from the early promise of black musicals.

Nevertheless by 1935 the white Negrophile Carl Van Vechten caught the excitement generated by small black penetrations of the inner layers of the Anglo-American psyche and transmitted it to his friend James Weldon Johnson. "Aren't the papers wonderful about Joe Louis," he wrote,

> and isn't Joe Louis wonderful? . . . I think this is likely to be a NEGRO WINTER. Headed by your book, there will be a lot of books. . . . Ethel Waters is starring in At Home and Abroad, Josephine Baker is arriving to star in the Follies. Bill Robinson is in Hollywood and Paul Robeson is arriving Tuesday for a concert tour and to do Showboat in Hollywood. Porgy goes on next week and Langston's [Hughes] play Mulatto is in rehearsal with Rose McClendon. There are lost [sic] of athletes and minor figures. A pretty good record, I call it, with James Weldon Johnson professoring at NYU for good measure![40]

The major hurdle remained the persistent white expectation that Negro professionals perform with quiet gratitude and avoid querulousness and complaint. As early as 1929 Andy Razaf's lyrics for Lew Leslie's *Blackbirds* suffered a loss of their most biting social protest, which might have clashed with the cardsharps and watermelons in the playbill sketches. And in the 1930s performers such as Ethel Waters with a reputation for being "difficult" sometimes lost jobs and regarded with suspicion Negroes such as Bill Robinson who got along too well with whites.[41] Besides, there were still whites in Hollywood like the producer who, responding to an angry, rejected writer's query, "What do you want—'Black Beauty'?," snapped back, "They ain't no market for them Nigger Operas!"[42]

Therefore moviemen continually searched for a bland, happy vehicle and at last put the guildmark of Hollywood black achievement in the mid-1930s on Marc Connelly's fable *The Green Pastures* (1936), a long-running Broadway musical show about rural Negro piety as interpreted by a white man with a good ear. Warner Brothers' picture made good use of a large company of appreciative black performers leavened by a massive cattle call that attracted a willing group of relative amateurs. It suited many black critics as well as the studio, for the picture was a depiction of black theological aspiration which depicted "sin" precisely as the traits of the old Southern metaphorical Negro that "De Lawd" tries to change into a more effectual moral and social vision. Rex Ingram, a good actor, played De Lawd, Adam, and finally Hezdrel, the black soldier who points the race toward a future of struggle and hope in the last reel.[43]

Throughout the depression decade moviemakers attempted to capture Afro-American life on the screen in some format outside of show business circles, but whether in two-reel form or as bits of feature films the Negro segments rarely gave a fully rounded appearance to their subject. In the ten years after *Hallelujah!* the great myth of black voices "better than white voices" led only to a few rumors of a production of *Porgy* or of some black revue, oddments such as the signing of Wallace Thurman and Langston Hughes to write scripts, and a decent living for a few groups such as the Hall Johnson Choir—at least until *The Green Pastures* appeared.

Though lacking the tone of *Hallelujah!*'s location shots, *The Green Pastures* rose above the common ruck, averted the worst taints of Southern metaphor, and brought black Southern folk religion to a wide and appreciative audience. Blacks, except for a few intellectuals, enjoyed it and lionized the players. Despite the tight control imposed by a stylized studio set, the sources in the tales of white writer Roark Bradford, the script by white Marc Connelly, and the direction of Connelly and William Keighley, the picture was a fair success. Indeed, it might have been a major hit except for the bland advertisements which opted for "taste" rather than electricity. Dozens of blacks besides Ingram, including the Hall Johnson Choir, George Randol of the "race movies," Ida Forsyne from black stage revues, Eddie Anderson from vaudeville, Slim Thompson from the Lafayette Players, Oscar Polk and other Hollywood Negroes, and the chosen minions from the cattle calls contributed their dignified presence to the picture which needed, according to witnesses, occasional cheerleading to break down the urbane reserve of the blacks and stir a bit of down-home foot-tapping and hand-clapping.

The result was a rich black version of the Old Testament fall of man

The ambitious treatment of Marc Connelly's fable *The Green Pastures* (© Warner Brothers Pictures, Inc.) stressed the extremes of the patient "Lawd" and the militant Hezdrel, both played by Rex Ingram. (Author's collection, Nederlands Filmmuseum)

set unobtrusively in an idyllic and occasionally musical heaven that man must first fall from and then fight to regain. The good and evil sides of the black world, cast as they were in terms of the old Negro and the new Negro, gave comic entertainment to whites and an epic of hope for blacks. As though to delimit the old Southern Negro from the "new Negro" Rex Ingram's three roles and Eddie Anderson's two grew progressively firmer and more commanding. Anderson appeared first as a down-home preacher but ended as a whimsically authoritarian Noah in dutiful command of his appointed Ark. Ingram's overpowering, gentle-by-turns, quietly anxious Lawd who wishes the best for his flock of mortals provided the moral thrust of a black theology toward a unified urban future. De Lawd first sees sin in the form of inattentive, dozing children in a rural Sunday school, uninspired by fussy matrons in picture hats, while a dull sermonizer drones through a string of "begats." De Lawd decides to test man against temptation so as to prove his hidden innocence. He determines to "rare back and pass a miracle," and create his Adam who needs Eve " 'cause in yo' heart yo' is a family man." Eons later Earth is seen as a Southern town, plausibly segregated, taken up with the pleasures of fishfries and the sins of gambling, wenching, and chewing tobacco—the sins against urban bourgeois norms. Following the lore of the Old Testament through the casting out of man from Paradise, De Lawd himself gradually changes from the angry tribal god Yahweh into the merciful figure described by Hosea, thus opening the way for New Testament prophesy. The new Negro, Hezdrel, Ingram's third role, is a soldier, barechested, fighting in a smoky battle against a nameless and presumably godless enemy who can only be racism. It was a powerful denouement for a movie that had opened on a Paradise framed as a grand fishfry.[44]

Although the picture, especially its fishfry, raised the hackles of black critics, few of them agreed on specific flaws. Indeed, Ralph Matthews in the *Afro-American* thought it "a disgrace to the movie industry and a reflection on the colored race" not so much for its message but because the Warner Brothers' production had rejected the cast of the long-running Broadway show in favor of Hollywood Negroes. Roi Ottley, a major figure among black newspapermen, called forth even less precise objections and settled for a rhetorical broad racial boosterism:

'The Green Pastures' will no doubt, receive magnificent and glowing accounts in the Negro press . . . and unhappily so for the Negro public. . . . Negro newspapers on the whole have a false sense of values. . . . They seem to work from the premise that anytime a Negro appears in a play or picture which the whites have produced it should be applauded regardless of its merits. . . . This department goes on record as feeling that Oscar Micheaux, with his inferior equipment, would have produced a better picture.

Nevertheless, his paper, the *Amsterdam News*, reckoned the opposite impact was truer to life—that Hollywood's depictions of Afro-American lore and problems in *The Green Pastures, Showboat*, and other major feature pictures drove the "race movie" producers from the screen. The compromise solutions offered by Hollywood in its slick, bright packages seemed enough for hungry Negro audiences. In fact, *Variety*, whose editors rarely asked bookers to take risks, challenged exhibitors to overcome the hot-weather opening of *The Green Pastures* with a vigorous campaign against "two mass-mentality handicaps—the all-colored cast and the complete absence of . . . a marquee name."[45]

But few black or white critics, producers, and writers shared those early hopes that had stirred Winnie Sheehan, King Vidor, and Marc Connelly. Because *Hearts in Dixie, Hallelujah!*, and *The Green Pastures* failed to do top-dollar business, the possibilities of black life on film were lost on moviemakers. The Warner Brothers had spent $100,000 alone on acquiring rights to the play *Green Pastures*, campaigned hard to "make their nut" in urban dates as a hedge against presumed rural losses, received praise for the sense of tragedy and "honest Negro humor" they had caught on film, and still a year later the sales departments of the major studios balked at an offer by the producer of the *Blackbirds* revues to do an all-Negro musical. So blacks settled back into musical shorts, and it would be a decade before their segregated status would really begin to change.

The moribund state of the art and of black accommodation to it may be fairly seen in three films of the late thirties. Sol Lesser produced *Rainbow on the River* (1936) and *Way Down South* (1937) using, in one way or another, the lyrics, dialogue, vignettes, and advice of Clarence Muse and veteran Harlem Renaissance wit Langston Hughes. The mammy in *Rainbow*, as played by Louise Beavers, emerged as a fully rounded figure with responsibility for her actions and a stiffbacked will to fight for custody of the orphaned white boy she had seen through the worst days of the Civil War. If the character seemed so tough-minded that the *Times* reviewer questioned her plausibility, nevertheless she was still a mammy in the grand tradition and profited little from Muse's presence. Besides, Lesser cast Bobby Breen, a shrill male rival of Shirley Temple, as the orphan, and managed to make the textures of New Orleans and the North barely distinguishable, so that Muse's contribution seemed negligible.[46]

Lesser and RKO gave over the studio a year later to a black team

that included Clarence Muse and George Randol and white director
Leslie Goodwins. And yet they chose the ante bellum Southern metaphor as a vehicle for depicting black humanity for a new generation in
Way Down South—and got nowhere. Their story followed "darkies"
picking cotton, toting sacks to the tallyman, and crooning the works
of Stephen Foster. The camera settles on Zeke and "Ca'line" in the
crowd as he stuffs her bag so she can make the weight. In broad dialect
they talk of their coming marriage, and the news of it flickers through
the faces of the pickers, who are saddened only by the demands of
picking that will keep them from raising a house for the lovers—saddened, that is, until the white boss paternally lets off the whole gang.
"Give 'em a nice wedding," he says. Quickly they flit through a country barbeque, fade into a church singing, "I've Been 'Buked" and "Ain't
Gwine Lay My 'Ligion Down," and out to the houseraising with a
chorus of "I'm goin' down dat lonesome road." They sing through a
wedding feast, a "gran' march," a "cakewalk," and a handclapping
"Way Down in Georgia." In the end they stand in a tight two-shot in
the doorway, the chorus doing "My Old Kentucky Home" as the camera pulls back in the half-light on the last words, ". . . far away."
Thus, no matter what Muse brought to the film, it never escaped its
time frame or its dependence on the dated style of the Hall Johnson
group. Two years later Lesser expanded the film into a feature and
added Hughes to the writers corps. Unfortunately whatever Hughes
might have brought to it was balanced by the return of Beavers, Breen,
and the Hall Johnson Choir and by a hoary slave who gratefully testi-
fies to his old master's kindness.[47] Thus the presence of blacks at every
level accomplished scant change in the studios' traditional rural vision
of black life and music.

The Marx Brothers' *A Day at the Races* (1937) revealed how low the
hopes of black audiences and critics had fallen. Like all of the Marx
movies the script provided no more than a vehicle for the team's zany
anarchy and hardly qualified as a source of black musical life. But it featured a minor, even gratuitous, yet buoyant, foot-stomping, hand-wring-
ing black romp from shack to poor shack in the Negro quarter behind
the horsebarns. Harpo Marx and the black singer Ivie Anderson led the
rousing chorus, which picked up tempo as more and more stablehands
emerged from their cabins and joined in the frolicking parody of a revival. In the midst of a drought of authentic musical motifs of black life
the *Amsterdam News* grasped at the small gesture and appreciatively
dubbed it "A Day at the (Negro) Races."[48] Their critic proved correct
in his praise of a small favor, for moviegoers would not again see a full-
scale reminder of the early black musical romances until the middle of
the Second World War.

Chapter Eleven

THE HOLLYWOOD NEGRO FACES THE GREAT DEPRESSION

During the Great Depression, Americans changed their race relations ever so subtly. The norms of daily life brought blacks and whites closer together as they stood in the same queues, moved along at prodding of police, and crumpled their caps as they sat on the hard chairs of grubby employment agencies. A slice of Southern etiquette intruded on the urban middle class as the wives of black men cooked and washed in white homes. Both learned a city version of the two poles of Southern paternalism: blacks and whites outwardly affectionate and mutually grateful for opportunity and for service rendered, but patronizing and resentful after they parted at the end of the day. Despite the clashing of social demands, of opposing forces, of muted outrage, a feeling of equanimity and uneven optimism spread through the columns on the back pages of the black press.

If racism persisted in popular science and in the universities, the cultural relativism of Franz Boas had spread a bit. Americans who had never heard of Boas believed that if Afro-Americans in the main could aspire to little, still there were exceptional Negroes. In white popular literature Booker T. Washington remained an icon of accommodation. George Washington Carver, an inventive agronomist, became such a folk hero to whites that his reputation among them far outstripped his actual scientific achievement. Joe Louis's quiet mien allowed him to serve double duty as a coolly effective boxing champion *and* an unthreatening metaphor for dogged black plodding against adversity.

Politically, blacks rose from the slough of President Hoover's laissez faire apathy in the face of economic decline and the revival of a "lily white" movement within the party of Lincoln. Roosevelt's New Deal, on the contrary, gave them so many symbols of hope that by 1936 many had taken the earlier advice of Kelly Miller of Howard and a scattering of black publishers and converted to the Democratic cause. If a few black critics carped at New Deal failings, especially those on Southern ground, most blacks took heart from omens such as Mrs. Roosevelt's role as ambassador to the race, the growth of an unofficial "black cabinet," the appointment of NAACP activist Harold L. Ickes as Secretary of the Interior, and the surface evidence that Negroes were nominally included in the ranks of the disinherited.

The renewal of Democratic faith in black circles eroded both nationalism and radicalism. The Communist Party made halting progress in the thirties despite genuine gestures such as vigorous defense of "the Scottsboro boys" and the nomination of a black Vice-Presidential candidate. But leftist waffling over the issue of "self-determination" by a fanciful black "republic" versus "integration" seemed no more than precious theorizing in contrast to the bourgeois NAACP, which grew a bit stronger by filling its ranks with anti-Communist leftists and integrationists. On the other hand the nationalist Marcus Garvey had fallen so far from grace after his imprisonment that two "race movies" parodied his life. The thirties style focused attention on demands that mayors repudiate police brutality, on impressing party bosses with the need for black district judges, and on, in Chicago at least, the successful campaign to elect Oscar Depriest, the first black congressman since George H. White departed in 1901. The icons of the new sensibility were those who were "a credit to their race"—Louis, Carver, and Jesse Owens, the shy victor in the "Nazi" Olympic Games of 1936.[1]

New York was not typical of black America, but it provides a useful profile of the larger outlines of social life. The *Amsterdam News*, including its hyperoptimistic New Year's round-up, revealed a striking degree of cohesive activity. To be sure, vestiges of old and antisocial behavior remained and recurred in the exposés of "voodoo" hustlers and flimflam artists. And flamboyant style made it difficult to sort out the good race men from the charlatans in the ranks of the Father Divines, Daddy Graces, and Sufi Hamids. But blacks survived them and perhaps took heart from them. There on the back pages, though, standing tall, were the intellectual survivors of the Renaissance: J. A. Rogers's popular history, Miller's acerbic politics, Dean William Pickens's social thrust, DuBois's graceful style, Carter Woodson's scholarship, and the show business and theater pieces of old Lester Walton, young George Norford, and Theophilus Lewis. Some, like Miller and DuBois, broadened their concern to include the darker peoples everywhere, even though at home they might debate the respective merits of economic nationalism and integrationism. Less cerebrally, but as proudly, blacks rooted for the new light-heavyweight champion, Kid Chocolate, registered in print the cool argot of the black streets—"freebie," "cool," "jive," "ofay"—or struggled to keep alive the Harlem Tenants Association, the Colored Merchants Association, and the Rockefeller-backed Dunbar Bank; or tingling with group feeling, they demanded that whites use an uppercase "n" and never say "Negress," debated the merits of "Negro" versus "colored" as a race cognomen, and kidded each other with outrageous in-group name-calling.[2]

The tenor of the times appeared on the screen in many small ways: fresh social themes, urbane comedy, a small black "star system" that supplanted the studio hangers-on of the twenties, and, of course the depression itself, treated with irony, humor, or cautionary homily. It was an easy matter for the black press to turn away from the bankrupt "race movies" toward the Hollywood that promised a major thrust away from mere divertissement. Audiences chose Hollywood films except when a "race movie" appeared at the bottom of a double bill or a "tab show" as padding. The racial stereotypes kept up with the times. The crooning black convict on death row, the earthy old darkey from whom the child star learned common wisdom, the Negro vaudevillian who played "herself" safely outside the white plot were, in the beginning at least, fresh intrusions upon movies. Each one of them made war upon older types like Stepin Fetchit and his exemplars who survived the "fading effect," the sociologists' term for the waning of a no-longer-meaningful symbol.[3] This is not to say that Negroes stood alone as symbols for an age. The studios regularly treated the social concerns of the day in films such as Vidor's *Our Daily Bread*, Frank Capra's *American Madness*, and the gangster films and musicals of Warner Brothers. And if they failed, *Variety* stood ready to warn exhibitors, as they did of the Cohens and the Kellys series, that this was just "another insincere attempt to sell sympathetic syrup to the Jewish public."[4]

Black critics, usually from the East, challenged the complaisance of Hollywood Negroes and demanded an end to the old types on which they earned their keep. But the black Hollywoodians argued that if their traditional roles were symbols of accommodation, they also served as symbols of success and adulation to the race while preparing the way for favorable social change by disarming white fears.

So at bottom the black cinema achievement of the thirties rested upon the cadre of black stars who would give their style and substance to the movies. Unlike the blacks of the twenties they held jobs because of experience and talent rather than the accident of living in Los Angeles or of incidental fame as an athlete. Bill Robinson was a street busker in Richmond, a "pick" in a roadshow, a top man in Harlem's

"Hoofers' Club," and a star of musical revues. Clarence Muse claimed, convincingly if not accurately, a law degree, and later a tour with the Lafayette Players. The point is not whether he had legal training but that whites believed it, so that even if he seemed a "pet actor" to some, he also was a trusted intelligence, a coach of other actors, a writer, an opinionmaker—anything but merely a lucky Negro on a hot streak. Rex Ingram also lived off his reputation both as a medical school graduate and a member of Phi Beta Kappa, neither one of which was supported by documents. But for actors appearances mean more than substance. Possessed of limited range, Ingram built a neat twenty-year career on his imposing presence. Eddie Anderson came to films with a well-traveled versatility acquired in a life on the vaudeville stage. The most stalwart of the women, Hattie McDaniel and Louise Beavers, came from straight-arrow middle-class families whose precepts of hard work held them in good stead. Stepin Fetchit and Mantan Moreland came to California as splinters off broken vaudeville teams. Very few of the blacks conformed to the twenties model actor who, like Wille Best, was "discovered" on the street.[5]

This new Negro as perceived by average whites who liked movies formed the central source of a stream of black film roles. They played servants or foils who were faithful *and* flippant, mannered *and* casual, distant *and* familiar. The most prolific among them brought some fresh style, talent, or twist on the old type to the screen. Beavers, McDaniel, George Reed, and others brought a querulous stubbornness to their jobs. Bill Robinson preserved a bit of the flicker-footed natural man of his stage career in his liveried butlers and "uncles" who danced with and protected the child star, Shirley Temple, in a string of Fox films. Fetchit stylized the slavey into a surreal mockery of the old stereotype.

The black press responded to the mood with overwhelming support of Hollywood movies. Although the studios spent scant advertising money in black newspapers, the local exhibitors bought space in which they billed star and title *under* the black performers. The papers also ran columns of boilerplate plugging movies, with or without Negro performers, and reporting gossip of the movie lots. The stories ranged from that of Muse's prying money from Mae West for an antilynching campaign after "he found that most of his 'brothers' were broke," to social-page pieces on "the colored 400 of Hollywood, . . . one of the wealthiest, most cultured and splendid" élites in America.

Thus the Hollywood Negroes in the thirties played larger roles in rounder and more varied scope. Any serious film profited from their presence, while, in contrast, during the twenties almost any film trailed generations of racist baggage impossible to discard. Compare, for example, the variety of Negro roles in *Gone with the Wind* with the blackface scarecrows in Griffith's era.

Meanwhile, within the ranks of the NAACP debate raged between those who supported DuBois's urge for black economic unity and others who feared that black solidarity would imply acceptance of segregation. In Hollywood, though, integration seemed a likely Negro stance because so many doors were opening a crack. Wallace Thurman spent the last months of his life doctoring film scripts. *Variety* argued for a movie treatment of Harlem life and reported several false starts. The *California Eagle* discovered Harold Garrison's "soon to be scenarized" black story. The NAACP discussed dramatizing Walter White's novel *The Fire in the Flint* with Paul Robeson as the star. Will Vodery did several musical arrangements. James Weldon Johnson sold the movie rights to his famous *Lift Every Voice and Sing*. And by the mid-1930s Muse, Langston Hughes, and George Randol had done treatments, lyrics, and scripts.[6] Hyperbolic press agentry, much of it directed at the black press, inflated the promises and celebrated the achievements. Fetchit became the "Greatest Colored Star"; Muse, the "expert in the making of pictures employing colored talent"; Robeson, a "powerful influence" on *Showboat*. Summing up the mood, Leigh Whipper declared, "Hollywood is a swell place."[7]

Protesting Negroes could only agree to flog the dead horse named *The Birth of a Nation*, and even then, as they forced the New York YMHA to cancel a 1935 showing, Roy Wilkins scribbled on a memo that he was "not sure we should issue publicity." On a specific point such as the role of Farina in *Our Gang*, a white leftist critic cried racism, while Lawrence Reddick, the curator of the Schomburg Collection of the New York Public Library's Harlem Branch, found the series "brilliant and winsome."[8] So minor complaints replaced concerted action, with Walter White grumbling over the use of "darkie" in lobby cards, or William Pickens of the NAACP feeling trapped between the "degrading nonsense" of *Imitation of Life* and the "superb" acting of its black actress. A survey of Negro "adult leaders" in Los Angeles in 1932 confirmed the division of opinion. Their opinions of the Amos 'n' Andy radio show ranged from sheer delight at the favorable racial propaganda to "marked resentment and emphatic disapproval." Loren Miller, a black jurist and writer, could only conclude that "the Negro's place and stage and screen has been fixed for so many years that tradition sways the judgement of Negroes themselves."[9]

Within the studios the dependent blacks, powerless and grateful for good and bad roles and their $7.50 per day as extras, would have none of the debate. Their bosses cultivated dutiful studio hangers-on equally with those blacks "distinguished by splendid artistry as well as fine personal conduct." In the guilds, because "even the apprentices were chosen by the union" and "usually they were the sons of the members," the few black members "just paid their dues and went along with whatever we said." At the bottom of the scale the Hollywood Negro might face the same fate as a hustler, such as the time when Raymond Turner, after a long career, joined his wife on a police blotter for allegedly maintaining a brothel. So it was understandable when an able character actor like Oscar Polk defended Warner Brothers against the charge that they paid Negroes below scale. Or when Louise Beavers defended "playing mother roles" because she wanted "my public to know me as playing these loving character parts."[10]

Thus if studios were susceptible to external social and political pressure, they were also riding at an anchor provided by the black acting establishment. The liberal drift of the thirties would have only a faint effect on Hollywood. Conservative forces in the studios were too strong. The depression brought on a mood of retrenchment, rigidity, and authoritarianism that the studios outlived only by cutting costs, shutting East Coast plants, trimming low-volume theaters, wages, ticket prices, and office budgets, and by using stock shots, postponing building plans, and pruning shooting schedules. With investments in sound equipment becoming a fixed cost, the entire system came to regard controversial pictures warily.[11]

The trend accelerated the decline of the director's control, strengthened the hand of studio bosses, sharpened the tension between New York backers and California producers, and prevented blacks from stoking up liberal fires fed by the success of the early black musicals. The MGM model, for example, proceeded along a chain from the Schenck-Loew group in New York to Culver City, where Eddie Mannix represented the East Coast in a studio run by Louis B. Mayer on the business end and Irving Thalberg in production. The marriage of assembly line and atelier allowed a strong man like Thalberg to develop scripts, shape them to "current thinking" and "the moods of the public," test them on preview audiences, and rework them in "Retake Valley"—a wit's label for the MGM studio. From his end Mayer saw to stabilizing the business by strangling independents who "might upset the system of a controlled product and a controlled market."[12] Small lots were tighter but held similar ambitions.

Therefore the Hollywood during the depression provided few new opportunities for blacks. Southern literary metaphor had eroded a bit, but no clear alternative emerged. So blacks were represented only by memorable bits in films not really dealing with their needs or problems. Black critics and audiences made do with a few "stars" and hints of "progress." Sadly for black performers the myth of superior Negro voices faded as sound engineers, New York actors, theatrical craftsmen such as George Cukor, and a rash of little interior comedies like his *Our Betters* took the play away from blacks. Instead of a rage for black films "talking pictures created a panic in Hollywood," recalled Adolph Menjou. Instead of black spontaneity there were sound men who scurried about the sets testing the mikes by muttering "Mississippi . . . Mississippi . . ."[13]

Thereafter Afro-Americans profitted from the common run of films only to the degree that their presence made some small point. In *Gabriel Over the White House*, for example, a mildly New Dealish film that outraged conservative Mayer, a black butler enters a cabinet meeting on the sound of the word "democracy." *The Big House*, an early statement that bad prisons bred criminals, started a line of crooning Negro convicts who sang Greek choruses over the tragic prisoners. Yet such a self-consciously social film as Vidor's *Our Daily Bread* placed no Negroes in the ranks of its heroic poor.[14]

The coming of sound brought a revival of the minstrel show, that most racist form of entertainment, on film. The success of Amos 'n' Andy's radio show undoubtedly continued strongly to the trend. The first two of the cycle should have warned off producers. Moran and Mack, a team of vaudeville imitators of Amos 'n' Andy, made a pair of grind house movies that failed to rise above the level of the "acceptable program picture that never gets very near to bigness." Then Amos 'n' Andy themselves, despite *Variety*'s giving four pages to their debut, which would bring "countless millions to the joy of honest laughter and the boon of hope and courage," failed to match their radio success on screen. In RKO's *Check and Double Check* the blackface team were so useless after the establishing shots in their Harlem taxicab office that the plot cut away to a tangle of lost deeds, Southern manses, white heavies, and a wasted appearance by Duke Ellington. Redundant sight gags punctuated by "yassuhs" and malapropisms filled the screen. RKO had misread the radio ratings, thought they had a winner, paid $1000 per day in line charges so the team could shoot on the West Coast while recording for radio, beefed up publicity, and covered up Ellington in the billing "due to the Southern angle." Yet after the first splash, grosses slumped and only the familial ties of RKO with radio assured a second film. In a year the radio team slumped into Sennett shorts. Ellington's claim that his role was a "crowning point" seemed to be the exact opposite of the true facts.[15]

Blacks had not minded—indeed, had enjoyed—Amos 'n' Andy on radio. But movies were different, for on radio one could fancy them in the mind's eye as genuinely black rather than as greasepainted Dybbuks,

The worst of the new sound films merely exploited well-worn roles, as here in *Check and Double Check* (© RKO-Radio Pictures, Inc.). (Author's collection)

played by two whites, Charles Correll and Freeman Gosden, under the blackface mask. Moreover, even though RKO had outbid two major studios for movie rights they doubted the team's ability to carry an entire movie. Not only were the starring blacks buried in a white plot; their strong women, Ruby and Sapphire, were gone, along with the urban ghetto environment (save for a brief Harlem establishing shot), and with them the opportunity for a black-centered dramatic conflict.

Meanwhile "major studios," said *Variety*, are awaiting the next story cycle without an idea as to what will be its nature."[16] While they fretted, their production units ground out films with particolored variety: the musicals, a freshet of Fetchit bits, prison exposés, Paul Whiteman's lily-white *King of Jazz*, *The Cohens and the Kellys* series stretched to embrace African cannibals who lose their ivory cache in a game of miniature golf, the birth of a rival to Fetchit—"Sleep 'n' Eat," nee Willie Best—in *Up Pops the Devil.* Josef Von Sternberg's *Thunderbolt* deviated most from convention when in a flash of Harlem ambience George Bancroft winks with knowing familiarity at Teresa Harris, his Negro girlfriend who sings in a saloon. Seventy-five blacks appeared, among them Sul-te-Wan, Oscar Smith of the shoeshine stand, Nathan Curry, and Mosby's Blue Blowers.[17]

Now and again in these ambivalent days after the first flush of black musical successes but before the studios knew their next step, a black presence redeemed Hollywood. Ethel Waters gave life to a small bit in Warner Brothers' and Alan Crosland's backstage melodrama *On with the Show* (1929) as "herself," a billing that would later offend Negroes. Along with the veterans of black theater circuits, the tap-dancing Covans, she does "Birmingham Bertha" and "Am I Blue?" thereby winning over hostile first-nighters and saving the show. Although defused by the show-within-a-show format, her numbers were exciting clever twists on the sexuality of blues. As Bertha, for example, her lament for her Chicago-bound lover precedes her transmogrification into a mean, black woman come to the city to claim her man and who intimidates even the police into releasing him. Her man is the perfect jazz dancer, lean and cool, in love with his woman, but deftly avoiding domestication.[18]

No one could be found outside of musical circles who would carry black imagery beyond the conventional outlines save for the producers of a few major releases to be examined presently.

Such B pictures as William Wellman's *Safe in Hell* (1931) offered the only source of employment for Nina Mae McKinney and other aspiring black actors and actresses. Either B pictures served as experimental labs or the studios ignored the opinions of matinee fans. In either case an occasional black got work in a role that did not represent the usual racial stereotype.

Safe in Hell, a trim little melodrama, a bit silly in spots, showed how to use Negroes in a "white" film. The plot is simple. A blonde hooker kills an old flame, flees New Orleans, takes up with a naïve sailor, reaches safety on a fetid Carib isle, becomes the sex fantasy of the local dregs, is befriended by a decent black woman, and at last confesses her crime in order to avoid becoming the sexual pawn of Bruno, the vicious local police chief. If they can do nothing else, the entire company joins in a charade to keep the impending tragedy from the sailor who leaves, expecting an eventual reunion. The shabby white crooks, escape artists, ticket-of-leave men, and at-liberty mercenaries in their dingy tropical suits are contrasted with Bruno, the cop, who knows too much about them; his steely, massive sergeant (Noble Johnson); Leonie

(Nina Mae McKinney), the slim brown waitress; and the very British and very black butler (Muse). The whites live off their past; the blacks off their carefully cultivated principles, hidden under their cool manners. They rise above the script. "I'm a New Orleans lady too," says Leonie when the writers ask her to say, "I's from N'Orleans myself." They are religious in their way and protect the woman from the locals. One white makes a pass which she rejects by accepting a light from Muse's steady black hand. Leonie sets a cocky example by waiting tables, singing, holding to her faith, and fending off the whites. In a contrived ending and a sham trial the white woman is convicted and chooses death rather than a life in the hands of Bruno. In the last sequence the blacks help her die in peace by steering her sailor away, Leonie embraces her in tears, and "Nobe" gives her a last cigarette. Together they turned a programmer into a neatly done piece of Wellman's best local color.[19]

But if a few new Negro roles appeared, the old ones still survived in Southern programmers and Will Rogers films. In the van were *Heaven on Earth* from a Ben Lucien Burman novel, with Sul-te-Wan as "Voodoo Sue"; Fox's remake of *Jubilo* with Beavers as mammy; Paul Green's *Carolina*, a tale of a marriage of proud Rebel and pragmatic Yankee with Fetchit's "Scipio" supporting; George Stevens's witless Wheeler and Woolsey vehicle, *Kentucky Kernels*, with Sleep 'n' Eat; *Judge Priest*, by Irvin S. Cobb with Rogers and Fetchit as fishing partners "in a sort of rose-colored Southern mist of the nineties"; the pair teamed again in George Ade's *County Chairman;* Paramount's *Virginia Judge* with Fetchit's prisoner in the dock providing "human touches"; and Fox's *In Old Kentucky* remake with Bill Robinson as "Wash Jackson."[20]

Their only merits were the salty whimsy and gentle kidding of race mores. Untouched by depression, fixed in their orbits, they spun out nostalgia as though it were jute. In one of the best, *Judge Priest*, director John Ford and the liberal writer Dudley Nichols created a crusty Southern ambience clothed in wisps of racial satire that must have satisfied them both. Negro women tote "white folks' washing"; a potbellied Kentuckian lazes on a verandah under the fanning of a black boy; blacks and whites doze in the courthouse square as a harmonica trills. Inside, a judge hears a "gangling, lazy mumbling negro" charged with chicken-thieving but acquits him because both would miss their fishing trip. In the same year another variant, Ford's *The World Moves On*, took a Louisiana family to France and war where the black servant is wounded in combat made real by Pathé-Natan newsfilm. A. Edward Sutherland's *Mississippi* contrasted Southern insult with Yankee patronizing. "Get on that box, you Senagambian!" says W. C. Fields to a black lackey while a Stephen Foster type shushes whites so as not to "spoil" a black chorus of "Swanee River." Wise servants came to be "in on every-thing" in many scripts, and in *Zenobia*, Fetchit's "stylized" servant is upstaged by "comic pickaninnies" who recite the Declaration of Inde-pendence.[21] But the cracks in the mold were faint.

In costume dramas the demand for authentic historical backgrounds produced all sorts of black appearances on the screen, especially in the works of Cecil B. DeMille. In 1938 his *Buccaneer* sketched the mélange of races on the eve of Jackson's fight for New Orleans. From servant boys and butlers in the White House the camera moves to Louisiana low country, where we meet servants, hawkers of pralines, and in an enfilad-ing truck-shot, Indians, an Arab at prayer, a Chinese honing a kris, blacks calling out to enlist, and Scipio, servant to the pirate LaFitte, who kisses a rabbit's foot in deference to DeMille's remembrance of things past.[22] So again the old monopoly broke a bit.

Unfortunately for blacks, the old roles survived in newer form in the genres of westerns, sporting movies, and jungle pictures. Westerns, in-

"B" movies depicted traditional roles with assembly line sameness, as here in *Thank You Jeeves* (© 20th Century-Fox Film Corp.). (British Film Insti-tute, hereafter BFI)

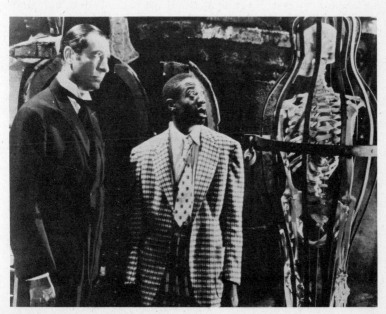

The old roles broadened slightly to include black social dimensions, featuring here the two perennials, Sam McDaniel and Louise Beavers, in *It Ain't No Sin* (© Paramount Productions, Inc.), retitled *Belle of the Nineties*. (Author's collection)

deed, provided a surrogate for Dixie because of their reliance on similar codes of single combat—the *code duello* and the shootout. So black sidekicks and barroom flunkies took on the values of the ante bellum servants, with illiteracy replacing servility as the caste mark. Edgar "Blue" Washington, a Los Angeles policeman, made a good living and sent his son to UCLA by playing the role. By decade's end the flagging genre perked up because of singing cowboys, such as Gene Autry, who varied their fare with occasional exotic settings where they took their blacks. Even so, trade reviewers complained of "the time worn plot, with the typical colored comic sequences taking away what strength it builds."[23]

Sporting movies became another successor to Southern metaphor because the most segregated activity in American life, with the exception of churchgoing, remained athletics. Blacks became only trainers and mascots, with Fetchit the model ever since *Salute* (1929), Ford's patriotic tale of Naval Academy football. Racetrack pictures, most of them cheaply made from stock shots, conformed to the segregation of white jockeys from black exercise boys. Among them were Fetchit's "Hustler" in *Neck and Neck* (1931); rare jockeys in *County Fair* (1932) and *Sporting Chance* (1931); Muse's singing flunky in Capra's *Broadway Bill* (1934); the Fetchit-Rogers team in a setting of trotting tracks in *David Harum* (1934); Bojangles's "Zephyr" in *Road Demon* (1938); George Reed and Sul-te-Wan in *Kentucky*, Fox's big Technicolor Christmas show of 1938; and dozens with titles like *Sweepstakes Winner*, *Pride of the Bluegrass*, *Racing Blood*, and *Saratoga*. In the stock ending the white principals embraced as their jockey booted home his mount and "Mose" or "Eightball" stumbled over a rake or put his foot in a feedbag and got the last laugh.[24]

In a way these movies reconstructed the old paternalistic slave relationships, where slave and master were physically close and bound together in strong emotional attachment. As social distance increased in contemporary settings, black roles would decline in substance because no one understood the limits of the new relationships. It was similar to the problem old Southerners had solved by creating Reconstruction's black codes to define what had once been known to all. Racetracks were then symbolic plantations. If this was so, then boxing pictures must have rendered surrogate master-houseservant relations: white boxers as cavaliers served by black Pompeys. From the silent *Patent Leather Kid* and *Leatherpushers* through a cycle of Toones and Moreland programmers in the 1930s until a revival of *Leatherpushers* replaced them with white Andy Devine's raspy comedy.[25]

Of all the genres, jungle movies were most spoiled by vestigial racism. *Trader Horn*, despite its flaws, effectively used Mutia Omooloo, a sensitive African; authentic location shots; and a plausible tension between colonized and *colons*. Afterward such films made do on the back lot and lost their African flavor.

Exotic locales had always appealed to, in Faisal's words to T. E. Lawrence, "the English hunger for desolate places." So in 1932 to exploit this market MGM decided to milk its outtakes from *Trader Horn* and revive *Tarzan*. The picture was a hit because of director W. S. Van Dyke's flair for the tropics, good outtakes from the *Horn* expedition, a good Burroughs premise, black ambience and dramatic conflict, whites who admired African life and beauty, and an honest wish to make romance out of Africa. It opens on a file of bearers sweating under the weight of ivory, the goal of the heavies. Jane, a young Englishwoman, washes off her makeup in respect for Africa's natural grandeur while her father, an old Africa hand, introduces her to the lore of the tribes. Their hard-lashing driver presses the bearers toward the elephants' graveyard in search of ivory. Along the way they engage in

In the thirties, *Tarzan* (© Metro-Goldwyn-Mayer Distributing Corp.) revived jungle melodrama based on conflict with tribal warriors. (Author's
collection)

plausible conflict with Pygmies defending their turf. Only the arrival
of Tarzan saves them from execution at the hands of a maddened ape.
Yet the point is less his white dominance than Jane's decision to reject
"civilization" in favor of pristine Africa.[26]
   Unfortunately the movie triggered a long cycle that never again
reached the stature of its sire because of the increasing use of stock
shots and the sediment of racism. The series slipped into the B ranks
under Bernard Hyman and then into a rival independent series produced by Sol Lesser. Gradually white motifs and conflicts predomi-
nated, and the nameless natives disappeared. The sequel in 1934 featured lily-white conflict with faithful bearer Nathan Curry as the sole
black credit. The pursuit of ivory was hardly interrupted by "gory
battles between bands of natives" before Tarzan settled the issue and
restored peace to his "domain." By 1938 a "villainous king" had become a European, black credits slipped to the bottom line, and a chim-
panzee stole the picture. That summer Burroughs himself released a

presumably faithful version but removed it to racially neutral Guatemala. To prolong the series MGM even considered a comic version.[27]

The products of lesser studios were even worse, trotting out grainy library footage of nondescript jungles, tendrils of plastic foliage, and brown-skinned veterans of cattle calls. Over-the-hill athletes, improbably light-skinned Negroes, and popular saloon singers joined polished veterans such as Noble Johnson and undermined authenticity. *Variety* griped of the African king in *Nagana* (1933): "Despite his appearance in trunks only, like a Minsky stripper, he talks perfect Lenox avenue." At their worst they fell to absurd comedy such as Wheeler and Woolsey's *So This is Africa* (1933) and *Africa Speaks English* (1933), a vehicle for ventriloquist Edgar Bergen.[28]

Black critics were helpless because of their duty to plug race actors. The *Courier* in 1930 praised Curry's long career from Louise Glaum's *Leopard Woman* through *Tarzan* and ignored the quality of the roles. The most fleeting black heavy peering from beneath the rubber plants drew a plug as "the colored star." Reporters knew that even able actors such as Rex Ingram lived off cattle calls between good jobs. Moreover, the removal of sexual conflict from jungle films because of the Breen Office proscription of miscegenation could have been taken for "progress" by some. As one MGM script reminded its director during a black ambush sequence, "No native is touching any of the white safari."[29]

As early as 1932 the studios discovered the South Seas romance as a vehicle for preserving the titillation of interracial sex without Negroes. "White man . . . brown girl," proclaimed the pressbooks of Vidor's *Bird of Paradise*, a tale of the tropics where "blood runs hot and the heart is free" and where the volcano must blow "because she broke the savage Taboo!" Thenceforward island princesses, halfcastes, heavy white traders, and tragic pearl divers undermined the African movies. The disinterested white *Times* could kid the trend. Black zombies were tolerable, wrote the *Times* man, because "They can carry off blondes without getting ideas in their heads, which helps in these mad days."[30] But the result was not only that overt racism withered, but that *all* black roles lapsed into tolerable blandness.

The racial-sexual neutrality of Micronesia allowed even a conservative such as John Ford to use the genre with maturity intolerable in a Negro setting. As African locales fell into B's, serials, and comedy, Ford's *Hurricane* (1937) transferred a Charles Nordhoff and James Norman Hall novel to the screen and took an Oscar for special effects. The mildly antiimperialist story follows a cruel European governor who unjustly jails an islander. The islander escapes, becoming an insular Zapata and the instrument through which the gods are angered

and the Europeans destroyed. Despite the implausible casting of Jon
Hall and Dorothy Lamour (in the first of her "sarong" roles), they
used good aboriginal actors, some of whom had been two years without work. Sadly, Ford's hit led to a worsening cycle of Lamour comedies and mindless plays on miscegenation.[31]

So awkward was it to penetrate the maze of barriers to black experience in tropical locales that a freak horror movie about a giant ape
came to stand as an underground allegory for black experience. *King
Kong* could have been dismissed as merely a racist nightmare—indeed,
in German it was *King Kong und die Weisse Frau*. But rather than a
mindless black brute, the fifty-foot-high title role was the kidnapped
king of an idyllic island lost in a prehistoric time-warp, ripped from
ecological harmony, set down and chained on a New York stage to be
gawked at by effete urbanites. "He has always been king of his world,"
says one of his tormentors, "but we'll teach him fear." He becomes a
tragic figure, colonized, enslaved, cut from bucolic roots, destroyed by
the city atop the empty engineering triumph, the Empire State Building, but to the end capable of love, cradling his miniature blonde co-
star aloft before his fall from the great tower. In the end Kong became
an enduring mythic figure, part "bad nigger" and part universal victim
of exploitation.[32]

The picture had everything—except perhaps, conscious design: a
whiff of Conan Doyle's *The Lost World*, a solid story by British mystery writer Edgar Wallace, the experience of Schoedsack and Cooper,
the enthusiasm of Selznick and RKO, and the special effects of Willis
O'Brien, who repeated his success of *The Lost World*. But myths are
difficult to sustain, and in the sequel the delicate balance of black rustic
and white urban icons set in romantic fantasy toppled, unnoticed by
serious critics, black or white. Cooper, whose visits to Africa fertilized
the germ of the idea, left the project; Wallace died; O'Brien suffered a
personal tragedy; RKO tightened the budget; and they shot locations
on prosaic Catalina Island. Except for a few actors, including Noble
Johnson, *Son of Kong* received little from his sire. He is discovered
helpless in a bog, an endearing clown in white fur, whimpering in a
half-language and handing over a treasure to the whites, a seedy lot of
down-and-out fugitives from a one-ring carney, the defeated of the
western world.[33] The makers had retreated from the implications of
their creation and settled for a broad wink.

Nevertheless exotic locales provided one last chink through which a
minimal black presence could be seen—a rash of authentically mounted
British colonial movies from Darryl Zanuck, head of Twentieth Century-Fox, and his imitators. Zanuck loved big, well-researched romances of personal success and triumph over adversity—*Clive of In-*

dia, *The House of Rothschild, Cardinal Richelieu, Mighty Barnum, In Old Chicago* (a family caught in the great fire), *The Affairs of Cellini, Lloyds of London, Suez, The Prisoner of Shark Island, The Story of Alexander Graham Bell*—and "Nineteenth Century-Fox" paid for them. Among them were colonialist pieces that supported the rightness of the quest for world markets. At their worst they provided work for blacks —"Zanuck's Central Avenue Beaters," they were called. At their best they gave a glint of insight into an occasional African such as the defeated chieftain in *Rhodes of Africa* (1936), a "genuine Matabele warrior."[34]

Even those that celebrated imperialism gave patronizing tribute to the defeated. If, as the *Times* said, George Stevens's *Gunga Din* was an "imperialist symphony," it also paid touching homage to the heroism of an East Indian whom Indians found "untouchable." And the leader of an unsuccessful Kali cult insurrection has a few moments to lecture the blustery British soldiers on "false pride" of race. In the same year, 1939, Alexander Korda's beautifully shot remake of A. E. W. Mason's *Four Feathers*, a tale of the British campaign against the usurper of the Mahdi in the Sudan, was made to seem a gesture to free the people. When imperialist-racism went too far as in the case of United Artists' *The Real Glory* (1939), a chauvinistic tale of the "always outnumbered, never outfought" Philippine Constabulary which brutally put down the Moro insurrection, critics compared it with Mussolini's assault on Ethiopia. In Zanuck's best work he struck a balance between violence and humanitarianism. *Stanley and Livingston* (1939), for example, is a dramatic conflict between the secular, cocky American, Stanley, whose speech before the royal geographers asks them to open Africa to exploitation, and the benign missionary who commands his guest to "never strike these simple people."[35] Within their limits these were good movies when they offered bright, human rivals to Europeans, and they flopped whenever all they could present were mindless, black straw men incapable of inciting dramatic conflict.

But to see only the persistent motifs of the thirties—the old fashioned, the ante bellum—is to throw away a useful micrometer that measures vernier-fine distinctions that pointed toward a more open future. Those movies that spoke to an urban sensibility—gangster movies, prisons, modern novels, Broadway plays, the increasing artistic products of the political left—tamed the facts of the depression with a cleverness, flippancy, and social optimism free enough of old racial baggage to allow greater freedom for blacks. In no sense revolutionary, or even shocking, the urban vista merely tolerated greater racial variety and imposed no Southern party line on ideas.

Reformist prison movies, at first no more than a few adaptations of

A genuine chieftain played in *Rhodes of Africa* (© Gaumont British Picture
Corporation of America). (GEH)

Broadway plays, developed into a cycle that became a benchmark of American urban culture. Wisecracking, antiauthoritarian, fast-paced, gritty with a scratch-ankle realism, they accepted Negroes as victims of color caste, rotting in dank prisons and in sweaty peonage.

Among the very first, *The Last Mile* (1930), with a bit by Daniel Haynes, and *The Big House* (1930) established a pattern of Negro convicts among the white, and the prototypic crooning black whose plaintive song served as an editorial. A black presence thus gave artistic form to social reportage. Often overdone, as in Columbia's *Guilty* (1930), when a summation of ten witnesses to a crime is suggested by a black trio doing "Swing Low, Sweet Chariot" and "Steal Away," they spurred the *Amsterdam News* to feel that no one could see such conditions without being "inspired to write a spiritual that would portray the feelings of the prisoners." The implied egalitarianism recurred in small ways. A Negro convict played by Everett Brown is the powerful instrument of the jail break in *I Am a Fugitive from a Chain Gang* (1932). Good and bad, the cycle spun through *Laughter in Hell*,

The prison film cycle spawned dozens of imitations like *The Getaway* (© Loew's Inc.). (Author's collection)

Popular hits like *I Am a Fugitive From a Chain Gang* (© Warner Brothers Pictures, Inc.) encouraged staunch black roles such as Everett Brown's convict, here with Paul Muni. (BFI)

Women without Names, and the others. The films missed their aim only when they averted their eyes from root-causes of social malaise or when the blacks served as mere atmosphere. *Ladies They Talk About* (1932), for example, was only a socially precise vehicle for Barbara Stanwyck as an inmate in a jail speckled with blacks, including a darkly ominous Sul-te-Wan. But *Hell's Highway* made more of a point in that Muse's road gang convict was a commentator on his situation. The Negro chorus crooning over the evils of the system was becoming common, but Muse was more pointed: when a guard orders the mules removed from the sun, Muse mutters that "mules cost a lot and convicts cost nothing."[36]

The same sensibility extended to movies of the streets, saloons, courtrooms, and city desks—the locales that accommodated a black presence. In small ways Negroes became a plastic material through which moviemakers shaped their vision of the city. Thus black roles profitted to the degree that white writers understood the difference between the blacks' place in urban life as opposed to Southern life. Not that the urban-toned films preached insurrection; they asked only for an urban awareness, not conversion to a holy cause. Only around the rims of Beverly Hills pools did the drift seem revolutionary. "Motion pictures," said the producer Walter Wanger, "reach the people whom the liberal needs to convert." But the Eastern, more socially conscious writers who made the pilgrimage to Hollywood—Ben Hecht of Chicago, the Algonquin wits, James Hilton, Fitzgerald, Faulkner, Britons such as Wallace, Christopher Isherwood, and Aldous Huxley, and leftists such as Clifford Odets—were drawn by money and would hardly jeopardize it by leavening their scripts with radical dogma.[37]

Besides, the most common black roles brought no more than arch whimsy to bleak movies. Early cases were Muse's Annapolis steward who livens a trip to the south Pole in *Dirigible* (1931), Beavers's "philosophic handmaiden to the ladies of easy virtue" in *Good Sport* (1931), and the blacks of *Night World* (1932), who seemed to one reviewer to go beyond the usual preternatural black folk wisdom toward genuine tragedy:

> Outside of Happy's place the Negro doorman stamps his feet in the snow and wonders if he can take an hour to see his wife in the hospital. He does not know it, but she is going to die, and the night has a sardonic end waiting for him.[38]

Servants held opinions, grumbled, counseled, had tastes, and aspired for success along with their striving employers. Often they and their masters had risen from the bottom together and were the closer for it, even, it seemed, off the screen. "Whenever I planned a show the first person I thought of was Louise," said Mae West of Beavers, who got the idea for her own radio show from her roles in West's *I'm No Angel* and *She Done Him Wrong*. Like the maids in Jean Harlow's movies and later in Dietrich's, she emitted a persona denied her sisters of the twenties. "Ah loves to work for you," says Pearl, the ambitious maid who helps set the red-flocked *fin de siècle* tone of *She Done Him Wrong*. "You got such pretty things." In *I'm No Angel* West has two maids who coolly appraise her lovers. "Great gals, eh?," she says, speaking of them as though they shared her sexuality and her trading on it. "You's a lady now," one reminds her, implying they have risen together from the bottom. Harlow's blonde *Bombshell* gives a negligee to her maid who reappears, her negligee torn at the shoulder, with a sexy leer in her eye. In a segregated world such moments were artful satires on social separation. Moreover, servants were more than confidantes to demimondaines. Sul-te-Wan's maid in the Chicago fire in *In Old Chicago* and Beavers's confessor to the anxiety-ridden cadet of

Brother Rat (1938) carried the roles away from Southern roots, as did Eddie Anderson, a Northern California vaudevillian whose brash "Rochester" boomed the career of radio comedian Jack Benny.[39]

Always, however, studios bought urban ambience, never racial reformism, from their writers. Blacks contributed to movies and profitted from them *only* to that extent in the thirties. Jack Warner remembered two traits of Wilson Mizner: he loved to lounge in the tony Brown Derby restaurant, and he wrote crisp citified dialogue. In *Five Star Final* (1931), Mizner's melodrama of newspaper corruption, a wisecracking Irish editor inquires into slumping Harlem circulation and is told that the city desk has stopped running page-one stories of Jack Johnson's love affairs and "clearing house reports" (one of the computation bases for Harlem gambling). In another case a Negro bootblack is among the bankrollers of a small-time gambler on his first foray against Gotham's big players in *Smart Money* (1931). [40]

Not only did such atmospheric bits help shatter the monopoly of Southern racial metaphor; they supported good black actors. Clarence Muse appeared in Capra's good-natured fables; in programmers such as *Attorney for the Defense, Criminal Court, New York Town, Winner Takes All, Laughter in Hell, Black Moon,* and *The Wrecker;* as a diminishing number of "diverting stable boys"; as the finely crafted mute Ali in *The Count of Monte Cristo;* or the blind vagabond of the mildly populist *Cabin in the Cotton;* and in a brace of good "race movies." In *The Mind Reader* he is everything he could not have been earlier: a quarrelsome, street-wise, turbaned shill for Chandra, a carney hustler; a smart bettor on horses—"cockroaches," he calls them with loving contempt—and a pusher of hair straighteners upon a motley crowd of Memphis Negroes. The comedy is at the expense of blacks only as they share equally the role of victim of Chandra.[41]

Stepin Fetchit, *né* Lincoln Perry, a Southern fugitive from vaudeville, bore most of the traits of the classic thirties black star, lasted longer, outraged more organized Negroes and liberal whites, and revealed both the richness of the older black roles and their limits as entertainment for sophisticated audiences. He started in the silent era as Carolynne Snowden's lover in Fox's *In Old Kentucky,* a success which endeared him to Fox executives, who made him a moneymaking mascot. For them he did everything in the canon of American racial romance and melodrama from Aphra Behn to Charles T. Dazey: foils, slaveys, flunkies, bumpkins, *enfants terribles,* coin-cadging br'er rabbits who eluded every tarbaby in the briar patch, all the while growing more stylized, surreal, and unintelligible. To John Ford he became a pet whose manner grew so personal as to be "undirectable" because his faith was in the survival powers of his profitable stereotype rather in than his current job. But he could alter his mask if so moved, as in *Hearts in Dixie,* in which his Gummy approached the outskirts of tragedy, and in Ford's *The World Moves On,* in which as a servant he follows his Louisiana master to Europe, to war, into the ranks of the French *poilus,* and was wounded in combat.

Fetchit took to cruising Central Avenue in a flashy car stenciled with the legend "Fox Movie Star," squandering his money, developing a "difficult temperament." To the black press he became "the Greatest Colored Star," even if he seemed to organized Negroes to be no more than an omen that the past would survive in the future. He cultivated white reporters with preposterous stories of his tastes and deeds such as his "staying up the entire night before he works so he will be properly tired and lazy" as required. To them he appeared to know his place so well that at the première of *Hearts in Dixie* he sat "upstairs in the gallery where I belong." He was just plain "Step":

> Nothing fancy. Nothing educated or emancipated. He typifies his race. All the traits and talents that legend gives to colored people are embodied in him. He has their joyous, child-like charm, their gaudy tastes, their superstitions. And as for singing, dancing, and strumming a mean banjo—he does them all. And would probably steal chickens if he hadn't promised the Lord never to do anything illegal again.

At the top of his form he and Will Rogers gave Fox a run of stylish rural hokum that helped the studio through the worst of the depression in such vehicles as *David Harum,* Irvin S. Cobb's Kentucky tales of *Judge Priest, The County Chairman,* and Ford's own fondly remembered tribute to Cobb's tales, *Steamboat Round the Bend,* starring the pudgy, horsefaced Cobb himself and Rogers as rival Mississippi steamboat skippers. Indeed, they got on so well as teammates that Rogers's death in a plane crash may have driven Fetchit to an early slump into programmers. In these films Fetchit's persona supports a mossy sentimental vision of Southern life and celebrates the close personal connections between the old bondmen and their masters. And by minimizing the cruel and punitive side, the pictures seemed to say that once upon a time when race relations were closer no one had needed laws and cops to remind him of place and status.[42]

Sadly for Fetchit, ever smaller audiences enjoyed his green glade of racial goodwill. In modern settings every obsequious tic stood out and grated on critical nerves. In his earliest films, even though critics liked him in *Hearts in Dixie,* they carped at his style when it appeared out of place in other pictures. Only six months apart the *Amsterdam News* blasted his paltering mumble in Fox's *Movietone Follies* and Ford's *Salute,* while the *Times* found him "slower and more indistinct than ever, [and] only mildly amusing" in a remake of the New Orleans melodrama *Cameo Kirby*. Even so, the chiding of critics failed to dampen his popularity among the black masses, who remembered that underneath his comic mask he had established landmarks, opened the way for others, and gave them a success model of whom they could be proud. Besides, his hyperbolic, shrill shuffling through *Stand Up and Cheer* with a penguin as a straight man or some other low plateau of achievement would be remembered against his best Rogers vehicles when his character wheedled his way out of jail, bilked coins from gullible whites, or otherwise burlesqued the black condition.

So in a small way he played for two audiences, giving to one a reassuring vision of Southern nostalgia, and to the other a covert, unstated metaphor for insurrection.[43] Despite his critics, Fetchit symbolized the thirties waffling on racial imagery. In the great bulk of movies, the producers failed to make the older figures speak to modern taste. But neither Fetchit nor his writers of Cobb's school should be blamed for this, for their creation was a genuine fable of Southern Americana: the whites deriving status and identity from their unquestioned paternal rule, the blacks salvaging theirs with whatever dignity they could cling to in a servile state. Besides, the most memorable character in *Steamboat Round the Bend* was neither Fetchit nor Cobb; he was "the New Moses," a ragged itinerant preacher who shouted his way through the sandflats with empty promises of a New South all knew would not come.

If Fetchit showed the way for black vaudevillians and Muse for thespians, their success in a way blunted Negro demands for a share of Hollywood. True, with the decline of dominant Southern attitudes, there was no longer any reason to deny blacks a place in a movie. But the spectrum of black imagery represented by the two poles of Fetchit and Muse provided white writers with a limited range of black roles—indeed, black women, for reasons taken up later, would stretch black roles to greater dimensions.

Perhaps for black actors to do more than merely contribute they would be required, not unlike black cavalrymen in the Spanish-American War, to prove themselves. The twin urges to prove one's black masculine ability and to contribute substance to American life had driven the black bourgeoisie for years, and the Hollywood Negro was no exception. Movie roles for blacks increased many times over compared to the slack twenties, in number, variety, substance, and quality. Sometimes they were a mere *non sequitur* presence as in Laurel and Hardy's early soundfilms *Pardon Us* and *Pack Up Your Troubles*. In the former the team breaks jail by inserting themselves in a parody of crooning fieldhands in blackface, and in the latter they search for the family of a dead war-buddy, along the way meeting a Negro who answers his door as the pair blurt a repressed, apologetic, "We thought you were Eddie's father." In *You Said a Mouthful* (1932) Joe E. Brown played his shy braggart against Allan "Farina" Hoskins's black straightman. Mistaken for a champion swimmer who is to test a new bathing suit by swimming to Catalina, Brown has his bluster tempered by Hoskins's baleful eye and his misguided plans steered from disaster by the kid's wit. *Variety* reported that "Farina, freed from his 'Our Gang' limitations, gives the story an added comedy flavor, the mournful eyed pickanniny drawing laughs on his own and not overplayed." A few months earlier upon the loss of his longtime place in "Our Gang," *Motion Picture Herald* had praised Hoskins for his black contribution to the sentimental children's series as "the perfect incarnation of poor, witless man's struggles against inscrutable, and very rough and dirty, fate." His style spurred imitators and induced stars such as Fetchit to play in short films.[44]

The trend reached every sort of film, including the snooty maid in *Morning Glory* (1933), who derives her own status from that of her *grande dame* mistress; the traditional whitecoated butlers like Sam McDaniel in Joe E. Brown's *Polo Joe* (1934) and their modern equivalents like Raymond Turner's elevator operator in *Weary River* (1932); the false ring of blackface in Wheeler and Woolsey's *Diplomaniacs* (1933); the blacks included in the militant children's army in Wellman's *Wild Boys of the Road* (1933), who throw watermelons instead of vegetables at the railroad cops; Philip Hurlic's stableboy and Sam McDaniel's liveried butler in Hearst's version of the Betsy Patterson-Jerome Bonaparte wedding in *Hearts Divided* (1936); Hattie McDaniel's maid who resists *Babbitt*'s (1934) attempts to modernize *her* kitchen with electric gadgets and asks merely for Sundays off; Buck and Bubbles's tutors of the white dancers in *The Varsity Show* (1937); the persistent convicts like the mulatto who croons "Nobody Knows the Trouble I've Seen" as Gene Raymond goes to the "chair" in *If I Had A Million* (1932); the protective black maid who symbolizes the fallen plight of Marlene Dietrich's *Blonde Venus* and wards off cops and snoops because underneath their different skins she and Dietrich are both women in a hostile world—and hundreds more contributions to their times.[45]

Unfortunately for blacks, the next step beyond mere contribution seemed too far to be seen by the naked eye. Etta Moten, for example, appreciated her director's "deliberately" casting a Negro in a 1933 film and Warners' seeming conscious urge to be "first" among liberals. But she fretted through the long waits "between jobs," the endless offers to do "specialties" in white plots, the need to accept jobs dubbing for white singers, the sure knowledge that even a "hot" property could ex-

pect no more than redundant bits. Fredi Washington also worked hard
to hang on in Hollywood but resented the casual racism of the crews.
So that "progress" appeared to be slower than expectations, at least until the rush of 1936.[46]

By that year Afro-Americans through luck and persistence restored
some of the bright optimism that had attended the 1929 "Dixies," while
they broadened their contribution to an unprecedented range. Even the
common run seemed changed. Bill Robinson gave both cool grace and
bright-eyed wit to the butlers in Fox's *The Littlest Rebel* and *The Little Colonel*. Who else could have survived in good style two movies
with Shirley Temple's strong presence—and follow them with still another half-dozen? And if other musical performers like the Cabin Kids,
Ellington, and the electrically agile young Nicholas Brothers began
more than ever to appear as "themselves," their urbane charisma itself broke new ground. The exotics and convicts survived in the persons of Daniel Haynes and Noble Johnson in Columbia's *Escape from*

The year 1936 marked a minor watershed. A subsequent burst of black roles
included Bill Robinson's agile butler in *The Little Colonel* (© Fox Film
Corp.). (Author's collection)

Devil's Island. Servants such as Sam McDaniel's "Pot Roast" in *Unwelcome Stranger* grew more flippant. Hattie McDaniel's career escalated with each new maid and mammy, Kitty and Mamie, giving rise to a cadre of bosomy broadbeamed imitators. Willie Best matched her rise with each new "Catfish" and "Brass," while Fred Toones metamorphosed into a permanent role as "Snowflake." The Hall Johnson Choir resumed its career singing on levees. And new blacks such as Etta McDaniel and Oscar Polk joined Muse and the other studio regulars.[47]

Black performers imposed a mid-thirties vision on the most traditional of vehicles. Even the remake of Charles Dazey's wheezing *In Old Kentucky* profited from Bill Robinson's bright vernacular dances. And in urbane pictures like *Hooray for Love* black bits appeared and caught the romance of the streets. In a playlet within the film Robinson is a kind of neighborhood "mayor" who saves Jeni Legon from eviction by interceding with a shadowy landlord, after which they celebrate with a vibrant dance sequence to Fats Waller's crooning of "Livin' in a Great Big Way." And when one of the older types appeared, Beavers could give it life, as she did in *Annapolis Farewell,* standing beside her employer, an old commodore, watching affectionately and unknowingly as his old ship rides at anchor before being towed as a target. By then audiences could enjoy them while knowing along with the *Times* critic that the old-style pictures were "adrip with magnolia and vast, unashamed portions of synthetic Dixie."[48]

The Civil War appeared as the clearest sign of eroded ante bellum imagery, for writers gave attention to black responses to their plight. The most modest of them, *Hearts in Bondage,* a Republic programmer spotted with muted blacks, rose above its evasive dedication to those "who fought for and against" the Blue and Gray, and focused on the construction of Union gunboat *Monitor.* At a higher notch, *Slave Ship* indicted the ocean-going "blackbirders" for their cruelty to captive future slaves without firmly accusing domestic slavery. Nevertheless, Carl Van Vechten appreciated the gesture and told his friend James Weldon Johnson. "Have you seen 'Slave Ship'?" he wrote. "This goes a little further in the direction of realism than most movies on this subject & you get a glimpse of how the Africans were packed into the holds of the ships & treated." The best of them, though not necessarily the most satisfying to black audiences, was John Ford's *The Prisoner of Shark Island,* a sympathetic portrait of Dr. Samuel Mudd, who set John Wilkes Booth's leg in the dark hours after Lincoln's assassination and suffered an awful term in the tropical squalor of Dry Tortugas prison. Mudd's fate slowly falls into the hands of Buck, a faithful black fellow-Marylander (Ernest Whitman) who joins the army in a classic gesture of the servant's duty to the master and follows Mudd to Florida.

His study in self-sacrifice treated the slave's role with evenhanded honesty while stiffening a bit when he becomes a blueback soldier. Ford and the Georgian Nunnally Johnson, who wrote the script, could do no more with Whitman's role, but they caught the black mood of Reconstruction with good, dimly lighted shots of mutinous black soldiers who refuse to minister to fever-ridden white soldiers. The resulting tight-knit drama saved an otherwise middling picture. Only black Buck and Mudd can move the mutineers at the height of a storm because, as one of them argues, Mudd is no legalistic Yankee but a "good" Southerner who understands their reluctance to take risks for an impersonal institution such as the United States Army.[49]

Unfortunately, the finest black roles served the worst of pictures, King Vidor's studio assignment made from Stark Young's novel of the bloody ground of Reconstruction, *So Red the Rose*. A dull rehearsal of Southern agonies away from the centers of combat, it included on its periphery a strong conflict between two boldly painted slaves, the stately house servant, William Veal (Daniel Haynes), and a hard-eyed fieldhand, the rebellious Cato (Clarence Muse), who beautifully represented the poles of black response to slavery—accommodation and insurrection.[50]

In the best of the mid-decade lot Negroes actually carried major parts of movies. If the overriding motif of the time was a cynical, despair-twisted success myth—Horatio Alger's *Jed the Poorhouse Boy* rendered by the Dead End Kids or Andrew Carnegie's secular puritanism seen through the prism of Al Capone—then black experience had moved closer to general American life. The best single expression of the times as far as blacks were concerned grew out of Robert E. Sherwood's play *The Petrified Forest*. It opens at the confluence of the lives of a dying poet and a rude gangster in a seedy gas station and diner on the edge of the "forest." There only the crass and the dull survive in a half-life from which Gabrielle, the ingenue, wants to escape so she can write in Paris. She and a wistful poet stand in the center between shimmering Paris and flat bourgeois desert, her choice between flight and torpor sharpened by the arrival of a gang of fleeing criminals.

Among them is a wisecracking black gunman flowing through the shots slim as a reed in contrast to the rough-edged Duke Mantee, their leader. "Hi, everybody!" he says, pushing through the screen door. " 'Bout time you got around to inviting me in." To the liveried, prissy black chauffeur of a rich hostage he says, too loudly, "Hi-yah, colored brother." "Good evening," says "Joseph," muffling his discomfort. Later the distinction in their lives is more explicit: Joseph must ask his employer if it is all right to accept a drink. "Listen to him," mocks Slim, the gunman. "Is it all right, Mr. Chisholm? Ain't you heard about

The struggle between Daniel Haynes's accommodating house servant and Clarence Muse's rebellious Cato in *So Red the Rose* (© Paramount Productions, Inc.) showed a broadening scope for black acting talents. (Author's collection)

Louise Beavers's Nellie Silvers, the numbers queen in *Bullets or Ballots* (©
Warner Brothers Pictures, Inc.), marks her most dramatic departure from
her bread-and-butter roles playing maids. (BFI)

the big liberation? Come on, take your drink, weasel!" Like Duke, the
cocky black gunman has chosen the way of the outlaw and freedom. If
his stakes were lower than those of the rich whites, he gave a black vision of better life to the sequence, dominated it, and gave it meaning.
Edward Thompson brought such strength to the role that the character's
name was changed from "Pyles" to "Slim," the actor's own nickname.[51]

Any good movie in 1936 might use black imagery to make a dramatic
point. In DeMille's *The Plainsman* we know immediately that Latimer,
the Indian agent, is the heavy dealing in smuggled rifles because he is
rough on the black dockers. Accommodating Louis Armstrong turned
upside-down the legend of Negro necrophobia in *Pennies from Heaven*
by pursuing a skeleton with his blaring trumpet and rasping, "That cat
don't want no more of me!" The black press labeled the movie "an important step for the whole Negro profession." *Bullets or Ballots*, a rare
treatment of the "numbers racket" sector of urban criminality, ac-

curately caught Negro motifs in the person of Beavers's "Nellie Silvers, the numbers queen," who uses the rackets to desert domestic servitude. She can boss her stocky gunman and her chauffeur, coolly wear a diamond bracelet, deliver the betting slips with smart professionalism, and still remonstrate with her servant successor for her fumbling effort to set her old mistress' hair. Unashamed of her beginnings, even fondly recalling them, she knows the racket is spreading through Harlem and her former mistress is correct in her advice: "You've graduated; keep on managing Harlem. You created the game; get your profit." The so-so movie would have been worthless without her.[52]

The spirit of the time can be fairly seen by contrasting Universal's two productions of Edna Ferber's melodramatic *Showboat* (1929 and 1936). A strong subplot that indicts American racial mores as the weight upon an interracial marriage is muted in the former as compared to the high relief it is given later. In the first film, Joe, a strong, even-tempered black deckhand, is played by Stepin Fetchit, in part because rudimentary sound techniques could not make use of the boom-

Paul Robeson's Joe in *Showboat* (© Universal Productions, Inc.). (Author's collection)

Robeson's fame in other media allowed him to sit on the right hand of
director James Whale (© Universal Productions, Inc.). (BFI)

ing voice of Jules Bledsoe's Broadway original; while the second version featured a good job by Paul Robeson. Bulky, black "Queenie" was
played first by temperate Gertrude Howard, then by sharply witty
Hattie McDaniel. Robeson's and McDaniel's familial comedy far out-
shone Fetchit's broad reading of the tense sexual role-rivalry. James
Whale's remake also restored Jerome Kern and Oscar Hammerstein's
angry black resentment of white privilege, in "Old Man River." For
their part, the writers gave the establishing shot to Joe, "the big smiling
sensitive-faced deck hand," and in their fashion, gave Julie, the mulatto,
her identity by penciling through all the "thats" in her "Fish Gotta
Swim, Birds Gotta Fly" number and changing them back to their original "dats," and changing "is" to "ain't." The *Amsterdam News* itself
was swept along by the "thrills" Robeson brought to the screen and by
the miscegenation theme that survived the Hays office scissors.[53]

These good black parts notwithstanding, the use of Negroes in Hollywood pictures did not always pull even with the standard set in 1936. A toughminded broadside against lynching. MGM's *Fury* softened, stammered, and finally lost sight of terror. The studio had only reluctantly agreed to do it, more or less as a lesson to a headstrong young producer, and grudgingly assigned its budding star, Spencer Tracy, and its new German director from UFA, Fritz Lang. With the naïveté of an émigré Lang took Norman Krasna's tough script on its face and planned for a white woman to be raped by a Negro so as to treat only the true issue of mob violence rather than the side issues of race and guilt. Gradually, though, every important reference to race molted in the cutting room, including a Negro woman absently singing about "a happy home where all de darkies are free." After every strong shot in the rushes Lang fretted outside Eddie Mannix's office awaiting the shrill reaction. In the end *Fury* became a modest hit and started a cycle that missed the point that Negroes were the historic victims of lynching. Still, the black critic Roi Ottley thanked God and Lang for a small favor. A year later Archie Mayo's flattering imitation, *Black Legion*, caught the crack of the whip, the meanness of lynching's bloody carnival, the weaseling of "responsible businessmen" who averted their eyes, and a parodied KKK, then, like *Fury*, failed blacks all the way to its lily-white courtroom summation. In the same year the worst of the waffling failures, Mervyn Leroy's *They Won't Forget*, brought Ward Greene's novel about an actual lynching case to the screen. But it set its viewers on a false trail because the first arrest after a Southern kidnapping is a terror-stricken black janitor (Clinton Rosamond) who appears only to point the way toward the eventual white victim of the mob. Thus if its theme is symbolized by stark images such as a steel hook snatching a mailsack from a passing train, the social point is wasted by its focus on whites. Appropriately, it opened in Manhattan in the heat of a dull summer and received bland, dutiful praise from the *Times* and the *Amsterdam News*.[54]

Taking one sort with the other, good black treatments were not so much self-consciously "liberal" or reformist as they were pictures in which the new Negro plausibly fit: Sam McDaniel's "Doc" in MGM's *Captains Courageous*, Noble Johnson's "Roustan" in the Boyer-Garbo Napoleonic romance, *Conquest*, Hattie McDaniel in the Gable-Harlow *Saratoga*, Sul-te-Wan as "Tituba" in *The Maid of Salem*, the flashy Harlem number in *Artists and Models*, the nameless bondmen in *Slave Ship*, or the reportage of Fox's programmer from Judge Ben Lindsay's story of a Negro mother who raises a white child only to lose him in a court fight.[55] Indeed, the good racial depictions and the bad sold equally well, all other things being equal. For example, when *Prestige*, a stale

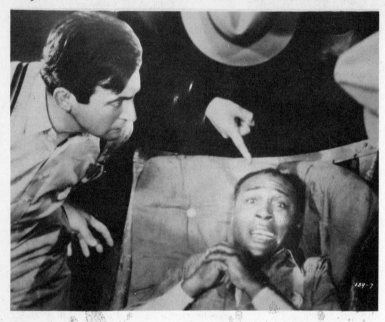

Rosamond's near-victim of a lynching in the evasive *They Won't Forget*
(© Warner Brothers Pictures, Inc.) presented a side of black life mostly
ignored by Hollywood in the 1930s. (Author's collection)

melodrama whose colonialist racism oozed from every sprocket-hole,
failed in Louisville, *Arrowsmith*, a derivation from a popular Sinclair
Lewis novel that deviated from racial custom, outgrossed it four-to-one;
the liberal, well-mounted, pro-Jewish *House of Rothschild* outdrew the
traditional Negroes of *Carolina* in Birmingham; and the Southern chauvinism of the uninspired *So Red the Rose* failed despite a round of splashy
Southern premières.[56] Throughout the depression blacks only occasionally made a real impact because success of a film usually depended on
other factors.

Nevertheless the black press gave ever more attention to movies in
the late thirties and grew touchier about their racial faults. As self-
appointed cheerleaders the newspapers applauded both the quantity
and merit of the new Negro roles, plugged "important" notches of
progress, and ran well-laid-out features on the stars which probably
boosted ad-space sales. As never before they could make hairline distinctions between the purported realism of a *March of Time* segment

on black magic, which was a "deliberate attempt," according to one story, "to characterize the people of Harlem as a group of primitive, ignorant savages devoid of any knowledge of the civilization surrounding them," and some "head-scratching" role on which they decided to avoid direct comment for fear of stirring a squabble between critics and Hollywood Negroes. In time they reached out from the movies themselves, complained of the MPAA's toleration of "coon" and "darkey" in scripts, and reported on incidents such as the Greensboro students who boycotted theaters that had refused to show *Artists and Models* and *One Mile from Heaven*. The Italian assault on Ethiopia raised blacks to new levels of consciousness which, along with the purchase of prestigious dramas and novels by the studios presumably for more literate liberal audiences, moved producers to break still more racial conventions.[57]

Thus by the time of Roosevelt's second inaugural self-conscious blacks had contributed to producing social and aesthetic change in concert with liberal whites. Overt and vicious racism slipped into the backwaters of the cinema, stuff made for habitual rather than selective moviegoers. Thoughtless newsreels, stylized cartoons, and opportunistic educational films also carried on the old prejudices.

Throughout the depression newsreel cameramen rarely shot more than Negro *curiosa* such as "Harlem Negroes Eating Watermelon," Elks parades, a freak who had married fifty-six times, chain gangs, colorful mass baptisms, Africans dancing, and among the worst, the golfer Joe Kirkwood driving a ball off a prone Negro's pursed lips. Another newsreel featured the psychiatrist A. A. Brill, intercut with clapping hands and flashing feet, explaining the racial basis of swing music. In their libraries they filed the footage under such cues as "C. U. of nigger children talking," "Old Tom . . . ," "C. U. of Uncle Joe," and so on. Here and there black humanity might peer from the sandbaggers during a Mississippi flood, from the ranks of a sad-eyed file of Missouri croppers camped along Highway 61 protesting their need for federal aid, from a circle of black workers celebrating a bumper crop of Virginia tobacco, from ringside where Jack Johnson hung on the fringes of the fight game while Joe Louis trained to box Tony Galento. Then as war approached, the all-black 99th Pursuit Squadron, black paratroopers, the old Negro 92nd receiving Purple Hearts, and Marian Anderson singing at Lincoln Memorial appeared on the screen. Even then the only shots of social malaise followed the Harlem riots of the 1930s as cameras scanned the damage and the prisoners to the exclusion of the preconditions.[58]

In contrast with feature films, documentaries seemed regressive. Save for a few attempts by Henry Luce's film-child, *The March of Time*, they avoided the black streetscape in favor of the safe paths of the jungle and the Southern furrow. Exotic locales had always been favored, so the topics were not new. Their sin was their near-uniform poverty of insight and their smug lack of cultural relativity. For every honest *Nanook* there were fraudulent *Ingagi*s; for every *Tabu*, dozens of *Nabonga*s; for every *Voyage au Congo*, ribbons of dull Martin and Osa Johnson travelogues and Frank Buck "animal pictures," all of which were produced by filmmakers with the advantage of personal observation of black cultures which they might have offered to their audiences' curiosity rather than pandering to their cultural chauvinism. For years they had masqueraded as anthropologists, safe from all but a tiny band of critics who charged them with grinding out the "unauthoritative, the supercilious, the patronizing, the wisecracking" bedrock of racism. Their sharpest critic, *Variety*, loved to twit them for their "semi-simian women," their "actionless, drab and draggy" footage, their "Westchester weeds," and their mock "Boy Scout thing."[59] *Untamed Africa* hid behind the scholarly aegis of a geographic society as it retailed images of blacks trading wives for salt, "superstitious" natives "jabbering and yelling in African," and in the end coyly announced: "Censorship forbids the pictured finish of this orgiastic dance, but it closes with the frenzied darkness of primitive night." By 1933 Frank Buck made *Darkest Africa* for Chicago's Century of Progress Exposition, trotting out still another generation of staged dances, firewalkers, Pygmies, and clattering spearbearers. In the classroom children could catch Edited Pictures' *Glimpses of Northern Brazil* (1937), where "halfbreed Negroes" live out lives "almost as primitive as their African ancestors . . . indolent and carefree" under the tutelege of "pure" European Brazilians.[60]

Treatments of voodoo in Harlem in *The March of Time* outraged the black press. But their best reached only slightly higher with segments on the raspy timbres of Huddie Leadbetter in 1935, and by 1939 a few bits of Father Divine and the boom-and-bust economics of Dixie. And in 1941 an "Americans All" sequence included not a single Negro. In the classroom American themes were little better. *The Old South* and *Dixie*, two prestigious films, stressed slave loyalty and contentment, the salubrious climate rather than the profit motive at the root of slavery, and slave frolics in the quarter rather than their ditching, chopping, cutting, picking, and hauling. The latter picture ignored revisionist historians who quarreled with the benign view of the old South yet marketed the product under the distinguished logo of the Yale Chronicles of America series.[61]

Given the conservative themes, motifs, and images in the standard fare offered by moviemakers, the major body of film that pointed to

more honest and sympathetic depiction of blacks came from Eastern
literary sources. These films allowed the boldest play to Negro aspiration and expression, provided opportunity for black contributions to
major artistic attainments, and at the least offered honest and forthright
reportage of some qualities of Afro-American life. Among this influ-
ential corporal's guard were Sinclair Lewis's *Arrowsmith*, Fanny Hurst's
Imitation of Life, Clifford Odets's *Golden Boy*, Paul Green's *Cabin in
the Cotton*, Booth Tarkington's *Alice Adams*, John Steinbeck's *Of
Mice and Men*, and Owen Davis's *Jezebel*, in addition to the works of
Southerners Nunnally Johnson and Lamar Trotti.

Arrowsmith (1931) provides a good case of the high hopes the lit-
erateurs held for their works as well as the tangled path to success. Directed by John Ford for Samuel Goldwyn, the picture episodically pursues the conflict between Dr. Martin Arrowsmith's personal integrity
and the snare of overintellectualized professionalism. Torn between

Clarence Brooks's Dr. Marchand intrudes into a white plot in John Ford's
Arrowsmith (1931), an omen of things to come (© Samuel Goldwyn-
United Artists). (BFI)

devotion to his frail wife, his grinding practice, and his yen for research, he at last breaks from the confines of the impersonal laboratory in order to help fight bubonic plague in the West Indies. There he meets Dr. Oliver Marchand (Clarence Brooks) of Howard University. Again opposites rear up in the form of a choice between science and healing. For brownskinned Marchand there is no choice between fighting the plague and his old mentor's suggestion that he create a black control group to whom he would deny serum so as to learn more of the disease. The only black doctor on an island beset by war between pantheistic voodoo and western medicine is forced by circumstance to opt for humane immediacy rather than long-run benefit.

Until Ford's Indies sequences came on, the picture limped. But the island with "plague raging" is, in the manner of his Dublin in *The Informer*, a tightly shot, mottled set with stark shadows against white walls, straw hats flecking the streets, drums over all. When a baby dies, there is a tight closeup of a black madonna; when a doctor dies, we hear wails from a circle of blacks. Potentially a cliché in other hands, Ford made it work as surely as he raised westerns above dull routine. But most significantly, the black presence in the Indies made Arrowsmith's dilemma come to life and made the movie greater than its other parts.[62]

But if *Arrowsmith* broke new ground in 1931 with its depiction of a black doctor, it also suffered the fate of avant garde literary movies, especially those with racial themes. *The New York Times* admired it. In big cities such as Chicago, even in the Southern towns like Baltimore, it had good grosses. And blacks praised it as a "first." But *Variety* reminded bookers of the historic low box office potential of such movies, and Brooks never got another good role in Hollywood. Nevertheless, even though the odds were long that it would be a hit, Lewis counted the sale of the novel to an independent producer such as Goldwyn as one of his most satisfying moments. And he regaled Negro sociologist Horace Cayton with the story of his personal pride when the black doctor makes his entrance, slowly turning and revealing his identity to the "startled audience." Almost anytime earlier Lewis could not have sold his novel, even to an indie, much less have Ford direct it, and have it released as a profitable film.[63]

In a month or so Clarence Muse joined the ranks of the lucky few who scored in literary movies. He had just come from *Prestige*, a tedious failure in which his tragic native servant, Nahum, helps a Foreign Legionnaire put down an insurrection of, in *Variety*'s words, "the most goshawful savage types ever gathered into one picture," thereby saving the "prestige" of the white race. But in *Cabin in the Cotton*, Paul Green's adaptation of Henry Kroll's indictment of sharecropping, he

played, said the *Amsterdam News*, "a poor blind old Negro whose unhappy lot is that he must beg alms of the poor white trash in the South
who are almost as destitute as himself."[64]

The picture only nicked its target, but some of its gritty Southern
populism survived. The white dramatic conflicts were spoiled by the
contrivance of placing the son of a "peckerwood" in the offices of a
planter. Thus the white action goes downhill after its opening sequence
in which a peckerwood shoots a planter and is harried through the
swamps. The young man under two flags sees his wizened father die,
learns of a double set of ledgers in the planter's store, but at the mass
meeting of the croppers he can only join in a plea to seek remedies, "not
fix guilt."

On the other hand, a good range of black roles gives strength to an
otherwise evasive picture. There is Muse's blind black beggar led about
by a singing waif. A rackety Memphis jazz band too brash for cracker
tastes symbolizes the historic disunity of the Southern poor on racial
lines when a lounging cropper complains of the "$400 for a jazz band
sweated out of my people." In the script idlers in the street haze the
white youth then working for the planter for playing "chambermaid
for a bunch of yellow saxophone players." A storekeeper accepts a bale
of cotton from a Negro who is symbolic of the croppers' plight, while
deducting thirty-four percent for back interest. "He took it easy," says
a hanger-on. "Nothing else for him to do," says the vaguely sympathetic clerk. He is not a toady, he seems to say, but a victim of "the
same old system." Nevertheless the theme is thrown aside because the
climactic mass meeting is nearly lily white.[65]

One of the best black roles almost saved a turgid "woman's picture"
made from Hurst's *Imitation of Life* (1934). John M. Stahl's tearful
unfolding of one of the oldest racial dilemmas in America, the decision
to "pass" across the line from black to white, worked largely because
of its interesting Negroes. A white widow and her cook market a favorite pancake mix and become rich, a situation into which the camera
neatly intrudes as though in a zoom shot—down into Atlantic City, to
Delilah's Place, under the Boardwalk lights, to Peola, the cook's light-
skinned daughter (Fredi Washington) snapping, "I'm *not* black! I'm
not!" Sadly, the best conflict is thrown away by Louise Beavers's urge to
be lovable. As the cook she finds her daughter's rejection and wish to
"pass" is no one's fault because "It can't be the Lord's." In school Delilah thoughtlessly exposes her passing daughter, who rails at the betrayal to which her mother can offer only history in rebuttal: Peola
is like "pappy"—"beating his head against life." Through ten years of
pancakes and wealth Delilah remains a diffident cook, while Peola
passes as a restaurant cashier. "You don't know what it is to look white

Literary sources such as Fanny Hurst's *Imitation of Life* (© Universal Pictures Corp.) raised formerly arcane issues such as passing across racial lines while giving infrequently decent work to fine black actors like Fredi Washington and Louise Beavers. (BFI)

and be black," Peola explains to her mournful mother, who feels as though she is being asked to "unborn my own child." In the end Delilah's only reward is her "hanker for a good funeral," for which blacks turn out in droves complete with wailing music, white horses, columns of Masons in plumes and regalia, and uniformed black sororities.[66]

The murky picture was a high notch of Hollywood racial vision and persuaded *Variety* to dodge its usual duty of warning off Southern exhibitors:

> Most arresting part of the picture and overshadowing the conventional romance between the late thirtyish white widow and Warren William is the tragedy of Aunt Delilah's girl born to a white skin and Negro blood. This subject has never been treated upon the screen before. Girl is miserable being unable to adjust herself to the lot of her race and unable to take her place among the whites. This is, of course, very grim and harsh stuff.

It seems very probable the picture may make some slight contribution to the cause of greater tolerance and humanity in the racial question. Its reception in the South, of course, cannot be judged or guessed by a northerner. Exhibs below Mason-Dixon will have to make their own decision.[67]

Its weaknesses lay hidden beneath the liberal surface. The middlebrow *Literary Digest* spotted the squishy-soft center: its wish to be "extremely careful to avoid its most dramatic theme, obviously because it fears its social implications." Also, Stahl seemed to regard Peola "with a bit of distaste," preferring Delilah "because she is of the meek type of old-fashioned Negro that, as they say, 'knows his place.' " Nevertheless, the picture offered abundant signs that depression attitudes were producing changes. Universal's decision to produce it, the astonishing prescience of white magazines, the enthusiasm of white audiences who found it "gripping and powerful," its "surprisingly" large grosses everywhere, topped by a $36,000 average for three weeks at the Roxy, and the predictable splash in Negro neighborhoods, where it "created a sensation," added up to a minor revolution in moviegoers' tastes.[68]

A year later a literary source provided still another, though less dominant, racial figure, and helped open the budding career of Hattie McDaniel. In Tarkington's *Alice Adams,* a treatment of the vanity of a small-town social climber and the tatty values of her middle class, McDaniel's maid is an editorial chorus. George Stevens's first decent picture gave blacks some of the most honest racial bits ever filmed. Taken together, they gave the plot a strong though muted underpinning.

The establishing shots dolly down Main Street settling on Alice (Katharine Hepburn) as she emerges from the five-and-ten. We know *its* clientele and *her* status when a Negro matron and her children follow her out of the shop. Later, we know Alice's brother is a rakish nonconformist because of his familiar ease among the blacks. "Hi ya, Sam," he snaps to a hat-checker at a dance. "What're you doin' up there, big boy?" he asks the fat bandleader with a knowing nod. In the shank of the evening Alice must hesitantly approach the coatroom and ask to speak to her brother, who by then is shooting dice with the blacks behind the coats. The black checker responds in two codes of diction: with due crispness to Alice, and with an over-the-shoulder black-toned, "Hey, your sister wants you!" to her brother. Thus in a few seemingly offhand black shots we know the opposite side of the distant racial etiquette of the decent white folks into whose circles Alice wishes to climb.

Everyone climbs the social ladder in his own way: Alice's mother cultivates formal manners, her father struggles with his glue factory, her brother looks to the turn of a card. Alice herself attempts the top rung by entertaining a well-placed bachelor at a dinner for which a maid has been engaged. The broad black maid has been through it all before, so she chews gum through the redundant instructions. "It's too hot for soup," she carps at Alice's choice. The whites are not used to servants close at hand; the maid is only a tool. When she stumbles, Alice needs only to ask: "Did she break any of our things?" The stiff evening grinds onward, the Adamses formal and wooden, the guest cool. The dining room doors stick with heat. The soup, Alice decides under the maid's baleful reproach, is wrong for hot weather. Contemptuously the maid snatches away the bowl with father's spoon still aloft. In bad French Alice tries to blame the evening on permissiveness with the servants. The maid sneers from the kitchen. Does she know French? "Here you!" someone barks like a sergeant, but she ignores it, revealing the Adamses' gentility as a fraud. The entire *tour de force* is given meaning and strength through McDaniel's craftsmanship and centrality. Not that anyone noticed. The *Times* applauded only "her hilarious bit."[69]

In a short time Hattie McDaniel enlarged the role in RKO's *The Mad Miss Manton* (1935), an urbane script by Philip G. Epstein which drags the maid, quirks and all, into a screwball plot. "I had to wake your maid," Miss Manton's doorman says, "and boy was she fried." Manton's (Barbara Stanwyck) liberal mugwump crusaders are often interrupted by the maid's judgments of callers and of the unseemly din. "Sounds like a pipsqueak to me!" she says, hand over the phone. "I ain't deaf," she shouts through the door to a caller. "Sometimes I wish I was." Still later, she speaks sharply to a woman, only to be reminded "She is our guest." But "I didn't invite her up," she snaps. Ordered to keep a suitor away, she hits him with a pitcher of water. "Orders is orders," she says, "but I used distilled water."[70] Clearly she had caught the spirit of thirties screwball comedy and had helped make a good script work to its fullest dimensions.

But a better measure of the period and its scripts would be the treatment of ante bellum servants. William Wellman's *Jezebel* (1938) seemed in the mood of Lillian Hellman's waspish assaults on the South, *The Little Foxes* and *Another Part of the Forest*. Black and white critics approved of the new naturalistic version of the ante bellum South and the wide range of blacks in slave-ridden, disease-ravaged, languishing New Orleans of 1852.[71]

Easily the best black role appeared in a film with a heavyhanded leftist social message, Clifford Odets's *Golden Boy*. If the boxing game was to be a symbol of heartless capitalism, then the fighters must succeed by climbing over the fallen, a point that is sharpened by having a black opponent die in the ring. His killer is Joe Bonaparte, the son of

A wider range of expression for black actors appeared in Clinton Rosamond's outraged head of the family at the brutal death of their boxer son in *Golden Boy* © Columbia Pictures Corp.). (Author's collection)

an Italian who prefers Joe to be a violinist. Instead, Joe fights Kid Chocolate in a smoky arena pulsing with shots of "the colored section of the gallery" where "the Harlem crowd is in distress" as Joe pummels their hero. After the Kid crumples and dies, his angry father (Clinton Rosamond) lashes out at whites; and when Joe is cleared of murder, the audience knows there is no justice for blacks. Even though Rouben Mamoulian focused on character rather than class, the message—"we just little people, and all of us got a burden"—is strengthened by its black source. Graham Greene wrote: "I would put the final boxing match, when the Golden Boy, with hate in his gloves for the sport and its exploiters, kills his black opponent in a cruel knockout, among the finest sequences of the talking film."[72]

But by the end of the Great Depression such bits remained isolated. For every movie that gained from a black presence, many more were neutral and said nothing, or worse, some good movies rested on ancient racial lore. The bland maid in Capra's *You Can't Take It With You;*

the bowdlerizing of Leigh Whipper's lines as the Negro, Crooks, in
Milestone's movie of Steinbeck's *Of Mice and Men;* the maudlin slavey
of Stevens's *Gunga Din,* which managed to find the humor at the core
of British colonialism, were merely thoughtless racist bits flecked
through otherwise superb movies.[73]

Moreover, the liberal tactic of inserting occasional Negroes into gratuitous shots was pointless, contributing neither to movies nor to
black recognition. A neat maid in *Destry Rides Again,* a bourgeois
Negro couple flashing past the eye in *The Maltese Falcon,* an unctuous
porter balanced by a wise circus hand in *Chad Hanna,* a black family
among the winners of a radio contest in *Christmas in July,* Noble Johnson as an Indian in *Juarez,* and the growth of Eddie Anderson's Rochester role pointed to no major change.[74]

Any firm attempt to bring black urban life to the screen met with
blindness and apathy. As late as 1940 the black musicians Andy Razaf
and Fats Waller were outraged when Fox's *Tin Pan Alley* implied by
omission that whites had written "Honeysuckle Rose." In the studios
producers resisted social themes. Harry Cohn of Columbia flatly refused Mamoulian's wish to film *Porgy.* Delmer Daves, a trusted craftsman, wrote a treatment of an urban slum story only to have a studio
memo smother it in an early draft. Hollywood would not change its
approach until the NAACP brought effective pressure against it during
the war years.[75]

Despite the importance of race and group in American life, movies
offered no better imagery or motifs of immigrant, Indian, or Oriental
life, save for Pearl Buck's *The Good Earth* and its imitators. Assimilation came to predominate ethnic opinion; few writers were inspired by
group tension; Hollywood wished to avoid friction with organized
groups. The decade ended with the masses enlisting in another war for
democracy in an army in which they seemed equally represented in
every platoon.

Early on, liberal pressure drove malevolent Orientals from the
screen, to be replaced by benign missionaries, just colonialists, or hapless flotsam caught in the crossfires of warlords. Whimsically clever
detectives in the mold of Earl Derr Biggers's *Charlie Chan* became popular, but box office considerations placed the roles in the hands of Europeans such as Warner Oland, Sidney Toler, Peter Lorre, and Boris
Karloff. Gradually, after the *Times* blasted Sax Rohmer's *The Mysterious Dr. Fu Manchu* (1930) as an inane melodrama of "mysterious
messages, daggers bathed in blood, opiate druggings, and much gun-
play" such villainy was matched by equal and opposite Oriental virtue,
and fell into disuse. Anna May Wong, Sessue Hayakawa, and other

former stars went to Europe, leaving the field to low-billed Toshio Mori, Tetsu Komai, Victor Wong, and Willie Fung, some of whom survived the dry spells by running restaurants. Even the excitement over the Sino-Japanese War failed to stir a revival.[76]

At the top, movies tried for greater fidelity to Asian culture and to East-West *Realpolitik*. Among the best was Thalberg's *The Good Earth*. As early as 1933 he tested Asians, built authenticity, and won the praise of the writer Lin Yu Tang for the award-winning story of Chinese duty, fatalism, and filiopiety.[77] Others—*The Bitter Tea of General Yen* (1933), *Shanghai Express* (1932), *The General Died at Dawn* (1936)—focused on politics through tendrils of fog, rough warlords, steamy train stations, wailing refugees, swaggering soldiery, and blondes living by their wits along the China coast. Only the coming of war restored the old heavies in the guise of Japanese enemies.[78]

The great conflict arising from pastoral Indians sharing a continent with industrial America was lost to 1930s audiences because assimilationism left Indians a perplexing anomaly. Western B pictures abandoned them in favor of tangled plots about water rights, deeds, and railroads often settled by the ritual *code duello*. Indians appeared as stolid victims more than sharp-etched enemies, and since federal policy was presumed correct, the heavies were usually crooked Indian agents or renegade halfbreeds. Even documentaries avoided root causes. A classroom film, *A Vanishing Race*, found that "the nobler qualities of the primitive Indian" shown with a shot of a lone mounted brave fording a stream were shattered by, the audience is assured, "the unscrupulous few" white men.[79]

MGM tried once. They bought Oliver LaFarge's Pulitzer Prize novel, *Laughing Boy*, and in 1932 set out in a tangle of mishaps led by Jim Thorpe's strike against the use of Mexican and Negro extras. Two years later it opened with—save for its two leads—an all-Indian cast, censor problems, and a *Variety* review warning that it "mixes races, something the screen has generally shied from." Warner Brothers chipped in with *Massacre*, an interesting failure that saw parallels in the treatment of Negroes and Indians. *Geronimo*, the only other major gesture of the 1930s, reminded a reviewer of *The Lives of a Bengal Lancer*. The others were epics of white achievement, such as DeMille's *Union Pacific*, peopled by Indian straw men with Noble Johnson in the van.[80]

So in a sense Negroes made more of an impact on the 1930s screen because at least they appeared in hundreds of roles that gave whites a cursory glance at black life and successfully broke the old Southern racial images. And if the impact seemed muted, then at least, as Etta Moten put it, "I educated my girls with it."[81] The clearest sign that for blacks quantity was not enough was in the late-thirties revival of

"race movies," which had been driven into bankruptcy after the first
flush of the early black operettas. Blacks had been denied so long
that they seemed to reject the mere inclusion proferred by liberal
studios; yet they sensed that the Hollywood Negro had gone as high
as he could go without help from outside the movie colony.

Chapter Twelve

MEANWHILE FAR AWAY FROM THE MOVIE COLONY

By the late thirties Afro-Americans were watching the New Deal for some sign of hope for a future within the nation. Black migration northward indicated that no viable Negro nation could develop on Southern ground. Yet Negroes with faith in the urban coalition of the Democratic Party had few opportunities for cheering. Although Roosevelt had shaped a "black cabinet," Mrs. Roosevelt maintained a social schedule that included black groups, and the New Deal often touched blacks while the black press covered the scene, the programs represented no tide of rising black fortunes. Moreover, NAACP branches suffered from apathy, uneven growth, and a slump in funds. Meanwhile, a small coalition of liberals and Marxists that eventually became the National Negro Congress momentarily gained strength in part because of its vaguely nationalist cast—the polar opposite of blacks supporting the New Deal.[1]

Blacks in Hollywood had a similar choice before them—whether to seek a Hollywood "new deal" or some sort of race nationalism apart from Hollywood. The choice was not casual. Hollywood had risked scarce cash on all-Negro pictures it could have avoided; the ante bellum *So Red the Rose* included balky rebels among its dutiful slaves; the women of *Alice Adams* and *Imitation of Life* broke new ground; Stepin Fetchit lost his early stature; and the most beastly black roles in jungle movies gave way to white heavies.

But the pace was too slow for a people coming to view themselves as a nation within a nation. Trapped into stasis by a friendly government, baffled by white flattery, reluctant to convert to a Communist sect, exhausted by the rigors of the Depression, black intellectuals waited for Godot. When a correspondent complained of Fetchit's influence on whites and asked for "a higher type Negro" on the screen "in order to hope for a leveling off of race prejudice," James Weldon Johnson could only plead that Fetchit was "a pretty good clown" who should not be taken so seriously. And Claude McKay, one of the poets of the moribund Harlem Renaissance, felt trapped between white "faddists" and his feeling that there was "no hope nor place for a Negro nation within the United States."[2]

At first European films held out greater social and artistic promise, perhaps because of Paul Robeson's well-publicized faith in them. The Depression had decimated "race movies" and opened the way to white promoters, while Europe offered a variety of possibilities including a residual faith in Soviet sincerity left after the Meschrabpom experience, Robeson's persistence, an appreciation of Josephine Baker's celebrations of black style, and news stories of occasional good black roles in European movies.

Black hopes rose even though Europeans were only marginally concerned with race. Coincident with Meschrabpom's abortive *Black and White* Sergei Eisenstein left Paramount for Moscow with a copy of John W. Vandercook's romance of the Haitian revolutionary Toussaint L'Ouverture in his baggage. He culled the literature of three languages, shaping Toussaint into an alloy of the oppressed American Negro and the spirit of revolution against racism. Along the way he must have written to Robeson as a prospective Toussaint, and at Christmas 1934 they met in Moscow to discuss a film. With Mrs. Robeson they talked over dinner and into the night and played records, with Eisenstein feeling classless and raceless and "knowing what it meant . . . to be a Negro in America." When the Robesons left, they felt the idea would soar out of Eisenstein's mind onto the screen. But with the finality of an interoffice memo from Zukor or Lasky, his political enemies reduced it to a bare mention at a meeting of the Soviet film industry, and he lived out his life using it as a classroom exercise at the State Cinema Institute.[3] As in America, black hopes rested on coincidence with white goals.

Later, perhaps because the Soviet Union wrestled with its own polyethnic problems, perhaps because its ideological rivals were mired in racism and colonialism, perhaps because of an attempt at diplomatic point-scoring, a few racial films appeared. Yet the best of them, G. V. Alexandrov's *The Circus* (1936), was never offered to Afro-American audiences. In it a white circus star is run out of the South because of her black baby, drifting northward, then eventually to Russia, where she is taken on by a circus. She becomes the object of a rivalry between a breezy Russian officer and Von Kneischitz, her leering Teutonic Svengali. After she chooses the Russian, the audience knows as the camera carries them to a great city, down onto their balcony and into their tiny flat, that the old German will cause them pain. Even before then the officer comes upon the child and spits out, "That kinky hair, that flat nose!" after which a parade of happenstance intercut with songs, circus acts, precision dances, and buoyant gymkhanas carries the plot to the center ring, where the German attempts to ruin the woman's career by exposing the child. Instead the Russian crowd cheers, grasps the boy, and bears him upward by hundreds of hands through the crowd as the German skulks off. In the finale all sing as though kneeling at the footlights in an operetta, and the child leads a parade.[4] There was no way of telling whether American Negroes would accept such artless propaganda, but neither were they given the opportunity.

Other continental film disappointed all the more because prints arrived in America and made a scant splash. The most likely candidate for black stardom was Josephine Baker because of her American roots and presumed following. But she could never move beyond her role as a brightskinned exotic dancer. Like Noble Johnson in Hollywood she was always Tam Tam or Zou Zou, languid under the palms. When *Princess Tam Tam* arrived in Brooklyn in 1938 the *Amsterdam News* dutifully plugged the Gauguinesque tale of a French novelist who leaves his wife for a heady season in the Casbah with Aouina, "who symbolizes the carefree joy of the natives." But few Afro-Americans troubled to see it.[5]

European documentaries were less glamorous, even less celebrated, and lost to all but a tiny cell of New York Negroes. Besides, even

Josephine Baker's exotic primitives departed little from American stereotypes and drew small audiences. (Author's collection)

though some were sponsored by anthropological societies, and attempted to humanize their black subjects, others bore badges of racism, dwelt on sensational efforts to find some lost tribe, and devoted inordinate closeups to the exposed dugs, filed teeth, and raised tattoos of nonwestern culture. Back in the twenties Marc Allegret and Andre Gide had imitated the manner of Flaherty in *Voyage au Congo* (1927), capturing a neat courtship between a slim black woman with a plate in her nose and a courtly, lean-muscled farmer who lived among the daub-and-wattle thatched huts and amidst the fetching and carrying of village life on a curving strand of an African river. But so few followed their path that when the Italians invaded Ethiopia, American studios had only a Swiss travelogue and a comedy titled *Laughing with Medbury in Ethiopia* in their vaults.[6]

All things considered, the best single continental film, as art, as event, and as black presence was Victor Trivas's *Niemandsland* (1932). In spite of censorship in its German homeland, probably because of its internationalism and its anti-Nazi production team, and in spite of its fable format and the spotty distribution accorded imports, the black press gave it prerelease space and friendly notices.[7]

War is Hell (its English title) was a kind of *Grand Hotel* of the trenches and a study of "little people" caught in war fever. A crescendo of rapid cutting carries a delegate from each nation away from his quiet life into the drumbeat of wheeling and marching platoons. The most rounded figures were a Jewish tailor (Vladimir Sokoloff) and a black vaudevillian (Louis Douglas). Leftist pacifism aside, the Negro contribution to the early reels remained a check-suited, gold-toothed, scat-dancing Bojangles whose last routine ends in a Zouave uniform, a crisp martial salute, a cheering vaudeville house, and a cut to war.

But once under the gun the tone changed. One at a time they seek shelter in a dugout, where a German and a Frenchman act out their historic anti-Semitism upon the Jew, who emits a silent scream of despair. Then the Negro enters, rescues a Briton, and unifies them as sufferers, although he retains his role as snappy waiter and hoofer. At last the *crump-wump* of exploding shells forces them to talk out the causes of the war that will kill them. Only the Jew and the Negro are free from the taint of colonialism, so it is the black who first sheds his uniform and forswears war. In the end he is still a jongleur and clown, but a tragic and wise clown weeping under his paint.[8] If blacks in New York saw the irony that he wore no paint but only brown skin, then that was the best that Europe could offer.

After 1935 black themes and roles came with a rush from European screens, yet international distribution tangles, muddled and even old-fashioned imagery, and formula tokenism spoiled them as surely as if Hollywood had ground them out. Pierre Chenal's *L'Alibi*, a piece of outrageously baroque Von Stroheim intrigue, owed its racial images to the eighteenth-century "Great Chain of Being," with humanity ranging downward from Von Stroheim's white, silken, Queen Anne-heeled dominance, to Anna May Wong's childlike slavey, to the muted trumpets of black jazzmen. Jean Renoir's *Toni* (1935) trailed through the lives of migrant workers in the South of France, where a fusion of many races had marked the land. They are seen through the prism of Toni, with a single Negro on the edge of the circle, as though a token sent by the Souilly-sur-Mer branch of the NAACP. Jean Benoit-Levy's *La Mort du Cygne* (1937) allowed a lightskinned Italianesque apprentice ballerina into its plot. Sacha Guitry and Christian-Jaque's *Les Perles de la Couronne* did no more than retail the stock roles of an *Aida*, exotic temple dancers, and black courtiers in a brief Abyssinian segment. And like the American films in which social equality occurs only in jail or on the bottom rail, Jacques Feyder's *Le Grand Jeu* asked its characters to cross racial lines only in the French Foreign Legion, and Jean Vigo's bargemen in *L'Atalante* tolerated black drinkers in their bars.[9]

If any European cinema tradition offered Afro-Americans a substantive departure from Hollywood, it was the British. Their colonial system resembled American racial arrangements in the way in which it encouraged cultural assimilation while denying social integration. Moreover, common language provided a bridge over which the powerful figure of Paul Robeson might carry British cinema to Afro-American audiences. That he eventually failed was testimony to the misplaced optimism of many black American intellectuals who believed the European culture could offer relief from American racial arrangements. Nonetheless, in the beginning the British saw only a major musical talent, an internationalist with a feel for African culture, and an amenable Anglophile.

Prior to Robeson's debut in 1936 British films had begun to shape an evenhanded, paternal, colonial cinema. Chinese missionaries, American Indians, and Africa all received attention in the years after 1900. Among the wide range were a jingoistic tale of the Zulu War, *How a British Bulldog Saved the Union Jack* (1906); Lt. Daring's rescue of "a girl from the unwelcome attentions of a Spaniard" *In a South American Port* (1911); the interracial triangle of *The Ring and the Rajah* (1914); a long series of Sax Rohmer's Oriental melodramas in the twenties; *The Drum* (1924), *If Youth but Knew* (1926), *Tommy Atkins* (1928), and others in which white conflicts emerge in an African setting; H. Rider Haggard's *She* (1925); *The Jungle Woman* (1926), a variant on the Tondelayo theme; *When Giants Fought* (1926), a gritty tale of Tom

Molyneux, the pioneer black boxer; *Palaver: A Romance of Northern Nigeria* (1926), shot on location; *Emerald of the East* (1929), in which the British Army rescues a kidnapped child of an Indian prince from rebels.[10] In their persistent casting of non-European peoples in a dependent, occasionally hostile, role they were reminiscent of American Indian movies.

With the coming of sound, British films matured to allow greater range and nuance, greater interracial personal conflict, and a British willingness to laugh at one's own customs. Orientals especially contributed good melodrama, such as a decent remake of *Broken Blossoms* (1936); E. A. DuPont's murky *Piccadilly* (1930), dense with Germanic mood, a tricky murder mystery, and Anna May Wong's touching kitchen slavey who turns variety performer; and *Tiger Bay* (1934), J. Elder Wills's misty colonial backwater served by the rusty tramps of the sealanes. Wills's camera peers through the dim alleys and rutted streets, over the heads of the Lascars, down-and-outers, and Arabs to black dandies with smart "foxes" on their arms. "Hey, boy, where you going all dress up. . . ?" they kid each other, and rattle dice, aloof from the poverty around them. Inside, Anna May Wong presides over her pub and her white ward behind its curtains, against the covetous, coarse English heavies. "When the name of Chang is threatened," she says, "I dare anything." Outside, a black chorus echoes her fear, mourning "the worn-out nigger on judgment day." In the end she kills the heavy—"an execution," she says—and takes poison from her ring.[11]

The dominant British trait was humor—perhaps, because unlike the Americans, they intended to shed their racial problems, and therefore could laugh at a presumably temporary condition. The Colonial Empire Marketing Board, for example, asked the documentarist Basil Wright to make *Men of Africa* (1939), which became a promise that British tutelege would give way to a "new Africa" ruled by "our fellow citizens" who would "conquer ignorance, poverty, and disease" with the British lion merely to "guide and develop." So *Timbuctoo* (1934) may kid racial mores by having its heroine bolt to Africa to marry a Negro in order to spite Uncle George. The pursuing comic safari is a pastiche of the usual pith helmets, shouting drivers and bearers, oozing snakes, and gutteral spearbearers; but also of the clattering golf clubs, clumsily flicked flywhisks, and a white hunter who proves his prowess by shooting a baby hippo. Meanwhile, the heroine has chosen a busride through motley African adobe cities, busy with robed, urbane blacks. The fun depended on a brazen kidding of both cultures that would have been lost on fretful Americans unhappy with their permanent racial scars. Later, in *Old Bones of the River* (1939), they burlesqued not only Edgar Wallace's heroic colonial novel, *Sanders of the River,* but the entire missionary-imperialist premises of African exploitation. "Darkest Africa" says the opening title—where "a handful of Englishmen" try "teaching the black man to play white man." Throughout, the Africans know too much to be ruled by "the Teaching and Welfare Institution for the Reformation of Pagans"—TWIRP —and they soon assume power.[12]

Of all the British possibilities Paul Robeson's movies seemed the richest vein, the creations most likely to unite mass audience and intellectuals with images capable of making artistic war on Hollywood racial assumptions. Shortly after the release of *The Emperor Jones* in 1933 Robeson met Zoltan Korda, the Hungarian producer of London Films, and together they screened film and played records of African music and dance gathered by Korda's company. Soon afterward Robeson agreed to do Bosambo, the black chief in Wallace's *Sanders of the River,* apparently believing his presence would damp down its imperialist tone.

After shooting in Africa and Shepperton studios the film opened in London's Leicester Square and revealed still another face of the black aesthetic problem. The movie had a split focus: first on a tribute to "the Keepers of the King's peace," the colonial officers whose rewards were mosquito bites rather than Victoria Crosses; and second, on the local black politics. Robeson's role could hardly loom large if Bosambo is under Sanders's tutelage, if he rules only under the gaze of the king's "beautiful face" on the coins, if he calls Sanders "Lord" (albeit with a knowing smile), and if the old king has turned slaver and must be done in. Can he impose a Pax Bosambo when Sanders goes on leave? No. Even as he teaches his son war, music, politics, and love, the drums beat out the false news that "Sandy-is-dead" and "There-is-no-law-anymore." White outlaws erode the peace with gin and guns, war and pillage, and Bosambo's own son is kidnapped. The message is clear: law can prevail only under the hand of "Lord Sandy." He returns with a handful of police in suntans and helmets and puts down the rebels. Throughout, Bosambo sings Sanders's praise. He is "My Lord Sandy . . . the hater of lies . . . the righter of wrongs," to whom the African sends his only son to government house to learn British ways and to become "a great, great chief." Within such limits Robeson fashioned a stalwart prince, who suffered dramatically for lack of tension and conflict. As his wife, Nina Mae McKinney seemed more a road-company "Bess" than an African queen.[13]

Poor Robeson. In place of the anticipated "black men living out their lives," there were only drums and shouts, "shots of grotesque and painted natives," and himself smirking and indolent, "a puppet on a string." It must have been the retakes and cutting at Shepperton. At

Paul Robeson (here with Nina Mae McKinney) and Alexander Korda
cooperated on *Sanders of the River* (© London Film Productions, Ltd.), an
unsuccessful attempt to do equal justice to black Africa and British colonialism. (Author's collection)

the première he seethed, refusing to rise and either speak or sing for
the audience. America too would have none of it. Even though Robeson "dominates" the film, *Variety* predicted failure because of thousands of feet of draggy jungle footage and unknown white actors who
added "nothing to the box offices except in the arty sure-seaters." The
ad men grew shrill. "A million mad savages fighting for one beautiful
woman!" they screamed. "Until three white comrades ALONE pitched
into the fray and quelled the bloody revolt!"

The black press bubbled with rage, perhaps because, like Robeson,
they had expected so much. After years of building European goodwill
in the fight against racism he returned home charged as a "white man's
n----r." The Baltimore *Afro-American* headlined its story "ROBESON
FILM CALLED PROPAGANDA JUSTIFYING BRITISH IMPERIALISM," and ran
Nancy Cunard's charge that it was "pure Nordic bunk." Roi Ottley
thought it an attempt to convert the "ofays" to Mussolini's side of the
Ethiopian invasion. Only the star-oriented *Amsterdam News* culled

press releases into praise of its "great drama" and "unusual excellence."[14]

Still Robeson could not quit the British. There must be a way to tell an African story on film. If only he could retain control. While on location for *Sanders* he had heard a curious African legend that might serve as a cinema source. First he worked off commitments and earned some cash in a brief London theater run, a fast turn in Hollywood as Joe in *Showboat*, and finally as Umbopas, the black chief of H. Rider Haggard's *King Solomon's Mines* (1937), who, like a deep-bass teddy-bear, leads the lagging whites over the mountains singing a booming paeon to white ambition: "Climbin' up, climbin' up, mighty mountain . . . mighty mountain . . . gonna climb you." Again, his vision of the great black figure set between the races who was much more than a "splendid savage" was bled out in the final cut.[15]

Meanwhile, Claude Wallace, who had told Robeson the African legend, helped shape it into a script which J. Elder Wills would direct. *Song of Freedom* (1937) told the story of an "ordinary" black, a stevedore, whose African heritage would not down. He hums an ancient song and wears an antique medallion as he works and soon he is "busking" in the streets and finally singing in concerts. Here Robeson began to share blame for the failure of his pictures. More improbabilities pile up: an anthropologist in an audience who identifies the tune as a regal chant; Zinga's (Robeson) smoothly polished wife (Elizabeth Welch), who rejects the London life for a sandy African strand; a grinning black bearer (Robert Adams) who goes with them to redeem Zinga's tribe. Over the miles and years they go, back to the tribe, dressed in missionary whites and pith helmets. They break up a witch doctor's dance, undermine his authority, use their talismans to take over. In the end the new king leaves to sing in Europe to raise money to bring white man's medicine to the tribe. Not even a friendly review in *Variety* could persuade bookers to buy the sentimental fable, so few blacks in America ever saw it.[16]

Robeson had expected so much of *Song of Freedom*. It was his test of himself as an actor, of the appeal of black themes, of the abandonment of racial sentimentality, and the "first step in my effort to break down the prejudice" of the cinema. He hovered over everything down to the final cut, nursing his ideal against "the rough-and-tumble of the film studio." Afterward Graham Greene found a fine film smothered by its own patronizing and "sentimental and absurd" story. Still, Robeson believed in his director and in the future of a black aesthetic, and they tried again a year later with *Big Fella*, a little movie of the denizens of the Marseilles waterfront which also failed to attract American exhibitors. In the same year he went to Cairo and, with his wife taking a firmer hand in the management of events, attempted one last African

Jericho (Buckingham) was one of many Robeson European vehicles with which he hoped to carry off major changes in black film imagery. (Author's collection)

tale. *Jericho* is an American soldier who takes up with a Tuareg tribe in order to avoid a death sentence. Like the hero of a well-made B movie, he becomes chief and rescues an American pursuer, who abandons the chase upon finding Jericho "leading a useful life." Again, the press refused to help it along. The blacks focused on Princess Kouka, an African actress, while Crowther of the *Times* guffawed at the posturing reminiscent of *The Sheik* and at Robeson's solemn singing of "Mamma's Little Baby Loves Shortnin' Bread." By then Robeson was forty and defeated, it seemed, not by racism, but by contrivance, bad melodrama, and low grosses.[17]

Indeed, if Robeson had looked at the careers of his co-stars, Elizabeth Welch and Robert Adams, he might have seen a drift of British cinema away from his faith. Welch, a sophisticated café singer at the height of her powers, could never get more than slick bits. Adams repeated his flunky of *Song of Freedom* in *Midshipman Easy*, Carol Reed's film of Captain Marryat's story. True, as he plays cabin boy to

Robert Adams, an able Guyana actor, brought quality to a string of good roles, as in *Midshipman Easy* (© British Lion) with Hughie Green. (BFI)

Hughie Green's *Easy*, he capers through a number of scraps, pulls the enemy's colors off the foretop, helps sail a prize back to their ship, rescues *Easy*, and kills the Latin heavy; but he is still the stripe-shirted slavey 'tween decks of HMS *Harpy*. In 1939 he did a comic Bosambo in the parody *Old Bones of the River*, and not until the end of World War II would he get a decent role in Thorold Dickinson's *Man of Two Worlds*.[18]

Robeson's last European feature film finally revealed the deeply running problems that would carry any racially inspired idea off course. The time was 1939. Fascism had become a clearcut enemy of liberals everywhere. Michael Balcon's small, inventive, and personally controlled Ealing Studio in London's western suburbs seemed ready for a project that would fuse Robeson's race pride, English working-class sensibility, Welsh nationalism within the United Kingdom, and later, tacked on by the coming of war, a clear call for resisting Fascism. Robeson felt close to one of the writers. Balcon had faith in young Pen Tennyson, who would direct. Mrs. Robeson hovered over the activity as a "protective wife." All of the actors genuinely liked and admired Robeson. And if progressive-liberal intentions mattered, nothing could go wrong.[19]

But *Proud Valley* fell victim to irreconcilable differences between European and American views of race. Europeans, living far from their darker-skinned colonials, saw injustice in terms of class distinctions rather than racial discrimination, while Americans knew from personal experience that race mattered more than class. When in European progressive circles, Robeson accepted their notions of socialist internationalism, discounting the weight of the safely remote American racial arrangements that had a life of their own and seemed impervious to appeals to working-class solidarity. Thus *Proud Valley* was, in Robeson's view, "the one film I could be proud of having played in," and yet it said nothing to Afro-Americans.

The movie opens on David Goliath (Robeson) ambling along a Welsh road where he meets a "busker," a streetsinger with whom he develops a shoddy act. After his voice is heard by a Welsh miners' choirdirector he is taken in as lodger, coal digger, bass voice, and good fellow. Thereafter, he becomes more Christlike and sacrificial. At the pit-head he diffidently retreats from a racist confrontation until his own gang expresses support. He makes a heroic fruitless attempt to save the choirmaster in a cave-in. At the Eisteffodd, the Welsh national festival, his voice booming out "Deep River" is the solo hit. Later, as depression shuts the mines, he offers to move on; and in the negotiations to reopen them he hangs back in the streets and anterooms while the Welshmen haggle. On their march toward London his voice is the

Many good European films, here Korda's *The Thief of Bagdad* (© London Films), offered Rex Ingram and other Americans little more than they could find in Hollywood. (Author's collection)

instrument that helps fill their outstretched hats with coins. Here, the coming war, literally bursting forth during the last days of shooting, gave the writers an angle that would reopen the mines—the need to fight the Nazis. So the collieries reopen, providing David with his final sacrificial gesture. Another accident traps miners who are saved because David lights the necessarily short fuse on the charge that will blow all to freedom. The only way out of the picture is an upbeat montage of miners, flags, and coalhoppers, gradually pulling back on the rolling hills of Wales with Robeson's booming voice over it all. So the sequence for Afro-Americans is about Welsh miners who express their militance to their bosses with a crisp "veddy good, sah!" a war in which Americans have not yet been enlisted, and a black man whose working-class solidarity hovers on the edge of obsequiousness. Except for the size of the role, he had advanced a black cinema presence no farther than the Negro convicts in prison movies or the black sailor in *Yankee Clipper*.

Moreover, *Proud Valley* faced a mixed reception. Even British critics divided. One of them found it the finest racial statement produced by his country's studios, while another pounced upon it as an overpraised bag of pithead clichés to which Robeson contributed no more than a "big, black Pollyanna, keeping everybody cheerful and dying nobly at the end." Even if it had received wide distribution, American audiences could have seen instead Carol Reed's *The Stars Look Down* and John Ford's *How Green Was My Valley*, both more highly polished coalfield epics. Of all of Robeson's films, although he liked it best, *Variety* gauged it lowest in box office appeal. The black press gave it no more space than other imports.[20]

The reasons for Robeson's failure to touch Afro-Americans from his foreign platform can only be guessed. Certainly the remoteness of European racial experience from American and the snubs American exhibitors would give *any* foreign film defused his message. But other more personal problems lay below the surface. Even his musical and theatrical work frustrated him. In 1938 he announced his retirement from London's West End theaters in order to "be himself" and to devote himself to "honest roles" and "protest songs."[21] So not only the cinema seemed to him off its target. Furthermore, Hollywood's product steadily broadened its black dimensions. A hidden key to Robeson's European frustration lay in the fact that he was moving closer to espousal of a kind of socialist international position while at the same time he continued to need the applause that came to him as a performer. He genuinely liked living among friendly neighbors in Chelsea. And in the familial circle of leftist coworkers he appeared a "friendly . . . lamb," as the British left migrated from little Soho film societies into the studio establishment on the eve of war. Together they felt as though they worked in the Lord's vineyard for social change, so Robeson could find little of substance to attack. Indeed, "His wife was probably the aggressive one," thought one actor. "Dear Paul, never."[22] Thus good feelings on the set concealed differences that could be exaggerated in the cutting room and blared forth in the première—too late for debate.

So in the depression decade Hollywood's liberal drift and Robeson's ambitions for racial honesty in European cinema were equally frustrated. If black audiences were to receive the rewards of a black cinema, then some third force would have to produce them. "Race movies," with all their imperfections of technique, artistic quality, and Hollywood-derived artifice, would revive as the hope of the thirties. Like all black hopes, they were threadbare. For the "race movies" could not begin to solve problems such as a suitable role for whites. Without whites, the requirements of dramatic construction created a world in which black characters acceded to the white ideal of segregation, and unreal black cops, crooks, judges, and juries interacted in such a way as to blame black victims for their social plight. Nevertheless, "race movies" could have deep meaning for blacks.

But unfortunately for them the black moviemakers barely staggered through the Great Crash. Indeed, before they could shape a black aesthetic of soundfilm all but Micheaux perished under the burdens of shrinking capital and fewer outlets. Soon white backers filled the void, forcing even Micheaux to turn to them for capital, thus frustrating Lincoln's old ideal of a black-controlled cinema.

The struggle may be seen in perspective in the early soundfilms of Micheaux and Harry Gant. By 1928 Micheaux, the greatest of the black "moguls," slipped into bankruptcy and began to live off his revivals. A year later he desperately tried to crash New York by rereleasing his silent films in the face of the craze for "talkies." Neglected by the black press, he turned to Frank Schiffman, the white manager of the Apollo, for backing of his first talkie, *The Exile,* a disaster that moved *Variety* to advise him to abandon drama in favor of more easily controlled and marketable comedy.[23]

Micheaux's *Ten Minutes to Live* (1932) typified the shoestring race movie, with its tangled racial theme, spare sets, snippets of vaudeville padding, and jagged continuity patched together with subtitles. If the old men of Lincoln aimed for the center of "a Negro's ambition," Micheaux's limited means allowed him only dimly to see the target. He lectured his audience on soundtracks fat with stilted verbiage that no American, black or white, ever spoke. He spliced three stories into a plot that ran nowhere over a road pot-holed with variety acts. The "action" was a string of one-dimensional café-table conferences on which the audience eavesdropped. With the dull rhythm of a coxswain's bark the action rolled on: a two-shot introduces a casting director; cut to a single male dancer fronting a chorus; cut to two lightskinned men who discuss a marriage; cut to two blackface comics who mimic folk Negroes with their scat song; cut to a stiff audience; cut to more talk of marriage; cut away to a stagey blues singer; cut back to the tables; cut to an exotic dancer; cut to agents discussing her for a movie; cut to talk of the murder of a doomed cad who had been "luring girls to their ruin"; cut to dancing patrons; pull back at last to a wide shot of a woman shooting her Svengali. Immediately after a title frame the action plunges into the next disconnected story through the dull device of a letter foreshadowing the action. It falls to its lowest by using a narrative title in a soundfilm. "What mystery here!" it asks. "Why has this beautiful girl been put 'on the spot'? Let us go back—" Yet without an occasional title it becomes impossible to follow its succession of trains, slamming cab doors, busy dance floors, and stilted dialogues. At its worst it seems to affirm color caste among Negroes. Sadly, Micheaux, black and isolated from the Hollywood technocracy, had committed Hollywood's greatest sin—he had made a bad, money-losing movie.[24]

Shortly before Micheaux's plunge into soundfilm Harry Gant, the white cameraman of the old Lincoln Company, demonstrated that whites were not immune from technical incompetence and that their bad movies would not stop them from slowly taking over race movies anyway. In the summer of 1930, after the splash made by *Hallelujah!* and *Hearts in Dixie,* he produced *Georgia Rose,* complete with derivative Hollywood-style glamour. His stars were Clarence Brooks, "the world's greatest Negro screen star"; Evelyn Preer, billed as Lenore Ulric's understudy in *Lulu Belle;* Roberta Hyson and Edward Thompson of Christie Comedies; Irene Wilson, a "new find" who, unlike the whites with voices that failed to "register," was "mike perfect." Their story played on the old theme of rural virtue tainted with urban vice as seen by a Midwestern black family "weeviled" off their land and reduced to tenancy. He raised money from whites but fronted his Aristo Studio with D. Ireland Thomas and Ira McGowan of Lincoln, which allowed the black press to portray it as black enterprise. After the first press puffs nothing went well. Micheaux clouded its Chicago opening by coming into town with his own *Daughter of the Congo* under his arm in quest of the tiny summer "take." The critic on the *Whip,* although he gave it modest praise, blasted its poor sound quality. When no one challenged the *Whip,* Gant wrote to William Nunn of the *Pittsburgh Courier* complaining of the inattention of the black press and their unfair comparisons with white films. But Nunn could not abide the draggy plot, the artless camera-consciousness, and the endless cutting to fields of cows (to symbolize black ownership, Gant said). In New York it may have been recut and renamed, but still *All Quiet on the Western Front* bumped it after two days.[25]

The film's most self-defeating trait was its inability to offer a black statement to counter Hollywood's grudging liberalism. After all, the star himself would appear the next year before the largest audience ever to see a Negro in a modern dramatic role in John Ford's *Arrowsmith.* Aristo promised a film "devoid of the usual racial propaganda," but asked Negro patrons to excuse "the technical defects" and to admire it as "the best effort put forth by Negro producers." Thus it made a special pleading for black indulgence without offering special black fare, thereby failing to provide a proper setting for a black cinema.[26]

Soon blacks were frozen out of race films. Until revived at the end of the thirties race movies would deserve the name only because of the players and audiences. After Micheaux's alliance with Schiffman, Gant turned over the Southern premieres of *Georgia Rose* to whites. By 1932

Georgia Rose (© Aristo) and other "talkie" race movies provided work for Spencer Williams, Evelyn Preer, Clarence Brooks, and others but struggled with the technical problems of sound recording. (George P. Johnson collection)

Bill Robinson's *Harlem is Heaven* was white from shooting script to release.[27]

The combination of black attrition and white invasion failed to enhance quality. Even though Jack Goldberg mustered the music and performers of *Shuffle Along*, along with James Baskette, Putney Dandridge, and the Cotton Club Revue, there were only ten days shooting in Fort Lee for *Harlem is Heaven*, Bojangles's debut in feature films. Despite a pressbook that promised "A Picture That Colored Patrons Will Be Proud Of," a midnight première, and a full soundtrack, the *Amsterdam News* sadly concluded that, although it might be the best race movie, "That is not saying much," and in parts found it "positively objectionable from a racial standpoint." Micheaux's *Exile* had a $15,000 "nut" that permitted partial dialogue, synchronized music, and Chicago exteriors, but it needed the padding of cabaret routines. His sermon on racism became tangled in mixed identities at the end of which the hero gets the light-skinned girl. Harlem audiences laughed in the wrong places. Romeo Daugherty defended *The Black King*

(1932), Donald Heywood's movie on the Garvey movement, under a glowing banner, although a trade reviewer found it muddled and poorly recorded with comedy indistinguishable from drama. Within a week of the première a film warehouse sued Heywood's company for overdue storage.[28]

Such flops ensured the ruin of the market for years, moving Daugherty, who had rarely admired race movies, to urge black actors to aspire to Hollywood. Race movies not only faced white technology and "well trained stars" with the dull weapons of "strained acting, poor staging and poorer scenery [which] discloses that another shoestring [black] article is on its way," wrote Daugherty; but blacks by 1932 probably preferred the Hollywood product.[29] For whatever reason—black support of Hollywood or apathy toward race movies—all-black production slumped and Negro audiences grew dependent on Hollywood polish. Race movies slipped into a slough of false press releases, static movies, misfired openings, split weeks, darkened houses, and white incursions.

In contrast Hollywood press puffs promised much: Stepin Fetchit signed for this, Nina Mae McKinney for that, a new film company blossoming in Louisiana, a Blackbirds writer signed up, another New Jersey studio dusted off for Negro shooting, a lightskinned "star" to become a "Negro Walter Huston," a picture that scored "throughout the South" and would come to 125th Street and raise black cinema attainment "a notch."[30]

Thenceforward black producers languished, with Micheaux suffering the ignominy of trial on a charge of misappropriating the funds of the Lafayette Players. Typical of the mid-thirties fare was *Drums O' Voodoo*, heralded as a genuine Negro folk play in 1933, but more a pastiche of its white producers, Robert Mintz and Louis Weiss, its white director, Arthur Hoerle, its white cameraman, and its source in an unsuccessful black play by J. Augustus Smith. It featured Smith, Laura Bowman, "amateurish" support, and an improbable string of brandished razors, heavies blinded by lightning, voodoo drums, a "snakehips" dance in a brothel, and a rousing revival meeting, all of which broke Loew's Harlem house into laughter.[31]

The cost of even these poorly lighted, jerky movies proved too much for most producers. Instead, they scraped by on revivals, shorts, compilations of Harlem stock shots, and old Signal Corps footage. Among them were Robert Rossen and Jack Goldberg's *The Unknown Soldier Speaks*, a celebration of the black soldiers' contribution to American wars; the Howard-Lincoln football game in Atlantic City, and other events retailed by Brown-America, Frank Schiffman, Al Lichtman, and Phil Slatko. The few originals, such as Micheaux's *Lem Hawkins' Con-*

Some race movies such as *Gig and Saddle* reworked old types even for black audiences. (Author's collection)

fession or Gramercy's melodrama of the "numbers" game, *The Vicious Circle*, suffered from choppy cuts, uneven acting, weak sound, and in some places, censor problems.[32]

Of all the players in the game Micheaux held the edge. But for all of his experience and fortitude, his light seemed less the gemlike flame of genius than that of the third man on a match. At every turn his freewheeling methods destroyed the confidence of coworkers and induced spying, the planting of agents, suspicion, charges of misappropriation and plagiarism. Therefore he could never muster the big "nut" that would overcome the complexities of sound and result in a well-mounted movie. Black audiences could not make out his message because he said it so poorly. He remained an untrained primitive who failed to reach beyond his limited means. He must have keenly felt his hobble, for in 1934 he plugged his latest movie as "his first story in which he will have adequate studio facilities and cast to do credit to his directorial genius." Yet *The Brand of Cain* or *Lem Hawkins' Confession*—it bore both titles —still suffered from poor cutting, barely adequate sound, and "decid-

edly overdone" acting. Micheaux lasted another ten years, never free of
shooting on a shoestring in friends' ill-lighted apartments and in shabby
disused studios.[33]

At last in 1937 the dream of an independent black cinema aesthetic
expired. An article in the *International Photographer* announced a new
trend toward collaboration between black talent and white angels and
bookers. The prototype company included George Randol, a veteran
of the black stage and Hollywood, where he worked on RKO's *Deep
South;* Ralph Cooper, who discovered he was too lightskinned to be a
Hollywood Negro; and Ben Rinaldo, a sometime agent and promoter.
They turned out *Dark Manhattan,* "the first all-colored cast motion
picture with modern story, setting, and costumes," and the first from
Hollywood. Production dragged on for two months of press releases,
but they got $3.50 tickets at the Harlem opening of the tale of "under-
world activity in happy, hearty Harlem."[34]

They dedicated their movie to Richard B. Harrison, "De lawd" in the
stage *Green Pastures*, Bert Williams, Florence Mills, a *Blackbirds* star
who had died prematurely, and other black actors. But thereafter Harry
Fraser, the B movie director, followed conventional Hollywood format.
The film's black vision consisted of its cast, its precise duplication of a
segregated city, and its attempt to depict a small group of blacks in
power—on both sides of the law. Unfortunately, the poor production
values and B-picture melodrama provided a flawed lens through which
to see black images. Urban crime is seen in its conventional division of
labor from the boss in a paneled office "down to the jungles," where the
soldiers wear checked suits and cocked derbies and men draw knives
over a poolroom tiff. Cooper is "Curly," the tough, bright kid being
brought along through the ranks. He does a time-step in farewell to his
"jungle" friends as he moves uptown to the plush den of the biggest
"policy" banker in all of Harlem. Curly is early for his first day on the
job and a bit too cool in light-checked Norfolk jacket. He marches
through the ranks of the clerks to the boss's chamber, where he learns
not to be needlessly hard. Crime is neither love nor war—it is business.
He soon learns to dress like a '38 Buick, catch the eye of a radio star,
and claw his way to the top. As the boss's health slips, Curly takes over
the business and his woman. The theme of old versus young breaks into
open conflict. The more highhanded Curly grows, the closer to *hubris*
and eventual tragedy he moves. In the end, deserted by friends, at odds
with his mentor, turned out by his woman, he carries the fight to a rival
gang and dies in a shooting scrape with the police, exchanging flippan-
cies with them despite the blood trickling from his mouth.[35]

In quick succession, imitators joined the new wave. Jed Buell, a white
exploiter of trends, announced a series of Negro singing westerns star-

ring Herb Jeffries. Dudley Murphy formed Associated Artists and announced the purchase of a Duke Ellington score for a movie that would feature Cab Calloway, Ethel Waters, and "other leading citizens of Swing Town."[36] And still more followed.

The best company among them was Million Dollar Productions because it combined the West Coast experience of Leo and Harry Popkin, an urban vision that had eluded Micheaux, and connections with distributors. By the end of the year they had absorbed Rinaldo, Cooper, and Randol. Moreover, the Popkins persuaded Loew's Theatres that their *Bargain with Bullets* was "up to the Loew standard," a coup that spurred Harry to make a promotional tour through the East. Afterward he closed still another deal with RKO, thus effectively building a circuit to exploit black northward migratory patterns that promised to increase income and lessen dependence on small Southern towns. For their première they took three-column boxes and hired Les Hite's Cotton Club orchestra.[37] Nevertheless, even at Million Dollar weaknesses remained: the eternal problem of budgets and facilities, Hollywood's hold on black audiences, "headaches" resulting from evading union rules, working odd hours, paying low wages, with late checks that sapped the actors' loyalty, balky "angels," and sometimes their mutual suspicions of each other.[38]

Having survived for the moment, they seemed like the Whig president who wondered what to do with the office after he had won it. They failed to develop a coherent black approach since Popkin was a Hollywood liberal who, like the black middle class, saw racial progress as the assimilation of middle-class values. For him the goal was not "race propaganda" but merely good movies with black casts. To "inject race" would have spoiled the premise of all-black casts, caused "trouble" in Southern markets, and closed off "extra juice" from white patrons. His enemy was not Hollywood racism but rather the old "so corny, so cheap" race movies that he could make better. Cooper presented still another barrier to shaping a black heroic iconography. A talented hoofer and a passable singer and actor, he had been "unfortunately too light to be a hit; too dark to be a white idol." For him race movies were a second choice over a job as Hollywood off-camera tutor of white stars. So he seemed to his coworkers unhappy, fitful, lacking in concentration, devoted to hustling better opportunities, and tinged with weathervaning loyalty.[39] At his best in race movies he faced the reverse of customary racism: his bronze skin had the same effect as a white hat in a western, so heroes remained light and heavies black.

To say more would be to blame the victim. Cooper was the sociologists' marginal man caught between two worlds. Hollywood had made many like him. Despite inchworm gains, Hollywood Negro roles—the butlers and the maids—demanded positive racial identity, so those with full lips, broad noses, and deep brown skins built their résumés at the expense of the Peolas. With American irony those of lightest complexion—Monte Hawley, Clarence Brooks, Frank Wilson, A. B. Comathiere, Laura Bowman, Cleo Desmond, Jesse Lee Brooks—drifted into race movies made for black folk. A single issue of the black *Western Informant* exposed the tension between the two sources of black cinema images. Although the magazine plugged the opening of Cooper's *Dark Manhattan* and took note of the Hollywood Negroes who turned out, it agreed with *Variety* that it was "slightly amateurish." But in another story on Carl Laemmle at seventy the *Informant* praised him for his pictures in which "the Negro actor was given the chance to emote to advantage," especially those in which he gave breaks to Louise Beavers, who then "skyrocketed to fame." In effect, the author, along with most black moviegoers, had preferred Hollywood, with its very gradual approach, to the possibility of a solely black cinema.[40]

For such reasons almost every race movie by 1938 dissolved into a mirror reversal of Hollywood. Even stereotyped mimics such as Stepin Fetchit and Mantan Moreland duplicated their Hollywood roles in race movies. Black gangsters, black molls, black heavies, black cowboys—all acted like their white counterparts in *Little Caesar* or *The Painted Desert*. If they scored with Negro audiences it was as icons of success. If they overcame flat direction, old stock shots, naïve motivations, and wooden characters, it was with a bit of good lighting, fast pacing, neat cutting, and tough black images of aggression. In Popkin's next, *Gang War*, for example, Cooper returned, this time as the kid who sets out to take over the jukebox racket and boasts to his girl he will "lay Harlem at your feet." The moral issue of success within the law or outside it is strong. In the end Jesse Lee Brooks's stern black cop prevails, and Cooper dies in a rooftop shooting.[41]

Micheaux followed with his version, *Underworld*, which he sold to Alfred J. Sack, one of the white bookers who had bought into the trend. Again, he reached inward to deep black roots of aspiration. But he could not match the Hollywood competence that "white" race movies showed. He neatly contrasted the demiurge of a graduate of a Negro college "somewhere in the Southland" with the underworld of Chicago, where he has gone to become the "live one," the new man in the gang. There he finds fights, conspiracies, silken women having breakfast in bed, erotic embraces, and ruin because of "bad liquor or reefers." In a streetscape of processed hair, sharp suits, streetcorner ease, obsequious, defeated shoeshine "boys," black men take success by force. Their lives are punctuated by dancehall and nightclub frolics and flashing moneyrolls. The winners are "black spasms" of sexuality and "cool pappas." But again Micheaux spoiled his aim with padding, poorly mounted vaudeville turns, amateurs who could barely read a line, tacky backdrops, narrative titles, and other makeshifts. Consequently, despite his attempts to sell his stars as equivalents of white success—Oscar Polk, who had appeared "on Broadway"; Bee Freeman, who "turns in a Mae West performance"; and Sol Johnson, who "photographs a la Clark Gable"—he could make only four days at the Harlem Opera House.[42]

The gangster genre had served Hollywood for years as melodrama, social commentary, popular sociology, morality play, urbanized western myth, and a vehicle for stars. Actors—even studios—built careers on them. But the black version's "immediate acceptance was dissipated" by progressively weaker imitations. The old burdens of debt, the labs that held "masters" as collateral, the split weeks, the actors who moved onto new jobs after their week's work, the amateurs who evoked such jibes as "we had to fake around her a lot" combined to strangle a potentially useful black cinema form.[43]

Among the worst were Bert and Jack Goldberg's International Road Show pictures, *Mystery in Swing* (1938) and *Double Deal* (1939), tacky pastiches by the Hollywoodians Arthur Hoerle and Arthur Dreifuss. They combined the cops-and-robbers format of Million Dollar with Micheaux's musical interruptions and added the old comedian Flournoy Miller. In *Mystery in Swing* Monte Hawley plays a flippant journalist-press agent who is cast aside by his client, a female singer who signs a Hollywood contract and no longer needs his "rag." The plot, which includes a murder, a dagger that pins a threatening note to a wall, Buck Woods's running gag as a comic valet, and Miller's interlude as a Fetchitesque cop, is all set in a saloon, which makes the vaudeville interruptions plausible. Only *Double Deal* attempted a racial message: Hawley's gambler reminds a young tough to start at the bottom and work up—"Some of our finest men rose from the ranks of the porter service." But the lame cutting, dull backdrops, confusing flashbacks, stagey fights, "talking heads," and lightskinned heroes, even though they eroded quality, may have soothed an urge of a small black audience untouched by Hollywood.[44] Ofttimes their black focus stopped at the pressbook. *Mystery in Swing* was offered as a behind-the-scenes look at "a colored newspaper office and what an important part the profession plays in the everyday life" of black America. Negroes, said the patronizing blurb, "through their papers, have proved that they will not tolerate being exploited and ridiculed on the screen, and feel that in order to produce successful all-colored pictures, a company must film stories showing the true side of the race."[45]

The worst exploitations spackled their cracks with smooth Hollywood Negroes, so that as·they reached their peak before the war, pictures such as *Midnight Shadow* (Randol Productions, released by Sack, 1939) offered no more than Napoleon Simpson, Ruby Dandridge, and Clinton Rosamond as "talking heads." As quality worsened, some of the companies exploited the black press by sending out press-release boilerplate, thus cutting advertising revenue and putting the burden of ad costs on the local exhibitors. Only the Popkins' Million Dollar studio retained control of the product from script to distribution.[46] Under such conditions it was impossible for them to make the quantum jump from mediocrity to black art.

It was as though the moviemen, black and white, imagined a shallow, gullible, sensation-prone Negro audience that could be cultivated, plucked, pressed of its life fluids like a cotton boll. The infrequent gestures at publicity were like medicine-show drumbeats. When *Double Deal* opened, the *Amsterdam News* ran its blurb as though it were a critical review datelined "Hollywood." "One of the best to come out of Black Hollywood," it said of a film produced by the Goldbergs, Hoerle, and Dreifuss, the latter two being "the Frank Capra and Richard Thorpe of the Colored motion picture industry." Everything was made to seem a "major production" with "sure-fire box office" prospects. Sometimes they stuck in the editor's craw so he would run the plugs, then blast the "weak" story, the "inevitable cabaret scene," and the parts that "seemed strange to average Negro life." By the middle of World War II interviews with Cooper and the others still puffed every picture as a "sensation" that "broke a record."[47]

Among the blacks first Randol and then Cooper attempted a break with the whites. Randol, an ex-Hollywood Negro, could do no better than a flop starring his California colleagues and an abortive musical called *Darktown Strutters' Ball*. But Cooper broke from the whites in 1939 and made a genuine effort to speak through the gangster genre in the manner of Warner Brothers. In his best movie, *Am I Guilty?* (1940), he portrayed a Harlem doctor who dreams of a free clinic. Although shortly into the picture it became "another cops and robbers affair," it remained interesting because of the moral choice of deferring the clinic in favor of ministering to a criminal gang. The press releases also cleaved to the idea of a new departure that caught the eye of "artists, community figures, and newspapermen" even though the ad mats hedged and focused on the gangsters and Pigmeat Markham. Nevertheless, the compromise between black cinema and black box office failed. When it opened in Brooklyn it shared a split week with two white B westerns. And in a few days Million Dollar, his old white company, merged with A. W. Hackle's white Supreme Pictures, and Cooper's independence came to an end.[48]

No black gangster movie truly succeeded either as box office hit
or artistic success that could overcome its disabilities and reflect black
life in a way that Hollywood never could hope to do. But two of them
—both by whites—showed how it should be done. *Moon Over Harlem*
(Meteor, 1939), by a German émigré, Edgar G. Ulmer, with music by
Donald Heywood, made a rare gesture toward making the gritty streets
of Harlem speak of the plight of Negroes. The social oppression that
turned blacks toward crime, "numbers," and in-group violence was
used as a dramatic motive. Its players were a nice mix of Hollywoodians
like Slim Thompson, stage performers like Cora Green, race movie vets
like Alec Lovejoy, and tolerable rookies, all of whom broke the monopoly of lightskinned Hollywood rejects and the old heads of the Lafayette Players. Stylized maintitles prepare the viewer for good established shots of nighttime Harlem—a long truck shot down 125 Street
past Blumstein's, the Apollo, the Alhambra, and into a wedding party.

Moon over Harlem (© Meteor Productions, Inc.) combined a social theme,
a black cast, Edgar G. Ulmer's direction, and a Frank Wilson story and
role. (The State Historical Society of Wisconsin)

Choppy cuts, varied shots, and visually interesting dissolves build epi-
sodic sequences that no race movie had ever attained.

In a coolly effective interior the players are thrown together in a
microcosm of urban in-group tension. Women quarrel over marriage
mores: one prefers a "high yella" man; another a man who can be held
by home life and "home cookin'." A little man pulls a knife in defense
when his machismo is impugned. Still another nags the band into playing black music.

The camera pulls back to pick up the exteriors of the tenements and
life on the hot fire escapes. There a young pair talk of love for Harlem
and making it better with a bit of "leadership." They quarrel with the
hoodlum who spoils the life of the ghetto. Bourgeois aspiration is re-
stated when a nightclub maid presses her daughter to leave the saloon
life, give up her flirtation with a gangster, and go home to study.
Clearly she is ambitious for her daughter because she sees her status as
an economic plight rather than a permanent state of mind.

Although dramatic conflict is stated as black bourgeoisie against
gangsters, the white hand on Harlem's noose is seen supervising the
counting of the spoils of a protection racket. "Dollar Bill," the coolest
of the blacks, wants to destroy the white protection racket—"the gangsters' last stand." Despite his friends' fears for his safety he preaches
solidarity. "When they stoop to chiseling poor colored folk they're
steppin' on my toes," he says. So the social theme and the personal story
move in parallel. For the people it is the "first time in the history of
Harlem they been with anybody so unanimously."

Like a Greek chorus, black women encourage "the voice of the new
Negro." At the club the men agree. "I sure like the way you talk,
Dollar," one of them says. "It makes us *all* feel like men." In the struggle
there can be no easy victory, and the picture touches the level of
tragedy when one of the women is killed in the gangsters' gun fight.

Throughout, the picture was leavened by nuances of Harlem life—
the rivalry between middle-class and street culture, the tight circles imposed by ghetto perimeters, the half-hidden white bosses, the subtleties
of male and female culture differences. Even in minor sequences, carefully sketched portraits appear. For years Harlem had been divided between West Indians, whose British manner intimidated Americans, who
in turn resented the Jamaicans' "dicty" style. One of Bill's toughest
rivals is given sparkling life, then, because he is "that Jamaican fool
who's been making stump speeches against me." Later, tragic death is
given comic relief by using a traditional black wake where food is
served. Amidst crackling laughter one man is accused of making the
rounds of undertakers seeking the best victuals.

The result was not great art. But all of the resources of programmers contributed to a tight little movie that made good use of black life in ways that Hollywood would never see.[49]

One of the last black gangster movies, *Murder on Lenox Avenue* (Colonnade [sic], 1941), was a near-miss directed by Dreifuss, adapted from a story—a modern version of Othello, according to its pressbook—by the Negro actor Frank Wilson, and scored by Heywood. It made good use of New York, opening on a jazzband rehearsing in a Harlem flat, enraging the tenants, and driving them to angry jostling on the stairs. The black bourgeoisie looks askance at the brawlers who "reflect on our reputations." But the class conflicts are dimly seen as matters of manners.

The flitting focus settled at times on "Marshall," who encourages black proprietorship as a panacea. He stirs a "pie woman" to move from street "Arab" to storekeeper. He boasts of his thriving "business league," which indeed matched the actual Harlem Colored Merchants Association or Booker T. Washington's National Negro Business League. Wilson's drama of social struggle became a tract that featured researchers who work for "the benefit of the South," marching black war veterans, rent parties dense with mutual self-help, old men who wish for the day when the ghetto will be "the prosperous Harlem it should be." Harlemites immerse themselves in the movement to "clean our house" of "all disturbing factions" and "forge ahead . . . with pride in our race." If the rhetoric grew shrill and intruded upon the plot, nonetheless it marked a return to the goal of using white techniques to shape an artistic statement to blacks, and called upon the black city experience to speak to black movie audiences.[50]

The flash of attention given the gangster pictures encouraged versions of other Hollywood genres: the biography, the western, the musical, and the documentary. By the late thirties the ambivalent black press boosted them with friendly reviews and big layouts. One paper sponsored a "Greater Negro Movie Month" that recognized the actors "who give the best of their talents to interpretation of the roles depicting true phases of Negro life," pointed toward "the future of the Negro in the motion picture industry," and boosted an "insatiable" desire for black productions.[51]

The musical in particular eluded the grasp of the race moviemakers, perhaps because its musical performers lacked acting experience, its cutters could not carry off the awkward shifts from realism to musical fantasy, and its budgets could not be stretched far enough to meet the increased requirements of the genre. Harry Popkin signed Lena Horne and Cooper to do one, but he could afford only a telephone call rather than an audition and so signed a plumpish Horne just out of a maternity ward. Then they failed to raise their nut and could not pay the cast.[52]

Although the NAACP used the film, *The Duke is Tops*, for a 1938 charity première in Pittsburgh, it eventually made a dreary round and died. Little more than a thin thread with vaudeville turns strung on it, the picture proved to be a flawed model for future race musicals, which seemed unable to grasp the essentials of pacing skits and music. Cooper avoided the opportunity to do another with Nina Mae McKinney and returned to gangster movies. Jack Goldberg and Randol promised a musical that would "end the era of the gangster films," but by the beginning of the war the only musical footage came from a few Eastern studios, one of them fronted by Fritz Pollard, the black football star who ground out "Soundies," or short loops of jazz numbers designed for jukeboxes. After the war the last race movies by Sackamuse, Ted Toddy, and Robert M. Savini, and the Goldbergs suffered from the same stunted production values.[53]

If a distinction may be made between the musical and a drama with a musical milieu, then *Broken Strings* (1940), a good-hearted but cloying melodrama starring Clarence Muse, pointed toward a more artful use of music. The theme concerns raising Negro music to the dignity of European music. Muse plays an effete classical violinist whose hands are damaged. Throughout the story he rides above the moil of the Negro world. Beneath his social pedestal blacks doze in his audiences and his daughter, a steno in the office of a hair-processor, is courted with a promise of "everything you'd need"—clothes, car, and a "swell home." From on high he remonstrates with a black pupil who jazzes up "Humoresque." "You are desecrating a classic," he snaps. His social equal, an aloof black doctor, agrees to take his case while on his way to his class reunion at the Sorbonne.

And that is the center of a neat irony. While he languishes in shabby gentility, wringing his broken hands, railing at black music, his pupil raises money for surgery with a jazz concert, even as the violinist rants. "I'll drive the spirit of the masters into you," he cries, "and drive out the spirit of jazz!" But the operation is a success, and he can play again. "My heart still belongs to the masters," he says. "But look what swing has done for me!" If the film patronized black music, it also paid it due and set a fair story in it, along with a tolerable smidgen of sermonizing on black solidarity.[54]

The late-thirties musicals achieved what was possible within their limited means. At the same time the western, one of the most visually exciting genres and one with the longest of cinematic pedigrees, abjectly failed to touch young black boys with the same impact as its white counterpart had upon white boys. Black westerns may have reached Southern audiences with greater effect than Northern, but they suffered from a reluctance to explore the realities of black life on the

As with many race movies, *Broken Strings* (© Goldberg, Sack) gave work to Hollywood fugitives like Clarence Muse and Stymie Beard. (Author's collection)

frontier. Instead they chose to mirror the most gimmicky white musical horse operas.

In the two years after 1938 four of them emerged from Jed Buell's Hollywood Productions: *Harlem Rides the Range*, *Bronze Buckaroo*, *Two Gun Man from Harlem*, and *Harlem on the Prairie*. With a few exceptions they offered reused costumes, old Republic programmer plots, "good guys" in white hats, shuffling, bug-eyed comedians, crooning commercial western music, a lightskinned café singer named Herb Jeffries, a week's shooting in the San Fernando Valley, and a pair of relatively darker heavies in one of them. As in white westerns of the thirties, there were no Indians; so dramatic conflict depended on rivalries over water rights and real estate leavened with a mildly star-crossed love story. Black addenda seemed no more than random accidents such as the comic "Dusty" (Flournoy Miller) doing a scat dance in the bunkhouse while others watch in hats and stylish mustaches much as they might at a jam session at the Hoofers' Club. The plots were remote from black interests, as in *Harlem Rides the Range*, in which the characters struggle over radium deposits. Moreover, as in white westerns they chose broad comedy for interludes between chases rather than testing their ability to create closeup love scenes. Because fight sequences in westerns depended on oft-rehearsed and choreographed bits of tightly cut film, they steered away from them in favor of improbable bits such as Jeffries's lassoing a heavy's pistol while it is still in its holster. Because, therefore, the fights and shooting scrapes lacked pace and conviction, they broadened out to montage chase sequences based on a surfeit of redundant wideshots that slowed the action. A black viewer would need to search for reasons to buy a ticket beyond the obvious fact that the principals were black. All else duplicated Monogram westerns. Even Mantan Moreland, Miller's comic partner, deviated only once from his pop-eyed passive stock role when he bashed a heavy with a skillet. So they failed to develop the West as an allegory for the black urban experience. All that remained was curious irony such as the stylish way in which Western lingo and manner— "C'mon boys, let's leather!"—blended with the cool vigor of the ad lib black talk; or the manner in which Jeffries gilded his modest success by imitating the white cowboys' penchant for ornamenting their cars with bronze Western motifs.[55]

Of all the late thirties genres documentaries offered the least to black audiences. Old Signal Corps footage, the grainy animal pictures, an occasional New Deal propaganda film were the best of the bad lot. Tight money blocked the aspirations of black producers. Fritz Pollard, who might have been a good risk in white circles, failed to raise white money for a proposed studio. The only exceptions to the blackout were the National Anti-Tuberculosis Association's *Let My People Live* (1938), a plea by Rex Ingram for the conquest of rural black TB, and Bryant's film biography of Carver, marred by amateur support. The NAACP refrained from producing films at least until the war years. "I don't think pure machine-made propaganda does much good," wrote Joel Spingarn, the President, to Walter White.[56]

By 1940 the race movies hung back, remote from the centers of Negro life. Save for the gangster movies, Hollywood genres had failed them. It mattered little whether the creators were the continentals Ulmer or Dreifuss, the exploiters Jed Buell or Alfred Sack, or the blacks Cooper or Randol. Indeed, it could be argued that the producer mattered most, with the West Coast having the better of it. Thus no amount of black dues-paying on the part of Spencer Williams could save his heartless, soulless *Dirty Gerty from Harlem, USA* (1946), a Negro version of *Rain*, from the shabby materials supplied by his producer.[57] Their accidental dependence on light-skinned actors opened them to the charge of racism. Their plots seemed forever tangled in criminal trivia or hollow Western lore. They stretched racial identity out of shape between the positive pole of bourgeois ambition and the negative pole of street-corner lethargy. "For the first time in screen history the life of the upper strata Negro will be paraded before audiences," boasted one of their blurbs that set class against black class.[58] Could any genre offer a heroic figure who could take on the system without the taint of exploiting the race? And if one appeared could the popular black press fill the void of criticism, see what was to be seen, and lay it before a prospective audience eager to know?

The first answer would be a tentative "yes," if a movie could successfully capture black struggle in a modern allegory without sneering at the black proles and without preaching. Two little movies pointed the way that few eyes saw: *The Spirit of Youth* (Grand National, 1937), a biography of Joe Louis; and *Keep Punching* (Sack, 1939), a biography of Henry Armstrong. The former, produced, written, and directed by whites—Lew Golder, Arthur Hoerle, and Harry Fraser—combined the surehanded craft of Edna Mae Harris, Cleo Desmond, Jesse Lee Brooks, and Clarence Muse with the understated persona of Louis himself. "Joe Thomas" drifts from Alabama to baggage-smashing in Detroit, where a fistfight in defense of a friend leads to the arena. Louis's impassive mien serves to set his firm Southern moral sense against the flashy city and its nightclub queens. With the help of his shrewd black backer (Muse), he overcomes a rebellious streak, avenges a single defeat, and cleaves to his goal "t'git ahead and be somebody and do things for mamma and pappa."

The stock shots from Golden Gloves bouts become marvels that result in a world with blacks on top and white opponents down. As the *Times* man put it, "Members of the so-called ruling white race enter it only to be knocked flat." Joe's manager confirms the point when he offers a handout to a down-at-the-heels white fighter.[59] Thus the prizefighting format provided an ideal scene in which to act out black ambition without blundering into fantasy. Compared to the westerns it was a fine attempt.

Henry Armstrong, another black champion, appeared in a boxing film with greater possibilities. Because Armstrong was more glib and a better actor, he might have added real significance to his role as gambler-hustler-womanizer who matures into a deeply pious champion. The resourceful boxer, with the help of the skilled Canada Lee, Dooley Wilson, Hamtree Harrington, and Francine Everett, turned out a good homely movie on the theme of "pluggin' away" at success. At its best there were ironic ambiguities between the monastic grind, the salty trainers, and the hangers-on of the training camp on the one hand and

The Spirit of Youth (© Grand National) starred Joe Louis in a thinly masked autobiography. (Author's collection)

the flashy women who are the prizes of the victors on the other. And it tried to make boxing into an allegory of "our community," a reasonable gesture in the flush days of the first black boxing champions since Jack Johnson.[60]

But two satisfying but flawed boxing movies that had scored more because of sincerity than talent were not enough. To carry the medium forward required a sure-handed knowledge of the prospective audience, North and South, urban and rural, poor and bourgeois; a keener awareness of Hollywood's failure to touch blacks even at its best; and a critical fraternity who could debate issues of quality with a broad audience.

Given the strictures imposed on blacks, the only possible black institution up to the task would have been the press because of its intimate historical connection with "show biz." And indeed, Romeo Daugherty, Abe Hill, Dan Burley and other writers honestly struggled with the problem of a black cinema aesthetic. Yet if the press was to be the instrument, it would need to overcome its dependence on bookers' ad space and on Hollywood boilerplate. They plugged Hollywood in gratitude for slow "progress" and because of ad revenue, but they loyally labeled every race movie that crossed the river from Fort Lee a "sensation," or a "fast moving, absorbing and gripping" tale. Moreover, those newspapers who printed the columns of the Westerners, Lawrence LaMar and Harry Levette, doomed their readers to press releases and a critical canon that extolled mere appearance and condemned only what seemed "undignified."[61]

Producers and press alike possessed little knowledge of the prospective audience. Not since the days of Lincoln had a black studio surveyed its viewers. The shrewd Burley asked the question in 1939:

> Why have most of the recent pictures based on Negro themes, using all-colored casts and written by colored authors, failed to make the instantaneous hit with the public as intended and what must be done before the Negro public will register a heavy enough demand for its own artists on the screen . . . in preference to the stars of Hollywood?[62]

How many Negroes thought of their culture as no more than a protective reaction to racism that would wane? How many thought of Negro

Despite Louis's limited range, the romantic story with Edna Mae Harris was effective. (Author's collection)

art as hokum and themselves as "lamp-blacked Anglo-Saxons?" How
many agreed with Micheaux that the race would not pay to see blacks
in manual chores? How many thought Hollywood's glacial change better reflected their true plight in America? How many could sort out
black Southern tastes from Northern? Only *Variety* tried. Of Cooper's
Am I Guilty? its reviewer guessed:

> It compares favorably in every respect with the B output of major
> lots. Only difficulty it may run into is its effort to reach too far. In
> endeavoring to get away from the usual obvious Negro comedy style,
> it risks being too high-brow. It was well-received by the comparatively
> sophisticated audience of Harlem, but whether the more poorly-
> educated Negroes of the South, on which, after all, the picture must
> depend for a major portion of its income, would not rather see low
> comedy than a story of mental conflict is something else again.[63]

Indeed, race movies may have shared a blind spot with Hollywood:
both of them testing their markets for racial themes with minorities,
either black New Yorkers or white Southerners. Race, region, and class
tastes eluded them. So their movies rarely touched on the centers of
life: the black family, interracial conflict, color stratification, the trials
of poor black institutions such as Southern colleges, celebrated events
such as Scottsboro, the intermingling of street culture and "square"
life, the charisma of folk preachers, the brassy life of jazz, or even
"Harlem's poor folks who work for the rich folks on Sugar Hill."[64] In
contrast was another electronic medium, radio, which covered Negro
life and included many musical traditions, as well as reportage on labor
and urban problems, the total consisting of more than a dozen black
programs per day in New York alone.[65]

Critics and producers alike fretted over the echoing laughter when
the love scenes came on. But no one knew whether the laughs muffled
inner tears of despair or whether some scenes deserved a horse laugh.
Reporters merely recorded that they "laughed at the escapades when it
should have been tense." But what could be funnier than the black cop's
homily that crime does not pay as Cooper's body slumps at the feet of
his girl? Crime, gambling, prostitution, and narcotics had paid well for
years in Harlem, and, indeed, counted as crime only if whites lapped
off the profits. Or why should the house not howl at the young black
about to be wrongly executed as the old convict tells him to "buck up"
and "take it" like a man. On the self-conscious left, Angelo Herndon's
Young Communist League picketed Micheaux's *God's Step Children*
as an impediment to race fulfillment because it "creates a false splitting
of Negroes into light and dark groups" and "It slandered Negroes,
holding them up to ridicule."[66]

Black press and trades sometimes blasted the most sincere failures.

The Popkins' *Reform School* (1939), for example, though technically sound, seemed an "over-dramatic" attempt to deal sympathetically with the "familiar pattern" of the black mother whose son brushes with the law. *Variety* flogged the Popkins' *One Dark Night*, a lame imitation of MGM's *Hardy Family*, for everything—lighting, pacing, "so-so" acting, jerky pans. But black critical awareness had broad tolerant ranges that may have thwarted the growth of a critical audience. Jed Buell, a graduate of the old Sennett Studios, exploited any gullible audience—religious pietists, Negroes, even midgets—and in 1940 he formed Dixie National Pictures with James K. Friedrich, his partner in a Jesus movement, and Ted Toddy of Atlanta. Their *Mr. Washington Goes to Town*, "a sort of colored 'Grand Hotel,'" was peppered with Moreland's and Flournoy Miller's wizened routines, the writing of whites, among them Walter Weems, a gagman for the "Two Black Crows"—lines such as "Pork chops is the fondest things I is of," and worse. And yet a Negro critic gave it "four bells minus" and a light slap on the wrist for a fight between two men which he considered "undignified."[67] Thus on the eve of yet another war for democracy race movies failed to give forward thrust to a black aesthetic, failed to overcome their white producers' preconceptions, failed to reach their audience, and failed to bridge black barriers of region and class, largely because the black press avoided the challenge of encouraging *both* race movies and progressive change in Hollywood.[68]

Consequently, as the economy crept out of depression, makers of race movies still lacked sufficient capital, never raising a nut higher than $40,000 or so. Their fixed distribution costs still allowed only tacky pressbooks filled with misspellings. Some sold territorial rights to avoid petty thieving by exhibitors. Their most famous performers refused to alter their typed roles for fear of spoiling their images. Thus only a few race movies could overcome odds, shuck free of stock melodrama and tabshow comedy, and draw dramatic conflict from the stuff of black life.[69]

In the end the old veteran, Oscar Micheaux, must stand as the exemplar both of persistence and of failure in the face of unyielding barriers. He had survived rural naïveté, conniving exhibitors along the Mississippi Valley circuits, the burdens imposed by disused studios, personal bankruptcy, charges of misappropriation, bad scripts, artless movies, indifferent actors, and the life of the road. Then on New Year's Day, 1940, he was about to have his finest hour. He had met Colonel Hubert Julian, the "Black Eagle" of the rickety Ethiopian Air Force, the jinxed follower in Lindbergh's flight path, the self-proclaimed victor in the fight to place Negro aviators in the Army Air Force. Together they planned movies that Julian claimed would "build up the morals of my race." Already they had two in the can, finished probably before the merger—*The Notorious Elinor Lee* and *Lying Lips*.[70]

Elinor Lee was to be a tribute "to the important part played by the Colored fighter" in restoring the popularity of boxing. The principals were Edna Mae Harris, who steered Joe Louis through the trials of moviemaking, and Robert Earl Jones, perhaps the most accomplished of the race movie actors. They opened at the RKO Regent complete with Julian in topper and cape. Only in the page-bottom ads could one detect the split week they had settled for.[71]

Julian's flair, the glitter of black stars, the homage paid by white showmen, Mayor Fiorello LaGuardia's wish to spur moviemaking, and the glowing speeches veiled the flaws on the screen. "Don't expect the perfection of a Hollywood picture," Julian told the crowd, "but know that we have done our very best." Then Micheaux came on and hinted that he would use whites in his movies, and "not as buffoons." Afterward they went to a party in the manager's office.[72]

On the screen, beside Jones and Harris, were the veterans Laura Bowman, Amanda Randolph, and Juano Hernandez. The story smelled of *Golden Boy*, but instead of that film's wisecracking class consciousness and social thrust, *Elinor Lee* stalled, ploughed along at dead slow, and settled on the bottom. The man who would have been Odets's Fuseli, the corrupt white manipulator of the puppet-boxer, was a limp, cigar-smoking caricature who seemed glued to his desk. The heavies conspire to prevent the rise of another black champion. Only Jones stands in the way, trim, forthright, at the ready, while Elinor Lee purely for pelf sets out to induce him to "take a dive." Her notoriety, then, grows out of the fact that she is a poor "race woman."

Then something went terribly wrong. Perhaps they had no cover shots for a botched segment, or an actor quit, or they lacked footage with which to cut smooth narrative. In any case, pacing crumbled, momentum faltered, and "talking heads" took over. Dull plottiness smothered character. A rehash of the ancient Afro-American myth of Staggerlee is told with Elinor at its center. A subsequent murder and a bit of half-remembered "low down business in Paducah" is revealed incredibly, even insultingly, to its black audience through a parrot who witnesses it and later tells the story. Without foreshadowing or motivation a low-key trainer (Hernandez) enters, convinced he can sharpen the boxer's talent. His efforts to crack the boxer's circle form a circumferential subplot that blurs focus on the main theme. Then at the crest of the action, the main bout, the boxers' introduction, smoky and fetid with the air of Madison Square Garden, is more visually interesting than the fight. The bout that should have redeemed Afro-

America's faith in its own is a flat succession of long shots and poorly choreographed closeups.

Julian and Micheaux had promised much and delivered nothing, because they could not overcome the historic disabilities of the medium. In the largest black city in the world they earned no more than a split week. Using fine actors and an old black myth they made them dull. The allegory of the prize fighting arena was thrown away. *Elinor Lee* had proven that for race movies to be viable they must be good or they are mere exploitation, and that Micheaux still suffered from his isolation.[73]

A few weeks later audiences saw a possible source of the fault. Micheaux released *Lying Lips*, a cautionary tale about men who show no respect to the women of the race, featuring all the players who had been in *Elinor Lee*. "You can get plenty of men of our race to do anything," says a character reproving the race's esprit. True, says a woman, in defense, but "We're so poor it's hard for our males to be real men any more." They debate whether one should "take care of a man" to avoid facing the consequences of his poverty and unemployment. In

Oscar Micheaux's later movies like *Lying Lips* (© Oscar Micheaux) departed from his personal style, relying more on Colonel Hubert Julian's flair for publicity rather than on their merits. (GEH)

The snapshot of the crew on the set of *Mystery in Swing* (© International Road Shows) revealed the heavy white contribution to race movies in their last years. (Author's collection)

the streets a black cop (Jones, again) sees proliferating saloons as the crime against black males, and it makes his "blood boil."

Again the dramatic issues waft off target and into paternity suits, broken families, hard drinking, overdrawn prison sequences, and shrill melodrama, ending in a haunted house where cops have taken a suspect to wring a confession from him. By the end even skilled actors muffed their ad lib lines and cast sidelong glances at the camera.[74] The only reasonable excuse for a tangle of images was that Micheaux patched together one film from the outtakes of the other and fobbed them off on a Julian eager to puff his own career. Whatever the cause, Micheaux joined the ranks of the blacks who had failed to overcome the insuperable.

Gradually race movies became the private preserve of a coterie of white entrepreneurs: Buell, Popkin, and Rinaldo in Hollywood; the Goldbergs in New York; Ted Toddy and the Sacks in the South; and an occasional poacher; along with their directors, Ulmer, Dreifuss, and

Fraser. Technicians remained lily white. When the war dried up production, the old ones came out of the cans with fresh titles. *Mr. Washington Goes to Town* exemplified the decline of black impetus: Buell produced; Dixie National released; Walter Weems, the old author of *Hearts in Dixie*, blackface routines, and the *Two Black Crows* radio show, wrote the script; Mantan Moreland, Flournoy Miller's replacement for the dead Aubrey Lyles, rehashed their old lines; Bert Sternbach was production manager; the crews were white despite the appearance of Harold Garrison, Vidor's assistant on *Hallelujah!*; and most press blurbs seemed to go to the white papers.[75]

Black criticism remained silent, perhaps in appreciation of Hollywood liberalism and perhaps because of the old rule against carping at a brother in public. No canon of criticism, no demand for quality, no community of opinion matured. The answers for one *Amsterdam News* writer were more "sex and glamor" in race movies and a "squawk to the high heavens" at a presumed white conspiracy to stifle Micheaux.

In their latter days race movies departed from melodrama and social themes in favor of musicals in the manner of *Ovoutie O'Rooney* (© Astor Pictures Corp.) with Slim Gaillard. (Author's collection)

According to Abe Hill, "amateurish filming, ludicrous situations, lousy sound recording and willful violation of movie techniques" spoiled films. The worst, he wrote, "should have been called LIFE IS A GREAT HUSTLE."[76]

As war came to America, race movies lapsed into a coma, and black actors and the NAACP both turned toward a changing Hollywood and a better place in the California sun.

Chapter Thirteen

THE POLITICS
OF ART

In World War II American rhetoric was directed against the racist theories of Nazi Germany. This in turn brought about a reaction against racism at home. As a result, there developed real pressure within American society to provide racial equality. The war years also became a seedtime for a heightened black political consciousness. These stirrings of change were reflected, at first timidly and tentatively, by Hollywood.

For most blacks in the movie colony it began with a page-one banner in *Variety* in the spring of 1942—"BETTER BREAKS FOR NEGROES IN H'WOOD."[1] The proffered promise resulted from meetings of studio heads, Walter White of the NAACP, and Wendell L. Willkie, the defeated Republican Presidential candidate and counsel for the NAACP. The negotiations codified some of the social changes that had occurred in America and thus marked a new beginning for Hollywood by eliminating the old racial stereotypes on the screen.

So the immediate future of black cinema would pass from the hands of the race-movie makers—the outsiders like Micheaux and the Goldbergs—to a liberal Hollywood under assault from the NAACP who, like Blucher's troops at Waterloo, arrived almost too late. For a dozen years whites, at least those on the left, had signaled their willingness to abandon racist attitudes. The strongest signs of change came from the American theater in all its aspects, commercial, experimental, and, later, the politicized Federal Theatre. The Afro-American penetration of the theater, wrote R. Dana Skinner in the liberal Catholic weekly *Commonweal*, at the end of the Harlem Renaissance, was "progressing

apace" and quickening the hopes of those who "feel the inner poign-
ancy of the Negro's handicap in the American environment." By the
thirties "drama was a weapon," and liberals used it to state the Negro's
case for equal treatment. Thus Paul Green's *In Abraham's Bosom*,
Frank Dazey and Jim Tully's *Black Boy*, DuBose Heyward's *Brass
Ankle* and *Porgy*, Julia Peterkin's *Scarlet Sister Mary*, Hall Johnson's
Run Little Chillun, John Wexley's *They Shall not Die*, and Langston
Hughes's *Mulatto* brought black themes to theater audiences and in the
process trained a new generation of actors who would be ready to take
advantage of the opportunities wartime Hollywood would hold for
blacks.[2]

The same thrust carried over into black and white popular media.
There were Harlem dance crazes, lindy hoppers, revivals of Miller and
Lyles, "hot colored clubs," Irving Mills's all-black vaudeville units, and
at the Harlem Opera House Ralph Cooper as "The Chocolate Stick of
Personality and His Kongo Knights." Whites and blacks alike enjoyed
Aimée Semple McPherson's gospel singers, radio's *Amos 'n' Andy*, stylized black events like *Green Pastures, The Hot Mikado, Porgy and
Bess*, and the waning small-time minstrel shows. Only backstage with
the lights down did Negroes bristle at the other side of success: the low
pay, the censorship of gritty black themes, and the clever white imitators such as Nora Bayes and her "I'm No Nigger" routine.[3] In a letter
to *The New York Times* the black actress Rose McClendon insisted
that "social realism" be used by dramatists to "deal with Negroes, with
Negro problems, with phases of Negro life, faithfully presented." At
the very least some smug matinee-goer might "send my colored maid
to see . . . one of her race who has made something of herself."[4]

But if movies were to take a lead from Rose McClendon and treat
Negro life with greater perception, it could be done only after direct
political action by blacks and their white allies. Already new black political styles had emerged. Adam Clayton Powell, a flashy Harlem
preacher, spoke from his pulpit in support of A. Philip Randolph and
his Brotherhood of Sleeping Car Porters' threat to march on Washington to demand a better share of jobs in war industry for blacks, a threat
that did indeed produce the desired result.[5] In Hollywood the studios
contributed to a white liberal tide by hiring many writers with Eastern
and leftist roots and by taking a much more skeptical attitude toward
the alleged power of the South's box office. Already Southerners had
bought tickets, not always in droves, to see *Emperor Jones, The Green
Pastures*, and other black-toned movies. Southern critics as far South as
New Orleans regularly judged black actors without regard to race.
And radio stations as far South as Charlotte pledged to censor racial
slurs on the air.[6]

Each new demand for equal treatment seemed to have a successful conclusion. Hollywood soon reflected the trend. The liberal consensus in the nation seemed to point the way for a new deal in Hollywood, too.

In no way could the liberal coalition be taken for a leftist coup, for its tenets were the high-flown sentiments of the Atlantic Charter and Roosevelt's "four freedoms" speech, which set the broadest possible boundaries on which the Western democracies could agree to fight fascism. Indeed, there were limits to the New Deal vision because the specific reformist remedies often split the coalition. For example, Pare Lorentz found that his two documentary pleas for the New Deal, *The Plow That Broke the Plains* and *The River*, nettled studio bosses who refused him stock shots, revived Will Hays's hostility toward message movies, and irritated Southern bookers. When Walter Wanger, John Howard Lawson, and William Dieterle made *Blockade*, a sympathetic view of the Loyalists in the Spanish Civil War, pressure from Congressman Martin Dies and other strong anti-Communists required them to leave the combatants nameless and to open in suburban Westwood instead of on Hollywood Boulevard. The *Times* man could only praise them for "doing the most we can expect an American picture to do." So in frustration Hollywoodians joined such committees as the Anti-Nazi League and the Motion Picture Artists Committee and lent their names to progressive causes. Leftist causes became fashionable, but their rhetoric was clearly not visible in the many potboiler films most left-leaning writers and filmmakers created in this period. "In such an epoch," said Andrew Sarris, "even an Irish Catholic conservative like [John] Ford could be mistaken for a progressive force."[7]

Meanwhile, blacks in Hollywood, although far more race-conscious than in the silent era, avoided criticising the studios and attempted to maintain good relations with them. "Hollywood is a swell place," said Leigh Whipper after visiting Muse's ranch and Bojangles's "fashionable" neighborhood. He echoed the good hopes of the cadre of actors in their neat bungalows in Pasadena, Perris, and Watts, as well as the friendly black press. The NAACP gave tacit approval by doing no more than offering praise for prosaic efforts to promote more work for Hollywood Negroes.[8]

The movie press took a liberal-centrist position. Along with continuing to print stories of black success in films, the papers were now prepared to discuss the plight of the Negro actor in Hollywood. One of them allowed Fetchit to defend himself against freshening criticism— "He's No Uncle Tom; Feels He Has Helped Race Relations." One paper as early as 1934 found that, although Hollywood was "still afraid of color problems," the "movies are growing up" and the era of "fat, black, and ugly" had ended. By the end of the decade the *Amsterdam News* could report two extremes of black experience with equal honesty. On the one hand it noted the old cattle calls still provided "several weeks with locations and good overtime for men, women, and children," and on the other, they let the embittered Paul Robeson protest that he was "no longer willing to identify myself with an organization that has no regard for reality . . . and entirely ignores the dynamic forces at work in the world today." If the first statement represented no more than a hedge against losing advertising revenue, the second represented good reportage. After all, the *Amsterdam News* concluded, pejorative comedy survived because "the public likes to believe minority groups are, in reality, just as movies paint them," a position shared by Hollywood Negroes, who believed with Eddie Anderson that the roles, although "fiction [and] someone's imagination," were sketched from a life he personally knew. And a survey of Negro audiences confirmed that *Tarzan* pictures were favorites along with Lena Horne, Anderson, Hattie McDaniel, and six white stars. Finally, the Hollywood Negroes wished to avoid the professional risks involved in broadening their range beyond the outlines of their familiar characters.[9]

Clearly some third force from the national Negro community would have to provide direction and a political aesthetic if blacks were to carry their awareness of social change beyond isolated complaints about movies, lyrics, segregated seating, and racial insults.[10] Other than continuing their fitful tilts with revivals of *The Birth of a Nation*, the NAACP provided scant leadership from their New York offices. Even then they sometimes achieved no more than free newspaper copy for the picture and for the Communist Party pickets searching for a racial cause. Therefore they chose easy targets such as college film classes and clubs or cities with ordinances prohibiting movies that "tend to stir up or engender race prejudice." And those campaigns offended white liberal allies, who often requested that they abandon their attempts at censorship "so that we won't have occasion in the future to take any of your locals to task."[11]

On the eve of war, with change in the air but direction lacking, Hollywood ground out more than a hundred films that gave greater prominance to blacks but represented little change in basic outlook. It is as if Hollywood was waiting for someone to tug its sleeve. And sometimes they still avoided the issue entirely by omitting Negroes. *The Story of Irene and Vernon Castle* (1939) substituted Walter Brennan for the smart Negro of Mrs. Castle's memoirs; *The Boy Slaves* (1939) indicted mainly white peonage; and *St. Louis Blues* (1939), *Blues in the Night* (1939), and *Strike Up the Band* (1940) couched black music in mindless white stories. Indeed, Orson Welles's *Citizen*

Kane, thought by many critics to be the finest movie ever made, may have been the residual product of an attempt to do Joseph Conrad's *Heart of Darkness*.[12]

The bedrock on which movie Negroes rested their careers was the stout black role of the confidante who knows where all the bodies are buried. The most accomplished blacks took up the role and gave it a deep-running humanity and made a living from it—either as serious craftsmen (Muse, George Reed, and Ernest Whitman), vaudevillians (Eddie Anderson and Mantan Moreland), or movie foils (Willie Best and Sam McDaniel). Best, for example, was a wide-eyed slim brown reed from Mississippi who bent himself into the shape of a Stepin Fetchit. He was Sambo, George, Algernon, Willie, Wellington, always hoping for a friendly mention "as the terror-stricken menial [who] garners the film's major acting honors." In the 1940s he was succeeded by Fred Toones, who appeared as First-and-Second-Thessalonians, Genesis, and Snowflake, which became his own name so that in his

During the war roles like Mantan Moreland's Birmingham Brown, here in *The Jade Mask* (© Monogram Pictures Corp.), fell into the ranks of "B" movies. (Author's collection)

later credits he recurred as "Himself." The racial overtones of these films derived from their Zeroes, Feets Johnsons, and Washes. Perhaps in another country with no racial past these parts would have appeared to be only benign humor. In America in 1940, however, they represented the easy, cheap way out of dealing with the problem of racial stereotypes. And old Noble Johnson still prowled as Elon or Tecumseh or Moukali or some other copperskinned heavy. Yet white critics loved them for their bits: Rochester's scene-stealing that saved Jack Benny's sputtering career; his rural folk-doctor in *Rainbow on the River;* Benny Carter as the "priceless find" of *Sporting Blood;* the "colored assistant . . . crack comedy role" of *Scattergood Baines;* Sam McDaniel's "sparkling bits" in *Bad Men of Missouri;* Best's "excellent laugh lines" in *Who Killed Aunt Maggie?;* Moreland's "popeyed porter," who was "fast becoming a fixture in Monogram's pictures."[13]

Perhaps because they represented less of a direct threat, the women gave sting to smartly witty lines in their roles as confidantes. Even younger women occasionally gave themselves to the craft—Hattie Noel, Dorothy Dandridge, Hilda Simms, Teresa Harris. Their most important role was as wisecracking, fey, abrasive rebels against caste. With sly winks they proffered advice or raised eyebrows at their employers' follies as though following the path laid down by Hattie McDaniel in *Alice Adams.* Libby Taylor, Lillian Yarbo, Marietta Canty, the Randolph Sisters—they all built careers on the role, which provided steady work and only rarely evoked the negative critical reaction that greeted their male-confidante counterparts. Like Sul-te-Wan's maid with the heart of gold in Zanuck's *In Old Chicago,* they gave folksy point to white plot incidents. A Louise Beavers could save her own dignity and sometimes a whole movie with a well-turned Aunt Lindy, Mammy, Selectine, Clotilda, Beulah, Clementine, Aunt Emmeline, or Petunia, so frequently that when she failed, *Variety* noticed she might have made more of "the colored slavey, but was held down."[14]

At the top of their form they insinuated fine nuances in the cracks of the old molds. In *Pride of the Blue Grass* (1937) Sam McDaniel, a groom, punctures the stuffed shirt of a French-speaking Oriental. "Don't give me that, big boy," snaps McDaniel, who has paid higher dues. "You ain't been around here dat long." In *Louisiana Purchase* (1941) he bends an old taboo by commenting blackly on the beauty of white women: "Boy, if she was black she'd be beautiful!" Dooley Wilson also made more of a line than it meant. In *Take a Letter Darling* (1942), a satire on career women, he milks the old racial etiquette for a modern laugh, addressing the feminist as "Boss."[15]

Images changed least in the most stylized Hollywood forms, the cartoons and musical shorts that depended on immediate recognition of surrealistic figures. Detail was sacrificed to fluidity, identity became stereotyped, and dialogue strung into one-liners and tag-lines—"Th-th-that's all folks!" and "What's up, Doc?" Thus the maids in MGM's *Tom and Jerry* cartoons shuffled and drawled a burlesque that no Negro actor could equal. In the 1940s George Pal's *Jasper* was a three-dimensional "puppetoon" of a Negro boy whose pop-eyed, lip-smacking addiction to watermelon leads him into *contretemps* with a shrewd black scarecrow and a hustling black crow. In seven minutes —with "Mammy's Little Baby Loves Shortnin' Bread" on the sound-track—Pal dragged in malaprops, a parody of *Green Pastures*, ghosts, knocking knees, sausage-lipped grins, and venal deacons. As late as 1944 Disney's Uncle Remus in the partially animated *Song of the South* owed much to road-company Tom shows.[16]

Like opera, film musicals followed necessarily stylized, well-worn images. Louis Armstrong fell victim to stereotyped musical roles after his musical shorts and his ground-breaking work in *Pennies from Heaven* and *Artists and Models*. Thereafter he lapsed into a musical "whitewing"—a uniformed streetsweeper in Mae West's *Every Day's a Holiday* (1937); the musical inspiration of a rhythmic racehorse in *Goin' Places* (1938); an "outtake" in *Dr. Rhythm* (1938); a musically rich Max Fleischer cartoon; and a clutter of shorts and soundies. Most Negro musicians—Horne, Count Basie, Dandridge, Calloway, the Hall Johnson Choir, the Mills Brothers, Meade Lux Lewis, and less frequently, Jimmie Lunceford, Coleman Hawkins, and others—played in segregated specialties that commercialized jazz and boogie woogie, although occasionally they contained a signature piece such as Calloway's "Minnie the Moocher." A few good shorts in the format of "tab-shows" bucked the trend. *King for a Day* (1934), for example, offered Bill Robinson, Muriel Rahn, Hattie Noel, Dusty Fletcher, and Babe Matthews doing everything from lindy hopping to "Ol' Man River." *Black Network* (1936) presented Nina Mae McKinney, the Nicholas Brothers, the Washboard Serenaders, Amanda Randolph, and Bill "Basement" Brown as founders of a Negro radio show. And *Carnival in Rhythm* (1940) mixed the Afro-Cuban and classical dance of Katharine Dunham, Archie Savage, and Talley Beatty. But to its white set decorators Harlem still meant dice, billiard cues, and razors.[17]

Two garden-variety musicals departed from the norm. *Panama Hattie* (1942) jumped with the lean, limber, shoulder-shaking, finger-snapping dances of the Berry Brothers in pearl-grey derbies or Afro-Cuban frills or top hats and tapping canes. Their dances tease the thematic question: "You mean down below the borderline [110th Street] they don't kick the gong around?" Lena Horne sings some innocently sexy Cole Porter music in her isolated bit. In *Star Spangled*

Rhythm (1942) Dunham and Eddie Anderson tear off a segregated bit in an army camp show, this time with a political message. They do a zoot-suited, silky-smooth scat dance outside Pinky's Place on 137th and Lenox. But the picture goes out on a chauvinistic montage of Mt. Rushmore with Bing Crosby explaining the soul of America, which includes red clay, watermelons, spirituals, and black church women singing "Sometimes I Feel Like a Motherless Child." We need all the Washingtons, says Bing: "George, Martha, and Booker T."[18]

By 1940 documentaries were also minimally accessible to blacks, but few of them reflected the New Deal racial attitudes. Louis DeRochemont's *The March of Time* series for Henry Luce reached the widest audience and placed the Negro in the most fairly drawn milieu, even though their feature length sermon on the manly art of "preparedness" was as lily white as MGM's Civil War segment of its *Land of Liberty* shown at the New York World's Fair. But their older-style Negro roles appeared with a certain fidelity. There were black Navy stewards, stately Southern Negroes waiting tables, crusty fishermen going after channel "cats," Southerners in a "brave struggle" with ignorance and pellagra and worn soil, hard-handed farmers signing up in the segregated Civilian Conservation Corps, families swaying in church, and downcast mourners at the fag-end of lynching fever. New urban roles were more baffling. Harlem appeared in the form of dance contests, voodoo cults, charismatic sects, and fire-hydrant baptisms. Except for Joe Louis's fights, nonfiction film received scant broadcast. Only Carver's biography, a Rockefeller-backed film on Georgia education, and government film such as the National Youth Administration's sketch of its Alabama and Georgia programs in which black youth learned domestic arts and "how to brighten up their homes" against the day when "life will be better for them and for all of us here in the South" broke the silence.[19]

Of all the genres of American cinema, Civil War movies came closest to combining the art of the screen, racial integrity, mythic verisimilitude, and a politesse that made them acceptable to the Southern box office. The finest and still unmatched masterpiece was *Gone with the Wind*—at least in the care and precision with which it defined the realities of Southern society. As an incident in American cinema history it did more to signal the changing racial arrangements than any other movie.

But first, racial issues that arose out of the Civil War had to be treated in a more mature, modern way by filmmakers. Ever since Vidor's *So Red the Rose*, filmmakers had begun to consider issues and antagonists in other than purely simplistic black and white terms. They sprinkled villainy among insolent Negroes, Southern rascals, and Yankee

Hazel Scott's participation in this scene in *Something to Shout About* (© Columbia Pictures Corp.) was unusual in that black entertainers usually appeared in film segments without whites so they could be cut when the film was shown in the South. (Author's collection)

adventurers, although they felt obligated in the title "crawls" to rehash older historiography and in the plots to minimize the presence of strong-willed blacks in the South.

A fine example was Paramount's *The Texans* (1938), which, like many of them, used the Southwest locale to introduce "western" fans to a turgid literary wave of the bloody shirt of Reconstruction myth:

> Reconstruction. . . . it is an era of lawlessness—of smoldering hates—of oppression after a Civil War fought for a great ideal. But hardly had the smoke of battle cleared before that ideal was forgotten. . . .
> The South was ruled as a conquered enemy. Northern politicians wallowed in an orgy of power—of plunder by organized mobs—of tribute and tyranny and death.[20]

Thus filmwriters easily passed over the revisionist historians' findings that the politicos rewrote old near-useless state constitutions, created public education where there had been none, broadened the tax base, encouraged investment, rewrote racist law, worked with the Freedmen's Bureau and Yankee philanthropists to encourage blacks to build their own social institutions. The establishing shots dissolve into the

Gradually the liberal mood altered old roles. In *The Texans* (© Paramount Pictures, Inc.) violent, unreconstructed rebels were at least as malevolent as the black Yankee troops. (BFI)

riverfront of "Indianola, Texas," where drunken black troopers shove gray veterans off the muddy duckboards, gruff Yankee sergeants slap stickers—"Confiscated Rebel Property"—onto chattels stacked upon groaning wharves, and strawbosses goad hungry Southerners into toting cargo—"nigger work." But then we are quickly into the plot: an uninspected wagon, a worn boot on the driver's box, a noisy croaking of "Dixie" which diverts a dull Yankee sergeant and allows a cargo of rifles to pass into town bound for Emperor Maximilian in Mexico and an intended revival of Southern fortunes. Unlike the movies of the age of Griffith, the end allows the hero to turn away from Southern fantasy—a plan "to drive the Yankees out of the South," in the words of the belle who proposes it. "This is America," he says artlessly, "We govern by law, not by nightriding." So the old racial fears open the movie, but it closes on a libertarian speech.

Jesse James and *Belle Starr*, two ambitious prewar Fox epics, rehearsed the same myth with the added dimension of strong black roles.

In the former Ernest Whitman repeated his confidant of *The Prisoner of Shark Island*. In the latter Belle, a Southern woman, follows the plow in the hard times after the war until Yankee bungling and corruption result in the burning of the old manse. She then lights out for the hills, reborn as the charred ruin dissolves into a guerrilla's campfire. A montage of signs—"Carpetbaggers Get Out of Missouri"—and of whooping raiders, accompanied by a muted "Dixie," who drive out the dandy blacks in checked vests and plug hats. The whole tale is told by grand black Mammy Lou, the staunch symbol of home to whom Belle returns for sustenance. Like Faulkner's Dilsey, *she* prevails. Belle and her legend die.

This is not to say that the Civil War lore was washed clean of its racist barnacles. *The Santa Fe Trail* (1940) cast the war as a polarity of the careers of Jeb Stuart and George Armstrong Custer, with the apparently mad Abolitionist John Brown pulling America apart against its will, first in "bleeding Kansas," then in the erroneously lily-white arsenal Harpers Ferry. Then Paramount's Technicolor *Virginia* (1941) brought the sections together in a union symbolized by Leigh Whipper, "the old slave returning home to die," still believing his master's kindness and not federal policy has freed him. "Honestly, we'd never have believed it if we hadn't seen it with our own eyes," moaned the *Times*, "that the bloody shirt could be waved, especially in this day and time, as seriously and as bluntly as it is in 'Virginia.'" As late as 1943 Walter Van Tilburg Clark's clean-lined, strong indictment of lynching, *The Ox-Bow Incident*, was changed to allow its heavy to masquerade as a Southern officer rather than *be* an actual Confederate, probably as a hedge against Southern reaction.[21]

How to account for the modest humanity of a few Civil War pictures as opposed to the ancient Southern metaphors of others? If executives indeed ruled, then it may be a matter of the hand on the telephone. At Paramount, the source of much timid racial imagery, Y. Frank Freeman, was a resident Southerner and a crusty "Lester Maddox" of his day. In contrast, at Fox, Lamar Trotti and Nunnally Johnson were trusted urbane Southerners, both of whom saw blacks in other than racist terms and were no longer prisoners of traditional Southern racial attitudes. As writers or producers they turned out *The Ox-Bow Incident, Slave Ship, In Old Chicago, Prisoner of Shark Island, Young Mr. Lincoln, Belle Starr, Tales of Manhattan*, and other pieces that dealt with the race problem.[22]

Gone with the Wind, however, most reflected its times, caught up in the tension of changing racial attitudes. That it appeared at all was a small miracle because the Lost Cause had been thought to be box office poison—and for good reason, since the gap between Northern and

Southern taste seemed unbridgeable. In the South *So Red the Rose* had eleven gaudy premières and the blessing of a gaggle of governors and the United Daughters of the Confederacy, a success apparently not matched in Northern markets. The Southern press had loved its vision of "plantation life, the charm and pleasantness of the people of the South, the courage of the women, and their acceptance of the misfortunes thrust upon them by ruthless Yankees." But Yankees balked at its crooning darkies and mint juleps as "spurious" pap. *Variety* gauged it somewhere between "fine and distinctive" and "draggy and uncertain," which was a notch higher than it had placed the "routine materials" and "the old hoke" of the crop of profitless thirties Civil War movies such as *Only the Brave* (1930), *Operator 13* (1934), and *General Spanky*.[23]

Gone with the Wind would be different. David O. Selznick had wished to break from his father-in-law, Louis B. Mayer. With aid from Thalberg and rich Eastern backers such as John Hay Whitney, John Hertz of Yellow Cab, and a brace of bankers he formed Selznick-International. In the summer of 1936 Selznick, prodded by Whitney, bought Margaret Mitchell's long mock-Victorian novel, *Gone with the Wind*, which had just been sold to the Book-of-the-Month Club. Caught up in the national rage over the book and taken by Mitchell's reverence for the South, he carried it with him on a Hawaiian holiday, where he trimmed it into a workable treatment. As a gimmick to keep it alive while he worked off prior commitments, his publicity director, Russell Birdwell, mounted a search for Scarlet O'Hara that included Hollywood's great ladies and a flock of eager amateurs.

As he moved toward the start of shooting Selznick went for the best. British Vivian Leigh won Scarlet's role. He surrendered a piece of the picture to get Clark Gable from MGM. George Cukor, then Victor Fleming and Sam Wood came on to direct. First Sidney Howard, then Scott Fitzgerald and, in a horrendous marathon, Ben Hecht and Selznick himself, wrote the screenplay. Selznick fretted over every aspect of production. The many changes and retakes drove up costs. Fleming's health broke under the strain. But Selznick maintained momentum and resisted surrendering his vision, although he once admitted, "I have even thought about D. W. Griffith for the job."

At first the weight of Southern influence was burdensome. Even Thomas Dixon, down on his luck and politicking in Tarheel courthouses, tried to muscle in with an offer to "write a study" of the novel which Mitchell rejected with a ladylike fan letter. But there were visits and consultations in Atlanta, Cukor's tests of actresses there and in New Orleans, the hiring of Southern "experts," and rumors of Mitchell's choice of Mrs. Roosevelt's maid as "Mammy." In addition, Fitzgerald had been hired to cull turns of phrase from the book to be used as patching plaster, a chore which resulted in restoring much of Mitchell at the expense of Howard's work.[24]

How could a fully rounded, historically sound portrait of Negroes be constructed from a novel that seemed to demand that the old Southern racist stereotypes be applied? First, Selznick intuitively wished "that the Negroes come out decidedly on the right side of the ledger." His urge for balance allowed him to minimize both the Ku Klux Klan and a party of Yankee house-burners. Second, he counted Mammy among the principals, as a "superb indication" of Scarlett's life, and asked to test many actresses before settling on Hattie McDaniel. Third, he imagined the rhythm of the slaves' day more like the peasants of *Viva Villa!* than ante bellum tradition.[25]

Moreover, unlike many of the extras on *The Green Pastures*, the blacks were professionals and craftsmen. Butterfly McQueen played a shrill, whining servant reminiscent of her "high stepping little dusky creature with a piping voice" in *Brown Sugar* on Broadway. But she remembered the decent manners, the camaraderie on the set, and the freedom to make suggestions. Between takes she read George Jean Nathan's column in *Esquire*, and after she gave her cry of "de Yankees is comin'" she plumped down with an anthology of Alexander Woollcott. Always, she balked at treatment less than professional. Cukor expected no more than a quick reading, and when she covered her face and fought to capture a mood, he barked, "Whoja think you are, Greta Garbo?" When the crew aped her trills she smiled them aside and called them "my imitators." And in the end she won in a small way. *Time* noticed her "sly humor," especially when the Yankees come to Atlanta and she sings "Jes' a few mo' days ter tote de wee-ry load."[26]

Every black responded differently to white manners, coaching, and direction. Hattie McDaniel, because she was a known Hollywood figure, received the greatest attention in the press. She was proudly used as a symbol to tell blacks that the role had been "coveted" and would lead to finer work because of the "dignity and earnestness" that would raise the role to "more than a servant." "She is confidante, counselor, and manager of the O'Hara household," said one blurb in the *Amsterdam News*. On the set she dutifully learned to drawl in the Southern manner (from her white tutor) and soaked up enough "fundamental Southern philosophy" to give motives to Mammy. If Oscar Polk, an old Hollywood hand, tommed a bit on the set, perhaps it was payment for getting the role. "We-all knows how folks act down south, don't we, Miss Myrick," he drawled to a consultant with exaggerated politesse. And between takes he rattled off his old routines and acted as self-appointed "house hand." But the black extras would have none of it. They played insiders' games, strutted in "Central Avenue overcoats,"

In spite of its antebellum setting *Gone with the Wind* (© Selznick-International Pictures, Inc.) calculatedly enlarged and humanized traditional black
roles such as Hattie McDaniel's mammy, here playing opposite Clark Gable's
Rhett Butler. (The State Historical Society of Wisconsin)

and applauded the takes of the blacks. Perhaps they helped inspire Mc
Daniel's great, earthen performance.[27] In any case, life on the set was
light-years away from a Griffith set.

In the middle of summer 1939 the shooting ended. It took three
months to cut and score the film. Then it was screened for happy
MGM backers, and then sneak-previewed, at over four hours running
time, in Riverside. Just before Christmas the producers mounted a première in Atlanta complete with Hollywood celebrities, prestigious Atlantans, Mitchell, a parade, and a nighttime gala. Everyone bubbled
with pride. In a few more weeks Yankee box offices clicked off millions. After three months at New York's Capitol it still averaged $65,000,
and only log jams of MGM releases moved it. In Philadelphia it brought
$650,000 in twenty weeks. The Northern press praised it as a "great"
film, and Southerners thought it "the biggest news event since Sher-

man." But the most important element of its celebrity was that critics of all regions and colors responded to *Gone with the Wind*'s moderate approach, which took into account the South's difficulties but also recognized, albeit indirectly, the harsh black experience in the Civil War period.[28]

Selznick's company had given life to the overblown novel by taking its best, blaring ante bellum music over it, fussing over accuracy, and rendering it on a broad social canvas in Technicolor. A grand romance, it follows the happy fortunes of Scarlet O'Hara until her father's old plantation is spoiled by war and the old life is "gone with the wind." Thereafter, like many landed Southerners she and her kind resort to most déclassé pursuit—they go "into trade." Victims of scalawags and carpetbaggers, they survive with a patch of the old dignity and a hint of the moral that those who change are able to prevail. For blacks there are parallels, though eventually lost: it is the tough black women who counsel and direct their old masters and who keep a bit of dignity. The town dandy who glowers from "darktown" crannies and who refuses the work of building a new South can live with no greater certainty than the old white family that cannot bring itself to work for wages. But because the black world is scarcely seen, there are only finely crafted black characters, lacking the substance that black connections would have given them. But that would be asking too much of a movie in a time of transition. No one noticed, though, for the bravura performances and colorful bits like the burning of Atlanta carried it over every gap and romantic implausibility. And even white critics noticed the blacks, especially McQueen's sly humor and McDaniel's "most moving scene in the film, her plea with Melanie that the latter should persuade Rhett to permit burial of his baby daughter."[29]

The black and liberal press were seduced by the quality of *Gone with the Wind* and took little notice of its confused ideological view that made it conservative and somewhat avant garde at the same time. If one wished to attack, there were weak spots. Under stress Prissy's (McQueen's) lines are hysterical and out of character; black fieldhands seem to have finer character than those in the big house; black women dominate men; life in the quarter is hidden; blacks hold no power in the new order; they have no subplot. But even the leftist press divided on the film's social-artistic merits.

The most astonishing split opened on the far left over the old politico-aesthetic question of whether or not fine work could be done for specious ends. The National Negro Congress, the Brooklyn Civic and Labor Committee, and the Communist Party's *Daily Worker* attacked the Southern mystique, the racism, and the dated view of Reconstruction shown in the film. But when Howard Rushmore wrote a mixed review on artistic grounds, he was sent back by Ben Davis, the Negro party leader, to produce a jeremiad.[30]

For Negro critics it was worse because of the popular acclaim for McDaniel. They tacked and veered and settled dead in the water, unable to shape a common aesthetic. DuBois waved it aside. *The Birth of a Nation* had been "a cruel libel," but *Gone with the Wind* was only "conventional provincialism about which Negroes need not get excited." The *Amsterdam News* gave a mixed review and depended on irate readers for its barbs. Edward G. Perry in the *Negro Actor* agreed with the *Pittsburgh Courier* that a period piece deserved higher tolerances, and indeed insisted he "was not offended or annoyed," but the *Courier* concluded "much of it was distasteful to the Negro race."[31]

Then they were betrayed by the Academy of Motion Picture Arts and Sciences, who gave McDaniel an Oscar, the first ever given to a black performer. A few black pickets appeared, but the euphoria attendant upon the award smothered them. McDaniel took her statuette from Fay Bainter, thanked God, and predicted a decent age that would let black kids "aim high and work hard." She pulled it off in the Hollywood style, fashionably late, wrapped in ermine, gardenias in her hair, seated at Selznick's table. Afterward Leigh rushed up and kissed her, and Gable pumped her hand.[32]

"Ye gads, what's happening to Hollywood?" asked Bill Chase of the *Amsterdam News*, of the new "temper of the times." McDaniel was for him the perfect symbol for a "times" that could accept the movie as "a true stage in the development of the South" without projecting its Negro roles onto the present. She was publicly grateful, lived in a big house on Jefferson Avenue, trained her voice, went on tour, won featured billings, gave patient interviews, and bought up her contract so she could be free to search for elusive jobs. Like every character actor she retailed a single trait, which in her case was matriarchal blackness. But Jimmy Fidler, a teletype-paced radio gossip-monger, detected the ache under the clutches of telegrams and flowers for Hattie McDaniel. "And where does this Negro artist go from here?" he asked.

> Why, back to playing incidental comedy maids, of course. An actress comparable with the immortal Marie Dressler has flashed across the screen—and now must disappear because Hollywood can't give her adequate parts. No one's to blame, least of all the producers who would ask nothing better than to capitalize on her ability. . . . But I don't think it will be easy for me to laugh at Hattie's comedy in the future, for I'll never be able to overlook the tragic fact that a very great artist is being wasted.[33]

The movie and the Oscar represented a watershed, after which blacks were owed some due in roles and in public attention to their feelings. If

Would-be black critics of *Gone with the Wind* were disarmed both by McDaniel's Oscar and the grace with which she received it. (The State Historical Society of Wisconsin)

On the eve of the period of the liberalism aroused by the war aims of World War II films only fitfully dealt with social change. Leigh Whipper's oldtime slave in the *Vanishing Virginian* (© Loew's Inc.) still wishes to be returned to the old plantation for burial. (Author's collection)

McDaniel was not a causal factor she represented a shift in racial arrangements. Fresh racial wit and character surfaced and meant more, perhaps, than writers intended. In the sentimentalized *Maryland* (1940) black stablehands live fully in both black and white circles. Old Shad must shoot a tragically lamed horse for master's sake. But at home he and his wife quarrel over Negro burial society premiums gambled away. Muse as a firm preacher topped a cast of a good dozen able black actors. In Preston Sturges's satiric *Sullivan's Travels* (1941) Sam McDaniel does his bit as a hapless cook, but Sullivan, a modern Candide, is thrown into a black church meeting led by Jesse Lee Brooks as they sing "Let My People Go" with the supreme irony of a cut to a black and white chain gang. *Blossoms in the Dust* recounted the founding of a Texas orphanage. The script asked Clinton Rosamond to provide "an ivory grin," but he was also allowed to be rightly fearful of "de river bottom whar de po' white trash live." "Rochester" and Teresa Harris interrupt a

Jack Benny movie with a satiric duet "masquerade party at the Harlem Social and Come-What-May-Club." Hope and Crosby are pursued by resolute black soldiers in a "Road" picture. Willie Best and Bob Hope toyed with the old types in *The Ghost Breakers* (1940): young Best introduces himself blandly as "the *old* family retainer"; as he fumbles with oars, Hope says, "I thought you rowed for Harlem Tech"; when they meet Noble Johnson as a zombie, Hope dismisses him as "only the colored caretaker"; and they reverse the old humor when they see an apparition and Hope panics while Best says, "I know better." In *Birth of the Blues* (1941) Eddie Anderson teaches whites that blues "tain't the minuet." Jimmie Lunceford does a brief piece in *Blues in the Night* (1941) after years off camera. McDaniel and McQueen repeated their *Gone with the Wind* roles in *Affectionately Yours* (1941), and McDaniel read her sharpest lines in *The Male Animal* (1942).[34]

The close confidantes grew closer. Hattie McDaniel's Violet in *The Great Lie* (1941) was plainly egalitarian and made the plot work. It is she who steers the rekindled love affair of Bette Davis and George

Jackie Cooper's callow white musician initiated into jazz circles by blacks in *Syncopation* (© RKO-Radio Pictures, Inc.) was a variation on the old motif of the natural man. (Author's collection)

The kids in *Banjo* (© RKO-Radio Pictures, Inc.) differed little from the old *Our Gang* films, and still Southern censors protested. (Author's collection)

Brent. "Don't come callin' that man things; he ain't comin' here no more," she warns of their separation. When the lover whistles through the door she snaps, "No use usin' *dat* whistle, Mr. Pete; dat sound belongs to a day that is *gone!*" She gives "advice," appeals to "conscience," and finally threatens "to use force" to keep them apart—all in shared two-shots. In Rene Clair's *The Flame of New Orleans* (1941) Teresa Harris plays the same role to Marlene Dietrich's bogus countess, and, like her mistress, she is traveled, sexy, too wise for her own good.[35]

The limits of liberal change could best be seen in self-consciously liberal vehicles such as Lillian Hellman's Broadway play *The Little Foxes* (1941); the best statement of American isolationism turned anti-fascist, *Casablanca* (1942); and *In This Our Life* (1942), John Huston's forthright attempt to mesh black and white Southern life into common tragedy. The Broadway origins of *The Little Foxes* encouraged Warner's to give it good workers: Hellman herself, Arthur Kober and Dorothy Parker for added dialogue, and William Wyler to direct. It opened by peering through the Spanish moss into the bedrock of Southern life, Negroes driving a wagon, wrestling laundry, polishing brass, serving a busy cotton gin, and in the big house a butler "yassuming" the whites and remonstrating with cook for serving cold grits. It is 1900 or so, and the crumbling Southern family is torn between the old graces and the need to "go into trade." The patriarch takes leave of his tippling Southern lady, strides past an old gray cannon, and tries to sell his business to a Chicagoan who wants cheap Southern labor. An impotent newspaper editor is the liberal voice who alone appreciates the changeless plight of the blacks and knows the North where the talk is of "people's rights." His mother's voice of the old South is worse than

In self-consciously liberal movies such as *The Little Foxes* (© Samuel Goldwyn) servants remained on the periphery of the action. (The State Historical Society of Wisconsin)

powerless; it is irrelevant. Through a useful dramatic trick her muted voice is lost in the clatter. The blacks are a memory-bank, knowing the old days and names, knowing the father's money came from cheating blacks, knowing the times when "there were people who ate the earth." But because the black proletariat could not act in its own behalf, except to snub a weak son, a leftist dramatist threw them away as a dramatic force by using them as mere atmosphere and chorus.[36]

Ellen Glasgow's *In This Our Life* won a Pulitzer Prize after Warner Brothers bought it, so the studio may have been tempted to style it into an "important" movie. But by assigning it to young John Huston the studio assured its treatment on a human scale and gave relatively greater weight to the opinions of its prestigious black actress and uncompromising black actor, but still contained racial vestiges in the script such as the "old darky [who] sits gorilla-fashion, his hands thrust through the bars, mumbling." The story of a selfish bitch whose compulsive scheming leads to her death, its Southern ambience is given an urbane twist by its black juvenile law student whom she blames for a hit-and-run accident.[37]

Ernest Anderson, by way of Northwestern University and radio, fresh from the studio service corps, played the lad as a studious presumptive lawyer. Hattie McDaniel played a strong mother and laundress whose unprepossessing house included a plausible telephone, a detail that rang true to black audiences. Still, Irving Rapper, the dialogue director, presumed business as usual during rehearsal, and attempted to impose a lazy drawl on Anderson. Script revisions confirmed Rapper's view until Anderson drove to Warner Brothers and complained to Huston, who pronounced the script a "mistake." Still, Rapper complained of Anderson's "British accent" until a showdown runthrough that Huston gauged as "perfect." In the final take Huston, on Anderson's counsel, departed from the script. The camera was to dolly in on Anderson's tears of rage at his false arrest and then pull back to smug Bette Davis impatiently turning from the cell. Instead, the camera pulls in tightly on Anderson, catching his rage *and* contempt. To Anderson it seemed evidence that the studio posture could be met by a black presence. Ignorance, not racism, shaped their work. To Jack Warner and Bette Davis the movie meant no more than the latest of their running spats, while Anderson remembered it as the movie that black soldiers on a segregated post stopped with their shouts and applause in order to rerun the jail scene.[38]

Of all the films following the *Gone with the Wind* thaw in racial depictions *Casablanca* (1942) reached the widest audience and probably had the strongest impact within the limits of liberal faith. Not only was the Warner Brothers film popular, it carried off two Academy Awards,

Appreciative black troops once demanded a rerun of Ernest Anderson's scene with George Brent and Bette Davis in *In This Our Life* (© Warner Brothers Pictures, Inc.). (BFI)

expressed American ambivalence caught between war and peace, and in succeeding years became a celebrated cult film for several generations of university students. Perhaps because the executives, Hal Wallis, Jerry Wald, and the Warners, wanted to rush through a stalled "property," the writers and the director, Michael Curtiz, were left alone to struggle between two poles of ambition for the picture—either harmless romance or a drama of "cynicism and political idealism." The result was a liberal, arcane, witty, well-made play in which a strong black role not only survived but gave dramatic underscoring to important themes and incidents.

Dooley Wilson played Sam, the piano player at *La Belle Aurore* in Paris, who under the guns of the Germans flees to Casablanca with Rick, an anti-fascist who has fought in Ethiopia and Spain in the cause of liberalism. Together they open "Rick's Cafe Americain" in Casablanca. Sam is in on everything. Stolen letters-of-transit with which to smuggle out anti-fascists are hidden in his piano. It is clear that he is to

Casablanca (© Warner Brothers Pictures, Inc.), with Dooley Wilson and Humphrey Bogart, became the classic liberal statement against isolationism and in favor of racial tolerance. (Author's collection)

be taken for an equal. Rick denies admission to a German officer with a wink at Sam, establishing, according to a draft of the script, "the fact that as far as Rick is concerned, the negro is a privileged person." Sam refuses an offer to play in a rival saloon, not with the grin of a loyal toady, but because of friendship, and in one script version, because he owns ten percent. When the Vichy cops raid the place, Sam's piano and voice lead a group-sing of "Old Noah, What Did He Do?" as a pan shot picks up "all types of people" tapping out the beat.

Sam's personal relationships are less sophisticated: the versions of the script seem torn between "Boss" and "Mr. Richard" as forms of address, with the former winning narrowly. And he will sing "Shine" if that is what it takes to win over an audience. Even so, when Rick's former lover arrives with her husband, an underground leader, with the Nazis in pursuit, it is Sam's point-of-view the camera takes. Ilse, the woman, and Sam exchange glances and enter a cryptic and painful reverie. "Play some of the old songs," she asks; and Sam does the theme song, "As Time Goes By," which becomes the central motif of the film's call for a break from isolationism. Sam, the love affair of Rick and Ilse, and the coming of war are intertwined. Thus Sam shares their pain. He had been the man who had gotten Rick aboard the last train from Paris before the Germans entered the city and separated them. In one version, Ilse and Sam do more than reminisce. She gives him well-meaning praise as a natural musician, but he will have none of it and reminds her of twelve years at Juilliard. "Well," she smiles, "all the best theories are going under these days."[39] If Sam seems to have no black connections, at least liberal Warner Brothers carried the theme as far as it could go given the milieu and the times. Liberal critics recognized what was there and praised Wilson as "a Negro 'find' " and "the best of the supporting players."[40]

Indeed, critics of all persuasions took notice of such racial bits as important signs and blasted the old stereotypes. Moderate critics on the *Times* and *Newsweek* found pictures like *Virginia* a "bad scene" that was "absurd" in its strident sectional chauvinism. One critic blasted the colonialist *Sundown* as the "Boy Scouts in Africa" because of "this stuff about . . . Africa being saved for the British." They found the old black roles "dog-eared," the *Belle Starrs* "neurotic unreconstructed rebels," and the blacks of *The Little Foxes* by way of contrast displaying rare "humor and dignity." As critics became more alert to such social data, even the annual fan magazine *Hollywood Who's Who* in 1941 asked black Jimmie Lunceford for a frank account of the changing plight of the Hollywood Negro. Black critics went so far as to take notice of the absence of Negroes in situations where they plausibly belonged. "You know they're there by their absence," said one of them about Ford's film of John Steinbeck's social novel *The Grapes of Wrath*.[41]

Nevertheless, if movies as popular art were to share in American racial change they would have to respond to more systematic pressure from the left and also to the tutelage of organized Negroes. By 1940 both forces began to have their effect on Hollywood. The forces of the left grew into the "popular front" against fascism. A few members were led by John Garfield, who addressed the National Negro Congress in an effort to reach out and mold an alliance. In writers' conferences they promised each other reformist movies and vowed to fight repressive forces abroad in the land. Out in the "nabes" the exhibitors felt that even their ticketbuyers shared the urge for liberal social themes to replace Hollywood's "all-too-familiar escapist fare."[42]

The Hollywood Negroes joined in the mood whenever they could. In December of 1939 a number of black civic leaders and performers led by Spencer Williams and Earl J. Morris met over luncheon on the set of *Horror House* to discuss demands for a national Negro censor. Clarence Muse, Laura Bowman, and the others debated "some sort of check" on the "derogatory types and stigmas" that no other race tolerated. But they knew they spoke from weakness, from the ranks of the Bs, from still prevalent servile roles, from an age when Amos 'n' Andy's ratings were high and when even a biography of Bert Williams timidly awaited "public reaction" to a trial balloon. Thus some conservative blacks saw the attacks from the left as threats to their livelihood. Moreover they counted the NAACP as a potential enemy because of Walter White's ability to crack the producers' offices while the black actors remained unconsulted and excluded. And indeed, one black Los Angeles adviser, quoting a third source, warned White off meeting with them because "most of them are ignorant; [and] can only fit in with the parts they have been playing anyway." Clearly if the NAACP were to become a third force proving solid direction to the movement in Hollywood, obviously they would need to move beyond their traditional arena of the courtroom and the mimeographed assaults on *The Birth of a Nation*.[43]

In the early months of the forties they could not yet move off dead center, and the Hollywood Negro community passed them. Too young to remember the *Birth of a Race* disaster, White discussed with Selznick, Wanger, and others "making a film about the Negro in which he would be pictured neither as a buffoon nor as a humble servant," but as a folksinger in the style of *Song of Freedom*. "With all the talk about democracy which is in the air these days," he tried to drum up interest among Southern white newspaper editors. But it was so far-fetched that Jonathan Daniels of the Raleigh *News and Observer* offered a jesting two-page script "if Mr. Selznick wants to buy." By summer's end White settled for inserting an NAACP bit in an Atlanta Life Insurance Company short inspired by an executive's witnessing a lily white patriotic film at the New York World's Fair.[44]

The most exciting sign of the changing times opened on the stage of the Mayan Theatre in Los Angeles in the summer of 1941. *Jump for Joy*, a liberal romp that ran for three months, benefitted from white angels such as John Garfield and Joe Pasternak; bright young performers like Dorothy Dandridge, Ivie Anderson, and Herb Jeffries; words and music by a team featuring Duke Ellington, Billy Strayhorn, Langston Hughes, and Mickey Rooney and casting by black Ben Carter; all held together by a young writer named Henry Blankfort. Every night Hollywood celebrities, "middle-class ofays," "dicty Negroes," and just plain folk turned out to see a satire in which Uncle Tom's deathbed is surrounded by his children singing "He lived to a ripe old age. Let him go, God Bless him!" as a brace of producers struggle to keep him alive by pumping adrenalin into his arms. The first act finale was a comic song in which Uncle Tom's Cabin becomes a drive-in "chicken shack" at Hollywood and Vine. In case anyone might miss the point, the program helped the "square" to become temporarily "groovy" by providing a handy glossary of black urbane idiom.

Sadly for Afro-American performers, no one realized how close they had come to capturing the social thrust of the next few years in one revue, even though comedians cried for joy as they came off stage, applause ringing in their ears, and proud of having worked without blackface for the first time in their careers. Avanelle Lewis Harris, a chorus girl in the show, remembered the sense of suspended animation:

> The importance of its message caused a wave of enthusiasm throughout the cast, which was well aware of its controversial impact. Everything, every setting, every note of music, every lyric, meant something. All the sketches had a message for the world. The tragedy was that the world was not ready for *Jump for Joy*.[45]

Meanwhile the NAACP seemed ineffectual and irrelevant to the real needs of blacks in Hollywood. White's infrequent cranky letters assaulted symptoms rather than causes and may have hurt black actors more than they affected white studios. On the one hand he complained that "My wife, son and I were inexpressibly shocked" at a pro-South "trailer" for *Santa Fe Trail*, but on the other he refused to endorse race movies because of their mediocrity. To the Hollywood Negroes he seemed a "phoney" merely "trying to be white" from the safety of New York offices. By spring a distributor claimed the New York office misrepresented the more flexible branches. "I do not take the National too seriously in its criticisms," she wrote.[46]

At last, early in 1942 the NAACP was finally forced into giving some direction. In February White and Wendell Willkie attended the annual convention of the NAACP in Los Angeles, a conference attended by thousands of Negroes in the area. There White met with David O. Selznick and other Hollywood executives. Knowing his mission was to shape the NAACP into a force to press them for black roles, the Hollywood leaders balked, missed appointments, and shunted White onto secretaries. He soon saw the need for glamorous connections, political support, and perhaps a big public meeting during which resolutions could be passed. "To do the job right," he saw, would require a month of politicking:

> I wired [Wendell] Willkie the facts and urged him to reinforce his request to Zanuck for the conference when Willkie gets here Wednesday. That, and a swell letter from Mrs. Roosevelt, may do the trick. Jimmy

Cagney is having a luncheon for me at the studio tomorrow, Melvyn Douglas, Jean Muir and others are being most helpful. But its the producers we've got to crack.[47]

After a spring and summer of luncheons and conferences White, Willkie, and the NAACP hoped to wed the contractual parties to some sort of agreement that would reflect the new mood.

Finally the studio heads met with White and Willkie, who had been retained as counsel, and promised over lunch to liberalize their depiction of Negroes on the screen in keeping with the changing times. Their action resulted in a mere soupçon of good movies, but they set forth new conditions to which Hollywood was asked to conform. *Variety*'s bannerline, "BETTER BREAKS FOR NEGROES IN H'WOOD," was echoed in the pages of the *Negro Actors' Guild of America Newsletter*. March 1942 became a date by which to measure the future against the past.[48]

Already much had transpired. Rumors flew among black actors. Dooley Wilson's option was picked up; Rex Ingram rushed to the coast; Robeson was to do MGM's all-Negro *Cabin in the Sky;* Katharine Dunham would choreograph movies; flagging careers were to perk up; *Porgy* would come to the screen; at last Eddie Anderson's *Bert Williams* would be shot. Southern exhibitors discussed ways of entertaining Negro troops. Some Southern critics treated black actors on their merit. The old roles had slipped into the B's. *Tarzan* shut down at MGM and went independent. More than ever the black press had begun to express systematic displeasure at stereotyped black roles and to mourn the dead end to which McDaniel's Oscar sometimes seemed to point.[49]

At first the bargain appeared to have no impact, but gradually it gave thrust and direction to the liberal drift and gave pause to purveyors of the old Southern attitudes. For the moment the old servile roles continued without threat to the Hollywood Negroes. The segregated musical bits increased to include the Chocolateers, the Golden Gate Quartette, and the calypso singer Sir Lancelot.[50] Nevertheless the agreement became a standard against which studios, Negroes, and even the white press gauged Hollywood's sincerity, if not its art. In the absence of a formal black aesthetic it was something.

Liberal magazine critics regularly used the new Negro roles as tests of presumptive white cupidity. The black press delighted in Southern mourning of the trend such as the Richmond *News-Leader*'s complaint against Ethel Waters' singing in MGM's *Cairo:* "It seemed the camera hunted her out to the exclusion of the other actors." Studios matched their old concern for Southern sensibilities with attention to Negro wishes, especially on such obvious targets as Thaddeus Stevens, a Reconstruction hero to Negroes, whom MGM intended as the villain of William Dieterle's *Tennessee Johnson*. The Negro columnists who were friendly to Hollywood explained away or accounted for failures of the promissory note that the bargain had become, while the more waspish among them set timetables, or, like Earl Dancer, sent politically unlikely scripts such as a Crispus Attucks (the black Revolutionary War hero) story around the movie lots. Others became cheerleaders for *Stormy Weather* and other all-Negro projects. "Now It's Up To Us To Improve on Hollywood-Made-Progress," insisted one. The *Daily Worker* was hard put to stay in the van, and by the end of the war did no more than nag Southern censorship and the NAACP for its past silence, while gingerly avoiding charging the Hollywood guilds with racist exclusion.[51]

The movie critics themselves were another matter. Lacking a coherent consensus of black aesthetic sense, most magazine critics fell into the American trap of mistaking liberal politics for good moviemaking. So the NAACP agreement served as a blue litmus paper with which writers tested film and pronounced this or that movie "in no sense represents the fulfillment of Hollywood's pledge to regard the Negro as an integral part of American life." Thus when politics replaced art in the critical canon, then *Casablanca* was liberal and good while *Dixie* was lacking in "social consciousness" and therefore merely tolerable. Indeed, critics sometimes disagreed on social grounds. Philip T. Hartung in *Commonweal* thought *Stormy Weather* flawed, blamed the whites, forgave the blacks, and snapped "Rain! No Game!" while a black paper headline blared approvingly that there were "NO BANDANNAS IN 'STORMY WEATHER.'" Or they found, as did the *Times* of *In This Our Life*, that "the one exceptional component of the film" was its "brief allusion to racial discrimination" and its "uncommon portrayal of an educated Negro." On the left, Manny Farber despaired at the zoot suits, good black singers forced to clown, and the survivals of old Negro roles that had masked the absence of change. "Obscene," he grumbled. "There is no other word for [the] rush the movies are now giving Negroes." Unfortunately, for black actors the high standards of leftist critics were at war with the professional hopes of the performers. Reviewing identical movies *PM* blasted the studios for segregating blacks "almost like zoo animals," while the grateful *Negro Actors' Guild of America Newsletter* praised the pictures as "an example of the much spoken 'new order' of roles for our people" and the performers as examples of the "'New Type' Sepia Movie Star." By 1943 the *Amsterdam News* could make hair-splitting distinctions based on the new standards, finding *The Ox-Bow Incident* a "rare opportunity" while complaining "it is too bad [Leigh] Whipper played in servile fashion."[52]

In the studios, even though the old Negro images continued to ooze forth, producers developed antenna with which to sense offending ma-

terial in films. Someone at Twentieth in the mid-career of *My Gal Sal*
caught Paul Dresser's old song, "I'se Your Nigger If You Wants Me,
Liza Jane," and saved the movie from bearing it as a cross. Frank Borzage's *Stage Door Canteen* made a gesture toward including black soldiers in its scenes. Sol Lesser's *Tarzan* used "the natives" in the fight
against Nazism. In his continuity sketches" for *The Very Thought
of You* Delmer Daves firmly defined a minor black role in detail: "A
Negro girl, fellow worker at the parachute plant. Married, husband is
a soldier, good-natured, open-hearted." On Alfred Hitchcock's *Life-
boat* the producer, Darryl Zanuck, fretted over making the Negro role
an "assistant steward" who sings, recites psalms, "boogies up" a song,
and admits to being a pickpocket. At Twentieth Century-Fox they reshot perhaps a third of *Stormy Weather* to avoid the appearance of re-
neging on the NAACP deal.[53]

MGM's *Shoe Shine Boy* (1943) was a good example of the feckless
combination of artlessness and sermons. The short "once upon a time"
tale opens on a kid, a trumpet fan, who buys a pawnshop bugle. Two
stereotyped impresarios come to his shoeshine stand, audition him, and
he in turn stops their show with his riffs. But his real ambition is "to
blow for Uncle Sam." "Blow one in Hitler's eye just for me," says one
of the producers, tossing him a tip. "Sho' will," he says as he dissolves
to a tilted-up one-shot in uniform, then to white assault troops and a
voice-over: "He loved his horn and his country."[54]

Outside the stucco fences of the movie lots a slow rise of organized
committee activity further caught the attention of filmmakers. Even
before the war, such groups as the Greater New York Committee for
Better Negro films and the Negro Cultural Committee surfaced, issued
press releases, and scheduled documentaries. By the middle of the war
the NAACP cooperated with some of them. The *Crisis*, for example,
ran Dalton Trumbo's speech to the Hollywood Writers Conference as
"Blackface, Hollywood Style." The progressive Hollywood Democratic
Committee ritually required that "prominent Negroes be invited to join
the Board" by 1944 so as to further the work of boosting racial liberalism, recruiting for the NAACP, and forcing apologies from exclusionist
Hollywood hotels. By the end of the War they had become the Hollywood Independent Citizens Committee on the Arts, Sciences, and Pro-
fessions, which supported fair employment practices and gave "Unity
Awards" to social movies. Horne, Canada Lee, Ingram, and Sir Lancelot sat on the board. White studio bosses sat with blacks on Brotherhood Week committees. When the Hollywood Canteen opened, the
Hollywood Victory Committee which represented many guilds announced that war aims required open admittance. At Harlem's Hotel
Theresa, Clarence Muse and forty Negroes under the auspices of the

National Negro Congress met in an "emergency conference" on "Negro Culture in Wartime" in order to hammer out a means of monitoring mass media and to promulgate a black alternative to the motion picture code. Such bodies at the National Negro Publishers' Association began to blast individual movies such as Walt Disney's *Song of the South* (1946). By 1945 the studios also faced Fredi Washington and Leon Hardwick of the Interracial Film and Radio Guild. And Jane White, Walter White's daughter and a budding actress, seemed to be as much Negro observer of the enforcement of her father's treaty as actress on film sets.[55]

One incongruous group contributed to the destruction of the old monopoly of Southern racial attitudes on the screen. Early in the war the Roosevelt government made tentative steps toward propagandizing its war aims, including a black version of its blood-donor drives, *The Negro College in Wartime*, and the Department of Agriculture's *Henry Brown, Farmer*. The latter featured a narration by Canada Lee linking the farmer's daily round with the war effort by the parallel threads of roughhanded farmwork and the training of a son in Tuskegee's 99th Pursuit Squadron. It seemed so powerful that Lawrence Reddick, curator of Harlem's Schomburg Collection, screened it to cool down the street crowds after the Harlem race riots of 1943.[56]

Gradually the Office of War Information assumed a role desired by organized Negroes: arbiter and censor of racial themes. By the end of 1942 they had issued a guidebook to the industry on matters of racial content and run an inspirational column in *Variety*. The enemy is racist, it claimed. "We must emphasize that this country is a melting pot,"

a nation of many races and creeds, who have demonstrated that they can live together and progress. We must establish a genuine understanding of alien and minority groups and recognize their great contribution to the building of our nation.

An OWI man nearly always sat through rough cuts and recommended deletions and modulations. Sometimes, as in the case of Warner Brothers' *Mission to Moscow*, the OWI literally commissioned movies. Indeed, *The New York Times* gave OWI the bulk of credit for the wartime cycle of Negro films.[57]

Until American cinema art could grow to fit the Negro, the single most significant marriage of art and politics was *The Negro Soldier*, a product of political pressures put upon the Army by John Houseman, formerly of Federal Theatre; William Hastie of FDR's "black cabinet"; and Carlton Moss, a young black writer and Houseman's successor in the Federal Theatre. Moss took an Army-approved script to

American war aims as expressed in the Atlantic Charter seemed oddly
served by the well-meant, segregated musical, *Cabin in the Sky* (© Loew's,
Inc.) with Lena Horne, Ethel Waters, Oscar Polk, and Rex Ingram. (Author's collection)

California for ten days' shooting at Paramount and Fox's old place on
Western Avenue. Then Hastie's successor Truman Gibson, a Negro
adviser to the War Department on matters of race, showed his dossier
of discriminatory acts against black troops in the South to Frank Capra,
the harried executive producer of the Army's *Why We Fight* series of
training films. Under the pressure from Washington Capra gave free
rein to the unit and its young black filmwriter. In disused studios in
Hollywood Stuart Heisler, a steady Hollywood hand, directed; Moss
wrote; they made an even-handed forty-five-minute tribute to Negro hope and aspiration—an intricate mixture of stock footage, thin
historical narrative, and fictive binder couched in the form of a Negro
preacher's sermon with Moss himself in the pulpit.[58]
  They shaped their project in isolation, putting Capra in the role of
salesman to both the Army and a preview audience of black journalists
who were asked to plug it if they wanted civilians to see it. They
praised it as a "brave, important and helpful event in the history of

U. S. race relations." Neither maudlin nor overstated, it was an unqualified hit. It ran in hundreds of houses—three hundred in New York alone—and one Negro magazine thought it so vital that it took Elder L. H. Michaux and Jack Goldberg to task for attempting to enjoin its distribution as unfair competition to their own compilation film, *We've Come a Long, Long Way*. "ARMY SHOWS HOLLYWOOD THE WAY," said the bannerline.[59]

The success of *The Negro Soldier* was reflected in a rash of equally appealing Hollywood integrationist movies and a pair of all-black films. The NAACP agreement, the government's war films, and an exciting revival of *Porgy and Bess* stimulated Vincente Minnelli's *Cabin in the Sky* (1943), and Twentieth's near miss based on Jim Europe's army experiences, *Stormy Weather* (1943). Hollywood rivals of *The Negro Soldier* included Twentieth's *Crash Dive* (1943), with Benny Carter in a role inspired by black Dorie Miller's heroism at Pearl Harbor; Columbia's *Sahara* (1943), with Rex Ingram's African soldier in the van of anti-Nazi soldiers; and MGM's *Bataan* (1943), with its uncontrived black soldier (Kenneth Spencer) who fought in the last thin lines.

But contributions were an easy step, and the white press found them as easy to praise. Each black seemed "one of the outstanding merits" of the pictures. The black press joined in the cheering of *Sahara* and the

Stormy Weather (© 20th Century-Fox Film Corp.) with Lena Horne, Bill Robinson, Dooley Wilson, and Ernest Whitman (as bandmaster Jim Europe) was another such all-black musical. (Author's collection)

Kenneth Spencer appeared as the token Negro in *Bataan* (© Loew's, Inc.).
(Author's collection)

others with occasional reservations, such as Abe Hill's feeling that *Life-boat* was only so-so because it failed to offer a "vital and realistic interpretation of the Negroes' part of Americana." Even Langston Hughes, whose every experience in the cinema from Hollywood to Moscow had been a bitter pill, blunted an attack on the old metaphorical roles by casting it in the form of a query: "Is Hollywood Fair to Negroes?" The organized black actors saw a future in which "We may look forward to great opportunities from other big companies" and in which even in the old roles they were "allowed to speak normally, like other extras." Old Lester Walton, who had observed blacks on the screen from the beginning, wrote:

> There is no excuse for any of us to say we have to do scripts as they are written. The writers and producers invite corrections and criticisms. They are tired as we are of these caricature dialogues. There are more instances where actors are asked to make these revisions than there is room to write them. Of course there are still times when the opportunity does not present itself but at least we have made a big step.[60]

It is here that the first part of the story ends. Although Walter White and the NAACP were not directly responsible for a single beautiful movie, their contractual codification of the social changes of the Great Depression and the second Great War finally destroyed the monopoly of Southern racial attitudes on the screen and made cinematic racism untenable. The next twenty-five years or so allowed blacks the opportunity to reshape and define a new black image still in process.

For the moment the turnbuckle tension amongst blacks was frightful. The politico-aesthetic struggle may best be seen in the responses to two good movies to which blacks gave talent: *Tales of Manhattan* and *The Song of the South*. In the former case an embittered Paul Robeson reached the end of his patience with Hollywood, not only because of its racism but because of the terrible split caused in black ranks. The latter film also caused recriminations and spoiled an innocently touching portrayal by old James Baskette, who was near death.

Julien Duvivier's *Tales of Manhattan* was good enough to be credited with reviving the anthology format. It was a string of gemlike stories held together by the presence of a money-stuffed coat and its

Canada Lee had a prominent part in *Lifeboat* (© 20th Century-Fox Film Corp.). (Author's collection)

impact on the lives of its possessors. In the end it falls from the grasp of an effete group of airplane passengers and into the rough hands of a village of Southern Negro farmers. Their enclave is sketched in stylized, almost hillbilly, imagery—as though Duvivier had reached the limits of French capacity for comprehending Southern American racial arrangements. The dramatic conflict was symbolized by Robeson's open-handed communal vision of a black sharecropper as opposed to Eddie Anderson's raspy-comic venal preacher who has a sharp eye for the main chance. In the end the seriocomic naïve piety of the croppers wins out over the grubbing of the burlesque preacher. If the sequence was broadly stylized, so too were the white parts of the picture.

Unfortunately, the liberal progress of Hollywood, combined with Duvivier's romantic Gallic image of Afro-America, stirred angry blacks, who turned on the picture as a betrayal. A few Hollywood Negroes stood by Robeson in the face of pickets under marquees. They met at Anderson's, where they rejected the charge of "Uncle-Tomming" and blasted the Negro press for ignoring racist speeches and Jim Crow conditions while aiming at a big target whose demise would deprive Negroes of a livelihood in white studios. The *Amsterdam News* did its best to mollify black critics under a headline proclaiming "NO UNCLE TOM DEPICTED IN 'TALES OF MANHATTAN.'" And *Time* granted Robeson credit for attempting to change the picture while on the set. But Robeson, despondent and bitter, told an interviewer that his film career was at an end, and thereafter he rejected a cinema Othello. Forced to choose between long-standing loyalty to cinema and his faith in the politics of the left, he chose the latter and blasted the picture he had liked enough to appear in and fight to change. "It was the same old thing," he complained, "the Negro solving his problem by singing his way to glory. This is very offensive to my people. It makes the Negro child-like and innocent and is in the old plantation tradition.[61]

Walt Disney's *Song of the South* presented still another problem of black aesthetics. How could blacks appreciate Baskette's Uncle Remus and his subsequent posthumous special Academy Award while protesting the outdated stylizing of Joel Chandler Harris's old Southern source of the movie? Months before production began, Tiny Bradshaw asked advice from columnist Leon Hardwick about Disney's offer of the Remus role, but then decided it would make him a traitor to the race. Disney countered, arguing that Remus would "help mould" white minds and that Negroes "will laud this film," but from New York to Hollywood pickets turned out and black politicians called for its suppression. Within its limits the movie gave Baskette a chance to do a bravura performance as the wizened and wise old black man who lives alone. True, his closest relationship is predictably with children, in keeping with

Harris's derivative tales. But he shares the center, and in his staunch rural balkiness he prevails over white wishes and converts them to understanding his closeness to the children who need him. Baskette's strength overcame almost every disability of dated sources and white blindness. But few blacks took Wendell Green's long view that the picture was "the greatest thing Disney has ever done" and deserved attention:

> The theme, flavor and fantasy of the Uncle Remus tales are caught with their full scope of human understanding. . . . The dialect used was rich and varied and of itself not offensive as it is fitted in with the mood and locale of the picture. . . . Hattie McDaniel played her usual greasy handkerchief head mammy role. From the standpoint of characters and voices the picture was superb.
> It was so authentic that one realized the extremely squalid and servial [sic] conditions that Negroes were forced to live under, and still do, after Reconstruction. The scene where two small boys not yet in their teens flaunt [sic] Uncle Remus as a man, their elder, and a human being is more searching than it appeared on the surface.
> The major objection to the picture from a race standpoint is that it is a throwback to an era that we strive every day to escape.

The white South would love it, he guessed, as relief from "those uppity darkies" who had gone to war, become educated, forgot their sense of place, demanded a vote, pressed FEPC for skilled jobs, and bucked lynching.[62] Old Baskette died with the issues still in the air, blacks and white liberals picketing under his name while Hollywood voted to give him an award.

If witnesses came to see the change in Hollywood by comparing before-and-after the increasingly famous "conference on the status of the Negro in a fighting democracy," there were other blacks who turned on each other to lay blame for past hurts. Many organized Negroes quarreled over McDaniel's and Baskette's awards for their renderings of ante bellum Southern stereotypes. New black critics, such as Abe Hill, who replaced the Daughertys, Waltons, Levettes, and LaMars, sometimes allowed their wish for "the greatest organized force ever set up to combat Hollywood tradition" to be expressed as a harsh call to cease "carrying a torch" for "a dozen or so full time actors in the movie industry."[63]

Typically, Walter White stood in the middle trying to make the center hold. He knew as much as anyone of the story of blacks in cinema from the days of Edison, the hard age of Griffith, the silent twenties, the buoyant early musicals, the low plateau of the depression years, the sputtering race movies, and the wartime identification of race with the progressive "popular front." And, like other black intellectuals,

The war years closed on another black dilemma: whether to picket the stereotypes in *Song of the South* (© Walt Disney Productions) or to pay homage to James Baskette for his posthumous special Oscar for his characterization of Uncle Remus. (Author's collection)

he had given his best thought to the thorny question of the future of race movies and found it dim. At last, at the end of the summer of 1942, he gave a "statement to the Negro public, particularly in Los Angeles," a kind of state-of-the-race message, at least with reference to movies:

> Our utmost wisdom and intelligence must be used by Negro actors, present and future, and by the Negro public generally on the pledges which have been made by the motion picture industry to broaden the treatment of the Negro in films. . . .
> Negroes must realize that there are three vitally important phases of the subject. First and most important is picturization of the Negro not as comic and menial figures but as normal human beings. Growing out of this is the second phase of more acting roles for Negroes in motion pictures. Third is the matter of employment of qualified colored men and women in the technical end of production.
> As for those actors in Hollywood who can play only comic or servant roles, I trust they will not let their own interests spoil the opportunity we now have to correct a lot of things from which Negroes have suffered in the past in the movies. . . .
> I can assure Negroes throughout the country that some extraordinarily fine things are in prospect in the moving picture world so far as Negroes are concerned which conceivably may play a large part in creating a new concept of the Negro.[64]

In a single stroke White's announcement signaled the end of the monopoly of Southern racial stereotypes for Negro roles in films, provided new standards for blacks in Hollywood to strive for, and provided a scenario for the race's future in movies—a slow fade to black.

AFTERWORD

The "final solution" to the Negro question in cinema satisfied no one. It was bourgeois, reformist, liberal, progressive, and finally soporific in its lack of drama and celebrity. To some degree the bargain struck by Walter White and the studio heads passed, like the myth of the Southern box office, into the legends of Hollywood. On the other hand, veteran black actors such as Ernest Anderson believed that White merely codified an inevitable trend.

Recent social historians, notably John Brooks, have implicitly come to agree with the Hollywood actors. For them the impact of the second Great War had become central to American life, indeed the life of the world, and forever altered the old bases of opinion, attitudes, and decision-making. In contrast to changes wrought by war, Roosevelt's New Deal seemed tentative rather than permanent, reactive rather than positive, halting rather than surefooted, and finally weakened by its dependence on a frail coalition. It was the coming of war that opened up American life.[65]

Afro-Americans caught the mood and exploited it for racial gain whenever they could. After 1936 most of them became Democrats. Walter White himself was a modish New Dealer—anti-fascist, aloof from the sects of the left, and holding close to the progressive center. In fragile concert NAACP legalists and hesitant New Dealers gingerly probed the surface racism of America. Hollywood also had its goads, notable among them the NAACP.

The legalistic and contractual changes wrung from a few willing Hollywood producers in 1942 paralleled and even anticipated concessions in the larger American society. Aesthetically what had been achieved by the summer of 1942 was the final step of a dissolution of the monopoly that Southern literary attitudes had held over the depiction of racial life in America. Each new black image upon the screen eroded further the old metaphors.

In previous generations pictorial and literary racism persisted in popular magazines, cartoons, and sketches, thus providing a wellspring of traditional imagery upon which racism fed. But after 1945 Americans sloughed off the icons of their racial past. So changes in racial arrangements were forced upon the postwar generation at least in part because the hagiography of racism had lost its popular oracles, scribes, and priests. Touchy Negroes and responsive liberal whites forced the old imagery from magazines, radio, and cinema. By 1952 the NAACP barely needed to clear its throat before CBS removed *Amos 'n' Andy* from television screens. Thus the old "ways of white folks" no longer were a firm pictorial tradition handed down to the children.

Unfortunately for blacks and for the country at large one problem remained unsolved. It had surfaced in cinema history only when a few blacks rode the tiger of "race movies" and when soundfilm made it possible for blacks to enter briefly the top ranks of performing in such pictures as *Hearts in Dixie* and *Hallelujah!* It was based on a dichotomy that developed from American racial arrangements: many vernacular forms of music and dance grew from segregated black sources, while movies were a pristinely white medium. So that American movies generally rested upon such white sources as polyethnic vaudeville, the Western experience as romanticized and transshipped back East in the form of wild west shows, and roadshow repertory melodrama. Blacks, then, isolated in their customary place, could contribute little to cinema except insofar as they were willing to depict traditional racial stereotypes or to imitate white forms in the negative images of "race movies." Moreover, because American racial arrangements themselves were changing, Afro-American leadership tended to affect a studied equalitarian assimilationism that discouraged attempts to emphasize black values and attitudes, for this might seem to support segregation. Therefore no one set about shaping a black rhetoric, an aesthetic, or a politics.

After the war, then, black artists needed to make a quantum jump toward a *new* black aesthetic that would build on the platform left by the 1942 agreement. After fifty years of struggle the iron black jockey was missing from the lawn; moviemakers would spend the future trying to grow fresh grass in its place.

NOTES

List of Abbreviations

AA: *Afro-American* (Baltimore)
AAS: A. A. Schomburg Collection, New York Public Library
AFI: American Film Institute
AN: *Amsterdam News* (New York)
BFI: British Film Institute
BTWP: Booker T. Washington Papers, Library of Congress
CD: *Chicago Defender*
CE: *California Eagle* (Los Angeles)
GEH: International Museum of Photography at George Eastman House
GPJC: George P. Johnson Collection, Special Collections, UCLA
JWJC: James Weldon Johnson Memorial Collection, Beineke Library, Yale
LAS: *Los Angeles Sentinel*
LC: Library of Congress
MCN: May Childs Nerney
MOMA: Museum of Modern Art
MPM: *Moving Picture Magazine*
MPN: *Moving Picture News*
MPW: *Moving Picture World*
NAACPR: Records of National Association for the Advancement of Colored People, Library of Congress
NYA: *New York Age*
NYT: *New York Times*
PAC: Performing Arts Collection, New York Public Library
PC: *Pittsburgh Courier*
Var.: *Variety*
VLP: *Vitagraph Life Portrayals*
WSHS: Iconography Collection, Wisconsin State Historical Society
ZC: Stephen Zito Collection, American Film Institute
Films with uncited sources are in general release, rental or television.

Notes to Introduction

1. Parker Tyler, *The Three Faces of Film: The Art, the Dream, the Cult* (New York, 1960), 105-14; David Grimsted, *Melodrama Unveiled: American Theatre and Culture, 1800-1850* (Chicago, 1968), vii; Albert F. McLean, Jr., *American Vaudeville as Ritual* (Lexington, Ky., 1965), passim.

2. On varieties of American criticism see Stanley Edgar Hyman, "Attempts at Integration," in *The Armed Vision: A Study in the Methods of Modern Literary Criticism* (New York, 1955); Marshall McLuhan, "Myth and Mass Media," in Henry A. Murray, *Myth and Mythmaking* (New York, 1960), 289, 293; Carl Bode, *The Anatomy of American Popular Culture, 1840-1861* (Berkeley and Los Angeles, 1960), 73, 191; E. Douglas Branch, *The Sentimental Years* (New York, 1934, 1965), 127, 133, 165-68, 172; John A. Kouwenhoven, *Made in America: The Arts in Modern Civilization* (New York, 1962), 2-4, 14-15, 84-88, 179, 215, 218.

3. George S. Schuyler, "The Negro Art Hokum," *Nation,* June 23, 1926, 662-63; Langston Hughes, "The Negro Artist and the Racial Mountain," *Nation,* June 16, 1926, 692-94.

4. A good anthology dealing with black aesthetics is Addison Gayle, Jr., *The Black Aesthetic* (Garden City, N.Y., 1971). See also Annette Powell Williams, "Dynamics of a Black Audience," in Thomas Kochman, ed., *Rappin' and Stylin' Out: Communication in Urban Black America* (Urbana, Ill., 1972), 101-9; Robert A. Bone, *The Negro Novel in America* (New Haven, 1965), 244, 249, 252-53; Leroi Jones, "The Myth of a 'Negro Literature'," in Raman K. Singh and Peter Fellowes, *Black Literature in America: A Casebook* (New York, 1970), 308-15; Roger D. Abrahams, "The Changing Concept of the Negro Hero," in Mody C. Boatwright, Wilson M. Hudson, and Allen Maxwell, eds., *The Golden Log,* "Texas Folklore Society Publications," XXXI (Dallas, 1962), 119-34; Herbert Hill, *Anger and Beyond: The Negro Writer in the United States* (New York, 1966).

Notes to Chapter One

1. A good list of types is in Sterling A. Brown, "Negro Characters as Seen by White Authors," *Journal of Negro Education,* April 1933, 179-203.

2. Terry Ramsaye, *A Million and One Nights* (New York, 1926, 1964), 73-83.

3. C. W. Ceram, *Archaeology of the Cinema* (New York, 1965), plates 157-64, 178-83, p. 156.

4. A. R. Fulton, *Motion Pictures: The Development of an Art from Silent Films to the Age of Television* (Norman, Okla., 1960), 10-17; Gertrude Jobes, *Motion Picture Empire* (Hamden, Conn., 1966), 24-25; Edward Wagenknecht, *The Movies in the Age of Innocence* (Norman, Okla., 1962), 16, who cites Charles K. Harris, "Song Slide the Little Father of Photodrama [*sic*]," MPW, March 10, 1917, 1520-21; Kleine Optical Company, *Complete Illustrated Catalogue of Moving Picture Machines, Stereopticons, Slides, Films* (Chicago, 1905), 25.

5. McLean, *American Vaudeville as Ritual,* x, 1, 4.

6. M. H. Vorse, "Picture Show Audiences," *Outlook* June 24, 1911, 441-47.

7. Lewis R. Marcuson, "The Irish, the Italians, and the Jews: A Study of Three Nationality Groups as Portrayed in American Drama Between 1920 and 1960" (Ph.D. dissertation, University of Denver, 1966), 11-17; McLean, *American Vaudeville,* 131; Kalton C. Lahue and Terry Brewer, *Kops and Custards: The Legend of Keystone Films* (Norman, Okla., 1968), 7-8.

8. Fannin S. Belcher, Jr., "The Place of the Negro in the Evolution of the American Theatre, 1767-1940" (Ph. D. dissertation, Yale University, 1943), 123.

9. *Ibid.*, 3-26, 77-82, 176-81; George Peck, manager, Rice's Comedians, to Mr. Holmes, Feb. 12, 1899, in JWJC; Frank Rahill, *The World of Melodrama* (State College, Pa., 1967), 182-83.

10. Harris, "Song Slide," 1520-21; Kleine, *Catalogue, 1905*, 25.

11. Ramsaye, *Million and One Nights*, 303.

12. Langston Hughes and Milton Meltzer, *Black Magic: A Pictorial History of the Negro in American Entertainment* (Englewood Cliffs, N.J., 1967), 4-48.

13. *A West Indian Woman Bathing a Baby* (Edison, *ca.* 1895), in GEH; *Buck Dance* (Edison, 1898) and *Watermelon Contest* (Edison, 1899), in LC, are a tiny sample of extant ethnic footage. For a montage of traditional roles see the still from *Oh! That Watermelon* (Biograph, 1896, 1902), in Gorden Hendricks, *Beginnings of the Biograph* (New York, 1964), fig. 13.

14. *Colored Troops Disembarking* (Edison, 1898); *The Ninth Negro Cavalry Watering Horses* (Edison, 1898), in LC; Amusement Supply Company [Catalogue, 1906], 358-59, 396, which also featured films of Negro chicken thieves.

15. *The Rout of the Filipinos* (Edison, 1899), in LC. The Anti-Imperialist League attributed increased racial violence to American adventures abroad.

16. *The Edison Minstrels* (*ca.* 1897-1900); *Minstrels Battling in a Room* (Edison, *ca.* 1897-1900); *Sambo and Aunt Jemima: Comedians* (Edison, *ca.* 1897-1900), in LC.

17. Amusement Supply Company [catalogue], 396, 358-59; [William Selig], *Special List of Films Made Expressly for Selig* (Chicago, 1900), 8-9, 20-24; S. Lubin, *Lubin's Films* (Philadelphia, 1903), 31-36; Kleine, *Catalogue, 1905*, 234-36; *A Nigger in the Woodpile* (Biograph, 1904) and *Chicken Thieves* (Edison, 1897), in LC.

18. Nicholas Vardac, *Stage to Screen: Theatrical Method from Garrick to Griffith* (Cambridge, Mass., 1947), passim, develops the idea that melodrama presaged cinema technique. *Ballyhoo Cakewalk* (Edison, 1903) and *West Indian Girls in Native Dance* (Edison, 1903), both in LC. See also *Gold Dust Cleansing Powder* (Biograph, 1903), in LC, and other examples of racially neutral commercials and topical pieces.

19. Peter Noble, *The Negro in Films* (London [1948]), 27-28. Neither Noble nor later writers such as Carlton Moss, "The Negro in American Films," *Freedomways*, III (Spring 1963), 134-42, agree on what *Echappés de Charenton*—its French title—meant.

20. *The Gator and the Pickaninny* (Edison, 1903); *A Scrap in Black and White* (Edison, 1903); and *The Tunnel Workers* (Biograph, 1906), first two in LC; last in Kemp R. Niver, *The First Twenty Years: A Segment of Film History from 1894 to 1912* (Los Angeles, 1968), 107; conversation with Stephen Zito.

21. *Uncle Tom's Cabin* (Edison, 1903), in LC; Lewis Jacobs, *The Rise of the American Film: A Critical History, with an Essay, Experimental Film in America, 1921-1947* (New York, 1939, 1968), 36, 42.

22. *Uncle Tom's Cabin* (Vitagraph, 1909), in BFI; interview with Jimmie Smith, Lowe's manager, Los Angeles, June 1970; J. Stuart Blackton, "Yesterdays of Vitagraph," *Photoplay*, July 1919, 32; Ralph Eugene Lund, "Trouping with Uncle Tom, *Century Magazine*, Jan. 1928, 329-37; *Motion Picture Story Magazine*, Jan. 1914, 76; Noble, *Negro in Films*, 31-32.

23. *Everybody Works but Father* (Biograph, 1905) and *A Bucket of Cream Ale* (Biograph, 1904), both in LC; Kleine, *Catalogue 1905*, 289, for his identity as a Dutchman.

24. [*The Negro's Revenge*] (Pathé Frères, *ca.* 1906), in BFI.

25. *Johnson vs. Ketchell, Colma, California, October 16, 1909* (Ringside Picture Corp., 1909) and *Jack Johnson vs. Jim Flynn* (Jack Curley, 1912), both in LC; NYT, April 16, 1915; on Kalem's *The Making of a Champion*, MPW, Feb. 20, 1909, 212-13.

26. *The Night I Fought Jack Johnson* (Vitagraph, 1913) and *Some White Hope*

(Vitagraph, 1915), both in BFI. In the latter film the boxer is "Lam Bangford" (Sam Langford), another black.

27. *Paul J. Rainey's African Hunt* (1912); *The Military Drill of the Kikuyu Tribes and Other Native Ceremonies* (Paul J. Rainey, 1914); *Capturing Circus Animals in the African Wilds* (Selig Polyscope Company, ca. 1913), all in LC; *Theodore Roosevelt in Africa* (n. p., n. d.); *African Natives* (n. p., n. d.); and *Theodore Roosevelt's Camp in Africa* (n. p., n. d.), in Roosevelt Memorial Association Collection, LC; NYT, June 23, 1914.

28. Of the rich literature of the period three essentials are C. Vann Woodward, *Origins of the New South, 1877-1913,* Vol. IX in "A History of the South (Baton Rouge, 1951); August Meier, *Negro Thought in America, 1880-1915* (Ann Arbor, Mich., 1964); and Rayford Logan, *The Betrayal of the Negro from Rutherford B. Hayes to Woodrow Wilson* (New York, 1954, 1965).

29. *The Fights of Nations* (Biograph, 1907), in LC; MPW, March 9, 1907, 9-10.

30. MPW, March 20, 1909, 348; March 6, 1909, 278-79; Jan. 30, 1914, 553, 626; June 12, 1909, 793; and other reviews in ZC. Another view, stressing the persistence of racism, is in Daniel J. Leab, *From Sambo to Superspade: The Black Experience in Motion Pictures* (Boston, 1975), which enlarges the list of "nigger subjects."

31. MPW, March 6, 1909, 278; Jan. 31, 1914, 626; and other trade journal clippings in ZC.

32. *Tuaregs in Their Country* (Pathé, ca. 1909) and *Life in Senegal* (Gaumont, 1910), both in BFI; *The Zulu's Heart* (Biograph, 1908) and *The Kaffir's Gratitude* (Biograph, 1915), both in LC; MPW, May 18, 1912, 614; May 7, 1910, 749; May 21, 1910, 833; April 11, 1908, 325; June 21, 1913, 1237, 1332; June 28, 1913, 1358, 1369.

33. Robert W. Fenton, *The Big Swingers: A Biography, Edgar Rice Burroughs, 1875-1950; Tarzan, 1912-* (Englewood Cliffs, N.J., 1967), 73; *Forbidden Adventure* (Mutual, 1915), in LC; *A Night in the Jungle* (Selig, 1915), in BFI.

34. MPW, May 31, 1913, 953-54; VLP, Nov. 1914, 47; *The Valet's Wife* (Biograph, 1908) and *Mammy's Child* (Crystal Films, 1913), both in LC.

35. *Swami Sam* (Lubin, 1915), in BFI; *Colored Villainy* (Keystone, 1915) and *Florida Enchantment* (Vitagraph, 1915), both in LC; VLP, Sept. 6-9, 1915, 8.

36. NYA, Aug. 26, 1909; Jacobs, *The Rise of the American Film*, 123; Noble, *Negro in Films,* 31; Mabel Rowland, ed., *Bert Williams: Son of Laughter* (New York, 1923, 1969), 150-55; Foster sources cited in full in chapter three below.

37. *Reception of President Taft at Petersburg, Virginia, May 19, 1909* (Edison, 1909), in LC; MPW, July 31, 1909, 160.

38. The most useful studies of Griffith are Robert M. Henderson, *D. W. Griffith: His Life and Work* (New York, 1972), his *D. W. Griffith: The Years at Biograph* (New York, 1970), and Russell L. Merritt, "The Impact of D. W. Griffith's Motion Pictures from 1908 to 1914 on Contemporary American Culture" (Ph.D. dissertation, Harvard University, 1970).

39. *In Old Kentucky* (Biograph, 1909); *His Trust* (Biograph, 1911); and *His Trust Fulfilled* (Biograph, 1911), all in LC; *The Battle* (Biograph, 1911), in BFI; Merritt, "The Impact of D. W. Griffith," 227-34.

40. *A Fair Rebel* (Klaw and Erlanger, 1914) and unidentified Civil War footage, both in LC; MPW, May 22, 1909, 686; June 1, 1912, 817; *Motion Picture Story Magazine,* May 1913, 65ff; MPW, Jan. 17, 1914, 320, and May 31, 1913, 940-41; VLP, Jan. 1-31, 1914, 35; *New York Dramatic Mirror*, Aug. 8, 1908, 7, and Feb. 1, 1911, 29, the latter serial cited in George C. Pratt, *Spellbound in Darkness: A History of the Silent Film* (Greenwich, Conn., 1973), 56, 86-87.

41. *The Soldier Brothers of Susannah* (Kalem, 1912) and *The Only Veteran in Town* (Vitagraph, 1913), both in BFI; MPW, May 15, 1909, 643; Sept, 5, 1914, 1377, 1381, and May 31, 1913, 926; *Kinetogram,* April 1, 1912, 8.

42. MPW, Feb. 12, 19, 1910, 227, 258.

43. *A Special Messenger* (Kalem, 1911), in BFI; *Kinetogram,* July 1, 1911, 9; MPW, May 27, 1911, 1206, and Aug. 5, 1911, 274.

44. *Motion Picture Story Magazine,* Aug. 1912, 123; MPW, Aug. 10, 1912, 582,

and July 26, 1913, 464; synopsis of *A Gentle Volunteer* in copyright file, LC; VLP, Feb. 1-28, 1914, 48; *The Informer* (Biograph, 1912), in LC.

45. MPN, April 26, 1913, 24, 35; MPW, Aug. 8, 1914, 813, and Dec. 13, 1913, 1320, 1322; *True to the Colors* synopsis in LC.

46. *Battle Hymn of the Republic* (Vitagraph, 1911), in LC; VLP, Feb. 1-28, 1914, 12; MPM, Aug. 1917, 13.

47. The social atmosphere that contributed to white Americans' fascination with Indian lore is too complex to deal with here, but several historians have illumined the period. On conservation see Arthur A. Ekirch, Jr., *Man and Nature in America* (New York, 1963), 88-95; on tourism, Earl Pomeroy, *In Search of the Golden West* (Berkeley, 1960), 123-36; on nature-worship and child-rearing, Peter J. Schmitt, *Back to Nature: The Arcadian Myth in Urban America* (New York, 1969), xix-xxii, 28-46, chap. VI, 108-9, 149-53, 186; Roderick Nash, *The Wilderness and the American Mind* (New Haven, 1967), 131-202; Roy Harvey Pearce, *The Savages of America: A Study of the Indian and the Idea of Civilization* (Baltimore, 1953, 1965), 8, 110, 136, 239, 169, 207, 213-14, 217; for documents, Nash, *The Call of the Wild (1900-1916)* (New York, 1970), 19, 36, 86ff.

48. John Drinkwater, *The Life and Adventures of Carl Laemmle* (London, 1931), 74-75; Merritt, "Griffith," 66-67; Kalton Lahue, *World of Laughter: The Motion Picture Comedy Short, 1910-1930* (Norman, Okla., 1966), 7; Balshofer, *Two Reels and a Crank*, 76, 80, 91; George C. Pratt, "See Mr. Ince," *Image*, May, 1956, 100-111; letterhead of Go-Won-Go Mohawk in JWJC.; Hart, *My Life East and West*, 14-15; Richard Andres, "An Actor and His Indian Friends," *MPM*, March 1910, 104, 106; *New York Dramatic Mirror*, Aug. 8, 1908, in Pratt, *Spellbound*, 56.

49. *Call of the Wild* (Biograph, 1908), in LC; *Back to the Prairie* (Pathé, 1911), in BFI; MPW, March 6, 1909, 279; Sept. 11, 1909, 356; Feb. 19, 1910, 269; and Jan. 17, 1914, 332, 336.

50. *Broken Doll* (Biograph, 1910), in LC. MPW, April 30, 1910, 690, praised *Fighting the Iroquois in Canada* (Kalem, 1910) for its authenticity, educational value, and research—while ignoring the point that the movie was about killing Indians.

51. *Ramona* (Biograph, 1910), *On the Warpath* (Kalem, 1909), *Iola's Promise* (Biograph, 1912), all in LC; *The Indian Vestal* (Selig, 1908), *The Blackfoot Halfbreed* (Kalem, 1911), *The Sepoy's Wife* (Vitagraph, 1910), all in BFI; Merritt, "Griffith," 109, 240; MPW, Feb. 21, 1914, 1022, Jan. 10, 1914, 204-6, Jan. 17, 1914, 332, and Oct. 5, 1912, 69; MPM, June 1913, 29ff. Themes include rescues, Oriental variants, and other standards.

52. NYT, May 21, 1914; June 2, 1914; *Curse of the Red Man* (Selig, 1911), in BFI.

53. Lahue, *Kops and Custards*, 72; Balshofer, *Two Reels and a Crank*, 77; *Kinetogram*, Jan. 15, 1913 and through teens for ethnic comment; *Nation*, Aug. 28, 1913, 193.

54. See for example *Ching Ling Foo Outdone* (Edison, 1900); *Happy Hooligan Surprised* (Edison, 1901); *How the Dutch Beat the Irish* (Edison, 1901); *Lady Bountiful* . . . (Biograph, 1903); *Alphonse and Gaston* . . . (Biograph, 1902); *Murphy's Wake* (Biograph, 1903); *The Black Hand* (Biograph, 1908); *Cohen's Advertising Scheme* (Edison, 1904); *The Fights of Nations* (Biograph, 1907), all in LC. See also Kleine, *Catalogue*, 1905, 298; MPW, March 9, 1907, 9.

55. *The Romance of a Jewess* (Biograph, 1908); *In Little Italy* (Biograph, 1909); *The Child of the Ghetto* (Biograph, 1910), all in LC; *A Female Fagin* (Kalem, 1914); *Levi and McGinnis Running for Office* (IMP, 1914), both in BFI; *A Natural Born Gambler* (Biograph, 1916), in author's possession; MPW, June 13, 1908, 515; and clippings, in ZC. Henderson, *Griffith*, 39, notes that in *Lonesome Junction* "a black hand dago" appears.

56. *The Gypsy's Warning* (Méliès, n. d.); *A Gypsy Duel* (Biograph, 1903), both in LC; *Rescued by Rover* in Niver, *Twenty Years*, 93.

57. *Greaser's Gauntlet* (Biograph, 1908), in LC; *The Mexican's Faith* (Essanay, 1910); *Her Wedding Bell* (Biograph, 1913), both in BFI. *Tony the Greaser* in VLP, April 1-30, 1910, 55.

58. *The Hindu Fakir* (Edison, 1902); *The Heathen Chinee and the Sunday School Teachers* (Biograph, 1904); *That Chink at Golden Gulch* (Biograph, 1910), all in LC. *The Mystery of Brayton Court* in VLP, Nov. 1-30, 1914, 5.

59. NYA, April 4, 1910; June 1, 1911; Aug. 26, 1909.

Notes to Chapter Two

1. NYA, July 10, 1913; April 23, 1914; Sept. 10, 1914; March 25, 1915. Charles Flint Kellogg, *NAACP: A History of the National Association for the Advancement of Colored People* (Baltimore, 1967), 142.

2. NYA, April 23, 1914; James Weldon Johnson, *Black Manhattan* (New York, 1930, 1968), 95-106.

3. *The Sultan's Dagger*, in MPM, Aug. 1913, 84.

4. George C. Pratt, "The Posse Is Ridin' Like Mad," *Image*, April 1948, 82-85.

5. Lillian Gish and Ann Pinchot, *The Movies, Mr. Griffith and Me* (Englewood Cliffs, N. J., 1969), 132.

6. Raymond Allen Cook, *Fire from the Flint: The Amazing Careers of Thomas Dixon* (Winston-Salem, N.C., 1968), 140.

7. *Ibid.*, 141.

8. Merritt, "Impact of Griffith," 284, 273; Roy E. Aitken and Al P. Nelson, *The "Birth of a Nation" Story* (Middleburg, Va., 1965), 40; Linda Arvidson, *When the Movies Were Young* (New York, 1925, 1969), chap. XIX.

9. Interview: Miriam Cooper and author (telephone), Autumn 1971; taped interview: Mme Sul-te-Wan and Raymond Lee, through courtesy of David Shepherd; D. W. Griffith manuscript autobiography, MOMA.

10. Griffith autobiography and Billy Bitzer typescript memoir, both in MOMA.

11. Merritt, "Impact of Griffith," 273ff; holograph script marginalia in Griffith papers, MOMA; Gish, *Griffith*, 136; Charles L. Hutchins, "A Critical Evaluation of the Controversies Engendered by D. W. Griffith's 'The Birth of a Nation'" (M.A. thesis, University of Iowa, 1961), 18. The recent memoirs of Karl Brown, *Adventures with D. W. Griffith* (New York, 1973), and Miriam Cooper with Bonnie Herndon, *Dark Lady of the Silents: My Life in Early Hollywood* (Indianapolis, 1973), corroborate this account.

12. Seymour Stern, "Griffith: 1—*The Birth of a Nation*," special issue of *Film Culture*, Spring-Summer 1965, 53-55.

13. Thomas Dixon, *The Clansman* (New York, 1907), 6, 23, 34, 38.

14. *The Birth of a Nation* (Epoch, 1915).

15. Vachel Lindsay, *The Art of the Moving Picture* (New York, 1915, 1922, 1970), 74-77.

16. Cook, *Dixon*, 167-68. In other versions the locale shifts or Griffith is given a place in it, but Dixon appears to have been the author of the title change. Aitken and Nelson, *The "Birth of a Nation" Story*, 46; Gish, *Griffith*, 154; Henderson, *Griffith*, 156.

17. Cook, *Dixon*, 167-70; Mrs. Thomas Dixon to Thomas Cripps, June 7, 1962; interview with Mrs. Dixon (telephone), June 6, 1962.

18. MCN to Eugene U. Scott, Janesville, Wisc., copy, Jan. 10, 1915; MCN to [?], Feb. 27, 1915, in NAACPR, in LC.

19. CE, Feb. 6, 1915; NAACP to Los Angeles City Council, Feb. 2, 1915; E. Burton Cerutti to MCN, Feb. 3, 1915, in NAACPR.

20. CE, March 11, 1915; April 3, 17, 1915. A. B. Spingarn to MCN, memo, March 9, 1915; Feb. 27, 1915; Mary Ashe Miller, San Francisco censor board, to

Gentlemen, March 3, 1915; W. A. Butler, *et al.*, NAACP, to Mayor James Rolph, Jr., copy, Feb. 26, 1915, in NAACPR.

21. Stern, "Griffith," 67. John E. Milholland to "Professor," March 1, 1915, in NAACPR.

22. Hugo Munsterberg, *The Photoplay: A Psychological Study* (New York, 1916); Lindsay, *Art of the Moving Picture*, 74-79.

23. The account here depends on Thomas R. Cripps, "The Negro Reaction to the Motion Picture 'Birth of a Nation'," *Historian*, May 1963, 244-62; NYT, Feb. 14, 1915.

24. Frederic C. Howe to [Joseph P.] Loud in NAACPR, *Fighting a Vicious Film*, 33; *Survey*, April 3, 1915, 4-5; W. D. McGuire, Jr., National Board of Review, "Censoring Motion Pictures," *New Republic*, April 10, 1915, 262-63.

25. "Fighting Race Calumny," *Crisis*, May 1915, 40-42. MCN to Jacques Loeb, copy, March 3, 1915, in NAACPR. *Post* (New York), March 10, 1915, carried the last advertisement; the review appeared March 13, 1915.

26. MCN to Baker, Copy, March 15, 1915; Selznick to NAACP, March 15, 1915; MCN to Chief Magistrate McAdoo (New York), copy, March 3, 1915; Malcolm Davis, *Post*, to MCN, n. d.; James H. Anderson, AN, to MCN, March 15, 1915; form letter to ministers, March 6, 1915; *Crisis*, May, 1915, 40-42, in NAACPR.

27. *Crisis*, June 1915, 87; NAACP, *Fighting a Vicious Film*, passim; AA, March 27, 1915; A. B. Spingarn *et al.*, to Mayor, copy, March 19, 1915; Alice [?] Patterson to Frederic C. Howe, copy, March 17, 1915, in NAACPR.

28. NYA, March 25, 1915; *Crisis*, May 1915, 40-42; AA, March 3, 1915; August Meier, "Booker T. Washington and the Rise of the NAACP," *Crisis*, Feb. 1954, 122.

29. Gish, *Griffith*, 155; souvenir program, The Strand, St. Paul, in WSHS; *This Book Contains a Wonderful Tale That Will Surprise and Fascinate You Read It!*, pamphlet in Griffith MSS; S. S. Frissell to MCN, March 30, 1915; Paul Cravath to MCN, March 19, 1915; MCN to John M. Glenn, April 9, 1915, and reply April 22, 1915, in NAACPR; NYA, June 3, 1915; *Pawtucket Times* clipping, April 3, 1915 in BTWP.

30. Dixon speech in *New York Commercial Advertiser*, April 1915, in Griffith MSS. Thomas Dixon to Rolfe Cobleigh, copy, March 27, 1915; Joseph Prince Loud to MCN, April 15, 1915, in NAACPR.

31. MCN to Lillian D. Wald, copy, March 9, 1915; MCN to "Our Branches and Locals," April 19, 1915, in NAACPR.

32. Typescript report; Joseph P. Loud to MCN, April 15, 1915, in NAACPR.

33. MCN to Gilbert D. Lamb, copy, April 13, 1915; MCN to Charles C. Allison, Jr., Urban League, copy, Dec. 17, 1915; Allison to MCN, Dec. 21, 1915, in NAACPR.

34. *Crisis*, June 1915, 87; NAACP, *Fighting a Vicious Film*, passim. See also *Sunday Post* (Boston), April 4, 1915; *Post*, April 5-8, 1915. The list included Dorothea Dix, Rupert Hughes, Booth Tarkington, Richard Harding Davis, Hugh Johnson, George Peabody, Senators James E. Martine, Duncan U. Fletcher, Henry Lee Myers, Thomas J. Walsh, and Wesley L. Jones, Representative Claude Kitchen, Rev. C. H. Parkhurst and Thomas Gregory. According to the NAACP, Dixon's method of soliciting approval was to pass out cards between the halves of the film, that is, before the racial theme.

35. NAACP, *Fighting a Vicious Film*, 26; *New Republic*, May 5, 1915, 17; *Broad Ax* (Chicago), June 5, 1915; *Post* (Boston), April 24, 1915; unsigned letter to "Mr. Spingarn," April 9, 1915, and Joseph P. Loud to MCN, April 17, 1915, in NAACPR; Stephen R. Fox, *The Guardian of Boston: William Monroe Trotter* (New York, 1971), 191.

36. *Sunday Post* (Boston), April 4, 11, 1915; *Post*, April 6-8, 1915.

37. Fox, *Guardian of Boston*, 191-93.

38. After the riot other Boston papers covered the story but none of them favored censorship or seemed concerned about the struggle. See *Transcript, Journal,* and *Herald,* April 18-26, 1915; Fox, *Guardian,* 193-96; Joseph P. Loud to MCN, April 23, 1915, in NAACPR.

39. Francis J. Garrison [?] to Oswald Garrison Villard, April 9, 1915, in Villard Papers, Houghton Library, Harvard.

40. William G. Willcox to BTW, copies of wires, April 13, 15, 1915; R. R. Moton to BTW, May 12, 1915; BTW to C. R. Miller, Oct. 14, 1915; Phil J. Allston to BTW, copy, April 12, 1915; BTW to Allston, copy, April 19, 25, 1915; Charles E. [?]llason to BTW, June 1, 1915; Samuel E. Courtney to BTW, copy, April 19, 1915; BTW to Courtney, copy, April 23, 1915; Rabbi Abram Simon to BTW, confidential wire, April 14, 1915; Emmett Scott to Simon, copy of wire, April 14, 1915, in Box 75, BTWP. BTW wrote one letter of protest to the Atlanta *Independent* (NAACP, *Fighting a Vicious Film,* 35-36). See *Post* (Boston), April 24, 1915, for hints that Allston may have expressed approval of the film; also BTW to Louis B. Anderson, copy, n. d., BTWP.

41. Charles H. Evans to BTW, Oct. 26, 1915, scrawled at bottom: "Please get this off today"; J. Mott Hallowell to BTW, June 1, 1915; BTW to M. H. Bidez, Palace Theatre, Jacksonville, April 21, 1913, on movies at Tuskegee; Dr. W. R. Watkins to Louis B. Anderson, copy, May 10, 1915; [E. J. Scott] to Watkins, copy, Aug. 6, 1912; George W. Broome to BTW, May 15, 1909; "Moving Pictures of Tuskegee," *Tuskegee Student,* Jan. 25, 1913, 2, in BTWP. Lent by Professor Louis R. Harlan.

42. *Post* (Boston), April 12, 18-19, 1915; *Crisis,* June 1915, 87; correspondence in NAACPR, *Fighting a Vicious Film,* 30-31.

43. Joseph P. Loud to MCN, April 23, 1915; May 10, 1915; Butler Wilson to "Sir," April 27, 1915, in BTWP; Hutchins, "Controversies," 23-24; *Boston Globe,* April 27, 1915.

44. Dixon to Wilson, Sept. 5, 1915; Dixon to Joseph P. Tumulty, May 1, 1915, in Wilson Papers, quoted in Arthur H. Link, *Wilson: The New Freedom* (Princeton, 1956), 253-54. "The Civil War in Film," *Literary Digest,* March 20, 1915, 608-9; Francis Hackett, "Brotherly Love," *New Republic,* March 20, 1915, 185; "After the Play," *New Republic,* Dec. 4, 1915, 123; June 5, 1915, 125.

45. *Post* (Boston), June 5, 1915; *Crisis,* July 1915, 147-48, insisted there had been no hearing; *ibid.,* Aug. 1915, 200-201; (Sept. 1915), 245; "The Negro Business League" (Oct. 1915), 280-81; "Social Uplift," 268; "The Birth of a Nation," 295-96; Harry Aitken cashbook and ledgers, in WSHS.

46. J. H. Harris to BTW, May 31, 1915, in BTWP.

47. "The Birth of a Nation," *Crisis,* Oct. 1915, 296; CE, May 22, 1915.

48. CE Aug. 22, 1915; MCN to F. S. Churchill, Chicago, copy, May 20, 1915; "Branches," *Crisis,* July 1915, 147; Aug. 1915, 200-201; G. W. Bradenburgh to NAACP, March 12, 1915; *Broad Ax* (Chicago), March 16, 1915; May 22, 1915; John S. Miller, Chicago, to MCN, April 12, 1915; *Chicago Tribune,* May 15, 1915; MCN to Dr. Charles Bentley, copy, April 9, 1915; Pvt. George Best to W. E. B. DuBois, April 9, 1915; MCN to Archibald H. Grimké, copy, April 22, 1915; John B. Jefferson, Oakland, to MCN, May 6, 1915; MCN to Judge Mayer Sulzberger, Phila., copy, June 10, 1915; Alonzo J. Bowling, Chicago, to *Crisis,* Nov. 1, 1916; Var. clippings, all in NAACPR.

49. Fragments of DeForest soundfilm, in AFI, including a singing sequence by Abbie Mitchell.

50. Aitken and Nelson, *Birth of a Nation Story,* 61, 91-93, 95.

51. Gish, *Griffith,* 162; Homer Croy, *Star Maker: The Story of D. W. Griffith* (New York, 1959), 108-9.

52. *The Coward* (Ince, 1915), in LC.

53. *The Governor,* program, Broadway Strand Theatre, Detroit, in GEH.

54. S. P. Keeble to MCN, April 11, 1915; *Bee* (Washington), May 1, 1915; Joe Brown, Des Moines, to MCN, May 29, 1915, in NAACPR.

55. *Gazette* (Cleveland), April 10, 1915; May 22, 1915. Frank B. Willis to Harry C. Smith, April 8, 1915 (copy to MCN), June 4, 1915; Della H. Fields to MCN, April 17, 1915; S. P. Keeble to MCN, wire, Aug. 2, 1915; H. J. Nichols to MCN, Aug. 3, 1915, in NAACPR.

56. MCN to John E. Brent, *et al.*, April 22, 1915; B. Johnson to MCN, April 13, 1915, in NAACPR.

57. CE, Aug. 22, 1915. Resolutions of Executive Committee, Boston Branch, NAACP, June 8, 1915; Thomas Dabney, Va. Union, to Joel Spingarn, Aug. 10, 1915; W. A. Butler, Pres., N. Calif. Branch, to MCN, Aug. 14, 1915; Charles A. V. Girard to W. E. B. DuBois; T. Edward Kinney to MCN, Sept 8, 1915, in NAACPR.

58. Inez Milholland, "Censorship," *Crisis*, Jan. 1917, 116-17; Walter White to S. L. "Roxy" Rothapfel, April 28, 1921, in NAACPR. In NAACP circles only Milholland urged action beyond mere censorship.

59. Kenneth T. Jackson, *The Ku Klux Klan in the Cities, 1915-1930* (New York, 1967), 271-72; Var., Feb. 21, 1924, 14. No one has ever seriously checked the KKK boast that its rolls were swelled by showings of *The Birth of a Nation*. Indeed, it might be argued that as the new Klan shifted toward the Middle West, and toward anti-Semitism, and anti-Catholicism, the picture became irrelevant. Furthermore, one might argue that the Klan's claims rested largely on the tribute paid the movie by the NAACP's persistent protests. The latest attempt surveys the literature and finds only that the movie and the Klan "reacted upon one another." See Maxim Simcovitch, "The Impact of Griffith's *Birth of a Nation* on the Modern Ku Klux Klan," *Journal of Popular Film*, Winter 1972, 45-54.

60. Affidavit of Louis T. Wright on Boston, 1915, Dec. 4, 1922; W. E. B. DuBois memo for Walter White's file, n. d.; memo on New York, 1922; "The Birth of a Nation," memo, Jan. 19, 1923; Walter White to Eugene Covington, Bloomington, Ill., copy, April 22, 1924; Blanche Watson to Film Arts Guild, copy, Oct. 21 [1926], in NAACPR.

61. Press release, Oct. 14, 1918; Percy Carter to NAACP, Feb. 25, 1919; Walter White to John E. Nail, copy, Dec. 6, 1922, in NAACPR.

62. Emory T. Morris to JWJ and Mary White Ovington, May 21, 1921; Lester Walton to JWJ, May 25, 1921, in NAACPR. Var., May 20, 1921, 47; July 1, 1921, 30; Sept. 23., 1921, 45; June 4, 1924, 24.

63. Var., Sept. 30, 1927, 38; "Free and Equal," memo, May 4, 1925, NAACPR.

64. White to Rev. Mr. Morrison, copy, Sept. 8, 1930; Alexander to Hays, copy, July 23, 1930; Carl E. Millikin, secretary to Motion Picture Association of America, copy, to Alexander, Aug. 9, 1930; White to Hays, copy, Aug. 12, 1930; White to J. Howard Butler, San Francisco NAACP, copy, Sept. 2, 1930; White "To the Branches," copy, Sept. 9, 1930; White to William Pickens, memo, n. d.; William Short, Motion Picture Research Council, to DuBois, Oct. 23, 1932; clipping, *News and Observer* (Raleigh), Oct. 22, 1937; Valdo Turner to White, Dec. 30, 1930, in NAACPR.

65. Bob Treman to White, wire, July 7, 1938; Roy Wilkins to Messrs. Houston and Morrow, memo, copy, May 4, 1938; *Daily Worker*, Dec. 10, 1938, clipping on CPUSA; Thurgood Marshall to Committee on Administration, memo, copy, March 4, 1940; White to Walter Winchell, copy, May 20, 1940; "N.A.A.C.P. Hits Revival of 'Birth of a Nation,'" press release, March 22, 1940; *Times-Herald* (Washington), March 13, 1940, clipping; press releases on various academic screenings; Arthur Garfield Hays to Nate Goldstick, copy, May 1, 1939; Roger Baldwin to Roy Wilkins, April 17, 1940, in NAACPR. Interview: Harry Aitken and author (telephone), Summer 1968, Waukesha, Wisc.

66. *Crisis*, Nov. 1915, 36; "The Slanderous Film," *ibid.*, Dec, 1915, 76-77; NAACP, *Fighting a Vicious Film*, passim; Rev. W. Bishop Johnson, *The Birth of a Nation; A Monumental Slander of American History, the Negro and the Civil War by Thomas Dixon Analytically and Critically Considered* (n. p., [1916]); Isaac L. Thomas, *The Birth of a Nation: A Hyperbole Versus a Negro's*

Plea for Fair Play (Philadelphia, 1916), all in the Moreland Collection, Founder's Library, Howard University, Washington, D.C. See also "Birth of a Nation Revived Draws Protest," *Crisis*, March 1938, 84.

Notes to Chapter Three

1. The fundamentalist position was reinforced by black boycotts of segregated Southern theaters. Interviews with Walter Fisher and George Sinkler, Morgan State University, Spring 1972. The literature of black urban migration is immense. See, for example, the implicitly urban material in Meier, *Negro Thought;* and the more explicit Constance McLaughlin Green, *The Secret City: A History of Race Relations in the Nation's Capital* (Princeton, 1967), chaps. VIII, IX; Gilbert Osofsky, *Harlem: The Making of a Ghetto; Negro New York, 1890-1930* (New York, 1968), passim; Seth M. Scheiner, *Negro Mecca: A History of the Negro in New York City, 1865-1920* (New York, 1965), passim; Allan H. Spear, *Black Chicago: The Making of a Negro Ghetto, 1890-1920* (Chicago, 1967), passim; Richard B. Sherman, ed., *The Negro and the City* (Englewood Cliffs, N.J., 1970), chap. I; Emmett J. Scott, *Negro Migration During the War* (New York, 1920, 1969), passim.

2. John Drinkwater, *The Life and Adventures of Carl Laemmle* (London, 1931), 174; "A Chameleon City," *Literary Digest*, March 27, 1915, 686.

3. Mrs. Mary Hallowell Loud to MCN, May 12, 1915; W. E. B. DuBois to the Motion Picture Committee; other correspondence in Box C-303, NAACPR.

4. MCN to Charles E. Bentley, copy, May 11, 1915; George Cook to MCN, May 11, 1915; MCN to William English Walling, copy, May 13, 1915; MCN to Joseph P. Loud, copy, May 17, 1915; confidential memo from Mary White Ovington, June 1915 in NAACPR; ——— to A. B. Spingarn, June 1, 1915; the writer hoped to enlist scholars, politicians, and veterans in filming a true story of Reconstruction; A. B. Spingarn Papers, LC.

5. See, for example, F. M. Smith, sales manager, Culinary Utilities Department of the Consolidated Safety Pin Company, Bloomfield, N.J., to Scott, Dec. 21, 1914 in BTWP, Box No. 10.

6. Jones and Baker, brokers, to Scott, Feb. 25, 1916, in Box. No. 11; BTW's correspondence with L. B. Anderson, May 1915, and with Phil. J. Allston, April 1915, in Box No. 75; and Rabbi Abram Simon to BTW, April 12, 1915; Scott to Simon, April 14, 1915; BTW to Allston, copy, April 25, 1915. Washington's expertise stemmed from the shooting of *A Day at Tuskegee*, a promotional film that was good enough to be screened in commercial theaters. See M. H. Bidez, manager, the Palace Theatre, Jacksonville, Florida, to BTW, April 17, 1913, in Box No. 923, BTWP.

7. Rose Janowitz to Scott, July 9, 1915, in BTWP.

8. Amy Vorhaus to BTW, July 9, 1915; BTW to Vorhaus, July 13, 1915, in BTWP.

9. Elaine Sterne to MCN, Aug. 16, 1915, in NAACPR; NYT, Aug. 15, 1915.

10. Vorhaus to Scott, Aug. 20, 1915; H. C. Oppenheimer to Scott, Sept. 10, 1915; Scott to Mirror Films Co., copy, Oct. 27, 1915 (marked personal), in BTWP; Ovington to ———, copy, Oct. 27, 1915; Carl Laemmle to Jacob Schiff, Nov. 2, 1915, in NAACPR. Contract is in Scott MSS, Morgan State University, Baltimore.

11. D. B. Griswold to Scott, Sept. 15, 1915; Scott to JWJ, Aug. 3, 1915, in Scott MSS; Ira Champion to BTW, July 31, 1915, in BTWP.

12. Scott to Barker, Oct. 18, 1915; Nov. 6, 1915; and contract, Dec. 20, 1915, in Scott MSS.

13. A copy is in GPJC.

14. GPJ to curator, Powell Library, Oct. 24, 1968; *The Birth of a Race News,* July 1917; Oct. 1917, in GPJC.

15. Var., Oct. 12, 1917, 29; March 22, 1918, 58; *Billboard,* March 23, 1918, the latter a clipping in GPJC.

16. Var., Nov. 22, 1918, 50; Dec. 6, 1918, 38; *Exhibitors' Herald,* May 1919, 1761; *Billboard,* Dec. 14, 1918; and undated clippings, in GPJC.

17. Memoir of Johnson, in GPJC.

18. Edith J. R. Isaacs, *The Negro in the American Theatre* (New York, 1947), 280; Ramsaye, *Million and One Nights,* lxix, chap. I; Tom Fletcher, *100 Years of the Negro in Show Business* (New York, 1954), 205; Belcher, "Negro in the Evolution of the American Theatre," 163; AA, Sept. 18, 1915; Vinton R. Shepard, ed., *The Ohio Nisi Prius Reports;* . . . *New Series,* XIX (Cincinnati, 1917), 476.

19. CE, July 31, 1915.

20. CE, survey, 1915-20.

21. CE, Aug. 22, 1915; Dec. 11, 1915; Jan. 1, 1916; June 24, 1924. H. L. Mencken to JWJ, Aug. 8, 1919, in JWJC.

22. Typescript synopsis, in GPJC.

23. Tony Langston to GPJ, Aug. 10, 1916; penciled on back: "proposition accepted. Make own contracts," in GPJC.

24. CE, Oct. 14, 1916. The firefight came at the height of Mexican-American tension, with America caught between German intrigue and Mexican outrage at the presence of 6600 American troops who had pursued Pancho Villa into Chihuahua. A dozen Americans died. See Barbara W. Tuchman, *The Zimmermann Telegram* (New York, 1958), 97.

25. Langston to GPJ, Oct. 10, 1916; clippings, dated July 1917; and typescript memoir, in GPJC.

26. CD and other clippings and typescript memoir, in GPJC.

27. As expressed here it is Bill Foster to Noble Johnson, June 1, in GPJC.

28. Based on GPJ's typescript memoir, in GPJC.

29. Langston to GPJ, Oct. 23, 1916; CD clipping, May 12, 1917; Pollard's defense to Johnson: "we proved to the public that colored players can put over good comedy without any of that crap shooting, chicken stealing, razor display, watermelon eating stuff" is in Pollard to GPJ, June 12, 1918; Monumental Pictures to "Friend," n. d., all in GPJC.

30. Langston to GPJ, Nov. 24, 1916; Oct. 23, 1916; May 24, 1917; CD, July 14, 1917, and other clippings, in GPJC.

31. "Information Blank (Theatres)," in GPJC.

32. CE, Jan. 21, 1921.

33. GPJ to Charles S. Hart, Director of Division of Films, Committee on Public Information, copy, Aug. 12, 1918, in GPJC.

34. "——— to see Scott," memo, in GPJC.

35. "A Report of a Trip Made to Chicago August 27 to September 6, 1918, in an Effort to Interest Eastern Capital . . . ," typescript in GPJC. See also J. J. Rabinowitz (Reol) to R. R. Moton, Tuskegee, Nov. 14, 1921, in Moton Papers, Tuskegee Institute (lent by Prof. John Wiseman, Frostburg State College).

36. On newsfilm see D. Ireland Thomas to Clarence Brooks, March 17, 1919; facsimile purchase order; Var. clipping, Dec. 6, 1918; on grosses, Thomas to Brooks, July 8, 1919; E. L. Cummings, Reol's Southern booker, to GPJ, June 21, 1921; on Jews, GPJ to Robert L. Vann, March 27, 1920, in GPJC.

37. Noble Johnson to GPJ, pencil, n. d., in GPJC.

38. Robert L. Vann to J. T. Smith, Jan. 29, 1920; Vann to GPJ, April 16, 1920, in GPJC.

39. GPJ to Vann, July 20, 1920; Vann to GPJ, July 21, 1920; GPJ to Harry Pace, copy, July 14, 1920; holograph memoir, "A Million Dollar Negro Film Deal Fell Through," all in GPJC.

40. Var., April 26, 1918, 45; Feb. 11, 1921, 9.

41. *Spying the Spy* (Ebony, 1918), in LC.

42. Tony Langston to GPJ [1918?]; Democracy Photoplay Corporation brochure; letter fragment filed with Delight Film Corp.; MPW, Aug. 10, 1918, in GPJC.

43. Democracy Film Corp. file includes shot list of black troops. Typescript memo, 1918; Frederick Douglass Co. brochure; Jack Johnson card file, Blackburn Velde Productions; Colored Feature Photoplays card file; *Los Angeles Times*, July 21, 1919; *Los Angeles Express*, July 21, 1919; and undated clippings; "Bookings in Justice Film" file; Unique Film Co. brochure; Toussaint Co. card file; *Sport of the Gods* card file; *Green Eyed Monster* file; *A Giant of His Race* file; Ker-Mar Producing Corp. file, in GPJC. Thomas, *Selznick*, 20-21.

44. NYA, May 24, 1917; Oct. 29, 1921.

45. Harry Gant budget, April 13, 1920; Charles P. Bailey to Gentlemen, March 6, 1920; *Oakland Post, California Voice*, AN clippings, all in GPJC.

46. "Los Angeles Showing (Trinity Auditorium) January 24, 1921," in GPJC.

47. *By Right of Birth* script continuity, June 1921; typescript memoir, in GPJC; CD, July 9, 1921; Sept. 17, 1921.

48. Typescript memoir, in GPJC.

49. Trinity Show accounts, in GPJC. A few feet of the film survive in AFI and in author's collection.

50. Most studios computed the breakeven point at two, or two-and-a-half times the "negative cost," that is, the final cost of production before distribution costs were added on.

51. Account sheets for 1921, in GPJC.

52. Interviews with Ted Toddy (telephone), Jan. 1971; Ben Rinaldo, and Bert Sternbach, both June 1970.

53. Account sheets for 1921; typescript memoir; shooting script for *The Black Americans*, apparently shortened and retitled *A Day with the Famous 10th*, in GPJC. CE, June 24, 1921.

54. List of companies in *Western Dispatch* (Omaha), n. d., Var., March 1919; May 1922, in GPJC; Thomas R. Cripps, "Movies in the Ghetto B. P. (Before Poitier)," *Negro Digest*, Feb. 1969, 24; interview with Anita Bush (telephone), Dec. 1971.

Notes to Chapter Four

1. Robert M. Fogelson, *The Fragmented Metropolis: Los Angeles, 1850-1930* (Cambridge, 1967), chap. I-II.

2. Var., July 7, 1916, 22; July 21, 1916, 17; Dec. 1, 1916, 22; Oct. 19, 1917, 31.

3. Gertrude Jobes, *Motion Picture Empire* (Hamden, Conn., 1966), 161-91; Var., Dec. 21, 1917, 50; Dec. 28, 1917, 234; March 22, 1918, 56; March 21, 1919, 27; Feb. 25, 1921, 47; July 16, 1920, 39; Oct. 8, 1920. 47; Jan. 7, 1921.

4. Ben M. Hall, *The Best Remaining Seats: The Story of the Golden Age of the Movie Palace* (New York, 1916), 16, 32; Abel Green and Joe Laurie, Jr., *Show Biz from Vaude to Video* (Garden City, N.Y., 1952), 144. On the appeal to the middle class I am grateful for demographic data provided by Russell L. Merritt.

5. Benjamin B. Hampton, *History of the American Film Industry from Its Beginnings to 1931* (New York, 1931, 1970), 167, 175ff, 204, 232.

6. Var., Nov. 23, 1923, 18; Jimmy Lloyd Ball, "Distribution of Theatrical Motion Pictures: The History and Contemporary Practices of Independent Producers" (unpublished M.A. thesis, University of Southern California, 1965), 14-19, 22, 26, 32, 36, 168, 210, 227; Hampton, *History of the American Film Industry*, chap. XII, 255.

7. Hampton, *History of the American Film Industry*, 338-42; Lewis Jacobs, *The*

Rise of the American Film: A Critical History with an Essay, Experimental Cinema in America, 1921-1947 (New York, 1939, 1967), 295-97.

8. Raymond Moley, *The Hays Office* (Indianapolis, 1945), 20-21, 240-243; Hampton, *History of the American Film Industry*, 297-99; Bob Thomas, *Selznick* (New York, 1970), 33, 49.

9. Of the many accounts of such men the most famous is Lillian Ross, *Picture; A Story About Hollywood* (New York, 1952), which detailed the work of Gottfried Reinhardt on the set of John Huston's *The Red Badge of Courage*. Bob Thomas, *King Cohn: The Life and Times of Harry Cohn* (New York, 1967), 142 (quoted); W. W. Hodgkinson, "Better Movies," *Collier's* (Dec. 16, 1922), 11-12; *Hallelujah!* pressbooks, NYPL. Var., Aug. 22, 1928, 7, reported that Vidor's film had been a pet project based on "his own observations in Texas and elsewhere on the everyday life of the Negro." A print of *Borderline* is in GEH. On Macpherson see *Close-Up*, V, 2 (Aug. 1929). Also based on correspondence between the author, Macpherson, and Winifred Bryher, Nov. 1968.

10. Var., Nov. 22, 1939, 4.

11. *Studio Tour of Inceville* (Thomas Ince, n. d., directed by Hunt Stromberg;), in LC.

12. Rudi Blesh, *Keaton* (New York, 1966), 153; Theodore Huff, *Charlie Chaplin* (New York, 1951), 52; Dagmar Godowsky, *The Lives of Dagmar Godowsky: First Person Plural* (New York, 1958), 84; on Baker: clipping in GPJC; Lillian Ross and Helen Ross, *The Player: The Profile of an Art* (New York, 1962), interview with Robert Preston, 404-5, 408; Louella O. Parsons, *The Gay Illiterate* (Garden City, 1944), 84; Fred Lawrence Guiles, *Norma Jean* (New York, 1969), 16. Even the gossip surrounding the death of director F. W. Murnau recapitulated the connection between sex and race in Hollywood: see Kenneth Anger, *Hollywood Babylon* (Phoenix, Ariz., 1965), 186ff.

13. R. J. Minney, *Hollywood by Starlight* (London, 1935), 130-31 (on Chaplin); Sylvia, *Hollywood Undressed: Masseuse of the Stars* (New York, 1931), 19 (on Colman); Robert C. Cannom, *Van Dyke and the Mythical City, Hollywood* (n. p., 1948), 137 (on Van Dyke); Colleen Moore, *Silent Star* (New York, 1968), 257; Joe Pasternak, *Easy the Hard Way* (London, 1956), 74; Marie Dressler, *The Life Story of an Ugly Duckling* (New York, 1924), 96; Harmony Haynes, "Mae West's Personal Maid Tells All!" *Hollywood*, 1, Jan. 1934, 32-33, 58 (Libby Taylor); Kenneth Anger, *Hollywood Babylon*, 185ff (on F. W. Murnau and his Filipino driver); Pola Negri, *Memoirs of a Star* (New York, 1970), 235.

14. Anita Loos, *A Girl Like I* (New York, 1966), 8-19 (on Hollywood Hotel); Adolph Menjou and M. M. Musselman, *It Took Nine Tailors* (New York, 1948), 79 (on housing); Margaret L. Talmadge, *The Talmadge Sisters: Norma, Constance, and Natalie* (Philadelphia, 1924), 116 (on housing); George Sanders, *Memoirs of a Professional Cad* (New York, 1960), 138-39, 131-32 (on luxury); Jane Ardmore, *The Self-Enchanted: Mae Murray, Image of an Era* (New York, 1930), (on night life); Rob Wagner, *Film Folk* (New York, 1918), 87 (on set); Anthony Quinn, *The Original Sin: A Self-Portrait* (Boston, 1972), chaps. XVI-XVII.

15. Cannom, *Van Dyke and the Mythical City*, 151 (on Washington); Shipp, *Mack Sennett: King of Comedy*, 233 (on the cemetery); Ali Hubert, *Hollywood: Legende und Wirklichkeit* (Leipzig, 1930), 230, 244, 252, 267 (on McPherson); Var., Jan. 7, 1942, 62, and Jaik Rosenstein, *Hollywood Legman* (Los Angeles, 1950), 151 (on racial humor); Robert Lewis Taylor, *W. C. Fields: His Follies and Fortunes* (Garden City, N.Y., 1949), 339; Jill Schary Zimmer, *With a Cast of Thousands: A Hollywood Childhood* (New York, 1963), 63; Dorothy Spensley, "A Few Stars Unwrap Their Favorite Rastus-and-Mandy Stories" (1929), ZC, is typical of a genre of fan magazine story.

16. Hubert, *Hollywood*, 230, 244, 252, 267; Irving Crump, *Our Moviemakers* (New York, 1940), 134; Martin and Osa Johnson, "Cannibals and Movies," *Asia* (May 1921), 425.

17. Ethel Waters with Charles Samuels, *His Eye Is on the Sparrow: An Auto-
biography* (Garden City, N.Y., 1951), 198-99; maid quoted in Kevin Brownlow,
The Parade's Gone By (New York, 1968), 36; Louis Sobel, *The Longest Street*
(New York, 1968), 268.

18. Griffith and Bitzer Papers, in MOMA. Associated Motion Picture Schools,
How to Write Motion Picture Plays (Chicago, 1913), Lesson VII; see also Mervyn
Leroy, *It Takes More Than Talent* (New York, 1953), 75.

19. Jack Warner, *My First Hundred Years in Hollywood* (New York, 1964),
62-63.

20. Var., May 30, 1923, 5.

21. Bertha Westbrook Reid, *Wallace Reid: His Life Story* (New York, 1924),
54-55, one of many biographies with Southern traces.

22. Southern anecdotes appear in Cecil B. DeMille, ed. by Donald Hayne, *Autobiography* (Englewood Cliffs, N.J., 1959), 359, 367; Hart, *My Life East and West*,
55, 89, 140; Bob Thomas, *Thalberg: Life and Legend* (Garden City, N.Y., 1969),
95; Brian Connell, *Knight Errant: A Biography of Douglas Fairbanks, Jr.* (Garden
City, N.Y., 1955), 37; Arthur Mayer, *The Story of the Movies from Long Chase
to Chaise Lounge* (New York, 1953), 95-96; Beth Day, *This Was Hollywood*
(London, 1960), 36; John McCabe, *Mr. Laurel and Mr. Hardy* (New York, 1966),
6; Alice M. Williamson, *Alice in Movieland* (London, [1927]), 67; Boyce House,
How I Took Hollywood by Storm (Dallas, 1942), 10-11; Bosley Crowther, *The
Lion's Share: The Story of an Entertainment Empire* (New York, 1957), 290;
Cannom, *Van Dyke and the Mythical City*, 137; Jesse Lasky, *I Blow My Own
Horn* (New York, 1957), 183 (on Katz); Var., Oct. 13, 1922, 46; March 15, 1923, 27
(on Lynch). Kuykendall attended E. V. Richards's Saenger Managers' School, Bay
St Louis, Miss., 1927; Richards ephemera, Drama Collection, University of Texas
at Austin.

23. Salka Viertel, *The Kindness of Strangers* (New York, 1969), 161, 175, 211;
John Bainbridge, *Garbo* (New York, 1961), 136-37; Edgar Wallace, *My Hollywood Diary* (London, n. d.), 195; Clarence Winchester, *An Innocent in Hollywood* (London, 1934), 23, 134; Errol Flynn, *My Wicked, Wicked Ways* (New
York, 1959), 213-15.

24. Ronald Reagan with Richard G. Hubler, *Where's the Rest of Me?* (New
York, 1965), 8, 64; Fred Astaire, *Steps in Time* (New York, 1969), 49.

25. *National News Gravure*, July 5, 1930, clipping, in AAS; *Chicago Bee*, Feb.
15, 1931, in GPJC; Crowther, *Lion's Share*, 169-70; Day, *This was Hollywood*, 59-
63; Cannom, *Van Dyke and the Mythical City*, 227.

26. Blaise Cendrars, *Hollywood: La Mecque du Cinema* (Paris, 1936), 15; Var.,
June 19, 1929, 55; CE, Aug. 26, 1921; Jan. 14, Feb. 11, March 11, 1922.

27. PC, Aug. 1, 25; Sept. 29; Dec. 15, 1923, for quotations; AN, Sept. 28, 1927;
NYT, July 24, 1968, clipping in PAC; "Hollywood's First Negro Movie Queen,"
Hue, March 1954, 40-42; CE, Oct. 14, 1927; Oct. 12, Nov. 5, March 15, 1929; Var.,
Feb. 8, 1927; interviews with Carolynne Snowden, Jimmie Smith, and Lawrence
LaMar, June 1970.

28. Interviews with Snowden, LaMar, Thomas Southern, Bill Walker, Los
Angeles, June 1970.

29. Interview with Lloyd Shackelford (telephone), April 1972.

30. Clippings and abstracts, in GPJC.

31. Clippings, in GPJC, especially PC, Oct. 1929; *Western Informant*, 1937.

32. Var., Sept. 19, 1928; Feb. 6, 1929; interview with Jimmie Smith, June 1970,
Los Angeles.

33. AN, Dec. 5, Aug. 8, Oct. 24, 1928; May 23, 1929. For a year's survey of
black activity and of Central Casting see Var., Jan. 16, 1929, 7.

34. Var. July 31, 1929, 10; May 22, 1929; AN, Nov. 6, 1929; April 23, May 7,
1930; March 6, 20, April 2, 1929; interview with Etta Moten (telephone), Nov.
1970.

35. AN, Aug. 13, 1930; July 9, 1930.

36. Clipping from *Silhouette*, in GPJC.
37. Muse's résumé and other correspondence with the author. Quotations from AN, April 23, 1923; Sept. 11, 1929; also May 7, 1930; April 13, 27, 1932; Aug. 8, 1933. For an NAACP officer's view that many blacks did not wish to see "what they consider lower phases of Negro life" dramatized, see JWJ to Mary Ruta, copy, May 7, 1932, in JWJC. For another black sideline see Irving Clark, "Leading a Dog's Life," *Kennel Review* (Dec. 1933), clipping on Noble Johnson in GPJC. Mrs. Anna Mary Walters, Registrar, The Dickinson School of Law, Carlisle, Pa., to Thomas Cripps, July 18, 1973.
38. Survey of CE and LAS, especially CE, Jan. 24, Oct. 30, 1952; May 5, 1949; Oct. 26, 1950; Nov. 19, 1953; LAS, May 8, 1947; Jan. 9, 1947 for enduring traits. *Silhouette* clipping in GPJC.
39. Interview with François André, June 1970; AA, May 26, 1945 and clippings on Fetchit, in GPJC; Var., April 2, 1930, 18. A good example of the tension between West and East was radio's *Amos 'n' Andy Show*, a broadly comic, sometimes touching serial of black life created by two facile white men. It was popular with both races, perhaps because of its locale in the mind's eye rather than the visual reality of the movie screen. But Bishop A. J. Walls complained of its blindness to the density of black life. Bert Williams, he wrote, had been "the pathetic symbol of the cramped powers of crushed perceptions and immeasurable resources and aspirations of a race waiting for a chance," while Amos 'n' Andy were no more than "a white man's backward look." See Walls, "What About Amos 'n' Andy?" *Abbott's Monthly*, Dec. 1930, 38-40, 72; see also Var., March 26, 1930; PC, Oct. 14, 1933.
40. See Thomas R. Cripps, "The Myth of the Southern Box Office: A Factor in Racial Stereotyping in American Movies, 1920-1940," in James C. Curtis and Lewis L. Gould, eds., *The Black Experience: Selected Essays* (Austin, Texas, 1970), 116-44.
41. Survey of trade papers in Cripps, "Myth of Southern Box Office."
42. Var., Oct. 5, 1927, 9, and Feb. 23, 1932, 23.
43. Richards Pressbooks, Drama Collection, University of Texas.
44. Derived from a survey of Var. by Alma Taliaferro Cripps.
45. Var., Aug. 12, 1925, 8 and Cripps, "Myth of Southern Box Office."
46. Var., May 13, 1925, 25. On black theater see John Selby, *Beyond Civil Rights* (Cleveland, 1966); Edith J. R. Isaacs, *The Negro in the American Theatre* (New York, 1947); Loften Mitchell, *Black Drama: The Story of the American Negro in the Theatre* (New York, 1967).
47. Var., Dec. 1, 1926, 4; June 14, 1923, 17; Nov. 17, 1922, 2; Jan. 18, 1928, 23; Jan. 29, 1935, 14; Jan. 26, 1938, 57; May 15, 1929, 3.
48. Derived from Cripps, "Myth of the Southern Box Office."
49. For minstrels see *Billboard*, Oct. 2, 1915, 20, 43, 50; Var., Jan. 5, 1923, 1; Feb. 19, 1930, 2; April 2, 1930, 19.
50. For an anthropological approach to isolation see Hortense Powdermaker, *Hollywood: The Dream Factory: An Anthropologist Looks at the Movie-Makers* (Boston, 1950); Leo C. Rosten, *The Movie Colony; The Movie Makers* (New York, 1941); Leo A. Handel, *Hollywood Looks at Its Audience: A Report on Film Audience Research* (Urbana, 1950); Margaret Farrand Thorp, *America at the Movies* (London, 1946); and with special reference to the South, Peter A. Soderbergh, "Hollywood and the South, 1930-1960," *Mississippi Quarterly*, Winter 1965-66, 15-19.

Notes to Chapter Five

1. E. M. W. Tillyard, *The Elizabethan World Picture* (New York, n. d.), 99.
2. For pre-war change see Henry F. May, *The End of American Innocence: A*

Study of the First Years of Our Own Time, 1912-1917 (Chicago, 1959, 1964); Oscar Cargill, *Intellectual America: Ideas On the March* (New York, 1941). The quotations are from Paul A. Carter, *The Twenties in America* (New York, 1968), 11-12, 24; see also Milton Plesur, *The 1920's: Problems and Paradoxes* (Boston, 1969), Part V; and George E. Mowry, *The Twenties: Fords, Flappers, and Fanatics* (Englewood Cliffs, N.J., 1963). Sample monographs are Lewis Atherton, *Main Street on the Middle Border* (Bloomington, Ind., 1954); Humbert S. Nelli, *Italians in Chicago, 1880-1930: A Study in Ethnic Mobility* (New York, 1970), chap. V-VI; Dale Kramer, *Chicago Renaissance: The Literary Life in the Mid-West, 1900-1930* (New York, 1966); Gilbert Osofsky, *Harlem: The Making of a Ghetto, 1890-1930* (New York, 1968).

3. Editorial in Elliott Rudwick, *W. E. B. DuBois: Propagandist of Negro Protest* (New York, 1960, 1968), 238.

4. Thomas, *Thalberg,* 19; Var., Feb. 11, 1921, 45; Edward Wagenknecht, *The Movies in the Age of Innocence* (Norman, Okla., 1962), 63-67, 74, chap. III, 167, 179; Alexander Walker, *Stardom: The Hollywood Phenomenon* (London, 1970), Part III.

5. NYT, April 16, 1924; June 6, 1924; Raymond Moley, *The Hays Office* (Indianapolis, 1945), 25-43, 240; Arthur Knight, *The Liveliest Art: A Panoramic History of the Movies* (New York, 1957), 115.

6. Jacobs, *Rise of the American Film,* 167-70; Murray Schumach, *The Face on the Cutting Room Floor: The Story of Movie and Television Censorship* (New York, 1964), 85; Warner, *My First Hundred Years,* 131, 136, 119; Bosley Crowther, *Hollywood Rajah: The Life and Times of Louis B. Mayer* (New York, 1960), 59, 70, 78; [Upton Sinclair], *Upton Sinclair Presents William Fox* (Los Angeles, 1933), 97; Phil Koury, *Yes, Mr. DeMille* (New York, 1959), 94, 117; Thomas, *Thalberg,* 113; Day, *This Was Hollywood,* 29, 45; Glendon Allvine, *The Greatest Fox of Them All* (New York, 1969), 81-86; Norman Zierold, *The Moguls* (New York, 1969), 256-57.

7. Wagner, *Film Folk,* 47; *The Big Parade* (MGM, 1925), script in Feldman Library, AFI, Los Angeles.

8. For example, Lester Walton in NYA, May 4, 1918, Nov. 11, 1918.

9. On Negro consciousness see note 32. For white advertising see NYA, March 3, 1920; June 14, 1917. H. L. Mencken to JWJ, Aug. 8, 1919, in JWJC.

10. NYA, June 14, 1917. See also NYA, Dec. 7, 1916; Jan. 4, 1917; Feb. 2, 1917; March 8, 1917; April 12, 26, 1917; June 6, 1917; Jan. 12, 1918; April 6, 1918; Aug. 24, 1918.

11. MPN, April 26, 1913, 24, 35; Esenwein and Leeds, *Writing,* 250, 285; Bertsch, *How to Write,* 171.

12. *The Crisis* (Selig, 1915), fragment, in LC; Var., Oct. 6, 1916, 25.

13. MPM, April 1917, 13-14; MPW, Aug. 8, 1914, 813; MPN, Dec. 20, 1913, 42; MPW, May 31, 1913, 953-54.

14. *The Kaffir's Gratitude* (Biograph, 1915), in LC. MPW, May 18, 1912, 614; June 21, 1913, 1251, 1275-76; June 28, 1913, 1369; Var., Sept. 20, 1918, 47; Robert W. Fenton, *The Big Swingers: Edgar Rice Burroughs, 1875-1950; Tarzan, 1912-* (Englewood Cliffs, N.J., 1967), 45, 62, 70-75, 80, 84-87, 10; Gabe Essoe, *Tarzan of the Movies: A Pictorial History of . . . Burroughs' Legendary Hero* (Secaucus, N.J., 1973), 1-15.

15. Fenton, *Big Swingers,* 62, 45.

16. NYT, Jan. 28, 1918; Oct. 14, 1918; Var., June 18, 1920, 29; Oct. 22, 1920, 43; *The Adventures of Tarzan,* chap. V (Great Western-Weiss Brothers, 1920), in LC; review of *The Return of Tarzan, Photoplay,* Sept. 1920, 74; Lahue, *Continued Next Week,* 88-98, 101-2; Essoe, *Tarzan,* 16-62.

17. *A Night in the Jungle* (Selig, 1915) in BFI; Var., Oct. 27, 1916, 28; June 6, 1919, 29; Oct. 8, 1920, 42; Feb. 22, 1923, 42.

18. Var., Nov. 10, 1916, 25; Dec. 8, 1916, 29; Feb. 1, 1918, 42; March 22, 1918, 4; June 15, 1917, 27; Aug. 16, 1918, 38; Oct. 4, 1918, 47; June 27, 1921, 35; Dec. 15,

1922, 42; April 5, 1923, 37, 36; July 7, 1923, 24. "Love conquers the pride of race" and other homilies blunted messages of tolerance. See *The Unbeliever* (Kleine, 1918), *The Tiger's Coat* (Dial, 1920?), and others, in LC. Conversely, *Billy and the Big Stick* (LC) used Haitians to mask race conflict.

19. *The Thief of Bagdad* (United Artists, 1924); Ralph Hancock and Letitia Fairbanks, *Douglas Fairbanks: The Fourth Musketeer* (New York, 1953), 204-6; Var., March 24, 1924, 26; July 16, 1924, 22; June 4, 1924, 26; Jan. 28, 1925, Feb. 11, 1925, clipping; June 15, 1927, 17.

20. *A Fool There Was* (Fox, 1915), in BFI; Allvine, *Greatest Fox of Them All*, 56; Zierold, *Moguls*, 219-22.

21. Var., Oct. 20, 1916, 27; Ramsaye, *Million and One Nights*, 704-6; Jacobs, *Rise of the American Film*, 201, 214; Rotha, *Film Till Now*, 209; Ezra Goodman, *The Fifty Year Decline and Fall of Hollywood* (New York, 1961), 361.

22. On Indians see Var., July 14, 1916, 19; April 6, 1917, 25; Aug. 3, 1917, 24; Nov. 2, 1917, 49; Feb. 2, 1917, 24; March 29, 1918, 46; Jan. 10, 1919, 45; Jan. 24, 1919, 45; Nov. 26, 1920, 34; Feb. 15, 1923, 43; Sept. 16, 1925, 40; Oct. 21, 1925, 34.

23. Var., April 20, 1927, 15; Aug. 7, 1929, 185; DeMille, *Autobiography*, 279, 282; Koury, *Yes, Mr. DeMille*, 118-27.

24. Credits in GPJC; interviews with GPJ, Carolynne Snowden, and Jimmie Smith; correspondence between Clarence Muse and author; taped interview: Raymond Lee and Mme Sul-te-Wan.

25. Résumés, flyers, and letterheads in GPJC. Johnson apparently never identified his race to white reporters even as blacks took pride in him. His available films include *The Leopard Woman*, *The Four Horsemen of the Apocalypse*, *Ben Hur*, *The Sea Beast*, *The Ten Commandments*, *King of Kings*, and *Vanity*.

26. See Chapter III and PC, July 14, 1923, and Aug. 4, 1923.

27. *Nanook of the North* (Revillon Frères, 1923), in Enoch Pratt Free Library; *Moana* (Zukor-Lasky, 1925), in MOMA; Richard Griffith, *The Worlds of Robert Flaherty* (New York, 1953), 36-44; Arthur Calder-Marshall, *The Innocent Eye: The Life of Robert J. Flaherty* (New York, 1963), 15-36.

28. Herbert J. Seligmann, "Moana of the South Seas," *Arts*, Nov. 1925, 255-59; Lasky, *I Blow My Own Horn*, 188, 203; Griffith, *Flaherty*, chap. II; Calder-Marshall, *Innocent Eye*, chaps. IX, X, 123; NYT, Jan. 25, 1925; Crowther, *Hollywood Rajah*, 135; Thomas, *Thalberg*, 185; Cannom, *Van Dyke*, 159-77.

29. *Chang* (Zukor-Lasky, 1927), in LC; Var., Oct. 12, 1927, 5; Edward K. Graham, "The Hampton Student Strike of 1927: A Case Study in Student Protest," *American Scholar*, Autumn 1969, 668; interview: author and G. James Fleming, Morgan State University; Var., Aug. 29, 1928, 5; Nov. 24, 1926, 18; March 30, 1927, 15; June 1, 1927, 24 (quotation); Oct. 19, 1927, 13; *Close-Up*, Oct. 1928, 57; Lasky, *I Blow My Own Horn*, 188-89.

30. *Mr. Miller's Economics* synopsis in Aitken Papers; Var., Feb. 14, 1919, 51; *The Cohens and the Kellys in Atlantic City* (Universal, 1927), screened in Corner Theatre, Baltimore, 1971.

31. Ann Charters, *Nobody: The Story of Bert Williams* (London, 1970), 130.

32. *Fish* (Biograph, 1916) and *A Natural Born Gambler* (Biograph, 1916), in Killiam Shows. Var., Feb. 9, 1917, 18, July 27, 1917, 24, and others reported Williams to be writing and directing. Noble, *Negro in Films*, 31, alleged that Williams's career began and ended with *Darktown Jubilee* which caused a riot at its Brooklyn opening.

33. *Jubilo* (Goldwyn, 1919), in MOMA.

34. *Some White Hope* (Vitagraph, 1915) and *The Night I Fought Jack Johnson* (Vitagraph, 1913), in BFI; *Pa's Family Tree* (E. & R. Jungle Film Co., [1916]), in LC.

35. *Hoodoo Ann* (Triangle-Fine Arts, 1916); *Manslaughter* (Zukor-Lasky, 1922), both in LC; *Mr. Miller's Economics* synopsis.

36. *By Stork Delivery* (Triangle, 1916), synopsis in Aitken Papers; Var., Feb. 14, 1919, 21; Dec. 27, 1918, 115; Dec. 20, 1918, 36; *Me and My Dog* (Roach, 1927),

in BFI; Monroe N. Work, ed., *Negro Yearbook* (Tuskegee Institute, 1925); AN, Sept. 26, 1928; Var., May 19, 1926, 20; Sept. 26, 1928, 11; Sept. 19, 1928, 21; Aug. 15, 1928, 22; Jan. 28, 1928, 20. William K. Everson, *The Films of Hal Roach* (New York, 1971), 35-36, disagrees.

37. Quoted in Walker, *Celluloid Sacrifice*, 28-29; Var., June 21, 1926, 1, on Porgy.

38. *The Ruby of Kishmoor* synopsis, Kleine files, in LC; *The Lion's Mate* (Selig, 1924), in BFI; *The Three Must Get Theirs* (United Artists, 1922), in LC.

39. Bits of black military film in National Archives, Baker Collection, and LC. MPM, March 1919, 74; Var., Jan. 3, 1919, 38.

40. Var. Sept. 13, 1923, 28; Jan. 28, 1928, 16; *The Jazz Bout* (No. 6 in "Flying Fists" series, 1924), in BFI.

41. For more or less conventional Negro roles: Var., Oct. 20, 1916, 27; March 25, 1925, 38; Jan. 27, 1922, 39; March 3, 1926, 38; July 22, 1921, 36; May 20, 1921, 41; June 20, 1922, 32; *Change of Spirit* (Biograph, 1912), in LC. New departures include: *Two in One* (Pathé, 1924), in LC; *California Straight Ahead* (Universal, 1925), in Yale Film Collection; *Seven Chances* (MGM, 1925), in which a slow-moving black messenger, in contrast to the woman, is barely noticed; Var., May 27, 1921, 35; May 16, 1919, 50; Sept. 18, 1922, 41; April 13, 1927, 22; Aug. 4, 1922, 36.

42. Var., Oct. 27, 1922, 40.

43. *One Exciting Night* (United Artists, 1922), in MOMA. Recent critics ignore the Kaffir and fix on Romeo. See Hughes and Meltzer, *Black Magic*, 303; Moss, "Negro in Films," 137-38; *Black History, Lost, Stolen, or Strayed?* (McGraw-Hill Films, 1968); NYT, Oct. 24, 1922; Kenneth W. Munden, exec. ed., *The American Film Institute Catalogue of Motion Pictures Produced in the United States*, Vol. F2 (New York, 1970), 568.

44. CD, April 1, 1922; E. Harry Martin to Griffith, Oct. 4, 1923, in Griffith MSS; Jacobs, *Rise of the American Film*, 392-93; Var., Dec. 1, 1922, 36.

45. *The White Rose* (United Artists, 1923), in MOMA; Jacobs, *Rise of the American Film*, 392-93; *Abraham Lincoln* (United Artists, 1930), in MOMA.

46. *His Darker Self* (G and H Pictures, W. W. Hodkinson, 1924), in BFI; Munden, *AFI Catalogue*, F2, 351. Alfred Grey to Griffith, July 26, 1923; Grey to Earl Hammons, July 20, 1923; Griffith to Hammons, copy, March 9, 1925; Jack White to Grey, July 7, 1925; White to Grey, wire, Sept. 10, 1925; Hammons to Grey, Sept. 15, 1925, in Griffith MSS. NYT, March 26, 1924; Var., May, 30, 1923, 1; June 14, 1923, 19; June 21, 1923, 18; July 28, 1923, 32; April 30, 1924, 5; Aug. 30, 1923, 32; May 26, 1924 (xerox); PC, Dec. 29, 1923. Noble, the eventual director, had directed the horrendous *The Birth of a Race*.

47. W. W. Hodkinson, "Better Picture," *Collier's*, Dec. 16, 1922, 11; AA, Dec. 20, 1924; PC, Dec. 29, 1923; "Pot Pourri," *Opportunity*, Feb. 1924, 61.

48. Locke, *New Negro*, ix-xvi (Robert Hayden's introduction to 1968 edition); Work, *Negro Yearbook*, index.

49. AN, Dec. 6, 1922; April 4, 25, 1923; May 23, 1923; June 13, 1923; July 16, 1923; Nov. 7, 1923; March 25, 1923, examples of black concern.

50. NYA, June 14, 1917; NYT, May 7, 1921; Nov. 7, 1921.

51. CD, June 23, 1923.

52. AN, July 22, 1925; Sept. 23, 1925; Aug. 5, 1925; NYT, May 23, 1921; Aug. 10, 24, 1921; April 9, 1923; Aug. 2, 1923; Carl Van Vechten to JWJ, Oct. 31, 1925, in JWJC; George S. Schuyler, *Black and Conservative* (New Rochelle, N.Y., 1966), 139-40.

53. NYT, Dec. 6, 1922; PC, April 5, 1924.

54. Var., Sept. 3, 1920, 4; Oct. 8, 1920, 3.

55. NAACPR, G-157 file, Nov. 2-22, 1920; Var., March 25, 1921, 47 (KKK); April 22, 1925, 44 (Woods).

56. NYT, Oct. 12, 1924 (Miss.); Oct. 13, 1924 (*Cannibal Island*); Dec. 30, 1924 (*Dixie Handicap*).

57. Irene Castle, as told to Bob and Wanda Duncan, *Castles in the Air* (Garden City, N.Y., 1958), 145ff; Wilson's letter in Ferdinand Lundberg, *Imperial Hearst: A Social Biography* (New York, 1936), 241. Kalton C. Lahue, *Continued Next Week: A History of the Moving Picture Serial* (Norman, Okla., 1964), 48; United States Congress, Senate, *Brewing and Liquor Interests and German and Bolshevik Propaganda* 66 Cong., 1st sess., Doc. 62 (Washington, 1919), II, 1675-76; James P. Mock and Cedric Larson, *Words That Won the War* (New York, 1939), 143-45, both cited in Jacobus Ten Broek, Edward N. Barnhart, and Floyd W. Matson, *Prejudice, War, and the Constitution* (Berkeley and Los Angeles, 1954, 1970), 139-40, 532, 668; W. A. Swanberg, *Citizen Hearst* (New York, 1961), 296-97; NYA, March 29, 1917; fragment of *Patria*, in MOMA; Var., Nov. 24, 1922, 34, 38.

58. On Asians: Var., Feb. 8, 1918, 41 (*Madame Jealousy*); Jan. 18, 1918, 43 (*Innocent*); Aug. 30, 1918, 38 (*A Japanese Nightingale*); Aug. 5, 1921, 26; March 18, 1921, 39; Jan. 21, 1921, 44; Aug. 23, 1923, 23 (*Drifting*); April 5, 1921, 40 (*Dream Street*); March 11, 1921, 32 (*Wing Toy*); Oct. 28, 1921, 34 (*The Cup of Life*); Sept. 23, 1921, 36 (*After Midnight*); April 22, 1921, 41 (*A Tale of Two Worlds*); Deems Taylor, Marcelene Peterson, and Bryant Hale, *A Pictorial History of the Movies* (New York, 1943), 85; Gish, *Movies, Mr. Griffith, and Me*, 217-27; Brownlow, *Parade's Gone By*, 80, 90, 93; Lahue, *Continued Next Week*, 48, 62, 94; on Chan in various media, Nye, *Unembarrassed Muse*, 229, 250, 257, 401; *Broken Blossoms* (United Artists, 1919), in BFI; *Heart of the Hills* and *The Mission of Dr. Foo* synopses in Kleine records, in LC.

59. Var., Oct. 26, 1917, 34 (*The Savage*); Oct. 28, 1925, 32-33 (*Strongheart*); *The Lost World* (First National, 1925); *The Dawnmaker* lobby sheet, in W. S. Hart Collection, in LC; John D. Hicks, *The Republican Ascendancy, 1921-1930*, "New American Nation" series (New York, 1960), 3; Harvey Wish, *Society and Thought in Modern America: A Social and Intellectual History of the American People from 1865* (New York, 1952, 1962), 515-16; John Collier, *Indians of the Americas: The Long Hope* (New York, 1947), 134-55; Hart, *My Life East and West*, 154; Olive Stokes Mix with Cedric Heath, *The Fabulous Tom Mix* (Englewood Cliffs, N.J., 1957), 141; Peter Bogdanovich, *John Ford* (Berkeley, 1962), 190ff; *The Iron Horse* (Fox, 1925), in MOMA; Daniel Blum, *A Pictorial History of the Silent Screen* (New York, 1953), 189, 272; George N. Fenin and William K. Everson, *The Western from Silents to Cinerama* (New York, 1962), 37-38; Allen Eyles, *The Western: An Illustrated Guide* (London, 1967), lists only one Indian actor by name; *Universal Monthly*, I (1924), 1-12, passim, for Hoot Gibson; Var., Nov. 17, 1922, 41 (Jack Hoxie's *Crow's Nest*); Oct. 20, 1926, 63 (McCoy); Munden, *AFI Catalogue Index*, F2; DeMille, *Autobiography*, 89, 303; Adolph Zukor with Dale Kramer, *The Public Is Never Wrong: My Fifty Years in the Motion Pictures* (New York, 1953), 122-23; Vardac, *Stage to Screen*, 218, 221; Brownlow, *Parade's Gone By*, 33.

60. For example, Chaplin's *The Immigrant* (United Artists, 1917), in Pratt Library; George Beban's *The Italian* (New York Motion Picture, 1915), in LC; Var., Oct. 11, 1918, 44 (*Tony America*); April 11, 1919, 55 (*Hearts of Men*); July 22, 1921, 36 (*Little Italy*); Dec. 23, 1921, 35 (*Vendetta*); Feb. 10, 1922, 34 (*Boomerang Bill*); Dec. 15, 1922, 40 (*Broken Chains*).

61. For sample comment and reviews, Var., June 4, 1920, 27; Aug. 3, 1927, 11; July 13, 1927, 22; Feb. 10, 1922, 35; Nov. 9, 1927, 19; Dec. 12, 1923, 38; Sept. 8, 1926, 4; Sept. 14, 1927, 4; Oct. 26, 1927, 24; Sept. 15, 1916, 25; Oct. 6, 1916, 25; June 6, 1920 (*Humoresque*); Aug. 31, 1921, 24; June 24, 1921, 34 (*The Golem*); Sept. 13, 1923, 28 (*Potash and Perlmutter*); Sept. 7, 1927, 21 (*Clancy's Kosher Wedding*); April 25, 1928, 28; Feb. 24, 1926, 42; Oct. 27, 1926, 68; Nov. 10, 1926, 14; April 13, 1927, 18; July 18, 1928, 4 (*Nize Baby*); May 2, 1929, 29 (*Mamma's Boy*); June 6, 1928, 22 (Irish societies); April 20, 1927, 15 (*King of Kings*). *Raggedy Rose* (Pathé, Roach, 1926), in Corner Theatre; *The Cohens and the Kellys in Atlantic City* (Universal, 1927), in Corner Theatre; *Abie's Irish Rose* (Zukor-Lasky, 1928), in BFI; *The Second Hundred Years* (Roach, 1927) and *Pardon Us*

(Roach, 1931); *Better Days* (Pacific Pictures, First Division Pictures, 1927), in Corner Theatre. MPM, Dec. 1916, 158 (*Irish Lass*); interview: John Ford and author, Los Angeles, June 1970; Bogdanovich, *Ford*, 24, 122; Judd L. Teller, *Strangers and Natives: The Evolution of the American Jew from 1921 to the Present* (New York, 1970), 23-24, 28, 32, 83, 94; Raymond Durgnat, *The Crazy Mirror: Hollywood Comedy and the American Image* (London, 1969), 102-3; Russel Nye, *The Unembarrassed Muse: The Popular Arts in America* (New York, 1970), 152, 196, 198; Green and Laurie, *Show Biz*, 293-94; Lasky, *I Blow My Own Horn*, 223; Taylor *et al.*, *Pictorial History of the Movies*, 209; *Frisco Sally Levy* pressbook, in PAC; DeMille, *Autobiography*, 279, 282; Koury, *Yes, Mr. DeMille*, 118-27.

Notes to Chapter Six

1. The quotation on Tom is in GPJ typescript. For a study of the barrenness of Southern myth for urbanites see Russell L. Merritt, "Dixon, Griffith, and Southern Legend," *Cinema Journal*, Fall 1972, 26-37. On 1920s see *Time-Life* eds., *1910-1920*, Vol. I in "This Fabulous Century: Sixty Years of American Life" (New York, 1969), 80 (quotation); F. Scott Fitzgerald, "Echoes of the Jazz Age," in Loren Baritz, *The Culture of the Twenties* (Indianapolis, 1970), 413-24; Carter, *Twenties in America*, 13, 22, 40, 46, 51, 63-64, 73, 88-89; John Hope Franklin, *From Slavery to Freedom: A History of Negro Americans* (New York, 1947, 1956, 1967), 486-512; Ralph J. Bunche, "The Programs of Organizations Devoted to the Improvement of the Status of the American Negro," in August Meier and Elliott Rudwick, eds., "The Making of Black America," Vol. II: *The Black Community in Modern America* (New York, 1969), 249; for local black protest, Emma Lou Thornbrough, "Segregation in Indiana During the Klan Era of the 1920s," 185-203; E. David Cronon, *Black Moses: The Story of Marcus Garvey and the Universal Negro Improvement Association* (Madison, Wisc., 1955), 170-201; for lily white progressiveism and blacks, Robert L. Zangrando, "The 'Organized Negro': The National Association for the Advancement of Colored People," in James C. Curtis and Lewis L. Gould, eds., *The Black Experience in America: Selected Essays* (Austin, Tex., 1970), 161; Alexander Saxton, "Race and the House of Labor," in Gary B. Nash and Richard Weiss, eds., *The Great Fear: Race in the Mind of America* (New York, 1970), 118; Richard Sherman, "The Harding Administration and the Negro: An Opportunity Lost," in Richard Resh, ed., *Black America: Accommodation and Confrontation in the Twentieth Century* (Lexington, Mass., 1969), 66-67; Harvey Deneroff, "A Historical Study of Early American Film Criticism: 1907-1915" (M. A. thesis, University of Southern California, 1968), 6-7, 12, 21, 27, 30ff, 37, 40, 56, 89.

2. Alphabetized files, in GPJC.

3. Résumé, letterheads, flyers, and GPJ to [Lincoln Co.], July 31, 1918 in GPJC; PC, July 14, 1923; Aug. 4, 1923, for early work. The trade press never revealed his identity; blacks never forgot it.

4. *A Devil Dancer* (Goldwyn-United Artists, 1927), in LC; sample reviews in Var., Nov. 9, 1927, 21; March 20, 1928, 27; Dec. 14, 1927, 26.

5. *West of Zanzibar* (MGM, 1929), in MOMA.

6. Var., Nov. 8, 1923, 20.

7. Griffith, *Flaherty*, chap. II; Calder-Marshall, *Innocent Eye*, chaps. IX-X; Crowther, *Hollywood Rajah*, 135; Thomas, *Thalberg*, 185; Cannom, *Van Dyke*, 159-77; *Close-Up*, Oct. 1928, 57 (*Four Feathers*).

8. *Ingagi* (Congo Picture Co., 1930), in LC; Var., April 16, 1930, 46; March 12, 1930, 55; May 6, 1931, 6; AN, Nov. 6, 1929; NYT, June 12, 1930.

9. AN, April 2, 1926.

10. *Vanity* (DeMille Productions, 1927), in LC.

11. NYT, July 24, 1968 (Fetchit Interview), clipping in PAC; NYT, Nov. 27, 1927; clippings in GPJC; Var., June 19, 1927, 22; interview: author and Carolynne Snowden, Los Angeles, June 1971.

12. Noble, *Negro in Films*, 30ff; Munden, *AFI Catalogue*, F2, 843; Var., Aug. 9, 1918, 32; Oct. 25, 1918, 25 (*When Do We Eat?*); Jan. 27, 1922, 40 (*Little Eva Ascends*); MPW, Oct. 24, 1925, 638 (*Uncle Tom's Gal*); *Uncle Tom's Cabin* (Vitagraph, 1914), in BFI.

13. Var., April 27, 1927, 20; July 27, 1927, 21; May 11, 1927, 23.

14. AN, Aug, 31, Sept. 7, Nov. 2, 1927; March 21, 1928.

15. Johnson, *Along This Way* (New York, 1933, 1968), 155; John H. Bracey, Jr., August Meier, and Elliott Rudwick, eds., *Black Nationalism in America* (Indianapolis, 1971), 367, 355.

16. Schuyler, "Negro Art Hokum"; Hughes, "Negro Artist and the Racial Mountain"; and J. A. Rogers, "Jazz at Home," in Locke, *New Negro*, 216-24; New Year's issues of AN in 1920s.

17. Var., Aug. 12, 1925, 1; Kennard Williams, "The Spotlight," AA, Aug. 29, 1925; AN, July 14, 1926; Nov. 3, 1926; Jan. 12, 1927.

18. AN, July 14, 1926; Nov. 3, 1926; Jan. 12, 1927; Feb. 3, 10, 1926; March 3, 10, 1926.

19. Interview: author and Jimmie Smith; AN, Sept. 15, 1926; Var., Oct. 27, 1926, 1; Feb. 16, 1927, 5, 18; March 9, 1927, 5; Hughes and Meltzer, *Black Magic*, 300; Williamson, *Alice in Movieland*, 170ff.

20. Var., Oct. 20, 1926, 53; Aug. 24, 1927, 46; Nov. 16, 1927, 25.

21. *Uncle Tom's Cabin* (Universal, 1927); interview with Jimmie Smith, 1970; clippings in GPJC and Jimmie Smith collection in author's possession; AN, Sept. 7, 1927; Dec. 21, 1927; Nov. 21, 1928.

22. Ephemera and stills, Jimmie Smith collection.

23. AN, Aug. 31, 1927; Sept. 7, 1927; Nov. 2, 9, 1927; March 21, 1928.

24. For examples see Var., Aug. 29, 1928, 7; Sept. 5, 1928, 9, 60; Sept. 12, 1928, 8; April 11, 1928, 4.

25. Var., April 25, 1928, 23.

26. Raymond Kline to Albert Banzhof, June 17, 1927, in Griffith MSS; *Topsy and Eva* (United Artists, 1927), in LC; interview: Vivian Duncan and author, Atherton, Cal., Spring 1970; Var., June 22, 1927, 36; July 20, 1927, 9.

27. Arun Kumar Chaudhuri, "A Study of the Negro Problem in Motion Pictures" (M.A. thesis, USC, 1951), 9; clippings in GPJC; AN, Dec. 19, 26, 1928.

28. *Beggars of Life* (Paramount, 1928), in GEH; Var., Sept. 26, 1928, 14.

29. *Old Ironsides* (Paramount, 1926), in LC.

30. *The Merry Widow* (MGM, 1925); *Man, Woman, and Sin* (MGM, 1927), in GEH; interview: author and Carolynne Snowden; Joel Finler, *Stroheim* (Berkeley, 1968), 114, 139; Joseph McBride, "Stepin Fetchit Talks Back," *Film Quarterly*, Summer 1971, 23; Louise Beavers, "My Biggest Break," *Negro Digest*, Dec. 1949), 21-2; Var., March 3, 1926, 38.

31. *The King of the Cannibals*, typescript in Ben Glazer Papers, Special Collections, Powell Library, University of California at Los Angeles; Var., May 27, 1927, 5; June 8, 1927, 9.

32. Constance McLaughlin Green, *The Secret City: A History of Race Relations in the Nation's Capital* (Princeton, 1967), 215-25; Fox, *Guardian of Boston*, chap. VIII; Osofsky, *Harlem*, 180.

33. From a survey of subject index, Munden, *AFI Catalogue*, F2; Fenin and Everson, *The Western*, 37-38.

34. Var., April 20, 1927, 17 (*Mr. Wu*); May 22, 1927, 21 (*Driven from Home*); April 18, 1928, 27 (*Crimson City*); March 27, 1929, 24 (*Ships in the Night*); April 3, 1929, 20 (*Chinatown Nights*); Jan. 16, 1929, 11 (*Manchu Love*).

35. Var., Feb. 25, 1925, 31; April 13, 1927, 22; Feb. 2, 1927, 18; July 4, 1928, 16. Blacks enjoyed a fleeting vogue as sidekicks as in, for example, *Haunted Range* (Davis, *ca.* 1926), in LC.

36. Interview: John Ford and author, June 1970; Bogdanovich, *Ford*, filmography, 109ff.

Notes to Chapter Seven

1. For a survey see Thomas R. Cripps, "Movies in the Ghetto, B. P. (Before Poitier)," *Negro Digest*, Feb. 1969, 21-27, 45-48.

2. Hortense Powdermaker, *Hollywood, The Dream Factory*, 305; Milton M. Gordon, *Assimilation in American Life: The Role of Race, Religion, and National Origins* (New York, 1964), 163-73; Andrew Billingsley, *Black Families in White America* (Englewood Cliffs, N.J., 1968), 10-15; E. Franklin Frazier, *Black Bourgeoisie: The Rise of a New Middle Class* (New York, 1957), passim; Ulf Hannerz, *Soulside: Inquiries into Ghetto Culture and Community* (Lund, Sweden, 1969), 177ff.

3. AN, Dec. 23, 1925; "Ofay" was Negro "pig latin" for "white man" or "foe." L J. Pollard to GPJ, n. d.; GPJ to "Nobe," typescript note, in GPJC.

4. Typescript memo on Creel Committee; [GPJ] to Charles S. Hart, copy, Aug. 12, 1918; [George E. Cannon?] to GPJ, Dec. 2, 1916, in GPJC; NYA, Oct. 8, 1914 (on lodges); Sept. 24, 1914.

5. Var., June 2, 1917, xerox; [Cannon?] to GPJ, Dec. 2, 1916; Douglass Co., herald, in GPJC.

6. NYA, Oct. 12, 1916; April 26, 1917; June 14, 1917; May 24, 1917.

7. *Doing Their Bit*, herald (Toussaint Motion Picture Exchange, [1918]), in GPJC; Var., March 7, 1919, 73; NYA, Nov. 30, 1918; Aug. 24, 1918. After the war blacks still tried to assemble and distribute military footage from Pathé and other sources. See *Journal and Guide* (Norfolk), Jan. 22, 1921 (lent by Prof. Robert Hill, Northwestern Univ.); and Edward L. Snyder to A. C. Holsey, in Moton MSS (lent by Prof. John Wiseman, Frostburg State College).

8. NYA, March 6, 1920; Dec. 13, 1919; Munden, *AFI Catalogue*, F2, index. *Dallas Express* clipping, Gumby Coll., Columbia.

9. CE, July 2, 1921; Aug. 12, 26, 1921.

10. Herald, in GPJC; NYA, March 13, 1920.

11. Democracy Photoplay Co., brochure; Var., June 6, 1919, 57; *Democracy, or A Fight for Right* and *Loyal Hearts* herald, in GPJC; CE, Aug. 8, 1921, May 5, 1918, on Pollard-Johnson talks.

12. Clippings and notes, in GPJC; NYA, May 21, 1921; Var., Oct. 7, 1921, 31; July 4, 1923, 18.

13. *Dallas Express, Billboard, Star,* and other clippings in Gumby Coll., PC, July 14, 1923. E. J. Scott to GPJ, Sept. 27, 1918; April 17, 1918; George Frederic Wheeler to Scott, April 23 [1919], in Scott MSS.

14. CD, April 1, 1922.

15. AA, May 18, 1923; CD, June 25, 1921; PC, Aug. 11, 1923.

16. Unique Film Co. brochure, in GPJC; survey of CD by Robert Bunn, Morgan State University; clippings in Gumby Coll.

17. Noble Johnson to GPJ, Nov. 20, 1924; and memoir in GPJC.

18. *The Lure of a Woman*, clippings; Ira [McGowan], Micheaux Co., to George [GPJ], Aug. 17, 1917; L. J. Pollard, Ebony Film Corp., to GPJ, Sept. 21, 1920; S. Simpson, Eureka to [Rosa] Dale, May 23, 1921; J. W. Clifford, Monumental, to GPJ, March 8, 1921; *Western Dispatch*, Dec. 1, 1921, and other letters and "paper" in GPJC.

19. Ira McGowan to GPJ, July 12, 1921; William Riely, Eagle Films, St. Louis, to Lincoln, May 4, 1922; *Western Dispatch*, Dec. 1, 1921, in GPJC; Var., May 19, 1922, 45 (Gate City); Dec. 3, 1924, 20.

20. Bill Foster file, GPJ.

21. Joseph Polansky, MGM, to GPJ, Oct. 31, 1927, in GPJC.

22. *Competitor* (Pittsburgh), Jan.-Feb., 1921, 61; (June 1921), 37-39, boasted of fifty Negroes under contract to the "majors." Robert L. Vann to GPJ, Sept. 11, 1921; May 5, 1921, in GPJC.

23. AA, Aug. 29, 1925; *Los Angeles Herald*, July 21, 1919, in Gumby Coll.; PC, Aug. 4, 1923.

24. AN, Dec. 23, 1925.

25. Untitled clipping, n. d., in GPJC.

26. MPW, Aug. 10, 1918; April 20, 1918, 355, clippings in GPJC; Var., April 26, 1918, 45.

27. NYA, Aug. 6, 1921; MPW, May 4, 1918, 745, and clippings in ZC; *Dark Lover's Play* (Keystone, 1915) and *Beauty Contest* (by Ernest Truex, 1921), synopses in LC; J. F. Decker, Brayco, to LC, Jan. 2, 1925, in LC; AA, June 16, 1927.

28. MPW, Oct. 8, 1921, 680, 690; *The Custard Nine*, synopsis in LC.

29. Clipping in Gumby Coll. (*Black Boomerang*); interview: Anita Bush and author (telephone), July 1971.

30. Munden, *AFI Catalogue*, F2, 27, 98, 104, 289, 316, 682, 722, 756-58, and "lost" films such as *A Child in Pawn* (D. W. D. Film Corp, 1921), 123; *A Fool's Promise* (White Film Corp., 1921), 262; *Hearts of the Woods* (Supreme Art Productions, 1921), 335; *The Jazz Hounds* (Reol, 1922), 393; *The Greatest Sin* (Trio Production Co., 1922), 315; *Foolish Lives* (Young Producers Co., 1922), 259; *The Lure of a Woman* (Progress Picture Association, 1921), 468; *The Man From Texas* (Ben Roy Productions, 1921), 480; *The Negro of Today* (C. B. Campbell Studio, 1921), 539; *The Perfect Dreamer* (Young Producers Filming Co., 1922), 599; *Square Joe* (E. S. & L. Colored Features Productions, 1921), 760; *Undisputed Evidence* (Cotton Blossom Film Corp., 1922), 845; *The Wife Hunters* (Lone Star Motion Picture Co., 1922), 932; Var., May 27, 1925, 40; *The Schemers* (Reol, 1922), script, in LC.

31. Clipping, Gumby Coll.; Munden, *AFI Catalogue*, F2, 2, 176, 519, 508, 250, 617, 684, 711, 790.

32. "Oscar Micheaux," typescript in GPJC.

33. Micheaux to GPJ, June 25, 1918; letter fragment, May 20, 1918; typescript memorandum of agreement, May 20, 1918, in GPJC.

34. Brochure in GPJC.

35. D. Ireland Thomas to Clarence Brooks and GPJ, July 2, 1919; Micheaux to Brooks, Sept, 13, 1918; Micheaux to GPJ, May 5, 1919, in GPJC.

36. "Booking Route" (Homesteader); Micheaux typescripts, in GPJC.

37. *Ibid.*, GPJC.

38. Goins to GPJ, wire, April 5, 1920, in GPJC.

39. Micheaux to GPJ, Aug. 14, 1920, in GPJC.

40. NYA, Dec. 25, 1920; Jan. 1, 1921; April 23, 1921; April 16, 1921; CD, April 30, 1921.

41. Goins to GPJ, July 21, 1920; Swan Micheaux to GPJ, Oct. 27, 1920, in GPJC; NYA, Sept. 11, 18, 1920.

42. [GPJ?] to Micheaux, Aug. 10, 13, 1920; Sept. 15, 1920; Micheaux to GPJ, Aug. 14, 1920, in GPJC.

43. Swan Micheaux to George P. Jones [*sic*], Sept. 17, 1920; Swan Micheaux to GPJ, Nov. 27, 1920; GPJ to "Dear Nobe," copy, Sept. 27, 1921; "Ira" [Goins?] to GPJ, Aug. 17, 1921; Micheaux Records, in GPJC.

44. Micheaux Records, in GPJC.

45. Micheaux to GPJ, Aug. 14, 1920, and other correspondence in GPJC.

46. NYA, Nov. 8, 1924; PC, March 22, 1924; Oct. 18, 1924; AN, Sept. 8, 1926; CD, April 2, 1921. Charles F. Gordon to D. Ireland Thomas, March 19, 1920; Capt. Theo Ray to Supt. Frank Mooney, New Orleans Police, copy, March 10, 1920, in GPJC.

47. "'The Symbol of the Unconquered,' New Play," *Competitor*, Jan.-Feb. 1921, 61.

48. NYA, March 24, 1923; Jan. 12, 1924; PC, July 14, 1923, for example.

49. Munden, *AFI Catalogue*, F2, index.

50. The versions appear in *Body and Soul* (Micheaux, 1925), in GEH; Var., Nov. 26, 1924, 1; Munden, *AFI Catalogue*, F2, 73; *Body and Soul* file, GEH.

51. Thomas R. Cripps, "Paul Robeson and Black Identity in American Movies," *Massachusetts Review*, Summer 1970, 468-85.

52. PC, Jan. 1, 1927; April 24, 1926; June 11, 1927; April 16, 23, 1927; April 21, 1928; Aug. 18, 25, 1928; AN, July 14, 1926; Aug. 8, 1928; AA, June 16, 1927; *Journal and Guide* (Norfolk), Jan. 8, 19, 1927; CE, Oct. 14, 1927; NYA, May 4, 1918; Var., Oct. 27, 1926, 1; Feb. 1, 1928, 2; xerox fragments of Garvey's *Negro World*, lent by Prof. Hill; interview with Eubie Blake, Baltimore, Feb. 15, 1971.

53. NYA, Jan. 8, 1927; Feb. 2, 1929; *Chicago Whip*, March 19, 1927; notes on CD by Robert Bunn in possession of author; Munden, *AFI Catalogue*, F2, 617, 790; PC, Jan. 2, 1926.

54. *Ten Nights in a Bar Room* (Colored Players Film Corp., 1926), in LC.

55. AN, June 5, 12, 1927; Var., Aug. 31, 1927, 18; *Philadelphia Tribune*, April 16, 1927, in GPJC; PC, June 25, 1927.

56. *Scar of Shame* (Colored Players Film Corp., 1927), in LC; interview: Lucia Lynn Moses and author, New York, Spring 1973.

57. AN, Dec. 7, 1927; Oct. 5, 1927; Var., Oct. 19, 1927, 19; Nov. 23, 1927, 10; July 6, 1927, 5; Nov. 13, 1929, Feb. 15, 1928, 10; March 14, 1928, 16, and other clippings in GPJC; Munden, *AFI Catalogue*, F2, 801, 508, 911; Swan Micheaux memorandum, in GPJC; *Eleven P. M.* (Richard D. Maurice, *ca.* 1928), in LC.

Notes to Chapter Eight

1. Walter White to "Mr. Bryher," Feb. 27, 1929, in collection of Prof. Norman Holmes Pearson, Yale University.

2. Var., Jan. 23, 1929, 10; conversation between Ernie Smith and the author, Oct. 1971; Munden, *AFI Catalogue*, F2, index; Hampton, *American Film Industry*, 320; Rotha, *Film Till Now*, 115; NYT, May 26, 1933.

3. *The St. Louis Blues* (RKO, 1930), script in LC, print in GEH; introductory talk by Bob Chatterton, Avenue Photoplay Society, San Francisco, Dec. 13, 1969; conversation with Ernie Smith; Derrick Stewart-Baxter, *Ma Rainey and the Classic Blues Singers* (New York, 1971), 44ff.

4. Var., Sept. 4, 1929, 12-13.

5. *The St. Louis Blues* (RKO, 1930).

6. Var., Sept. 4, 1929, 12-13.

7. *Black and Tan* (RKO, 1930), script in LC, print in John Baker Coll., Columbus, Ohio; AN, Aug. 13, 1930.

8. AN, July 9, 1930; Aug. 13, 1930; Edward Kennedy Ellington, *Music Is My Mistress* (Garden City, N.Y., 1973), 77.

9. *Black and Tan* (RKO, 1930), in Baker Coll.

10. Richard Griffith, "Introduction: The Film Since Then," in the reissue of Rotha, *Film Till Now*, 417, 422.

11. Harry Alan Potamkin, "The Jew," *Liberator*, March 28, 1931, 7; Potamkin, "Movie: New York Notes," *Close-Up*, Feb. 1930, 99, 101, 109-10.

12. Quotations from Kenneth Macpherson, "As Is," *Close-Up*, 1930, 293-96; Walter White to "Mr. Bryher," Feb. 27, 1929; Elmer Carter to ed., *Close-Up*, May 22, 1929; Langston Hughes to Macpherson, Sept. 24, 1927; March 12, 1929, in Pearson Coll.

13. Eslanda Goode Robeson to Macpherson, Feb. 27, 1929; Mrs. Robeson to "Dear People," April 12 [1930], in Pearson Coll.

14. Mrs. Robeson to Macpherson, Feb. 19, 1930; Mrs. Robeson to Mr. and Mrs. Macpherson, Feb. 19, 1930; "Essie" to "Dear People," April 12, [1930], in Pearson Coll.

15. [Hilda Doolittle?], *Borderline: A Pool Film with Paul Robeson* (London, 1930), 5, 7-8, 23-24, 28, 33 (a pamphlet).

16. *Borderline* (Pool Films, 1930), in GEH; [Doolittle?], *Borderline*, 2-3.

17. *Studio Cinaes; La Veu de Catalunya; La Nau; La Publicitat,* Jan. 3, 1931; *Today's Cinema,* Oct. 14, 1930; *Manchester Guardian,* Oct. 14, 1930; *Observer,* Oct. 14, 1930, Herman G. Weinberg, Little Theatre, Baltimore, to W. Bryher, Oct. 16, 1931; in Pearson Coll., correspondence between the author, Macpherson, and Bryher, Nov. 1968.

18. [UNESCO], *Premier Catalogue Selectif International de Films Ethnographiques sur L'Afrique Noire* (Bruges, 1967), 378-79; Henri Gautier, *Jazz au Cinema,* "Premier Plan: Hommes, Oeuvres, Problemes du Cinema," No. 11 (n. p., n. d.), 17, 21-24, 30-35; NYT, June 25, 1935; Thomas Cripps, "Native Son in the Movies," *New Letters,* Winter 1971, 49-63; Cripps, "Robeson and Black Identity"; Réné et Charles Ford, *Histoire Illustrée du Cinema,* I "Le Cinema Muet, 1895-1930" (Paris, 1967), 135; Georges Sadoul, *Dictionnaire des Cinéastes* (Paris, 1965), 10.

19. AN, Feb. 15, 1928; Nov. 20, 1929.

20. AN, Jan. 22, 1930; PC, Jan. 11, 1930; Oct. 5, 1929.

21. Var., June 9, 1931, 19; June 7, 1932, 25.

22. AN, March 9, 16, June 8, 1932; interview: Ted Poston and author, May 1972.

23. Interview: Ted Poston and author, May 1972.

24. Poston interview; Langston Hughes, *I Wonder as I Wander: An Autobiographical Journey* (New York, 1956, 1964), chap. III; AN, Oct. 5, 1932; Var., Sept. 20, 1932, 39; Paul Babitsky and John Rimberg, *The Soviet Film Industry* (New York, 1955), 117, 164, 168, 205, 209, 258-59; Eugene Lyons, *Assignment in Utopia* (New York, 1937), 508-9.

25. Herman G. Weinberg, "The Emperor Jones," *Close-Up,* Dec. 1933, 351-52; Var., April 18, 1933, 2; NYT, Sept. 13, 24, 1933; AN, Feb. 22, 1933.

26. JWJ to Mary Ruta, copy, May 7, 1932, in JWJC. They cut costs by taking little; O'Neill, $25,000 for rights, Robeson, $15,000 and overtime.

27. NYT, May 26, June 11, 1933; *Time,* Sept. 25, 1933, 31-32; interview: John Krimsky and author, Spring 1973, New Brunswick, N.J.

28. *The Emperor Jones* (United Artists, 1933), in AFI.

29. Var., Oct. 3, 1933, 11; Nov. 7, 1933, 8, 10; clippings, Gumby Coll. PC, May 6, 1933; NYT, Sept. 20, 1933; *Literary Digest,* Oct. 7, 1933, 31; *Commonweal.* Oct. 6, 1933, 532; AN, Sept. 27, 1933; Weinberg, "Jones," 251-52.

30. Dudley Murphy to Walter White, Oct. 6, 1933; White to Murphy, copy, Oct. 9, 1933; memo, White to Roy Wilkins, copy, Sept. 21, 1933, in NAACPR.

31. Gordon W. Allport, *The Nature of Prejudice* (New York, 1954, 1958), 196ff.

32. Langston Hughes, *The Big Sea: An Autobiography* (New York, 1940, 1963), 334; White to "Mr. Bryher," Feb. 27, 1929, in Pearson Coll.

33. JWJ to William Foster, copy, Aug. 15, 1929, in JWJC.

Notes to Chapter Nine

1. Frederic Thrasher, *Okay for Sound: The Screen Finds Its Voice* (New York, 1946), 75-77.

2. *The Jazz Singer* (Warner Brothers, 1927), in BFI; pressbooks (photocopies) in author's possession.

3. Thrasher, *Okay for Sound,* 77-79; "First All-Negro Talkie," typescript in GPJC.

4. Typescripts in GPJC; *Talking Pictures,* a prospectus of Foster Photoplay Company; JWJ to Bill Foster, copy, Aug. 15, 1929, in JWJC.

5. Clipping and Foster-GPJ correspondence, in GPJC.

6. Foster to JWJ, n. d., in JWJC. His reference is to Fox's *Hearts in Dixie* and MGM's *Hallelujah!*, two all-black features.

7. Arthur M. Schlesinger, Jr., *The Crisis of the Old Order, 1919-1933*, Vol. I in *The Age of Roosevelt* (Boston, 1957), 141, 168, 171, 212, 217, 222, 251; David A. Shannon, *Between the Wars: America 1919-1941* (Boston, 1965), 194-96.

8. AN, July 29, 1925; Aug. 5, 1925; Sept. 30, 1925; Oct. 25, 1925; Oct. 30, 1925; Dec. 23, 1925 and a survey from Aug. 1928 to March 1935.

9. Isaacs, *Negro in Theatre*, IV; Johnson, *Black Manhattan*, 182-208; interview: author and Eubie Blake, Baltimore, Feb. 15, 1971.

10. AN, Aug. 31, 1927; CE, March 15, 1929; PC, Oct. 8, 1927; Sept. 3, 1927; undated clippings in JWJC and GPJC.

11. JWJ to Mary Ruta, copy, May 7, 1932; Herbert V. Gellendre, director Repertory Playhouse Associates, to JWJ, May 13, 1932; undated clippings (Muse); Bishop W. J. Walls, "What About Amos 'n' Andy?" *Abbott's Monthly*, Dec. 1930, 38-40, 72, all in JWJC; AN, May 5, 1926 (Hall Johnson).

12. NYT, Oct. 6, 1928; Var., Aug. 22, 1928, 7; July 18, 1928, 4; Oct. 3, 1928, 4; Feb. 24, 1926, 35; AN, May 5, 1928; Tono Films clipping in GPJC; *Night in Dixie* (DeForest Phonofilm, n. d.), fragment in LC; PC, Dec. 15, 1928; Sept. 7, 1929; AN, Oct. 3, 1928; May 5, 1928.

13. MPN, Jan. 12, 1929, 125; April 5, 1930, 49; Feb. 9, 1929, 436; May 11, 1929, 1646; pressbooks and Spencer Williams file, in GPJC.

14. *Oft in the Silly Night* (Christie, 1929), in possession of Robert Stendahl, East Gary, Ind.

15. *Brown Gravy, The Lady Fare, The Framing of the Shrew*, scripts in LC; MPN, Jan. 12, 1929, 125.

16. Roberta Hyson file, in GPJC.

17. Floyd C. Covington, "The Negro Invades Hollywood," *Opportunity*, April 1929, 113-14; Elmer Anderson Carter, "Of Negro Motion Pictures," *Close-Up*, Aug. 1929, 119; Geraldyn Dismond, "The Negro Actor and the American Movies," 90-97; Harry Alan Potamkin, "The Aframerican Cinema," 107-17; Kenneth Macpherson, "As Is," 90; Robert Herring, "Black Shadows," 104; "Letter from Walter White," 105-6; Elfa McWilliam Porter, "The Curve of Retention in Moving Pictures for Young Children" (M.A. thesis, Iowa State University, 1930). 45, 70.

18. AN, May 23, 29, 1929; NYA, Sept. 28, 1929.

19. *Jimtown Speakeasy* and *The Mayor of Jimtown* (MGM, n. d.), scripts in LC; Ernie Smith, "Hot Filmography," *Record Research* (Aug. 1960), 6-11.

20. *Jailhouse Blues* (Columbia-Victor Gems, 1929), in John Baker Coll.; Var., May 8, 1929, 23.

21. *Film Daily*, Feb. 23, 1930 (*Low Down* and *Darktown Follies*) March 16, 1930, 9 (*Honest Crooks*); and Dec. 1, 1920, 11 (*Black Narcissus*), in ZC; MPN, Dec. 21, 1929, 40 (*Foul Play*); Feb. 8, 1930, 76 (*High Toned*); MPN, Feb. 22, 1930, 9 (*Darktown Blues*); Oct. 26, 1929, 33 (*In and Out*); MPN, Sept. 14, 1929, 989.

22. *Cotton Pickin' Days* (Tiffany, 1930), in Baker Coll.

23. Clippings in ZC.

24. In like fashion the synopses of *Yamacraw, Dixie Days*, and *They Know Their Groceries* reflect casual scripting. All in LC.

25. *Melody Makers* (Wardour Films [British distributor], 1932), in BFI. See also *Night in Dixie* (DeForest Phonofilm, n. d.), fragment in LC; Var., Sept. 5, 1928, 12.

26. *After Leben* (Paramount, 1929), in Baker Coll.; Marshall and Jean Stearns, *Jazz Dance: The Story of American Vernacular Dance* (New York, 1968), 201.

27. *I'll Be Glad When You're Dead, You Rascal, You* (Paramount, 1932), in possession of Robert Pike, Van Nuys, Cal.

28. *Minnie the Moocher* (Max Fleischer-Talkertoons, 1932), in Baker Coll.

29. *Uncle Tom's Cabin* (Walter Lantz, 1926), in LC; *Out of the Inkwell* (Paramount-Zukor-Fleischer, 1938), in Pike Coll.; and clippings in ZC.

30. *Amos 'n' Andy's Rasslin' Match* (Van Beuren Corp., 1934), in LC; *Who Killed Cock Robin?* (Walt Disney, 1935), screened in AFI series, "50 Years of Animation" (1972); Var., March 25, 1931, 3, 16; March 18, 1931, 14; May 6, 1931, 6, 22; Nov. 28, 1933, 13; March 21, 1933, 16. Pal received a special Academy Award in 1943 "for the development of novel methods and techniques." Leslie Halliwell, ed., *The Filmgoer's Companion: An International Encyclopedia*, 3rd ed. (New York, 1970), 750.

31. *Yamacraw* (Vitaphone, 1930), in Baker Coll.; *Film Daily*, April 27, 1930, 13.

32. *Smash Your Baggage* (Vitaphone, 1932), in Baker Coll.; interview: author and Ernie Smith, New York, Summer 1971. In the cast were many stars of the Negro stage, including Doris Rubbottom, Lew Payton, Small's Paradise Entertainers, Mabel Scott, Rubberlegs Williams, and Babe Wallace.

33. *That's the Spirit* (Vitaphone, 1932), in Baker Coll. The Washboard Serenaders and and Cora La Redd played and danced.

34. *Barbershop Blues* (Vitaphone, 1932), in Baker Coll.; script in LC.

35. *A Rhapsody in Black and Blue* (Paramount, 1932), in author's collection.

36. Typescript and holograph files of Baker and Smith; *Black Network* (Vitaphone, 1936); *All-Colored Vaudeville Show* (Vitaphone, 1934); *Hi De Ho* (Vitaphone, 1937), in Baker Coll.; *Cab Calloway's Jitterbug Party* (Zukor-Lasky, 1935), in author's collection. The players were overexposed early; Buck and Bubbles were released from their contract in 1930: Var., July 16, 1930, 39. *King for a Day* (Vitaphone, 1934) and *Carnival in Rhythm* (Warner Brothers, 1940), in Baker Coll.

37. Telephone interview with Fritz Pollard, Summer 1970; conversations with Baker, Smith, and Dave Dixon (Vancouver); "Juke Box War," *Business Week* May 18, 1940, 52-53; NYT, April 7, 1940; AN, March 21, 1942; Aug. 21, 1943; Var., July 23, 1941, 10, and GPJC clippings. Many of the sets detracted from the music: Armstrong in picker's overalls doing "Sleepy Time Down South," Louis Jordan in western get-up doing "Cow Cow Boogie," and other distractions dimmed stars like Una Mae Carlisle and Meade Lux Lewis.

38. Billie Holiday with William Duffy, *Lady Sings the Blues* (New York, 1956, 1972), 52.

Notes to Chapter Ten

1. King Vidor, *A Tree Is a Tree* (New York, 1953), 175-76; telephone interview: Vidor and author, Summer 1970.

2. JWJ to "Horace" Dietz, copy, July 9, 1929, in JWJC; telephone interview: Wanda Tuchock and author, Autumn 1971.

3. NYT, Feb. 24, 1929.

4. Allvine, *Greatest Fox of Them All*, 85; Clarence Muse to Robert Bunn, Jan. 5, 1966; Muse to Cripps, March 7, 1970; "Actors Replaced by Other Actors," typescript in GPJC.

5. Var., Aug. 1, 1928, 5; clippings in GPJC.

6. *Hearts in Dixie* (Fox, 1929), in MOMA series, 1972; Var., March 6, 1929, 18; March 13, 1929, 14.

7. NYT, March 10, 1929; AN, April 2, 1929; May 15, 1929.

8. AN, Sept. 11, 1929; NYT, Feb. 28, 1929.

9. Sample in GPJC, including Los Angeles *Record, Examiner*, and *Express; Cleveland Plaindealer, New York World, Sun;* Var., March 6, 1929, 12.

10. Henry Dobbs, "Variations on the Same Theme," *Close-Up*, Aug. 1929, 79ff; *Chicago Whip*, May 18, 1929.

11. *Dirigible* (Columbia, 1931), in Los Angeles County Museum, Spring 1970; *Cabin in the Cotton* (Warner Brothers, 1932), in WSHS.

12. Thomas, *Thalberg*, 163; Var., Aug. 22, 1928, 7.

13. PC, Dec. 14, 1929; Vidor and Tuchock interviews with author.

14. *Telegram*, Feb. 23, 1929, and other clippings in PAC; *Tatler*, Aug. 24, 1929, in AAS; Var., Sept. 5, 1928, 12; PC, Dec. 15, 1928; AN, Oct. 3, 1928.

15. Samuel I. Brooks in *Tatler*, Aug. 24, 1929.

16. *Commercial Appeal* (Memphis), Oct. 30, 1928; other clippings in PAC; Mary Astor, *A Life on Film* (New York, 1971), 27; Vidor, *A Tree Is a Tree*, chap. XIV.

17. *Charleston Gazette*, Dec. 9, 1928; other clippings in PAC, for example, Dorothy Manners, "Enter the Dixies," *Motion Picture Classic*.

18. Crowther, *Lion's Share*, 164-65; Jacobs, *Rise of American Film*, 458; Thomas, *Thalberg*, 163-64; Vidor, *A Tree Is a Tree*, chap. XVI; Siegfried Kracauer, *Theory of Film: The Redemption of Physical Reality* (New York, 1960), 130-31; Dorothy B. Jones, "The Language," in Allen Rivkin and Laura Kerr, *Hello Hollywood* (New York, 1962), 342.

19. Interviews between Tuchock, Walter Fisher, and author.

20. Vidor, *A Tree Is a Tree*, 184-86.

21. *Hallelujah!* (MGM, 1929); Charles Higham, "King Vidor," *Film Heritage*, Summer 1966, 15-25.

22. Clippings in PAC, AAS, Gumby Coll.; *Literary Digest*, Oct. 5, 1929, 42.

23. Var., Aug. 28, 1929, 18.

24. James Agate, *Around Cinemas (Second Series)* (Amsterdam, 1948), 29; Harry Allan Potamkin, "The White Man's Negro," *Liberator*, March 28, 1931, in JWJC; Var., Jan. 22, 1930, 22; Feb. 12, 1930, 5; Feb. 19, 1930, 12.

25. *World*, Oct. 11, 1928; PC, Sept. 7, 1929; *Photoplay*, May 1929, in GPJC; *New York Mirror*, Aug. 23, 1928; Samuels, *Waters*, 198; AN, Aug. 28, Sept. 25, 1929; Var., Aug. 14, 1929, 4; Oct. 23, 1929, clipping. See also Herbert Howe, "Stepin's High-Colored Past," *Photoplay* (June 1929), 31, 123-25.

26. *Negro World*, Jan. 17, 1931.

27. AN, Nov. 20, Sept. 18, Oct. 2, 1929; *West Indian News*, Aug. 24, 1929, and clippings in PAC; Johnson, *Black Manhattan*, 229.

28. *Mammy* (Warner Brothers, 1930); Var., Dec. 12, 1928, 5; Dec. 26, 1928, 4; NYT, Sept. 13, 1930.

29. *Big Boy* (Warner Brothers, 1930), in WSHS.

30. *Dixiana* (RKO, 1930), in KDKA-TV; NYT, Sept. 5, 1930; CE, April 5, 1929; AN, Oct. 8, 1930.

31. *Sunny Side Up* (Fox, 1929); Munden, *AFI Catalogue*, F2, 273.

32. *Golden Dawn* (Warner Brothers, 1930), and script, both in WSHS.

33. *Hallelujah, I'm a Bum* (Warner Brothers, 1933); interview: Lewis Milestone and author, Hollywood, Spring 1970; John Kobal, *Gotta Sing Gotta Dance: A Pictorial History of Film Musicals* (London, 1971), 115-16.

34. *Kid Millions* and *The Kid from Spain* (United Artists, 1934, 1932), in KDKA-TV; AN, Dec. 14, 1932. Cantor's films often used black foils.

35. *Gold Diggers of 1933* (Warner Brothers, 1933); Al Dubin and Harry Warren song quoted in Kobal, *Gotta Sing Gotta Dance*, 125-26.

36. Interview: Etta Moten and author, telephone, 1971; *Flying Down to Rio* (RKO, 1934); *Duck Soup* (Paramount, 1933); *Wonderbar* (Warner Brothers, 1934); *Footlight Parade* (Warner Brothers, 1933); *Swingtime* (RKO, 1936); *Go Into Your Dance* (Warner Brothers, 1935).

37. *Artists and Models* (Paramount, 1937); AN, May 5, 22, 1937; Var., Aug. 4, 1937, 18.

38. *Stand Up and Cheer* (Fox, 1934), in KDKA-TV; Norman J. Zierold, *The Child Stars* (New York, 1965), Chap. III.

39. *The Little Colonel* (20th Century-Fox, 1935); *The Littlest Rebel* (20th Century-Fox, 1935), both in KDKA-TV.

40. Carl Van Vechten to JWJ, Sept. 27, 1935, in JWJC.
41. Interview: Eubie Blake and author; Stearns, *Jazz Dance*, 182-84.
42. Var., May 13, 1931, 6; April 29, 1931, 4.
43. Marc Connelly, *Voices Off Stage: A Book of Memoirs* (New York, 1968), chap. V; G. James Fleming to Cripps [n. d.]; Northwestern Medical School to Cripps, in possession of author.
44. *The Green Pastures* (Warner Brothers, 1936).
45. Var., July 29, 1936, 12 (Matthews); July 22, 1936, 12; April 8, 1936, 16; Aug. 18, 1937, 1; AN, June 20, 1936; *New York Sun*, April 1, 1936; taped interview with Marc Connelly in WSHS; NYT, March 8, May 24, June 7, 1936; James P. Cunningham, "Green Pastures," *Commonweal*, June 5, 1936, 160; "Follow the Films," *Scholastic*, Sept. 19, 1936, 17; *Literary Digest*, July 18, 1936, 18-19; *Canadian Magazine*, April 1936, 56-59; *Time*, July 29, 1936, 38-40.
46. *Rainbow on the River* (RKO, 1936), in KDKA-TV; NYT, Dec. 18, 1936.
47. *Way Down South* (RKO, 1937), script in LC; Var., March 10, 1937, 14; Aug. 23, 1939, clipping; NYT, Aug. 18, 1939; AN, July 29, 1939; May 14, 1939; interview: Sol Lesser and author, Los Angeles, Spring 1970.
48. *A Day at the Races* (MGM, 1937); AN, April 10, 1937; Allen Eyles, *The Marx Brothers: Their World of Comedy* (London, 1966), 103-4, 166; Joseph Adamson, "The Seventeen Preliminary Scripts of *A Day at the Races*," *Cinema Journal*, Spring 1969, 2-10.

Notes to Chapter Eleven

1. Theodore Draper, *The Rediscovery of Black Nationalism* (New York, 1971), 64; Wilson Record, *Race and Radicalism: The NAACP and the Communist Party in Conflict* (Ithaca, 1964), chap. III; and his *The Negro and the Communist Party* (Chapel Hill, N.C., 1951), passim; Dan T. Carter, *Scottsboro: A Tragedy of the American South* (London, 1969), chap. III; Gilman M. Ostrander, *American Civilization in the First Machine Age, 1890-1940* (New York, 1970), chap. VIII on ethnic dominance.
2. The foregoing account is derived from an AN survey of 1928-33. On the social critics see also Leslie H. Fischel, Jr., "The Negro in the New Deal Era," in Eric Foner, *America's Black Past: A Reader in Afro-American History* (New York, 1970), 392-413; Osofsky, *Burden of Race*, sect. VIII; Raymond Wolters, *Negroes and the Great Depression: The Problem of Economic Recovery* (Westport, Conn., 1970), part III.
3. Gordon W. Allport, *The Nature of Prejudice* (Garden City, N.Y., 1954, 1958, abridged), 197.
4. NYT, Oct. 5, 1929; March 8, 27, 1930; Var., June 12, 1929, 1.
5. Correspondence between the author and officials of Dickinson College and Dickinson School of Law and the Medical School of Northwestern University, July 1973 and Jan. 1974. See also alphabetical biography files, GPJC.
6. A sample of the activity may be seen in Allan Schoener, *Harlem on My Mind: Cultural Capital of Black America, 1900-1968* (New York, 1968), 165; AN, April 13, 1932; Feb. 21, 1934; March 10, 1934 (Muse and Wallace Thurman); CE, April 5, 1929; Var., March 27, 1934, 6; April 3, 1929, 35; Feb. 5, 1930, 12-13; Jan. 22, 1930, 63; Nancy Cunard, *Negro* (New York, 1933), 298 (on Will Vodery); JWJ to E. B. Marks, copy, Feb. 29, 1936; JWJ to Emelyn Wyse, copy, April 18, 1936, JWJC; folder on *Fire in the Flint*, C-303, NAACPR.
7. AN, Sept. 25, 1929; Oct. 8, 15, Nov. 5, Dec. 10, April 23, Sept. 24, May 7, March 19, 1930; Nov. 1, 1933; Feb. 24, March 10, 1934; March 16, 1935; Aug. 1, 22, 1936; June 5, 26, July 10, 17, 31, Sept. 4, April 10, 1937; *Flash*, May 3, 1938, 26.
8. Correspondence in C-302, especially White to YMHA members, copy, Sept. 4, 1935, NAACPR; Harry Allan Potamkin, "Aframerican Cinema," *Close-Up*

(Sept. 1929), cited in Chaudhuri, "Negro in Motion Pictures," 17; Lawrence D. Reddick, "Educational Progress for Improving Race Relations: Motion Pictures, Radio, the Press and Libraries," *Journal of Negro Education*, July 1944, 367ff.

9. Pickens to ———, copy, March 25, 1935, C–299; White to YMHA, copy, Sept. 4, 1935, C–302, NAACPR; Loren Miller, "Hollywood's New Negro Films," *Crisis*, Jan. 1938, 8–9; AN, March 5, 1938.

10. AN, March 5, 1938; Feb. 24, 1934; April 6, 1935; June 8, 1940; Aug. 15, 1936; Singer Buchanan, "A Study of the Attitudes of the Writers of the Negro Press Towards the Depiction of the Negro in Plays and Films, 1930-1965" (Ph.D. dissertation, University of Michigan, 1968), 27-28; Herbert Sorrell, taped memoirs, University of California, Berkeley, 42, 44, 142.

11. NYT, Oct. 10, 1928; Dec. 20, 1931; Var., June 16, 1931, 24; June 23, 1931, 1; Jan. 5, 1932, 61; May 20, 1931, 21; May 27, 1931, 5; March 13, 1929, 1; July 5, 1932, 1; July 12, 1932, 6; Nov. 15, 1932, 19, 25; Jobes, *Motion Picture Empire*, 256-304.

12. Thomas, *Thalberg*, 90-91, 94-95, 122; quoted, 126, 139; Thomas, *Selznick*, 65; Var., May 13, 1931, 6; April 29, 1931, 4.

13. *Our Betters* (RKO, 1933); Thomas, *King Cohn*, 69; Menjou and Musselman, *It Took Nine Tailors*, 189; Gavin Lambert, *On Cukor* (New York, 1972), 29ff.

14. Crowther, *Hollywood Rajah*, 178-79; *Our Daily Bread* (MGM, 1933), Yale; Charles Higham and Joel Greenberg, *The Celluloid Muse: Hollywood Directors Speak* (London, 1969), 234-35.

15. Var., April 9, 1930, 1; April 16, 1930, 23; *Check and Double Check* (RKO, 1930), in KDKA-TV; Var., July 16, 1930, 15; Oct. 9, 1929, 31, 34; Aug. 20, 1930, 4; Jan. 24, 1933, 41.

16. Var., April 15, 1931, 33; April 29, 1931, 4, through Spring 1931.

17. See Jolson's redundancy in *Mammy* (Warner Brothers, 1930); AN, Dec. 25, 1929 (*Jazz Heaven*); NYT, Sept. 5, 13, 18, 1930; Dec. 20, 22, 1930; Var., April 30, 1930, 8 (*Mammy* as a draw); April 9, 1930, 8; May 20, 1931, 17 (*Up Pops the Devil*); *King of Jazz* (Universal, 1930), in LC; *Thunderbolt* story line from Ernie Smith.

18. *On With the Show* (Warner Brothers, 1929).

19. *Safe in Hell* (First National, 1931), in WSHS; dialogue in box 61, United Artists Coll., WSHS.

20. NYT, Dec. 19, 1931; Dec. 3, 1932; Nov. 29, 1935; Jan. 19, 1935; Aug. 18, 1939; Feb. 16, 1934; Var., Feb. 13, 1934, 14, 25; Oct. 23, 1935, 13; *Kentucky Kernels* (RKO, 1934), in KDKA-TV; *Judge Priest* (20th Century-Fox, 1934); *County Chairman* (20th Century-Fox, 1935); *Literary Digest*, Oct. 27, 1934, 17; *David Harum* (20th Century-Fox, 1934).

21. *Judge Priest*, script in USC; *The World Moves On* (20th Century-Fox, 1934), in National Film Theatre, London, 1972; *Mississippi* (Paramount, 1935); see similar unproduced script in Delmer Daves MSS, Stanford.

22. *Buccaneer*, script in USC.

23. Var., Jan. 17, 1933, 15; Nov. 6, 1940, 18; Feb. 2, 1938, 17; Feb. 9, 1938, 15; June 22, 1938, 14; Feb. 16, 1938, 17; Aug. 4, 1937, 19; Jan. 20, 1937, 30; AN, July 22, 1931 for survey of "B" westerns with black roles; *Go West, Young Man* (Paramount, 1935).

24. Var., Aug. 21, 1929, 18; Nov. 17, 1931, 26; May 31, 1932, 15; Jan. 19, 1932, 9; Sept. 29, 1937, 15; Dec. 14, 1938, 15; June 28, 1939, 14; *Broadway Bill* (Columbia, 1934), script in USC; *David Harum* (20th Century-Fox, 1934); *Saratoga* (MGM, 1937); *Racing Blood* (Conn, 1938); *Pride of the Blue Grass* (Warner Brothers, 1939); NYT, Dec. 24, 1938.

25. *The Patent Leather Kid* (First National, 1927), in WSHS; *Leatherpushers* (Universal, 1950); Var., May 25, 1938, 13; Jan. 21, 1942, 18.

26. *Trader Horn* (MGM, 1930); Ethelreda Lewis, *Trader Horn: Being the Life and Works of Aloysius Horn* (New York, 1927); Var., March 15, 1929, 27; March 19, 1930, 20; June 13, 1929, 4; June 9, 1931, 9; April 22, 1931, 9; Jan. 22, 1930,

10; March 29, 1932, 25; NYT, Oct. 6, 1929; Dec. 8, 1929; March 31, 1929; Feb. 15, 1931; AN, July 15, 1931; *Tarzan the Ape Man* (MGM, 1932); Crowther, *Lion's Share*, 170; Fenton, *Big Swingers*, 102, 167-74, 181-82; Essoe, *Tarzan of the Movies*, 69ff. The MGM script for *Horn* went so far as to establish white blame for African conditions: *Horn's* cargo is "kegs of rum and crates of bibles." Script in Feldman Library, AFI, Beverly Hills.

27. *Tarzan and His Mate* (MGM, 1934); *Tarzan and the Green Goddess* (Dearholt, Stout, and Cohen, 1938); Var., July 15, 1936, 2; April 24, 1934, 14; Jan. 12, 1938, 14; June 1, 1938, 12; Thomas, *Thalberg*, 212; Essoe, *Tarzan of the Movies*, 70 and passim.

28. *Nagana* (Universal, 1933), in LC; *Zanzibar* (Universal, 1940), whose implausible colors included dark Muse, Polynesian Ray Mala, and white Abner Biberman; Var., Feb. 21, 1933, 14, 21; Feb. 28, 1933, 15; July 22, 1942, 8; April 3, 1940, 14.

29. PC, March 29, 1930; AN, Oct. 28, 1931; NYT, Sept. 20, 1969; interview with Bill Walker, Spring 1970; Var., April 16, 1930, 46, through summer. Noble Johnson's 1930s exotics included *East of Borneo*, a "native chief" in *King Kong*, Ran Singh in *Lives of a Bengal Lancer*, the Amhaggar chief in *She*, a thug in *The Murders in the Rue Morgue*, a Tartar in *The Most Dangerous Game*, a Nubian in *The Mummy*, and a boatman in *Nagana*. Cyril Hume's *Tarzan* script is in AFI.

30. NYT, July 29, 1932; Var., Aug. 16, 1932, 12-13; Oct. 12, 1938, 15.

31. *Hurricane* (United Artists, 1937); *Jungle Princess* (Paramount, 1936); *Her Jungle Love* (Paramount, 1938); Var., May 22, 1937, 18; Oct. 27, 1937, 19.

32. German title from still in Memory Shop, N.Y.; Wallace, *Hollywood Diary*, 143ff; Andrew Bergman, *We're in the Money: Depression America and Its Films* (New York, 1972), 72ff; Var., March 7, 1933, 14; *New York Post*, March 2, 1933; NYT, March 3, 1933.

33. *Son of Kong* (RKO, 1933), in KDKA-TV; Carlos Clarens, *An Illustrated History of the Horror Film* (New York, 1967), chap. IV.

34. On reinforcement of colonialist attitudes see Robert R. Stillwell, "A Study of the Effects of Motion Pictures on the Attitudes of Seventh Grade Students" (M.A. thesis, Ohio State University, 1939), 19-45; NYT, Nov. 20, 26, 1936 ("beaters"); *Time*, March 9, 1936, 44; Mark Van Doren, "The Higher Jingoism," *Nation*, Jan. 30, 1935, 360; *Rhodes of Africa* (20th Century-Fox, 1936), in BFI.

35. *Gunga Din* (RKO, 1939); *Four Feathers* (United Artists, 1939); *Stanley and Livingstone* (20th Century-Fox, 1939); *The Real Glory* (United Artists, 1939); NYT, Aug. 4, 1939; Jan. 27, 1939; Var., April 26, 1939, 12; James P. Cunningham, "You're a Better Man Than . . . ," *Commonweal*, Feb. 10, 1939, 441; *Nation*, Feb. 4, 1939, 158-59; Gussow, *Don't Say Yes*, chap. II.

36. *I Am a Fugitive from a Chain Gang* (Warner Brothers, 1932); *Hell's Highway* (RKO, 1932), in AFI; *Ladies They Talk About* (Warner Brothers, 1932), in WSHS; Var., April 9, 1930, 35; Sept. 27, 1932, 21, NYT, Feb. 25, 1933.

37. John Schultheiss, "The 'Eastern' Writer in Hollywood," *Cinema Journal*, Fall 1971, 13-47.

38. *Dirigible* (Columbia, 1931); NYT, Dec. 12, 1931; quoted May 28, 1932.

39. Beavers and Anderson, in GPJC; *I'm No Angel* (Paramount, 1933); *She Done Him Wrong* (Paramount, 1933); *Bombshell* (MGM, 1933); *In Old Chicago* (20th Century-Fox, 1938); *Brother Rat* (Warner Brothers, 1938); Lamar Trotti and Sonya Levien, *In Old Chicago* (Beverly Hills, 1937), 71, 73, 78, 172-73, 257.

40. *Five Star Final* (Warner Brothers, 1931) and *Smart Money* (First National, 1932), Stanford Freshman series, Clive Miller, director.

41. *The Count of Monte Cristo* (United Artists, 1934) and *Cabin in the Cotton* (First National, 1932); *The Mind Reader* (First National, 1933), in WSHS; Muse résumé in GPJC; NYT, Nov. 24, 1934; AN, Aug. 8, 1934; April 20, 1932; Sept. 1, 1934; Var., May 31, 1932, 18.

42. Résumés in GPJC; John Ford interview, Spring 1970; *The World Moves On*

(20th Century-Fox, 1934); AN, Aug. 2, 1929; Var., March 22, 1929, 3; Myrtle
Gebhart, "The Chocolate Comedy," *Extension Magazine*, Nov. 1929, 17-18, 42, 44;
Cal York, "Gossip of All the Studios," *Photoplay*, Nov. 1929, 46; NYT, March 8,
1930; Elisabeth Goldbeck, "Stepin Fetchit . . . ," *Motion Picture*, July 1929, 76,
92; Howe, "Stepin's High-Colored Past," 32, 123-24.

43. *Stand Up and Cheer* (20th Century-Fox, 1934); NYT, March 8, 1929; AN,
Aug. 2, 1929.

44. *You Said a Mouth Full* (First National, 1932); *Pardon Us* (MGM, 1931);
Pack Up Your Troubles (MGM, 1932); Var., Nov. 22, 1932, 17; "paper" for
Father's Son (Vitaphone, 1931), in Blair MSS, WSHS; *Motion Picture Herald*,
May 30, 1931, 54.

45. *Morning Glory* (RKO, 1933); *Polo Joe* (Warner Brothers, 1936); *Weary
River* (First National, 1932), in WSHS; *Diplomaniacs* (RKO, 1933); *Wild Boys
of the Road* (Warner Brothers, 1933), in WSHS; *Hearts Divided* (Warner
Brothers, 1936); *Babbitt* (Warner Brothers, 1934), in WSHS; *The Varsity Show*
(Warner Brothers, 1937), script in WSHS; *If I Had a Million*, script in UCLA;
Blonde Venus (Paramount, 1932).

46. Interview with Etta Moten.

47. For example, *Gold Diggers of 1935* (Warner Brothers, 1935); *The Littlest
Rebel* (20th Century-Fox, 1935); *O'Shaughnessy's Boy* (MGM, 1935); Var., Oct.
9, 1935, 14; *The Little Colonel* (20th Century-Fox, 1935); *Mississippi* (Paramount,
1935); *Charlie Chan in Egypt* (20th Century-Fox, 1935); NYT, June 24, 1935;
Annapolis Farewell (Paramount, 1935); *In Old Kentucky* (20th Century-Fox,
1935); *Hooray for Love* (RKO, 1935); NYT, July 13, 1935; *Escape from Devil's
Island* (Columbia, 1935), NYT, Nov. 25, 1935; *Helldorado* (20th Century-Fox,
1935), in *Herald-Tribune*, Nov. 25, 1935, in PAC; *Bachelor of Arts* (20th Century-
Fox, 1935), Var., April 17, 1935, 13; *Stolen Harmony* (Paramount, 1935), Var.,
April 24, 1935, 13; *Reckless* (MGM, 1935), and Var., Oct. 16, 1935, 23; *County
Chairman* (20th Century-Fox, 1935), and NYT, Jan. 19, 1935; *One More Spring*
(20th Century-Fox, 1935), and NYT, Feb. 22, 1935; *Unwelcome Stranger* (Co-
lumbia, 1935), Var., April 10, 1935, 17; *Big Broadcast of 1935*, Var., May 1,
1935, 3; *Gentle Julia* (20th Century-Fox, 1935), in Var., April 1, 1935, 23; *Mur-
der on the Bridle Path* (RKO, 1936), in Var., April 15, 1936, 16; *Bullets or
Ballots* (Warner Brothers, 1936), and Var., June 3, 1936, 15; *The Lawless Nineties*
(Republic, 1936), and Var., July 11, 1936, 23; *The Bride Walks Out* (RKO, 1936),
and Var., July 15, 1936, 31; *High Tension* (20th Century-Fox, 1936), in Var.,
July 15, 1936, 55; *Postal Inspector* (Universal, 1936), in Var., Sept. 9, 1936, 17;
Banjo on My Knee (20th Century-Fox, 1936), and Var., Dec. 16, 1936, 14; *Make
Way for a Lady* (RKO, 1936); *Mummy's Boys* (RKO, 1936), and Var., Dec. 16,
1936, 15; *Rainbow on the River* (RKO, 1936), and Var., Dec. 16, 1936, 20; *Guns
and Guitars* (Republic, 1936), and Var., Jan. 20, 1937, 30; *Libeled Lady* (MGM,
1936); *Go West, Young Man* (Paramount, 1936); *King of Burlesque* (20th Cen-
tury-Fox, 1936), and NYT, Jan. 16, 1936; *Laughing Irish Eyes* (Republic, 1936), in
NYT, April 4, 1936; *The Singing Kid* in NYT, April 4, 1936; *Muss 'Em Up*
(RKO, 1936), in NYT, Feb. 3, 1936; *Hearts Divided* (Warner Brothers, 1936),
and NYT, June 13, 1936; *Valiant Is the Word for Carrie* (Paramount, 1936), and
NYT, Oct. 8, 1936; *Dimples* (20th Century-Fox, 1936), and NYT, Oct. 10, 1936.

48. NYT, March 22, 1935; *Hooray for Love* segment, in Baker Coll.

49. *Hearts in Bondage* (Republic, 1936); *Slave Ship* (20th Century-Fox, 1937);
The Prisoner of Shark Island (20th Century-Fox, 1936); interviews between John
Ford and Nunnally Johnson (telephone), Spring 1970; JWJ-Van Vechten cor-
respondence in JWJC.

50. *So Red the Rose* (MGM, 1935); interview: author and Vidor.

51. *Petrified Forest* (Warner Brothers, 1936); clippings in GPJC; Andrew
Bergman, *We're in the Money: Depression America and Its Films*, passim.

52. *The Plainsman* (Paramount, 1936); *Pennies from Heaven* (Columbia, 1936);
Bullets or Ballots (Warner Brothers, 1936), in WSHS and BFI, script in WSHS.

53. *Showboat* (Universal, 1936), in BFI; *Showboat* (Universal, 1929), Filmarchiv der Deutsche Demokratische Republik, Berlin; script in UCLA; AN, June 19, 20, July 4, 1936.

54. *Nation,* Oct. 18, 1933, 459; AN, June 13, 1936; *Literary Digest,* May 30, 1936, 28; NYT, July 18, 1937; AN, July 17, 1937; Var., July 14, 1937, 8; *Time,* July 26, 1937, 23; *Fury* (MGM, 1936); *Black Legion* (Warner Brothers, 1937); *They Won't Forget* (Warner Brothers, 1937).

55. NYT, Aug. 19, 1937. *Captains Courageous* (MGM, 1937), in AFI, for example, featured, along with Sam McDaniel's ship's cook, black mourners who toss flowers into the sea in a ritual shared with white families.

56. Cripps, "Myth of the Southern Box Office," passim; Var., May 24, 1932, 35; May 8, 1934, 27; May 29, 1934, 11; Dec. 4, 1935, 7.

57. Buchanan, "Negro Press and Motion Pictures," 211-12, 240-41, 284; AN, June 5, 26, 1937; July 10, 17, 31, 1937; Sept. 4, 1937; March 27, 1937; March 5, 1938; Feb. 19, 1938; *March of Time* segment in BFI.

58. Samples of the newsfilm are (or were) in the Fox-Movietone and Hearst warehouses in New York; the Sherman Grinberg Library; the National Archives; and LC, with many gaps and negative footage.

59. Comments on films like *Ingagi, Jango, Africa Speaks,* and *Congorilla* are in NYT, Feb. 28, 1928; Sept. 24, 1930; Var., June 19, 1929, 6; June 12, 1929, 35; April 3, 1929, 27; July 24, 1929, 39; April 16, 1929, 46; Jan. 22, 1930, 17; July 19, 1932, 6; July 26, 1932, 17; Potamkin, "The White Man's Negro," 81.

60. *Untamed Africa* dialogue transcript, in WSHS; NYT, July 29, 1932; Var., Aug. 16, 1932, 12-13; Oct. 12, 1938, 15; *Glimpses of Northern Brazil* (Edited Pictures, 1937), in LC. *Dark Rapture* (Armand Denis, 1938), in BFI, featured "childlike," "innocent," "harmless," "mysterious," "weird" Africans often with a "pungent aroma."

61. *The Old South* (Eastman Teaching Films, 1932); *Dixie* (Yale, 1924), in LC and MOMA; Raymond Fielding, "The March of Time, 1935-1942" (M.A. thesis, UCLA, 1956), 21, 90, 142, 148, 155-56, 168, 175, 217; most issues of *The March of Time,* in BFI.

62. *Arrowsmith* (United Artists, 1931), in a BFI series, Aug. 10, 1972; Ford, notorious for hazing interviewers, once pretended to have forgotten making the film.

63. Var., Dec. 15, 1931, 14; Feb. 16, 1932, 8; *The New York Times Directory of the Film* (New York, 1971), 37; *Philadelphia Tribune,* Dec. 24, 1931, in GPJC; Mark Schorer, *Sinclair Lewis: An American Life* (New York, 1961), 568; Horace R. Cayton, *Long Old Road: An Autobiography* (Seattle, 1964), 298; Bogdanovich, *Ford,* 55, 125.

64. *Prestige* (MGM, 1932), in KDKA-TV; *Cabin in the Cotton* (Warner Brothers, 1932); Var., Feb. 9, 1932, 19; AN, May 25, 1932; Harry Allan Potamkin, "The Year of Eclipse," *Close-Up,* March 1933, 30-39.

65. Script in WSHS.

66. *Imitation of Life* (Universal, 1934).

67. Var., Nov. 27, 1934, 15.

68. *Literary Digest,* Dec. 8, 1934, 23, praised Beavers's "excellently" done job and Fredi Washington's "vital, straightforward, and splendidly in earnest" Peola; AN, Dec. 29, 1934; Jan. 19, 1935; Feb. 2, 1935; NYT, Nov. 24, 1934; Var., Dec. 11, 1934, 8; Dec. 4, 1934, 9.

69. *Alice Adams* (RKO, 1935); NYT, Aug. 16, 1935.

70. *The Mad Miss Manton* (RKO, 1935). Such roles were valued by Hollywood Negroes. Louis Armstrong thought, after his job in *Pennies from Heaven,* "I do believe that all the colored people in the world loves Papa Bing [Crosby]." Max Jones and John Chilton, *Louis: The Louis Armstrong Story, 1900-1971* (Boston, 1971), 142-43.

71. *Jezebel* (Warner Brothers, 1938); Otis Ferguson, "Two in Fiction," *New Republic,* March 23, 1938, 280; AN, Jan. 21, 1939.

72. *Golden Boy* (Columbia, 1939), script in USC; Tom Milne, *Mamoulian* (Bloomington, Ind.), 116; interview: Mamoulian and author, Spring 1970; Var., Aug. 16, 1939, 14; *Spectator*, Dec. 1, 1939, 776.

73. Interview: Lewis Milestone and author, Spring 1970; Var., Sept. 7, 1938, 12; *Gunga Din* (RKO, 1939); Otis Ferguson, "It's Criminal," *New Republic*, Feb. 27, 1939, 73-74.

74. *Destry Rides Again* (Universal, 1939); *The Maltese Falcon* (Warner Brothers, 1941); *Chad Hanna* (20th Century-Fox, 1940); *Juarez* (Warner Brothers, 1939); *Christmas in July* (Paramount, 1940).

75. AN, Dec. 28, 1940; Jan. 18, 1941; Milne, *Mamoulian*, 116; Hal to Henry Blanke, Warner Brothers, copy, Feb. 19, 1940, in Daves MSS.

76. Ethnic films and reviews include: Var., July 30, 1930, 16; March 20, 1929, 12 (quotation); May 2, 1929, 15, 29; March 8, 1932, 23, 24; May 22, 1929, 16; Aug. 21, 1929, 18; March 12, 1930, April 5, 1930, 15; Feb. 14, 1933, 21; April 8, 1936, 16; Nov. 15, 1939, 18; NYT, March 10, 1930; Dec. 20, 1930; May 25, 1929; July 21, 1929; May 3, 1930; *Symphony of Six Million* (RKO, 1932); *The House of Rothschild* (Fox, 1933); *Fisherman's Wharf* (RKO, 1939); *Hell's Kitchen* (Warner Brothers, 1939); Ethel Rosamond, "On Topa Da World" [Henry Armetta] *Picture Play* (March 1935), 46ff, in Blair MSS, UCLA. Among the titles were *Schlehmiel*, *The Callahans and the Murphys*, *The Cohens and the Kellys*, *Smiling Irish Eyes*, *Ginsberg from Newberg*, *Clancy on Wall Street*, *George Washington Cohen*, *East Side Sadie*, *Two Gun Ginsberg*, and *Laughing Irish Eyes*.

Non-white roles, news, and reviews include: NYT, April 14, 1930; July 21, 1929; Oct. 1, 1932; Var., March 18, 1932, 2; Jan., 26, 1932, 23; Nov. 24, 1931, 21; Dec. 6, 1932, 15; Dec. 8, 1931, 6; May 3, 1932, 21; Aug. 16, 1932, 15; Oct. 10, 1933, 23; June 21, 1932, 4; June 13, 1933, 17; Jan. 26, 1938, 2; May 22, 1929, 24; May 29, 1929, 26; July 24, 1929, 35; Feb. 5, 1930, 19; Nov. 5, 1930, 30; Nov. 24, 1941, 19; Jan. 3, 1933, 27; Feb. 28, 1933, 39; Jan. 20, 1937, 26; March 22, 1939, 20; April 12, 1939, 18; *The Mysterious Dr. Fu Manchu* (Paramount, 1930); *Hatchet Man* (First National, 1930); *Charlie Chan* series (20th Century-Fox, 1930's; Monogram, 1940's); *Think Fast Mr. Moto* (20th Century-Fox, 1937); *Chandu* (Fox, 1932), in N.Y. Cultural Center.

77. Var., Nov. 14, 1933, 1; *The Good Earth* (MGM, 1937); Philip McKee, "The Good Earth," *Asia*, April 1937, 314-15; BFI, *Monthly Film Bulletin*, April 30, 1937, 80.

78. *The Bitter Tea of General Yen* (Columbia, 1933); *Shanghai Express* (Paramount, 1932); *The General Died at Dawn* (Paramount, 1936); Var., Aug. 10, 1938, 4 (on Chan); Nov. 16, 1938, 15; Nov. 23, 1938, 14; Dec. 21, 1938, 15; NYT, Oct. 16, 1938; on Hollywood life for Asians, interview: Merv Griffin and Keye Luke, CBS-TV, 1972; Var., Oct. 20, 1937, 1; Dec. 7, 1938, 12; Feb. 14, 1940, 20 (on changes in themes induced by the coming of war).

79. *A Vanishing Race* (Edited Pictures, 1936); *Ramona* (20th Century-Fox, 1936); sample reviews, Var., Oct. 22, 1930, 35; May 27, 1931, 6; Jan. 23, 1934, 13; Sept. 27, 1932, 21; NYT, Jan. 18, 1934.

80. Var., May 10, 1932, 6; June 14, 1932, 3; June 21, 1932, 6; May 15, 1934, 14; Nov. 22, 1939, 14; May 3, 1939, 16; and as an example of a white epic, *Union Pacific* (Paramount, 1939).

81. Interview: Etta Moten and author, Spring 1971.

Notes to Chapter Twelve

1. Record, *Race and Radicalism*, chaps. III-IV; Draper, *The Rediscovery of Black Nationalism*, chap. IV.

2. Claude McKay to JWJ, Aug. 8, 1935; July 9 [1935]; Harry B. Gordon to JWJ, Sept. 14, 1935; JWJ to Gordon, copy, Oct. 22, 1935, in JWJC.

3. Jay Leyda, *Kino: A History of the Russian and Soviet Film* (New York,

1960), 299; Marie Seton, *Sergei M. Eisenstein: A Biography* (New York, 1960), 316-17, 326-28 (quotation), 334, 366; Vladimir Nizhny, *Lessons with Eisenstein*, trans. by Ivor Montague and Jay Leyda (New York, 1962), chap. II, 27, 58, 166, 170-71; Ivor Montague, *With Eisenstein in Hollywood* (New York, 1967), 346.

4. *The Circus* (Mosfilm, 1936), in Royal Belgian Film Archive.

5. AN, Feb. 15, 1929; Nov. 20, 1929; Jan. 22, 1930 (quotation); Var., March 27, 1934, 61; Dec. 4, 1934, 11; April 24, 1935, 60; AN, May 21, 1938 (quotation).

6. *Peaux Noires* (Osso, 1932), in Royal Belgian Film Archive; Var., June 13, 1929, 1; Oct. 8, 1930, 23; Oct. 16, 1935, 60; AN, Oct. 19, 1935; *Voyage au Congo* or *The Courting of Djinta* (Gide-Allegret, 1928), in BFI.

7. AN, March 29, 1933; Feb. 7, 14, 1933.

8. *Niemandsland* or *War Is Hell* (Resco, 1932), in Royal Belgian Film Archive.

9. *L'Alibi* (Eclair-Journal, 1936), *Toni* (Les Films D'Aujourd'ui, 1935); *La Morte du Cygne* (Kosmo, 1937), all in Royal Belgian Film Archive; Noble, *Negro in Films*, 136ff and appendix; *Les Perles de la Couronne* (Guitry, 1937), in Staatliches Filmarchiv der Deutsche Demokratische Republik.

10. All titles in BFI; credits in National Film Archive, *Catalogue*, part III, "Silent Fiction Film, 1895-1930" (London, 1966), 72, 81, 91, 114, 121, 124-27, 129, 130, 134, 136-39, 145, 147.

11. *Piccadilly* (British International, 1930), screened in AFI series; *Tiger Bay* (British Lion-Wyndham, 1933), in BFI; Rotha, *Film Till Now*, 140, 317.

12. *Men of Africa* (Colonial Marketing Board, 1939); *Timbuctoo* (British International, 1934); *Old Bones of the River* (Gainsborough, 1939), all in BFI. European critics differ on the merit of their films. Noble, *Negro in Films*, 138, finds some of them liberal "landmarks." But Siegfried Kracauer, *From Caligari to Hitler: A Psychological History of the German Film* (Princeton, 1947), 236, sees one of Noble's favorites as evidence that "German militarists did not have to fear" such "timid heresies." The voyeur, Lo Duca, *L'Erotisme au Cinema* (Paris, 1962), Vol. I, 118, sees the documentaries as "Le Prétexte Exotique" for "l'usage de l'éxotisme pour justifier le nu." See also Jean Rouch, "Situation et Tendance du Cinema en Afrique," in *Premier Catalogue Selectif International de Films Ethnographiques sur l'Afrique Noire*, 374ff.

13. *Sanders of the River* (London, 1935), in Royal Belgian Film Archive.

14. The foregoing account is from Cripps, "Paul Robeson and Black Identity in American Movies," supplemented by interviews with Elizabeth Welch and Sir Michael Balcon, London, Sept. 1972, and by a telephone conversation with John Laurie, Chalfonte St. Giles, Sept. 1972. *King Solomon's Mines* (Gaumont-British, 1937), fragment in BFI; AA, July 6, 1935, in Gumby Coll. For black opinion see AN, Feb. 29, 1936; July 27, 1935; May 9, 1939; Oct. 10, 1936; Dec. 12, 1936; Jan. 3, 1937.

15. *King Solomon's Mines*, fragment in BFI.

16. *Song of Freedom* (British Lion-Hammer, 1937), Mogull Films, New York; Cripps, "Robeson and Black Identity," fn. 33; interview with Elizabeth Welch.

17. Noble, *Negro in Films*, 117; Cripps, "Robeson and Black Identity," 482-84; interview with Elizabeth Welch.

18. *Midshipman Easy* (British Lion, 1936); *Old Bones of the River* (Gainsborough, 1939); *Man of Two Worlds* (Two Cities, 1946), in BFI.

19. *Proud Valley* (Ealing, 1940), in Filmarchiv der Deutsche Demokratische Republik, Berlin; interviews with Balcon and Laurie, 1972.

20. Cripps, "Robeson and Black Identity," fn. 37; *Spectator*, March 15, 1940, 361.

21. AN, July 2, 1938.

22. Interviews with Balcon, Welch, Laurie, and Michael Powell, England, Sept. 1972.

23. Clippings and lists in GPJC; AN, Oct. 2, 1929; Nov. 6, 13, 1929; PC, April 12, 1929; Nov. 15, 1929; Var., May 13, 1931, 4; May 27, 1931, 57; interview with Lester J. Sack, Dallas, June 1970.

24. Press releases in GPJC; *Ten Minutes to Live* (Micheaux, 1932); see also *The Girl from Chicago* (Micheaux, ca. 1933), both in LC. In the former, one of the "bananas" has heard of the middle-class heroes of the race, Washington and Douglass, and he admires Lincoln, but at the zionist, Garvey, he can only sneer "that nigger . . ." Early on, Theophilus Lewis complained of Micheaux's "high yeller fetich" manifested by the situation in which "all the noble characters are high yellows." "Now, when the white folks [in Hollywood] are giving it up," he wrote, "is no time for colored producers to begin dallying with it." AN, April 16, 1930.

25. Var., May 14, 1930, 13; PC, Sept. 27, 1930; Aug. 30, 23, 1930; July 26, 1930; May 3, 1930; AN, Oct. 29, 1930; Sept. 17, 1930.

26. Clippings in GPJC.

27. Var., May 13, 1931, 4; May 27, 1931, 57; interview with Lester J. Sack; AN, June 8, 19, 1932.

28. AN, June 8, 19, 1932; May 25, 1932; April 27, 1932; July 13, 20, 1932; Var., May 31, 1932, 29; June 7, 1932, 20; July 19, 1932, 25; March 27, 1931, 57.

29. AN, June 22, 1932.

30. Var., March 15, 1932, 4; April 19, 1932, 2; May 31, 1932, 4; AN, March 15, 1933; Feb. 24, 1932. Negro leaders such as JWJ received bright prospectuses in their mail, promising "a show that would captivate the world" or break Hollywood's "death hold," in JWJC.

31. Var., May 15, 1934, 27; AN, March 15, 1933; Oct. 6, 1934; April 26, 1933.

32. AN, April 7, 1934; June 28, 1934; April 27, 1935; Oct. 31, 1936; Sept. 26, 1936; Aug. 1, 1936; July 11, 1936; Var., April 10, 1934, and March 27, 1935, clippings; Dec. 30, 1936, 4; May 29, 1936, 14.

33. AN, Dec. 1, 1934; April 27, 1935; and impressions culled from conversation with Ruby Dee, Annville, Pa.; and telephone conversations with Lorenzo Tucker and Lewis Jacobs, in 1970 and 1972.

34. Interview with Ben Rinaldo, Hollywood, Spring 1970; AN, Jan. 16, 1937; March 13, 1937; Feb. 13, 20, 1937; advertising in GPJC; James Asendio, "History of Negro Motion Pictures," *International Photographper*, Jan. 1940, 16-17.

35. *Dark Manhattan* (Sackamuse, 1937), through anonymous collector.

36. Var., Oct. 13, 1937, 4; AN, April 24, 1937; NYT, July 18, 1937.

37. AN, Oct. 9, 23, 1937; Nov. 20, 27, 1937; Dec. 4, 18, 1937.

38. Interviews with Ben Rinaldo; Ted Toddy, telephone, Spring 1970; Thomas Southern, Los Angeles, Spring 1970; Bert Sternbach, telephone, Spring 1970.

39. Interviews with Rinaldo and Harry Popkin, telephone, 1970.

40. *Western Informant*, I (May 1937), 11, 14, in JWJC; Var., March 17, 1937, 15.

41. *Gang War* (Million Dollar, 1938?), through anonymous collector.

42. *Underworld* (Micheaux, 1938?), in LC; clippings in GPJC.

43. Interview with Ben Rinaldo.

44. *Double Deal* (International Road Shows and Argus Pictures, 1939); *Mystery in Swing* (International Road Shows, 1938), through anonymous collector. See also *Dirty Gertie from Harlem, USA* (Alfred Sack, 1946), directed by Spencer Williams, in GEH.

45. AN, Jan. 13, 1940.

46. *Midnight Shadow* (Randol Productions-Sack 1939), through anonymous collector; interview with Popkin; AN, Aug. 5, 1939; Nov. 18, 1939; Dec. 2, 1939.

47. AN, Dec. 2, 1939; Aug. 26, 1939; Sept. 2, 1939; Nov. 18, 1939; May 8, 1943; and clippings in GPJC.

48. Madison Thomas, "He Started It All"; Glenn Douglas by-line, Oct. 12, 1940, clippings in GPJC; Var., Oct. 2, 1940, 25.

49. *Moon Over Harlem* (Meteor Productions, 1939), in LC; AN, Feb. 4, 1939.

50. *Murder on Lenox Avenue* (Colonnade Pictures Corp., 1941); *Paradise in Harlem* (Goldberg, 1938), in LC.

51. AN, Jan. 8, 22, 29, 1938; April 9, 1938; May 14, 1938. A side-effect was the growth of get-in-the-movies ads: July 16, 1938.

52. Lena Horne and Richard Schickel, *Lena* (Garden City, N.Y., 1965), 89-90.

53. Horne and Schickel, *Lena*, 89; AN, Feb. 26, 1938; March 5, 1938; July 23, 1938; Sept. 3, 24, 1938; Oct. 15, 1938; Nov. 12, 1938; Var., July 20, 1938, 12; *Negro Actor*, I, July 15, 1938, 4; clippings in GPJC; interview: Fritz Pollard and author, telephone, Spring 1971.

54. *Broken Strings* (Goldberg, Sack, 1940), in LC.

55. Interview with Thomas Southern; *Harlem Rides the Range* and *Harlem on the Prairie* (Hollywood Productions, both 1938); *Two Gun Man from Harlem* (Merit, 1939); *Bronze Buckaroo* (Sack, 1939), through anonymous collector. Besides Buell the company included director Richard C. Kahn; Bert Sternbach; the old Yale athlete, Sabin W. Carr; the white writer, Lew Porter; and Maceo B. Sheffield, a black actor, nightclub owner, and policeman; AN, April 15, 1939; Oct. 1, 1938; *Time*, Dec. 13, 1937, 24.

56. AN, May 14, 1938 (*Let My People Live*); July 2, 1938; Feb. 12, 1938 (Pollard). Joel Spingarn to Walter White, memo, Jan. 27, 1933, in NAACPR; Var., April 17, 1940, 16 (Carver).

57. *Dirty Gertie from Harlem USA* (Sack, 1946), in GEH.

58. AN, Oct. 21, 1939; April 16, 1930 (Lewis on "high yeller fetich").

59. *The Spirit of Youth* (Grand National, 1937); *Keep Punching*, through anonymous collector; *Time*, Jan. 31, 1938, 35; NYT, Feb. 2, 1938.

60. *Keep Punching*; AN, Sept. 30, 1939; Dec. 9, 1939; Var., Jan. 5, 1938, 16. Million Dollar made a football film with Kenny Washington, UCLA.

61. AN, Dec. 2, 1939; Aug. 26, 1939; Sept. 2, 1939; Nov. 18, 1939; May 8, 1943; and clippings in GPJC; interview: author and Lawrence LaMar, Spring 1970.

62. AN, Aug. 19, 1939.

63. Var., Oct. 2, 1940, 25.

64. A sample of later productions, in LC: *Of One Blood*, *Murder with Music*, *Beware*, *Go Down Death*, *Souls of Sin*, *Killer Diller*, and *Big Timers*.

65. Survey of AN radio log, 1930's.

66. For examples, see AN, Aug. 19, 1939; Var., April 3, 1940, 16 (*Gang War*); July 8, 1942, 16 (Toddy's *Take My Life*); Young Communist file in GPJC.

67. AN, June 17, 1939; Var., May 3, 1939, 16; Dec. 6, 1939, 16; Nov. 29, 1939, 14; and clippings in GPJC.

68. *Harlem on the Prairie* pressbook, in PAC; AN, Feb. 10, 1940; April 20, 1940; May 18, 1940. Debate continues over recent "blaxploitation" movies and their paltering social thrust and shoddy aesthetics despite increased funds, distribution, audiences, and access to studio skills.

69. *Harlem on the Prairie* pressbook; Rinaldo and Popkin interviews.

70. *Time*, Jan. 29, 1940, 67.

71. AN, Jan. 13, 1940; John P. Nugent, *Black Eagle* (New York, 1971), 111-14.

72. AN, Jan. 20, 1940.

73. *The Notorious Elinor Lee* (Micheaux, 1940), through anonymous collector.

74. *Lying Lips* (Micheaux, 1940), through anonymous collector.

75. Interview with Don Malkames, telephone, Spring 1970. A Toddy post-war sales brochure included: *Eddie Green's Laugh Jamboree*, *Professor Creeps*, *Lucky Ghost*, *One Round Jones*, *His Harlem Wife* (ex-*Life Goes On*), *Murder Rap* (ex-*Take My Life*), *Prison Bait* (ex-*Reform School*), *Pigmeat's Laugh Hepcats*, *Racket Doctor* (ex-*Am I Guilty?*), *Night Club Girl* (ex-*One Dark Night*), *The Bronze Venus* (ex-*The Duke is Tops*), *Mantan Messes Up* (probably a pastiche of bits), *Voodoo Devil Drums* (possibly ex-*Drums O'Voodoo*, a curious filmed play by J. Augustus Smith, in University of Illinois), *Gangsters on the Loose* (ex-*Bargain with Bullets*), *Gun Moll* (ex-*Gang Smashers*), *Crooked Money* (ex-*While Thousands Cheer*, a football story featuring UCLA's Kenny Washington), and *Buck and Bubbles Laff Jamboree* (a string of bits from their ancient Christie comedies). *Mr. Washington Goes to Town*, Dixie National pressbook in author's collection.

76. AN, Nov. 17, 1945; Dec. 15, 1945. Hill's mail was so heavy he devoted another column to his charge. AN, Sept. 30, 1939 ("sex and glamor"). The producers did their best to preserve a black image and to ask "constructive rather than

destructive" criticism from organized Negro groups. James Asendio, Argus Pictures and International Road Shows, to "Friend" [Dec. 4, 1939]; and Flournoy Miller to Walter White, Jan. 11, 1938, in NAACPR.

Notes to Chapter Thirteen

1. Var., March 25, 1942, 1.
2. *Commonweal,* March 6, 1929, 514; Belcher, "Negro in Theatre," 217-82, 239.
3. Interview with Eubie Blake, Feb. 1971; Var., Nov. 21, 1928, 1; Nov. 28, 1928, 1; June 19, 1929, 55; Jan. 22, 1930, 33; Feb. 12, 1930, 14; Feb. 5, 1930, 34; March 13, 1929, 57-58; June 4, 1930, 67; June 18, 1930, 18-21; April 2, 1930, 4; Feb. 19, 1930, 35; Dec. 15, 1931, 24, 45; Oct. 25, 1932, 41; Nov. 8, 1932, 33; Nov. 28, 1933, 52; NYT, Feb. 28, 1929; March 15, 1929; AN, Feb. 24, 1932; March 23, 1932; Walls, "What About Amos 'n' Andy?" 38-40, 72; Hughes and Meltzer, *Black Magic,* 116-25; JWJ to Frances Hunt, copy, Dec. 29, 1932, in JWJC.
4. NYT, June 30, 1935; John T. Gillard, "Mamba's Granddaughters," *Commonweal,* Jan. 5, 1940, 241-42.
5. Herbert Garfinkel, *When Negroes March: The March on Washington Movement in the Organizational Politics for FEPC* (Glencoe, Ill., [1959]).
6. Saenger clipping books, in University of Texas; Var., Oct. 31, 1933, 77 (radio); Nov. 28, 1933, 52; interview: John Krimsky and the author, New Brunswick, N.J., Spring 1973.
7. Snyder, *Pare Lorentz,* 32, 39, 47, 56, 59, 64-65; Viertel, *Strangers,* 227, 239; interview: Ernest Anderson and author, Los Angeles, Spring 1972; Ella Winter, "Hollywood Wakes Up," *New Republic,* Jan. 12, 1938, 276-78; AN, Oct. 2, 1937; BFI, *Monthly Film Bulletin,* June 30, 1938, 156; NYT, June 17, 1938 (quotation); April 30, 1939; June 4, 1939; John Howard Lawson, "Comments on Blacklisting and 'Blockade'," *Film Culture,* Nos. 50-51 (Winter 1970), 28-29; Sarris, *American Cinema,* 45, 46-48; *Blockade* (United Artists, 1938).
8. JWJ to J. R. Johnson, copy, April 27, 1938, in JWJC; *Negro Actor,* Nov. 1, 1939, 1; AN, Nov. 11, 1939; June 17, 24, 1939; Oct. 7, 1939; March 15, 1941; May 31, 1941.
9. *Flash,* May 3, 1938, 26; *Western Informant* (March 1937), 15; AA, May 26, 1945; PC, April 13, 1935; *Journal and Guide* (Norfolk), March 23, 1935; NYA, Feb. 23, 1935; AA, Dec. 15, 1934; AN, March 11, 1939; March 15, 1941; May 31, 1941, and clippings in AAS and GPJC; NYT, Feb. 24, 1935; Var., March 31, 1943, 44 (Tarzan survey); interview with Ernest Anderson, telephone, May 1970.
10. For protests see Var., Dec. 4, 1935, 1; Dec. 8, 1937, 48; Feb. 23, 1938, 52; April 13, 1938, 17; March 18, 1942, 3; Dec. 30, 1942, 7; Feb. 17, 1943, 20; *Daily News* (New York), Nov. 8, 1942.
11. New York University, Division of General Education, "History and Appreciation of Cinema" (New York, mimeo. syllabus, 1937), 1; *New York Post,* Oct. 5, 1937; *News and Observer* (Raleigh), Oct. 22, [Walter White] to Jonathan Daniels, Raleigh, copy, Nov. 22, 1937; [Roy] Wilkins to Messrs. Houston and Morrow, memo, copy, May 4, 1938; *Daily Worker,* Dec. 10, 1938; *Boston Guardian,* Aug. 13, 1938; Bob Treman to Walter White, wire, July 7, 1938; Roger [Baldwin] to Walter White [received] April 26, 1939; W. F. Turner to Thurgood Marshall, Oct. 4, 1939; Marshall to Committee on Administration, memo, copy, March 4, 1940; "N.A.A.C.P. Hits Revival of 'Birth of a Nation'," press release, March 22, 1940, with fragment of NAACP letter to Will Hays; George E. Haynes, Federal Council of Churches, to Walter White, March 28, 1940; Stephen S. Wise, American Jewish Congress, to Walter White, March 26, 1940, all in NAACPR. The campaigns also drew cranks such as the Feldmans, Harry and Joseph, amateur cinéastes who would expose *The Birth of a Nation* as a fraud. Feldmans to White, Nov. 27, 1940, in NAACPR.

12. *The Story of Irene and Vernon Castle* (RKO, 1939); *The Boy Slaves* (RKO, 1939); *St. Louis Blues* (Paramount, 1939); *Blues in the Night* (Warner Brothers, 1939); *Strike Up the Band* (MGM, 1940). The Kane case is persuasively argued, if circumstantially, in Hubert Cohen, "The *Heart of Darkness* in *Citizen Kane*," *Cinema Journal*, Fall 1972, 11-25.

13. A Willie Best sample: *I Take This Woman* (MGM, 1940); *Flight from Destiny* (Warner Brothers, 1940); *High Sierra* (Warner Brothers, 1940); *Road Show* (United Artists, 1941); *Highway West* (Warner Brothers, 1941). A Fred Toones sample: *The Biscuit Eater* (Paramount, 1940); *Seventeen* (Paramount, 1940); *One Man's Law* (Republic, 1940); *Frontier Vengeance* (Republic, 1940); *Texas Terrors* (Republic, 1940); *Missouri Outlaw* (Republic, 1942). A Noble Johnson sample: *The Mad Doctor of Market Street* (Universal, 1940); *Aloma of the South Seas* (Paramount, 1941); *Ten Gentlemen from West Point* (20th Century-Fox, 1942). NYT, June 6, 1939. Critical quotations: NYT, June 2, 1939; July 22, 1940; Var., Feb. 14, 1941, 14; March 12, 1941, 16; Aug. 6, 1941, 9; Nov. 6, 1940, 16. A general sample: *Kentucky* (20th Century-Fox, 1938); *Zenobia* (United Artists, 1939), with "comic pickaninnies" reciting the Declaration of Independence; *Gambling Ship* (Universal, 1938); *TV Spy* (Paramount, 1939); *I Take This Woman* (MGM, 1940); *Parole Fixer* (Paramount, 1940); *Quiet Please* (Warner Brothers, 1939); *Congo Maisie* (MGM, 1939); *Destry Rides Again* (Universal, 1939); *Swanee River* (20th Century-Fox, 1939); *Buck Benny Rides Again* (Paramount, 1940); *Young America* (20th Century-Fox, 1942); *Robin Hood of the Pecos* (Republic, 1941); *Life with Henry* (Paramount, 1941); *Pride of the Bowery* (Monogram, 1941); *Topper Returns* (United Artists, 1941); *Ellery Queen's Penthouse Mystery* (Columbia, 1941); *You're Out of Luck* (Monogram, 1941); *Thieves Fall Out* (Warner Brothers, 1941); *The Getaway* (MGM, 1941); *Broadway Lights* (United Artists, 1941); *South of Panama* (PRC, 1941); *Hello Sucker* (Universal, 1941); *Dressed to Kill* (20th Century-Fox, 1941); *Kisses for Breakfast* (Warner Brothers, 1941); *New York Town* (Paramount, 1941); *Dr. Kildare* series (MGM, 1940s); *Our Wife* (Columbia, 1941); *The Pittsburgh Kid* (Republic, 1941); *Sign of the Wolf* (Monogram, 1941); *The Thin Man series* (MGM, 1940s); *Women Without Names* (Paramount, 1940); *Millionaire Playboy* (RKO, 1940); *In Old Missouri* (Republic, 1940); *On the Spot* (Monogram, 1940); *I'm Nobody's Sweetheart Now* (Universal, 1940); *Earl of Puddlestone* (Republic, 1940); *Boys of the City* (Monogram, 1940) an integrated "Dead End Kids" vehicle; *I Want a Divorce* (Paramount, 1940); *Money and the Woman* (Warner Brothers, 1940); *I Can't Give You Anything But Love, Baby* (Universal, 1940); *Calling All Husbands* (Warner Brothers, 1940); *Charter Pilot* (20th Century-Fox, 1940); *Murder over New York* and others in Chan series (20th Century-Fox, 1940); *Dark Command* (Republic, 1940).

14. AA, May 18, 1935, in AAS; Trotti and Levien, *In Old Chicago*, 71, 78, 123; clippings in Gumby Coll.; Var., March 17, 1943, 23; April 9, 1941, 16; March 1, 1939, 15; *Affectionately Yours* (Warner Brothers, 1941), with McQueen and McDaniel; *Reap the Wild Wind* (Paramount, 1942); *Mokey* (MGM, 1942); *The Toy Wife* (MGM, 1938); *The Gentleman from Dixie* (Monogram, 1941); *Among the Living* (Paramount, 1941), with Negro murder victim; *Panama Hattie* (MGM, 1942); *Holiday Inn* (Paramount, 1942); *Syncopation* (RKO, 1942); *A Night in New Orleans* (Paramount, 1942); *My Old Kentucky Home* (Monogram, 1938); *Just Around the Corner* (20th Century-Fox, 1938), the fag-end of the Temple-Robinson team.

15. *Pride of the Blue Grass* (Warner Brothers, 1939); *Louisiana Purchase* (Paramount, 1941); *Take a Letter Darling* (Paramount, 1942); *Talk of the Town* (RKO, 1942), with Rex Ingram's scholarly butler.

16. *Tom and Jerry* (MGM, 1940s); *The Song of the South* (Disney, 1944); *Jasper* series (George Pal, 1940s), sample in LC.

17. Alphabetical clippings in GPJ, on Horne and Scott (MGM), Sullivan (Paramount), Legon (RKO), Joyce Bryant (Monogram); Ernie Smith filmogra-

phies; *King for a Day* (Vitaphone, 1934); *Black Network* (Vitaphone, 1936); *Carnival in Rhythm* (Warner Brothers, 1940), Baker Coll.; *Big Broadcast of 1936* production memos, in Ben Glazer MSS, in UCLA.

18. *Panama Hattie* (MGM, 1942), in BFI; *Star Spangled Rhythm* (Paramount, 1942).

19. Var., Feb. 14, 1940, 18; May 22, 1940, 4; July 24, 1940, 14; Jan. 15, 1941, 114; NYT, April 17, 1940; *March of Time* segments, III on Navy, XIII on Dixie, XII on "The Land of Cotton," etc., in BFI. *Henry Brown, Farmer* and *The NYA and Negro Youth*, in LC.

20. *The Texans* (Paramount, 1938), in BFI.

21. *Belle Starr* (20th Century-Fox, 1940), in BFI; *Ox-Bow Incident* (20th Century-Fox, 1943); *Jesse James* (20th Century-Fox, 1943), LC; *Sante Fe Trail* (Warner Brothers, 1940), in BFI; Var., Jan. 15, 1941, 8, 14; NYT, Jan. 29, 1941; George Bluestone, *Novels into Film* (Los Angeles and Berkeley, 1957), 184.

22. *New York Times Directory of Film*, index; interview: Nunnally Johnson and author, telephone, Spring 1972. Lincoln as an icon of national unity contributed little to black imagery because his film biographers, Robert E. Sherwood, Ford, and Griffith, and others, focused on his early life in Illinois.

23. *Literary Digest*, Nov. 23, 1935, 26; *Newsweek*, Nov. 30, 1935, 27; *Time*, Dec. 2, 1935, 40; Var., Dec. 4, 1935, 15 (*So Red the Rose*); Var., March 12, 1930, 33 (*Only the Brave*); June 26, 1934, 16 (*Operator 13*); March 3, 1937 (*General Spanky*); Jan. 18, 1939, 13 (*Lincoln in the White House*); *Newskeek*, Feb. 10, 1941, 63.

24. Crowther, *Lion's Share*, 215, chap. XXIX; Var., March 3, 1937, 29; July 14, 1937, 5; March 31, 1937, 7; Mitchell to Dixon, Aug. 15, 1936, in Nelson and Aitken, *Birth of a Nation Story*, 9; AN, May 22, 1937; Jan. 8, 1938; Thomas, *Selznick*, 146ff; Ben Hecht, *A Child of the Century* (New York, 1954), 488ff; Aaron Latham, *Crazy Sundays: F. Scott Fitzgerald in Hollywood* (New York, 1971), 213ff; Gavin Lambert, *On Cukor* (New York, 1972), 88ff; "Interlude: On David O. Selznick," in Rudy Behlmer, ed., *Memo from David O. Selznick* (New York, 1972), part 6, 148; see also Gavin Lambert, *GWTW: The Making of Gone with the Wind* (Boston, 1973).

25. Selznick to Mr. Ginsberg, Dec. 12, 1938, in Behlmer, *Memo*, 187.

26. NYT, Dec. 3, 1937; *Time*, Dec. 25, 1939, 30-32; Victor Shapiro, "Diary of Gone with the Wind," in Special Collections, UCLA. "We were all conscientious people," McQueen said on *Betty Robley Show*, taped, Feb. 28, 1971, WRC-TV, Washington. AN, Feb. 18, 1939: Negroes on the set attempt to delete "nigger" from early drafts.

27. AN, Jan. 21, 1939; March 18, 1939; Shapiro, "Diary."

28. NBC Special, *Hollywood, The Selznick Years*, March 21, 1969; Day, *This Was Hollywood*, 194; Var., March 6, 1940, 6, 9; July 17, 1940, 10; Frank Daniel, "Cinderella City: Atlanta Sees 'Gone with the Wind'," *Saturday Review of Literature*, Dec. 23, 1939, 9; *Commonweal*, Jan. 12, 1940, 246, 267; *Atlanta Constitution*, in Charles Samuels, *The King: A Biography of Clark Gable* (New York, 1962), 227ff, 233-34.

29. *Gone with the Wind* (Selznick International-MGM, 1939); Var., Dec. 20, 1939, 20.

30. Clippings, n. d.; NYT, Dec. 22, 1939; *Daily Worker*, Dec. 20, 1939, all in AAS.

31. AN, Jan. 6, 13, 1940; March 2, 1940; Dec. 30, 1939; *Daily Worker*, Dec. 20, 1939; Jan. 9, 1940, in AAS. The CPUSA position waffled on *Gone with the Wind* because of two precious party tenets: that Negroes were a nation moving toward liberation and that American economic oppression of the masses remained largely unremitting during the age of the movies from 1915 to 1949. To show that workers were better off, no matter how slightly, or to show that GWTW was more liberal than *The Birth of a Nation*, opened the way for liberals to claim "progress" had taken place in the face of Marxist-Leninist predictions to the contrary. Thus Marxist-Leninist aesthetics seemed to lack historicity, verisimilitude, and relevance.

See, for example, V. J. Jerome, *The Negro in Hollywood Films* (New York, 3rd printing, 1952), 64: "Scientific criticism of film dealing with Negro life requires as its basis the Marxist-Leninist teaching on the relationship of art and society and especially the teaching on the national question, with its concrete application to the national-liberation movement of the Negro people." See in contrast the *Daily Worker's* clean-lined indictment of *Stanley and Livingstone*, "With Gun, Camera and Zanuck Through Africa," Aug. 7, 1939, in AAS, perhaps because the obvious case of colonialism lacked the ambiguities of American racial custom. Edward G. Perry, "Impressions," *Negro Actor*, Feb. 15, 1940, 4; PC, quoted in Var., Feb. 14, 1940, 27. See also John D. Stevens, "The Black Reaction to *Gone with the Wind*," *Journal of Popular Film*, Fall 1973, 366-71.

32. AN, March 9, 16, 23, 1940.

33. AN, Dec. 30, 1939 (Fidler); Feb. 10, 1940; March 9, 23, 1940; April 19, 1940; March 1, 1941; May 18, 1940; *Merv Griffin Show*, CBS, Sept. 7, 1971; *Herald-Tribune* (New York), July 21, 1940, in AAS.

34. *No Time for Comedy* (Warner Brothers, 1940); *Maryland* (20th Century-Fox, 1940); *Northwest Mounted Police* (Paramount, 1940); *The Road to Zanzibar* (Paramount, 1941); *Ghost Breakers* (Paramount, 1940); *The Return of Frank James* (20th Century-Fox, 1940); *Tin Pan Alley* (20th Century-Fox, 1940); *Meet John Doe* (Warner Brothers, 1941); *Nothing But the Truth* (Paramount, 1941); *Ten Gentlemen from West Point* (20th Century-Fox, 1941), script in UCLA; *Birth of the Blues* (Paramount, 1941), script in UCLA; *The Maltese Falcon* (Warner Brothers, 1941); *Blues in the Night* (Warner Brothers, 1941); *They Died with Their Boots On* (Warner Brothers, 1941); *Sundown* (United Artists, 1941); *Sullivan's Travels* (Paramount, 1941), in MOMA; *Blossoms in the Dust* (MGM, 1941); Var., Dec. 25, 1940, 16 ("Rochester"); March 19, 1941, 16; July 30, 1941, 8; *Affectionately Yours* (Warner Brothers, 1941), in WSHS; *Male Animal* script in WSHS.

35. *The Great Lie* (Warner Brothers, 1941); *Flame of New Orleans* (Universal, 1941), both in BFI; compare Harris with Dandridge in *Lady from Louisiana* (Republic, 1941).

36. *The Little Foxes* (Warner Brothers, 1941); interview: author and John Marriott, Baltimore, 1967.

37. *In This Our Life* (Warner Brothers, 1942); script in Howard Koch MSS, WSHS.

38. Interview with Anderson; Warner, *My First Hundred Years in Hollywood*, 255; Bette Davis, *The Lonely Life: An Autobiography* (New York, 1962), 208-9; Var., April 8, 1942, 8; Rapper to Cripps, Feb. 5, 1974, remembered the scene as a "neutral" one intended to do no more than preserve Huston's style.

39. *Casablanca* (Warner Brothers, 1942); script in Koch MSS, in WSHS.

40. NYT, Nov. 27, 1943; "Notes on the Production of 'Casablanca'," typescript memoir in Koch MSS, in WSHS; Julius J. Epstein, Los Angeles, to editor of *New York* n. d., *New York*, May 28, 1973, 5; Howard Koch, *Casablanca: Script and Legend* (Woodstock, N.Y., 1973), passim; *Commonweal*, Dec. 11, 1942, 207.

41. NYT, Jan. 29, 1941 (*Virginia*); Dec. 26, 1941 (*Sundown*); *Commonweal*, Feb. 28, 1941, 476; Feb. 7, 1941, 402; Dec. 12, 1941, 199-200; NYT, Feb. 12, 1942 ("dog-eared"); Nov. 1, 1941 (*Belle Starr*); Otis Ferguson, "The Man in the Movies," *New Republic*, Sept. 1, 1941, 278, (*Little Foxes*); *Newsweek*, Feb. 10, 1941, 63 ("absurd"); AN, Feb. 3, 1940 (*Grapes of Wrath*); Jimmy Lunceford, "Colored Actors," *Hollywood Who's Who* (1941), 28-29. Southern critics, at least those along the Saenger circuit, reported on racial roles with studied neutrality and near blindness. See Saenger clipping books, University of Texas.

42. NYT, April 30, 1939 (progressives); June 4, 1939 (New School); June 1, 1941; Feb. 3, 1940 ("escapist fare"); *Daily Worker*, April 1, 1940.

43. AN, Dec. 23, 1939; Aug. 21, 1940; Var., Nov. 6, 1940, 3; Oct. 2, 1940, 1; May 22, 1940, 4; Dec. 4, 1935, 1; Dec. 8, 1937, 48; Feb. 23, 1938, 52; April 13, 1938, 17; March 18, 1942, 3; Dec. 30, 1942, 7; Feb. 17, 1943, 20; Norman O. Houston, Los

Angeles, to Walter White, Sept, 16, 1943, in NAACPR; interview: Eddie Anderson and author, telephone, Los Angeles, May 1970.

44. White to Virginius Dabney, copy, April 8, 1940; Dabney to White, April 13, 1940; Grover C. Hall to White, April 14, 1940; Jonathan Daniels to White, April 12, 1940; [White] to J. Richardson Jones, YMCA, copy, Sept. 18, 1940; Jones to White, Sept. 21, 1940; White to Jones, copy, June 16, 1941; White to Roy Wilkins, memo, May 21, 1941; White to Wilkins and Marshall, May 20, 1941; Robert Huebach to White, n. d., in NAACPR. Within the New York circle they could not agree on *Proud Valley*. A. Philip Randolph thought it imperialist (Randolph to White, Feb. 6, 1941), while others declined a hasty invitation to preview it: "must go to oculist," ". . . things to do," "thanks, but really need rest." White to Pickens, Jones, Morrow, and Reeves, interoffice memo, Jan. 31, 1941, in NAACPR.

45. Ellington, *Music Is My Mistress*, 175-180.

46. Interview with Eddie Anderson; Walter White to "Warner Brothers," Feb. 4, 1941; White to J. H. Hoffberg, Feb. 24, 1941; Mary Warner to William Pickens, April 29, May 2, 1941, in NAACPR.

47. White to Wilkins, Feb. 23 [1942], in NAACPR.

48. On shifting movie themes see Martha Monigle, "A Survey of Story Purchases by Twentieth Century-Fox During 1939-1940" (USC, M. A. thesis, 1942), 2, 5, 11, 13, 45, 4, 8, 50.

49. *Negro Actors Guild Newsletter*, March 1942, 2; Walter White, *A Man Called White* (New York, 1948), 200ff.

50. Saenger clipping books, in University of Texas; Var., Feb. 4, 1942, 3; *Negro Actors Guild Newsletter*, April 1942), 1.

51. NYT, July 2, 20, 1942; Oct. 2, 10, 16, 1942; Aug. 5, 1942; Nov. 6, 27, 1942; Sept. 18, 1942; Jan. 14, 1943; Var., Feb. 23, 1942, 8; March 4, 1942, 8; April 8, 1942, 8; May 13, 1942, 8; June 24, 1942, 8; July 8, 1942, 2; Aug. 12, 1942, 8; Sept. 23, 1942, 8; March 10, 1942, 15; March 24, 1943, 3.

52. NYT, Oct. 10, 1942; Sept. 13, 1942; Nov. 11, 1943; April 2, 3, 6, 30, 1942; Jan. 5, 24, 1942; Feb. 7, 12, 19, 1942; July 20, 1942; March 28, 1942; Sept. 18, 25, 1942; Var., Dec. 16, 1942, 16 (*Tennessee Johnson*); *Herald-Tribune* (New York), Nov. 29, 1942; *Daily Worker*, March 10-17, 1946; July 1, 1945; Feb. 2, 3, 17, 1946; Feb. 27, 1947; April 6, 1947; July 25, 1947; Sept. 27, 1947, in AAS; PM (New York), Feb. 28, 1943; Ezra Goodman, "Hollywood and Minorities," *Asia*, Jan. 1943, 34-5; AN, Sept. 26, 1942; Jan. 1943 (clipping on Dancer in AAS); July 31, 1943; Aug. 7, 1943; May 15, 1943 (*Ox-Bow Incident*); March 27, 1943; Feb. 20, 1943 (*Stormy Weather*); June 20, 1942 ("sepia star"); PM (New York), Feb. 28, 1943 ("integral part"); Nov. 11, 1943; *Negro Actors Guild Newsletter*, II, Oct. 1942, 2; *Commonweal*, Dec. 11, 1942, 207; July 9, 1943, 302; July 23, 1943, 344-5; Manny Farber, "To What Base Uses," *New Republic*, March 1, 1943, 283-4; AN, Jan. 9, 1942 (on Dancer); July 18, 25, 1942; Aug. 1, 15, 1942; Dec. 12, 26, 1942.

53. PM (New York), March 22, 1943; Jo Swerling's *Lifeboat* script and Zanuck's notes, in WSHS; continuity sketches for *The Very Thought of You* and *Stage Door Canteen* script, in Daves MSS; Var., Jan. 20, 1943, 9 (*Tarzan*); on Dresser, clipping, n. d., in AAS. Still, whites were baffled by Fetchit and Best whom they found "undirectable"—the word, in this context, is John Ford's. "I didn't do much to affect it [Best's performance] one way or the other," said Vincent Sherman. Interviews between John Ford and Vincent Sherman (telephone), Spring 1970. The stylized cartoon continued to reach for some of the texture that Fetchit and Best imparted to their roles, though without the range or human scale of the originals.

54. *Shoe Shine Boy* (MGM, 1943), in LC.

55. CE, Sept. 30, 1938; Jan. 22, 1948; Council Minutes, HICCASP, Aug. 18, 1947, in WSHS; Hollywood Democratic Committee minutes, June 16, 1944; June 14, 1945, May 18, 1945, Dec. 20, 1945; Executive Board minutes, Nov. 27, 1944; Helen Gahagan Douglas to George Pepper, June 12, 1944; Revels Cayton, Minorities Director, California CIO Council, to Pepper, July 20, 1944; Pepper, HDC, to

Hollywood Roosevelt Hotel, Dec. 21, 1944, all in WSHS; *Daily Worker,* July 1, 1945, in AAS; Dalton Trumbo, "Blackface, Hollywood Style," *Crisis,* Dec. 1943, 365-67, 378, reprinted from Hollywood Writers' Congress proceedings; AN, Aug. 14, 29, 1942; Sept. 22, 1945; Var., Dec. 2, 1942, 43; Aug. 10, 1944, clipping in Academy Library, Los Angeles; Gwendolyn Bennett, Greater New York Committee for Better Negro Films, to "Dear Friend," May 30, 1939 (discussing using *My Song Goes Forth* [Ambassador, 1939], in BFI); William Alexander to White, Sept. 20, 1937; John Velasco, Negro Cultural Committee, to "Dear Friend," March 30, 1938; press release, "Movie Producers Still Libel Negro in Films Says Film Survey," (mimeo., n. d.); Emmet May, Greater New York Committee, to George Murphy, Jr., NAACP, Oct. 10, 1939, all in NAACPR; *New Jersey Herald News,* May 16, 1942, in AAS; PC, Sept. 8, 15, 1945; LAS, Aug. 30, 1945 (Jane White). Even in the South exhibitors offered to entertain Negro troops: John S. Arthur, 2nd Lt., to E. V. Richards, April 22, 1942; George Hunter, Brig. Gen., to Richards, April 24, 1942; A. W. Dent, Dillard University, to Richards, April 24, 1942, in Richards MSS, in University of Texas.

56. *Army and Navy Blood Donor Project; Henry Brown, Farmer; Negro Colleges in Wartime,* all in LC; Var., Dec. 2, 1942, 22; Lawrence J. Reddick, "Movies in Harlem," *Library Journal,* Dec. 1943, 981-82.

57. NYT, Jan. 23, 1943; Harry Albert Sauberli, "Hollywood and World War II: A Survey of Themes of Hollywood Films About the War 1940-1945" (M.A. thesis, USC, 1967), 321, 323, 336, 348-49; NYT, Sept. 13, 1942.

58. "Army Shows Hollywood the Way," *Negro,* Sept. *ca.* 1944, 94-95, in JWJ.

59. Var., April 8, 1942, 3, 22; *Cabin in the Sky* (MGM, 1943), in LC; *Stormy Weather* (20th Century-Fox, 1943), in Baker Coll.; *Crash Dive* (20th Century-Fox, 1942); *Sahara* (Columbia, 1943); *Bataan* (MGM, 1943).

60. NYT, June 4, 1943; *Los Angeles Daily News,* June 12, 1943; PM (New York), March 22, 1943, in GPJ; AN, Feb. 5, 1944; April 29, 1944; *Negro Actors Guild Newsletter,* July 1944, 3; Langston Hughes, "Is Hollywood Fair to Negroes," *Negro Digest,* April 1943, 19-21; *Negro Actors Guild Newsletter,* Jan. 1943, 1, and clippings in GPJ.

61. *Tales of Manhattan* (20th Century-Fox, 1942); Cripps, "Robeson and Black Identity," 483ff; AN, Aug. 29, 1942.

62. *Song of the South* (Disney, 1944), in revival, 1972; PM (New York), Dec. 24, 1946, in AAS; Var., Aug. 10, 1944; *Pilot,* May-June 1966, latter two clippings in Academy Library; AN, April 14, 1944; Aug. 26, 1944; Richard Schickel, *The Disney Version: The Life, Times, Art and Commerce of Walt Disney* (New York, 1968), 276-77; Hedda Hopper, *From Under My Hat* (Garden City, N.Y., 1952), 286.

63. *New Jersey Herald News,* May 16, 1942, AAS; AN, March 31, 1945.

64. "STATEMENT TO THE NEGRO PUBLIC, PARTICULARLY IN LOS ANGELES," by Walter White, Sept. 19, 1942, in NAACPR.

65. John Brooks, *The Great Leap: The Past Twenty-Five Years in America* (New York, 1966), chap. I.

SUBJECT INDEX

Vann, Robert L., 80-83, 180
Variety, 3, 75, 110-11, 113, 119, 133, 138,
140, 145-46, 148, 153, 157, 163, 168-69,
199, 205, 212, 250, 256, 261, 267, 269,
287, 298, 300, 302, 307, 330, 342, 349,
360, 376, 379
Verwayen, Percy, 182
Vidor, King, 98, 104, 111-12, 119, 208,
236, 243-44, 246-47, 249-50, 252, 265,
269, 277, 290
Vitagraph, 21-22, 24, 33, 72, 109, 118, 199,
228
Vitaphone, 167, 198, 219-20
Vodery, Will, 113, 220, 224, 267
Von Sternberg, Josef, 166, 271
Von Stroheim, Erich, 100, 120, 166, 313

Wallace, Edgar, 278, 283, 314-15
Waller, Fats, 234, 289, 306
Walton, Lester, 6, 10, 25, 40, 42, 57-58,
67, 85, 120, 143-44, 173-75, 180, 186,
189, 382
Wanger, Walter, 283, 351, 374
Warner Brothers, 97, 120, 167, 219, 242,
253, 258, 265, 271, 287, 307, 370, 373
Washington, Booker T., 20-21, 42, 57,
61, 72, 86, 89, 145, 158, 182, 263
Washington, Edgar, 96, 154, 165, 274
Washington, Fredi, 207, 216, 232, 288,
301-2, 379
Waters, Ethel, 97, 220, 231, 234, 254, 257,
271, 329, 376, 380
Weems, Walter, 237, 240, 343, 347
Welch, Elizabeth, 317, 319
Wellman, William, 165, 271-72, 287, 304
West, Mae, 96, 283, 355

Westerns, black, 88, 274, 292, 328-29,
336-37
Wheeler and Woolsey, 272, 277, 287
Whipper, Leigh, 177, 267, 306, 351, 359,
366, 377
White, Jane, 379
White, Walter, 67-68, 108, 204, 209, 217-
18, 225, 242, 267, 349, 374-76, 387-88
Whitman, Ernest, 289-90, 353, 359, 381
Wilkins, Roy, 68, 217, 267
Williams, Bert, 11, 25, 38, 76, 134, 174,
221, 328, 374, 376
Williams, Spencer, 106, 129, 151, 222-24,
325, 338, 374
Williams, Zach, 101, 129, 240
Willkie, Wendell, 349, 375-76
Wills, J. Elder, 314, 317
Wilson, Dooley, 339, 354, 371-72, 376,
381
Wilson, Frank, 216, 228, 330, 333, 335
Wilson, Tom, 138, 142
Wilson, Woodrow, 41-42, 47, 52, 62,
145-46
Wong, Anna May, 128, 147, 168, 306,
313-14
Woods, Frank, 43, 45
World War I, 80, 82, 117, 172
World War II, 349

Yarbo, Lillian, 109, 354
Young Communist League, 167, 342

Zanuck, Darryl, 119, 278-79, 378
Zukor, Adolph, 37, 94, 118

TITLE INDEX

Additional titles appear in the notes.